THE PAPERS OF

WOODROW WILSON

VOLUME 8
1892-1894

SPONSORED BY THE WOODROW WILSON
FOUNDATION
AND PRINCETON UNIVERSITY

THE PAPERS OF
WOODROW
WILSON

ARTHUR S. LINK, *EDITOR*

JOHN WELLS DAVIDSON AND DAVID W. HIRST
ASSOCIATE EDITORS

JOHN E. LITTLE, *ASSISTANT EDITOR*

JEAN MACLACHLAN, *CONTRIBUTING EDITOR*

M. HALSEY THOMAS, *CONSULTING EDITOR*

Volume 8 · 1892-1894

PRINCETON, NEW JERSEY
PRINCETON UNIVERSITY PRESS
1970

QUANTITY	STOCK NO.	TITLE	CODE
1	1260	VOL. 8 PAPERS OF WOODROW WILSON	
		PUBLICATION DATE JUNE 10	

FROM: **PRINCETON UNIVERSITY PRESS**
PRINCETON, NEW JERSEY 08540

NO. 54496
PACKING SLIP

INTRODUCTION

THIS eighth volume of *The Papers of Woodrow Wilson* covers the period from June 1892 through August 1894. It seemed then that the United States was careening from crisis to crisis—from the Homestead Strike and Populist revolt of 1892, to the Panic of 1893 with all its baleful consequences, to the Pullman Strike of 1894 and its bloody eruptions.

Woodrow Wilson went through a crisis of political identity under the impact of these events. The man who had earlier acknowledged Walter Bagehot as his mentor found a new master, Edmund Burke, to guide him through the troubled political seas. In the summer of 1893, in the midst of the domestic convulsions, Wilson wrote his first lecture on the great Anglo-Irishman. It is printed in this volume in the form in which it is believed that Wilson wrote it. Also printed are addresses in which Wilson echoed Burke's exaltation of expediency and order as the guides to and prerequisites of progress, and his maledictions against impatient utopian reformers.

As the documents in this volume abundantly reveal, the years 1892-1894 were a time of remarkable development for Wilson as a scholar, publicist, and teacher. Completing his first major historical work, *Division and Reunion*, in 1893, he immediately embarked upon a more ambitious undertaking, a "Short History of the United States." At the same time, he secured his reputation as a trenchant reviewer of scholarly books. His bibliography of legal studies and suggestions for a special collection in political science for the Princeton University Library, both printed herein, give more than an inkling of his progress toward mastery of his special fields. All the while he was gaining pre-eminence as a teacher in the eyes of Princeton undergraduates. He enriched his undergraduate offering by adding courses in the history of law and in the history of the English common law. His notes for his course in American constitutional law and for selected lectures in the history of the English common law are printed in this volume; they give clear evidence of the level of his undergraduate instruction. At The Johns Hopkins University, Wilson completed his new three-year cycle of lectures on administration. His notes for these lectures, printed herein, complete the series begun in Volume 6. During the period covered by this volume, Wilson also emerged on the national scene as a leader in discussions about educational philosophy, objectives, and methods.

This volume is rich in personal letters, many of which have been recovered from collections scattered across the United

States. No brief comment can adequately describe these letters; it can only be said that they shed brilliant new light upon Wilson in his various relationships as husband, professional colleague, author, and friend.

We have adopted only one important editorial innovation in preparing this volume. It is to abandon use of the symbol for letterpress copies, LPC, and to use the more descriptive symbols of ALS, TLS, etc., accompanied, of course, by a reference to the letterpress books from which the copy was obtained.

Readers are reminded that *The Papers of Woodrow Wilson* is a continuing series; that persons, institutions, and events that figure prominently in earlier volumes are not usually reidentified in subsequent ones; and that the Index gives cross references to fullest earlier identifications.

Librarians and curators continue to answer our queries and to send us new materials when they can be found. Ellen B. Ballou of Dublin, N.H., and Carolyn E. Jakeman of the Houghton Library of Harvard University deserve special thanks for their help in finding new materials in the Papers of Horace Elisha Scudder and of the Houghton Mifflin Company in the Houghton Library.

The Editors are grateful to Mrs. Bryant Putney of Princeton University Press for copyediting and other assistance, and to Marjorie Sirlouis and Colonel James B. Rothnie, U.S.A., Ret., for their continued expert work in deciphering Wilson's shorthand.

THE EDITORS

Princeton, New Jersey
October 13, 1969

CONTENTS

CONTENTS

ILLUSTRATIONS

Following page 326

TEXT ILLUSTRATIONS

ABBREVIATIONS

AL	autograph letter
ALS	autograph letter(s) signed
API	autograph postal initialed
EAW	Ellen Axson Wilson
enc(s).	enclosed, enclosure(s)
env.	envelope
hw	handwriting or handwritten
JRW	Joseph Ruggles Wilson
L	letter
sh	shorthand
T	typed
TCL	typed copy of letter
TDS	typed document signed
tel.	telegram
TLS	typed letter signed
WW	Woodrow Wilson
WWhw	Woodrow Wilson handwriting or handwritten
WWsh	Woodrow Wilson shorthand
WWT	Woodrow Wilson typed
WWTLS	Woodrow Wilson typed letter signed

ABBREVIATIONS FOR COLLECTIONS AND LIBRARIES

Following the National Union Catalog of the
Library of Congress

CtW	Wesleyan University Library
CtY	Yale University Library
DLC	Library of Congress
Ia-HA	Iowa State Department of History and Archives, Des Moines
ICU	University of Chicago Library
MB	Boston Public Library
MdBJ	The Johns Hopkins University Library
MH	Harvard University Library
NcU	University of North Carolina Library
NIC	Cornell University Library
NjP	Princeton University Library
RSB Coll., DLC	Ray Stannard Baker Collection of Wilsoniana, Library of Congress
ViU	University of Virginia Library
ViW	College of William and Mary Library
WC, NjP	Woodrow Wilson Collection, Princeton University
WHi	State Historical Society of Wisconsin, Madison
WP, DLC	Woodrow Wilson Papers, Library of Congress
WU	University of Wisconsin Library

[Sept. 8, 1892] publication date of a published writing; also date of document when date is not part of text

[*Sept. 8, 1890*] latest composition date of a published writing

[[Aug. 23, 1894]] delivery date of a speech if publication date differs

THE PAPERS OF

WOODROW WILSON

VOLUME 8

1892-1894

THE PAPERS OF
WOODROW WILSON

From Ellen Axson Wilson

My own darling,   Princeton June 16/92

It is ten o'clock and we have all separated for the night, but before I go to bed I will send a tiny little message to my love.[1] I meant to have written in time to mail it, but somehow I have been very busy today gathering up various broken threads and getting domestic affairs in thorough order after the late turmoil. Then of course there had to be the "long talk" with Anna[2]— impossible in the midst of the commencement rush.

Your telegram came safely to hand;[3] am *so* sorry about the tiresome delay. I hope however that it gave you a comfortable night's sleep in Washington.

We are getting on nicely. I am making a brave struggle against the blues. I think I am successful on the whole, but I find it will be best not to write a "love-letter"—not to dwell just yet on how much I miss you, and need you, and *love* you. Oh my darling, my darling,—life itself seems to stand still when you are gone! I wonder that my heart does not stop beating. But no—this *must* not be! I must try to harden that same heart a little,—to try to turn philosopher, or indifferentist, or *something* less intense,— more comfortable than a loving woman separated from the dearest, noblest, tenderest, most perfect, most *wonderful* husband in the world!—Dearest love to all.

Your own   Eileen.

ALS (WC, NjP).

[1] Wilson had just left for Columbia, South Carolina, for a visit with his sister and brother-in-law, Dr. and Mrs. George Howe, Jr., his father, his brother, Joseph R. Wilson, Jr., and Joseph's bride, Kate Wilson.
[2] Anna Harris of Rome, Georgia, who was visiting Ellen.
[3] It is missing.

To Ellen Axson Wilson

My own darling,   Columbia, 17 June, '92

One consequence of my delay was that I found the bridal party already here when I arrived. They reached here last night at 12 o'clock.—I, this morning at a quarter past six. I feel now (at eleven o'clock) as if it were afternoon; but I am *quite well*—it is not intolerably hot—and we are serene. Sister Annie[1] is pulled down, by nursing first brother George and then Jimmie![2] but *considering that*, looks quite well.

Our new sister is really lovely—if anything prettier than her photograph, for she has a bright colour and her face has a great deal of expression. She is, of course, silent with embarrassment; but she seems very attractive both in speech and manner, nevertheless.

Ah, my darling, how sad it is to be away from you—already I am feeling *divorced*, maimed, hurt—it is such a wrench to come away from my precious, my indispensable, my matchless little wife. They all love you so much here, my pet. *I* love you more than I could tell you, even if I were a poet! Happy as I am to be here with these dear ones, I would give the world to be back in your arms! My love, my queen, I am altogether

Your own   Woodrow

ALS (WC, NjP).
  [1] The reader is reminded that this is a continuing series, and that persons referred to by familiar names and diminutives who have appeared in earlier volumes are identified in the Index of this volume under the form of the name used.
  [2] James Hamilton Woodrow, whose fatal illness is described in WW to EAW, June 18, 1892.

From Ellen Axson Wilson

My own darling,   Princeton June 17/92

Your telegram[1] has come and I am indeed glad to get it. I hope you had a comfortable journey but I fear it was very hot. It is almost as hot here as it was on Tuesday. We have been loafing most of the day; at about eleven we went to the college library and staid until one; in the afternoon we "lay around" reading and embroidering, rather used up by the heat. We got "Cranford"—Mrs. Gaskell[2]—from the library and are enjoying it very much. Late this afternoon I relieved my conscience of a long-standing prick by calling on the Aikens.[3] Leroy Gresham and John Wilson have just been in to say "goodbye";—this morning we met Bowdre Phinizy[4] who said that he was just coming here on the same errand. He wanted your address so as to write and beg you to go to "Grove-something" to see them. Wilson wanted his essay, which he said you had told him was on your desk. I went up to get it and found that La Dowaline[5] had *closed the desk*! That will prevent my getting that check, by the way. (I suppose you have the key of the desk with you.) Perhaps you had better send me another check from Columbia.

Your *"prize"* has come from Baltimore,[6] and is quite striking. The head is about as large as my fist in very high relief; then there is a wide background of bronze and a wide frame of oak; so that the whole thing is rather large.

How anxious I am, dear, to get your first letter. I want so much to know in detail how you do, and also to hear about all the rest,—how Bro. George is and Sister Annie & the baby,—all about Jimmie and his poor, poor wife,—and *all* about the new sister too. You have a great deal to write about in order to satisfy my sympathetic inquiries. I am so pleased, dear, to think that two days of this separation are gone now; never before have I counted them so eagerly or with such intense longing to have them pass. I fear that is not the best mood for coaxing them into haste,— contrary things that they are! Indeed I find they do but "creep withal" though they fly fast enough when one is intensely happy. There is some comfort though—however spiteful they may be they *can't* stand wholly still!

Goodbye 'till tomorrow dear heart. I *love* you—oh *how* I love you! Best love to all the dear ones,   Your own   Eileen

ALS (WC, NjP).

1 Wilson's telegram from Columbia is missing.

2 Elizabeth Cleghorn Gaskell, *Cranford* (London and New York, 1853); a new edition, with a preface by Anne Thackeray Ritchie, appeared in 1891.

3 Ellen was probably referring to Sarah E. Aiken, widow of Professor Charles Augustus Aiken of the Princeton Theological Seminary, who lived at 31 Steadman Street. Aiken had died on January 14, 1892, and some members of her family were probably still with her.

4 LeRoy Gresham, '92, and John Glover Wilson, '92, both of Baltimore, and Bowdre Phinizy, '92, of Augusta.

5 Presumably a new servant.

6 In 1892, The Johns Hopkins University began awarding the John Marshall Prize—a bronze portrait of the Chief Justice—to the "Ph.D. graduate who had produced during the year the best work on some subject in historical or political science, ancient or modern." Four initial awards were made in 1892 to Henry Carter Adams, Charles Herbert Levermore, John Martin Vincent, and Woodrow Wilson. John C. French, *A History of the University Founded by Johns Hopkins* (Baltimore, 1946), pp. 348-49.

To Ellen Axson Wilson

My own darling,   Columbia, S. C.   18 June, 1892

I can now give you the particulars of Jimmie's death. The disease was typhoid fever—and the collapse did not come so suddenly as we were led to suppose. He had been overworking himself *terribly*, cousin Kate [Woodrow] says, not going to bed, for example, more than three times during one week, soon before the breakdown. Marion Woodrow says he looked dreadfully for two or three weeks before he went to bed—was really ill then, but would not give up. He got up and went to his office to attend to his business correspondence after he had had a touch of fever which brought his temperature up to 104°. In short he had been making a silent (and fatal) fight against the illness for a long time. He had not taken a vacation of so much as a day's duration since entering the printing office, except when he went off for a two or three days wedding journey; and all the time he had worked *inordinately*, keeping no clerk of any kind, and doing the labour of two or three men. After hearing it all, I can only say, 'no wonder he died'!

The blow has been terrible, overwhelming to all concerned, as you may imagine—and yet they are bearing up under it with a Christian fortutude which is admirable.

This is Saturday afternoon, my pet, and no letter from you yet: I pray God to keep you from all harm—my heart stands still so long as no letters come from you. I am perfectly well—and could be quite happy, did I know that you, too, were all right. You are continuously in my thoughts, my sweet one. Even this lovely new sister of ours makes me think, not so much what a lucky dog 'Dode' is, as what rare happiness is *mine*, to have the loveliest wife of all, made of the finest clay, with the loveliest womanly ways, so beautified by every gift of *mind*, as well as of every other sort. Kate evidently has plenty of mind as well as plenty of spirit and sweetness and beauty. I have seen nothing about her that I do not thoroughly like and admire. But how my heart thrills when I think of what you are! You are so entirely *of your own species*—so unlike other lovely persons in your loveliness—and so superior to them all in the manner and *charm* of your loveliness!

All seem well here. Brother George seems to have recovered entirely. Father is much better than I expected to find him. The weather is really quite pleasant—*breezy* as well as warm. With a heartful of love.   Your own   Woodrow

Warmest regards to Miss Harris.

ALS (WC, NjP).

From Ellen Axson Wilson

My own darling,   Princeton June 18/92

I have just had the nicest letter from Mrs. Bird,[1] full of apparently very genuine enthusiasm over all of us and our "ideal home" and her visit. How charmingly warm-hearted she is! I am tempted to send you the letter but remember your objection to receiving enclosures in my letters! By the way, she says Judge Gresham[2] tells her that the C. R. R.[3] will pay its interest on the debentures, soon to be due. She sent me a newspaper article on the railroad situation which I havn't had time to read yet. Have been busy writing letters—to Miss Sayre and others and sewing while Anna reads that delightful "Cranford."

So you see dear we are getting on very pleasantly and comfortably. It is a good thing for me that Anna is here. We are enjoying each other and it would be sadly lonely without her;—though I *should* like some long quiet hours to write you the long, *full* letters which failed to get themselves written during my southern tour! However I still have an uneasy conviction that it would not be good for me to "invite my soul" *too* much just now.

I am in danger of taking this separation all too tragically. There is something *terrible* in having so much at stake in life; it involves sometimes an acute agony. May God help me,—make me a better Christian,—more spiritual-minded! There is no other help *possible* for one who loves so intensely. How else may she hope to win *peace*? *Joy* indeed she has in fullest human measure, but *peace*,— *security*—who save the infinitely Great,—the infinitely Merciful can ensure her that?

But I am called away,—and none too soon perhaps. I love you dear,—oh how I love you!   Your little wife   Ellie

ALS (WC, NjP).
  [1] The Wilsons' old friend, Sarah, or Sallie, Baxter Bird (Mrs. William Edgeworth Bird), of 22 East Mt. Vernon Place, Baltimore.
  [2] Judge J. J. Gresham of Macon, Ga.
  [3] The Central Railroad of Georgia.

To Ellen Axson Wilson

My own darling,   Columbia, 19 June, 1892

Your note of Thursday night reached me this morning—*it*, too, like myself, must have been delayed over-night in Washington. It comforted me so much! My spirits were going steadily down with the lengthening of the time since I had had a word from my sweet one, and I was sorely in need of that dear little note.

I wish you could have heard the enthusiastic (and yet really discriminating) praises Mrs. Bird heaped upon you, my darling, on our ride together to Baltimore! It made me glow with happiness to hear her. For she did not praise you for the wrong things, but for the very beauties and graces and gifts that you possess, and that make me admire you so profoundly and love you so passionately. It was a pure delight to listen. And yet it was a keen source of pain, too: for was I not being hurried away from you as fast as the train could carry me: was I not *needing* you more every moment? Every time I am separated from you, my own Eileen, I seem to see one more element of my dependence upon you—of my devotion to you. This time I am afraid that it is a *selfish* element I see. *Here*, where I love everybody and everybody loves me, I seem to miss you as sorely as I did at the Hotel during those dreary weeks in Princeton[1]—perhaps even *more* sorely: for I feel that no one is devoted *particularly to me*; and the feeling makes me so forlorn! The feeling is not *wholly* selfish: it is *you* I miss. It would not satisfy me to have somebody else devoted particularly to me. It is *your* devotion only that can satisfy my infinite longing for love: for that devotion is backed by *your mind* with its subtle, delightful power to understand, by *your heart* with its infinitely various power of sympathy, by your lovely, altogether indescribable, because incomparable, *personality*, with its penetrating charm, "to haunt, to startle, and waylay." Is it selfishness, darling, thus to admit the *demand* of my nature for the infinite gifts you have lavished upon me? Is it unreasonable to *need* what it would have been unreasonable to expect *before* you opened your heart and nature to me? Is it not just an admission of the enlargement you have brought about in my nature. You have made it *need* perfect delights by giving it such.

But I must stop. All send unbounded love to you. I am quite well, and live on thoughts of you and the babies. Give my warmest regards to Miss Harris.   Your own   Woodrow

ALS (WC, NjP).
    [1] Wilson refers to his stay at the Nassau Hotel in Princeton from early March to early May of 1892, while Ellen and the children were on an extended visit with relatives in the South.

From Ellen Axson Wilson

My own darling,   Princeton, June 19/92

I wonder how all you dear people in Columbia are spending this Sunday. I *hope* you all had an opportunity to hear Father preach. Or did you all hear Dr. Smith,—and how did you like him?[1] We went to the first church and heard Dr. Worden![2] What he said was really not so bad barring a few absurdities that seemed to be due to a lack of humour, but the man *looks* so in-

tolerably *smug* that everything he says sounds like cant. He reminds one constantly of one of Dickens characters.

It is still extremely hot and moist. I fear you are suffering, dear.
This 'spell of weather' has inaugurated my summer campaign
against the *flies*. They bid fair to be as bad as ever, though Ed
[Axson] has put up the doors and windows and I have been hard
at work. Suppose you see if Bro. George's inventive genius can't
think of some way to close that space at the top of the windows
so that our screens will be of some real service. I have jumped up
three times since I began this in pursuit of the wretches.

We are of course having an absolutely quiet time now,—no
visitors, no letters even. The only mail has been two wedding
announcements Miss Jean Fine's[3] and a certain Mr. and Mrs. J.
R. Wilson's. Who *can they* be?

You must kiss the dear little bride especially for me, and tell
her how very *very* much I wish that I were there with you all. I
feel quite left out in the cold when I think of that dear Columbia
party. I wonder if your first letter will reach me tomorrow in spite
of that delay in reaching your destination. Oh how I hope it will.
I am *wearying* for it—and for *you*, my own, own love. How exactly
that word 'wearying' expresses the peculiar pain that *separation*
brings! But it would be a shame to lament when there are so
many worse things, and when the separation this time is to be
so short, only eight or nine more days after this I suppose even
if you come by sea. Ah how happy beyond words will I be when
those days are all past!

Darling you will tell me, will you not?—*exactly* how you are?
You will not keep things from me as you did when I was South.
Remember I must have now the truth, the whole truth, and noth-
ing but the truth. With dearest love to all, I am as ever,

Your own,   Eileen

ALS (WP, DLC) with WWhw notation " 'Crokinole' " on env.
    1 The Columbia *State*, June 20, 1892, reported that Dr. Smith (identified in
EAW to WW, April 27, 1892, n. 1, Vol. 7) had preached a "strong sermon"
at the First Presbyterian Church on June 19.
    2 The Rev. Dr. James Avery Worden, superintendent of the Sunday School
Training Department of the Presbyterian Church, U.S.A., who was living at 10
Nassau Street in Princeton in 1892.
    3 Sister of Henry B. Fine, who had just married Charles Barzillai Spahr.

To Ellen Axson Wilson

My own darling,   Columbia, S. C., 20 June, 1892
    You will find a key to my desk, you know, in the little drawer
inside my small desk—just in front of the catalogue cards which
the drawer contains.

Your second letter reached me this morning, and I proceed at once to answer the questions it puts about the dear ones here.

Bro. George seems quite well again, and *is*, I believe quite as strong as when you were here, barring, perhaps, a somewhat increased liability to fatigue. Sister Annie, too, is better than I expected to find her. It is wonderful how much she can stand. After nursing bro. George for a couple of weeks, she nursed Jimmie! and still she does not seem any worse than when you were here,—is bright and playful, and most of the time *seems strong*.

Dinner was so late that this note was not begun till too late— and now they are calling me to come and take a ride. I must break away in spite of the pulling of my heart. Sister tells me to say that *we all* of us miss you dreadfully every minute—and 'tis so, darling—you are loved here almost as much as you deserve. As for myself, I fairly pant for my darling, my matchless little queen. I am counting the hours, as well as you, my sweet one, which separate you from   Your own   Woodrow

I am finding, you see, what it is to write a letter away from home.

W.

ALS (WP, DLC).

From Ellen Axson Wilson

My own darling,   Princeton June 20/92

Your dear letters, two of them, reached me this morning and I cannot tell you how welcome they were. How delightful that the new sister is such a complete success! You make me feel "desolated," as the French would say, to think that I am not to know her for nobody knows when! Is there absolutely *no* chance of inducing them to come here?

Poor poor Jimmie! What madness in him to work as he did! And it surely was not necessary. If I had been his wife I would not have *allowed* him to, for a million dollars! I heard something of it while there,—how he would sit up the whole of every night while the legislature was in session in order to see to the state printing. How much harder it must make it for them all to think that it was a needless sacrifice of his life. How does Josie seem— in health—and in general development too? You know we have not seen him since he became a man? Have you talked over his prospects with him? Is there any future for him on that paper?[1] & will marriage bind him hopelessly to that business?

What do you think of George and Wilson?[2] I suppose of course you will talk over George's plans and studies with him carefully. And what are Father's plans, and when will we see him here?

I am glad that you find the weather tolerable; my one consolation in the heat here is that at least you are not losing anything pleasant by being away, and that it *can't* be much worse there. Yet it does seem a most unseasonable 'change of base,'—and oh, I shall be glad beyond measure to have you back again. You do not know, dear, how constantly my thoughts dwell on you,—never about you, how my heart turns *always* to you, "as a dove to her window";—and how that heart "thrills at thought of what *you* are"—you incomparable one!

And not only is the heart thrilled but the *mind* as well. To think of you, dear, is a pleasure like that derived from a perfect picture or poem. It is as if a master artist had conceived a grand ideal, "had seen it steadily and seen it whole," and then with truly majic skill had been able to *realize* his vision. How often the grand conception is there while the execution shows only rude strength; and there again the details are exquisite but the design petty. Yet we are told on good authority that "all *great* art is delicate";—and Shakspeare greatest of all,—beyond all others in largeness and clearness of vision, grasp of his subject, power of insight and sympathy and characterazation,—every element of *strength* in short,—has also the most exquisite touch, the passages of most fairy-like beauty, of most melting tenderness. So too the masterpiece which it is the delight of my life to contemplate has the strength of the strongest without that taint of the *brutal* that sometimes attends it; the *power* of genius and of the born leader with the added fascinations of a sympathetic nature, of sensitiveness, and of a refined taste. And added to all that again a *beauty* of character—a tenderness and *charm* and lovableness beyond the power of words to describe. "A mouth for mastery and manful work, a certain brooding sweetness in the eyes, a brow the harbour of fair thought."[3] Ah truly such a man is the noblest work of God,—grander than a whole material universe. To see such a one and *realize* what one sees makes one catch one's breath with the wonder of it,

> "like some watcher of the skies,
> When a new planet swims into his ken."[4]

Ah I know you think that my love is the medium through which you loom so large. But why then, sir, does the most casual visitor to the house speak in exactly the same strain? With all of them the wonder is the same, viz., the perfect union in your mind and character and disposition of those elements of *magnificent* strength and *exquisite* beauty usually found dissociated. Truly you are an instrument fit for the gods,—steel of the finest temper, strongest yet keenest and most beautiful of weapons!

And by the way, methought that in a dream I heard that good blade lament because, forsooth, it was not a—*hammer*! It may have been the hammer of *Thor* that it envied, yet *that* hammer though it made some noise in the world *achieved* but little. And Thor himself was but a burly brute;—not exactly the god one would choose to serve. But how I run on. It is high time to say goodnight, dear heart. With love unspeakable I am now and forever   Your own   Eileen.

ALS (WC, NjP).
    [1] The Clarksville, Tenn., *Progress-Democrat.* See J. R. Wilson to WW, June 21, 1891, Vol. 7.
    [2] She refers of course to Annie's sons.
    [3] For Ellen's earlier use of this quotation, see EAW to WW, April 3, 1892, n. 1, Vol. 7.
    [4] From Keats's "On First Looking into Chapman's Homer."

To Ellen Axson Wilson

My own darling,   Columbia, S. C., 21 June, 1892
    I begin betimes to-day—to finish my letter of yesterday.
    Cousin Kate bears up as well as could have been expected. Father and I went to see her Saturday morning, and the interview was, of course, intensely painful: but she talked very sensibly and bravely. Her children[1] are, for the present, with Aunt Felie:[2] she herself with a cousin. She will probably go back into her own little house again in a few weeks. We went to see uncle James, Aunt Felie, and Marion the day I got here. Uncle James bears the terrible blow he has received with the quiet fortitude of a Christian of the highest type—nobly, beautifully, touchingly; and Aunt Felie and Marion with much more dignity than I expected.
    Dear father began his restless vacation career by leaving yesterday for New York—going, as usual, to 33 East 22nd. St.[3] He seems really much stronger in health: I had not hoped even to find him so well, after what he has gone through. He does not seem to have any definite plans as yet.
    I think I will reserve till I reach home my full description of our new sister. I like her thoroughly, and admire her sincerely—and she is certainly a rare little tid-bit of pretty flesh and blood. She has great good sense and delicacy of feeling, I find; and I am immensely pleased that Josie should have such a wife: I believe she will manage him just enough and in just the right

way. The only 'but' to the characterization is, that she would hardly satisfy an *intellectual* man. For all her sense and attractiveness, she is neither literary nor suggestive—wise and bright, but not wise and bright delightfully—not an image or a spirit to haunt, to startle, or waylay—but simply a fine little woman, pretty, affectionate, modest, and wise in practical affairs. Fortunately (though quite inexplicably) 'Dode' is not an intellectual or literary man, but simply a fine sensible fellow, needing just such a wife,—and no more.

I have just engaged passage, sweetheart, in a steamer which leaves Charleston on Friday afternoon at 5:50, and which will be due in New York about the same time on Sunday, or eight or ten hours later: the passage is from 48 to fifty-six hours. I can't telegraph from New York, of course, even if I get into New York early enough Sunday afternoon, Princeton being hermetically sealed on the day; but you may expect me (God willing) sometime on Monday—of course the train I take will depend upon the steamer's time of arrival. I keep perfectly well, darling, barring a little of my familiar bowel trouble, which is very slight—almost *normal.* All join me in the warmest possible expressions of love. As for myself, I love you in a wise which I shall try to particularize next time. It's too long—& too pleasant—a story to hurry through with. My whole life is wrapped up in you, my wife, my darling!   Your own   Woodrow.

ALS (WP, DLC).
    [1] Fitz William, identified in EAW to WW, May 6, 1892, n. 2, Vol. 7, and James Woodrow, born June 9, 1889. Mrs. Woodrow would bear a daughter, Katharine Hamilton Woodrow, on December 23, 1892.
    [2] Felie or Melie Baker Woodrow, wife of Dr. James Woodrow.
    [3] That is, to visit his friend, Elizabeth Bartlett Grannis. Dr. Wilson had just resigned from the Southwestern Presbyterian University.

From Ellen Axson Wilson

My own darling,   Princeton June 21/92

Another day has almost gone—the end of the first week is at hand, and there will not be at most more than another week in all! Ah, how glad I am! I hope tomorrow's letter will tell me your plans. If as you expected you take the steamer on Saturday no letter from me after tomorrow's would reach you. That sounds delightful, for it makes the time of your home-coming seem nearer. We are thinking of having an excursion ourselves. Anna has never seen the ocean and has set her heart on it. I have been making enquiries and Miss [Henrietta] Ricketts and others say that Long Branch is the most accessible place and the cheapest to reach. It is $2.50 for the round trip. You go at nine o'clock and get back at seven. So we are thinking of going with Ed & all the children—leaving the servants at home. But I havn't decided,—am also thinking of sending her alone with Ed. I hate to start out again with those children. We are waiting to see if the weather will get a little cooler, before we decide. I wish I knew if it would be very inhospitable to let her go with Ed. It is an easy trip though, takes no longer than to go to Phila.

By the way I should like it, dear, if you would call on Mrs. Dr. [Theodore M.] Dubose. You know it [is] very near Bro. George's? And it would be next best to seeing Rose, for Bev. could tell her about you!

What about that lot?[1] You remember you were to do all you could to secure the title?

But it is tea-time (we are having early tea) and I must close this hasty scrawl. We are all perfectly well, dear,—oh how I hope you are the same. Give my dearest love to Father and to *both* the dear sisters and both the dear brothers. How charming it would be to have a majic mirror and to be able to watch that loved Columbia circle, especially to see *my own own* darling: oh how sweet is that word 'mine'! To think that after all you belong more to me than to all those others, and that I belong *altogether to you.* Am now and forever   Your little wife   Eileen

ALS (WC, NjP).
[1] The lot in Buena Vista, N. C., that Wilson had purchased through Dr. George Howe, Jr. See G. Howe, Jr., to WW, July 30, 1891, Vol. 7.

To Stockton Axson

My dear Stock.,   Columbia, South Carolina, 22 June, 1892

I am down here to meet Josie and his bride. They were married last Wednesday, the 15th, just one week ago; arrived here Thursday night; and your humble servant joined the family party on the following morning, Friday. They seem extremely happy, and certainly Josie is a lucky dog to get a wife so attractive and so sensible. You have seen her, and know that she is very pretty: she is also sweet, sensible, and modest, capable, I think I perceive, of ruling Josie just enough and in just the right way. We like and admire her sincerely—and feel very comfortable about the future of the young couple. Kate is not literary or suggestive, but neither is Josie: so that part of it is all right. On the other hand, Josie is not always wise and prudent, and Kate seems to be both—and to be able to supply Josie with what he needs in that line gently, sweetly, without irritation—all of which is de-lightful.

I leave for home on Friday, the 24th, by way of Charleston, on the New York steamer. This ought to get me in Princeton by Monday morning, if we have ordinarily good weather for the voyage. I am anxious to hear that you will join us there the latter part of the week, to spend just as much of the Summer with us as you can possibly spare us. Ellie and I have been wondering very anxiously what plans you have formed, if you have formed any, for next year—and we have been hoping very earnestly that you have formed some plan which will spare you to us for the vacation. Write to me as soon as you can.

Miss Anna Harris and Mrs. Bird, of Baltimore, spent Com-mencement with us—and Miss Harris is, I am glad to say, with Ellie still. Ed. arrived all right and seems in excellent shape.

Sister Annie, bro. George, Josie and sister Kate—*all* join me in warmest love. They love you here as you would wish to be loved.

Your affectionate brother,   Woodrow Wilson

ALS (WP, DLC).

To Ellen Axson Wilson

My own darling,   Columbia 22 June, '92

Your sweet letters are such a comfort to me: you are so much needed in this little family company! We all love you and want you so earnestly and so constantly! As for your poor lover, his separation from you at this particular time, and under these particular circumstances is peculiarly tragical. Seeing this dear young couple here in their first happiness of married love in-evitably makes me think of another bride of seven years ago: and the yearning with which thoughts of her fill my heart keeps it on a tense strain which it is sometimes almost impossible to en-dure! It is not that I want my *bride* again: I want my little *wife* of the present. All that she has been and become to me *since* that happy season seven years ago crowds in upon my heart and makes it seem impossible that I should be able to do without her for a single moment more. Ah, if I had known *then* what I had gained—what accession of life and strength and joy—what infinite intimacy of sympathy—how my joy was to grow and my life to be increasingly beautified and dignified by the sweet companion-ship I had gained—how much more even than I did should I have striven to make my darling happy. I feel that I have now some-thing so much better than a charming bride—a perfect wife, who has brought untold treasures of sweet experience into my life; and yet all that experience seems to go back to and adorn that precious little bride of several years ago; and it all makes me yearn for the peerless little *woman* who is still my bride—always my bride—and yet so much more besides—her charm ever *fresh*, as if she were but just won, and yet her power old, deep and ineradicable as if it had been penetrating my heart for a whole life-time. A wife like my darling is so much sweeter than a bride, so much *more* than a bride, and yet so *like* a bride, so fresh and surprising in her charm, so constantly disclosing new provocations to love and new sources of delight. Ah, darling, was there ever so perfect a union as ours—so sweet a love, so perennial a joy! I am filled with wonder and with a sort of awed rapture whenever I think of it all.

All send unbounded love to you, my sweet pet. Two more letters, and then I start for the sweetest home, the loveliest wife in the world!   Your own   Woodrow.

Warmest regards to Miss Harris—kisses uncounted for the children.

ALS (WC, NjP).

From Ellen Axson Wilson

My own darling,   Princeton June 22/92

I enclose two letters received this morning thinking you might wish to answer them at once.

You remember we decided to hold that land at $25.00 a front foot for the upper two hundred feet and $20.00 a front foot for the rest. Do you know who this would-be purchaser is?[1]

Mr. Haskins letter is interesting, is it not? It is nice that he and Mr. Turner are getting on so well.[2] The Wis. catalogue came too. That University seems to be on a regular "boom." What *do* you suppose possessed Mr. Chamberlin to leave when things were so flourishing?[3] By the way, when you answer this *please* tell Mr. Haskins how you thought a little this spring of "going West" and mention your Ill. offer.[4] It would be *such* fun for you to have this one too.[5] I should like to keep the Princeton trustees in the hottest kind of water on your account until they were shaken out of their selfish lethargy in the matter of salaries.

I have had no letter from you this morning, dear, and feel of course very blank, but I hope it will come by a later mail. Have been re-reading for consolation the sweet one received yesterday—

the one written on Sunday. I am certainly obliged to Mrs. Bird for speaking so kindly of me. And as I told you I had exactly the same experience with her; she praised you to me in just the right way and for just the right things. She is a clever woman as well as a sweet one.

Oh I am *so glad*, love, that you miss me even there, among all those so near and dear to you. Speaking of selfishness I fear it is *very* selfish to feel actually a thrill of delight because my husband says he is "forlorn"! But after all I know he is not *too* forlorn,— just forlorn *enough*! For besides the love and companionship of all that dear circle he knows that somebody *is* "particularly"— *passionately*—devoted to him,—is thinking of him every moment and wearying for him, more than she ought I fear,—is counting the days and hours 'till his return—is *loving* him with all the depth & strength & tenderness and passion of which woman's heart is capable. With best love to all & kisses for dear little Annie

Your own   Eileen

I will not write again unless I hear of some change of plan in today's or tomorrow's letter. May you have a voyage all that is pleasant and prosperous, dear heart, and reach me safe and well— and soon!

ALS (WC, NjP).
  1 This letter referring to the Wilsons' property on Washington Street is missing.
  2 This letter from Charles Homer Haskins is missing. "Mr. Turner" was Frederick Jackson Turner.
  3 Thomas Chrowder Chamberlin had resigned the presidency of the University of Wisconsin to accept the chairmanship of the Department of Geology at the University of Chicago.
  4 That is, the offer of the presidency of the University of Illinois, about which there is much correspondence in Vol. 7.
  5 Haskins had obviously expressed the hope that Wilson might succeed Chamberlin.

Two Letters to Ellen Axson Wilson

My own darling,   Columbia, South Carolina   23 June, 1892

What a precious letter this is that reached me this morning, that extravagant letter of Monday, in which my love pours forth so delightfully her estimate of her husband—with so sweet an eloquence, and with such circumstance of clear detail that I almost believe what she says, as I read! It is all too beautiful and too delightfully said not to be true,—with such a ferver of passionate love and such an elevation of generous admiration as almost to make it too *sacred* to be disbelieved. My love! my precious little queen! how shall a man repay such perfect devotion as yours! Mrs. Bird was telling me on my way down to Baltimore with her that you had told her that your mission in life was to give me faith in myself, confidence of my own powers. Whether you will succeed in doing that or not I cannot foretell—even if you were to succeed, I do not believe that I could bring myself to tell you so, so sweet is it to have you try! But you do abundantly and constantly succeed in exhilerating me with a delight in being loved and believed in which is rewarding beyond all expression. I could wish for no greater reward in the world, my darling, than the devoted love and support which you give me. Another woman's admiration and devotion might offend me: so few women have sufficient *delicacy* of admiration—sufficient mind—or, rather, the right sort of mind—to admire with. But your mind is so near, so strangely near, kin to mine that its praises are a pure delight. You love and praise me so exactly according to my own ideals: what you believe me to be is so perfectly *in tune* with what I could wish to be, that my heart thrills with perfect satisfaction at every word you speak! But I must not run on indefinitely. I must give *one* page to news and plans. The sum of the whole matter is, that I have given over my whole nature to the exquisite pleasure of loving you!

Josie and Kate left this morning, to return home by way of Asheville, Knoxville, etc, etc. Josie does not feel that he can stay away from his work longer than the first of July and he must have a day or two for straightening up the house, and moving the furniture which father left. They expect to reach home Saturday morning. I leave for Charleston to-morrow, Friday, morning at 6:50, reach C. at about eleven o'clock, and sail about 5:30 P. M. I will of course write to you from C. to-morrow.

All the dear ones here join me in love messages that ought to make your heart warm. I love you, ah how *passionately* I love you, my darling!   Your own   Woodrow

Cordial messages to Miss Harris

                                                  Charleston Hotel,
My own darling,   Charleston, S. C. 24 June 1892

I've just taken my dinner here and am about to go down to the steamer. I suppose—I fervently hope—that I shall reach you as soon as this letter does. But I *cannot* omit to write on this particular date, the seventh anniversary of our marriage! Ah, my darling, the day is just such a one as that on which we were married—and it would not be difficult for me to imagine this Savannah. My thoughts are full of you and of that sweet time— now made so much sweeter by a thousand tender memories! How can I sufficiently thank God for his infinite goodness to me in giving me *such* a wife for my strength and delight. If I am any of the wonderful things you say I am in that precious letter of Monday, it is almost wholly because of what you did for me seven years ago in acknowledging me—adopting me—as your own, and giving your life to me. Oh that I had you in my arms, my Eileen, my darling, that I might look into your eyes and tell you the thoughts of this anniversary. I will tell you when I come. This is just a preliminary confession, to mark the date itself.

I am perfectly well and looking forward to a pleasant voyage.

Your own   Woodrow

ALS (WC, NjP).

From Elijah Richardson Craven

My dear Sir: Philadelphia June 30th, 1892.

It gives me great pleasure to inform you that at the meeting of the Board of Trustees of the college of New Jersey held on the 13th instant, your salary was fixed at three thousand dollars ($3,000) per annum, with an allowance of five hundred dollars ($500.) for house rent.

I remain,   Yours, very truly,   E. R. Craven.

TLS (WP, DLC).

From Stockton Axson

[Cambridge, Mass.]

My dear Brother Woodrow: Monday [July 18, 1892].

Havent I heard you say that you know (either personally or in a business way) some of the officials of the Boston Public Library? It has occurred to me that if you do know any of them you might give me a note of introduction whereby the doors, now closed very tight against me might be opened.

I am not built in such a way as to be able to study one thing seven or eight hours a day. After giving of my morning to French I am not in condition to accomplish much in that line in the afternoon or evening. I dont want to study German at present because I want to keep my head quite clear for the French; in studying two languages at the same time I am always getting the various grammatical characteristics confused.

Thus I have on hand considerable time for other study, and if I could only get the books I should begin at once reading for my thesis.

The officials at the library however say that they cant let me have books—not even though I make a fifty-dollar deposit which I offered to do. True they referred me to the chief, a Mr Grey, saying that it is barely possible that I may be able to make some special arrangement with him. I have been unable as yet to find Mr Grey in his office. If you know Mr Grey or any of the other librarians, and could give me a note stating that I want to do some work that is not altogether child's play I might be better able to make the "special arrangement."

I dont know whether it is Harvard "atmosphere" or what it is, but some remarkable change has suddenly come over me in the matter of learning a language. I never got along so swimmingly in my life. The other evening I picked up a novel (French)—not the one that I am studying—and began to read without the dictionary, and found that I could read (of course skipping some words) from 25 to 30 pages an hour which is almost as fast as I can read English. I am afraid that there is something factitious about it, and that I will come to the ground with a thud soon.

I have had several rather remarkable encounters with old friends. I took my seat at the breakfast table a few mornings since and presently raising my eyes saw sitting opposite me an old class-mate and club-mate from the university of Ga. I got in a street car and found sitting there one of my fellow seminary men at Hopkins. I went into a hotel washroom and found one of the boys from Wesleyan. Notwithstanding these casual meetings however I am so much alone that I am almost forgetting how to talk. My own voice sounds strange to me when I am called upon to speak a chance word to some one.

You see I have no boarding house—only a room in a house where I never see the people. For two meals a day I go to the Foxcroft eating house here in Cambridge where I get a meal for from 12 to 20 cents. I get one square meal a day in Boston at some restaurant. So I am not thrown in personal contact with anyone.

I have another room in which I am forbidden to smoke—this thing is growing monotonous.

I send my best love to all.

Very affectionately yours   Stockton Axson
30 Irving St   Cambridge

P.S. I received the mail which you forwarded. I am much obliged to you.

ALS (WP, DLC) with WWhw notation on env.: "Ans. 20 July, '92."

To Stockton Axson

My dear Stock.,   Princeton, New Jersey, 20 July, 1892

It was a great pleasure to get your letter of Monday and read its exhilerating account of your progress towards being a Frenchman. From *you*, you self-distrustful rascal, such acknowledgments of success are positively exciting. I am more delighted than I can say.

I know Judge [Mellen] Chamberlain, the chief Librarian of the 'Boston Public'—no one else connected with it—and I enclose a letter to him[1] which I hope will serve your purpose. If he is out of town, suppose you serve it on his next subordinate in charge, who may have heard of me, and be ready to relax discipline upon proper introduction. I also enclose a note of introduction to Mr. [Horace Elisha] Scudder, editor of the *Atlantic*. You will find him at Houghton & Mifflin's, 4 Park St. I hope you will deliver it. He is genuinely cordial and thoroughly natural and delightful—and I am really anxious to have you meet him. I know he will be glad to see you,—particularly this dry season.

A letter from Ellie is one mail ahead of this one. We are all well; but there is absolutely no news. The Epoch[2] goes slowly and painfully forward without accident or incident. I hope you will be able to write often: for we love you and think about you more than you are at all likely to believe.

In a tired man's haste, but with the freshest possible affection.

Your affectionate brother   Woodrow Wilson

ALS (MB).

[1] Wilson's letter to Chamberlain has not been found.

[2] That is, Wilson's book, *Division and Reunion*. For a summary and review, see the Editorial Note, "Wilson's *Division and Reunion*."

From Joseph Ruggles Wilson

My precious son—   33 East 22nd St. N. York, July 29 [1892]

Your dear good letter is just received and is fully appreciated you may be sure. Love is too scarce an article with me these days to be treated otherwise than as a big bank bill by a poor fellow. In you I have immense comfort, for your heart is always in the right place—and after all it is heart more than head that controls the happiness of people. A great heart is—genius.

I saw Woodbridge[1] a moment yesterday in the street. The mercurial little fellow darted up to me, & said something about his family which I failed to comprehend perfectly—and was off again.

I went to Saratoga last week, but didn't care for it much except that its waters *are* good for me, & so may go again before the season ends.

I am expecting to go to you before many days—if only I can see the *Minutes*[2] fairly out which I look for each current hour. Yes—it is pretty hot, but my rooms here are truly comfortable at all hours even when 90° afflict. Be certain I love you & Ellie with all the heart I have. Give her all love accordingly

Your affc   Father.

Is there anything I can send you from this big town

ALS (WC, DLC).
   [1] The Rev. Samuel I. Woodbridge, identified in JRW to WW, May 25, 1892, n. 1, Vol. 7.
   [2] Dr. Wilson was still Stated Clerk of the General Assembly of the southern Presbyterian Church.

From Horace Elisha Scudder

My dear Wilson,   [Cambridge, Mass.] 9 August 1892

Are you a faithful reader of the Atlantic? If so, you may have observed an effort I have made this past year to have political subjects discussed not from a party point of view, but in a spirit which believes it possible to treat of great public questions philosophically and temperately. It will not do to make the Atlantic an organ of any party or of no party. Still less do I wish to have it a mere colorless medium for the transmission of political views of each side. I wish it to speak, when it does speak[,] in the interests of serious politics.

All this is preliminary to an enquiry whether you will not write a paper for the November number on The Two Programmes which shall be a critical examination of the platforms of the two parties in the light of party and presidential action in the past and of current political speeches. I know it is customary to treat these platform utterances with some contempt as if they were merely insincere catch-vote proclamations. Nevertheless they are the only documentary creeds with which we have to do; only interpreted carefully by the acts of the parties, whatever insincerity they may exhibit will come out; whatever political creed they announce will be tested.

It has occurred to me that I might go farther, and after I had your paper in print, without signature, I might ask for the annotation of an intelligent and representative man in each party. What do you say? I should be glad if I could have the paper by the end of August. It should be, I think, about eight pages in length.

I have assumed that it would be like other papers I have had anonymous,—an Atlantic editorial, just as the literary judgments are anonymous and adopted by the magazine. I should like it to read so that the person who examines it is unable to say whether it was written by a Republican or a Democrat. He might even fancy it was by Mr. Bryce!

With the best wishes, I am

Sincerely yours,   Horace E. Scudder.

ALS (Houghton Mifflin Letterpress Books, MH).

To John Franklin Jameson

My dear Jameson,   Princeton, New Jersey, 10 August, 1892

It is to speak only the sober truth to say that we were *delighted* by the news of your engagement.[1] We both think that you *deserve* a good wife; we both think it evident that you are going to *get* a good one, and one who is more than good, that is, delightful; and we both feel the circumstances a substantial contribution to our own happiness. You make us very anxious to meet Miss Elwell, by what you tell us of her: for we are actually willing to take what you say as true even when you are not speaking as an historian, but as a lover: I think we both, being lovers ourselves, are the *readier* to believe you, and like you better than ever, *because* you speak as a lover. If we can't see her as Miss Elwell, cannot we see her *very* soon after she becomes Mrs. Jameson? Can't you—won't you, bring her to see us then? My dear fellow, you have our heartiest, our gladest congratulations. It makes us very happy to know that you are happy in a way which seems to us the best and most elevating of all ways!

Yes, I am 'Epoch'-making, and that's all I am doing: there's no fun to be had in this dry little town in the summer. I am drawing near to the end of my task, having fought the war through; and, after I finish it, I shall probably take a couple of weeks 'off' in some manner of recuperation. Mrs. Wilson went South, as she expected, from Baltimore and spent about two months in a round of visiting among our relatives in Georgia and South Carolina. You can imagine my state in the meantime much better a year hence than you can now! After our term closed I spent ten days in the South with my brother and his bride. Ten days in Carolina in June were hardly refreshing; but my sea trip homeward, from

Charleston to New York was very invigorating indeed. Since then the 'Epoch.'

Mrs. Wilson joins me in all I have said, as well as in warmest regards to both yourself and your family. Will you not let us extend our messages of regard and congratulation to Miss Elwell, too? We are decidedly of the opinion that she, too, is to be congratulated.

Affectionately Yours,   Woodrow Wilson

ALS (J. F. Jameson Papers, DLC).

[1] Jameson's letter telling about his engagement to Sara Elwell is missing.

To Horace Elisha Scudder

Princeton, New Jersey,

My dear Mr. Scudder,   11 August, 1892.

Your kind and interesting letter of the 9th reached me last evening. It is a genuine, and very keen, disappointment to me that I *must* say that I cannot write the article you propose, on the Two Programmes. Yes, I have noticed, and noticed with very deep interest, the development of your plan of giving a place in the *Atlantic* to the sober and dispassionate discussion of the larger sort of political questions; and I have more than once wished that I might be a contributor. But I am spending this summer "vacation," as I spent the last, writing the "Epoch" of American history, 1829-1889, for the series of the Messrs. Longmans, Green, & Co. which Hart, of Harvard, is editing. It will take every bit of my time, from now till the moment I *must* seek a few days relaxation before our college term opens, to finish it—as it took all last Summer to write the first half of it. For it must be done before the "Autumn Printing." The writing of it puts one in excellent form for comparison of present programmes and policies with those of the past; but I dare not spare from it either the time or the *spirit* that would be needed for the composition of such an article as I should like to send you or you would like to publish.

I say it's a severe disappointment to me to decline because I think the plan of discussion you propose, and the tone you suggest for the main article, alike admirable, and just what ought to be desired, for such a campaign as the present promises to be, by the better sort of readers. I should be proud to be so employed.

I hope you have found some cool retreat from this overwhelming heat for your nights at least, and that you keep very well. I think I shall want a fan whenever I see or think of the little volume I am now writing.

With warmest regards,

Sincerely yours,   Woodrow Wilson.

TCL (RSB Coll., DLC).

To Robert Bridges

My dear Bobby,   Princeton, New Jersey, 18 August, 1892

I conclude, from the post-mark on the photographs you so thoughtfully sent me, that you are back from your jaunt abroad, and I want to write you a word of welcome and of thanks. I hope you enjoyed your trip as much as you expected—and a great deal more; and yet I am so accustomed to take comfort from the fact that you are so near as 743 Broadway that I can't help feeling glad that you are back, and that I *can* see you next time I go to New York. I am sincerely obliged to you for the photographs: they are a most welcome addition to my little collection. Write to me soon and give me a hint of how you are and how you fared while away.

I've carried out my programme for the 'vacation,' and am now nearing the end of that wretched little 'Epoch'—at least of the first draft of it. I trust it will need very little revision to be the final draft. I've put into it already almost everything I know—and some things that I don't *know*, but only believe. I am well and doing as well as might be expected.

I've also a matter of business. I send, by Express, this afternoon, the *mss.* of a story entitled "Thornton vs. Thornton," written by Mrs. Wilson's brother, Stockton Axson. I send it because I think it really worth publishing, and I send it addressed to you simply because I want to say a word about it.[1] The plot is commonplace; but the way in which it is handled is not; and I think that you will agree with me that the situation to which it leads up, so far from being commonplace, is both dramatic and treated with the fine simplicity of direct dramatic power. I believe you will like it.

Mrs. Wilson joins me in cordial regards,

As ever,   Affectionately Yours,   Woodrow Wilson

ALS (WC, NjP).

[1] It was never published in *Scribner's Magazine*, or, insofar as is known, elsewhere.

To Horace Elisha Scudder

My dear Mr. Scudder,   Princeton, New Jersey, 24 August, 1892.

The invitation so cordially and generously extended to me by Mrs. Scudder and yourself in your last letter[1] has gratified me more than I can say, and warmed me most delightfully in the region of the heart. It now appears, alas! as if I were not to be able to get away from home after all, so greatly do my tasks multiply as I seek to wade to t'other side of them; and I am afraid that I must, however keen the disappointment, decline the invitation. That it would be delightful, and wholly delightful, to come to you I have not a moment's doubt. The companionship, the quiet, and the recreation you offer me are all equally seductive to my taste. It requires real courage, and fortitude in labour, to decline. But, since it must be done, I can only thank you, and hope for some other chance to see you and to make Mrs. Scudder's acquaintance. *Some* day, I trust, I may become more of a circulating medium.

Most sincerely yours,   Woodrow Wilson.

TCL (RSB Coll., DLC).
[1] This letter is missing.

To Albert Bushnell Hart

Princeton, New Jersey,
My dear Professor Hart,   24 August, 1892.

No indeed, it is not now at all disagreeable to be asked how I come on with my 'Epoch,' inasmuch as I can report progress of which I am not ashamed,—unless, indeed, it be *too* rapid.

I am well into the heart of the next to the last of the twenty-one divisions, or chapters, into which I have divided my volume. I am summing up Grant's two administrations; and shall not tarry long on those which follow. They are "too contemporary."

It is true that this is in a sense my first draft; but I have made it with great pains, and very little revision will convert it into 'copy.' I think, therefore, that I can live up to my last promises, and send the whole thing to you, perhaps, by the first of October.

Portions of the proof of your own volume[1] came to me to-day. I shall look them over with great interest; in order to see, among other things, how much I can do in the way of following your plan of division. I don't know what hopes I can hold out to you in that matter. I have laboured all along to weave and knit my narrative together as closely as possible; and I have kept the pattern big and single; so that I do not know what dividing up it will bear. But I will deal honestly with you and make real test of the possibilities.

Do you desire the return of the proof you have sent me, or is it duplicate? If you wish it back, drop me a card and I will make haste.

Very sincerely Yours,   Woodrow Wilson

TCL (RSB Coll., DLC).
1 The second volume in the "Epochs of American History" Series, *Formation of the Union, 1750-1829* (New York and London, 1892).

A Notebook

[Aug. 28, 1892-June 5, 1899]

Inscribed on cover (WWhw): "THE STATE / NOTES."
Contents:

(a) WWhw and WWsh outline of "The Philosophy of Politics," printed below.

(b) WWT outline, "STATESMANSHIP. Studies in Politics," dated June 5, 1899, to be printed in a future volume.

(c) Random WWhw and WWsh memoranda printed at Jan. 26, 1895, Vol. 9.

(d) WWhw outline, *"Modern Politics: Studies in Political Philosophy."*

(e) WWhw outline, "The Idea of the State as affected by Modern Political Conditions."

(f) WWhw outline, *"Statesmanship: Studies in Politics."*

(WP, DLC).

A New Outline of "The Philosophy of Politics"[1]

Mem. 28 Aug., '92

I. *The Life of States.*
   (1) History of States
   (2) Their Nature
   (3) Their Structure
   (4) Their Ends and Functions.
II. *Political Stability:*
   The Nature, Sources, and Functions of Law.
III. *Political Liberty* (Obedience to the laws of the social organism)
IV. *Political Privilege* (Selection of those prepared to rule)
V. *Political Progress* (Modification by experience) Authority
VI. *Political Prejudice* (The statical force added to the law in society)

VII. *Political Expediency* (Political therapeutics)
VIII. *Political Morality* (Obedience to the laws of political prog-
ress)
IX. *Practical Politics* (The use of political means)

WWhw and WWsh memorandum in notebook described above.
    [1] See the earlier outline printed at Jan. 12, 1891, Vol. 7, and the Editorial
Note, "Wilson's First Treatise on Democratic Government," Vol. 5, pp. 54-58.

To James Cameron Mackenzie[1]

Princeton, New Jersey,
My dear Dr. Mackenzie,   9 September, 1892.
    I was sincerely obliged to you for your very kind letter about
my young brother-in-law;[2] and I am sorry that I have to trouble
you, thus late, about another case. I was in Lawrenceville on
Wednesday,[3] but you were away and I was unable to see you.
I have, therefore, to trouble you with a letter.
    I have a young nephew, George Howe, of South Carolina, who
is to enter here, if prepared, next year (1893-'4), and who deserves the best training he can get. Though a youngster, it is
already his ambition to make a scholar of himself and some
day occupy a college chair in the classics. Would it, do you
think, be possible to obtain for him, too, as well as for my
brother-in-law, to obtain [sic] a tolerably liberal scholarship at
Lawrenceville this year? The matter of expense is a critical one
with him, as with most southern boys; but I can give you an account of him (and I am sure he could give an account of himself
in the school work) which would qualify him for any such
assistance.
    I know that this is a very tardy application, and I am not
even sure yet that he is prepared for the Fourth Form. But, if
he could get a scholarship and a room either in the Fourth
Form House or with Mr. Raymond,[4] it would assist his parents
greatly in their decision; and it is possible that he might come,
if a few days late.[5]
    Pray pardon the haste and irregularity of this letter and be-
lieve me, with warm regards,

                        Very sincerely Yours,   Woodrow Wilson

WWTLS (WC, NjP).
    [1] Born Aberdeen, Scotland, Aug. 15, 1852. A.B., Lafayette College, 1878;
Ph.D., Lafayette, 1882; student, Princeton Theological Seminary, 1882-83; or-
dained to the Presbyterian ministry, 1885. Organized the present Lawrenceville
School in 1882 and served as headmaster until 1899, when he resigned to be-
come director of the Jacob Tome Institute in Port Deposit, Md. Founded the
Mackenzie School at Dobbs Ferry, N. Y., in 1901. Died May 10, 1931.

² Their previous correspondence, which concerned a scholarship for Edward Axson, is missing.

³ To see about enrolling Edward Axson and George Howe III in the School, which opened on September 15.

⁴ Charles Henry Raymond, who taught elocution at the School.

⁵ He did indeed come, even though he did not receive the scholarship, as WW to J. C. Mackenzie, Jan. 4, 1893, reveals.

EDITORIAL NOTE
WILSON'S TEACHING AT PRINCETON, 1892-93

The Department of Philosophy was once again reorganized in 1892,[1] and Wilson's courses and those offered by Winthrop More Daniels were listed in a new Section V, "Jurisprudence and Political Economy." For the catalogue for 1892-93, Wilson made sufficient changes in his copy for the preceding year to justify printing the altered version here:

3 I. Outlines of Jurisprudence: an exposition of Jurisprudence as an organic whole, exhibiting the nature of its subject-matter, its relationship to cognate branches of study, the inter-relationship of its several parts to each other, and their proper function and aim. Lectures and collateral reading. Junior and Senior Elective; first term [2], alternating with course 3 II. Given 1893-94. Professor Wilson. *Holland*: Elements of Jurisprudence.

4 I. International Public Law. Text-book, lectures and collateral reading. Junior and Senior Elective; second term [2], alternating with course 4 II. Given 1893-94. Professor Wilson. *Hall*: A Treatise on International Law, 3rd edition, 1890.

3 II. General Public Law: its historical derivation, its practical sanctions, its typical outward forms, its evidence as to the nature of the state and as to the character and scope of political sovereignty. Lectures and collateral reading. Junior and Senior Elective [2], alternating with course 3 I. Given 1892-93. Professor Wilson.

4 II. Comparative Constitutional Law. Lectures and collateral reading. Junior and Senior Elective; second term [2], alternating with course 4 I. Given 1892-93. Professor Wilson. *Cooley*: American Constitutional Law.

5. History of Law: in general, and as exhibited in the growth of typical national systems. Lectures and collateral reading. Senior Elective; first term [2]. Professor Wilson.

Students are advised to consult with Professor Wilson before taking course 5.

6. Administration. Lectures and collateral reading. Senior Elective; second term [2]. Professor Wilson. . . .[2]

In public law, Wilson repeated the course of 1890-91 and used the notes described and referred to in the Editorial Note, "Wilson's Teaching at Princeton, 1890-91," in Volume 7. For his course on

[1] For its organization in 1891, see the Editorial Note, "Wilson's Teaching at Princeton, 1891-92," Vol. 7.

[2] *Catalogue of the College of New Jersey at Princeton . . . 1892-93* (Princeton, n.d.), pp. 40-41.

what he now–in 1892–called "Comparative Constitutional Law," he used the notes for his course of 1891 on American constitutional law, adding notes for new lectures on legislatures and the courts, state and federal.[3] In administration, Wilson also repeated the course that he had given during the two preceding years.[4] His assignments and recommended collateral reading for his courses in administration and constitutional law are printed at January 17 and 25 and April 18, 1893.

Wilson's Course in the History of Law

Wilson put most of his energy during the first semester of 1892-93 into his new senior elective course in the history of law. There is in his papers a two-page bibliography of works on the history of law.[5] Preparation of this bibliography may have marked the beginning of his systematic research for the course. In addition, he took, apparently at about the same time, extensive notes on Rudolph Sohm, *The Institutes of Roman Law*, cited earlier in this series, and on Samuel Epes Turner, *A Sketch of the Germanic Constitution from Early Times to the Dissolution of the Empire* (New York and London, 1886).[6] He also drew up what seems to have been a rough outline of his course.[7] Then, probably in mid-September, he began to type his notes, completing them on January 16, 1893. Midway in his labor, on November 28, 1892, he wrote to Albert Bushnell Hart: "I never had less time in my life, for *anything* [outside]. I am preparing and delivering from day to day a course of lectures on the History of Law, and you can imagine the enormous amount of reading and sifting I have to do to make such a course even a tolerably adequate and suggestive one. It takes every pound of power I have."

Wilson repeated his history of law course in 1893-94 without, it would appear, making any significant changes in or additions to his notes. However, when he gave the course again in 1894-95, he wrote a number of new notes for lectures and revised or, as he put it, "recast" some of his 1892-93 notes for the first two thirds of the course of 1894-95. For the final third of the course that year, he used notes from 1892-93. In December 1895 he added new notes for a lecture or lectures on French law. The notes were now complete, and Wilson continued to use them as long as he gave the course. This reconstructed and expanded set will be published at September 22, 1894, in Volume 9.

Since there were only about thirteen students enrolled in the history of law in 1892-93, no syllabus was printed for the course. Indeed, none seems ever to have been printed. No student classroom notes seem to have survived from 1892-93, or from the next year. And since Wilson also apparently destroyed about two thirds of his

[3] This course is described in the Editorial Note, "Wilson's Teaching at Princeton, 1890-91," and the notes, including the additions made in 1893, at March 10, 1891, all in Vol. 7.

[4] Again, see the Editorial Note, "Wilson's Teaching at Princeton, 1890-91," Vol. 7.

[5] WWhw MS. beginning, "Leist, W. B., 'Alt-Arisches Jus Gentium,' Jena (Gustav Fischer) 1889."

[6] These are on loose pages in WP, DLC.

[7] Loose pages, WP, DLC, beginning "*Definition* of Law. *Possibility* of having *a* history of Law."

1892-93 notes after recasting them in 1894, it is impossible either to reconstruct his notes accurately and fully or to list his lecture topics for the course of 1892-93. However, the examinations printed at December 13, 1892, and at February 2, 1893, give a good overview of Wilson's coverage and emphases.

It might be said in conclusion that Wilson originally designed his course in the history of law as one for a limited enrollment of advanced undergraduates and as the capstone of his undergraduate curriculum at Princeton. However, in 1894 he added a course in the history of English common law because his history of law course covered only ancient law and its spread and transformation in western continental Europe.

A Book Review[1]

[October 1892]

THE PLATFORM: Its Rise and Progress. By Henry Jephson. In two volumes. New York: Macmillan & Co.

Mr. Henry Jephson has zeal and industry, but no sense of humor. We are told in an advertisement by his publishers that he has been private secretary to the late Mr. Forster and to Sir George Otto Trevelyan; and doubtless the capacity for taking pains seriously and without too keen a perception of the ridiculous is an excellent quality in a private secretary. It is not, however, so serviceable an endowment for authorship,—unless, indeed, there be genius to elevate it above the commonplace. Burke was secretary to that lucky man "Single Speech Hamilton"; he had a capacity for taking pains which no man ever surpassed, and as little sense of humor as an Irishman could possibly have; but he had a genius for understanding political subjects, of which no trace can be found in Mr. Jephson's useful volumes. That he has no sense of humor is evident without opening the book. His "Platform" is not the American party document, but the English "stump,"—the hustings, in short; and it gives one's imagination whimsical exercise enough to conceive the "rise and progress" of this structure, its "birth," "suppression," "revival," and "emancipation." It requires a robust tolerance in matters of language to endure without wincing the bold imagery of such titles, to admit "platforming" into your mind as a synonym of speech-making, and to rejoice soberly in its "ultimate triumph."

The worst of it is, that a man who does not scrutinize and test his words seldom discriminates in his thought. Mr. Jephson's careless audacity in the use of phrases is but a counterpart of his reckless and superficial manner of thinking. This is the way he begins:

"A century and a half ago, three, and only three, great political institutions were in existence in this country, dividing between them the government of the kingdom—Crown, Lords, and Commons. In process of time there arose the fourth—the Press. . . . And still later, almost, in fact, within the memory of living men, there has arisen one more—the Platform." "The Platform" [he adds] "is the feature of our political constitution which distinguishes us alike from all the forms of government that the wit of man has contrived in the past, or that the civilized states of Europe have attained to in the present.["]

This "institution," too, is of a most broad and general character. "As a comprehensive definition," says our author, "I should say that every political speech at a public meeting, excluding those from the Pulpit, and those in Courts of Justice, comes within the meaning of 'the Platform.'" Of course there is a wide and liberal significance much in vogue of late for the word "institution." In this catholic sense afternoon teas are an institution, and swallow-tailed coats, and silk hats, and prize fights. But the word, when used after that fashion, is too big and vague to be of service to anyone but a newspaper reporter; and it must sadly discourage Mr. Jephson's judicious readers to find him upon the very first page of his two volumes speaking as if the Press and the Platform were institutions of the same sort as Crown, Lords, and Commons,—integral and organic parts of the political institution of the kingdom, not playing upon the government, but themselves constituting part of it. What place can such crude and shallow reasoning have in the elucidation of politics? Mr. Jephson often quotes Burke, but it is hard to believe that he has ever read him; quite impossible to believe that he has ever understood him. If he really knew his Burke, he would find it difficult to conceive of occasional public gatherings of no fixed or certain membership as forming parts of the ordered constitution of the kingdom. Let the government be never so sensitive to public opinion, public opinion still remains an influence,—does not itself become the government. The thermometer is exceedingly sensitive to temperature, but the temperature does not on that account become the thermometer. The wind sends a ship prosperously on her voyage, or disastrously upon the rocks, without becoming sails and hull and keel,—such mechanism as the helmsman can steer. Platform speakers thunder at the government, and more or less directly affect its action; but they neither coöperate nor agree: they may furnish the data for legislation, but they do not legislate; they may signal the steersman, but they do not steer; they may insist, but they do not conclude.

The real subject of these volumes is the history of political agitation in England, and of the intercourse, or rather inter-communication, between members of Parliament and their constituents on the hustings. Its theories and doctrines are foolish, but its material is full, its treatment consistent, and its usefulness unmistakable. The history of the public meeting, and of the various stages of its legal recognition, as well as of the slow establishment of a tolerant feeling towards it as a means of political agitation on the part of the ruling juntos and the conservative class in England, is clearly and intelligently told. The author's exposition of the legal aspects of the right of public meeting and free discussion needs to be given adequacy and distinctness by the perusal of such clarified explanations of the same matters as are to be found in Professor Dicey's "Law of the Constitution," and his treatment of the public meeting as a factor in English politics gains proper perspective only when read in connection with the other phases of constitutional development during the same period; but, if thus corrected and correlated, his descriptive and explanatory matter is sound and safe enough.

The book is an English book, and of course has nothing to do with the American "Platform," which one would have expected a thorough writer at least to mention. But Mr. Jephson says not a word about it. Doubtless it would have been awkward to mention American public meetings, and the careful documentary embodiment of their conclusions which we know as the "Platform," after committing himself to the judgment that such meetings embody the feature of the English constitution which distinguishes it from all others. His other conclusions would have been not a little strengthened if he could have seen far enough away from home to descry us here upon our distant continent. The organization of opinion outside of Congress is probably as perfect here as he could desire for any thesis that his book contains. It is in America, no doubt, that public opinion comes as near governing, and yet as subtly differs from the government itself, as anywhere in the world. But no man who lacks a sense of humor could considerately be advised to study us.   WOODROW WILSON.

Printed in the Chicago *Dial*, XIII (Oct. 1, 1892), 213-14.
 1 For the correspondence relating to this review, see F. F. Browne to WW, Feb. 10, 1892, Vol. 7.

From the Minutes of the Princeton Faculty

5 5' P.M., Wednesday, Oct. 5th, 1892.

. . . Prof. Woodrow Wilson was appointed a member of the Committee on Out-Door Sports.[1]

[1] Wilson served on this committee until he became President of Princeton University in 1902.

5 5' P.M., Wednesday, Oct. 12, 1892

. . . *Resolved* That a Committee consisting of the Dean [James O. Murray], the President ex officio, Prof. [Henry C.] Cameron, Prof. [William M.] Sloane & Prof. Wilson be appointed to consider the question of the proper date for celebrating the *One hundred and fiftieth Anniversary of the College* with a view to recommending the observance on that date to the Trustees.[1]

College of New Jersey, "Minutes of the Faculty, 1888-95," bound ledger book (University Archives, NjP).
[1] This committee's report is printed at Oct. 26, 1892.

A News Item

[Oct. 22, 1892]

COLUMBUS DAY.

The 400th anniversary of the discovery of America was appropriately celebrated to-day, with the following exercises: The orator of the day, Dr. Woodrow Wilson, of Princeton, was escorted to the flagpole by the School. . . .[1]

Printed in the Lawrenceville, N.J., *Lawrence*, XIII (Oct. 22, 1892), 1.
[1] This report goes on to give the program, including an "Oration by Dr. Wilson." An editorial in *The Lawrence*, XVIII (Feb. 12, 1898), 2, later recalled: "It was in 1892 that it was decided to celebrate Columbus Day. On a bright October morning Professor Woodrow Wilson, in the presence of a large company of people, made a notable patriotic address on the discovery of America. On this occasion the School flag was run up for the first time."

To Albert Bushnell Hart

Princeton, New Jersey,

My dear Professor Hart,   25 October, 1892.

I have been expecting almost daily to write to you, ever since the receipt of your last letter, and the proofs of portions of your book: because I have been daily expecting to have something to write to you about.

I have hung fire because of tribulations with my MSS. After I finished the first draft of it, I found that it was a great deal too long. I have gone over it again and again in search of matter to cut out; and I have found a great deal. I have cut out somewhat over eighty pages. To cut it any further would mutilate the whole. Rather than do that, I would keep it until next Summer, and re-write it. For there is no possible chance, I find once more, for any-thing of that kind in term time. I have been sorely put to it to re-vise the stuff in term time, and supply the pedagogical machinery of bibliographies and side notes. This must be my excuse for all delays.

I sincerely hope that you will like the result of my work. I send you to-day, by Express, the first two chapters, the Preface, and the Suggestions. The Preface will explain my principle of division into chapters. Treating the subject as I have done, it has proved impossible to increase the number of chapters; but I have made the number of sectional divisions very great indeed, meeting your suggestions in that matter, I believe, fully.

The Introductory chapter seemed to me indispensable, if the book was to stand on its own legs as an independent work.

The manuscript I send you is ready for the printer, and I stand ready to read proof at once. I shall write the publishers to that intent to-day. The other chapters lack only their 'machinery,' and may be expected to follow very shortly.

Still in great haste,

Very sincerely Yours,   Woodrow Wilson

TCL (RSB Coll., DLC).

From the Minutes of the Princeton Faculty

5 5' P.M., Wednesday, Oct. 26th, 1892

. . . The Committee appointed to consider the question of the proper date for celebrating *The One hundred and fiftieth Anniversary of the Founding of the College* made the following report which was adopted and ordered to be communicated to the Board of Trustees:

Report of the Committee on the 150th Anniversary.

Your Committee, consisting of the President, the Dean, and Professors Cameron, Sloane and Woodrow Wilson, appointed to consider the proper date for the celebration of the one hundred and fiftieth anniversary of the founding of the College, beg leave to submit the following report:

The facts upon which the decision of the Committee was based are these: The Colonial records of the State show that the first Charter of the College passed the Great Seal of the Province, and was attested by the President of His Majesty's Council, on the 22nd of October, 1746. No official records of the first Board of Trustees remain to us, and it is impossible to fix the date of the actual organization of the College. It is probable that it was actually organized at some time between February and April of the year 1747. The second Charter of the College bears the date the 14th of September, 1748, and was accepted by the Trustees the following month. There is no question of the continuity of the College under the two Charters. The second was but an amendment and enlargement of the provisions of the first.

The one hundredth anniversary of the founding of the College was celebrated, by direction of the Board of Trustees, on Commencement Day, the 30th. of June, 1847.—a date which, it will be observed, corresponds with none of the dates already mentioned.

Inasmuch, therefore, as the date of the legal creation of the College is clearly determined, and the date of its actual organization impossible of determination; and inasmuch as the 30th. of June, 1847, seems to have been fixed upon by the Trustees as the one hundredth anniversary of the foundation of the College for reasons of convenience simply, and not because it was in fact the anniversary of any ascertained date connected with the early history of the Institution, your Committee is strongly of the opinion that the proper date for the anniversary of the founding of the College will be the 22nd. of October, 1896. Its decision in the matter is the more confirmed by reason of the consideration that such a celebration can be given no really distinctive character if connected with the exercises of a regular College Commencement; whereas October recommends itself by reason of the beauty of the season, the convenience of foreign visitors, and the fact that the College is at that time living its characteristic life and is on that account the more interesting to strangers.

Your Committee therefore recommends that the Board of Trustees be requested by the Faculty to fix the 22nd. of October, 1896, as the date for the celebration of the one hundred and fiftieth anniversary of the founding of the College.[1]

[1] The Trustees, at their meeting on November 10, 1892, accepted the report of the faculty committee and authorized President Patton to appoint, "at his convenience," a committee to plan for the sesquicentennial celebration. Patton appointed a special trustees' committee on the sesquicentennial on February 9, 1893. "Minutes of the College of New Jersey, Vol. VII, February 10, 1887-February 8, 1894," bound ledger book (University Archives, NjP).

An Essay[1]

[Oct. 27, 1892]

THE TRUE AMERICAN SPIRIT.

The true American spirit is a spirit that chooses and does not
obsequiously submit. If the American spirit is different from the
spirit of any other nation it is so because of the history of America. That history has been a history of choice and independence.
A high-spirited and adventurous people chose a pioneer life on a
new continent in preference to submitting to opinions and institutions of which they did not approve, and having subdued that
new continent to the uses of civilization they established upon
it a government which was meant to have as its fundamental doctrine the right of every man to choose his own principles and his
own life.

This is sometimes said to be simply the spirit of democracy,
but it is worth observing that American democracy, if interpreted
by its history, is a democracy with a character quite peculiarly
its own. It is not the same either in principle or in practice as
the democracy of France or the democracy of a South American
republic. It is not a democracy which has been thought out, but
a democracy which has been lived out to its present development.
It has been wrought by struggle rather than by meditation. It
rests upon what has been achieved, not simply upon what has
been believed. It is, in brief, a continuation of the institutional
history of England—English institutions developed upon an
American scale and with American modifications.

The principle of other democracies is that the majority governs
and has the right to govern. The principle of our democracy is
that the majority decides between parties, and even sometimes
between measures, but that officers and the law govern. This is a
distinction which deserves more attention than it generally receives. Majorities, of course, as a matter of fact, never govern,
unless we are to use the word govern in a sense so loose that it is
no sense at all. The only use of majorities is to show how the
people are disposed toward those who do govern—their representatives and rulers. The people, under our system, choose men
for office according as their personal preferences are for one candidate or another, or because of their preferences concerning
the opinions and purposes of one candidate as contrasted with
another. Or, rather—for this we know to be much nearer the
actual truth of the matter—they assent to the selections of candidates made by this or the other small group of men belonging to a party organization. They vote sometimes, also, at long

intervals, upon the question whether or not some new provision or set of provisions shall be put into a State constitution or into the Constitution of the Union. But in these latter
cases they vote simply either "Yes" or "No," taking the whole
amendment or set of amendments together, without opportunity
to discriminate in their voting between the good and the bad
features contained in what the legislature or a convention has
proposed. And if the negative votes prevail, and the changes suggested are defeated, that is the last of their direct participation
in the matter; they cannot suggest other changes which they
would like better no matter how strong may be their desire that
some reform should be accomplished.

To select one of two candidates designated by party leaders
is not to govern. Neither is it governing to say "Yes" or "No"
simply to the choice which a few men have made of constitutional
provisions. The governing in a democracy, like the governing in a
monarchy or an aristocracy, is done by a very small body of persons, legislators and executive officers. The difference is that in
an aristocracy or a monarchy those who govern can get on for
long periods together without the sympathy and support of the
mass of the people until an insurrection calls halt upon them or a
revolution strips them of power and drives them out, whereas in
a democracy the means are provided by the standing arrangements of the government for frequently, even periodically, testing
the temper of the people upon questions of policy, and parties
are formed for the purpose of keeping the government squared
in conduct with the assent of the people. There is no less a government in the one case than in the other. But in a democracy
legislators and governors are chosen with a view to acting for
the people rather than for themselves, with an eye to their being
representative rather than autocratic. The difference lies in the
principle and method by which governors are chosen.

In a democracy those who govern are leaders also. In a monarchy or aristocracy they are masters. In the latter case they sub-
sist upon the tolerance and submission of the people, in the
former upon their agreement and co-operation. The key to the
conduct of a democracy, therefore, is leadership. Under every
other polity it is determined by blood or by hereditary power who
shall assume leadership, the masterful part, in the conduct of
affairs; but the true principle of a democracy is that leadership
is open to any man who is capable of leading. The vital principle
of development is that there is an opportunity to lead; the indispensable element of health and power for the political body as a
whole is that there exist a good average capacity among the

people for choosing leaders, a high average of independence in rejecting them when they cease to lead wisely or in the right paths. It is normal, under such a system, that leaders should be "men of the people," but it is noteworthy that no man who remains upon the general level of the people will ever lead. He must emerge from the general body of the people, by reason of masterful qualities of mind or will, in order to govern the people, in order to get their assent to the execution of his purposes. He must come out from among the people and go ahead of them. His peculiarity is that he can mold to his own mind the judgments of the "indistinguishable mass of common men." He has the same antecedents as they but he does not resemble them.

It is of the true essence and spirit of democracy, therefore, that you should have a mind of your own. The American spirit is born of a race that curbed kings in order that it might act through parliaments, that substituted parliamentary ministries for king's councils, that avoided revolution by having its own way steadily instead of suddenly. The laws which we obey were most of them passed long before we were born; the constitutions we live under are full of old principles having only a new formulation. We are obedient to custom and perpetuate the habits of races of free men, having discovered the principle of liberty long ago, when we discovered the principle of legality and substituted debate for warfare. We should not be Americans or possess liberty were we not conservative and thoughtful in reform, for we know order to be the fragile vessel which contains liberty. But the spirit that is to keep us true to American ideals is the spirit of temperate but independent and fearless choice.

We will be leaders if we can, but we will choose in which direction we shall lead. We will be followers in most things, for we can accomplish social objects only by moving in bodies, but we will choose in which direction we shall follow. Carlyle had caught the true conception of liberty. For proof take the story which Mr. Birrell repeats. In the year 1819 Scotland fell upon troublous times in politics. Armed political disturbance was feared and good citizens of the conservative sort began diligently to acquire the military habit. Carlyle tells how one day he met a friend hurrying with his musket to the drill. "You should have the like of this," said the friend, cheerily, patting his gun. "Yes," replied Carlyle, "but I have not yet quite settled on which side." Democracy is the privilege of settling on which side you will shoulder gun and jeopard life. It consists, in singular combination, of respect for law and for institutions and belief in the right sort of

change. It examines changes and approves or rejects them, acting not upon impulse but upon conviction.

What has been said implies rather than excludes the notion,
however, that the true democratic or American spirit is a spirit
of co-operation as well as a spirit of independence. Men must act
upon principle, but they cannot act nation-strong unless they
act in bodies. That is the argument for parties, and it is, of course,
a conclusive argument. But it is an argument for the formation
of new parties, when those already established go astray, as well
as for stanch adherence to bodies of principle or of men already
approved. The progress of a democratic nation is made in disciplined hosts, not by the speed of individual runners; but the
hosts may choose their leader and their cause; need not obsequiously submit even to authority once wholesomely respected.
A man is a true American only when he acts upon conviction.
The true American spirit is the spirit of choice and of independent choice.

Printed in the Boston *Congregationalist*, LXXVII (Oct. 27, 1892), 347.
    [1] There is a shorthand draft of this essay in WP, DLC. For earlier correspond-
ence concerning this essay, see H. A. Bridgman to WW, July 10, 1891, Vol. 7.

Two Letters to Albert Bushnell Hart

                                          Princeton, New Jersey,
My dear Prof. Hart,   2 November, 1892.

Your postal card, asking about the addition of inclusive dates
to chapter and section headings, reached me two days ago; but
the "letter of yesterday" of which it speaks has not yet turned up.
I am afraid it has miscarried.[1] I am perfectly willing to insert
dates: I had not noticed that feature in Nos. 1 & 2. I will put in
the dates in the proof of what you have and in the *Ms.* of what
I have not yet sent.

Please tell me, when you write, the number of the last page of
the *Mss.* I sent to you. I forgot to note it before I sent it off—and
can't go on with the continuous numbering of what I have.

              Very sincerely Yours,   Woodrow Wilson

    [1] Hart's postal card and letter are both missing.

                                          Princeton, New Jersey,
My dear Prof. Hart,   3 November, 1892.

Your letter has reached me at last. The stenographer had addressed it to "Prof. *John* Wilson" (thinking, doubtless, of the

printer)[1] and it had been on a hunt for such a person. I hasten to reply.

I shall of course make no objection to the insertion of my titles and the name of my books on the title page, if you desire it. It was simply a matter of personal preference with me that the name should stand without titles; but the preference is not strong enough to dispose me to insist upon it. It should read, with the additions you desire, "Woodrow Wilson, Ph.D., LL.D., Professor of Jurisprudence and Political Economy in Princeton University, Author of 'Congressional Government,' 'The State: Elements of Historical and Practical Politics,' etc., etc."

As for the other matters of change in my manuscript, I hardly know what to say—and shall propose what I think you will regard as a fair compromise.

When I began to write the 'Epoch'—indeed, until my *Mss.* was about half finished in the first draft,—I had no idea that the pedagogical use of the little volume was the use the publishers had principally in mind. It would have had almost no attractions for me, if I had. I conceived it as a *literary sketch* of the period—i.e. a sketch in the literary, rather than the text-book method. I so planned it, and for the most part, so wrote it. The subsequent introduction of paragraph headings—breaking the text, as they do, much more formally than the writing justifies—did great violence at best to my method of treatment. I feel, therefore, that I have done as much in that direction as is at all possible.

The book, too, was planned in five parts and I do not feel that I can give that division up, without obscuring that plan. I propose, therefore, the following compromise. Let the side notes remain, in lieu of more frequent paragraph headings; and let the book be divided into five parts, as shown on the enclosed sheet.[2] The parts not to be formally called such, but indicated as I have them on that sheet. Let the bibliographies come *under these five headings*, to avoid repetition and save space. Five bibliographies for sixty years are certainly enough. Let the titles of these divisions be the running headlines of the left-hand pages. The chapters, increased in number to 13, will appear as subdivisions, for convenience of the teacher.

If more than this were to be done, I should not feel that the book was mine at all, unless I should re-write it entirely, *as a text-book.*

Even these changes will necessitate some new wording of the Preface.

I have written with perfect directness because I knew you would understand all that I have said, as proceeding, not from any foolish unwillingness to change what I have written, but simply from the conviction that my *Mss.* can't be so radically changed in arrangement without depriving the treatment of the character I meant it to have.

I shall prepare bibliographies for the other divisions at once; and then only the insertion of paragraph numbers and dates and side notes will remain to be done.

I cannot estimate at all accurately the total length of my *Mss.*, because of the way it is cut up, but I do not think it will run much over the limit. It would be best, I should say, to go ahead with the printing; for the detail that remains to put into the rest of the *Mss.* will take a good deal of time, because of the very few odd moments I have at my disposal for such purposes.

Thanking you for your kind words about the *Mss.*,

Always in haste.   Faithfully Yours,   Woodrow Wilson

TCL (RSB Coll., DLC).
1 John Wilson of John Wilson & Son, University Press, Cambridge, Mass.
2 Wilson's enclosure is missing.

To Moses Coit Tyler[1]

Princeton, New Jersey,
My dear Prof. Tyler,   5 November, 1892

The publishers have announced the little volume about which you inquire for December.[2] It is most of it ready for the press and I see no reason why its publication should be later than the first of January. There ought to be no possibility of its being kept back till the first of March. I am ready for the printer at my end.

I am very much complimented that you should think of using my book.

With sincere regards,

Faithfully Yours,   Woodrow Wilson

ALS (NIC).
1 At this time Professor of American History at Cornell University.
2 The "announcement" probably appeared in a printed circular. The Editors have been unable to find any announcement of *Division and Reunion* in the journals of this time.

From Albert Bushnell Hart

My dear Prof Wilson: Cambridge, Mass. Nov 12, 1892.

Tonight is the first time that I have been able to give a critical examination to your MS. I have carefully read and annotated the preliminary matter and the first chapter. With two exceptions I find no statement of fact to which exception can be taken. Magruder's Marshall[1] seems to me the weakest of all the American Statesmen—and at any rate not within the field of your volume: I have therefore substituted Sumner's Jackson.[2] Have you a similar prejudice against that book? It seems to me also that Johnston's American Orations[3] ought to be admitted. You mention neither Wilson's Slave Power nor Blaines Twenty Years[4] —which latter is very useful on reconstruction: but that is your choice.

In the chapter I have rewritten a half page on commerce and manufactures in 1829, you will see why. Beyond that, I have only corrected a few phrases and words here and there—and that as a new reader to whom ambiguities and tautologies appear more quickly than to one who has already worked over the text

My candid editorial opinion of your style in the MS. is that it is too rugged and uneven, that it lacks finish, and the patient selection of the precise word to fit your meaning.

But, my dear Professor Wilson, I dare not make many suggestions, because I would not for any consideration pare away that strong, individual, original, forceful way of putting things. The book is alive, and more than that it will live. To my mind, this first chapter is the best thing you have ever written. I have been reading passages to my keenest critic, *viz.* my wife, and they have quite electrified her. And you drive the nail straight from the head: you have in your mind the true explanation of Jacksonianism—the rise of a national democracy which swept over its own local boundaries. I must sincerely pray that the Cleveland Democracy may not go the same way. In the humble judgment of the editor your book will do you great honor.

It is not worth while to send the MS. twice to and fro, for your inspection of such changes as I have suggested: you can easily "uneradicate" any that seem to you unfounded, in the galleys. The printers are cranky, and I shall send the whole to press at once. My changes are all in red ink and you can leave them or revert as you please, when you see it in print.

Editorship is a light task when the writer so far perfects his work, and takes in such good part the suggestions of one less experienced than himself.

Sincerely yours,   Albert Bushnell Hart

ALS (WP, DLC) with WWhw notations on env.: "Ans. 15 Nov., '92" and "Critical estimate of Mss. of Epoch."

1 Allan Bowie Magruder, *John Marshall* (New York, 1885). Wilson accepted Hart's suggestion about eliminating mention of this volume.

2 William Graham Sumner, *Andrew Jackson as a Public Man* (Boston and New York, 1882). Wilson permitted this addition to stand.

[3] Alexander Johnston (ed.), *Representative American Orations to Illustrate American Political History* (New York and London, 1884). Wilson cited this work.

[4] Henry Wilson, *History of the Rise and Fall of the Slave Power in America* (3 vols., Boston, 1872-77), and James Gillespie Blaine, *Twenty Years of Congress: From Lincoln to Garfield* (2 vols., Norwich, Conn., 1884-86). Wilson added citations of both works.

To Albert Bushnell Hart

Princeton, New Jersey,
My dear Professor Hart,   15 November, 1892.

The rest of my *ms.* is ready and I forward it to you to-day by Express. It has been finished several days, but, expecting that you would send the first part of the *ms.* back for some revision, I have waited to make a single package of the whole. Since you are going to send the other to press, however, I forward the remaining chapters for your examination at once.

I thank you very much for your frank letter received yesterday. I regard it as nothing but a compliment to be credited with the sanity of submitting to criticism without irritation or misunderstanding, and I believe that the compliment is in this case not undeserved. I shall be only grateful for corrections and suggestions; and I will adopt them whenever it is possible. I think, with you, that changes or additions by another hand will involve dangers, and that it will be best to leave alterations to the author himself, who *perpetrated* the style of the volume in the first place. Otherwise, there would not be homogeneity in the style, and the changes would *look* like patches.

I hope that you will like the other chapters as much as you seem to have liked the first. The first would have been better than it is in manner had it not suffered so much from excision. It was, as originally written, about twice as long, and I shortened it by cutting out sentences. I am sincerely glad that you like it as much as you do.

I am perfectly willing to leave out Magruder's Marshall; I put it in only because Jackson comes into collision with Marshall, and the two influences overlap. Sumner's Jackson was included in the first of the two lists in the preliminary matter. Did I omit it in copying? As for Wilson's Slave Power, it seems to me too grossly partisan to deserve recommendation in a general list; and Blaine's Twenty Years too unauthoritative. I quote the latter in the bibliography of the chapter on Reconstruction.

With sincere regard,

Faithfully Yours,   Woodrow Wilson

TCL (RSB Coll., DLC).

To Robert Bridges

My dear Bobby,   Princeton, New Jersey, 18 November, 1892

Alas, no! There's not a ghost of a chance of our beating Yale.[1] If the 32-0 experience[2] is not repeated, I shall be thankful. This is not because Penn., the despised Penn., beat us;[3] but because (this is in confidence) incredibly stupid coaching,[4] without invention or even a decent understanding of the possibilities of the game, has thrown admirable material—admirable in spite of hurts and mishaps—away. I would not say this to anybody else. The boys may take a brace and *hold* Yale; but as for *doing* anything against her, or any other strong opponents, that is out of the question. I am going to see the game; but I shall know what to expect.

I enjoyed this letter of Charlie's immensely[5]—tell him so when you write,—with my love. I was so sorry to find you out of town the Sunday I called. I am, if possible, harder at work now than ever before. My little book has gone to the printers.

In haste, late at night, but with love,

Yours as ever   Woodrow Wilson

ALS (WC, NjP).
    [1] Bridges' letter to which this was a reply is missing.
    [2] Yale had defeated Princeton 32 to 0 in their football game on November 27, 1890.
    [3] By the score of 6 to 4 on November 5, 1892.
    [4] There was no organized coaching of the team in 1892. As one writer has put it: "In the fall of 1892, the captain [Philip King, '93] selected a committee of three, who with himself, should hold weekly meetings during the course of the football season, map out the work for that week, and notify those coaches who were best fitted to carry out the plan of work. This committee was composed of A. Moffat, '84, T. H. Harris, '86, and D. Edwards, '85." [T. H. Harris *et al.*], "The Princeton Style of Play and System of Coaching in Football," in Frank Presbrey and James Hugh Moffatt, *Athletics at Princeton: A History* (New York, 1901), p. 401.
    [5] Probably a letter from their classmate, Charles W. Mitchell, which Wilson returned.

From Caleb Thomas Winchester

Wells College

My dear Professor Wilson,   Aurora New York   Nov. 19th '92.

I was very glad, of course, to write to President Patton in commendation of Axson;[1] and before I came away from home I spoke to Mead[2] about it, making sure that he would write too. I'm sure I hope our letters may be of some service. I wish I never had to tax my ingenuity more in writing a letter in behalf of any one than I do for Axson. I wonder how he is getting on at Burlington.[3]

I am hoping to hear from him before long, but as yet have had no letter.

As you see, I am making my annual "retreat" in this chaste nunnery—the only male creature, save a superannuated negro servant, that may lodge in this great building. Sometimes I take Mrs. W. along to be my natural protector, but this year she was unable to come. When I first began to visit here it really put quite a strain upon my native timidity: but I am getting used to it now. Besides, I am nearly ten years older than when I came first—and that, too, makes a difference doubtless.

I do not come to the Hopkins this year—principally for the same reason that accounted, in the song, for Ophelia's failure to marry: " 'cause nobody had *asked* her." I had, indeed, a feeling last spring that it was doubtful whether I had any course of lectures remaining that was well suited to Baltimore or could find time to write a new course. Moreover, I am a little tired of lecturing, and feel that I ought to do more of another kind of work. Yet I might very probably have gone to Baltimore to lecture again if I had been asked early enough. I shouldn't wish to be thought at all aggrieved or disappointed that I was *not* invited. Of course I didn't expect to be asked *every* year, and was, in fact, rather glad that the invitation didn't come. This, you know, is my first year at Middletown on an advanced salary—a salary which I fear some of the powers above think a little extravagant and partial: and I must *seem*, at least, to do a full quota of work at Middletown *this* year.

I rather wished that you and Mrs. Wilson could have been with the Hazens[4] and our family in the Adirondacks this summer. If I say I "rather wished" it, any lack of earnestness in my phrase does not spring from a lukewarm desire to have you along, but from some doubt whether you would have found the particular place where we were exactly suited either for work or play. But it was restful, and a little experience we had of *camping out* in the woods made us hungry for more. Next summer I think we shall turn our backs upon the Chicago Exposition and take to the woods. Won't you go too? The following year—if one may look so far ahead—I want to go to Europe.

The bell is ringing—"Hy-Zy-Hine" as Browning has it in the "Spanish Cloister": a rendering of the sound of a bell that always seemed oddly inappropriate till I heard the tinkle of this one—it's a kind of female bell. It means lunch—"refection" one ought to say here, I suppose. And I go to eat with sixteen girls. If I were younger what a happy fate—as it is, I rather prefer the dinner of herbs where love is.

Remember me most kindly to Mrs. Wilson, and were I at home
I am sure Mrs. Winchester would wish to send her kindest recollection to both of you.

                    Yours very cordially   C. T. Winchester.

By the way, Hurrah for Grover![5] Wasn't that a turn over!

ALS (WP, DLC).
    [1] Apparently Wilson had asked Winchester to support Stockton Axson's ap-
plication for a fellowship at Princeton.
    [2] William Edward Mead, at this time Associate Professor of the English Lan-
guage at Wesleyan.
    [3] Stockton Axson was an Instructor in English at the University of Vermont.
    [4] The Rev. Dr. and Mrs. Azel Washburn Hazen.
    [5] A reference, of course, to Cleveland's victory.

A News Item

                                                    [Nov. 21, 1892]

                    PHILADELPHIAN MEETING.

Professor Woodrow Wilson addressed the Philadelphian Society[1] in Murray Hall on Saturday evening [November 19] on
"Individuality."
Professor Wilson emphasized the fact that the complete Christian must not only be kind and firm, but must also have a certain
audacity born of individuality. The successful man in life is he
who has individuality; he must be steadfast in purpose, regardless of the comments of other men.

Printed in the *Daily Princetonian*, Nov. 21, 1892.
    [1] About which, see the news item printed at Nov. 1, 1890, Vol. 7.

Ellen Axson Wilson to Anna Harris

My dear Anna,   Princeton Nov. 22/92
    . . . They [the children] are all well, except for slight colds, and
very jolly. They have been taking a great interest in politics lately
and it is too funny to see Nellie hurraing for Cleveland. Isn't it
a glorious victory! I am so *thankful* for the size of it; the *moral*
effect of a close election would have been slight but now that the
people have "risen in their might, &c." one renews one's faith in
democracy. I for one find myself for the first time in my life
heartily patriotic.
    We needed something as great as this victory to enable people
here to endure the overwhelming football calamity, and defeat
by the U. of Pa.—our first defeat, of course, by any college except
Harvard (once or twice) and Yale.[1] Really, I think Woodrow

would have had some sort of collapse if we had lost in politics too! But the great victory saved him, and indeed made us forget the defeat so entirely that it was quite a shock to find that with the students the game was still the all-important thing. One of them lunched with us the Friday after the election & when I asked him if the boys were much excited over it he said with the utmost simplicity and sincerity, "No, they can still think & talk of nothing but the *game*." The Yale-Princeton game comes off you know in New York on Thursday,[2] and night before last the *students* (!) stood, or rather *sat*, in line on the campus all night (as usual!) to secure tickets! The line of chairs twisted itself all over the campus; there were hundreds of them. This year they introduced a new feature in the shape of a covered wagon which some of them placed in the line. They of course were not allowed to "sit double" in it, but seven of them occupied it in a single row! . . .

Stockton we hear indirectly has had a brilliant success already in his teaching. . . . He will be down for the Xmas holidays with Ed, of course and George Howe. The two latter are busy at Lawrenceville. George, you know, is sister Annie's son. Sister Annie herself with the baby[3] and nurse were here for a month this fall, and Bro. George too for a part of the time. Their visit was a great treat to us. Father has just left us & will go South in a few days. We also had a delightful visit from Uncle Tom[4] last week. Minnie Hoyt you know, is here now, and looking *splendidly*. I am excessively disappointed that she cannot stay with us until her return to college. Do excuse this wretched scrawl. I am really so tired tonight and sleepy too "that I scarcely know what I am doing.["] But Woodrow went to a "stag party" . . . and I am sitting up for him. . . .

Your aff friend,   Ellen A. Wilson

ALS (WC, NjP). P.S. omitted.
    [1] Ellen was referring to defeats in earlier years. Princeton did not play Harvard in football in 1892, and the Yale game was yet to be played.
    [2] Princeton lost to Yale, 12 to 0.
    [3] Annie Howe, born in 1891.
    [4] The Rev. Dr. Thomas A. Hoyt of Philadelphia.

From the Minutes of the Princeton Faculty

5 5′ P.M., Wednesday, Nov. 23, 1892.

. . . *Resolved* That the Dean and Professors [William A.] Packard and W. Wilson be appointed a Committee to examine into the condition of the Glee Club.[1]

1 The anonymous introducer of this resolution was undoubtedly motivated by the concern, which other faculty members must have shared, that the Glee Club was doing much too well, that is, that it was taking too many trips away from the campus. The special committee does not seem to have reported back to the faculty.

Four Letters to Albert Bushnell Hart

Princeton, New Jersey,

My dear Professor Hart,   28 November, 1892.

I finished reading the first batch of galley proofs so long ago as last Wednesday, and have been keeping them only because I hoped before returning them to have the advantage of seeing the galleys you had read. I will send them on almost immediately, looking over them again for pieces to cut out.

The length of the *mss.* startles me quite as much as it does you; and I am in one sense thoroughly willing to cut *ad libitum*. I have no affection for any particular part of the old monochrome; and I was quite sincere when I said that I would, if you desired, spend part of another Summer in re-casting it upon a reduced scale. My trouble is, that before I sent it to you I cut out some eighty pages of *mss.,*—every passage, every sentence, which then seemed to me unnecessary to the separate intelligibility of the little volume. Further cutting out, without re-writing, would, it seems to me, be a truncating process; and I am shy of it. At the same time I share to the full your desire to shorten the book, and I am more than willing to draw my pen through any sentences that can be spared, as shown in the galleys. A certain amount of repetition of matter contained in the other volumes of the series seems inevitable, even if those volumes were within the same covers, inasmuch as a reference hardly completes an explanation, which ought expressly, even if very briefly, to contain all its own elements. I promise you very willingly, however, to be on the look out for victims among my sentences. They shall be sacrificed without mercy. My only fear is that I can't see them.

It is principally upon the ground that it will increase still further the length of the volume to give each chapter its separate bibliography that I object to that plan. It would involve a great deal of repetition of titles, with changes only of pages. I hope very much that you will consent, therefore, to confine the number to five. At the same time I am sincerely grateful to you for your offer to make them more complete; and I hope that you will amend them in any way you please,—particularly by way of addition. Five very full lists ought, surely, to be enough. I have not had a chance to examine Rhodes[1] yet, except in the book stalls, and if you have a chance to send it to me I should be very much indebted to you for the kindness. Of course you will add it to the proper bibliographies. Might it not very properly be added also to the general list in the prefatory matter?

By the way, I struck out Sumner's Jackson from the place where you inserted it because I had already named it in the *short* list, to which the longer one was *additional*.

And this leads me to speak of your emendations, so far as I have seen them. Many of them seem to me admirable, and I have accepted them with pleasure. Those which I have rejected I have declined for special reasons, which did not concern their excellence, but only an author's feeling for his own style. The passage about manufactures etc., for instance, in the first chapter, I did not retain because it seemed to me different in style. I do not mean style, here, in the rhetorical sense, but *style of statement*. It had a *sort* of detail and definiteness which neighbouring passages did not have. I recognize the short-comings of my (rhetorical) style very keenly, and am unaffectedly obliged to you for your watchful criticism of it.

I wish I had time for real revision; but I never had less time in my life, for *anything*. I am preparing and delivering from day to day a course of lectures on the History of Law, and you can imagine the enormous amount of reading and sifting I have to do to make such a course even a tolerably adequate and suggestive one. It takes every pound of power I have.

I want to add my expression of appreciation of your own volume in the series to those which you have already received. The engrossing engagements to which I refer have prevented my reading more than portions of it; but I have read enough to discern its admirable characteristics, and I wish to tell you of my own very keen satisfaction in your success. You have certainly earned it; and you have my hearty congratulations.

Most sincerely Yours,   Woodrow Wilson

1 Wilson was referring to the first two volumes of James Ford Rhodes, *History of the United States from the Compromise of 1850* (New York, 1893), copyright 1892, which had just appeared.

Princeton, New Jersey,
My dear Professor Hart,   30 November, 1892

I received this morning your set of galley proofs, and have gone over them very carefully. I had already sent back to the printers the galleys of the prefatory matter, the first chapter, and a portion of the second (through section 18); but fortunately

there were no essential corrections noted by you in those portions that I had not myself made,—except in the bibliography of
the prefatory matter. I will write to the printers asking them to
send me a 'revise' of that, so that I may add Rhodes and select
a twenty dollar list, as you request. I don't think that it would be
wise to add Nicolay and Hay.[1] It seems to me that the chaff in
those volumes is vastly more abundant than the wheat. They
demand *very* judicious reading.

A word or two about certain statements in the text, about
which you have noted a query. I remembered the uproar which
Quincy's remarks created in the House; but you will recollect
that, although he was required to reduce the obnoxious phrases
to writing, the House declined to subject him to censure. I have
changed the phrase to read "the House had seen nothing in the
speech to warrant a *formal* censure."

There were indeed protests by the federalist States against the
Virginia and Kentucky Resolutions; but my phrase is that such
doctrine was not regarded as "treasonable" or as in derogation of
"constitutional" (i.e. legal) duty; however much it may have been
censured upon grounds of political morality.

I should be obliged if you would drop a hint to Wilson's proof
reader that I am inclined to insist upon my own spelling, capitalization, and punctuation. I would like to insist even upon the
'u' in such words as labour, harbour, etc., and upon single quotation marks in the case of slang or current phrases of no particular
or ascertained authorship; but I suppose it is too late now. I
notice that you change my guarant*ee* to guarant*y*. I think the
English usage of double 'e' much more classical. I observe, too,
that you change 'on *the* great scale' into 'on *a* great scale.' I venture to maintain that you will find 'on *the* great scale' the conventional form among standard writers.

I am afraid that I may seem stubborn to you in the matter of
separate bibliographies for the several chapters; and it must appear specially gratuitous and ungracious when you so generously
offer to take all the trouble of their preparation. But really I
think five a generous supply; and the repetitions and consumption
of space involved seem to me weighty considerations.

Let me express again my appreciation of your editorial kindness and tact. I doubtless need supervision,—especially when writing in a field which is not strictly the field of my professional
studies,—but I have always been shy of it. With you, however,
it loses its terrors.

I am very much relieved that a recount shows a reduction in
the probable length of my little volume. I was much concerned

at finding it so much beyond the limit. In the proofs which have been sent me I have cut out matter amounting, I suppose, to about three or four printed pages, choosing principally points of repetition: as, e.g. the Indian and tariff difficulties of the opening years of Jackson's term. I am much obliged to you for calling my attention to them.

Please be kind enough to give the printers very definite instructions about the management and arrangement of *Parts*, *references*, and *Chapters*. I have marked the insertion of chapter headings in the proof I have had; but I am anxious that, if the page proofs are to be made at once, no mistake should be made which would be expensive to correct.

It is very gratifying to think of meeting you on the "conference" on entrance examinations and school programs.[2] For what time and place has the meeting of ours been appointed, do you know?

With much regard,

Very sincerely Yours,   Woodrow Wilson

[1] John G. Nicolay and John Hay, *Abraham Lincoln: A History* (10 vols., New York, 1890).
[2] A conference in Madison, Wisconsin, about which see the Editorial Note, "The Madison Conference on History, Civil Government, and Political Economy."

Princeton, New Jersey,

My dear Professor Hart,   3 December, 1892.

I return once more the first two batches of galley proofs that were sent me. The third set I retain until your own copies are sent me, for comparison. I have willingly gone over the whole of the first sets again with your own, considering again the conclusions I had come to as to accepting emendations, and in some instances changing my mind about adhering to my original form of the matter. I have altered, as you will see, several of the side notes.

I do not like to seem to insist unduly upon the phrases I originally employed; but, whatever may be said against my style, which is far from impeccable, I think that it is at least consistent. Every author, I suppose, has a definite feeling for his style, which would enable him to perceive incongruities in changes suggested by others, who naturally do not have the same sort of sympathy with his particular forms of phrase. It is in accordance with such subjective standards that I have, always with hesitancy, rejected many of the emendations which you have suggested. I have all my life been a close student of style,—appearances to the contrary, notwithstanding!—and I beg you will believe that my choice in this matter is neither haphazard nor a result of weak fondness for what has come from my own pen. "The style is the man," after all; and, in my opinion, (as I should like to tell Wilson's reader) punctuation is a part of style,—and capitalization, too, for that matter. Unless I could control even the detail of style, to which I am very sensitive, in the case of the style of others, as well as in the case of my own style, I should not feel that I was in real fact the author of my own works. I say this, I am sure you will understand, not at all by way of protest to anything that you have suggested, but only by way of explanation of my own apparent persistency in matters of no great moment.

I retain the proofs of the prefatory matter for a few days for the insertion of the changes of which we have already spoken.

With sincere regard,

Faithfully Yours,   Woodrow Wilson.

My dear Professor Hart,

Princeton, New Jersey,
5 December, 1892.

I have been trying my hand to-night at a twenty dollar list of books for the Suggestions to Teachers and Readers, but I find that it is 'no go.' It may be my ignorance, but there do not seem to be enough books of the briefer and more obtainable sort for such a list. There are very few of the right kind or of the right price. I think we shall have to be content, for this volume, with the two lists, as amended.

The following seem to be appropriate headings for the left-hand pages in the five Chapters:

Stage of Development
Period of Critical Change
The Slavery Question
Secession and Civil War
Rehabilitation of the Union

By the way, in making the book up into pages, please see to it that the five major divisions are not called 'Parts' or 'Sections,' or given *any names*. It seems to me that they ought to be *called* nothing; but simply numbered with Roman numerals, placed above their titles.

I received the copy of Rhodes this evening, and I wish to express to you, and to the author,[1] my very cordial thanks for your courtesy in sending it. I shall examine it with the greatest interest, and I have no doubt with equal pleasure.

I have read your own galleys 20-40, and I am only awaiting your own corresponding proofs to return them. Do I understand you aright, that I need not return hereafter your galley proofs?

Will you not be kind enough to have duplicate page proofs sent to me, so that I may begin betimes on the index?

Madison, Wisconsin! Phew! That's a long pull! But perhaps it seems so to me now only because I am sleepy:—which must also explain the appearance of this letter.

Very sincerely Yours,   Woodrow Wilson

TCL (RSB Coll., DLC).
[1] Rhodes must have given the volumes to Hart to send to Wilson. They are in the Wilson Library in the Library of Congress and are not inscribed.

From the Minutes of the Princeton Faculty

5 5′ P.M., Wednesday, Dec. 7, 1892

. . . The Committee on Out-door Sports made a report recommending certain action in reference to students playing on other than the College Teams which was made the 2nd order of business for the next meeting.[1] . . .

[1] See the Princeton Faculty Minutes printed at Dec. 14, 1892.

Two Letters to Albert Bushnell Hart

Princeton, New Jersey,

My dear Professor Hart, 7 December, 1892.

I received your copies of galleys 20-40 yesterday afternoon, and I have gone over them (eclectically, as usual) with great care.

I wish I could accept your suggestions about the curtailment of the portion on the Bank, and the transposition of its sections; but really it is impossible. I cut out about one-third of it in *mss.*, and I do not think that its present proportions are extravagant. That little piece of history is really, I think you will agree, the most typical piece of the Jacksonian story: it is altogether the best key to the temper and methods of the man, and carries with it, by implication, the explanation of a great many other things of the time. It seems to me the heart topic of the period. As for the arrangement of the sections, it could not be changed without re-writing. For, you know, with me the division into sections came after the writing, and is simply a series of breaks in the text. I took great pains in weaving that narrative together, and a change in the order of its parts at this stage would cost me more

labour and reconsideration than there is now time for,—or opportunity on my part. It is too late to do anything so radical now:
the poor thing will have to stand as it is.

I have made marginal answers to several of your other suggestions on your galleys, which are in a fair way to become manuscript curiosities by reason of this new method of correspondence.

Before the page proofs come I want to ask the meaning of a
sentence in your letter of Dec. 2. You say "The right page heading
is set in a few words between the contents of the opening, that
is of the left and right pages. I have together." Apparently some
words have been left out, and I am at a loss.

I return galleys 20-40 by the same mail that bears this.

Very sincerely Yours,   Woodrow Wilson

Princeton, New Jersey,
My dear Professor Hart,   13 December, 1892.

I return to-day galleys 41-57. A short absence from home[1]
delayed my reading of Nos. 41-47.

I gave very careful consideration to the changes and additions
which you suggested, and I have modified several passages in
accordance with your notes. In the passage about the seizure of
New Mexico and California I restored the original phrases, somewhat altered, in order to give the right general impression of the
character of those extraordinary transactions without making
specific charges of motive against Polk and his advisers. I have
tried to make the narrative a narrative of measures, and of the
actions of groups of men and parties, rather than of the acts of
individual men; and it does not seem to me just to throw in sudden bunches of detailed matter as to personal motive unless you
can give the whole picture of the men concerned, and so maintain the right balance of judgment.

For the same reasons,—because it is an *incidental* charge without anything in the surrounding narrative to bring Calhoun's connection with the affair fully into view,—I have left out the words,
"with Calhoun's connivance." I have preferred in all cases to construct a narrative which will convey the right suggestions and
impressions rather than a narrative of incomplete detail,—which
must necessarily be out of perspective.

I hope that you will suffer this volume to differ from the
others in the small matter of capitalization.

When and by what route do you go West on our expedition?

Sincerely Yours,   Woodrow Wilson

P.S. It does not seem to me necessary to put in Mexico's *temporary* decree about slavery.

W.W.

TCL (RSB Coll., DLC).
    ¹ Wilson had delivered "Democracy" at Vassar College on December 9, 1892. See the news report printed at January 1, 1893.

A Written Recitation in the History of Law

[Dec. 13, 1892]

III.

Roman Law in Middle Ages.

1. Name, date, and characterize the principal barbarian codes. Which of these was the most important, and in what parts of Europe was it longest used?
2. What was the character of German public law, on the one hand, and of German private law, on the other, before the reception of Roman law? What did Roman law supply that it did not have?
3. What general influences induced the study of Roman law in Europe? What special influences in the Italian cities?
4. Who were the glossators? What was their method and whence derived? What their material?

WWhw MS. (WP, DLC).

From the Minutes of the Princeton Faculty

5 5′ P.M., Wednesday, Dec. 14, 1892

. . . The regulation in reference to students playing on other than College Teams as proposed by the Com. on Out-Door Sports was considered, adopted and is as follows, viz:

No student desiring to contend in Intercollegiate Sports of any kind as a representative of the College of New Jersey is permitted to contend in Athletic Games as a representative of any outside organization whatsoever.

A Newspaper Report of a Meeting of the Princeton Alumni of Delaware

[Dec. 17, 1892]

PRINCETON MEN AT DINNER

Although it is not quite one day old the Princeton Alumni Association of Delaware is a sprightly infant, and if its present rosy life continues it will indeed have a bright future. Its organization was effected last evening at the Wilmington Club, No. 1006 King Street. Immediately after the work of organizing had been completed the association gave its first annual dinner, and from then until after midnight the cosy club house resounded with praises of Princeton and the songs and tiger of old Nassau. The attendance was large and the occasion decidedly pleasant.

Officers as follows were elected: President, William C. Spruance, '52, Wilmington; Vice-president, Hon. George Gray, '59, Wilmington; Executive Committee, Judge J. Frank Ball, '76, Wilmington; Henry B. Thompson, '77, Wilmington; ex-Attorney-general, John Biggs, '77, Wilmington; Arthur W. Spruance, '91, Wilmington; Andrew C. Gray, '92, Wilmington; James Pennewill, '75, Dover, and Secretary of State David T. Marvel, '73, Georgetown; Secretary and Treasurer, Willard Hall Porter, '75, No. 300, Equitable Building, Wilmington.

The dinner began at 8.30 o'clock. . . .

The table was in the form of a capital "T" and was set in the parlor. Its ornamentation consisted of candelabra and plants. Princeton's colors, orange and black, were seen everywhere. The chandelier was entwined with orange and streamers of that tint extended from the chandelier to the corners of the room. Festoons of orange and black ornamented the side walls and the college colors adorned the menu cards. At the head of the table there was a pennant, orange tinted and inscribed "Princeton." President Spruance occupied the seat of honor, while on his right was Professor Wilson and on his left Senator Gray. Following was the menu:

Blue Points.

Cream of Celery.

Lobster Neuberg.

Truffled Turkey.

Olives.   Peas.

Sweetbread Patties.

Roman Punch.

Red Head Duck.

Salad, French Dressing.

Roquefort.   Crackers.   De Brie.

Frozen Plum Pudding.

Cake.

Coffee. . . .

The toast "The Faculty" was responded to by Professor Wilson. He said he supposed he ought to feel a maternal solicitude in the birth of the new child. He rejoiced in the formation of the society. The names on its roll ought to be weighed instead of numbered. The indications of its life were very much out of proportion to its size. It seemed more interesting that a small number of men should interest themselves in this way than a large number. When a small body like this associated itself it meant business. There is a great deal to be done for Princeton. It was never made what it is by any government or individual, but by a combination of individuals, generation after generation of interested men. He never goes in the old quadrangle without feeling his responsibility as a tutor. When he looks out on Princeton he does not see big men, but substantial men, men who are not heard of much in the public press, but who are relied on in private business. He wanted to make the institution more literary. It has produced statesmen but not many writers. It ought to produce more writers. A school of technical science has no business there. It is not essentially a scientific institution. It should be a literary institution, a college out of which you can turn your hand like a gentleman and a scholar to the duties of life. If the public is to be made to believe that Princeton is a vital institution the college must be made to do something. A law school should be founded there and commercial law should be taught along with the history of commerce. If such a law school is originated it will make the hit of the generation. He felt in a certain sense that the education of this country depends on Princeton. If it is given the means and support of its alumni it will lead as it has done in the past. . . .

Printed in the Wilmington, Del., *Every Evening*, Dec. 17, 1892; some editorial headings omitted.

From Joseph Ruggles Wilson

My precious son—   Columbia, S. C. Decr 18/92

Your letter received at Wilmington [N. C.] was a true heart-warmer, and I thank you for it. I am compelled to cry peccavi in view of the fact that I did not write you of my plans before leaving N. York. I had so resolutely intended to inform you of my prospective movements, as that I must have mistaken the strong intention for the doing—a mistake sometimes made, I think.

Well, I reached Wilmington in *time* to rest awhile before the three or four days' celebration[1] was to begin—but there was no rest possible. Upon learning that I was in town, the "clans began to muster," and I found myself at once in a state of siege, which had no let-up until I left. Never did a returning pastor receive a more flattering welcome; it was to all intents and purposes an *ovation* wherein no element of seemly enthusiasm was lacking. The "reception" proper was perfectly arranged with no appointment missing which could lend it interest or impressiveness. One would have supposed me a conquering hero restored to a grateful people who could not make enough of him in the way of affection and honor. If kisses were measurable entities, I had at least one mile of them. Or if hand-shaking be weighable, I had a ton. The people did every thing except *sleep* with me!

As to the public exercises which I was appointed to lead as "magna pars"—the one a presentation of bibles to the two oldest living members of the church—the other the Sunday morning's sermon—I am incompetent to speak through *partiality* (!) for the speaker. But I had no difficulty in gratifying my audience or in holding their attention perfectly. The sermon was extemporaneous as to its wording—lasted for 45 minutes—and was all that even I could have wished, or even *you*, my dear one, could have desired. The newspapers, for some reason, had almost no reports as to the proceedings from day to day—only brief outlinings.

I hope to hear that your visits to Vassar & to Wilmington Del.[2] were all that could have been expected, even by *me*. As to the "german"[3] you of course acquitted yourself well!

Many enquiries were made as to "Mr Tom," and lots of gratulation heaped upon me because I have such a son. I went to Augusta, from Wilmington, for a day or so. Love big & big to dear Ellie & to yourself all the heart of

Your affc   Father.

All here send love—much & mucher

ALS (WP, DLC).
[1] Dr. Wilson refers to the celebration of the seventy-fifth anniversary of the First Presbyterian Church of Wilmington, North Carolina, held December 8, 9, and 11, 1892. Dr. Wilson preached at the main service of commemoration on Sunday, December 11. His sermon, entitled "Yesterday, To-Day and Forever," is printed in *Memorial of the First Presbyterian Church, Wilmington, N.C. Seventy-Fifth Anniversary. 1817-1892* (Richmond, 1893).
[2] For an account of Woodrow Wilson's visit to Vassar, see the news item printed at Jan. 1, 1893; for an account of his speech in Wilmington, Delaware, see the news report printed at Dec. 17, 1892.
[3] An obscure reference. Perhaps Woodrow Wilson had been supporting the *Daily Princetonian*'s effort to spur the seniors to begin to make plans for the annual Senior Dance. See the *Daily Princetonian*, Nov. 30, 1892.

To Albert Bushnell Hart

Princeton, New Jersey,

My dear Professor Hart,   20th. December, 1892.

There are one or two points about the galleys which I return to you to-day which need a word or two of comment or explanation, besides those which I have noted in the margins.

You were right in calling my attention to the phrase about Sherman's cruelty, and I have modified it a little; but really there is no more deliberately considered phrase in the book. I am painfully familiar with the details of that awful march, and I really think that the words I used concerning it ought to stand as a piece of sober history. Sherman was aware of the cruelty involved in his policy of devastation, and declared, in answer to protests, that it (the policy, cruelty and all) was deliberate.

As for the treatment of prisoners in the southern prisons, that was doubtless heartless upon occasion; but the heartlessness was not part of a system, as Sherman's was. It was no greater than was to have been expected under the circumstances from any captors; and, as being incidental, I do not think it ought to be mentioned in such a sketch as I have written,—from which I have tried to exclude every harsh adjective that was not absolutely needed.

I shall send the copy of the bibliographies back to you, as well as the proof, for your comparison. By the way, I do not understand the transformation of the "Special" into "General" and the "General" into "Special" Histories in the first Bibliography. Was not that an inadvertence? Surely von Holst, Schouler, & Co. are "general" accounts. I am very much obliged to you for the trouble you have taken with the bibliographies.

I will try to catch you at Chicago on my way to Madison; but it would hardly be possible for me to go by way of Buffalo. I may not be able to reach Madison before Wednesday morning.

I want to thank you very cordially for your praise of my work on the little "Epoch." I am particularly sensible of your judgment that I have been successful in my attempt to maintain an impartial balance of judgment in the controversies which led to the war. It relieves me not a little of my present disgust with the whole thing (I am *so* tired of it, and so keenly sensible of its defects both big and little!); and I only hope that your judgment is not too generous.

I have feared more than once that you would deem me a bit stubborn and perverse about some of the changes of phrase or matter which you have suggested as the copy and proofs have passed through your hands; but I have trusted to your generosity not to look at my insistences in that light. In most instances I was simply contending for the maintenance of the original within the lines of the conception, as to style, treatment, etc., upon which I had in the first place constructed it.

With sincere regard,

Faithfully Yours,   Woodrow Wilson

TCL (RSB Coll., DLC).

To Charles Kendall Adams

My dear Sir,   Princeton, New Jersey, 23 December, 1892.

Allow me to thank you very cordially for your kind letter of December 13. I expect to reach Madison in time for the first session of the Conference; though I cannot say just at this moment by what train.

I hope you will not trouble yourself to have any one meet me at the train; for I expect to stay with my old friends Turner and Haskins[1] of your Faculty.

I am looking forward with much pleasure to my visit to Madison.   Very cordially Yours,   Woodrow Wilson

WWTLS (President's File, WU).

[1] Frederick Jackson Turner and Charles Homer Haskins. Wilson stayed with the Turners, and Wilson and Turner continued their discussions, long since begun, of the influence of sectionalism and of the West in American history. Turner had just completed a draft of his famous paper, "The Significance of the Frontier in American History." He read the paper to Wilson, and Wilson, Turner later remembered, "suggested the use of the word '"hither" side of free land' for which I had been hunting!" F. J. Turner to W. E. Dodd, Oct. 7, 1919, in Wendell H. Stephenson, "The Influence of Woodrow Wilson on Frederick Jackson Turner," *Agricultural History*, XIX (Oct. 1945), 253.

EDITORIAL NOTE

THE MADISON CONFERENCE ON HISTORY, CIVIL GOVERNMENT, AND POLITICAL ECONOMY

In response to nation-wide concern about the lack of proper standards in American secondary schools, the National Council of Education of the National Educational Association on July 9, 1892, appointed a Committee of Ten, headed by President Charles W. Eliot of Harvard, to arrange for a series of conferences "to consider the proper limits of its subject, the best methods of instruction, the most desirable allotment of time for the subject, and the best methods of testing the pupils' attainments therein. . . ."[1] The Committee of

[1] *Report of the Committee on Secondary School Studies Appointed at the Meeting of the National Educational Association July 9, 1892* . . . (Washington, 1893), pp. 3-4.

Ten, meeting in New York from November 9 through November 11, decided to hold nine conferences on various groups of disciplines in cities throughout the country on December 28; it also selected the members of the conferences, and prepared a list of questions for each to consider.

The members of the Conference on History, Civil Government, and Political Economy were, in addition to Wilson,[2] President Charles Kendall Adams of the University of Wisconsin; Edward G. Bourne, Professor of History at Adelbert College, Cleveland; Abram Brown, Principal of the Columbus, Ohio, High School; Albert Bushnell Hart, Assistant Professor of History at Harvard; Ray Greene Huling, Principal of the New Bedford, Mass., High School; Jesse Macy, Professor of Political Science at Iowa College, Grinnell; James Harvey Robinson, Associate Professor of European History at the University of Pennsylvania; William A. Scott, Assistant Professor of Political Economy at the University of Wisconsin; and Henry P. Warren, Headmaster of the Albany Academy, Albany, N.Y. The members invited to their meetings Frederick Jackson Turner, Professor of American History at the University of Wisconsin, Charles Homer Haskins, Professor of European History at Wisconsin, John Barber Parkinson, Professor of Civil Polity and Political Economy at Wisconsin, and Oliver Elwin Wells, Wisconsin State Superintendent of Public Instruction.

The conference met in the Seminary of Political Science located in the Fuller Opera House in Madison at ten o'clock in the morning of December 28. Professor and Mrs. Turner entertained the members at luncheon on that day. George Wilbur Peck, Governor of Wisconsin and better known to history as an author and journalist, gave a reception on December 29; and the Madison Business Men's Club honored the conferees and the President, faculty, and resident regents of the University of Wisconsin at a banquet on December 30, the final day of the conference.[3] "The members," the *Madison Democrat* said on December 31, "report themselves as charmed with Madison's beauty and hospitality, and the university and historical society called out their admiration. It is doubtful if the citizens of Madison ever entertained a more scholarly and delightful body of men."

The minutes of the conference, written by Hart and printed below, constitute the only piece of evidence that discloses the participation of individual members. The historian of the Committee of Ten and its movement to upgrade American secondary education has concluded that Wilson was the "key mover" of the Madison conference.[4]

Hart later expanded his minutes into a report that was printed in the *Report of the Committee on Secondary School Studies*, cited earlier, pages 162-203. The Committee of Ten distilled Hart's record in the section of its own report printed in the same volume on pages 28-31.

2 The letter of invitation to Wilson and his letter of acceptance are both missing. However, the correspondence had occurred by late November, as WW to A. B. Hart, Nov. 30, 1892, reveals.

3 *Madison Democrat*, Dec. 28, 30, and 31, 1892; Madison *Wisconsin State Journal*, Dec. 31, 1892.

4 Theodore R. Sizer, *Secondary Schools at the Turn of the Century* (New Haven and London, 1964), p. 109.

About the significance of the report of the Committee of Ten, it suffices to quote the evaluation of its historian:

"This *Report*—commonly referred to as 'the Report of the Committee of Ten'—has had a profound influence on American education. For fifteen years after its publication it served as gospel for the curriculum writers of the burgeoning high schools; in our own time it serves as the explicit rallying point for those who feel that our secondary schools have forgotten their central role in training the intellect. Called in 1894 'the educational sensation of the New Year,' it was termed in 1958 'the embodiment of the most profound, practical, and democratic philosophy of education ever enunciated in America.' While there were and are those who contest these assessments, it is clear that the *Report* carved a niche for itself in American school history, something that its scores of cousins written by similar committees and conferences failed to do."[5]

[5] *Ibid.*, p. xi.

Minutes of the Madison Conference

Minutes of the Historical Conference.
Madison, Wisconsin, December 28-30, 1892.

The Conference met at ten oclock on Wednesday, December 28th, in the rooms of the Seminary of Political Science, Opera House Block, Madison, according to the call. The following members were present:

President Adams, Professor Bourne, Mr. Brown, Professor Hart, Mr. Huling, Professor Macy, Mr. Warren, Professor Wilson.

President Adams called the conference to order.

On motion *Professor Hart* was chosen Secretary.

On motion *President Adams* was made permanent Chairman.

The Chairman invited with unanimous consent *Professors Haskins, Parkinson,* and *Turner* of the University of Wisconsin and *Mr. Wells* of the Wisconsin State Department of Education to sit with the Conference.

On question of making any report of the proceedings to the press it was agreed without a vote that no report be made except at the pleasure of the general Committee of Ten.

Mr. Huling moved that a committee be appointed to report on programme for the Conference: *Messrs Hart, Huling,* and *Wilson* were so appointed.

An exchange of views on the subjects before the Conference was now invited.

President Adams mentioned the disadvantages of poor history teaching in that it leads to a dislike of the subject. Hence, from the college standpoint, it is a question whether history might not well be ommitted in the lower schools. Poor teaching again gives indefinite ideas which are perhaps worse than none, and text book work is rote-teaching, police work.

He saw some improvement in the school methods of the last ten years, but not much, and thought our methods of teaching not comparable with those of the German schools. The subjects best taught were United States history and local history, on account of the personal interest of the pupils; and the history of Greece and Rome, which is taught in classical schools. He was not disposed to ask for more time on history until better teaching could be assured. As for pupils who did not intend to go to College, he was inclined to let them pick up their historical information indirectly.

Mr. Warren described the method pursued in the Albany Academy which he thought[,] however, was not in touch with other schools about it. He believed in interesting children in history by presenting to them heroic men and heroic deeds and thought there was no difficulty in arousing enthusiasm; but he avoided minute discussion of depraved characters such as Alcibiades and Napoleon. . . .

Professor Macy looked upon history as a branch of polite literature and art. The practice in the Iowa schools was to take up United States history side by side with arithmetic; when children had finished arithmetic they supposed they had also mastered United States history; but the instruction was now much improving, coordinate reading was spreading and in many places topical methods were used.

His view of history he thought had not yet been stated; he looked on history as a record of the movement of organized society. This view he contrasted with history as a part of politics, that is as a record of character; he thought both views ought to be regarded, but that the former was the more important. He found among children an intense interest in national life and in private life and institutions; sometimes an interest carried to absurd lengths as the case of a class in which Lorna Doone was read aloud as an illustration of history.

Mr. Brown described a different set of conditions in Ohio. . . .

Mr. Huling described the system of the New Bedford high schools, to which children come at fifteen with some knowledge of United States history. . . .

Professor Hart looked at the subject before the conference from three points of view: from that of a college teacher; of a college examiner for entrance; and of a person interested in the public schools. . . . He desired in the Conference to put aside the question of the colleges and to consider only how far history could be made a part of a good education in the lower schools. History to his mind was one branch of philosophy—a study of man and of motives—an attempt above all to find out what people had thought, and especially what they had thought about government. He thought the subject within the compass of the schools. The methods of historical teaching seemed the same from the lowest to the highest point in the schools. But in suggesting methods for schools, account must be taken of the fact that most of them had very limited apparatus. He then read an account of the school work at Thayer Academy, Braintree, Massachusetts . . . as an example of what might be done by vigorous and well directed teaching.

Professor Bourne spoke of the Ohio schools as a system established with little reference to Eastern colleges; only four high schools in Ohio, with a population of four millions, have a regular course in Greek. Furthermore there are many children of foreigners in Ohio who must be educated and especially who must be taught civil government since they do not absorb the principles of government from their fathers[,] . . .

Professor Wilson said they were not preparing for college in the secondary schools, but for life. We must remember that throughout the country almost no girls go to college and we must provide for them in the schools. We must avoid introducing what is called scientific history into the schools, for it is a "history of doubt[,]" criticism, examination of evidence. It tends to confuse young pupils: in Roman history for instance it was more important to teach what Livy thought was history than what Mommsen thinks was history; above all he desired a literary teaching of history. English history can be taught for instance through Chaucer, Shakespeare, Tennyson; what we need is to put children into the spirit of the times which they are studying. Scientific critical history is college work and not school work.[1] The idea of society as an organization should be reserved until we reach civil government. What we need to study in schools is the united effort, the common thought, of bodies of men; of the men who make public opinion, that is of the uncritical and conservative rather than of the educated classes. A striking example of the growth of institutions from this point of view is set forth in Johnson's Rudimentary Society Among Boys.[2] Civil government, he thought, ought to be a general subject. He objected to the

[1] Wilson expressed the very same sentiments in WW to M. S. Slaughter, Aug. 2, 1888, Vol. 5, p. 759.
[2] John Hemsley, Jr., *Rudimentary Society Among Boys*, Johns Hopkins University Studies in Historical and Political Science, Second Series (Baltimore, 1884).

government of any one political community because it became a study of the text of constitutions. He had known one case where the Constitution of the United States had been put into rhyme and learned by heart.

Second session, Wednesday afternoon, December 28th.

The Conference met at four o'clock. *Professor Robinson* appeared; *Professor Scott* was appointed by the Chairman on the authority of the Chairman of the Committee of Ten to take the place of *Professor Folwell*[3] who was unable to attend. The Chairman presented the invitation of the Governor of the State to his reception on Thursday night; and of the Madison Business Club to a banquet on Friday night. The Committee on Programme reported as follows:

Session I. Wednesday, 10 A.M.
    An account of methods now pursued.
Session II. Wednesday, 4 P.M.
    Selection of historical subjects (Questions of Committee of 10. No. 4)[4]
Session III. Thursday, 10 A.M.
    Arrangement of historical studies. (Questions 1, 2, 3, & 5.)
Session IV. Thursday, 3 P.M.
    Methods of historical study (Question 9).
Session V. Friday 10 A.M.
    Connection of schools with colleges in historical work (Questions 6, 10, 7, 8).
Session VI. Friday 2 P.M.
    Civil Government and Political Economy.

Professor Haskins by request spoke of the system of historical study in Wisconsin. The high schools have usually a one year's course which is of little account in preparation for college. The University advises high schools not to try general history but rather to attempt one half year of ancient history and one half year of English history; the latter to be accompanied by some sketch of other European history. This system has been tried in some cases and worked fairly well. He laid a special stress upon the importance of classical history especially in schools where there is no classical instruction. A good two years course in his judgment would be one year divided between ancient history and French history (as suggesting general European history)

3 William Watts Folwell, Professor of Political Science, University of Minnesota, and Acting President of the American Economic Association in 1892.
4 These questions are printed in *Report of the Committee on Secondary School Studies*, p. 6. Question 4 read: "What topics, or parts, of the subject may reasonably be covered during the whole course?"

and one year divided between English and United States history, with civil government.

Professor Turner of the University of Wisconsin, by request, said a few words of the tendency in Wisconsin to increase instruction in history in the high schools; but a system of two years divided well has not yet taken root.

Professor Robinson urged special attention to the teaching of European history which is very inadequately and imperfectly taught in the schools at present. He thought that great advantage could be derived from a somewhat minute study of some brief historical subject. Students when they come to college have little specific knowledge of anything in history. . . .

The Conference then proceeded to a general discussion of the nature of its recommendations: first, whether it would recommend different programmes for the different kinds of schools; and, second, whether it would recommend an ideal programme representing the maximum of historical work in the very best schools, or a practicable programme such as might be carried out in course of time in any good school. The burden of opinion was in favor of the latter suggestion.

On the motion of *Professor Hart* it was voted that history and (Res. 1) kindred subjects ought to be a substantial study in each of at least eight years.

The question of American history was then taken up. Mr. Warren desired to include a study of the French and Spanish history both in the colonial and constitutional period. It was finally voted on motion of Mr. *Huling* that American history be a part (Res. 2) of the programme and on motion of *Mr. Brown* that English his- (Res. 3) tory should be a part of the programme.

Third session Thursday morning, December 30th[29th].

In the temporary absence of the Chairman *Professor Macy* was made chairman *pro tem.* till President Adams appeared.

On motion of *Professor Bourne* it was voted that Greek and (Res. 4) Roman history be included in the programme. Professor Robinson then brought up the question of the study of European history and suggested that a part of the course be devoted to intensive study of the period of the French Revolution and Napoleonic era. The Conference discussed at large the question whether it was necessary to spend any part of the course in the detailed study of a chosen period; and further, what period was suitable for such a study. The question was settled for the time being by the adoption of the following vote moved by Professor *Robinson*: (Res. 5) that one year of the course be devoted to intensive study of history.

(Res. 6)   On motion of *Professor Wilson* it was voted that French history be made a part of the programme.

(Res. 7)   On motion of *Mr. Warren* it was voted that Greek and Roman history be taught with their oriental derivations.

Professor Wilson moved that the special periods for intensive study be preferably in European history, or in the absence of proper material, in American history.

Professor Hart moved as a substitute that the special period be usually in some field of American history, or in English history since 1600, or, in favorably situated schools in modern European history.

The two motions were withdrawn and a substitute proposed
(Res. 8)   by *Mr. Huling* adopted: (8) That the year of intensive study be devoted to the careful study of some special period, as for example the struggle of France and England for North America, the Renaissance etc. etc

Professor Hart moved that *Mr. Huling* be requested to prepare a list of suitable subjects with a preference for suitable American subjects. Lost 3 to 4.

Professor Robinson moved that a preference be given to European subjects. Lost 2 to 6.

It was informally agreed that *Mr. Huling* prepare a list without indicating a preference, and report on Friday morning.

Fourth session. Thursday afternoon, December 30th[29th].

The Conference proceeded to discuss the question of the distribution of subjects throughout the years of study.

Mr. Huling moved that the first four years of study be devoted to mythology and biography based on general history and American history.

(Res. 9)   *Professor Wilson* (9) moved to substitute three years for four years. Carried 6 to 3. The motion as amended was then adopted.

(Res. 10)   After long discussion the Conference adopted the following general programme submitted by *Professor Wilson*:

1st year, Biography and Mythology.

2nd year, Biography and Mythology.

3rd year, American history.

4th year, Greek and Roman history with its Oriental connections.

5th year, French history, Mediaeval and Modern, with connections of general history.

6th year, English history, Mediaeval and Modern, with connections of general history.

7th year, American history.

8th year, A special period pursued in an intensive manner and Civil Government.

Professor Bourne moved that the Conference proceed to frame an alternative six years programme, informally agreed to *(Res. 11)*

Professor Wilson moved that if it be necessary to reduce the course in any case to six years the French history and the special period be left out and that the Givil [Civil] Government go in with American history.

On motion of *Professor Hart* it was voted that the eight years course be consecutive. *(Res. 12)*

Professor Wilson moved that in no year ought the time to be less than the equivalent of two fifty minute recitation periods. Lost 4 to 6.

Professor Hart moved to substitute two periods of forty-five minutes. Lost

Professor Wilson's motion was then adopted as follows: That, in no year ought the time devoted to these subjects to be less than three forty minute periods per week, throughout the year *(Res. 12ᵇ)*

Professor Wilson then moved the following as an alternative's six years programme: adopted

1st year, Biography and Mythology. *(Res 13)*

2nd year, Biography and Mythology.

3rd year, American history.

(At this point the pupil would naturally enter the high school)

4th year, Greek and Roman history.

5th year, English history, mediaeval and modern, with connections of general history

6th year, American history and Civil Government.

Further, reading of historical literature in the schools to be recommended

Professor Robinson moved that the point of departure in stating the requisitions be fixed at the beginning of the high schools course. Carried *(Res. 14)*

Mr. Macy moved to make the minimum time three forty minute periods in each week throughout the course, instead of two periods of fifty minutes. Adopted. *(Res. 15)*

Professor Wilson moved that formal instruction in Political Economy be excluded from the school programmes. Adopted. *(Res. 16)*

Professor Scott moved that Economic subjects be treated in *(Res. 17)*

connection with other pertinent subjects as: Political History[,] Civil Government, and commercial geography[.] Adopted.

Professor Macy moved that *Professor Scott* be a committee to prepare a list of suitable economic topics. Adopted.

Fifth session, Friday morning, December 31st [30th].

(Res. 18)   Mr. *Huling* submitted a report of suitable topics for the special period which after discussion and modification was adopted as follows:

1. The Struggle between France and England for North America.
2. Spain in the New World.
3. The French Revolution and the Napoleonic Period.
4. Some Phase of the Renaissance.
5. The Puritan Movement in the Seventeenth Century.
6. The Commerce of the American Colonies during the 17th & 18th Centuries.
7. American Political Leaders from 1825 to 1830.
8. The Territorial Expansion of the United States.
9. American Politics from 1783 to 1830.
10. The Mohammedans in Europe.
11. The Influence of Greece upon Modern Life.
12. Some Phase of the Reorganization of Europe since 1848.
13. Some Phase of the Reformation.
14. Some Considerable Phase of Local History.

(Res. 19)   On motion of Mr. *Huling* it was voted that the Chairman and Secretary be authorized to append such notes upon these subjects as they deemed proper.

Professor Scott reported a list of subjects in Political Economy which was laid over for the time.

(Res. 20)   *Professor Macy* moved to add to American history in the first group the elements of Civil Government. Carried.

The Conference then proceeded to discuss the question of historical methods and the results of the discussion were embodied in the following resolutions:

(Res. 21)   *Resolved*, That in the first two years oral instruction in biography and mythology should be supplemented by the reading of simple biographies and mythological studies.

(Res 22.   *Resolved*. That after the first two years a suitable text-book or text-books should be used, but only as a basis of fact and arrangement, to be supplemented by other methods.

(Res. 23)   *Resolved*. That a collection of reference books, as large as the means of the school allow, should be provided for every school, suitable for use in connection with all the historical work done in that school.

Resolved. That a committee of two be appointed to draw up (Res 24) lists of suitable reference books, based on careful investigation of the subject, and conference with teachers.

Resolved. That pupils should be required to read or learn one (Res 25) other account beside that of the text-book, in each lesson.

Resolved. That the method of study by topics be strongly rec- (Res 26) ommended, as tending to stimulate pupils, and to encourage independence of judgment.

Resolved. That the teaching of history should be intimately (Res 27) connected with the teaching of English; first, by using historical works or extracts for reading in schools; second, by writing English compositions on subjects drawn from the historical lessons; third, by the committing to memory of historical poems and other short pieces; fourth, by outside reading of historical sketches, biographies and novels.

Resolved. That in all practicable ways an effort should be made (Res 28) to teach the pupils in the later years to discriminate between authorities, and especially between original sources and secondary works.

Resolved, That so far as practicable pupils should be encour- (Res 29) aged to avail themselves of their knowledge of ancient and modern languages, in their study of history.

Resolved. That the study of history should be constantly as- (Res 30) sociated with the study of topography and political geography and should be supplemented by the study of historical and commercial geography and the drawing of historical maps.

Resolved. That in all schools it is desirable that history should (Res 31) be taught by teachers who have not only a fondness for historical study but also have paid special attention to effective methods of imparting instruction.

Sixth session Friday afternoon, Dec 30.

The report of *Professor Scott* on instruction on Political Economy was made in typewriter. The Conference discussed the question of inserting as a subject the arguments for protection and free trade, and finally agreed to omit that phrase and to substitute a phrase with reference to international values and international trade. With that change the report of *Professor Scott* was adopted as follows (See papers of the Conference)[5]

The Conference then proceeded to discuss the question of a Insert No 32 separation between pupils preparing for college and others. It

---

[5] They are missing.

was the general sentiment that no such distinction should be made, and the opinion of the Conference was summed up in the following resolutions:

(Res 33)   *Resolved.* That the instruction in history and relative subjects ought to be precisely the same for pupils on their way to college or the scientific school and for those who expect to stop at the end of the grammar schools, or at the end of the high schools.

The Conference then discussed the relation of college examinations and came to the following vote:

(Res 34)   *Resolved,* That the examination in history for entrance to college ought to be so framed as to require comparison and the use of judgment on the pupils part, rather than the mere use of memory.

(Res. 35)   *Resolved,* That satisfactory written work done in the preparatory schools ought to be accepted as a considerable part of the evidence of proficiency.

(Res. 36)   *Resolved.* That the examination in history for entrance to college ought usually to be a part of the final examinations for college rather than the preliminaries.

The Chairman appointed as the committee of two to draw up the list of refer[ence] books *Professor Robinson* and *Mr. Huling.*

The Conference next took up the subject of Civil Government which had already been much discussed in connection with history. The result of the deliberation is summed up in the following votes—

(Res. 37)   *Resolved,* That Civil Government in the grammar schools should be taught by oral lessons with the use of collateral text-books and in connection with United States history and local geography.

(Res. 38)   *Resolved,* That Civil Government in the high schools be taught by using a text-book as a basis with collateral readings and topic work; and with observation of and instruction in the government of the city or town and state in which the pupils live; and with comparison of American Government with foreign systems.

On motion of *Professor Warren* it was:

(Res. 39)   *Resolved,* That the Conference extend their thanks to the University and citizens of Madison for their gracious hospitality.

(Res 40)   It was informally agreed that the report prepared by the Chairman and Secretary should be submitted to all the members of the Conference for their suggestions and revision and that a revised report be submitted for a second criticism before finally sending it to the committee of ten.[6]

6 This undoubtedly was done before the report of the Madison conferees,

Every member of the Conference was present at every meeting except the first. *Professor Haskins, Professor Turner,* and *Mr. Wells* attended most of the sessions. The Conference visited the buildings of the University at the invitation of the President, and the State Library at the invitation of the Librarian, Mr. Thwaites. There was no dissenting vote in any one of the thirty nine formal resolutions   Albert Bushnell Hart   Secretary.

---

printed in *Report of the Committee on Secondary School Studies*, pp. 162-203, was published. However, no correspondence relating to these exchanges survives in the Wilson Papers or has been found in other collections.

Typed MS. with hw emendations (C. W. Eliot Papers, University Archives, MH).

Two Letters from Ellen Axson Wilson

My own darling,   Princeton, Dec. 28/92

I have been puzzled to know what to do with the enclosed letter[1]—to forward or not to forward;—it seems to require an immediate answer so I will write and explain your silence. I think on the whole I will send this to Chicago.[2] It might do just as well for me to answer it myself & put the poor man's mind at rest!—for of course you can't give the lectures in Jan. with the book and the Hopkins lectures both on your hands! I think I *will* explain to him why the 10th and the 16th (Mon. & Tuesday) are in any event impossible dates.

Your telegram arrived last night and was a great, albeit only partial, relief.[3] I am now waiting eagerly for the one from Madison. Oh how I hope and pray that this terrible cold will do my darling no harm,—that he may reach home quite safe and well. I am trying not to borrow trouble—to be as happy as I can, but I find that a very different thing from being as happy as I *have* been; but when I get my darling safe in my arms again, then I will indeed be the happiest girl in the world.

The cold has not abated in the least here as yet, indeed I think it is colder; and we read terrible accounts of the weather in the north-west. It is 30° below zero at Burlington. But it has not reached zero here. The boys[4] are busy just now in covering those two nursery windows with the canton flannel.

Both the boys are coming tonight together with Miss Harris and Miss Owen.[5] I asked Miss Gaston[6] but found she was to leave for Boston today. We are perplexed because Stock has not his dress suit with him. If I had known it before I asked the girls I would not have had them. I hope that one or both of the other boys will come without. We went to the Murrays yesterday but had an unsatisfactory visit. Dr. Murray had just been sitting *four* hours in the Catholic church helping to make Father Moran a "Monseigneur"[7] and he was so bored and *sleepy* he hadn't a word to say for himself,—kept gaping in our faces! We will go to Dr. Patton's this afternoon. Of course you will have seen in the papers Gen. Kargé's sudden death.[8] It seems Mr. Fine was with him. He was struck down in the car and died before they could get him to the Astor House.

We are all quite well except Nellie who is about the same. Jessie does not cough at all now. They are still very happy over their toys. The dolls from Anna [Harris] arrived, also beautiful books for them from Sav. & a lovely little ring for each of them from Sister Annie. The latter are too small, they will barely get on their "little" fingers. I dare say we can change them.

I see from the New York paper that Prof. E. B. Wilson[9] & Mr. Conn[10] are both in Princeton;—would [like] to invite them to dine, but as you are not here I think I won't. It is very hard for me to reconcile myself to the fact that my darling is not here on his birthday! I long for you dearest with a longing unspeakable. You are not out of my thoughts one moment of the day or even of the night,—for I have had the good fortune of late to *dream* of you. Here are some pretty lines to the point which I came upon just before I went to bed last night—

> Goodnight! goodnight! Ah good the night
> That wraps thee in its silver light.
> Good-night! no night is good to me
> That does not bring a thought of thee.
> > Goodnight!
>
> Goodnight! Be every night as sweet
> As that which made our love complete;
> Till that last night when death shall be
> One brief good-night for you and me.
> > Goodnight![11]

May all your nights and days too, dearest, be as 'good' as brave, true living and happy loving can make them and may your birthdays be many and happy and may never another of them all be spent away from the one who loves you best,—loves you with all her heart and soul and mind,—your little wife and lover,

> Eileen.

Best love to Jessie & kind regards to Mr. Brower.[12]

1 It is missing.
2 Wilson was stopping in Chicago on his way to Madison to see, among others, Jessie and Abraham Brower.

³ This telegram is missing.

⁴ That is, Stockton Axson, Edward Axson, and George Howe III.

⁵ As her next letter makes clear, Ellen was having a party. "Both the boys" were undergraduates spending the vacation in Princeton. The only one who can be identified was James Maclin Brodnax, '94, of Mason, Tennessee. "Miss Harris" was Elizabeth P. Harris of 342 Nassau Street. "Miss Owen" could have been either Alice or Isabel Sheldon Owen, identified in WW to EAW, May 8, 1892, n. 2, Vol. 7.

⁶ She may have lived in Boston.

⁷ The Rev. Thomas R. Moran, pastor of St. Paul's Roman Catholic Church in Princeton for more than twenty-five years. He was invested with the Purple and given the title of Monsignor on December 27 in what the *Princeton Press*, December 31, 1892, called "one of the most imposing ceremonies which, perhaps, ever occurred in Princeton." Dean Murray made an address on behalf of the college.

⁸ General Joseph Kargé, Woodhull Professor of Continental Languages and Literature, who died in New York City on December 27.

⁹ Edmund Beecher Wilson, then Adjunct Professor of Biology at Columbia. He had taught at Bryn Mawr during the years when Wilson was there.

¹⁰ Herbert William Conn, Professor of Biology at Wesleyan University.

¹¹ From Silas Weir Mitchell's "Good-night."

¹² JRW to WW, Jan. 16, 1893, suggests the reason for Ellen's differential greetings.

My own darling,   Princeton Dec. 29/92

It seems scarcely worth while to write today when there is so much doubt of *any* letter reaching you—(you know I havn't Jessie's address,) still I will write a few lines on the chance. Your telegram reached me this afternoon and was a great comfort,—after the first thrill of terror during which I was sure that you were violently ill with pneumonia; a calamity which has been as it were haunting my thoughts ever since you left. So you may imagine how happy I was to learn that you are still well and having a "good time." Your friends out there must indeed be charming if they can entice you into feeling "jolly" with the thermometer at 30° below. George [Howe] returned today,—still well in spite of everything. The Dr. had lent him an overcoat while in New York and here I am making him wear an old "cut-away" of yours under his mackintosh & over his coat!

That suggests the dress-coat perplexity of last night. It all ended well, for neither of the boys had on dress suits. I should have known beforehand it would be so if I had ever met them; they are *very* nice boys but quite unused to society. You should have seen Mr. Broadnax trying to lead the way to the dining room! It was only in the door-way that Miss Harris succeeded in pulling him up and letting Stock and Miss Owen get ahead! But we had a jolly evening after all—sitting in a circle round the fire telling stories and "fortunes."

Stock left this afternoon. He had gotten a limited ticket and was obliged to,—most unwillingly. We went to Dr. Patton's and had a very pleasant call,—an agreeable contrast to the one on Dr. Murray.

Gen. Kargé is to be buried tomorrow from the house. Mrs. Fine's sister died the day before yesterday too; it was an exciting day for Mr. Fine; you know he was with the Gen! There has been only one little package of proof—no other mail of importance. Nellie is about the same—the rest well. Give my love to Jessie & tell her she *must* come to see me. How much I want to see the dear girl & to have some nice long talks with her about old times & new! Among other things I want to thank her for having a "Cousin Woodrow"! Be sure to get pictures of the family for me including Helen & dear Marion.[1] Goodbye dearest love, *my* Woodrow. I wonder if you know how *constantly* my thoughts are travelling that long bleak way that divides us. If they could materialize suddenly the whole air would be white with them, little tender, loving, fluttering things. Do you ever feel their presence about you?   Your own   Eileen

ALS (WC, NjP).
    [1] Jessie's sisters, Helen Woodrow Bones and Marion McGraw Bones.

A Report of Wilson's Address at Vassar College

[January 1893]

Professor Woodrow Wilson's lecture on "Democracy,"[1] given in the chapel on the evening of December 9th, was heard and enjoyed by a large number of students. A large, complex democracy like the United States, is hard to explain, but the fundamental idea is that the people are sovereign. Yet we cannot assume one prevalent opinion in this day of hard labor and little time for reflection, nor, when we take into account the prejudices, personal jealousies and other such forces, can we assume an average, instinctive, safe opinion. Moreover, history shows that the concurrence of majorities does not always express the general will. By the sovereignty of the people then, we mean that the people agree to be governed by individuals chosen from themselves; the people govern well when they use discrimination in this choice. This conception of liberty is higher and nobler than the common one. Political parties are useful for promoting consistency in belief and vigor in reform. The people have true liberty when they are obedient to law and to standards of character, and this law of liberty is the law of progress. It is a more serious matter to live under a democratic government than under any other. Citizenship is exalted, has the greater opportunities, and must be the nobler.

Printed in the Poughkeepsie, N. Y., *Vassar Miscellany*, XXII (Jan. 1893), 207-208.
¹ For this address, he used the text printed at Dec. 5, 1891, Vol. 7.

To Albert Bushnell Hart

My dear Prof. Hart,   Princeton, New Jersey, 3 January, 1893.

I hope you reached home comfortably (as I did, arriving last night), and not too much fatigued. You certainly deserve the heartiest thanks of the Conference, for undertaking the onerous duties of secretary,—to say nothing of your very great contributions to its debates and conclusions. I enjoyed the meetings thoroughly, and value the acquaintances and friendships it helped me to form more than I can say. It was a very great pleasure to see so much of you, and form so much closer ties of friendship with you than any amount of correspondence could have enabled us to form.

And now once more to the old business. Fearing you were not going to send me any more of your page proofs, I sent mine back to the printer just before leaving for Madison. I find the only corrections you make affect the Bibliography on p. 117. I send that page back to-day, with the last galley proofs. Please make the additions you have noted there.

Please call the attention of the printer, too, to the fact that the first chapter heading of each Part should come *after* the Bibliography, which is for the Part, not for that particular chapter.

In haste,   Most cordially Yours,   Woodrow Wilson

TCL (RSB Coll., DLC).

To James Cameron MacKenzie

                           Princeton, New Jersey,

My dear Dr. Mackenzie,   4 January, 1893.

Thank you for your kind note of yesterday. We are extremely gratified to learn of the bestowal of a full scholarship upon Axson, and wish to thank you for your kind consideration of his case. Although we are of course disappointed that Howe could not also secure some assistance, we hardly expected that he could, applying when he did, and perfectly appreciate the reasons.

I hasten to write a word or two in answer to your inquiry about Dr. Thomas B. Harrison.¹ It gives me genuine pleasure to be able to express a very high opinion of him. I may say that I know him very well. I have had no direct means of judging of his scholarship; but I had excellent indirect means. My brother-in-law, Ed. Axson's older brother, himself a scholarly fellow of the best type, was in the same department with Harrison for a year at the Hopkins, and expressed the highest opinion of his attainments. I myself found him a charming fellow and evidently a man of real spirit and genuine cultivation,—besides being a gentleman. Of course I do not know how well he can *teach*; but I feel sure that he is thoroughly worth trying. I should like to see him at Lawrenceville.

Faithfully Yours,   Woodrow Wilson

ALS (WP, DLC).
  [1] Thomas Perrin Harrison, who had received his Ph.D. in English from the Johns Hopkins in 1891 and was at this time Associate Professor of English at Clemson Agricultural and Mechanical College.

From Joseph Ruggles Wilson

My precious Woodrow—   Columbia, S. C., Jany 16/93

Geo. received your letter to-day, and I take advantage of this first news of your home-getting after the Western trip, to write a line or so to inform you of my comparative welfare. I was fortunate in having been in this *tolerable* latitude while those "cold waves" were sweeping over the land, the effects of which you experienced to your discomfort and are still feeling I dare say. It has been bad enough even here—for never has this region had such an extended or such a severe visitation from the spirit that rules at the north pole. And it is not yet over. It has brought rheumatism to myself and lots of other evils to many about me.

Geo. will no doubt write at once with respect to Mrs. Brown's ear complaint, in your account of which he seems to have taken a decided interest.[1] Poor, isolated, good, old lady—I wish George had her here for a week or more! He would fix her up I am sure.

You said nothing in your letter about having been in Chicago; so that I suppose you did not visit that windy city at all where you might have found nothing warm except Jessie's welcome: Brower's would have made the weather colder. I do hope that you will all have a contenting time at Baltimore next month: but am sorry that I shall not be able to see you before you go. It is quite probable that, to relieve my restlessness, I will go to N. York about the first prox.—i.e. if Boreas and his family of Arctics shall permit. Of course I must incur no needless risks. It will not be long until the last of this world's risks is exchanged for everlasting certainties. And I am ready whenever it shall please God—for indeed, indeed, to say nothing else, I fear that I have already become an unconfessed bore here. Present my love to daughter Ellie, and also accept for yourself my heart.　　　Your affc　Father

ALS (WP, DLC).
　[1] Woodrow Wilson had apparently written to Dr. Howe for advice to convey to Ellen's aunt, Mrs. Warren A. Brown, about her ear trouble.

An Announcement

[Jan. 17, 1893]

PROF. WILSON'S COURSES.

Prof. Wilson is to give a course of lectures at Johns Hopkins University in February and will not meet his classes during that month. He has assigned the following subjects upon which examinations will be given during the week beginning March 5. For the Junior and Senior Elective in American Constitutional Law; Cooley's General Principles of Constitutional Law.

For the Senior Elective in Administration; Bryce's American Commonwealth, Part 2, "State Government."

Printed in the *Daily Princetonian*, Jan. 17, 1893.

From the Minutes of the Princeton Faculty

5 5′ P.M. Wednesday, Jany. 18, 93

... *Whereas* it appears that there has been a strong and growing Student Sentiment against the practice of Cheating in Examinations, and further that the Students desire to have the Examinations so conducted as to be put upon their honor as Gentlemen,

Resolved, That until due notice be given to the contrary, there shall be no Supervision of Examinations, each Student simply subscribing at the end of his paper the following *Declaration*,

I pledge my honor as a gentleman that during this Examination I have neither given nor received aid.[1]

　[1] This resolution inaugurating the honor system at Princeton was adopted (even though the Clerk of the Faculty, Henry Clay Cameron, failed to note the fact in the Minutes) and published in the *Daily Princetonian*, January 19, 1893. There had been much agitation among the undergraduates for an honor system, and a strong plea for its institution by the *Daily Princetonian* on January 13 seems to have brought the matter to a head. The Faculty Minutes do not reveal the identity of the author of the resolution, but there is no reason to doubt the tradition that he was Dean Murray, who was presiding in the absence of President Patton. The Faculty Minutes indicate that there was no debate on the resolution and that it was adopted unanimously.

To Albert Bushnell Hart

Princeton, New Jersey,

My dear Professor Hart,   20 January, 1893.

The same day I sent you the last proof sheets of the third Epoch I sent the copy for the Index to the printers. The making of that index was perhaps the most vexatious part of the whole job; and I am deeply thankful it is over with. I shall ask the printers to send the proofs of it to Baltimore, where I begin my lectures on the 26th. of this month,—next week, in short.

It is a genuine pleasure to know that I shall see you in Baltimore again this time, and that I shall have an opportunity to meet Mrs. Hart. I hope that you will keep me informed of your movements when you are in that neighbourhood so that I may be sure not to miss you. I shall remain in Baltimore until the 4th. of March.

I want to thank you very cordially for your kind letter written since your return from Madison.[1] It warmed my heart not a little. Your favourable estimate of "Division and Reunion" is doubtless too partial; but it cheers me none the less. Just at present I am too weary of the tiresome little thing to think of it with any degree of allowance. In great haste,

Most cordially Yours,   Woodrow Wilson

TCL (WP, DLC).
[1] It is missing.

An Announcement

[Jan. 25, 1893]

ELECTIVE IN ADMINISTRATION.

The senior elective class in Administration for the second term will be expected to be ready for examination on Chapters VII., VIII., X., and XI. of Wilson's "The State" during the week beginning March 5. Bryce's *American Commonwealth* is temporarily out of print.   Woodrow Wilson.

Printed in the *Daily Princetonian*, Jan. 25, 1893.

From the Minutes of the Princeton Faculty

5 5' P.M., Wednesday, Jany. 25, 1893.

. . . Professors [Alexander T.] Ormond, W. Wilson and [Charles G.] Rockwood were appointed a Committee to present to the Faculty any thing further that may be necessary in connection with the recent action in reference to the Supervision of written Examinations. This Committee was really appointed at the last meeting.

EDITORIAL NOTE

WILSON'S LECTURES ON ADMINISTRATION AT THE
JOHNS HOPKINS, 1893

This particular note is an addendum to the general Editorial Note, "Wilson's Lectures on Administration at the Johns Hopkins, 1891-93," printed in Volume 7.

The Wilson family went to Baltimore on about January 25, 1893, at the end of the first Princeton term, and stayed with Mary Jane Ashton at 909 North McCulloh Street. Beginning on January 26, Wilson lectured twenty-four times, concluding his series on March 1.

The notes printed below are obviously incomplete, but the existence of a complete set of classroom notes taken by Louis T. Clark[1] enables us to reconstruct the complete set of notes that Wilson used in 1893. Once he had worked through the notes with the composition date of February 15, 1893, printed below, Wilson began to use his notes for his Hopkins administration lectures in 1890, commencing with the section entitled "Place of Municipal Government in Administration" and intending to go through the last section of this series, the one entitled "Administrative Justice."[2] Clark's classroom notes make it clear that Wilson actually only got through the section entitled "Central Control: Administrative Integration" in 1893. These classroom notes also reveal that the section of notes printed below with the composition dates of February 7, 1895, and February 13, 1896, were only slight revisions of the notes that Wilson had used for the same subject in 1893.

[1] They are now deposited in the library of The Johns Hopkins University.
[2] These sections are printed in Vol. 6, pp. 487-521.

Notes for Lectures at the Johns Hopkins

Third Year Course)   [Jan. 26, 1893-Feb. 13, 1896]

ADMINISTRATION

I. *Resumé* of Several Topics of Previous Year:

Our topic this year, *Local Government*; but by what *criteria* are we to distinguish local from central government?
1. *Nature of the Problem*:[1]

[1] Comp. F. J. Goodnow, "*Comparative Administrative Law*," Bk. I., Chap. VI., "Territorial Distribution of Administrative Functions." [See the Editorial Note, "Wilson's Lectures on Administration at the Johns Hopkins, 1891-93," Vol. 7, for an explanation of the treatment of notes and references. (Eds.' note)]

Evidently one of the widest and most important, and at the same time one of the most complex and difficult, questions connected with the study of government. It is *not a single, but a double*, question, concerning

(a) *The life of the State* as a whole, as a political unit;
(b) *Individual initiative* and the vitality of local gov't., coming very near indeed to qus. of *liberty* and the diffusion of *political capacity.*

2. *General Considerations*:

Supervision there must be, for the sake of the life of the State as a whole; but it must be exercised upon the principle also that *local autonomy and variety* are to be given full leave up to the point at which they clearly come into collision with the interests of the State as a whole—a supervision which is *not interference*, or direction, or guidance even; which is *not presidential, but prudential*, and for the sake of the country, not for the sake of the community.[2]

But, while it is easy to go on in this general way, *is it easy to find the line?* General remarks are not generalizations.

We may go further, however, and be somewhat more instructive, by saying that, if the units of local gov't. are to have a way of their own, they *ought to be homogeneous* in make-up and interest.

Not city *plus* country; or mining *plus* agricultural

Since there are some interests, too, which are larger than the smallest area of local gov't., and yet not so large as the State, there ought to be *divisions intermediate in size* between the commune or township and the State, with a corresponding set of intermediate officials. (Militia, certain roads chartered for national highways, school inspection, local incidental taxation, forests, etc., for example)

3. *Various Solutions of the Question*:

A. *The French Answer*: An argument for complete *national unity, uniformity* both in the provisions of law and in their application. The *solidarity and glory* of France: *the general good and united vigour of the country.* Liberty, says *M. Aucoc*, is no doubt a very precious thing, but the other good things which society can procure for us must not be sacrificed for it.

M. Aucoc urges three faults on the part of local authori-

---

2 This is simply the principle of individual liberty extended.
It is possible even to pick out obvious examples of functions to which authorities larger than the merely local should look: care of highways; protection from contagious diseases (though here the argument is hardly more than that of *knowledge*); regulation of poor relief; care of incapables and the insane,—among a great many others.

ties which he conceives it to be the duty of the central authorities to correct:

Violations of liberty and equality before the law.

Negligence in function.

Extravagance.

He would practically leave no field for local spirit or conscience.

He *urges a stronger reason* when he desires the defence of local minorities

Napoleon's dictum: "The personal proprietary interest is ceaselessly on the watch, bears fruit continually; on the contrary, the interest of the community is by nature somnolent and sterile: personal interest needs nothing but its instinct; the interest of the community requires virtue, and that is rare." *Mem. dictated to Ministry of Interior, 1800.*

Simon Patten's answer would be: the impracticability of uniform law in view of the almost infinite economic variety amongst communities.[3] But this proves too much. It is probably now too late to carve out economic units.

General answer: the French argument unquestionably *misses the principle of life*, which is *not uniformity, but diversity*. This is conclusive negatively; but it constructs nothing: it does not find the law or the limits of variety.

N.B. The effort has been made (e.g., in Prussia) to serve the purpose of variety by entrusting the peculiar interests of distinct localities to the supervising direction of distinct central Bureaux: but only to the confusion of all classification by reason of a cross-sectioning of divisions according to kind and divisions according to locality—geographical by [rather than] logical.

B. *Experimental Classification*: according to the breadth or universality of interests as revealed by experience. *Result: Trial Lists* of functions appropriate for uniform direction from the centre. *E.g., this, from Aucoc*: National roads; the greater railways; navigable rivers; canals; sea ports; post and telegraph; part of public education; certain matters concerning public worship; and

---

[3] See his article on "Decay of Local Government in America" in Annals Am. Acad. Pol. & Soc. Sci., i., p. 26. Points of the paper[:]
  Arbitrary creation of States and townships by Surveyor. Illustration drawn from Illinois. (p. 33)
  Wholesale imitation in law-making
  Neglect of actual separation of interest and type between great cities and the rest of the State to which they belong.

much of administrative police (including sanitation, I
suppose).

But what of national differences of development?

Such classifications lack vitality because empirical.
They are *pieces of pragmatic policy*, not statements of
principle

C. *'Political' distinguished from 'Economic' interests.*

Meier suggests this in his distinction between *'magisterial'*
functions and *'economic.'* He conceives the economic
functions of local authorities to be much more characteristic and much more intensive than the economic
functions of the central authorities. *The budget* is *much
more central to local than to imperial legislation.*

It is on this ground that he *justifies the three-class system of voting*, while questioning its justice when applied
to national affairs.

Sarwey embodies a similar idea in his suggestion that,
for the sake of unity in administration, and for the sake
of definiteness of responsibility to the representatives of
the people in their national body, *each branch of administration should have at its summit some central organ*
in which 'government' and 'administration' are united.

'Government'—those organs (or that organ) of the
State by wh. its unity is represented, as over against
foreign powers, or as over against the representatives
of the people: *the 'Responsible Executive,'* in a word, in
whose hands the *Administration is an instrument.*[4]

This much the most satisfactory suggestion.

4. *Summary of Suggestions:*

(1) *Solidarity*: a uniform will for the nation.

(2) *Convenience*, as shown in a general way by the size of
the function.

(3) *House-keeping vs. supervision* and the determination of
policy.

5. *Summary of General Considerations:*

1. *We are dealing*, on the one hand *with a general life*, with
its questions, primarily, of *positive law and assured political privilege*, of order and freedom; and its questions,
secondarily, of commerce, general intercourse, common

---

[4] *The French writers* make a distinction also between *'Gouvernement,'* the
direction of those affairs for which the name political is reserved, that is to
say, the relations of the head of the State with the 'great bodies' of the State,
and *'Administration,'* which they regard as *something "altogether different,"* viz.
the power which acts for the "collective needs of the citizens," where individual or private corporate initiative does not suffice.—*Aucoc*, I, 94, 95.

facilities and securities of life. Its economic questions are *questions of principle and policy rather than questions of practical means and institutions.*

2. *We are dealing,* on the other hand, *with communal life,* local *resources, occupations, natural advantages,* needs, tastes, pleasures, necessity for order and capacity for development. Its questions are *not so much questions of principle as questions of practical living*—means and institutions. (See extract fr. Hening.)[5]

Conclusion:

(1) The distinction bet. *political* and *economic* functions supplies us with the *subject-matter* of Local Government.

(2) The range of *sound policy* in respect of the distribution of functions bet. central and locallauthorities [local authorities] is determined by the consideration, that the relations bet. central and local government should not be such as in any degree to involve the *conduct* of local affairs by central authorities, but only such as to secure a nice adjustment of local administration to national aims and conveniences.

E.g.,—Militarizing of local police by means of a common organization and discipline.

Navigation Acts *vs.* a tea tax: &c. &c.

6. *Three types of government* serve to *illustrate* the several degrees in which this distinction is actually observed:

1. *The Prussian system,* under which elected local authorities are kept within bounds by the *supervision* of appointed *officials* who are themselves in a sense independent, inasmuch as they are *subject to removal only by judicial process.*

2. *The French system,* under which neither the central nor the local authorities are really independent. The more important *officials* are *appointed,* almost all are *subject to administrative removal. The local bodies are under tutelage* rather than under supervision (v. Sarwey, 105, 2, 3.).

3. *The English system* (now in a transitional stage), under which there is, in some branches, constant *inspection* by the central authorities, in all *occasional inquiry* and *potential supervision and even intervention;* but under which local offi-

---

[5] The "extract" is missing, but Wilson is probably referring to a passage in William W. Hening's *The Statutes at Large; Being a Collection of all the Laws of Virginia* (13 vols., New York, 1823) or in Hening's *The Virginia Justice* (Richmond, 1825). Both works are in the Wilson Library, DLC. The inscription on the title page of the first volume of *The Statutes at Large* indicates that Wilson acquired this series in 1881. [Eds.' note]

cials, whether appointed or elected, can be *held only to their statutory duties* and are not subject to arbitrary removal.

7. *Centralization vs. Concentration*:

Centralization—the *direct dependence* of officials of all grades and functions upon the central authorities, because appointed and subject to removal.

Concentration—an equal integration and an equally systematic organization, it may be, but also *a certain independence of tenure* on the part of local officials. They may be elected, and, *if subject to oversight*, are *not the creatures* of the central authorities.—*Concentration is integration.*

8. *Differences between Legislation, Adjudication, & Administration in respect of centralization, both historically & essentially.*

1. *In legislation*, centralization *modern*, a product of modern unifying, universalizing tendencies.

Unity a characteristic mark of the modern time

2. *In adjudication more ancient*, though almost unknown to the mediaeval world. Has *sprung from the growth of the monarchical power* in modern States.

3. *In administration*, though not more recent than in legislation, *much less natural*, much more difficult to justify. *Uniformity in legislation* secures uniformity and certainty in private rights and the major principles of public law; *uniformity in adjudication* fixes the legal habit, facilitates the legal life, and promotes a common national consciousness and feeling for the principles of liberty; *but uniformity in administration* may fatally *disregard healthful varieties* of economic and social condition.

Plan of following lectures:

TOPICS:

I. *Local Administrative Organization*, its conditions, principles, and (historical) development: *treated by taking four systems*, the English, American, French and Prussian, *and considering*
   (1) *The different conditions and historical stages* of their development.
   (2) *The different principles or conceptions* upon which they are based.
II. *Brief descriptions of these four systems.*
III. *The administration of the modern industrial city*, by way of fixing its place (whether distinct or not) in the general plan of administrative organization.
IV. *The Executive and the Courts: Administrative Justice.*

26 January, 1893

I. *Local Administrative Organization,* Its *Conditions, Principles,* and (*historical*) *Development,* as Illustrated by *four representative systems,* the English, American, French, and Prussian:

I. *The Different Conditions and Historical Stages of Development,*

IN ENGLAND:

A. *Conditions:*

(a) *Complete supremacy of the Crown.* This is the characteristic mark of English development: a comparatively *weak baronage* in the presence of an *exceptionally powerful monarch* (strong chiefly because of his power outside England).

(b) *Creation of a great middle class,* by a meeting halfway and ultimate fusion of the claims of smaller *tenants-in-capite* and of the claims of lesser barons or knights. The greater feudal barons drew apart to become that peculiar class, the "Lords" or political nobility, of England. *Result: "a resident provincial upper class,* comprising all the petty tenants-in-chief of the Crown and the inferior barons, and *a political aristocracy* comprising all the great barons and the counsellors summoned by the king." (*See* M. *Boutmy's* "The *English Constitution,*" p. 38)

(c) *Destruction of the old feudal nobility* (during the Wars of the Roses) and the *subjection of the Church* to the Crown by the English "Reformation," produced *the modern English classes, the Commons* (who had established many precedents of authority in the troublous times of the wars of the roses); *the Lords,* now *recruited from the Commons,* the great middle class referred to above; and the King, subject to no control but that of the nation as a whole.

(d) *The Industrial Revolution* of the eighteenth century and the establishment of *the Oligarchy.* The *yeomen driven out* by *latifundia,* and at the same time attracted to *the cities* by the prospect of commercial wealth.

Property qualifications doubled, at the same time that no recognition at all was accorded the commercial wealth of the cities. (*Temp. Anne*) *Decline of parochial government.*

(e) *The democratic revolution* of the present century, beginning with the *Chartist agitation* and the *Reform Bill of 1832,* with its enfranchisement of the city population. The completion of this reform in 1867, 1884-1885,

Thi'd Yea. Course)

ADMINISTRATION.

I. Local Administrative Organization, Its Conditions, Principles, and [historical] Development, as Illustrated by four representative systems, the English, American, French, and Prussian:

I. The Different Conditions and Historical Stages of Development,

IN ENGLAND:-

A. Conditions:-

(a) Complete supremacy of the Crown. This is the characteristic mark of English development: a comparatively weak baronage in the presence of an exceptionally powerful monarch (strong chiefly because of his power outside England).

(b) Creation of a great middle class, by a meeting halfway and ultimate fusion of the class of smaller tenants-in-capite and of the class of lesser barons or knights. The greater feudal barons drew apart to become that peculiar class, the "Lords" or political nobility, of England. Result: "a resident provincial upper class, comprising all the petty tenants-in-chief of the Crown and the inferior barons, and a political aristocracy comprising all the great barons and the counsellors summoned by the king". (See M. Boutmy's "The English Constitution", p. 58)

(c) Destruction of the old feudal nobility (during the Wars of the Roses) and the subjection of the Church to the Crown by the English "Reformation", produced the modern English classes, the Commons (who had established many precedents of authority in the troublous times of the wars of the roses); the Lords, now

A page of Wilson's Johns Hopkins lecture notes for January 1893,
showing an early use of his first Hammond typewriter,
with its interchangeable styles of type

made the old order of government by the Justices, however admirable in itself, *anomalous*, and its continuance impossible.

B. *Stages: Never* since Norman times has there been *representative self-government* in England; but only service self-government.

(a) *Government through the* SHERIFF *and the* COUNTY COURT. The *sheriff*, under this system was the *direct and universal agent and deputy* of the King, in financial, military, and civil affairs; though in most of these he was assisted by the county court (in which the freeholders did compulsory service). "*This court*, which the prelates, earls, barons, and free proprietors were expected to attend, in addition to the reeve and four men of each village, *presented those democratic features which are found in so many institutions of the middle ages.* Its functions were many and various; it was at once *a court* of criminal and of civil jurisdiction, *a registry* for the transfer of lands, the *place of publication* of royal ordinances, and an *office for the receipt of taxes*" (*Boutmy*, p. 58).

Notwithstanding the fact that the wealthier members of this court purchased exemption from attendance, and the less important shirked it as often as possible, *the importance of this court was maintained* even after the importance of the sheriff had considerably declined *by the fact that the royal Judges on circuit made constant and various use of commissions made up from its membership. The knights*, especially, were summoned to this service. This practice may be said to have inaugurated the stage next to be mentioned. (CONQUEST *to* RICHARD II).

(b) *Official self-government by the great body of* (middleclass) *gentry.* (*Since* TUDOR *times*, TO PRESENT CENTURY). *No officers elected except* the Coroner and the churchwardens.

Justices of the Peace appointed 1360, from among the knig[h]ts. the body of knights *ultimately merged in the general body of landowners*, squires, gentlemen, until, rank having disappeared, property qualifications were required (fifteenth century).

Waxing and waning of the Parish. It was under the Tudors that the importance of the Parish was increased by addition. *After the destruction of the monasteries* the *care of the poor* was entrusted to the churchwardens (one appointed by the pastor, one elected by the Vestry, two or three others appointed by the Justices of the Peace: 27 Hen. VIII & 43 Eliz.). *Then* (temp. Philip & Mary) *the care of highways* was entrusted to the Parishes, under the administration of *surveyors*, at first elected by the constables and churchwardens, but afterwards appointed by the Justices. Afterwards the *Parish waned* again in importance *because of* the constant increase of the the [*sic*] supervisory *powers of the Justices.*

The organization of the Justices into Quarter Sessions with the largest powers completed the development on the side of organization; but *the Justices* were for most of the period *subject to be controlled by the courts* through the writs of MANDAMUS, CERTIORARI, and PROHIBITION. In th*e time of the oligarchy* this *judicial control was abandoned,* and the Justices became autocratic.

The system from the first POPULAR.

(c) *The Oligarchy.* Another nation, the industrial of the midland and seaport towns, grew up alongside the old urganization [organization], and unrecognized by it; and every effort of legislation was made to strengthen and perpetuate its supremacy, until it grew odious.

(d) THE *Industrial Revolution,* the *first result* of wh. was the *Reform Bill of 1832;* but whose first result in the field of local government was the *Poor-Law Amendment Act of 1834.,* which created the Poor-Law Unions and introduced the *principle of representation* in the constitution of the Boards of Guardians. Its latest result has been the *Local Government Acts* of 1888-1889.

This *revolution consisted,* moreover, in part in the *introduction of a new principle of voluntary service.* The Guardians were permitted to act through salaried subordinates. (*Service as Sheriff, compulsory; service as* J.P., obligatory at first, but paid *per diem; now neither obligatory nor paid*).

These changes were accompanied, moreover, by the *introduction of central control,* and of the system of *multiple votes* in the choice of the Guardians.

B. [C.] *Brief Description of English Local Government*:

I. *As it was before the Reforms of this century:*

Principal Divisions, the COUNTY, the PARISH, and the chartered CITY.

Of these *the* COUNTY *was by far the most important* in local administration; and during much the greater part of the period the *Justices of the Peace* were the *all-important governing authority.*

The SHERIFF *was reduced* (as we have seen) (*a*) by the *absorptions* of jurisdiction on the part of the royal courts, (*b*) by the *discipline* of HENRY II., who (1170) brought the great baronial sheriffs to book, and put mere Exchequer officials in their places; (*c*) by the *appointment,* in 1194, *of "custodians of pleas of the Crown,"* Coroners, and (*d*) by the *prohibition* in Magna Carta (which applied also to the Coronors) to hold pleas of the Crown.

Rise of the Justices and the cumulation of functions in their hands. (*Read* from *"The State"* p. 413[)]

THE PARISH (the *"ecclesiastical"* Parish, the *"civil,"* the *"Poor-Law,"* the *"Highway"*).

The POOR-LAW PARISH *acts through the Vestry* (common or select) in the choice of churchwardens, waywardens, and assessors; and had charge, before the reforms of the present century, among other things, of *the relief of the poor and the care of highways.* Now changed in area and subordinated in function.

The CITIES and *the new towns.*

Nothing done by way of reconstruction until—

II. *Reforms of the present Century:*

(1) *Poor-Law Amendment Act of 1834* grouped the parishes into *"Unions"* for the purposes of poor-law administration under a Commission which subsequent legislation presently constituted a permanent *Poor Law Board,* supplanted, under an *Act of 1871,* by the present *Local Government Board*

BOARD *of* GUARDIANS, *consisting* of at least one from each Parish (though Parishes of less than 300 inhabitants may be merged by the Local Government Board in larger Parishes for purposes of poor relief) *elected* by the rate payers of the several Parishes, *under the multiple system of voting* (one vote for every £50 of rated property up to six votes). *Term* of the Guardians one year unless the Local Government Board, upon the vote of the rate payers, make it longer.

Powers of the Board:

Administer poor relief (except that urgent cases may be relieved by the pahish [parish] overseers);

Appoint the relieving and medical officers, the work-

house masters, chaplains, schoolmasters; and the regis-
trars of births and deaths.

ARE *the rural sanitary authorities*; the *rural sanitary Districts consisting* of such parts of the Unions as are not
within the limits of incorporated urban areas. (*The
boundaries of Unions* are run without regard to urban
areas.)

Hear appeals from the decisions of the overseers in respect of valuations and assessments for the poor rates.

Enforce Vaccination and the Bakehouse Regulation Acts.

OVERSEERS: (*a*) The churchwardens ex officio, where
the civil Parish is co-incident with the ecclesiastical; and,
(*b*) *besides*, in every Parish, *appointed overseers*, "four,
three, or two substantial householders" (says the statute
of Elizabeth) or one only (subsequent legislation). *Appointed by the Justices.—Paid deputies* or assistants
may be appointed by the Justices upon the election of the
Vestry of the Parish.

THEIR DUTIES are:

To *make and levy the poor rate;*

To *prepare jury lists, lists of* parliamentary *voters*, etc.

(2) *Municipal Corporations* Act of 1835 (amendments codified 1882) *Incorporation by petition* to the *Privy Council*, which also determines the area of the new borough,
the number of members who shall constitute its Council, etc. *Make-up of the Council*: (*a*) *councillors* elected
for three years, one-third of whom go out every year;
(*b*) one-third as many *Aldermen* elected by the councillors for a term of six years, one-half retiring every
two years. (*c*) *A Mayor* elected by the Council and salaried. *The councillors are elected by the resident ratepayers of the Borough.* "*Every person* who occupies a
house, warehouse, shop, or other building in the Borough, for which he pays rates, and who resides within
seven miles of the borough, is entitled to be enrolled
as a burgess."

POWERS *of the* COUNCIL: All the powers once belonging to the *county Justices* except those strictly judicial
in their nature, all the *sanitary powers* of urban sanitary
authorities, often the powers of school administration,—
all reguladtive and administrative functions *except* those
of *poor relief*, the Union spreading its jurisdiction quite
irrespective of differences between town and country.

Action through Committees.

ACTION AS AN ADMINISTRATIVE WHOLE.

Various changes in the organization and status of boroughs by the legislation of *1888.*

(3) *Public Health Act,* 1848 (1875) provides for the creation of URBAN SANITARY DISTRICTS which are, as the result of various Acts practically a subordinate species of municipalities. "The boundaries of poor-law unions are the boundaries of rural sanitary districts, and the guardians are the rural sanitary authority. The urban districts *are carv*[ed] *out of the rural districts according to the exigencies of population.*" these exigencies of population are *determined by the Local Government Board,* either upon its own observation and initiative, or in answer to the petition of "the owners and ratepayers of any district having a definite boundary"; and *an order of the Board* creates the District just as an order of the Privy Council creates a borough.

Once created, the authorities of the District *exercise a number of powers* not simply sanitary in their character.

The Board of the District is elected by the ratepayers, upon a *cumulative system of voting* like that by which the guardians of the Union are chosen.

(4) *The Education Act of 1870* (1876, 1880) divides England into *School Districts* whose administration is under the supervision of the *Education Department of the Privy Council.* These districts coincide for the most part with parishes or boroughs, and have either an *elective School Board* or an *Attendance Committee* which is a sub-committee of some previously existing body.

(5) *The Local (County) Government Act of 1888-1890*:
(*For the details* of this legislation *see* "The State" pp. 415-424; 431-433. *For the confusion* to be rem[ed]ied, see "*State*" p. *415.*)

This legislation *applies the principles of the Municipal Corporations Act* of 1882 *to the* government of *Counties,* and affects, directly, nothing but the Counties. It also affects the boroughs themselves, inasmuch as *boroughs of 50,000 inhabitants* are made entirely independent of county administration, while smaller boroughs are more or lass [less] merged with the Counties in various matters.

Erects "*Administrative Counties*" (the historical counties being in several instances cut up into two or even three of these new areas.)

Councils made up (of *councillors* and *aldermen*) in the same proportion and upon the same principle as the borough council. *Elected by the ratepayers.*

Every person not an alien or otherwise specially disqualified, who is actually resident within the county or within seven miles of it, paying rates in the county and occupying within the county, either jointy [jointly] or alone, any house, warehouse, countinghouse, shop, or other building for which he pays rates is entitled to be enrolled, if his residence be of twelve months standing, and to vote as a county elector.

POWERS *of the County Councils*, speaking roughly, *those of the Justices* so far as not judicial in character (or semi-judicial, like the licensing function); *except that* the control of the *constabulary* is left with a *joint committee* of the Council and Quarter Sessions.

Boroughs which are not "County Boroughs," i.e. which have *less than fifty thousand inhabitants*, are merged with the Counties in which they lie in such matters as the maintenance of *main roads* and the *costs of the assizes* (borough having separate Quarter Sessions and more than ten thousand inhabitants); the maintenance and management of *various public institutions*, such as pauper lunatic asylums, reformatory and industrial schools, etc., in the regulation of *explosives* and *locomotives*, and the appointment of *Coroners* (Quarter Sessions boroughs with less than ten thousand inhabitants); or in all matters not of strictly local interest and importance. (boroughs having neither Quarter Sessions nor ten thousand inhabitants.[)]

D. *Principles of Local Government in England*:
  I. *Under the Old System*:
  Electoral representative system not only new but revolutionary in conception.

  (1) *The original conception* of English local government, as modified by the Normans, may be said to have been *government by direct representatives of the Crown* (first the *Sheriff* then the *Judges*) through the *instrumentality* and with the assistance of the *responsible classes of the community* doing compulsory service (the knights and the freemen).

  (2) *The direct delegation of the public authority* to

these same responsible classes in all matters not falling within the jurisdiction of the Judges on circuit.

This is *the second stage* already described[.] The *old conception* of self-goversnment *disappears entirely*, except from such retreats as the little Parish, and even there the authority of the Justices becomes more and more dominant and determinant.

(3) *Property qualifications* for office. Even since the democratic revolution we find the Guardians of the poor required to possess a property qualification, and both they and the authorities of the urban Sanitary Districts elected by *the cumulative system of votes.*

Multiple votes are *no doubt* a *tempora[r]y* arrangement, however, a transition to an entirely democratec system.

(4) *Statutory enumeration of powers* the rule from the first: upon the principle that *the powers* of the local authorities were *not self-determinative*, but fixed both in character and extent by explicit delegation from the central government.

Until the recent reforms, however, *the central authority* was *never actually present* in local government and exercised its only functions of control through legislation and the courts.

II. *Under the Reformed system* now in course of construction:

(1) *Representative self-government*: a democratic organization.

(2) *Central Control.* In some cases this is very complete, as, for example, in the oversight of the poor law and sanitary authorities. But *in most cases* it is practically of this character: *the advice of the central authorities always accessible* by the local officers or bodies, and *its consent necessary to certain* classes of local *undertakings.*

EXAMPLES:

Acco[u]nts of all local authorities, except thosa [those] of the boroughs, audited by agents of the Local Government Board.

Consent of the Local Government Board must be obtained by the County Councils *to the borrowing of money* "on the security of the county fund." THE BOARD gives or withholds its consent only after a local inquiry, and, in case it assents, *fixes the period* within which the loan must be repaid, being itself limited in this last particular by a provision of the law that *the period must never exceed thirty years.*

Same in the case of loans to be raised by borough Councils.

May give *imperative directions in* all mattars of *sanitation,* and the *local medical officers,* though commonly appointed by the local authirities, *report,* not to them, but *to the Board.*

Control as complete is given to the Board also in all questions *of poor relief.*

This by way of *general characterization:*
"All these are *functions of system, rather than of centralization. Co-ordination* is sought in matters of poor relief, that relief being given under national statutes; and *co-operation* of central with local judgment in financial matters, local debts constituting a very proper subdivision of national finance. But *the spirit in which the control is exercised,* as well as the absence of permanent officials representing the central authority in local government, and even of permanent instrumentalities for the administration of financial oversight, bespeak a system of co-operation and advice rather than of centralization." (The "State," p. 438).

2nd. February, 1893.

II. *Local Government in the* UNITED STATES:

I. *Conditions* of development:
  (1) A *Deliberate, consciously Selective* development.
      This *true from the first,* even though also consciously imitative.
      Perhaps in a sense *more minutely selective* in New England than in the South.
  (2) *At first a slowly constructive development,* proceeding *from small to larger* by almost *insensible stages.*
      "Nothing in progression can rest on its original plan" (See *quotation from Burke,* The State, p. 463).
      This *development none the less natural* and indigenous *because* bearing either essential or formal *resemblances* to other institutions, not of our own race in some instances.
      Mistake of looking always and so closely and exclusively *at the anatomy of institutions.* You can in that fashion find resemblances to anything. It must be

remembered that there was *a common European development* in many particulars of Public Law.

It is *doubtless because* the development was slow, *deliberate, and selective* that it has proved possible to discover *so many prototypes* of the various parts of our local governmental structure.[6]

(3) *A development with a free local variety*; and so suited to local needs.

This true, however, *only during the earlier periods.* The *later periods* have been characterized by a degree of *indiscriminate imitation* which sharply differentiates them.

In this development, *not preconceived ideas*, so much as *practical habit* and *imperative conditions of life* were the determinate elements of choice.

This variety, however, has for the most part been *State-big*; and this fact has led, *particularly in the West*, to a *large degree of artificial uniformity.* Much more genuine and natural variety in the early than in the later periods of settlement.

(4) *A development by Statute*, as in the case of England.

But *in England* this erection by statute has been piecemeal, *not systematic*; whereas *in this country* it has been systematic, *even constitutional*, planned by the fundamental law of the land.

By state, not by national *statute*. This process, however, takes place among us *by the action of authorities whose almost exclusive function is that of legislation.* All the more conspicuously is this the case when the arrangements of local government are made by a constitutional convention. *In* the case of *England, the "Government" resides* in the central administrative authorities, and *legislation is an instrumentality of administration.* Under our system the central government, consisting almost entirely of a law-making body, furnishes

[6] "In comparison with other men of their time, the Americans were distinguished by the possession of new political and social ideas, which were destined to be the foundation of the American commonwealth. One of the strongest and most persistent elements in national development has been that inheritance of political traditions and usages which the new settlers brought with them. . . . The chief source of the political institutions of the colonies was everywhere the institutions with which they were familiar at the time of their migration from England. It is not accurate to assert that American government is the offspring of English government. It is nearer the truth to say that in the middle of the seventeenth century the Anglo-Saxon race divided into two branches, each of which developed in its own way the institutions which it had received from the parent stock."—[A. B.] Hart, "Formation of the Union," pp. 5, 6.

the regulative provisions upon which the local bodies are to live their virtually independent lives. *In short,* the only vital *law-making authority* is *at the centre* of the system; the only vital *administrative authority in commission* among the outlying bodies of local government.

The State is by this process, not integrated, but *created in a "plat."*[7]

In the later stages, this process has been, not development, but *creation by statute*. This particularly true of *the West*. Here, too, the creation has been in the same sense disintegrate, *on the "plat."*

II. *Stages* of Development:

(1) *Stage of* SETTLEMENT:

The settlement of the contry *not at all like the settlement of Britain* by the Jutes and Saxons. The settlers did *not* come with *armies to a conquest*, but in *small*, and often *separate, groups for peaceful settlement; not to establish states*, but to better their *economic* circumstances as colonists.

Sometimes, also, for *religious reasons*: to free themselves from an old system in only one particular.

There was no transplanation of a State, or political system *entire*, as in the case of the Saxon occupation or the Norman conquest; *but a slow working out through hardship and by various device*, as finally in the construction of the present federal government.

(2) *First stage of Expansion*:

Townships thrown out, and *such States as Kentucky* and Tennessee. *Same process* as that of the stage of settlement, *with experience added, and without* direct traditions of the systems of the old country. In this sense a *more characteristically American* process even than that of the period of settlement.

Perhaps a *less deliberative* and self-conscious development than that which preceded it.

These frontiersmen had something more imperative to do in their contest with Nature and the savage *than debate constitutions*. They were *not of the old world* and its contests, moreover, and did not feel so directly the practical significance of such debates. They simply *took for granted the conclusions of the early settlers* on

---

[7] That is, created more or less arbitrarily by survey. [Eds.' note]

these heads, *and imitated* the institutions with which they had been familiar in the East.

(3) *Second stage of Expansion*:

Deliberate planning and planting of States in the West. The constitutions of the Territoroes [Territories] taken ready-made from Congress; but *the later state constitutions made with a free hand*, and *upon a large scale of imitation*; (though in some cases with *local option* in respect of forms of organization.)

It is *in this stage*, perhaps, more than in any other that *the characteristic American ideas concerning the constitution of local government*, and the relations of the several parts of the state government to each other are *to be discerned*.

(4) *Stage of the creation of great Industrial Cities*:

Special charter vs. general (constitutional) *system* administered by the courts.

The false analogy upon which we have proceeded in organizing our great municipalities has been, that except for their smaller scale, they ewre [were] *exactly like the State itself* and ought to be constituted upon a similar plan; with *balanced "powers."*

This *the period also of hot enmity between city and country*, complete incompatibility of temper, and of the *pestilent interference and dickering* with the government and affairs of certain large cities on the part of the state legislature; *keeping them constantly in the false atmosphere of politics*, and making their control a matter of political strategy. (*See later lectures* for a development of this theme).

III. *Conceptions concerning Local Government in the U.S.*:

(1) *In the earlier periods no essential distinction observed between central and local government*.

It is *the earlier periods*, of course, which are significant for the *development of theory*. The ideas, as well as the structural models, were made in those periods of beginnings.

Beginning with the smaller units of government, as they did, it was natural that *the founders* of our governments should *regard them as political*, rather than merely administrative, parts of the structure as a whole; and that they should *give them the same degree of constitutional elaborateness*, and the *same basis of theory*, as the larger units, wh. were never allowed to swallow up the smaller.

The process, as it turned out, was *like a deliberate repetition of the historical order* of development, from the village community up, *minus* the process of the absorption of the less by the greater.

(2) *Entire absence of the Distinction* between *Law-making* (in the proper sense of the term) and *Administration*: and an organization consequently inconsistent with that distinction. Hist. explanation: Eng. const. history one of struggle to control (vested) Executive by means of popular rep. and so make *legislation* the whole vital and formative force of gov't.

E.g., the theory already referred to above (Stages, [4]) as to the proper analogies for the constitution of the government of a *municipal corporation*.

(3) *No conception of integration*, consequently, but that of *legal provision*, and *restraint by the courts*, whose processes of appeal furnish the only guarantees of uniformity.

This process of restraint, moreover, *put into operation*, not by representatives of any central authority, but *by officials of local choice* and attachments.

6 Feb'y, 1893

III. *Local Government in* FRANCE:

I. CONDITIONS of development:

(1) *A royal power beginning* simply as a ducal power; *built up piecemeal by* the slow addition of other feudal properties (by purchase, intrigue, marriage, conquest); wh. *finally became master of each piece* of France, treating separately (governing as it were separately) each old-time portion of it.

Even the great Carolingian monarchy had been *unequal* to the task of keeping its parts together. *Feudalism* in France *sprang* "*in part* from the want of proportion between the vast extent of the Carolingian monarchy and the weakness of the administrative machinery with which the monarchy sought to control a still barbarous society."

Boutmy's English Constitution, p. 4.

Note (*a*) *the territorial wholeness of the great feudal estates in France*, as contrasted with their division and dispersion in England, and (b) *the great extent of*

France, as contrasted with the relative smallness of England.

In France, "in the middle of the *thirteenth century,* we find the *distinction* in full force between *provinces* '*obedient to the king*' and '*not obedient to the king*'; *the latter,* in which the king had no real power, comprising all the domains of the great feudatories, *nearly two-thirds of the France of to-day*" (p. 11)

The government consequently amorphous.

(2) *No judicial integration* similar to that which took place in England.

In France judicial itineraries were never developed into a system as they were in England, but remained *occasional merely* and incidental to particular purposes or occasions.

The royal court of final appeal was '*portable*' (to be brought) *in England,* and '*querable*' (to be sought) *in France.*" (p. 14).

Variety of local custom; distinct judicial districts each with its own *separate parlement*: subject no doubt to the same appeal, but not to the same principles or system of law.

(3) *Absence of a real national life*:

States General, with their separate representation of *classes* not only, but their separate representation of provinces, or *Governments,* and the occasional secession of representatives of particular Governments.

States Provincial, too, standing for the system of separate dealings on the part of the Crown with each great Province. *Certain "Pays d'Etats"* retained at least a semblance of this old system of separateness long after it had really lost its vitality, notably *Languedoc and Brittany.* Read Boutmy, p. 19, n. 2.

Sharp separateness (and even hostility) *of the three estates* in France. "There was *nothing in England which answered to the 'third estate'* in France, a class both isolated and close, composed exclusively of towns-people, enjoying no commerce with the rural population, and at once detesting and dreading the nobility by whom it was surrounded." (P. 56).

(4) *No middle class*:

There was *a class of freemen, but not in the rural districts.* "In France, the class of freemen practically consisted of the burghers." (P. 44). *In the rural districts,* but two social grades, the feudal noblesse and those dependent upon them.

Contrast the make-up and character *between the English and French nobility*: a nobility of office vs. a nobility of blood.

Consequences: Read Boutmy, p. 40, n.

(5) *A levelling and systematizing Revolution*:

The *levelling* done *by the revolutionists*, the *systematizing by Napoleon*. Present French administration a creation of this century, *not* of *the ancien regime*. All that the latter established was the spirit that made that system possible.

II. STAGES of the Development of Local Government in France:

(1) *Before there was any central control* at all.

This *the period of the break-up of the Carolingian monarchy*; when not only great kingdoms like Germany and France fell apart from each other, but those kingdoms themselves became disintegrate.

This was *the period which gave the Capets their opportunity* to establish a titular headship which could afterwards be transmuted into real power.

(2) *The Period of the Drawing together* and Building up of the Central Power, by various means:

The means and instrumentalities of concentration. *Bailli* we find from a very early time; but they were somply [simply] the stewards of the sovereign in the administration of his own dsmesnes [demesnes]. Other feudal lords had also their stewards of the same title and functions.

Intendants were sent out from time to time for the settlement of the affairs of disturbed districts, oftentimes in the company of conquering generals; and it was long before their occasional and extraordinary powers became permanent and part of a fixed and somewhat uniform civil establishment. (*Read Boutmy*, p. 20, n.).

"*The re-union* of the several great provinces of France with the Crown was a gradual process; it was brought about in some ceses [cases] by *conquest*, in many by *marriage, inheritance, or treaty*; in almost all under *terms which safe-guarded their ancient privileges*. The king having taken the place of the former lord, treated directly and separately with each province, whether for the granting or the method of collecting the taxes." (pp. 18, 19).

A very great variety, consequently, characterized the central control, both in its amount and in the means of its exercise. *The result* of the drawing together of the various pieces of the kingdom under the royal power was *by no means a systematic organization* of administration.

(3) *Absolutism: uniform instrumentalities,* for the most part, in local administration, and the *same central organs of control,* generally, for all parts of the kingdom; *but variety, nevertheless,* in local administration:

This the *period of active evocation of suits* to the royal courts in Paris, and *of the portentous activity of the Comptroller General of the Finances,* to whom all *the Intendants* resorted for instructions in the exercise of their function of universal, providential oversight in the "Generalities." *The tyrrany* of this system *consisted in its capricious variety* rather than in its absolutism of authority.

(4) *Napoleon: first period of real System:*

Basis, the uniform *Departments* that the Constituent Assembly had created for the better obliteration of demoralizing memories. *All parts of France organized and dealt with alike,* by this consummate master of organization.

(5) *Period of the Present Republic:*

Characterized by a number of *liberal reforms* in local government: *but apparently transitional.* Reform hindered and made problematical by the existence of *the spoils system* of appointment to office. Hardly less a period of centralization than those which have preceded it.

III. *Brief* DESCRIPTION of the existing System of Local Government in France:

(1) *The Units of local government* and their relations to each other:

The chief units are *the* DEPARTMENT and *the* COMMUNE. The two other divisions of the country, the *Arrondissement* and the *Canton,* are *mere administrative sub-divisions,* with no vital independent existence of their own

The Arrondissement serves as a district for the detail of Departmental administration; as the *electoral district*

for the choice of members of the Chamber of Deputies; and as *judicial districts* for the courts of first instance.

The Canton is an *electoral* district for the election of the members of local administrative councils; a *registration* district; a *military muster* district; and a *road administration* district. It has no separate administrative organization of its own.

(2) *Magistrates*, their *Appointment and Functions*:

In each *Department a Prefect*; in each *Arrondissement a sub-prefect* (merely a Prefect's deputy); and in each *Canton a mayor*. Prefect and sub-prefect are appointed officials, the *mayor is elected* by the Council of the Commune; *but, whet[h]er appointed or elected, the magistrate is the direct agent in local affairs of the central government*. It is merely a question whether they shall choose or receive him.

The mayor, like the Prefect and his subordinates, *may be removed* by the President of the Republic. The Prefect, as well as the Minister of the Interior, may *disallow* the acts of a mayor; the Prefect may *suspend* him *from office* for a mnoth [month], the Minister of the Interior for three months; and, *if he refuse certain duties* imposed upon him by law, the Prefect may delegate someone else to do them, or even do them himself.

(3) *Administrative Councils*:

Administrative Councils, *elected by universal suffrage*, are associated with the Prefects in the *Departments*, with the sub-prefects in the *Arrondissements*, and with the mayors in the *Communes*; and in the Communes, as stated, these councils elect the mayors. *But their association* with the magistrates *does not relieve* the latter *of* their *direct responsibility* for the conduct of local affairs. They are simply *the advisers of the agents* of the Government.

Their functions are *administrative* simply, and supervisory, not originative. *They are in no sense law-making bodies*. They control the local *budgets*, but the moneys which they appropriate are derived from taxes which they do not lay. They direct the management of *local administrative property*; regulate the pay of the *police*; supervise *local public works*; oversee the management of *lunatic asylums* and the *relief of the poor*.

But all the acts of these local councils are subject to

be disallowed by the central authorities; and by presidential decree they can be dissolved.

(5) The two sides of local gov't. (a) Service of the Central Administration (b) Administration of Local Affairs.

(5) [6] *Central Control*:

The *completeness of* the *control* exercised by the central Government is thus abundantly evident: is indeed the most prominent and characteristic feature of the system. *All magistrates* are the *direct agents* of the Minister of the Interior; all the councils may be dissolved by decree; *the acts of* the General *Councils* of the Depertments are valid unless disallowed, but those of communal councils must, for a certain term at least, await confirmation.

This is Centralization, not Concentration merely.

IV. PRINCIPLES observed in the organization of Local Government in France:

(1) General, not specific, statutory grant of powers. (*Central* functions reserved, specific).

(2) *Direct responsibility* of all officials to the central Government.

This principle, of the direct delegation of all administrative authority by the central to the local authorities is the most ancient and most deep-rooted principle of all. And, *in contrast to the English case*, this delegation is not accompanied by any loss of control. It is *not self-governing authority* as in the case of the English Justices of the Peace.

It *must be understood*, of course, that this control, though legally so complete, is *not exercised* to the upsetting of local self-direction *except occasionally and under exceptional circumstances*. The confirmation of the actions of local councils, where required, is generally a matter of matter-of-course routine. *Though ordinary in point of law*, interference is *extraordinary in point of fact*.

(3) *The association of a Council* (of recent years of popular constitution) with every responsible officer of local administration:

This principle accepted by Napoleon in his origin[al] construction of the system of French administration. With him it *meant*, not the association of a committee with the official in authority and responsibility, but *simply* the guidance of the responsible executive officer by *counsel.*

In the Department, a standing committee of the General Council acts as the executive council of the Department. This is *the "Departmental Commission."*

The validity of elections to t[h]ese councils is determined (except in the case of the General Council) by the administrative courts.

The *councils are kept strictly within their jurisdiction* by administrative oversight.

(4) Central administrative oversight of Budget (esp. the budget of the Commune) (a) to secure interests of cent. govt. (b) to prevent extravagance.

(5) *Taxation by the Chambers alone*:

The *national legislature determines* both the *amounts* and the *sources* of local taxation; and the funds at the disposal of the local councils are put at their disposal by the Chambers.

The distribution of taxation, however, is effected in a measure by local authorities. *The General Council apportions* the direct taxes voted by the national Chambers among the Arrondissements; *the councils of the Arrondissements* among the Communes.

(6) *Division of Powers*:

French political theory is *very absolute* in its insistence upon the division of legislative, executive, and judicial powers.

Result: separate administrative courts; no such judicial control as the English.

7 February, 1895.

13   "   1896

IV. *Organization and Development of Local Government in Prussia.*

Deserves our closest attention both because most carefully studied and elaborated at home and because generaaly regarded as a model abroad.

Comp. Bornhak, Preussisches Staatsrecht, I, pp. 1-62.

I. *CONDITIONS* under which Local Government has developed in Prussia:

(1) *Consolidation of the royal power*: *Circumstances* and *Method*:

Settlement of the Mark, its thorough *Germanization* and its organization under the *direct authority of the*

Markgraf, but not under the direct authority of the Empire. Thus made a thoroughly German district, and yet *not under the ordinary political conditions of the Empire*, but with outside, independent conditions of itr [its] own.

Norman parallel of conquest and organization.

Consolidation (keeping together) *of the territories* of the Mark by the "Dispositio" or "Constitutio Achilea" (Markgraf Albert "Achilles," 1471-1486), which established the principle of *the indivisibility of the several pieces of the Hohenzollern possessions* (Ansbach and Bayreuth on the one hand, and Brandenburg on the other).

           (1473)

A policy in marked contrast with that of any other of the feudal pieces of the Empire.

Judicial concentration, which began to show itself (*as in the Norman case* in England) just as soon as outside princes, the Hohenzollern, were invested with supremacy in the Mark. *Provinziallandgerichte* were established which secured judicial oversight for the Markgraf; *the Roman Law* was added to the confused customs of the feudalized Mark as a body of "common" (i.e. customary) law; *the University of Frankfurt* an der Oder, established in 1506, became a nurse to the Roman Law; *general laws were promulgated*; and *a central court* was organized (das Kurfursten Kammergericht) with a permanent membership and a Chancellor as president, which held *quarterly sessions* in some of the cities of the Mark. *By the end of the seventeenth century* a very thorough organization of the administration of justice had been effected, the full *"privilegium de non appellando"* having been granted to the chief portions of the Mark that lay within imperial limits.

Suppression of the independence of the Church. The acceptance of the *Protestant faith* by the Hohenzollern princes had very much the same effect upon their political power (though upon a smaller scale) as *the "Reformation" in England* had upon the political power of Henry VIII. It not only constituted the Elector the titular head of the Church, but also placed its property and its patronage in his hands, to the curtailment of the patronage hitherto enjoyed by the feudal proprietors and to the enhancement of his economic independence of the Estates.

Ne[ce]ssity for military power. The exigencies of mak[ing] and perpetuating the conquest of territories and of the period of the *Thirty Years' War* rendered it necessary that Prussia should become and remain a military power, maintaining *a standing force* and giving the Elector the means of maintaining the integrity and independence of the State. *Hence*, after while, *permanent excise taxes* (Biergeld, etc.) instead of occasional grants and contributions.

Fixed Taxation became one of the most influential and pervasive means of extending and centralizing administration. Finally it became *a matter altogether independent of the votes of the Estates*; and *the economic direction of the kingdom fell wholly into the hands of the central authorities*, until they became as truly providential as those of France.

(2) *Prussia a Military Power*; and that fact determinative of both the forms and the substantial functions of her Administrative Organization.

The principal interests of such a State centred in the economic efficiency of the Nation.

In 1651 the *administration of the public Domains*, which extended with extensions of conquest and annexation, was *organized under the direct agents of the royal power*, and under a central Commission at the capital.

Military Intendants with power in the Provinces in all matters concerning the raising and organizing of troops, *presently gave place to commissions (Kommissariate)*, which had, besides, the duty of administering *the excise taxes* which took the place of the stated contributions of the Estates.

Then came that system of economic administration which was carried to so high a point of perfection under Frederic the Great. Industry and mechanical skill, the development of riches, of every independent resource, and the cultivation of all economic capacities, pushed to the farthest possible limit in order *to increase the tax-paying capacity of the people*. The country farmed for the benefit of the throne and the army. *Programme: riches and taxes; administrative efficiency and economy;* in all things *strict oversight and effectiveness. Hence,* among other things, the establishment of a general

"Schulpflicht" and of a general *"Wehrpflicht."* for all Prussians.[8]

(3) *Feudal Conditions of Communal Local Government*:

In exchange for a permanent system of taxation the crown had given to the greater land-owners large independent powers in local government. Creation of *separate Proprietary Communes*, in which the great proprietors exercised direct administrative authority, by delegation, appointing mayors, controlling police, etc.

This system lasted in completeness down to the times of the reforms of Stein and Hardenberg; and its last *remnants* were not destroyed *until* the passage of *the Country Communities Act of 1891-1892. The peasantry* were thus kept in a two-fold subjection to the land-owning class: a subjection both economic (for their tenure was still feudal) and political. They were *serfs and subjects.*[9]

Note the combination, therefore, of a *military central government* and a *feudal local organization.*

The cities, for the most part, were in direct subordination to the central government.

No middle class like the English. A class of feudal lords; a class of free burghers; and a subject class of serfs made up the nation.

(4) *Creation of an official Organization and Class*, The *"Beamtenstaat."*

The *decisive steps* in this process taken *by Friedrich Wilhelm I.* Commissioners drawn wholly from the burgher class were put into the several *Kommissariate* and these Kommissariate began to *absorb* all the functions of *interior administration* into their own hands. This brought them into conflict with the older bodies, the various Chambers for the administration of Domains, which in a way stood for the older order of things, and were backed accordingly by all the influences of opposition. *Friedrich Wilhelm* therefore *fused the administration* of the two kinds together (*War and Domains*), under a common central organ which was likewise conglomerate.

He sent *commissioners into the cities*, moreover, to regulate their debts, to the *upsetting* there of *the former*

---

[8] *Note the exemption of the more important industrial classes* from military service: its consequent confinement to *the lowest classes and foreign recruits.*

[9] See Bornhak, "Local Government of Country Communities in Prussia," in *Annals* of the Am. Acad. of Pol. & Soc. Sci., *Jan., 1893.*

supremacy of city patriciates. The whole State was thus centralized and officialized.

Two Stages:

(a) Under Friedrich Wilhelm, *the creation of a burgher official class* which was, and was intended to be, an offset to, and a direct check upon, the feudal class, whose power it was Friedrich's object to nullify;

(b) Under *Frederick the Great*, the *substitution of the feudal aristocracy for the burghers in the offices,* and the consequent fusion of the feudal and the official classes. *Result*: "Burgher and peasant stand outside public life and most naturally regard the State as foreign to themselves."

We have, therefore, under Frederick the Great the *highest development of the feudal-official State*; the most complete subjection of the peasant class; the most thorough *stratification* of the State into classes.

(5) *Scientific Reform*, systematically *planned*; advanced through its *first stages* by the initiative of great ministers like Stein and Hardenberg; but *completed* only the the [*sic*] use of the *piecemeal* and compromise processes of the constitutional State.

The object of these reforms was to create *a suitable social basis* for reconstruction by cutting away the legal foundations of the distinctions between class and class; and then build upon that new basis *a modern self-governing and homogeneous State.*

II. STAGES of the Development of Local Government in Prussia:

(1) *Creation of the State*:

This stage includes two periods and two processes:
First, the Germanization and organization of the Mark;
Second, the in-vestiture of the Hohenzollern with the markgrafship, and the creation of the modern State of Prussia.

(1) In the times preceding the Hohenzollern *the military Mark degenerated* into an ordinary feudal principality, in which *the Estates commanded both the money and the military forces* (the knights and their following, and the militia of the towns);

(2) *After the investiture of the Hohenzollern* with authority, *a steady drawing together of the power* of the State into the hands of the central government took place; to yield to centrifugal forces again (because of the need of grants in aid from the Estates) *until the neces-*

sities of war and conquest created the military State, with its imperious necesiities and its imperial power.

This final stage witnessed the *creation of those instrumentalities* for the administration of the Domains and of the army which supplied the machinery *of the absolute monarchy.*

(2) *The Absolute Monarchy*: the *Military and Official State* and its Organization: (1713-1807):

The administration of this period included *domains; military affairs; taxation; public works; economic subsidizing* and supervision; all interior administration.

It included legislation, too, as well as all executive functions. The Administration made, modified, annulled, as well as carried out the laws.

In the hands of Friedrich Wilhelm, who may be said to have created this organization, it was very efficient. *Frederick the Great* displayed little capacity for administrative organization on the civil side: the administration of his time was efficient because he carried it all on his own shoulders, seeing to an incredible number of details himself. *Under the successors* of these men *the whole organization degenerated,* given over to formalism and professionalism.

(3) *Reconstruction under Absolute Monarchs*:

Utter collapse of the feudal State during the *Napoleonic wars.* The ground cleared for reconstruction.

The plans for the reconstruction originated, but only in part carried out by *Baron vom Stein. He wished* to reproduce in Germany the leading conceptions of English government. To this end he desired to see all feudal political privileges abolished, a national legislature established, and the principle of the obligatory service in local government of the propertied classes. *What he accomplished* was, (1) the *abolition of serfdom,* and the establishment of the universal right to acquire and hold property in independent tenure; and (2) the realization of his principal ideas with regard to local government in *the great Municipal Corporations Act* of 19 Nov., 1808. He did, however, accomplish some important things in the re-organization of the existing administration, creating (3) the *organization by Government Districts (Regierungsbezirke)* which is so central to the the present structure of Prussian local administration.

Hardenberg changed the direction of the reform. He

meant to keep the centralized administration for the purpose of *working out the social reforms* which were necessary conditions precedent to any permanent administrative changes.

He abolished feudal and guild privileges and *freed trade* from vexatious restrictions; he originated the *policy of the Zollverein,* and established a *uniform system of taxation* in place of the old feudal three class system.

In the field of administration he *introduced the present Provincial organization* as an instrument of the central authority.

After his death, in 1822, there came a decided *reaction;* and then the *revolution of 1848.*

(4) *The Constitutional Monarchy: Compromise reforms:*

After protracted struggles over the question of the influence of landed vs. that of capitalistic property in local government, *there came forth the great Prussia* of the times succeeding 1866-1870; and in 1872 *reforms suggested by Gneist* were *carried out by Bismarck* in the *County Government Act (Kreisordnung)* of December 13 of that year. During the subsequent legislation completed these reforms.

Object and Means of these measures (Comp. Pol. Sci. Quarterly, IV., 662):

1. The *extension of local self-government.* This was sought to be effected by a reorganization of the *circle* and the *province* as administrative districts for the purposes of general state administration.

2. The introduction of a *judicial control over the actions of administrative officers.* To this end a reorganization of the administrative courts was effected.

3. *Decentralization and* the introduction of *a non-professional lay element* into the administration of state affairs. It was an essential part of this plan that matters hitherto administered by the agents of the central authorities should *devolve upon the local* administrative bodies.

III. *A Brief Description* of Prussian Local Government:

(See Goodnow, Pol. Sci. Quart., v., pp. 124-158).

Confusion of areas somewhat like the confusion in England, there being oftentimes non-coterminous areas for *general administration,* for *justice,* for *military* organization, and for *taxing or postal* arrangements.

(1) *Units of Prussian Local Government:* 12 *Provinces,* divided into thirty-five *government Districts,* divided into

464 *Counties,* or Circles, (of which number 37 are towns), divided into *Amtsbezirke.*

Respects in wh. the Government District stands apart from the rest in character. Not a local corporation, but simply *a division for* the exercise in detail of the functions of the *general govt.* The *other units both* divisions of central administration and corporations for local self-government.

The Province retained as a section of the State *because* historically such, like the *English counties* and the *French Provinces,* with characters and an institutional history of their own.

The Counties the original tax districts of the medieval monarchy.

Sharp differentiation and clear separation of functions of the *general state administration* and those of *local self-management.* Former understood to include such matters as *Taxation, police, educational administration, ecclesiastical affairs, military* affairs, and the maintenance of *highways. The latter,* such matters as *neighbourhood roads, local public works, agricultural improvements, asylums, museums,* the general field of *bye-laws,* etc.

In the Province two sets of organs to exercise these two sets of functions: *in the County, one set* of organs with double functions.

(2) *Magistrates:*

In the Province, Superior President, a permanent and *professional* officer, representing the Ministers at Berlin. *Appointed* by the Minister of the Interior. Exercising *a final jurisdiction* in most matters as *the Ministers' deputy and proxy.*

The Landeshauptmann, chosen to preside over local self-govt. by the *Landtag*

In the Government District, the *President of the Administration,* who is *a separate magistrate* in respect of his service of the Interior (police, and the supervision of inferior authorities), but merely *a presiding officer* (over the "Administration" as a whole) in other matters.

In the County, the *Landrath,* nominated by the County Diet, is, like the *French maire,* both an agent of the central and of the local directing bodies. *Cities of over* 25,000 inhabitants are organized as distinct *Counties:* the *Burgomaster* is *the elected president* of the municipal council. In some *smaller towns* there are burgomasters who constitute the executive, though generally associated, at least, with boards or committees.

In the Amtsbezirk, the *Amtsvorsteher*, chosen by the County Diet. ("Appointed in the name of the Crown by the Governor of the Province from the list drawn up and presented by the Circle Diet.")

(3) *Councils: Lay participation*: These *are either*

    (a) *Consultative*, associated with the magistrates as executive committees, or

    (b) *Directive* of the measures of local self-govt.

The former in all units, associated with officers having a considerable range of discretionary power; *the latter only in Province and County* (rural or urban), as the originative organs of local self-government.

A. Associated with the superior President, a *Provinzialrath*, with one professional member, besides the *Oberpräsident* himself (who presides) and five lay members who are elected. (Term, 6 yrs.) (*See* below for method of election).

Associated with the President of the Administration, in his individual functions (chiefly connected with the Ministry of the Interior) *a District Committee*, consisting of two professional life members and four lay members elected for a term of 6 yrs.

Associated with the Landrath a County Committee, consisting, besides the Landrath himself of six elected members chosen for a term of 6 yrs.

Associated with the Amtsvorsteher a Magisterial Committee (*Amtsausschuss*) wh. consists of the chiefs of rural communes.

The functions of these Committees much more important in Prussia than in France. *Their sanction necessary* for the validity of the ordinances, orders, etc., for the support, in general, of all the discretionary functions of the officers with whom they are associated. *The Committees of the Counties and of the District* are *also administrative courts*, besides (in the county grade) the *City Committee* which, though chosen by the city authorities, has no lay element, consisting, besides the Burgomaster, of four professional functionaries, chosen for a term of 6 yrs.

The Provinzialrath is *a supervisory administrative council*, as well as an authoritative advisory board.

B. *The Councils which direct measures of local self-government are*, the *Provincial Diet*, (*Landtag*) which is served executively by the the [sic] *Landeshauptmann* and the *Provincial Committee*, an officer and body of its own choosing; *and the County Diet*, served, as the central govt. also is, by the *Landrath* and the County Committee.

The cities to be separately considered, in connection with general consideration of city govt. *Their constitution* dates back to *the Municipal Corporations Act of 1809* (Stein) wh. has served (*as in England*) as a model for the reconstruction of local govt. in the other (rural) areas.

(4) *Electoral Processes*:

People (3 class system of interests)
> 1. *Cities* (less than 25 thousand inhabitants) electing thr. councils or (if in groups) thr. electors.
> 2. *Unions of great landowners*.
> 3. *Rural Communes* acting in groups thr. electors.

Elect *County Diet*
> Nominates *Landrath* & *Amtsvorsteher*
> Elects *County Comm.* and (in conjunction with other Diets) the *Landtag*,

[the Landtag]
> wh. elects *Landeshauptmann* & *Prov. Com.*

[Prov. Committee]
> Elects *Provinzialrath* (5 out of 7 members) and District Comm. (4 out of 6 members)

Note the *central position* in this scheme *of the County*.

(5) *Central Control*: (*a*) *In the administration of matters deemed to concern the State as a whole*, direct professional action, generally thr. the boards or committees of the District Administration. *But where officers act singly* in important functions, the sanction of a Committee predominantly of lay constitution.

(*b*) *In the field of local self-govt.*, a somewhat *indefinite authority to intervene*, in the general interest in restraint of the choice of measures by local authorities within the (indefinite) field of self-direction assigned to them.

IV. *Principles* of Local Government in Prussia:

(1) *A general field of local govt.*, not a minute statutory catalogue of powers.

But *consequent* enlargement and *indefiniteness* of the field *of central interference.*

(2) *A professional service,* with practically *life tenure,* subject to only *judicial* (legal) *responsibility.*

Checked, however, wherever *single officers exercise discretion* by—

(3) *Compulsory lay participation* in local government. *Lay judgment* served by *expert* (professional) *knowledge* and training.

(4) *Concentration rather than Centralization*: a restraining, rather than constraining, supervision; *though perhaps too indefinite* in its range.

15 February 1893

WWT and WWhw notes with WWsh additions (WP, DLC).

To Winthrop More Daniels[1]

My Dear Daniels,   Baltimore, Maryland, 30 January, 1893.

I have just received your letter of Saturday, and hasten to reply. It would not at all endanger the thoroughness of the required course to add a recitation elective; the only serious question in my mind is, whether it would not be too much for you. I would urge you not to overburden yourself; and if this additional course will overburden you, by all means decline it. Since you have committed yourself, say that I vetoed the proposal: as I do, under the above "if." If, on the contrary, you feel fully equal to it, I should be very glad indeed to see it given. Certainly you have every reason to be complimented by the demand for it. The men who took Finance with you have expressed to me the heartiest satisfaction with your instruction, and the sincerest admiration of it.

With very warm regards from us both,

Woodrow Wilson

WWTLS (W. M. Daniels Coll., CtY).
  1 This seems to have been the first document that Wilson typed on his new Hammond typewriter. See the Editorial Note, "Wilson and His Caligraph," Vol. 2, p. 368.

909 McCulloh Street,

BALTIMORE, Maryland,

30 January, 1893.

MyDear Daniels,

I have just received your letter of Saturday, and hasten to reply. It would not at all endanger the thoroughness of the required course
to add a recitation elective; the only serious question in my mind is,
whether it would not be too much for you. I would urge you not to overburden yourself; and if this additional course will overburden you, by
all means decline it. Since you have committed yourself, say that I
vetoed the proposal: as I do, under the above "if". If, on the contrary, you feel fully equal to it, I should be very glad indeed to see
it given. Certainly you have every reason to be complimented by the
demand for it. The men who took Finance with you have expressed to
me the heartiest satisfaction with your instruction, and the sincerest
admiration of it.

With very warm regards from us both,

Woodrow Wilson

Prof. W. M. Daniels.

*The first letter known to have been typed by Wilson
on his Hammond typewriter*

A Final Examination in the History of Law[1]

February 2nd, 1893.

College of New Jersey.

HISTORY OF LAW.

1. What materials exist for the study of the origins of law, and what is the relative value of the several sorts of material? Give a summary characterization of the origins of law.

2. Why did the office of judge emerge earlier in political development than the office of king?

3. What evidences have we of an original system of self-help in the maintenance of rights. Describe, compare, and (especially) contrast the Roman *pignoris capio* and the English Distraint. How far did Distraint belong to all Teutonic and Celtic practice?

4. Did the XII Tables constitute a complete code. Upon what conceptions did they rest as to the nature and transfer of property, and upon what four *legis actiones*. Explain and distinguish the terms *Mancipatio* and *Nexum*.

5. What was the Roman four-fold classification of Contracts? Explain the character of each of the four forms of contract.

6. What were *res mancipi*, and what was the ground of distinction between *res mancipi* and *res nec mancipi*? How were transactions affecting *res nec mancipi* effected?

7. Summarize, in outline, Maine's chapter on "The Early History of Contract."

8. Name, date, and characterize the principal barbarian codes. Which of these was the most important; what gave it its superior importance; and in what parts of Europe was it longest used?

9. What general influences induced the study of Roman law in Europe? What special influences in the Italian cities; and with what results?

10. What was the character of German public law, on the one hand, and of German private law, on the other, before the reception of Roman law? What need had Germany for the Roman law?

11. When, why, and how was Roman law received in Germany? What form of Roman law was received? In what fields did it most nearly supersede German law altogether?

12. Give the main points of the contrast which Maine draws between "Ancient and Modern Ideas respecting Wills and Successions."

"I pledge my honor as a gentleman that, during this examination, I have neither given nor received assistance."

Printed examination (WP, DLC). Att.: WWhw list of students and their grades.
[1] There is a WWhw copy of this examination in WP, DLC.

Notes for a Talk to the Baltimore Alumni

[Feb. 2, 1893]

Topics:

Feel like a Baltimorean this time a year as well as Princetonian—proper combination.

What in common among graduates of so many ages—each age remembering a different college from that remembered by the others—the common sentiment and refrain.

I remember a great many colleges but only one with an unsophisticated love—the first

Alumni Ass'n first of all an ass'n for enjoyment and good fellowship, no doubt—but its functions ought to extend to something more than reminiscences of early love—"Children obey your parents"—If you don't see what you want, ask for it—be ready to give it.

Something even more to be admired reserved for the recollection of those who are to come after—a college of *honour*—in examinations—men and gentlemen all along the line.

I see something I want—provision for graduate courses in the literary departments

And I want a law-school. "Prof. Wilson which is the best Law-School in the country?" The one to be established at Princeton.

Those repeated quiet investments of piety—courage, manliness ought to be maturing now, the conservative classes rallying to their college and make the progress *which assures the past*.

WWhw MS. (WP, DLC).

Stories:

(1) Every man some place (2) Some places better than others (3) Look out or you'll go to a place you don't like (4) few remarks on infant baptism.

Jane Colliard, a faithful and loving wife to the seven following persons.

We are looking *forward* at P.—and the steering is difficult—North Star—"not going that way"

Reminiscences: "Mought a hearn a toot or two."

Block-heads studying.

"This is no place to get religion"

A Newspaper Report of an Alumni Dinner in Baltimore

[Feb. 3, 1893]

IN PRINCETON'S HONOR.

"There is an ancient faculty, most ancient in renown,
That rules an ancient college built in an ancient town;
The town is in the inland, far from ye ancient sea.
About the middle of the State of New Jersee.

"We spend four years in college; we go with startling speed
On the precious little 'pony,' which he who rides must read.
If we get through our finals we take the proud degree
Of 'Baccalaureus Artium' in New Jersee."

A hundred lusty voices made this and more than a dozen other old college songs ring out last night and announced to all who passed the Lyceum Theatre between 8 and 11 o'clock that the members of the Princeton Alumni Association of Maryland were holding their annual banquet in the theatre parlors. The banquet was a characteristic one. A common tie bound all who were there. Every man, the gray-headed veteran and the beardless youth fresh from the college, regarded his neighbor as his brother and acted accordingly. It was a great big family gathering. Some names were represented by three generations at the same table. Formality was at a discount. Everybody went in for a good time. College songs were sung from the beginning of the dinner until the last man left the rooms and college stories were told, and, in fact, the diners paid more attention to these than they did to the excellent menu that Harris set before them.

A crowd of the younger alumni happened to get together at one of the tables and immediately established themselves as a "choir," with Johnson Poe as choirmaster. This "choir" led the singing, and under its leadership dignified business men, wise lawyers and eloquent clergymen threw their heads back and shouted out the familiar old words as they did twenty and thirty and even forty years ago. But the youngsters got somewhat beyond their seniors' depth when they interspersed the college songs with those telling of the achievements of the "Man Who Broke the Bank at Monte Carlo," and of the strange things that are seen and done "On the Bowery." This was also the case when they organized themselves into a troupe of trousered Lottie Collinses and sent "Ta-ra-ra-ra Boom de-a-a" ringing through the building.

Mr. E. J. D. Cross, the retiring president, presided. . . . After something more than two hours of music and mirth, with Lynn Haven oysters, boiled salmon, sweetbreads, terrapin, redhead ducks, sauterne, white seal,[1] old Solera sherry, Roman punch, cigars and other good things, the speeches began. . . .

Prof. Woodrow Wilson, one of the non-resident lecturers of Johns Hopkins University, represented Princeton College, the first college from which he was graduated. He spoke to the toast, "Our Alma Mater." The tie which binds us, he said, might be told in the sermon of an old hard-shell Baptist preacher. He told his congregation that his sermon would be under four heads. The first was that everybody had some place in this world; the second was that some people have better places than some others; the third was that some men would have a worse place after a while than others, and the last was a few remarks on infant baptism. ["]It is on this last point we find a common standing ground—some recollections of infant baptism. We all have our recollections of Princeton, and we all have recollections of a different college, and the students now at Princeton will have recollections of an entirely different nature than any of us have. For we are now abolishing all surveillance in examinations." [Cheers.] Someone called out, 'We are twenty years late.'

"It seems to me," continued Prof. Wilson, "that the most contemptible thing a man can do is to try to find out how contemptible other men are. We are trying now to put every man on his honor. And the fruit of this movement is being shown already. 'Why,['] said a man to me the other day 'the blockheads are studying now as they have never studied before. They are learning that there is such a thing as carrying the contents of books in their heads, something that they never seemed to think of before.' The recollections of the Princeton boys of today will be of a different Princeton than that which we knew. If there is anything you alumnists would like to see in Princeton for its development, ask for it, and if it is not forthcoming furnish the means to bring it about.

"We need money. We cannot steer by reminiscences. One of the things I am most anxious to see at Princeton is a law school. I want it to be better than any other law school in the country. I want a distinctive Princeton school. We all want to make the Princeton law school a historical and philosophical one. The legal profession of today is becoming, not a learned profession, but a profession of technical experts. We want to rescue it from this condition." . . .

Printed in the Baltimore *Sun*, February 3, 1893; some editorial headings omitted.
  [1] Probably a wine.

To Winthrop More Daniels

My dear Daniels,   Baltimore, Maryland, 4 February, 1893.

I am very much obliged to you indeed for all your kind services in the matter of my examinations,[1] and I should have written before to thank you and to answer the question or two your letters have contained, had I not been pressed beyond measure for time in the preparation of my tasks (not the least of which has been attendance at two Alumni dinners).[2]

I am perfectly willing that you should sign the schedules of the Specials for me. The only care I should take in the matter, were I there, would be to crossquestion as many as might be out of the purpose of taking Administration. Perhaps you can do a little of that good work for me.

The examination papers came to hand all right, and I shall try to make returns on them next week.

I think it was certainly wise not to burden yourself with the elective in the history of Political Economy; and I do not at all mind being saddled with a part of the responsibility for the refusal.

In haste.   Cordially Yours,   Woodrow Wilson

WWTLS (W. M. Daniels Coll., CtY).
    [1] The examination in the history of law is printed at Feb. 2, 1893. A printed copy of the final examination in public law, dated Jan. 31, 1893, is in WP, DLC.
    [2] An account of his speech to the Baltimore alumni on February 2 precedes this letter. Wilson spoke on the following evening to the Philadelphia alumni. A brief report of this affair is printed below.

A News Item

[Feb. 9, 1893]

The Princeton Alumni Association of Philadelphia and vicinity gave its annual banquet at the Art Club, Philadelphia, last Friday evening. . . .

Prof. Woodrow Wilson concluded the speech-making in a witty and humorous address on "Princeton—Past and Present."

Printed in the *Daily Princetonian*, Feb. 9, 1893.

To Robert Bridges, with Enclosure

My dear Bobby,   Baltimore, Md., 14 February, 1893

I am sincerely glad to hear that your sister is better than you had supposed and that the little plan I proposed may prove of some service to you. I enclose the letter to Dr. Howe. I believe

"Wrights Hotel" in Columbia is small and comfortable. You might try it until brother George advised you in the matter. I am sorry I must be always writing "in haste"—but I must.

Most affectionately Yours,   Woodrow Wilson

His house is on Blanding St.
P.S. Diseases of the eye, ear, and throat are Dr. Howe's specialty.

W.W.

ALS (WC, NjP).

E N C L O S U R E

To George Howe, Jr.

My dear brother George,   [Baltimore, c. Feb. 14, 1893]

This is to introduce my dear friend, Mr. Robert Bridges, of New York, assistant editor of *Scribner's Magazine*. Mr. Bridges was a classmate of mine at Princeton and is one of the truest and dearest friends I have in the world. He comes South with his sister, whose health is delicate and he wants your advice as to the best place to take one in her condition.

I have taken the liberty to send him to you and I know that you will treat him as if he were his affectionate friend and

Your loving brother,   Woodrow Wilson

ALS (WP, DLC).

EDITORIAL NOTE

WILSON'S WORKING BIBLIOGRAPHY ON LAW

By the early months of 1892, Wilson was already deeply immersed in the sources and authorities in the fields of administration, public law, jurisprudence, the history of law, and related subjects. Being constantly reminded (particularly while preparing the notes for his course on the history of law) of the need for a systematic bibliography for these fields, Wilson compiled the one printed below.

It is impossible to be absolutely certain about the precise date when he put this bibliography together. However, the physical appearance of the cards strongly suggests that Wilson compiled it over a fairly brief span of time. For example, the ink and writing are uniform throughout. In addition, the publication dates of certain titles cited and the use to which Wilson put some of the volumes strongly indicate that he could not have compiled this bibliography before the late summer of 1892. It seems highly dubious that he had either the leisure or the library resources at Princeton to have prepared the list at that time, or even before he went to Baltimore in January 1893.

Since Wilson almost certainly did not make up the bibliography later than the spring of 1893, it seems reasonably certain that he compiled it during the last two or two and a half weeks of his stay in Baltimore in 1893—that is, between mid-February and early March. Having completed all the new notes for his administration lectures by February 15, his time was relatively free until his return to Princeton in early March. Moreover, in Baltimore he had access to two great libraries and their resources for the compilation of the bibliography.

Wilson made his entries in longhand on approximately 300 2 x 5 ruled cards and put them in a tin file box. Each card begins with a subject heading, followed by a bibliographical citation which is usually complete. Some cards contain more than one title; a very few contain comments either by Wilson himself or copied from other authorities.

Wilson attempted to organize this bibliography into eleven broad categories, which he listed on a separate card: Encyclopaedias, General Theory, History, Customary Law, Roman Law, Public Law, International Law, Criminal Law, Procedure, Private Law, and Periodicals. However, while compiling his bibliography he kept making further sub-categories under the subject headings until his system of classification broke down. Moreover, a group of miscellaneous cards at the end of the file, as well as many individual cards interspersed among the main groups, simply do not fit into Wilson's general categories at all. Indeed, it may be that Wilson's order was subsequently disturbed.

In light of the above facts, the Editors have decided not to reproduce the file cards as they found them, but rather to provide an alphabetical listing by author of all titles included, giving complete bibliographical information according to modern usage. There are seven titles which the Editors have been unable to locate and check for accuracy; these are printed in a separate list at the end.

The original bibliography is in the Wilson Papers in the Library of Congress. Books on the list that remain in the Wilson Library have been marked with an asterisk.

In conclusion, it might be said that there can be no doubt that Wilson made extensive use of this bibliography: titles included in it appear frequently in his writings, research notes, and lecture notes of the late 1880's and of the 1890's. This bibliography, along with the one printed at March 27, 1890, Volume 6, shows the scope of Wilson's command of the literature of political science and of law and in particular gives further evidence of his dependence upon German scholarship for much of his factual knowledge as well as ideas.

Adickes, Franz Burchard Ernst Friedrich, *Zur Lehre von den Rechtsquellen* (Cassel and Göttingen, 1872).

Ahrens, Heinrich, *Juristische Encyclopädie, oder, Organische Darstellung der Rechts- und Staatswissenschaft, auf Grundlage einer ethischen Rechtsphilosophie* (Vienna, 1855).

Ahrens, Heinrich, *Naturrecht, oder Philosophie des Rechts und des Staates*, 6th edn. (2 vols., Vienna, 1870-71).

Amos, Sheldon, *A Systematic View of the Science of Jurisprudence* (London, 1872).

Archiv für die civilistische Praxis (1818-   ).

Encyclopaedia
Holtzen- 12   Encyclopädie der Rechtswissenschaft
dorff, F.v.   in systematischer und alphabetischer Bear-
(Editor).   beitung.   Leipzig: Erster systematischer
                        Theil, 5 ed., 1890. Zweiter Theil, Rechts-
                        lexikon   3 ed., '80-'81, 3 vols.

History of Law = Its Development.
Ihering,   Geist des römischen Rechts.
R. v.   Der Zweck im Recht, 2 vols. Leipzig, 2 ed.
                                1884, 1886.
                Der Kampf um's Recht, Wien, 1872 + nu-
                        merous subsequent editions.
                trans. Chicago, 1879.

Public Law, - German.
Laband,   Das Staatsrecht des deutschen Reiches,
P.,   3 vols., Tübingen, 1876-'82
                2 ed., 2 vols. Freiburg i. B.,
                        1888-'91.

Roman Law - System (modern)
Savigny,   System des heutigen römischen Rechts
F. C.,   9 vols.: Berlin 1840-1849,
                Sachen-Register by O.L. Heuser,
                                Berlin, 1851.

Samples of Wilson's cards for his bibliography on law

Arnesberg, Karl Ludwig Arndts von, *Grundriss der juristischen En-cyclopädie und Methodologie* (Munich, 1843).

Arnold, Wilhelm, *Cultur und Recht der Römer* (Berlin, 1868).

Arnold, Wilhelm, *Cultur und Rechtsleben* (Berlin, 1865).

Bähr, Otto, *Der Rechtsstaat* (Cassel and Göttingen, 1864).

Bar, Karl Ludwig von, *Die Grundlagen des Strafrechts* (Leipzig, 1869).

Bar, Karl Ludwig von, *Das internationale Privat- und Strafrecht* (Hanover, 1862).

Bar, Karl Ludwig von, "Die juristische Beurtheilung der Zustände geistiger Krankheit und Störung," *Zeitschrift für das privat- und öffentliche Recht der Gegenwart*, II (1875), 1-77.

Baumann, Johann Julius, *Handbuch der Moral, nebst Abriss der Rechtsphilosophie* (Leipzig, 1879).

Baumann, Johann Julius, ed., *Die Staatslehre des h. Thomas von Aquino* (Leipzig, 1873).

Baumert, Georg, *Ueber die Zurechnungsfähigkeit und Bestrafung jugendlicher Personen* (Breslau, 1877).

Behrend, Jakob Friedrich, *Lehrbuch des Handelsrechts* (2 vols., Berlin, 1880-81).

*Behrend, Jakob Friedrich, "Die neueren Privatrechts-Kodifikationen und der Entwurf eines bürgerlichen Gesetzbuchs," Franz von Holtzendorff, ed., *Encyklopädie der Rechtswissenschaft in systematischer Bearbeitung*, 5th edn. (Leipzig, 1890), pp. 387-422.

Bekker, Ernst Immanuel, "Zur Lehre vom Rechtssubject: Genuss und Verfügung; Zwecksatzungen, Zweckvermögen und juristische Personen," *Jahrbücher für die Dogmatik des heutigen römischen und deutschen Privatrechts*, XII (1873), 1-135.

Bentham, Jeremy, *Traités de législation civile et pénale*, ed. and translated by Étienne Dumont (3 vols., Paris, 1802).

Berner, Albert Friedrich, *Grundlinien der criminalistischen Imputationslehre* (Berlin, 1843).

Berner, Albert Friedrich, *Wirkungskreis des Strafgesetzes, nach Zeit, Raum und Personen* (Berlin, 1853).

Bernhöft, Franz, *Staat und Recht der römischen Königzeit im Verhältniss zu verwandten Rechten* (Stuttgart, 1882).

Bierling, Ernst Rudolf, "Ueber die Benutzung von Landtags- und Synodalverhandlungen zur Auslegung der neuern Deutschen Staats- und Kirchengesetze," *Zeitschrift für Kirchenrecht*, X (1871), 141-212.

Bierling, Ernst Rudolf, *Zur Kritik der juristischen Grundbegriffe* (2 vols., Gotha, 1877-83).

Binding, Karl, *Der Entwurf eines Strafgesetzbuchs für den Norddeutschen Bund* (Leipzig, 1870).

Binding, Karl, *Die Normen und ihre Uebertretung* (2 vols., Leipzig, 1872-77).

Bluhme, Friedrich, *Encyclopädie der in Deutschland geltenden Rechte* (4 vols., Bonn, 1847-58).

Bluhme, Friedrich, *Uebersicht der in Deutschland geltenden Rechtsquellen*, 2nd edn. (Bonn, 1854).

*Bluntschli, Johann Caspar, *Geschichte der neueren Staatswissen-

schaft, allgemeines Staatsrecht und Politik, 3rd edn. (Munich and Leipzig, 1881).

*Bluntschli, Johann Caspar, *Lehre vom modernen Staat*, 5th edn. (3 vols., Stuttgart, 1875-76).

Bluntschli, Johann Caspar, and Carl Brater, *Deutsches Staatswörterbuch* (11 vols., Stuttgart and Leipzig, 1857-70).

Bornhak, Conrad, *Preussisches Staatsrecht* (3 vols., Freiburg im B., 1888-90).

Brie, Siegfried, *Der Bundesstaat*, Vol. I (Leipzig, 1874).

Brinz, Aloys von, *Lehrbuch der Pandekten*, 2nd edn. (4 vols., Erlangen, 1873-95). [Wilson's card reads "2 ed., Erlangen, 1872-'76."]

Bruck, Felix, *Zur Lehre von der criminalistischen Zurechnungsfähigkeit* (Breslau, 1878).

*Brunner, Heinrich, "Quellen und Geschichte des deutschen Rechts," Holtzendorff, ed., *Encyklopädie der Rechtswissenschaft*, pp. 213-302.

*Brunner, Heinrich, "Ueberblick über die Geschichte der französischen, Normannischen, und Englischen Rechtsquellen," Holtzendorff, ed., *Encyklopädie der Rechtswissenschaft*, pp. 303-47.

*Bruns, Carl Georg, "Geschichte und Quellen des römischen Rechts," Holtzendorff, ed., *Encyklopädie der Rechtswissenschaft*, pp. 95-183.

Canstein, Raban von, *Lehrbuch des Wechselrechts* (Berlin, 1890).

Caspar, Johann Ludwig, *Handbuch der gerichtlichen Medicin*, 7th edn. (2 vols., Berlin, 1881-82).

Comte, Auguste, *Cours de philosophie positive*, Vol. VI (Paris, 1842).

Dahlmann, Friedrich Christoph, *Die Politik auf den Grund und das Mass der gegebenen Zustände zurückgeführt*, 2nd edn., Vol. I (Leipzig, 1847).

Degenkolb, Carl Heinrich, *Einlassungszwang und Urtheilsnorm* (Leipzig, 1877).

Dilthey, Wilhelm, *Einleitung in die Geisteswissenschaften*, Vol. I (Leipzig, 1883).

Dupont-White, Charles Brook, *L'individu et l'état*, 2nd edn. (Paris, 1858).

Eichhorn, Karl Friedrich, *Deutsche Staats- und Rechtsgeschichte*, 5th edn. (4 vols., Göttingen, 1843-45).

Endemann, Wilhelm, ed., *Handbuch des deutschen Handels-, See- und Wechselrechts* (4 vols., Leipzig, 1881-84).

Eötvös, József, *Der Einfluss der herrschenden Ideen des 19. Jahrhunderts auf den Staat* (2 vols., Vienna and Leipzig, 1851-54).

Fichte, Immanuel Hermann von, *System der Ethik*, Vol. I (Leipzig, 1850).

Frantz, Gustav Adolph Constantin, *Die Naturlehre des Staates als Grundlage aller Staatswissenschaft* (Leipzig and Heidelberg, 1870).

Fricker, Karl Viktor, "Das Problem des Völkerrechts," *Zeitschrift für die gesammte Staatswissenschaft*, XXVIII (1872), 90-144, 347-86.

Friedländer, Alexander, *Juristische Encyclopädie, oder, System der Rechtswissenschaft* (Heidelberg, 1847).

Gabba, Carlo Francesco, *Della retroattività in materia penale* (Pisa, 1869).

*Gareis, Carl von, *Allgemeines Staatsrecht* (Freiburg im B., 1883). Vol. I, Pt. 1 of Heinrich von Marquardsen, ed., *Handbuch des öffentlichen Rechts der Gegenwart in Monographien* (4 vols., Freiburg and Tübingen, 1883-1906).

Gareis, Carl von, *Das deutsche Handelsrecht*, 3rd edn. (Berlin, 1888).

Gerber, Carl Friedrich Wilhelm von, *Grundzüge eines Systems des deutschen Staatsrechts*, 2nd edn. (Leipzig, 1869).

Gessler, Theodor von, "Zur Lehre von der Zurechnungsfähigkeit," *Der Gerichtssaal*, XXII (1870), 245-74.

Geyer, August, *Geschichte und System der Rechtsphilosophie in Grundzügen* (Innsbruck, 1863).

Gierke, Otto Friedrich von, *Das deutsche Genossenschaftsrecht* (4 vols., Berlin, 1868-1913).

Gierke, Otto Friedrich von, "Die Grundbegriffe des Staatsrechts und die neuesten Staatsrechtstheorien," *Zeitschrift für die gesammte Staatswissenschaft*, XXX (1874), 153-98, 265-335.

Gierke, Otto Friedrich von, *Johannes Althusius und die Entwicklung der naturrechtlichen Staatstheorien* (Breslau, 1880).

Gierke, Otto Friedrich von, *Die Staats- und Korporationslehre des Alterthums und des Mittelalters und ihre Aufnahme in Deutschland* (Berlin, 1881).

Gierke, Otto Friedrich von, "Ueber Jugend und Altern des Rechts," *Deutsche Rundschau*, XVIII (Feb. 1879), 205-32.

Giron, Alfred, *Le Droit administratif de la Belgique*, 2nd edn. (3 vols., Brussels.

Gneist, Rudolf von, *Der Rechtsstaat und die Verwaltungsgerichte in Deutschland*, 2nd edn. (Berlin, 1879).

Gneist, Rudolf von, *Selfgovernment; Communalverfassung und Verwaltungsgerichte in England*, 3rd edn. (Berlin, 1871).

Gneist, Rudolf von, *Verwaltung, Justiz, Rechtsweg; Staatsverwaltung und Selbstverwaltung nach englischen und deutschen Verhältnissen* (Berlin, 1869).

Gneist, Rudolf von, "Verwaltungsjurisdiktion, Verwaltungsjustiz," Franz von Holtzendorff, ed., *Rechtslexikon* (3 vols. in 4, Leipzig, 1880-81), III, 1113-24.

Goldschmidt, Levin, *Handbuch des Handelsrechts*, 3rd edn., Vol. 1 (Stuttgart, 1891).

Goldschmidt, Levin, "Von der Verpflichtung der Unmündigen," *Archiv für die civilistische Praxis*, XXXIX (1856), 417-59.

Göppert, Heinrich Robert, *Das Princip: "Gesetze haben keine rückwirkende Kraft" geschichtlich und dogmatisch entwickelt*, E. Eck, ed. (Jena, 1883).

Göring, Carl, *Ueber die menschliche Freiheit und Zurechnungsfähigkeit* (Leipzig, 1876).

Gumplowicz, Ludwig, *Rechtsstaat und Socialismus* (Innsbruck, 1881).

Guyau, Jean Marie, *La Morale anglaise contemporaine, morale de l'utilité et de l'évolution* (Paris, 1879).

Hälschner, Hugo, *Die Lehre vom Unrecht und seinen verschiedenen Formen* (Bonn, 1869).

Hälschner, Hugo, "Nachmals das Unrecht und seine verschiedenen Formen," *Der Gerichtssaal*, xxviii (1876), 401-31.

Hänel, Albert, *Studien zum deutschen Staatsrechte* (2 vols., Leipzig, 1873-80).

Hare, John Innes Clark, *The Law of Contracts* (Boston, 1887).

Hartmann, Eduard von, *Phänomenologie des sittlichen Bewusstseins* (Berlin, 1879).

Hartmann, Wilhelm, *Das deutsche Wechselrecht* (Berlin, 1869).

Harum, Peter, *Von der Entstehung des Rechts* (Innsbruck, 1863).

*Hastie, William, compiler, *Outlines of the Science of Jurisprudence* (Edinburgh, 1887).

Hegel, Georg Wilhelm Friedrich, *Grundlinien der Philosophie des Rechts* (Berlin, 1821).

Held, Joseph von, *Grundzüge des allgemeinen Staatsrechts* (Leipzig, 1868).

Held, Joseph von, *Staat und Gesellschaft* (3 vols., Leipzig, 1861-65).

Herbart, Johann Friedrich, "Zur Lehre von der Freiheit des menschlichen Willens," *Sämmtliche Werke*, G. Hartenstein, ed. (12 vols., Leipzig, 1850-52), ix, 241-385.

Hertz, Eduard, *Das Unrecht und die allgemeinen Lehren des Strafrechts* (Hamburg, 1880).

Heyssler, Moriz, *Das Civilunrecht und seine Formen* (Vienna, 1870).

"Dr. Moriz Heyssler" [obituary notice], *Zeitschrift für das privat- und öffentliche Recht der Gegenwart*, x (1883), 770-78.

Hildenbrand, Karl, *Geschichte und System der Rechts- und Staatsphilosophie*, Vol. i, *Das klassische Alterthum* (Leipzig, 1860).

*Hinschius, Paul, "Geschichte und Quellen des Kanonischen Rechts," Holtzendorff, ed., *Encyklopädie der Rechtswissenschaft*, pp. 185-211.

*Holtzendorff, Franz von, "Das deutsche Verfassungsrecht," *Encyklopädie der Rechtswissenschaft*, pp. 1041-153.

Holtzendorff, Franz von, "Einige Bemerkungen über die Nichtbestrafung jugendlicher Personen," *Der Gerichtssaal*, xxvi (Stuttgart, 1874), 401-12.

*Holtzendorff, Franz von, ed., *Encyklopädie der Rechtswissenschaft in systematischer Bearbeitung*, 5th edn. (Leipzig, 1890).

Holtzendorff, Franz von, ed., *Handbuch des deutschen Strafrechts* (4 vols., Berlin, 1871-77).

Holtzendorff, Franz von, *Die Principien der Politik* (Berlin, 1869).

Holtzendorff, Franz von, ed., *Rechtslexikon*, 3rd edn. (3 vols. in 4, Leipzig, 1880-81).

Hrehorowicz, Thaddaeus, *Grundfragen und Grundbegriffe des Strafrechts* (Dorpat, 1880).

Humboldt, Wilhelm von, *Ideen zu einem Versuch die Gränzen der Wirksamkeit des Staats zu bestimmen* (Breslau, 1851).

Jahrbücher für die Dogmatik des heutigen römischen und deutschen Privatrechts (1857-1942).

Jellinek, Georg, *Die Lehre von den Staatenverbindungen* (Vienna, 1882).

Jellinek, Georg, *Die sozialethische Bedeutung von Recht, Unrecht und Strafe* (Vienna, 1878).
*Jhering, Rudolf von, *Geist des römischen Rechts auf den verschiedenen Stufen seiner Entwicklung*, 5th edn. (3 vols. in 4, Leipzig, 1888-98). [Wilson's card reads "Leipzig, 1852-1884."]
Jhering, Rudolf von, *Der Kampf um's Recht* (Vienna, 1872).
Jhering, Rudolf von, *Das Schuldmoment im römischen Privatrecht* (Giessen, 1867).
Jhering, Rudolf von, *The Struggle for Law*, translated by John J. Lalor (Chicago, 1879).
Jhering, Rudolf von, "Unsere Aufgabe," *Jahrbücher für die Dogmatik des heutigen römischen und deutschen Privatrechts*, I (1857), 1-52.
*Jhering, Rudolf von, *Der Zweck im Recht* (2 vols., Leipzig, 1877-83). 2nd edn. (2 vols., Leipzig, 1884-86).
Jodl, Friedrich, *Geschichte der Ethik in der neueren Philosophie*, Vol. I (Stuttgart, 1882).
Juraschek, Franz von, *Personal- und Realunion* (Berlin, 1878).

Karlowa, Otto, *Das Rechtsgeschäft und seine Wirkung* (Berlin, 1877).
Kirchmann, Julius Hermann von, *Die Grundbegriffe des Rechts und der Moral* (Berlin, 1869).
Knies, Karl Gustav Adolf, *Die politischen Oekonomie vom geschichtlichen Standpunkte*, 2nd edn. (Braunschweig, 1883).
Kozak, Theophil, *Rodbertus-Jagetzow's socialökonomische Ansichten dargestellt* (Jena, 1882).
Krafft-Ebing, Richard von, *Grundzüge der Criminalpsychologie*, 2nd edn. (Stuttgart, 1882).
Krafft-Ebing, Richard von, *Lehrbuch der gerichtlichen Psychopathologie*, 2nd edn. (Stuttgart, 1881).
Kuntze, Johannes Emil, *Deutsches Wechselrecht* (Leipzig, 1862).

Laas, Ernst, "Die Causalität des Ich," *Vierteljahrsschrift für wissenschaftliche Philosophie*, IV (1880), 1-54, 185-224, 311-67.
Laas, Ernst, *Idealistische und positivistische Ethik* (Berlin, 1882).
Laas, Ernst, "Vergeltung und Zurechnung," *Vierteljahrsschrift für wissenschaftliche Philosophie*, V (1881), 137-85, 296-348, 448-89; VI (1882), 189-233, 295-329.
*Laband, Paul, *Das Staatsrecht des Deutschen Reiches* (3 vols., Tübingen and Freiburg, 1876-82).
*Laband, Paul, *Das Staatsrecht des Deutschen Reiches* (Freiburg im B., 1883). Vol. II, Pt. 1 of Marquardsen, ed., *Handbuch des öffentlichen Rechts der Gegenwart*.
Laboulaye, Édouard René Lefebvre de, *L'État et ses limites*, 5th edn. (Paris, 1871).
Landmann, Rudolph, *Hauptfragen der Ethik* (Leipzig, 1874).
Lassalle, Ferdinand Johann Gottlieb, *Das System der erworbenen Rechte*, Vol. I, *Die Theorie der erworbenen Rechte und der Collision der Gesetze*, 2nd edn. (Leipzig, 1880).
Lasson, Adolf, *System der Rechtsphilosophie* (Berlin and Leipzig, 1882).
Laurent, François, *Études sur l'histoire de l'humanité* (18 vols., Paris, 1850-70).

Lecky, William Edward Hartpole, *History of European Morals from Augustus to Charlemagne*, 2nd edn. (2 vols., London, 1869).

*Leoni, Albert, *Das Staatsrecht des Reichslande Elsass-Lothringen* (Freiburg, 1883). Vol. II, Pt. 1 of Marquardsen, ed., *Handbuch des öffentlichen Rechts der Gegenwart*.

Lieber, Francis, *Manual of Political Ethics*, 2nd edn., Theodore D. Woolsey, ed. (Philadelphia, 1875).

Lieber, Francis, *On Civil Liberty and Self-government* (2 vols., Philadelphia, 1853).

Liman, Carl, *Zweifelhafte Geisteszustände vor Gericht* (Berlin, 1869).

Lindgren, W. E. von, *Die Grundbegriffe des Staatsrechts* (Leipzig, 1869).

Liszt, Franz von, "Der Zweckgedanke im Strafrecht," *Zeitschrift für die gesamte Strafrechtswissenschaft*, III (1883), 1-47.

Loening, Edgar, *Lehrbuch des deutschen Verwaltungsrechts* (Leipzig, 1884).

Loewe, Aloys, *Einleitung in das Studium der Rechtswissenschaft* (Zurich, 1835).

Lotze, Hermann, *Microcosmus: An Essay Concerning Man and His Relation to the World*, translated by Elizabeth Hamilton and E. E. Constance Jones (2 vols., Edinburgh, 1885).

Lotze, Hermann, *Mikrokosmus. Ideen zur Naturgeschichte und Geschichte der Menschheit*, 3rd edn. (3 vols., Leipzig, 1876-80).

*Marquardsen, Heinrich von, *Politik* (Freiburg im B., 1884). Vol. I, Pt. 2 of *Handbuch des öffentlichen Rechts der Gegenwart*.

Martitz, Ferdinand von, *Betrachtungen über die Verfassung des Norddeutschen Bundes* (Leipzig, 1868).

Martitz, Ferdinand von, review of Paul Laband, *Das Staatsrecht des deutschen Reichs*, in *Zeitschrift für die gesammte Staatswissenschaft*, XXXII (1876), 555-73.

Maudsley, Henry, *Responsibility in Mental Disease* (London, 1872).

*Maurer, Konrad, "Ueberblick über die Geschichte der Nordgermanischen Rechtsquellen," Holtzendorff, ed., *Encyklopädie der Rechtswissenschaft*, pp. 349-85.

Meier, Ernst von, *Die Rechtsbildung in Staat und Kirche* (Berlin, 1861).

Meier, Ernst von, *Ueber den Abschluss von Staatsverträgen* (Leipzig, 1874).

*Meier, Ernst von, "Das Verwaltungsrecht," Holtzendorff, ed., *Encyklopädie der Rechtswissenschaft*, pp. 1155-255.

Meili, Friedrich, *Geschichte und System des internationalen Privatrechts im Grundriss* (Leipzig, 1892).

Mejer, Otto, *Einleitung in das deutsche Staatsrecht*, 2nd edn. (Freiburg, 1884).

Merkel, Adolf, "Analogie und Auslegung des Gesetzes," Holtzendorff, ed., *Handbuch des deutschen Strafrechts*, II, 65-84.

Merkel, Adolf, "Die Auslegung des Strafgesetzes," Holtzendorff, ed., *Handbuch des deutschen Strafrechts*, IV, 73-86.

*Merkel, Adolf, *Juristische Encyclopädie* (Berlin and Leipzig, 1885).

Merkel, Adolf, *Kriminalistische Abhandlungen*, Vol. I (Leipzig, 1867).

Merkel, Adolf, "Recht und Macht," *Schmollers Jahrbuch für Gesetz-*

gebung, Verwaltung und Volkswirthschaft im Deutschen Reich, v (1881), 439-65.

Merkel, Adolf, "Rechtsnorm und subjectives Recht," *Zeitschrift für das privat- und öffentliche Recht der Gegenwart*, vi (1879), 367-96.

Merkel, Adolf, review of Hugo Meyer, *Lehrbuch des deutschen Strafrechts*, 2nd edn., in *Zeitschrift für das privat- und öffentliche Recht der Gegenwart*, v (1878), 633-42.

Merkel, Adolf, "Über 'Das gemeine deutsche Strafrecht' von Hälschner und den Idealismus in der Strafrechtswissenschaft," *Zeitschrift für die gesamte Strafrechtswissenschaft*, i (1881), 553-96.

Merkel, Adolf, "Ueber Accrescenz und Decrescenz des Strafrechtes und deren Bedingungen," *Juristische Blätter*, ii (May 4-18, 1873), 209-11, 221-23, 236-38.

Merkel, Adolf, "Ueber das Verhältniss der Rechtsphilosophie zur 'positiven' Rechtswissenschaft und zum allgemeinen Theil derselben," *Zeitschrift für das privat- und öffentliche Recht der Gegenwart*, i (1874), 1-10, 402-21.

Merkel, Adolf, "Ueber den Begriff der Entwicklung in seiner Anwendung auf Recht und Gesellschaft," *Zeitschrift für das privat- und öffentliche Recht der Gegenwart*, iii (1876), 625-32; iv (1877), 1-20.

Merkel, Adolf, "Ueber vergeltende Gerechtigkeit," *Kriminalistische Abhandlungen* (2 vols., Leipzig, 1867), i, 104-15.

Merkel, Adolf, *Zur Reform der Strafgesetze* (Prague, 1869).

Meyer, Georg, *Lehrbuch des deutschen Staatsrechtes* (Leipzig, 1878).

Meyer, Georg, *Lehrbuch des deutschen Verwaltungsrechts*, Vol. i (Leipzig, 1883).

Meyer, Georg, *Staatsrechtliche Erörterungen über die deutsche Reichsverfassung* (Leipzig, 1872).

*Mill, John Stuart, *Considerations on Representative Government* (New York, 1882).

Mill, John Stuart, *On Liberty* (London, 1859).

Mill, John Stuart, *Utilitarianism*, 2nd edn. (London, 1864).

*Mohl, Robert von, *Encyclopädie der Staatswissenschaften*, 2nd edn. (Tübingen, 1872).

Mohl, Robert von, *Die Geschichte und Literatur der Staatswissenschaften* (3 vols., Erlangen, 1855-58).

Mohl, Robert von, *Das Staatsrecht des Königreichs Württemberg*, 2nd edn. (2 vols., Tübingen, 1840).

Mohl, Robert von, *Staatsrecht, Völkerrecht, und Politik* (3 vols., Tübingen, 1860-69).

Mohl, Robert von, "Die völkerrechtliche Lehre vom Asyle," *Staatsrecht, Völkerrecht, und Politik*, i, 637-764.

Mollat, Georg, ed., *Lesebuch zur Geschichte der deutschen Staatswissenschaft von Engelbert von Volkersdorf bis Johann Stephan Pütter* (Tübingen, 1891).

Namur, Parfait Joseph, *Cours d'encyclopédie du droit* (Brussels, 1875).

Neuner, Carl, *Wesen und Arten der Privatrechtsverhältnisse* (Kiel, 1866).

Oettingen, Alexander Konstantin von, *Die Moralstatistik in ihrer Bedeutung für eine christliche Sozialethik*, 2nd edn. (Erlangen, 1874).

Oettingen, Alexander Konstantin von, *Die Moralstatistik und die christliche Sittenlehre* (2 vols., Erlangen, 1868-74).

Pernice, Alfred, "Rechtsgeschäft und Rechtsordnung," *Zeitschrift für das privat- und öffentliche Recht der Gegenwart*, VII (1880), 465-98.

Perthes, Clemens Theodor, *Das deutsche Staatsleben vor der Revolution* (Hamburg and Gotha, 1845).

Pfaff, Leopold, and Franz Hofmann, *Commentar zum österreichischen allgemeinen bürgerlichen Gesetzbuch* (2 vols., Vienna, 1877-87).

Pfenninger, Heinrich, *Der Begriff der Strafe* (Zurich, 1877).

Pollock, Frederick, *Essays in Jurisprudence and Ethics* (London, 1882).

Post, Albert Hermann, *Die Anfänge des Staats- und Rechtslebens* (Oldenburg, 1878).

Post, Albert Hermann, *Bausteine für eine allgemeine Rechtswissenschaft auf vergleichend-ethnologischer Basis* (2 vols., Oldenburg, 1880-81).

Post, Albert Hermann, *Der Ursprung des Rechts* (Oldenburg, 1876).

Pözl, Joseph von, *Lehrbuch des bayerischen Verfassungsrechts*, 5th edn. (Munich, 1877).

Puchta, Georg Friedrich, *Cursus der Institutionen* (3 vols., Leipzig, 1841-47).

Puchta, Georg Friedrich, *Das Gewohnheitsrecht* (2 vols., Erlangen, 1828-37).

Puchta, Georg Friedrich, *Grundriss zu Vorlesungen über juristische Encyclopädie und Methodologie* (Erlangen, 1822).

Renaud, Achilles, *Lehrbuch des allgemeinen deutschen Wechselrechts*, 3rd edn. (Giessen, 1868).

Rintelen, Victor, *Ueber den Einfluss neuer Gesetze auf die zur Zeit ihrer Emanation bestehenden Rechtsverhältnisse* (Breslau, 1877).

Rohland, Waldemar von, *Das internationale Strafrecht*, Pt. 1 (Leipzig, 1877).

Rönne, Ludwig Moritz Peter von, *Das Staatsrecht der preussischen Monarchie*, 4th edn. (4 vols., Leipzig, 1881-83).

Rönne, Ludwig Moritz Peter von, *Das Staatsrecht des Deutschen Reiches*, 2nd edn. (Leipzig, 1876).

Rösler, Carl Friedrich Hermann, *Lehrbuch des deutschen Verwaltungsrechts* (2 vols., Erlangen, 1871-73).

Roussel, Adolphe, *Encyclopédie du droit*, 2nd edn. (Brussels, 1871).

Rümelin, Gustav, *Juristische Begriffsbildung* (Leipzig, 1878).

Rümelin, Gustav, *Reden und Aufsätze* (Freiburg im B., 1875).

Rümelin, Gustav, "Ueber die Idee der Gerechtigkeit," *Reden und Aufsätze*, New Series (Freiburg, 1881), pp. 176-202.

Sarwey, Otto von, *Das öffentliche Recht und die Verwaltungsrechtspflege* (Tübingen, 1880).

*Savigny, Friedrich Carl von, *System des heutigen römischen Rechts* (8 vols., Berlin, 1840-49).

Savigny, Friedrich Carl von, *Vom Beruf unserer Zeit für Gesetzgebung und Rechtswissenschaft* (Heidelberg, 1815).

Schäffle, Albert Eberhard Friedrich, *Bau und Leben des socialen Körpers* (4 vols., Tübingen, 1875-78).

Schaffrath, Wilhelm Michael, *Theorie der Auslegung constitutioneller Gesetze* (Leipzig, 1842).

Schall, Richard, *Der Parteiwille im Rechtsgeschäft* (Stuttgart, 1877).

Schlossmann, Siegmund, review of Ernst Zitelmann, *Irrtum und Rechtsgeschäft*, in *Zeitschrift für das privat- und öffentliche Recht der Gegenwart*, VII (1880), 543-77.

Schlossmann, Siegmund, *Der Vertrag* (Leipzig, 1876).

Schmid, Reinhold, *Die Herrschaft der Gesetze nach ihren räumlichen und zeitlichen Grenzen* (Jena, 1863).

Schmoller, Gustav, "Die Gerechtigkeit in der Volkswirthschaft," *Schmollers Jahrbuch für Gesetzgebung, Verwaltung und Volkswirthschaft im Deutschen Reich*, v (1881), 19-54.

Schopenhauer, Arthur, *Die beiden Grundprobleme der Ethik*, 2nd edn. (Leipzig, 1860).

Schulte, Johann Friedrich von, *Lehrbuch der deutschen Reichs- und Rechtsgeschichte*, 3rd edn. (Stuttgart, 1873).

Schultze, August Sigismund, *Privatrecht und Prozess in ihrer Wechselbeziehung* (Freiburg and Tübingen, 1883).

Schulze, Hermann Johann Friedrich, *Einleitung in das deutsche Staatsrecht*, new edn. (Leipzig, 1867).

Schulze, Hermann Johann Friedrich, *Das preussische Staatsrecht auf Grundlage des deutschen Staatsrechts dargestellt* (2 vols., Leipzig, 1872-77).

*Schulze, Hermann Johann Friedrich, *Das Staatsrecht des Königreichs Preussen* (Freiburg, 1884). Vol. II, Pt. 2 of Marquardsen, ed., *Handbuch des öffentlichen Rechts der Gegenwart*.

Schvarcz, Julius, *Montesquieu und die Verantwortlichkeit der Räthe des Monarchen in England, Aragonien, Ungarn, Siebenbürgen und Schweden (1189-1748)* (Leipzig, 1892).

Schwartzer, Otto, *Die Bewusstlosigkeitszustände als Strafausschliessungsgründe* (Tübingen, 1878).

Schwarze, Friedrich Oscar von, "Zur Lehre von der Fragstellung an die Geschwornen," *Der Gerichtssaal*, xx (Erlangen, 1868), 10-25, 125-34.

Schwarze, Friedrich Oscar von, "Zur Revision des Strafgesetzbuchs," *Der Gerichtssaal*, xxvi (Stuttgart, 1874), 577-89.

Schwarze, Friedrich Oscar von, "Die Zurechnung der im Zustande hochgradiger Trunkenheit begangenen Handlungen," *Der Gerichtssaal*, xxxiii (Stuttgart, 1881), 430-72.

Scrutton, Thomas Edward, *The Influence of the Roman Law on the Law of England* (Cambridge, 1885).

Seeger, Hermann von, *Ueber die rückwirkende Kraft neuer Gesetze* (Tübingen, 1862).

Seydel, Max von, *Commentar zur Verfassungs-Urkunde für das deutsche Reich* (Würzburg, 1873).

Seydel, Max von, *Grundzüge einer allgemeinen Staatslehre* (Würzburg, 1873).

Sickel, Wilhelm, *Geschichte der deutschen Staatsverfassung bis zur*

Begründung des constitutionellen Staats, Part 1, *Der Freistaat* (Halle, 1879).

Sigwart, Christoph von, *Der Begriff des Wollens und sein Verhältniss zum Begriff der Ursache* (Tübingen, 1879).

Skrzeczka, Dr., "Die Geisteskrankheiten im Verhältniss zur Zurechnungslehre," Holtzendorff, ed., *Handbuch des deutschen Strafrechts*, II, 219-66.

Sohm, Rudolf, *Die altdeutsche Reichs- und Gerichtsverfassung*, Vol. 1 (Weimar, 1871).

Sohm, Rudolf, *Institutionen des römischen Rechts* (Leipzig, 1884).

Sontag, Carl Richard, *Die Redaktionsversehen des Gesetzgebers* (Freiburg, 1874).

Späing, W., *Französisches, belgisches und englisches Wechselrecht* (Berlin, 1890).

Spencer, Herbert, *The Data of Ethics* (London, 1879).

Stahl, Friedrich Julius, *Die Philosophie des Rechts nach geschichtlicher Ansicht* (2 vols. in 3, Heidelberg, 1830-37).

*Stahl, Friedrich Julius, *Die Philosophie des Rechts*, Vol. 1, *Geschichte der Rechtsphilosophie*, 5th edn. (Freiburg im B., 1878).

Stein, Lorenz Jacob von, *Geschichte der sozialen Bewegung in Frankreich*, Vol. 1 (Leipzig, 1850).

Stein, Lorenz Jacob von, *Die Verwaltungslehre* (7 vols. in 4, Stuttgart, 1865-68).

Stephen, Leslie, *The Science of Ethics* (London, 1882).

Stintzing, Roderich von, *Geschichte der deutschen Rechtswissenschaft*, Vol. 1 (Munich and Leipzig, 1880).

Stobbe, Otto, *Geschichte der deutschen Rechtsquellen* (2 vols., Braunschweig, 1860-64).

Taine, Hippolyte Adolphe, *The French Revolution*, translated by John Durand (3 vols., New York, 1878-85).

Thöl, Heinrich, *Einleitung in das deutsche Privatrecht* (Göttingen, 1851).

Thöl, Heinrich, *Das Handelsrecht*, 6th edn. (3 vols., Leipzig, 1878-80).

Thon, August, "Der Rechtsbegriff," *Zeitschrift für das privat- und öffentliche Recht der Gegenwart*, VII (1880), 231-63.

*Thon, August, *Rechtsnorm und subjectives Recht. Untersuchungen zur allgemeinen Rechtslehre* (Weimar, 1878).

Thudichum, Friedrich Wolfgang Karl von, *Verfassungsrecht des norddeutschen Bundes und des deutschen Zollvereins* (Tübingen, 1870).

Tocqueville, Alexis de, *L'ancien régime et la révolution*, 6th edn. (Paris, 1866).

Trendelenberg, Friedrich Adolf, *Naturrecht auf dem Grunde der Ethik*, 2nd edn. (Leipzig, 1868)

Turner, Samuel Epes, *A Sketch of the Germanic Constitution from Early Times to the Dissolution of the Empire* (New York and London, 1888).

Tylor, Edward Burnett, *Primitive Culture* (2 vols., London, 1871).

Volkmar, Wilhelm Volkmann von, *Lehrbuch der Psychologie*, 2nd edn. (2 vols., Cöthen, 1875-76).

Vorländer, Franz, *Geschichte der philosophischen Moral-, Rechts-, und Staatslehre der Engländer und Franzosen* (Marburg, 1855).

Wächter, Oscar Eberhard Siegfried von, *Encyclopädie des Wechselrechts* (2 vols., Stuttgart, 1879-81).
Wahlberg, Wilhelm Emil, "Grundzüge der strafrechtlichen Zurechnungslehre," *Gesammelte kleinere Schriften und Bruchstücke* (3 vols., Vienna, 1875-82), I, 1-67.
Wahlberg, Wilhelm Emil, "Die Strafmittal," Holtzendorff, ed., *Handbuch des deutschen Strafrechts*, II, 429-544.
Waitz, Georg, *Deutsche Verfassungsgeschichte* (8 vols., Kiel, 1844-78).
Waitz, Georg, *Grundzüge der Politik nebst einzelnen Ausführungen* (Kiel, 1862).
Walter, Ferdinand, *Deutsche Rechtsgeschichte*, 2nd edn. (2 vols., Bonn. 1857).
Walter, Ferdinand, *Juristische Encyclopädie* (Bonn, 1856).
Walter, Ferdinand, review of Hugo Hälschner, *Die Lehre vom Unrecht*, in *Kritische Vierteljahrschrift für Gesetzgebung und Rechtswissenschaft*, XI (1869), 289-301.
Warnkönig, Leopold August, *Juristische Encyclopädie, oder, Organische Darstellung der Rechtswissenschaft mit vorherrschender Rücksicht auf Deutschland* (Erlangen, 1853).
Wharton, Francis, *A Treatise on Mental Unsoundness* (Philadelphia, 1873).
Wharton, Francis, *A Treatise on the Conflict of Laws* (Philadelphia, 1872).
Williams, James, *The Institutes of Justinian Illustrated by English Law* (London, 1883).
Windscheid, Bernhard Joseph Hubert, *Lehrbuch des Pandektenrechts*, 5th edn. (3 vols., Stuttgart, 1879).

Zeitschrift der Savigny-Stiftung für Rechtsgeschichte (1880-   ).
Zeitschrift für Civilrecht und Prozess (1828-65).
Zeitschrift für das gesamte Handelsrecht (1858-   ).
Zeitschrift für das privat- und öffentliche Recht der Gegenwart (1874-1916).
Zeitschrift für Rechtsgeschichte (1861-78).
Zeitschrift für vergleichende Rechtswissenschaft (1878-   ).
Zitelmann, Ernst, *Begriff und Wesen der sogenannten juristischen Personen* (Leipzig, 1873).
Zitelmann, Ernst, "Gewohnheitsrecht und Irrthum," *Archiv für die civilistische Praxis*, LXVI (1883), 323-468.
Zitelmann, Ernst, *Irrtum und Rechtsgeschäft* (Leipzig, 1879).
Zöpfl, Heinrich Matthias, *Deutsche Rechtsgeschichte*, 4th edn. (3 vols. in 2, Braunschweig, 1871-72).
Zorn, Philipp Karl Ludwig, *Das Staatsrecht des Deutschen Reiches* (2 vols., Berlin, 1880-83).

Items for which no further information could be found or which could not be checked for accuracy (printed exactly as Wilson cited them):
Aloria, *Della retroattività delle leggi* (1868).

S. & R. Löning, *Ueber geschichtliche und ungeschichtliche Behandlung des deutschen Strafrechts* (Berlin and Leipzig, 1883).

Makower, H., Hahn, *et al., Kommentare zum deutschen Handelsgesetzbuch.*

Adolf Merkel, "Ueber den Begriff der Strafe in seinen geschichtlichen Beziehungen," *Oesterreichischen Wochenschrift,* 1872, pp. 513 *et seq.*

H. Meyer, *Die Gerechtigkeit im Strafrechte* (Stuttgart, 1881).

Meyne, *Essai sur le rétroactivité des lois répressives* (Brussels, 1863).

R. C. von Wächter, "Ueber Gesetzes- und Rechtsanalogie im Strafrechte," *Archiv des Strafrechts,* 1884, pp. 413 *et seq.,* 535 *et seq.*

From the Minutes of the Seminary of Historical and Political Science of The Johns Hopkins University

Bluntschli Library, February 17, 1893.

Professor Adams called the Seminary to order at 8.10 P. M. . . .

Mr. John Haynes read the second paper on the "Blending of National and State Politics." He said in part: An American is subject to two sovereign powers. If he be a voter, he is a partner in two governments. The principle of the distinctness of national and state governments is firmly intrenched in constitutional law. We might logically expect to find the same division in the politics of the land, national politics centering about national questions and state politics about questions falling within the jurisdiction of each State. But we find the exact reverse. State parties do not exist and never have existed with few exceptions. In State elections the vote is divided between the same parties as in national elections. The reasons for this are plain. Men who are associated in one line of effort tend to associate in others. Those who work together in national politics, by reason of their acquaintance with one another and with the voters of the community come to coöperate in local politics. Thus we have two strong political organizations in every election. Amelioration may be looked for through the action of independent voters. But a separation of these spheres of action is prevented by constitutional and statute law. The Constitution provides that United States senators shall be elected by the legislatures of the respective states, and the statutes provide that the several legislatures shall divide the states into congressional districts, and thus the legislative department of the States is given a direct and vital relation to national politics.

But, granting that the indirect method has some advantages, they are not sufficient to compensate for the disadvantages of the intrusion of national affairs into state politics. Often the voter must choose whether he will express himself on State or national matters; one or the other must be sacrificed. This blending often causes senators to sit in the National Legislature who misrepresent the convictions of the major part of their constituency. The most pernicious influence of the law [is a] tendency to divert the attention of the law-makers and people from vital state matters. Hence legislators are chosen with regard to their national policy, and not from any superior ability in legislation. What is the remedy? Let the people elect the senators and put the duty of dividing the States into congressional districts somewhere else than in the legislative department of the States. A commission might be chosen by popular vote for this purpose.

Professor Woodrow Wilson was invited to comment on the subject discussed by Mr. Haynes, and spoke as follows: It is extremely detrimental that we mix State and national politics. But what are we going to do about it? State questions are not suitable for bases of parties. In a few weeks the basis of formation has disappeared. The field of choice is national and there only do we have fields fit to base parties upon. The only way to divide the two sets is to separate the elections. In this case the frequency of voting would become an intolerable burden. It is useless to complain except we have a remedy to offer. . . .

A. C. Bryan,   Secretary

Typed entry, bound ledger book (MdBJ).

Two Letters to Winthrop More Daniels

My dear Daniels,   Baltimore, Maryland, 23 February, 1893

I am sincerely obliged to you for your careful letters about the '83 gift,[1] and I would have acted immediately in the matter, had it seemed possible for me to do so; but it has simply been out of the question amidst the very great and confusing variety of engagements which have pressed upon me here. Richardson wrote to me at last; but of course not at all to the purpose. Nothing, I am convinced, could be accomplished through correspondence with him. I shall make up a short list here and leave the rest until my return to Princeton, for a final rush,—if necessary by cable in the case of foreign books.[2]

As to the case of the man who wishes to change from my course to another, I have no objection at all. I always wish to leave all such matters entirely to the man's own choice and the Faculty's sanction from the point of view of general policy. Please refer all such cases to the Faculty, and say that I have no objection whatever to such changes.

I am sorry that I have to write always in a hurry. Thank you very much for the welcome items of news. I know nothing besides of what is happening in Princeton except what the Princetonian contains.

Mrs. Wilson joins me in warmest regards.

Faithfully and cordially Yours,   Woodrow Wilson

P.S. Will you not kindly fill out the blank from our English friends which I send with this?   W. W.[3]

1 "The Class of '83 propose to found and endow a Library of Political Science and Jurisprudence as their Decennial Class Memorial. Several thousand dollars have been raised and it is expected that about one thousand volumes will be purchased at once, the remainder of the money to be kept for a permanent endowment fund. The collection will be placed in the College Library." *Daily Princetonian*, Feb. 28, 1893. It seems a safe assumption that Wilson had been consulted by the officers of the Class of 1883, and that he had suggested the gift of a library of political science. However, documentary evidence to support this assumption is missing.
2 See the Editorial Note, "Wilson and the Class of 1883 Library of Political Science and Jurisprudence."
3 Daniels must have sent the blank on to the "English friends."

My dear Daniels,   Baltimore, Maryland, 27 February, 1893.

I send, by the same mail that carries this, a notice to the *Princetonian* announcing an examination in Public Law for Monday evening, March 13, and one in the History of Law for Tuesday evening, March 14. I am sincerely obliged to you for reminding me about the matter.

You can imagine with what emotions your recital of the difficulties of carrying out the verdict of the student committee on cheating filled me; I dare not trust myself to say anything yet by way of comment. But my thankfulness that the vote of the younger men saved the college from irreparable disgrace is simply inexpressible.[1]

Most Cordially and Sincerely,   Woodrow Wilson

I almost wish '83 had done something else with their money!

WWTLS (W. M. Daniels Coll., CtY).
1 The honor system, instituted during the mid-year examinations in January 1893, met, according to the *Daily Princetonian*, February 9, 1893, with "*unqualified* success" in the two upper classes. However, two freshmen and two sophomores were charged with having deliberately broken the pledge. On Monday, February 6, a student mass meeting was held to ascertain "the will of the college regarding cases of abuse of the new examination rules." A nine-man committee, representing all four classes, was formed "to constitute a court to try cases of men charged with dishonorable conduct" and was empowered to "impose penalties according to the nature of the offenses." *Daily Princetonian*, February 9, 1893. The *Princetonian*, in an editorial in this issue, recommended

ostracism of the culprits and warned that Princeton's reputation was, "in a larger sense than we may realize, at stake in its [the honor system's] success or failure."

The *Princetonian* announced on February 17 that the student committee had decided that the four men proved guilty should be given the alternative of applying to their professors for re-examination or having their names recommended for expulsion. However, the committee recommended instant expulsion in future cases.

The faculty meanwhile, on February 15, had ruled that students found guilty of cheating should receive a grade of zero for the examination involved and also be conditioned. Princeton Faculty Minutes, February 15, 1893. Then, following the report of the special student committee, the faculty at its meeting on February 24 adopted the following resolution: "Resolved, That the thanks of the Faculty be conveyed to the Committee of the Students, appointed at a mass-meeting of the College, who conducted the investigation into the cases of cheating at the late Examinations, for the fidelity and efficiency with which they discharged their office." Princeton Faculty Minutes, February 24, 1893.

All the records are silent about the disposition of the cases of the four offenders. Moreover, the records shed no light on the meaning of Wilson's statement about being thankful that the vote of the younger men saved the college from irreparable disgrace. To say that he was referring to younger men on the faculty would be mere conjecture, as the Faculty Minutes give no indication whatsoever of any debate on the resolutions adopted on February 15 and February 24.

An Assignment of Copyright[1]

[Feb. 28, 1893]

FOR VALUE RECEIVED I, Woodrow Wilson, of Princeton, New Jersey, hereby assign to Longmans, Green & Co. of 15 East 16th Street, New York, all my right, title and interest, present and future, including all copyrights or renewals thereof, in my work entitled DIVISION AND REUNION, *1829-1889*, written under agreement with Messrs. Longmans, Green & Co. dated June 24th 1889, for publication in a series of books to be issued under the general title of Epochs of American History, and edited by Dr. Albert B. Hart.

Dated this 28th day of February, 1893

Woodrow Wilson

Witness: F. Ross Payne

TDS (David McKay Co., New York).
  [1] This was apparently sent to Wilson for his signature before Longmans made the $500 payment for the manuscript of *Division and Reunion* as stipulated in the contract for the book.

To Albert Shaw

My dear Shaw: Baltimore, Maryland.   28 February, 1893.

Your long, interesting, and beguiling letter[1] has been forwarded to me here, where I am approaching the close of my lectures on Administration. If I were at home,—or were to be at home when

I get there, I would jump at your proposition to "do" the new Cabinet. There certainly has not been a Cabinet for a long time which so invited comment from a man studiously and dispassionately interested in public affairs. Moreover I have none of the usual professorial distaste for "off-hand and journalistic" work of the kind you propose.

But for the next eight or ten weeks I am to be only nominally at home. The early part of each week I shall spend in Princeton engrossed with classes, and the middle part in fulfilling engagements away from home; so that I shall have almost literally no time at my disposal for connected work. I have never yet learned to write on the fly.

I am sincerely sorry to decline the job, both because you want it done and I love you, and because I am interested immensely in the idea and want to do it for my own sake. But it is really out of the question.[2] By the way, I practiced at the same bar with Hoke Smith[3] and despise him as heartily as all the other men I knew at the Atlanta bar did. In his case, I opine, Mr. Cleveland has been woefully taken in!

Why not write the article yourself? You could do it vastly better than I could.

I shall be in New York next week, and will come in to have a talk with you. Forgive me for declining, it is inevitable under the circumstances; and believe me, as ever,

Your affectionate friend,   Woodrow Wilson

TCL (in possession of Virginia Shaw English).
    [1] It is missing.
    [2] But see WW to A. Shaw, March 4, 1893, in which Wilson agreed to write the article printed at March 17, 1893.
    [3] Secretary of the Interior in Cleveland's Cabinet.

EDITORIAL NOTE

WILSON'S *DIVISION AND REUNION*

The provenance and development of Wilson's first full-scale historical work, *Division and Reunion*, is chronicled in almost complete detail in letters and other documents printed in this volume and the preceding two, and the following summaries of the most important of these documents afford a clear guide to Wilson's progress:

April 23, 1889: Albert Bushnell Hart, editor of a new "Epochs of American History" series, to be published by Longmans, Green, invites Wilson to write the third volume, covering the history of the United States from 1829 to 1889, and sets the deadline as "a year hence."

May 1, 1889: Wilson tells Hart that he has to write his high school text on civil government during the coming months and could not possibly meet Hart's deadline.

May 2 and 10, 1889: Hart presses Wilson for a positive reply and says that Longmans are willing to postpone the deadline to September 1890.

May 13, 1889: Wilson declines, saying that he would need about two years to write the book because he would have to cover so much new historical ground.

June 1, 1889: Hart accepts Wilson's delivery date and adds that he is particularly eager to have Wilson write the book because he could impartially judge the South both before and after the Civil War.

June 3, 1889: Wilson accepts and says that although he is of southern birth and rearing, he has non-southern parents and has been a Federalist ever since he had independent political opinions.

June 12, 1889: Wilson accepts the title for his book, *Division and Reunion*, which Hart had suggested.

June 28, 1889: Longmans, Green acknowledge receipt of a signed copy of the contract for the book from Wilson.

August 9, 1889: Wilson, in a letter to Robert Bridges, indicates that he has done nothing on *Division and Reunion* during the summer but says that he will devote his course in American history at Wesleyan during the coming year largely to the period covered by the book.

August 23, 1889: Wilson writes to his former student at the Johns Hopkins, Frederick Jackson Turner, now at the University of Wisconsin, recalling their conversations in Baltimore about the importance of the West and asking Turner for evidence of the development of a self-conscious western sectionalism during the antebellum period.

August 31, 1889: Turner in reply says that he regrets that he will not have time to do the research required to find the materials that Wilson needs but will try to put one of his students on the project. (Turner was apparently unable to find a student to do this work.)

February 7, 1891: Wilson tells Horace E. Scudder that he has written only the first chapter of *Division and Reunion*, "after a fashion."

May 19, 1891: In reply to a letter from Hart of March 12, 1891, Wilson confesses that he has written only a preliminary draft of the first chapter and promises to spend the summer in Princeton in the hope of completing the first draft of the book.

July 1 and August 14, 1891: In letters to Richard Heath Dabney and John Franklin Jameson, Wilson writes that he is hard at work "Epoch-making" in spite of the intense heat.

August 21, 1891: Wilson tells Hart that about one half of his manuscript is "in some sort of shape."

September 11 and 22, 1891: Wilson, in letters to Hart and Bridges, says that about two thirds of his manuscript is "now in pretty good shape."

January 20, 1892: Wilson tells Hart that he has not been able to do anything on *Division and Reunion* during the past semester; encloses a copy of the chapter and section headings for the entire book; and offers to send the chapters already more or less completed to Hart for his criticism.

January 24, 1892: Hart in reply suggests a more detailed outline but does not ask to see the chapters.

July 20 and August 10, 11, and 18, 1892: In letters to Stockton Axson, Jameson, Scudder, and Bridges, Wilson chronicles his "painful" progress in writing during the summer.

August 24, 1892: In a progress report to Hart, Wilson says that he is well into the next-to-the-last chapter, and that his present draft, although a first one, is in such good shape that it can easily be converted into copy for the printer. Thinks that he can send complete copy to Hart by October 1.

October 25, 1892: Wilson tells Hart that he has completed his manuscript, which was much too long, that he has succeeded in cutting about eighty pages from it, and that if the publishers will not accept it in its present form he will have to defer the necessary rewriting until the next summer. He also sends to Hart the Preface, the first two chapters, and a section on bibliography.

November 2 and 3, 1892: Wilson discusses certain technical matters with Hart and makes it plain that he will not permit *Division and Reunion* to be put into a straitjacket insofar as format is concerned.

November 12, 1892: Hart reviews the entire manuscript, saying that he has made certain substitutions in and additions to the bibliographical sections, rewritten half a page on commerce and manufactures in 1829, but otherwise "only corrected a few phrases and words here and there." Hart, after making certain critical comments about Wilson's style, says that the book is original, forceful, and alive.

November 15, 1892: Wilson sends the balance of the manuscript to Hart and makes it clear that he, Wilson, must have the last word as to style.

November 28, 1892: Wilson tells Hart that he has finished the galley proofs, that he agrees that the book is too long, and that he will shorten it where he can without damaging the fabric but is not hopeful about the possibility of any extensive cuts. Wilson also makes it plain that usually he will insist upon phrasing things (including the paragraph on commerce and manufactures in 1829) in his own way.

November 30 and December 3, 5, 7, and 20, 1892: In letters concerning the final editing and revision, Wilson says that he has been able to cut three or four pages from the galleys and makes certain concessions to Hart. However, Wilson says that he prefers to use the English spelling of certain words and insists upon retaining his own style.

December 29, 1892: Ellen Wilson writes to her husband that a little package of proof (it seems to have been the last of the page proofs) has arrived.

January 20, 1893: Wilson, having already returned the last page proofs to Hart, tells the editor that he has just sent the

index for *Division and Reunion* to the publishers. Wilson adds
that he will do the final work on the book in Baltimore.

February 28, 1893: Wilson assigns the copyright of *Division
and Reunion* to Longmans for the fee of $500 stipulated in the
contract.

March 4, 1893: Wilson presents one of the first copies of
Division and Reunion to his wife.

The correspondence between Hart and Wilson makes it clear why
Hart was the greatest editor of historical series of his generation. He
had a genius for selecting able authors, which he revealed more
fully in his choice of contributors to his later American Nation
Series. He maintained pressure on his authors without, however,
alienating them. He was also meticulous in his attention to details,
whether they involved organization, the choice of maps, bibliographical citations, or style. Most important, he was content to give advice
and then to leave the final decisions to his authors.

The record printed sequentially above, complete though it is on a
certain level, can be so enriched by reference to other evidence as to
give us a remarkably intimate view of how Wilson went about writing
Division and Reunion.

As it happened, Hart in April 1889 asked Wilson to write about a
period that Wilson had already covered in his course, "Special Topics
in American History," at Bryn Mawr College in 1886-87.[1] The notes
for this course,[2] which Wilson seems to have used again at least in
part at Wesleyan in 1889-90,[3] were by no means complete enough to
serve as a first draft of *Division and Reunion*. However, Wilson had
at least surveyed the field by the the time that he received Hart's
invitation. And his Bryn Mawr lecture notes, generally speaking, did
constitute the embryo of a book. One finds in them more or less
developed concepts and ideas that would reappear in *Division and
Reunion*. For example, Wilson's view in *Division and Reunion* of
Jackson as the first presidential sovereign because he was the leader
of a national democratic movement that swept over local boundaries
is clearly forecast in the Bryn Mawr notes. So also is the emphasis
on the development of the West and of western sectionalism; so, too,
is Wilson's thesis that the South in 1860 was holding to an old view
of the nature of the Constitution, while nationalism had transformed
the northern concept of the Union. On a few occasions—as for example, in the section on the Cherokee cases and the resettlement of
the southeastern Indians—Wilson was able to use the text of his Bryn
Mawr notes—in heavily revised form, of course—in *Division and
Reunion*.

As has been said, Wilson seems to have relied upon his Bryn
Mawr notes when he gave his course in American history at Wesleyan in 1889-90; but he undoubtedly did a good deal of new reading
in the sources and authorities of the period to be covered by *Division
and Reunion*. However, the move to Princeton, entailing as it did the

[1] This course is described in the Editorial Note, "Wilson's Teaching at Bryn
Mawr, 1886-87," Vol. 5.
[2] Described at Oct. 4, 1886, *ibid.*
[3] See the Editorial Note, "Wilson's Teaching at Wesleyan University and the
Johns Hopkins, 1889-90," Vol. 6.

working out an entirely new course program, caused postponement of systematic work on *Division and Reunion* for virtually a full year. Wilson had roughed out in longhand a fairly complete draft of his introductory chapter by February 1891,[4] but this, apparently, is all that he was able to do on the book during the academic year 1890-91.

As the chronological guide reveals, Wilson began work on *Division and Reunion* in earnest soon after the Commencement of 1891. There is not sufficient documentary evidence to describe his method of working in complete detail. He almost certainly must have prepared a more or less detailed outline, or what he would have called "Analysis," before he began writing. However, he did not save this outline, if, indeed, he wrote one at this time.[5] Moreover, he does not seem to have taken any extensive notes before he began writing; at least only a few fragmentary jottings on loose pages (of what Wilson, in a letter to Hart of May 19, 1891, called "numerous scraps of paper") survive in the Wilson Papers. One can only assume, therefore, that he wrote from his outline by referring when necessary to the printed sources and authorities.

Wilson of course began in the summer of 1891 with the longhand draft of his first chapter, which included what became in his final draft the opening section of Chapter II. He apparently then made a typed copy of this first chapter and the beginning of the second. Once he had typed this manuscript, Wilson cut its regular-sized pages in two and began composing in shorthand on the versos of these half pages. Perhaps he decided to adopt this more rapid method of writing at this point simply because he was under the heavy pressure of his deadline. In any event, he wrote in shorthand on these versos through what later became Section 42 of Chapter II, and, additionally, Section 52 of Chapter IV of *Division and Reunion*.

Having used up the half sheets, Wilson continued composition on regular-sized stenographic sheets. It is possible to conjecture that Wilson's discovery that he could produce historical text quite easily in his Graham shorthand, while writing on the half sheets, caused him to continue to compose the balance of his first draft in shorthand.[6]

Wilson had completed his shorthand draft through what became the first part of Chapter VII, "The Territories Opened to Slavery (1848-1856)," by the end of the summer, perhaps by September 11, 1891, when he told Hart that he had about two thirds of his manuscript "in pretty good shape."[7] He had also gone back through his

---

[4] WWhw MS. beginning "I. *The Stage of National Development*" (WP, DLC). Only a fragment of this draft remains. It bears the marks of extensive revision, but Wilson had at least found his opening sentence for his book: "Many circumstances combine to mark the year 1829 as a turning point in the history of the United States."

[5] He sent a complete outline to Hart later, on January 20, 1892.

[6] This portion of the shorthand draft is described in the Editorial Note, "Wilson's Study and Use of Shorthand, 1872-92," Vol. I, pp. 17-19.

[7] This conclusion is based upon two facts: first, it was reasonable for Wilson to have assumed that these chapters of his shorthand draft would constitute about two thirds of his final copy; second, Wilson did not affix composition dates for the portion of the shorthand draft that he wrote during the summer of 1891 but did affix such dates for the chapters that he wrote during the following summer.

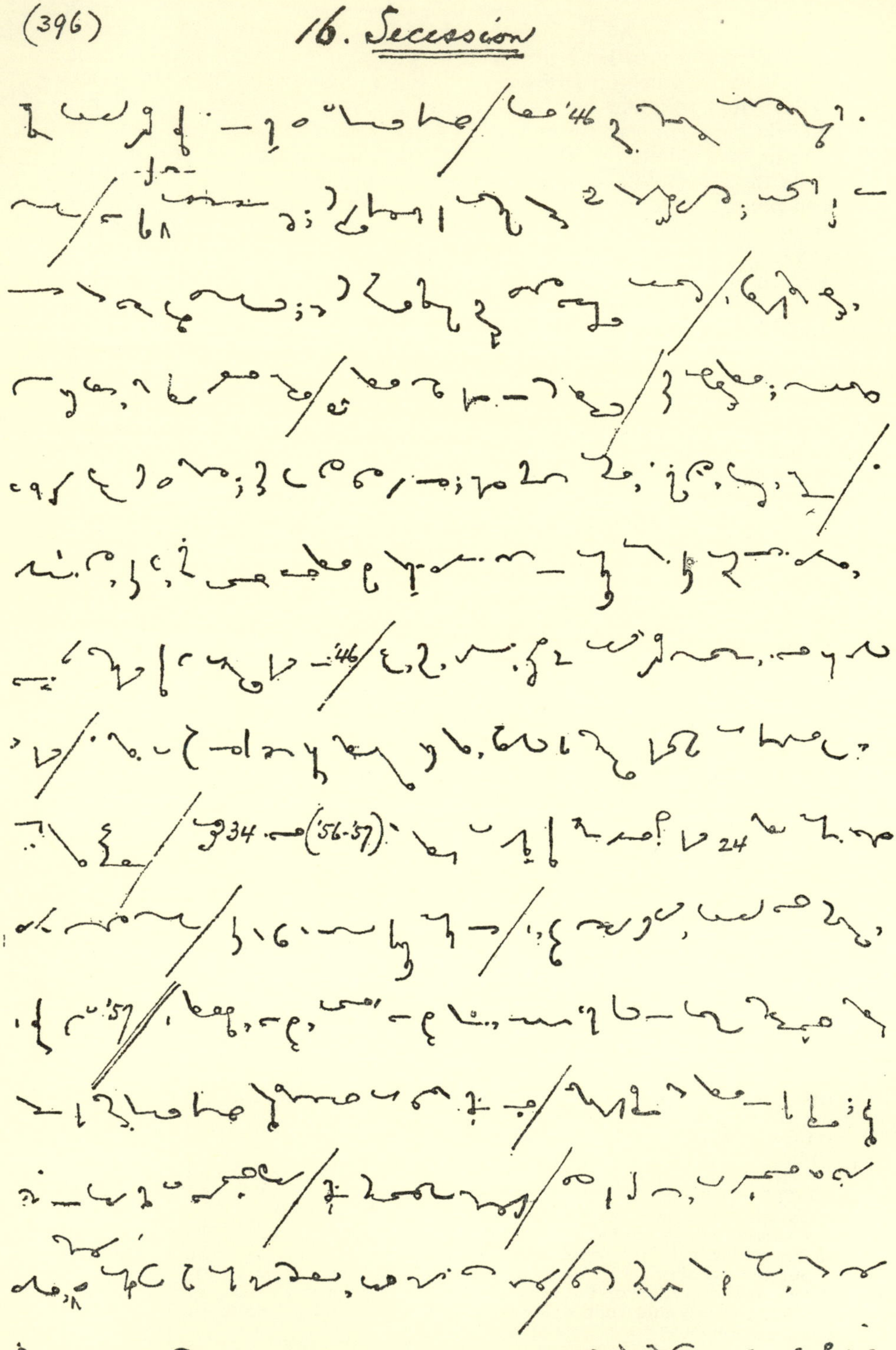

A page of Wilson's shorthand draft of Division and Reunion

manuscript, editing it in shorthand, and had probably prepared a typescript of it by the time he wrote this letter to Hart. If not, he typed up his shorthand draft during the autumn, for on January 20, 1892, he offered to send these chapters to Hart for his review.

Wilson returned to *Division and Reunion* in June 1892. Still composing in shorthand, he completed what became in the book a portion of Chapter VII (on the crisis and Compromise of 1850) on July 12. He completed his narration of the repeal of the Missouri Compromise on July 22. Working relentlessly, he completed the final chapter on August 31. Meanwhile, he may have been typing up these chapters as he went, for we find him writing to Hart on August 24 that he was well into the next-to-the-last chapter, and that his present draft could easily be converted into copy for the printer.

By the early autumn, Wilson certainly had a complete typescript in hand, but one about 575 pages long, not counting bibliographies, which Wilson had not yet prepared. During September and October he went through the painful process of cutting what was already a highly compact manuscript. He eliminated a number of paragraphs and pages by excising them with scissors and pasting up new pages, often, of course, adding connective sentences. He was also able to eliminate sentences and paragraphs by emending pages that he did not cut. At the end, he had a typescript of about 495 pages and estimated that he had managed to eliminate about eighty pages.[8]

Wilson's letter to Hart of November 3, 1892, makes it clear that Wilson was then in the final stages of preparing the bibliographies. He sent the entire typescript (except for the portion that he had already submitted on October 25) to Hart soon afterward. Hart had gone through the copy by November 12. He added a number of marginal headings, made a number of minor stylistic changes, and rewrote a portion of the paragraph on manufactures and commerce in 1829 in Chapter I.

Hart, as his letter to Wilson of November 12 reveals, sent the revised copy straight to the printer on the understanding that Wilson could accept or reject his, Hart's, changes while reading the galley proofs. It would be easy for any analyst interested in undertaking it to compare the typescript with the printed version of *Division and Reunion*[9] and make an exact count of the number of Hart's changes that Wilson accepted and rejected. Wilson accepted virtually all of Hart's marginal headings. He went back to his own version of the portion of the paragraph relating to commerce and manufactures. However, he accepted more of Hart's purely stylistic changes than his, Wilson's, letters would indicate. Hart had a tendency to change an active sentence into a passive one. Most of these changes Wilson rejected. However, Wilson let stand a large number of changes that improved his prose through the use of synonyms and more vivid language. In addition, Wilson yielded to the printer, John Wilson (or to Hart), in the matter of using the American form of the spelling of labor, favor, etc. Wilson received first copies of *Division and Reunion* on about March 4, 1893, for the copy that he presented to his wife is inscribed: "E.A.W. from W.W. 4 March, 1893."

[8] The complete typescript is in WP, DLC.
[9] There are no galley or page proofs in the Wilson Papers.

Much has been written about *Division and Reunion* as an historical work and its place in the historiography of the United States. Much has also been said about what the book reveals regarding Wilson's own social and political views, for example, his attitude toward slavery.[10] It must suffice here to say that historians have assigned an important place to *Division and Reunion* in the mainstream of American historical writing because it was the first scholarly synthesis of the period between Jackson's election and Reconstruction; it introduced an important new interpretation concerning the causation of the Civil War (that is, the view that by 1860 the North and South had entirely different understandings of the nature of the Constitution); and it anticipated the development of a whole new historical literature on sectionalism generally and on western sectionalism in particular. One other new interpretation, which historiographers have entirely missed, was pointed out by a contemporary reviewer: "Mr. Woodrow Wilson has first brought out very clearly that the United States at first were not only not democratic, but that the Constitution was very carefully framed in the interests of money and monopoly. The 'glittering generalities' of the Declaration of Independence found a strong counteractive in the conservative legal mechanism which Hamilton devised for preventing the people from having their own way."[11]

To these assessments the Editors can only add that *Division and Reunion* revealed Wilson at his best as a writer of historical prose, and that the book stands in striking contrast to Wilson's later historical writing for a popular audience, in particular his *George Washington* and *History of the American People*.

Wilson began the process of correcting and updating *Division and Reunion* almost as soon as the book was off the presses.[12] He made minor changes and bibliographical additions and substitutions in numerous reprintings of the first edition. Edward S. Corwin of Princeton University brought out a new and enlarged edition in 1909 and again in 1921. There were several reprintings of the 1909 edition and one of the 1921 edition in 1926.

The Preface and bibliographies of the first printing of the first edition are reproduced below because they reveal both Wilson's reflections upon the book and the range of his reading and research:

AUTHOR'S PREFACE.

In this volume, as in the other volumes of the series to which it belongs, only a sketch in broad outline has been attempted. It is not so much a compact narrative as a rapid synopsis—as rapid as possible

---

[10] Abundant contemporary opinion—in reviews, letters, etc.—will appear later in this volume. For the judgment of later historians, see, for example, Louis M. Sears, "Woodrow Wilson," in William T. Hutchinson, ed., *The Marcus W. Jernegan Essays in American Historiography* (Chicago, 1937), pp. 102-21; C. E. Cauthen and Lewis P. Jones, "The Coming of the Civil War," in Arthur S. Link and Rembert W. Patrick, eds., *Writing Southern History: Essays in Historiography in Honor of Fletcher M. Green* (Baton Rouge, La., 1965), pp. 231-32; and Henry W. Bragdon, *Woodrow Wilson: The Academic Years* (Cambridge, Mass., 1967), *passim*.

[11] From the review in the London *Daily Chronicle*, printed at April 21, 1893.

[12] See Longmans, Green, & Co. to A. B. Hart, April 19, 1893, n. 1, and WW to A. B. Hart, June 19, 1893.

—of the larger features of public affairs in the crowded space of sixty years that stretches from the election of Andrew Jackson to the end of the first century of the Constitution. The treatment of the first twelve years of that period I have deliberately expanded somewhat beyond the scale of the rest, because those years seem to me a most significant season of beginnings and of critical change. To discuss the events which they contain with some degree of adequacy is to simplify and speed all the rest of the story.

I have endeavored, in dividing the matter into five parts, to block out real periods in the progress of affairs. First there is a troubled period of critical change, during which Jackson and his lieutenants introduce the "spoils system" of appointment to office, destroy the great Bank of the United States, and create a new fiscal policy; during which the tariff question discloses an ominous sectional divergence, and increases the number of unstable compromises between North and South; when a new democratic spirit of unmistakable national purpose and power comes on the stage, at the same moment with the spirit of nullification and local separateness of feeling. Then the slavery question emerges into sinister prominence; there is a struggle for new slave territory; Texas is added to the Union, and the Mexican war is fought to make Texas bigger; that war results in the acquisition of a vast territory besides Texas, and the old question of slavery in the Territories is re-opened, leading to the sharp crisis and questionable compromise of 1850, and finally to the fatal repeal of the Missouri Compromise. Then there is secession and civil war, which for a time disturb every foundation of the government. Reconstruction and a new Union follow, and the government is rehabilitated. These seem to me the natural divisions of the subject.

That the period covered by this volume has opposed many sharp difficulties to any sort of summary treatment need hardly be stated. It was of course a period of misunderstanding and of passion; and I cannot claim to have judged rightly in all cases as between parties. I can claim, however, impartiality of judgment; for impartiality is a matter of the heart, and I know with what disposition I have written.

WOODROW WILSON.

PRINCETON, N. J., October 24, 1892.

◇

SUGGESTIONS FOR READERS AND
TEACHERS.

The fact that this volume is small and contains a mere outline of events is expected to make it the more useful both to teachers and to the "general reader"; for no subject can be learned from a single book. Only a comparison of authors and a combination of points of view can make any period of history really familiar. The briefer the preliminary sketch the better, if only it be made in just proportion. The use of this book should be to serve as a centre from which to extend reading or inquiry upon particular topics. The teacher should verify its several portions for himself by a critical examination, so far as possible, of the sources of information. His pupils should be made to do the same thing, to some extent, by being sent to standard authors who have written on the same period. The bibliographies prefixed to the several chapters are meant for the pupil rather than for the teacher. They are, for the most part, guides to the best known and most accessible secondary authorities, rather than to the original sources themselves. They ought to be acceptable, therefore, to the general reader also, who is a pupil without a teacher. If he wishes to seek further than these references carry him, he will find the books mentioned a key to all the rest.

The following brief works may serve for reference or comparison, or for class use in the fuller preparation of topics. The set should cost not more than ten dollars.

1. ALEXANDER JOHNSTON: *History of American Politics.* 3d ed. New York: Henry Holt & Co., 1890.—Best brief outline of purely political events.

2-4. JAMES SCHOULER: *History of the United States of America under the Constitution.* Vols. iii.-v. New York: Dodd, Mead & Co., 1889-1891.—A careful narrative, brought down to 1861. It should be used with caution, because of its strong bias of sympathy in the sectional controversy.

5, 6. CARL SCHURZ: *Life of Henry Clay (American Statesmen).* 2 vols. Boston & New York: Houghton, Mifflin & Co., 1887.—Covers the period 1777-1852.

7. EDWARD M. SHEPARD: *Martin Van Buren (American Statesmen).* Boston & New York: Houghton, Mifflin & Co., 1888.—Critical of political influences.

8. EDWARD STANWOOD: *A History of Presidential Elections.* 4th ed., revised. Boston & New York: Houghton, Mifflin & Co., 1892.—An account of the political events of each Presidential campaign, with the platforms and a statement of the votes.

9. WILLIAM G. SUMNER: *Andrew Jackson (American Statesmen).* Boston & New York: Houghton, Mifflin & Co., 1882.—Full account of financial questions.

To make up a very good working library of standard reference books, the following works may be added, at an additional cost of probably not more than one hundred and twenty dollars.

10, 11. THOMAS HART BENTON: *Thirty Years' View; or, A History of the Working of the American Government for Thirty Years, from 1820-1850.* 2 vols. New York: D. Appleton & Co., 1861, 1862.

12, 13. GEORGE TICKNOR CURTIS: *Life of James Buchanan.* 2 vols. New York: Harper & Brothers, 1883.—The best account of the disordered times immediately preceding the Civil War.

14, 15. JEFFERSON DAVIS: *The Rise and Fall of the Confederate Government.* 2 vols. New York: D. Appleton & Co., 1881.

16. RICHARD T. ELY: *The Labor Movement in America.* New York: Thomas Y. Crowell & Co., 1886.

17. WILLIAM GOODELL: *Slavery and Antislavery: A History of the Great Struggle in both Hemispheres; with a View to the Slavery Question in the United States.* New York: William Goodell, 1855.—A judi-

cious estimate of the movements of opinion, based upon extracts from authoritative records.

18. HORACE GREELEY: *A History of the Struggle for Slavery Extension or Restriction in the United States, from the Declaration of Independence to the Present Day. Compiled from the Journals of Congress and other official records.* New York: Dix, Edwards & Co., 1856.

19, 20. HORACE GREELEY: *The American Conflict. A History of the Great Rebellion in the United States of America,* 1860-64; *Its Causes, Incidents, and Results.* 2 vols. Hartford: O. D. Case & Co., 1864-1867.—Abounds in extracts from speeches and documents.

21-23. ALEXANDER JOHNSTON: *Representative American Orations to illustrate American Political History,* 1775-1881. 3 vols. New York: Henry Holt & Co., 1884.

24-26. JOHN J. LALOR: *Cyclopædia of Political Science, Political Economy, and of the Political History of the United States.* 3 vols. Chicago: Rand, McNally & Co., 1883, 1884.—Contains invaluable articles on the history and politics of the United States, by the late Professor Alexander Johnston.

27. JUDSON S. LANDON: *The Constitutional History and Government of the United States. A Series of Lectures.* Boston & New York: Houghton, Mifflin & Co., 1889.—An excellent brief constitutional history.

28-31. JOHN T. MORSE, JR., EDITOR: *American Statesmen Series.* Boston & New York: Houghton, Mifflin & Co., 1882-1891. In addition to those already mentioned: HERMANN VON HOLST: *John C. Calhoun,* 1882; HENRY C. LODGE: *Daniel Webster,* 1883; THEODORE ROOSEVELT: *Thomas Hart Benton,* 1887; ANDREW C. MCLAUGHLIN: *Lewis Cass,* 1891.—Lives of Lincoln, Seward, Sumner, Charles Francis Adams, and Chase are also announced.

32. EDWARD A. POLLARD: *The Lost Cause; A New Southern History of the War of the Confederates. Drawn from Official Sources.* New York: E. B. Treat & Co., 1866.

33. HENRY J. RAYMOND: *Life and Public Services of Abraham Lincoln, together with his State Papers.* New York: Derby & Miller, 1865.

34, 35. JAMES FORD RHODES: *History of the United States from the Compromise of* 1850. New York: Harper & Brothers, 1893.—The two volumes published cover the period 1850-1860, with an introductory chapter on Slavery.

36, 37. ALEXANDER H. STEPHENS: *A Constitutional View of the War between the States. Its Causes, Character, Conduct, and Results.* 2 vols. Philadelphia: National Publishing Co., 1867.—An exceedingly able argumentative statement of the Southern side of the slavery and State sovereignty controversies.

38. WILLIAM G. SUMNER: *History of American Currency.* New York: Henry Holt & Co., 1875.

39. F. W. TAUSSIG: *The Tariff History of the United States. A Series of Essays.* New York & London: G. P. Putnam's Sons. Revised edition, 1892.

40. GEORGE TUCKER: *The History of the United States from their Colonization to the End of the Twenty-sixth Congress, in* 1841. Vol. iv. Philadelphia: Lippincott, 1857.—A Southern history of admirable temper.

41-46. Hermann von Holst: *The Constitutional and Political History of the United States* (1750-1861). Translated from the German by A. B. Mason, J. J. Lalor, and Paul Shorey. Vols. ii-vii. Chicago: Callaghan & Co., 1877-1892.—The narrative begins at about 1828, and ends in 1860.

◇

I.

INTRODUCTORY.

1. *References.*

Bibliographies.—Hart's Formation of the Union, §§ 69, 81, 93, 106, 118, 130; Lalor's Cyclopædia of Political Science (Johnston's articles on the several political parties); Foster's References to the History of Presidential Administrations, 22-26; C. K. Adams's Manual of Historical Literature, 566 *et seq.*; Gilman's Monroe, Appendix, 255; Winsor's Narrative and Critical History of America, vii. 255-266, 294-310, viii. 469 *et seq.*, 491 *et seq.*

Historical Maps.—Thwaites's Colonies, Map 1; Hart's Formation of the Union, Maps 1, 3, 5 (Epoch Maps, Nos. 1, 6, 7, 10); Scudder's History of the United States, Frontispiece (topographical); MacCoun's Historical Geography of the United States, series "National Growth" and "Development of the Commonwealth;" Scribner's Statistical Atlas, Plates 1 (topographical), 13, 14; Johnston's School History of the United States, p. 218.

General Accounts.—Johnston's History of American Politics, chaps. i.-x.; Stanwood's History of Presidential Elections, chaps. i.-xi.; Henry Adams's John Randolph, 268-306; J. T. Morse's John Quincy Adams, 226-250; A. C. McLaughlin's Lewis Cass, 86-129; Carl Schurz's Henry Clay, 258-310; Theodore Roosevelt's Thomas H. Benton, 1-87; Tucker's History of the United States, iv. 409-515.

Special Histories.—Pitkin's History of the United States; McMaster's History of the People of the United States; Von Holst's Constitutional and Political History of the United States, ii. 1-31; Schouler's History of the United States, iv. 1-31; Henry Adams's History of the United States, ix. 175-242; W. G. Sumner's Jackson, 1-135 (chaps. i.-vi.); Henry A. Wise, Seven Decades of the Union, chap. v.

Contemporary Accounts.—Michel Chevalier's Society, Manners, and Politics in the United States; Albert Gallatin's Writings, ii.; Josiah Quincy's Figures of the Past; Daniel Webster's Correspondence; Thomas H. Benton's Thirty Years' View, i. 70-118; John Quincy Adams's Memoirs, vi. 5-104; Alexander Johnston's Representative American Orations; Alexis de Tocqueville's Democracy in America, Bowen's Translation, i. 1-72; Ben Perley Poore, Perley's Reminiscences, i. 88-199; Sargent's Public Men and Events, i. 116-171; Mrs. Frances Trollope's Domestic Manners of the Americans; Martin Van Buren's Inquiry into the Origin and Course of Political Parties, chapters v., vi.; W. W. Story's Life and Letters of Joseph Story, i.

◇

II.

A PERIOD OF CRITICAL CHANGE

(1829-1837).

11. *References.*

Bibliographies.—Sumner's Andrew Jackson, *passim*; Foster's References to the History of Presidential Administrations, 22-26; Lalor's Cyclopædia of Political Science (Johnston's articles, "Democratic Party," "Nullification," "Bank Controversies," "Whig Party," etc.); Adams's Manual of Historical Literature, 566 *et seq.*; Winsor's Narrative and Critical History, vii. 255-266, 294-310; viii. 469 *et seq.*; W. F. Allen's History Topics, 109-111; Notes to Von Holst's United States and Schouler's United States.

Historical Maps.—A. B. Hart's Formation of the Union, Map 3; this volume, Map 1 (Epoch Maps, 7, 8); MacCoun's Historical Geography of the United States, series "National Growth," 1821-1845; series "Development of the Commonwealth," 1830, 1840; Scribner's Statistical Atlas, plates 1 (topographical), 15, and series ix.; H. E. Scudder's History of the United States, frontispiece (topographical).

General Accounts.—H. von Holst's Constitutional and Political History of the United States, ii.; James Schouler's History of the United States, iii., iv., chaps. xiii., xiv.; George Tucker's History of the United States, iv., chaps. xxvi.-xxix.; Alexander Johnston's History of American Politics, chaps. xi.-xiv.; Edward Stanwood's History of Presidential Elections, chaps. xii.-xiv.; John T. Morse's John Quincy Adams, 226-291; Theodore Roosevelt's Thomas Hart Benton, 69-183; A. C. McLaughlin's Lewis Cass, 130-169; Andrew W. Young's The American Statesman, chaps. xxviii.-liv.; Josiah Quincy's Memoir of the Life of John Quincy Adams, chaps. viii., ix.; Henry A. Wise's Seven Decades of the Union, chaps. vi., vii.

Special Histories.—Carl Schurz's Henry Clay, i. 311-383, ii. 1-127; W. G. Sumner's Andrew Jackson, 119-386; Ormsby's History of the Whig Party; Patton's Democratic Party; Hammond's History of Political Parties; Holmes's Parties and their Principles; Byrdsall's History of the Loco-foco, or Equal Rights, Party; F. W. Taussig's Tariff History of the United States; W. G. Sumner's History of American Currency; James Parton's Life of Andrew Jackson; H. Von Holst's Calhoun, 62-183; E. V. Shepard's Martin Van Buren; Mackenzie's Life and Times of Van Buren; B. T. Curtis's Life of Webster; H. C. Lodge's Daniel Webster; R. T. Ely's Labor Movement in America.

Contemporary Accounts.—John Quincy Adams's Memoirs, vii.-ix. (chaps. xv.-xviii.); Thomas H. Benton's Thirty Years' View, i.; Amos Kendall's Autobiography and Life of Jackson; Martin Van Buren's Origin of Political Parties in the United States; Nathan Sargent's Public Men and Events, i., chaps. iii., iv.; Chevalier's Society, Manners, and Politics in the United States; Harriet Martineau's Society in America; Josiah Quincy's Figures of the Past; Daniel Webster's Correspondence; Private Correspondence of Henry Clay; J. A. Hamilton's Reminiscences; Ben Perley Poore's Perley's Reminiscences, i. 88-198; Alexander Johnston's Representative American Orations, ii.; Garrisons' William Lloyd Garrison, i.

◇

III.

THE SLAVERY QUESTION.

(1842-1856).

59. *References.*

Bibliographies.—Lalor's Cyclopædia, Alexander Johnston's articles, "Slavery," "Whig Party," "Democrat Party," "Annexations," "Wars," "Wilmot Proviso," "Compromises," "Fugitive Slave Laws," "Territories," "Republican Party;" Justin Winsor's Narrative and Critical History, vii. pp. 297-310, 323-326, 353-356, 413 ff., 550 ff.; W. E. Foster's References to the History of Presidential Administrations, 26-40; C. K. Adams's Manual of Historical Literature, 566-581, 602 ff. 652-654, 657-659, 663-666.

Historical Maps.—Nos. 1, 2, this volume; Epoch Maps, Nos. 8, 11, 12; MacCoun's Historical Geography of the United States, series "National Growth," 1845-1848, 1848-1853, and series "Development of the Commonwealth," 1840, 1850, 1854; Labberton's Historical Atlas, plates lxix., lxx.; Scribner's Statistical Atlas, plates 15, 16.

General Accounts.—James F. Rhodes, History of the United States from the Congress of 1850, i., ii. 1-236; Schouler's History of the United States, iv. pp. 359 ff., v. to p. 370; H. Von Holst's Constitutional History of the United States, ii. 371 ff., iii., iv., v., vi. 96; Carl Schurz's Henry Clay, chaps. xxii.-xxvii.; Johnston's American Politics, chaps. xv.-xviii.; J. H. Patton's Concise History of the American People, chaps. l.-lvii.; Bryant and Gay's Popular History of the United States, iv., chaps. xiii.-xvi.; Ridpath's Popular History of the United States, chaps. lvi.-lix.

Special Histories.—Nebel's War between the United States and Mexico; Stanwood's History of Presidential Elections, chaps. xvi.-xix.; Colton's Life and Speeches of Henry Clay; Stephen's Constitutional View of the War between the States; Greeley's American Conflict, i., chaps. xi.-xx.; W. Goodell's Slavery and Antislavery, pp. 143-219, 272 ff.; G. T. Curtis's Life of James Buchanan, i. pp. 458-619, ii. pp. 1-186; Tyler's Lives of the Tylers; F. W. Seward's Seward at Washington, 1846-1861, chaps. i.-xxxviii.; Hodgson's Cradle of the Confederacy, chaps. x.-xiii.; P. Stovall's Life of Toombs, pp. 1-139; Merriam's Life and Times of Samuel Bowles, i. pp. 56-178; Olmstead's Cotton Kingdom; Draper's History of the Civil War, i., chaps. xxii-xxv.; E. A. Pollard's Lost Cause, chaps. i.-iv.; T. N. Page's The Old South; Sato's Land Question in the United States (Johns Hopkins University Studies), pp. 61-69; Taussig's Tariff History of the United States, pp. 109-154.

Contemporary Accounts.—Benton's Thirty Years' View, ii. 209 ff. (to 1850); Sargent's Public Men and Events, ii., chaps. vi.-ix. (to 1853); Frederick L. Olmsted's Seaboard Slave States, Back Country, and Texas Journey (Condensed reprint as Cotton Kingdom); Clay's Private Correspondence; Webster's Private Correspondence; McCulloch's Men and Measures of Half a Century; G. W. Curtis's Correspondence of J. L. Motley; F. W. Seward's Seward: An Autobiography, chaps. xxxiii.-lxvi.; Chevalier de Bacourt's Souvenirs of a Diplomat (temp. Van Buren, Harrison, and Tyler); Herndon's Life of Lincoln, chaps. ix.-xii.; Thurlow Weed's Autobiography, chaps. xlviii.-lxi.

◊

IV.

SECESSION AND CIVIL WAR

(1856-1865).

95. *References.*

Bibliographies.—Lalor's Cyclopædia (Johnston's articles on "Secession," "Dred Scott Case," "Rebellion," "Confederate States"); W. E. Foster's References to the History of Presidential Administrations, 40-49; C. K. Adams's Manual of Historical Literature, 566-581, 602 ff., 663-666; Bartlett's Literature of the Rebellion; T. O. Sumner, in Papers of American Historical Association, iv. 332-345; A. B. Hart's Federal Government, § 40.

Historical Maps.—Nos. 3, 4, this volume (Epoch Maps, Nos. 12, 13); MacCoun's Historical Geography, series "National Growth," 1848-1853, 1853-1889; series "Development of the Commonwealth," 1861, 1863; Labberton's Historical Atlas, pl. lxxi.; Scribner's Statistical Atlas, pl. 16; Comte de Paris's History of the Civil War in America, Atlas; Scudder's History of the United States, 375, 378, 386, 396, 401, 403, 411; Theodore A. Dodge's Bird's-Eye View of the Civil War, *passim*; Johnston's School History of the United States, 293.

General Accounts.—Johnston's American Politics, chaps. xix., xx.; Patton's Concise History of the United States, chaps. lvii.-lxv. (to p. 963); Bryant and Gay's History of the United States, iv., chaps. xvi.-xxiii.; Ridpath's Popular History of the United States, chaps. lx.-lxvi.; H. von Holst's Constitutional History of the United States, vi., vii. (to 1861); J. F. Rhodes's History of the United States, ii. (1854-1860); James Schouler's History of the United States, v. 370-512 (to 1861); Jefferson Davis's Rise and Fall of the Confederate Government, vol. i. (parts i., iii.), vol. ii.; Henry Wilson's Rise and Fall of the Slave Power in America, ii. (chaps. xxv.-lv.), iii. (chaps. i.-xxxi.) James G. Blaine's Twenty Years of Congress, i. (chaps. vii.-xxvi.) J. G. Nicolay and John Hay's Abraham Lincoln, a History, vols. ii.-x.

Special Histories.—Edward Stanwood's History of Presidential Elections, chaps. xx., xxi.; Horace Greeley's American Conflict, i. (chaps. xxi.-xxxviii.); E. A. Pollard's Lost Cause (chap. v. to end); Joseph Hodgson's Cradle of the Confederacy (chaps. xiv. *et seq.*); G. T. Curtis's Buchanan, ii. 187-630; Henry J. Raymond's Life of Lincoln; F. W. Seward's Seward at Washington, i., xxxix.-lxvii, ii., i.-xl.; L. G. Tyler's Lives of the Tylers; G. S. Merriam's Samuel Bowles, i. 179-419; P. Stovall's Toombs, 140-285; John W. Draper's Civil War, i., chap. xxvi. *et seq.*, ii., iii.; Edward McPherson's Political History of the Rebellion; Comte de Paris's Military History of the Civil War; William H. Seward's Diplomatic History of the Civil War; F. W. Taussig's Tariff History of the United States, 155-170; J. J. Knox's United States Notes; A. S. Bolles's Financial History of the United States, ii., chaps. xv., iii. book i.; Theodore A. Dodge's Bird's-Eye View of the Civil War; John C. Ropes's History of the Civil War (in preparation); Leverett W. Spring's Kansas; N. S. Shaler's Kentucky; C. F. Adams, Jr.'s Charles Francis Adams (in preparation); John T. Morse, Jr.'s Abraham Lincoln (in preparation); J. K. Lothrop's William H. Seward (in preparation); F. L. Olmsted's Seaboard Slave States, Texas Journey, and Back Country (or Cotton Kingdom); Marion G. McDougall's Fugitive Slaves; Mary Tremain's Slavery in the District of Columbia.

Contemporary Accounts.—Appleton's Annual Cyclopædia for the several years (particularly under the titles "Congress of the United States," "Congress, Confederate," "Confederate States," "United States," "Army," "Navy"); Horace Greeley's American Conflict, ii., and History of the Great Rebellion; Herndon's Life of Lincoln (chaps. xii. *et seq.*); L. E. Chittenden's Recollections of President Lincoln and his Administration; O. A. Brownson's American Republic (chap. xii.); Alexander Stephen's War between the States, ii. 241-631, and appendices; George W. Julian's Reminiscences; George Cary Eggleston's A Rebel's Recollections; Jones's A Rebel War; Clerk's Diary; J. H. Gilmer's Southern Politics; Thurlow Weed's Autobiography (chaps. lxi.-lxv.); G. T. Curtis's Correspondence of J. L. Motley, i. (chaps. xiii.), ii. (chaps. i.-vi.); Hugh McCulloch's Men and Measures of Half a Century (chaps. xiv.-xviii., xxi., xxii.); U. S. Grant's Personal Memoirs; W. T. Sherman's Memoirs; S. S. Cox's Three Decades of Federal Legislation, 1855-1885 (chaps. i.-xvi.); Ben: Perley Poore's Perley's Reminiscences, ii. (chaps. i.-xvi.); Henry A. Wise's Seven Decades of the Union (chap. xiv.); James S. Pike's First Blows of the Civil War, 355-526 (to 1861); Alexander Johnston's Representative American Orations, iii. (parts v. vi.); William H. Seward's Autobiography.

◇

V.

REHABILITATION OF THE UNION.

(1865-1889).

124. *References.*

Bibliographies.—Lalor's Cyclopædia (Johnston's articles on "Reconstruction," "Impeachments," "Crédit Mobilier," "Disputed Elections"); Foster's References to the History of Presidential Administrations, 49-58; Bowker's Reader's Guide, *passim;* John Fiske's Civil Government, 275; A. B. Hart's Federal Government, § 469.

Historical Maps.—No. 5, this volume (Epoch Maps, No. 14); MacCoun's Historical Geography of the United States, series "National Growth," 1853-1859, and series "Development of the Commonwealth," last two maps; Scribner's Statistical Atlas, plate 17; Johnston's School History of the United States, frontispiece.

General Accounts.—Johnston's American Politics, chaps. xxi.-xxvi.; Patton's Concise History, pp. 963-990 (through Grant's administrations); Ridpath's History of the United States, chaps. lxvii.-lxx. (to

1881); Henry Wilson's Rise and Fall of the Slave Power in America, iii. 434-740 (1865-1869).

Special Histories.—Edward Stanwood's Presidential Elections, chaps. xxii.-end; Edward McPherson's History of Reconstruction; Walter Allen's Governor Chamberlain's Administration in South Carolina; R. H. Wilmer's Recent Past, from a Southern Standpoint; F. W. Seward's Seward at Washington, ii., xli.-lxxiii.; Taylor's Destruction and Reconstruction; E. B. Callender's Thaddeus Stevens; G. S. Merriam's Bowles, ii.; Pleasant Stovall's Toombs, pp. 286-369; O. A. Brownson's American Republic (chaps. xiii.-xiv.); J. C. Hurd's Theory of Our National Existence; J. J. Knox's United States Notes; F. W. Taussig's Tariff History, pp. 171-256; Albert Bolles's Financial History, iii., book ii.; J. C. Schucker's Chase; D. B. Warden's Chase; Moorfield Story's Charles Sumner (in preparation); E. L. Pierce's Charles Sumner.

Contemporary Accounts.—Appleton's Annual Cyclopædia; Edward McPherson's History of Reconstruction, and Political Handbooks (biennial); Hugh McCulloch's Men and Measures of Half a Century (chaps. xxiii.-end); Autobiography of Thurlow Weed (chaps. lxvi.-lxviii.); S. S. Cox's Three Decades (chaps. xvii.-xl.); J. G. Blaine's Twenty Years in Congress (1865-1885); Ben: Perley Poore's Perley's Reminiscences (chaps. xvii.-xlvii.); Alexander Johnston's Representative American Orations, iii. (parts vii., viii.); G. W. Cable's Silent South, Negro Question; Works of Charles Sumner; contemporary periodicals, especially Atlantic Monthly, Forum, North American Review, Nation, Political Science Quarterly.[13]

13 *Division and Reunion, 1829-1889* (New York and London, 1893), pp. vii-xii, 1-2, 22-23, 116-17, 194-95, and 253-54. A number of errors and misprints have been corrected silently in the Index.

An Announcement

[March 1, 1893]

SPECIAL NOTICE
IN PROFESSOR WILSON'S COURSES.

Those who were conditioned in Public Law or absent from the examination will have an opportunity to pass the subject off on Monday evening, March 13, at half-past seven o'clock, in the English room;[1] those who failed in the History of Law or were absent from the examination, at the same place and hour on Tuesday evening, March 14.[2]

Printed in the *Daily Princetonian*, March 1, 1893.
1 A large lecture room in Dickinson Hall.
2 In WP, DLC, there is a WWT copy of the condition and make-up examination in public law dated March 13, 1893, and a WWT copy of the special examination in the history of law dated March 27, 1893.

To Albert Shaw

Princeton, New Jersey. 4 March 1893.

I surrender at discretion [.][1] Send clippings of biography and commentary [.]
                                                   Woodrow Wilson

TC tel. (in possession of Virginia Shaw English).
  [1] Shaw's letter, urging Wilson for a second time to write an article on Cleveland's Cabinet for the New York *Review of Reviews*, to which this telegram was a reply, is missing, but see WW to A. Shaw, Feb. 28, 1893.

To Albert Shaw

My dear Shaw,   Princeton, New Jersey, 4 March, 1893.

As I remarked in my telegram, sent just now, I surrender at discretion, and beg for such clipping materials as your office may afford. I shall myself await the result with not a little wonder and anxiety. I am not afraid of my reputation (may Heaven help the poor dear little thing!) but what the effect will be upon the fame of the Review of Reviews its friends must seriously speculate upon! I do the thing simply because my affection for you is so great that I find it practically impossible to refuse you anything you so ardently desire.

In haste,

Your affectionate & indiscreet friend
                                                   Woodrow Wilson

TCL (in possession of Virginia Shaw English).

From Cyrus Hall McCormick

My Dear Wilson: [Chicago] March 8th 1893

I am requested by the Princeton Club of Chicago to enquire as to the time it would be convenient for you to come out here to attend our Annual Princeton Dinner, which we would like to have during the latter part of this month, or the early part of April. We would however, be quite willing to suit the time of our dinner to your engagements. Will you kindly inform me at your earliest convenience whether you will be able to come to us this spring, and if so, as to the various times at which it would be most convenient for you to be absent from Princeton?

Remembering the circumstances which prevented you from being with us last winter, we are especially anxious that you should represent the Faculty and the University at the Dinner, and the Executive Committee hope that you will be able to respond favorably to this request.

Yours sincerely,   Cyrus H. McCormick

TLS (C. H. McCormick Letterpress Books, WHi).

From John George Bourinot[1]

Dear Professor Wilson,   Ottawa, 9th March, 1893.

I am extremely obliged to you for your kind reference to my monograph on Parliamentary Government which has just been printed by the Am. Historical Association at Washington.[2] Your writings have been so great a source of pleasure and profit to me for some years past, that I am much delighted to merit your commendation. Your work on the State has been extremely useful to me & others in Canada; and it is not often one can find in a compendium, covering so large a ground, that freedom from inaccuracies & that fullness of knowledge which make a work an authority in the full sense of the word.

I have often told my friends [R. T.] Ely and H. B. Adams, on the occasions of my visits to Washington & Baltimore, how much pleasure it would give me at any time to meet a student of political science from whom I have already learned so much.

If at any time I can be of use to you do not hesitate to ask my aid

Believe me,

Sincerely yours,   Jno. Geo. Bourinot

P.S. Professor James Bryce spoke highly of the State when he was visiting me; he studied it, as a professor, while with me; he had not seen it before.

ALS (WP, DLC) with WWhw notation on env.: "Ans. 17 March, '93."
    [1] Chief Clerk of the Canadian House of Commons, 1880-1902, and author of many works on the history and constitutional law of Canada.
    [2] "Parliamentary Government in Canada: a Constitutional and Historical Study," in American Historical Association, *Annual Report . . . 1891* (Washington, 1892). The nature of Wilson's "kind reference" to this monograph remains mysterious. Perhaps he had spoken about it to Herbert Baxter Adams, and Adams had passed on the comment in a letter to Bourinot.

From George Howe, Jr.

Dear Woodrow,   Columbia, S. C., Mar 11 1893

I write a little note to ask you to make application for a scholarship for George [Howe III] at Princeton whenever it is the proper time to do so. I do not hesitate to say that I cannot pay his expenses[.] The only way I can do so is to borrow the money hoping to pay at some future day. I write now so as to be in full time. He may fail to get in at Princeton. His reports from Law-renceville are good, which is an indication that he will pass the examinations.

As we have never heard that he passed any of the examinations last Summer or rather Fall, I take it for granted that he failed.

Annie has just recovered from a severe neuralgic attack which had pulled her down very much.

I hope you are all well.

Annie joins me in unbounded love to you all.

Yrs affly   Geo. Howe

How did Mrs Brown's ear trouble turn out?[1]

ALS (WP, DLC).
    [1] See JRW to WW, Jan. 16, 1893, n. 1, and George Howe, Jr., to WW, July 15, 1893.

From Annie Wilson Howe

[Columbia, S.C., March 11, 1893]

Thank you *very* much, dear Woodrow, for the book.[1] I would have written at once—but have not been able.

With love to all   Annie.

ALS (WP, DLC) written on George Howe, Jr., to WW, March 11, 1893.
    [1] *Division and Reunion*, which had just appeared.

From the Minutes of the Princeton Faculty

5 5′ P.M., Wednesday, March 15, ″93

. . . The Dean reported from the Committee on Discipline that Messrs. —— & —— who had been intoxicated on a recent eve-ning had been sent to the President for a reprimand, their parents had been informed of the fact of their intoxication & that if guilty of the offence a second time they will be sent from College. The action of the Committee was approved.[1]

    [1] Hearings on these cases, dated March 14, 1893, are recorded in the body of WWsh notes described in Princeton Faculty Minutes, Sept. 23, 1891, n. 1, Vol. 7.

An Article

[c. March 17, 1893]

MR. CLEVELAND'S CABINET.

There is much to arrest attention and challenge comment in Mr. Cleveland's cabinet appointments. He has so evidently chosen his advisers with independence of judgment, not upon conventional lines, but upon lines of individual choice, that the make-up of the cabinet furnishes us with a fresh test of his interesting character as a leader and ruler. The career of Mr. Cleveland has been an individual career from the first. He has been a leader among citizens rather than a leader of parties. He has dominated his party because he represented a great force of unpartisan opinion. His career, too, has been exclusively executive within the field, not of the choice of measures, but of the choice of men and of just means for the conduct of the government on its business side. Equipped with an admirable practical judgment from the outset, and with an extraordinary capacity for understanding the larger aspects of great questions, he has yet, apparently, come slowly into the possession of general views regarding the legislative policy of the government.

These views, moreover, would seem to have come to him as to a very thoughtful man of affairs rather than as to a natural student of policy, as the result of the direct contact of a strong and sagacious judgment with the practical conduct of the business of the government. No one can doubt for a moment his extraordinary powers of mind. Those powers do not seem brilliant because they operate without display of force. They are equable, unhurried, moving, it would seem, through a certain inevitable course of judgment to conclusions which do not take them by surprise; and the reason he has so riveted the attention and engaged the admiration of his countrymen is that he possesses in perfection that largeness and candor of view, that strong sagacity in affairs, and that solidity of judgment which characterize the best Americans. He is a typical American, albeit of the best type, and his countrymen believe in him without always knowing why.

He approached his present exalted station, nevertheless, through a series of almost exclusively executive offices, which he had occupied, not as a man who had chosen a public career, but as an independent citizen who had consented to lend his individual character to the task of bettering the methods of public administration. He has always disconcerted the politicians by selecting, for such offices as he had to give, men like himself in their disconnection from politics—men whom the politicians had never heard of, and consequently found it difficult to reckon with. His conception of the way in which government ought to be conducted is identical with the conception which thrust him forward to occupy offices of the greatest influence within the gift of the people—the conception which gave Andrew Jackson the presidency. He believes that what the government needs at moments of apparent lethargy or demoralization is the infusion of new blood, the disinterested service of men untainted by party management. He has chosen his present cabinet on that plan. He would not have been true to his career or to his character had he not done so. He does not regard it as important that the country at large should know the men he has selected. The country has trusted him with the organization of the government, and, with his customary courage, he has assumed all the responsibility of the choice, taking, not men sifted out of the general mass by the processes of public life, but men whom his own judgment approved; and no one need be surprised or chagrined.

That he has chosen well in all cases no one can safely say until the four years of his administration shall have made full test of the men. With one exception, Mr. Richard Olney, who may, perhaps, be reckoned the scholar of the little group, the members of the new cabinet are all practical men, like Mr. Cleveland himself, with minds formed by experience, rather than by books or by the observation of affairs lying beyond the immediate sphere of their own lives. With two notable exceptions—Mr. Carlisle and Mr. Herbert—they have none of them had any such direct acquaintance with public questions as would be necessary to give them ease and steadiness of judgment in the exercise of the functions which they have now undertaken, unless Mr. Lamont busily hived wisdom in such matters while he served Mr. Cleveland as private secretary. With but a single exception—Mr. Lamont—they have all had the training of lawyers, though Mr. Carlisle and Mr. Herbert have doubtless added a great deal to that training during their long connection with the public business in Congress, where they have played no narrow rôle. Mr. Morton is said to have found the law too "unpractical" to satisfy his full-blooded ardor to be doing something that would tell at once; he, therefore, has made it only one instrument among many to enable him to live his hard pioneer life in Nebraska. Mr. Hoke Smith is not suspected of knowing more than enough law to serve the practical purposes of his professional engagements from day to day. It is a cabinet of lawyers, nevertheless, and two of its members, Mr. Gresham and Mr. Olney, may fairly be called great lawyers—men fit to be jurists if they would but take the pains. As a body of practical men they are accustomed to overcoming difficulties, and the ignorance of the majority of them as to what exactly they will have to do in their several departments will be but a new difficulty to surmount. They may be counted on to learn rapidly.

They are, at any rate, men of uncommonly fine physique and can easily outlive their sentence of four years at hard labor. The reporters have amused themselves and us with specific details as to their weight, which is most of it, they assure us, in bone and sinew, very little of it in mere adipose tissue, which might not stand the strain of too close application to executive routine. A stalwart set of men, with the good humor of giants for the most part,—until too outrageously assaulted by office seekers. And no part of the country, it would seem, has a monopoly in the production of giants. These big men come from widely separated States. Mr. Smith, of Georgia, is as large as Mr. Bissell, of New York, and each of these is bigger than Mr. Carlisle, the Kentuckian, who comes from a region where the men notoriously grow tall and full chested. Mr. Olney, too, is said to be of a height, an athletic build, and a distinction of bearing striking enough to have entitled him to be noted and known long ago outside his profession. You would know such men not to be insignificant, wherever you might chance to see them. It is a humorous way of estimating importance, not set down in any ethical manual; but it has its obvious usefulness as a standard for the general eye.

Compared, man for man, with their predecessors in Mr. Cleveland's official counsels, they afford material for some marked contrasts. The first time he filled the office of Secretary of State Mr. Cleveland followed time-honored precedents. Mr. Bayard represented the oldest and best traditions of American public life. He came of a race of statesmen, and had fair claim to rank with his forebears in the notable line of family succession. He was, by common consent, one of the foremost men on the Democratic side of the Senate; he had served on several of the most important committees of that body, the President's Great Council in foreign affairs; and when he assumed the duties of Secretary of State he only passed from one branch of the public service into another not far removed. The grave question was, Did not the Senate lose too much by his transference? He had as great familiarity with the policy of the government as Mr. Blaine, his immediate predecessor, and greater familiarity than Mr. Evarts, the predecessor of Mr. Blaine. His knowledge of the course of policy, moreover, was more a knowledge of questions considered upon their merits than Mr. Blaine's, whose close acquaintance with public affairs consisted in a knowledge of men in their groupings rather than in any mastery of questions considered apart from men. Judge Gresham has usually lived at a considerable remove from such business as his forerunners were immersed in. His fine qualities of mind, his engaging liberality of temper and elevation of moral view, have been manifested chiefly upon the bench in the West. For all his reading, his knowledge of men and of the history of the country, his wide sympathies and quick insight, he will be a novice in adjusting the foreign relations of the country. Mastery in such matters cometh not by observation merely. Besides the wishes of the President, he will have only his own legal capacity and his own natural apprehension of right and wrong to guide him. Fortunately our foreign relations are generally simple enough to require little more. But the experienced officials of the State Department will find their new chief very *naïf* and ignorant about many things which seem to them obvious arrangements of Providence.

It seems a pity, too, to waste so fine a Secretary of the Interior, as it seems certain Mr. Gresham would have made, on the novel field of foreign affairs. Other Presidents have taken their Secretaries of State from the interior of the country; but Henry Clay was already the leading spirit in public affairs before he took that post; Lewis Cass was a Nestor among the statesmen of his day when Buchanan called him to the cabinet; Elihu Washburne had served in Congress until he led, by sheer force of good service, in almost everything that it undertook. He was Secretary of State but a week (but six days, to be very accurate), but he had had experience enough in the conduct of the government's business to have remained Secretary of State for all the eight years of General Grant's terms. Mr. Gresham brings with him from the interior a minute knowledge of the questions of the interior, the questions of interstate commerce, of railway monopoly on the grand scale, of land grants and agricultural depression,—to enter, not the Department which deals with such matters, but the Department which looks away from home to questions affecting the exterior interests of the country. He was Postmaster-General for a year and a half in the cabinet of President Arthur, and the Post Office, the world supposes, demands little more of its chief than a talent for business; but the Secretaryship of State? This is certainly an appointment to provoke comment! It would seem a pity, I say, to lose so fine a Secretary of the Interior in order that a man of brilliant gifts may have the honor of the chief post in the Administration.

But not only, or chiefly, because it is in such wise out of the line of previous appointments, is this elevation of Judge Gresham to the office of Secretary of State remarkable. Mr. Gresham may do well or ill as Secretary of State—his talents fit him to do brilliantly even with a novice's hand. The startling feature of the ap-

pointment, as everybody knows, is that until last summer he was
a Republican, and a Republican of such influence and importance
in the West that he was seriously thought of as a candidate for
the Republican presidential nomination! When the issue was
squarely joined between the parties on the tariff question he declared that he could not act with his former party, but must vote
for Mr. Cleveland; and his announcement of his purpose to do so
was one of the notable incidents of the campaign. It was reckoned
widely influential in changing votes in the great States of Indiana
and Illinois, where his name stands for courage, sagacity, integrity and public spirit. Finding this notable man thus on his
way to the Democratic party, Mr. Cleveland called upon him to
make the whole journey at a single stage and accept at the hands
of a Democratic Administration the post that stands first on the
list of cabinet appointments. It was a bold step to take, both for
Mr. Cleveland and for Judge Gresham. It is the most original
thing Mr. Cleveland has done in all his striking career of independent choice. The politicians had grown accustomed to being
surprised by his appointments; this time they were dumfounded.

What the result will be a prudent man should be slow to predict.
Signs are not wanting that the Republican party is going, or at
any rate may presently go, to pieces; and signs are fairly abundant that the Democratic party is rapidly being made over by the
stirring and disturbing energy of the extraordinary man who is
now President. It may be that Mr. Gresham's accession to the
Democratic cabinet means that great interest and great forces of
thought in the Northwest are now turning about to the assistance
of the Democratic party, Judge Gresham being their gift to the
counsels of that party. Mr. Cleveland has been steadily effecting
a revolution in the purposes and methods of the Democratic party
by drawing so many new men about him, by assisting to shelve
so many older men of the Democratic party of former days. The
party has grown bold and aggressive and certain of its own mind
in consequence of the change. Mr. Cleveland's present term of
office may afford him time and opportunity to complete the transformation. Young men are eager to serve him; and a Democratic
party of young men is the most formidable danger the Republicans have to fear—the best hope that the Democrats have to
cherish.

There is a singular and quite admirable mixture of conservatism, however, in the new President's methods. Mr. Carlisle and
Mr. Herbert are living examples that he has not broken with
tradition in filling the great offices of State, and very important
examples indeed they are. In both of these appointments Mr.

Cleveland has followed some of the oldest and very best traditions of the government. Except for the Hawaiian matter, no questions of delicacy now press for immediate attention in the Department of State, but there is every reason to believe that its financial policy will be the most important feature of this Administration, and Mr. Cleveland has shown real statesmanship in placing at the head of the Treasury Department a man who is not only a real leader of his party, but its leader first of all and most notably in the field of financial legislation. Together with Mr. Morrison and Mr. Mills, he prepared it, by long and doubtful parlimentary battle, for the policy which it has now accepted from Mr. Cleveland himself. In poise and in the quiet masterfulness that makes a leader he is superior to both his comrades in that struggle. His elevation to the post of Secretary of the Treasury, moreover, redresses the balance of authority within the party which was for a time disturbed by the election of Mr. Crisp to the Speakership of the House two years ago. Mr. Manning and Mr. Fairchild, of Mr. Cleveland's former cabinet, were admirable business men; but something more than mere business capacity is needed in the Treasury at this juncture. Questions of financial policy have become exigent, and it was proper that a past master in financial legislation should be called to preside over the Department.

It is doubtful, indeed, whether the Treasury should ever be considered a mere business department. General Grant, it is understood, once invited Mr. A. T. Stewart, of New York, to occupy the post of Secretary of the Treasury, upon the theory that the Treasury Department was not essentially different in kind from a great commercial establishment. But the financial legislation of Congress is so dependent upon the Treasury for its wise effectuation, the policy of the department so intimately touches at every point the most sensitive business interests of the country, the Secretary of the Treasury has so often to determine questions which really fix a financial programme on the government, that it is always hazardous to put any man at the head of the Treasury who does not possess tested political judgment as well as approved business capacity. The appointment of Mr. Carlisle is a better appointment than that of Mr. Manning was, wise and efficient an officer as Mr. Manning proved himself to be. Mr. Manning was no statesman, as Mr. Carlisle is. The two appointments illustrate in their contrast the development of Mr. Cleveland himself. When he first became President he had no determinate or constructive views with regard to the general policy of the government, but came in to perform a purpose for the executive rather than for the legislative branch of the government: to reform the civil service, not to preside over a party programme. Now, on the contrary, he is conscious of a wider mission. His views broadened to the whole extent of his function as President during his first term of office; the interval of four years during which he has been out of official place has strengthened and particularized those views. He began by regarding the Treasury Department as a business branch of the service, like the post office; he now regards it as possessing a presidential function in respect of the general financial policy of the country.

Mr. Herbert has long had a very important part in administering the Navy Department. No one has had a more influential share than he in the legislation by which Congress has of late years sought to build up the navy into real effectiveness; and as chairman of the Committee on Naval Affairs in the House of Representatives of the Congress which has just expired he has been, as it were, the legislative representative and head of the Navy Department—a sort of American parliamentary secretary. He will now manage the Department from the inside instead of from the outside, that is all. His success in Congress has been marked, but it has been so quietly achieved that the country at large has hardly heard of it. Except that the public eye has not much noted him, he has won a cabinet place quite after the English fashion, by a steady course of eminently useful parliamentary service. He has come forward by that process of self-selection which is the most stimulating and significant feature of free institutions under parliamentary forms of government. Previous Secretaries of the Navy, being obvious heads of the Department, have gotten the credit for many things planned, proposed and accomplished by Mr. Herbert. He is now Secretary of the Navy himself, and may realize both his plans and the reputation which those plans ought to bring him.

But there is something else about Mr. Herbert which is even more interesting. He is not only a Southerner, but served with distinction in the Confederate army, and now he is put at the head of one of the war departments of the federal government, having been confirmed by the Senate, apparently without a dissenting voice: for it took the Senate only fifteen minutes to confirm the whole list of cabinet appointments of March 6. Mr. Lamar, of Mr. Cleveland's former cabinet, had also espoused and served the cause of the Southern Confederacy, and he became Secretary of the Interior and a Justice of the Supreme Court of the United States. But here is a man who fought against the Union; who has already spent many years in assisting to build up the warlike strength of the very government he resisted; and who is now made one of the war ministers of the government! Who can regard such facts without wonder and pride? Such is the healing and amalgamating force of fair fight, and of the sovereign determinations of policy under free institutions! The war is indeed a long way behind us—and yet these men are of the very generation that fought it!

The other appointments may be dismissed with much briefer comment—must be so dismissed, in fact, for we know too little of the men to make the commentary long. The selection of Mr. Richard Olney, of Massachusetts, for the office of Attorney-General may safely be pronounced excellent. No lawyer who knows him doubts that Mr. Olney stands at the front of his profession, not by arrogation, but by merit. Certainly the Department of Justice is the least political of the Departments. It is of little consequence whether the Attorney-General have the training and experience of a statesman or not. His functions, outside the cabinet meetings, demand, not a knowledge of public affairs, but a knowledge of the laws and a judicial fairness of mind in applying them to the law business of the government, and it cannot be reckoned unjust to Mr. Garland to say that Mr. Cleveland has made a better selection this time for this important office than he made eight years ago. Mr. Garland was a shade or two too much of a politician for that particular post. Mr. Olney, it may be taken for granted, has no entangling alliances by which to be embarrassed.

So far as we know anything about Mr. Morton, the new Secretary of Agriculture, his selection, too, seems a very happy one. There were no precedents to follow in filling this office—for even Mr. Rusk is hardly venerable enough to be a precedent—and Mr. Morton seems unquestionably a representative man for the post in the best sense of the term. A pioneer and yet a student, it is said; a man of hard sinew and acquainted with all weathers, with all moods of mother earth, he has yet taken time to think and act upon public questions; a good farmer whose mind has developed much beyond the limits of his farm, he ought not to find it difficult to be an excellent officer in the position of advice which he now occupies.

The other three men of the cabinet the public has been inclined to regard as curiosities in the line of cabinet appointment. Two of them Mr. Cleveland had long known and had doubtless sufficiently tested. Mr. Lamont was his private secretary during his first administration, and Mr. Bissell was his law partner twelve or thirteen years ago. Very sagacious politicians have known and trusted Mr. Lamont. He stood close in Mr. Tilden's confidence; he

earned great favor as editor of a political newspaper; Mr. Whitney, whose political talents every one now doffs his hat to, recognized the same ability, the same worthiness of confidence in him.
There can be no reasonable doubt about his ability to administer
the War Department with success, as there would have been
little doubt about his ability to occupy almost any other high
administrative post with credit and efficiency. The only criticism
which his appointment prompts is, that he was, so far as we are
able to ascertain, no more fitted for the War Department than
for any other. He is, in short, simply a very capable man of unusual executive talents. He has had no special training to be war
minister.

The management of the Post Office Department is not very
like "chamber practice," and Mr. Bissell has never been anything
but a lawyer; but the law is not now a learned profession, though
there are still men of eminent learning in it. Lawyers, nowadays,
in the great cities at any rate, are simply experts in a technical
business. Mr. Bissell is doubtless such an expert. The conduct of
the Post Office Department is also a technical business; no doubt
Mr. Bissell can learn all that it is necessary for the Postmaster
General to know readily enough. The trusted counsel of the Le-
high Valley Railroad must of course have a head for business.

But what is one to say of the appointment of Mr. Hoke Smith?
In selecting him Mr. Cleveland depended, not upon his own judgment, but upon the judgment of others; and upon the advice of
others he has entrusted him with some of the most delicate and
important interests of the Administration. This is the fact that
places Mr. Smith's appointment in sharp contrast with all the
others—neither the country nor Mr. Cleveland knew him when he
was selected. There is no Department, unless it be the Treasury,
whose mistakes can so easily or so quickly discredit the Administration as the mistakes of the Interior Department can. Mr. Cleveland last time appointed to this difficult office, with its nice tests
of character and judgment, a man of the highest attainments
both as a public servant and as a student of institutions, the
scholarly, earnest, enviably honored L. Q. C. Lamar. Mr. Lamar
had no quick executive capacity; his habit fitted him for contemplation rather than for action; he was doubtless better suited
for the place he subsequently took on the Supreme bench than
for service in one of the most complex and exacting of the administrative Departments. He made frequent mistakes in his
minor appointments, and, seeing his own errors of judgment in
such matters, often found it hard to make up his mind to sign any
commissions at all. But the making of appointments, important

matter as it is for the proper administration of the government, is not the whole duty of the Interior; and Mr. Lamar had that chastened and judicial cast of mind which the intensely and wholly practical man knows nothing of, and was the better fitted on that account for the dispassionate determination of delicate questions of policy which rest upon considerations of justice, but which the practical man might have regarded as based wholly upon considerations of expediency.

Expediency is a short-sighted counselor; and yet Mr. Smith's training has been such as disposes a man habitually to resort to her for counsel. His intellectual discipline has been intensely practical and upon a very narrow field of practice. Leaving college while still a boy, he went immediately to the bar, with only such an acquaintance with the principles of law as would enable him to pass the easy examination for license. Once admitted to practice, he made an eager, astute, unremitting, successful effort to get business. He prepared his cases diligently, became known by the number of cases he got and the number he won; devoted himself particularly to what one may call anti-corporation law, representing anybody, and presently everybody, that had a grievance against any railway especially, and finally grew to be so considerable a corporation lawyer that, just before he discovered himself to Mr. Cleveland's friends, he had begun to be employed by corporations. He had added meanwhile, of course, immensely to his knowledge of the law on its case side, to his ability to make his large figure and his flexible voice, his familiarity with the facts of the case, and particularly with the weak points of his opponent's position, tell upon the minds of the jury and the opinions of the court. It is a familiar story at the American bar; Mr. Smith's version of it is simply on a somewhat bigger scale than usual. Such men very often make very efficient and sometimes very useful practitioners. But they seldom make more. Their training is narrow, their apprehension specialized; their conceptions of justice are technical, their standards of policy too self-regardful. If they broaden, when opportunity is offered, to the scale of judgment required by more liberal functions, it is because of qualities which have lain latent in them, not because of qualities already developed in them by experience. The Department of the Interior will make a heavy drain upon Mr. Smith's latent qualities. If he turn out to have none, Mr. Cleveland will have to carry the heavy responsibilities of the Department for himself.

Taken altogether, this is certainly a very unconventional cabinet. Mr. Harrison's was made up much more after the conventional manner. His appointments were many of them open to very grave criticism, but they represented an attempt, made after the fashion set by previous Presidents, to bring the different elements of the party together into the council of the Administration. Until Mr. Cleveland, it may be said to have been habitual with our Presidents to regard the cabinet as a council of party leaders. Mr. Arthur, for example, unquestionably averted premature party calamity by putting aside his personal preferences in the choice of his cabinet and broadening its membership much beyond the ranks of the stalwart wing, to which he himself belonged. Other Presidents have followed a like course of conciliation and coöperation. Only men like Jackson have hitherto put their personal preferences foremost in supplying the Departments with heads and themselves with assistants.

In this case Mr. Cleveland has combined the two methods in a way which may turn out to have been significant of the future course of the Government under him. If he had put a man of real party consequence and of some political capacity of which we could be sure at the head of the Interior Department, instead of Mr. Hoke Smith, this would be plain enough to be taken for granted. The public questions which now press for solution lie within the fields of the Treasury and of the Interior. The policy already finely begun, which needs to be carefully and intelligently completed, lies with the Navy Department; it is the construction of an efficient modern navy. The immediate questions of the time affect the tariff, the coinage, the policy of the government with regard to its public lands, the administration of the Pension Bureau, and the realization of the purposes of our later legislation in respect to the settlement and civilization of the Indians. Mr. Carlisle can be counted on for sound and reasoned purposes concerning the tariff and the coinage; Mr. Herbert, we may be sure, will carry forward the plans for the navy; it may be that Mr. Smith will do what he is directed to do in the Department of the Interior. Let us hope that such will be the arrangement, for fear of miscarriages. If he were a man like Mr. Carlisle, it would seem clear enough that this Administration was prepared to play the difficult, but now imperative, part of guiding legislation: that a tariff bill and an explicit coinage policy might be expected to emanate from the Treasury Department, with distinct suggestions of the course to be pursued from each of the departments likely to be affected by legislation. As it is, we are left to surmises, for all the Administration is so strong and so truly representative in one or two departments. What will Mr. Cleveland do with this cabinet? for nothing can be clearer than that he purposes to do something. Will the Treasury submit a programme of reform? Will the Administration assume the leadership in revising the tariff laws, reforming the coinage, extending the provisions of the civil service law, as Mr. Whitney did in developing the navy? Is this a legislative as well as an administrative cabinet? Is it a cabinet with purposes as well as with capabilities? If so, how does Mr. Cleveland stand for strength in such courses, with a Cabinet constituted as this one is, not as a party counsel, but rather as a body of personal counsellors? Is it strong enough for leadership, or is Mr. Cleveland relying entirely on his own strength to carry his purposes to successful completion?

Probably he is depending upon himself, taking his cue from the country, which undoubtedly depends upon him to exercise an active guidance in affairs for the next four years. If so, it is a fine display of courage and resolution. It commits the country, it must be said, in a hazardous degree, to the understanding and capacity of a single man; but it will, at any rate, make capital test of our idea that the President, constitutionally viewed, constitutes the Executive Department of the government; that he is, not simply the directing head, but the efficient embodiment of the administrative function.

For, after all, one cannot avoid, if he would, putting general questions with regard to the character of the government at a time when appointments are being made to its chief administrative offices. Much as they are irritated by the appointment of irregular party men like Judge Gresham, and unknown party men like Mr. Bissell and Mr. Smith, the politicians fall back with resignation upon the consideration that "it is Mr. Cleveland's cabinet, and its make-up, after all, no body's business but Mr. Cleveland's." This is the view which Mr. Cleveland himself apparently takes—not arrogantly, but with a grave sense of responsibility for the manner in which the executive business of the country is to be carried on. It may be called the literally constitutional view of the cabinet. The constitution vests the executive power of the government in the President in perfectly plain terms. It takes it for granted in an occasional phrase that there will be "heads of departments," and it authorizes Congress to place the appointment of the minor officers of the government in the hands of such principal officials. But it offers no hint that they are to be more than heads of departments; they receive no cue from it to speak as if they had legal share in the exercise of executive power. Statute, indeed, may give them a certain degree of independence of the President. The statute which erected the Treasury Department, for example, gave Andrew

Jackson no little trouble because it rendered it necessary for him to obtain the assent of the Secretary to the withdrawal of the deposits of the government from the Bank of the United States. He had to make two removals before he found a pliant Secretary. But such statutes must be acknowledged to strain the tenor of the Constitution. The President may make what selections he will in providing the administrative departments with their chief officers, and keep indisputably within his literal constitutional powers. The Senate must, indeed, confirm his appointments; but it has long regarded its function in this respect, not as a right to assist or dictate to the President in his choice of cabinet officials, but merely as a check upon the nomination of men touched in some degree by scandal or known in some way to have shown gross incompetency for assuming public trusts. No man who has followed Mr. Cleveland's career ought to have the slightest disposition to curtail his freedom of choice, or can have sufficient reason for distrusting his judgment of men, and his strength to bear the whole executive responsibility of the government.

But no President dominates more than eight years of our national life. Whatever his individual talents, he is only one in a long line of chief magistrates. He does not make his own Administration merely; he gives a precedent to his successors, who may not have like ability and discretion. He contributes an example to the general development; he determines a section of the general institutional growth of the country. He is responsible, not only to the Constitution, which, besides being a legal document, is also a vehicle of life, but also to the general sense of the country regarding its institutions. We possess the right not merely, but must feel the duty also, of friendly criticism. We must take care to know very clearly what sort of a development we are having.

What kind of a government are we to have? Are we to have a purely administrative cabinet, and individual choice of policy by the President; or are we to have responsible party government, parties being made responsible not only for the choice they make of Presidents, but also for the character and motives of the men they bring forward to give him counsel? The choice between these two methods is a fundamental one in the constitution of government. Either system would be constitutional under the existing provisions of our fundamental law; the former literally constitutional, the latter within the permissions of the Constitution. The practice of our Presidents, too, whenever at least they have not been mere military chiefs like Jackson and Grant, with imperative preferences of their own, has been in the direction of the latter system, until Mr. Cleveland, a man as truly taken from outside the regular lines of civil promotion as either Grant or Jackson. He has broken more than most Presidents with what I may call the historical method of appointment. That method has unquestionably regarded the cabinet as a party council. Mr. Carlisle is the only Democratic leader Mr. Cleveland has put into his cabinet. Eminent and admirable as the services of Mr. Herbert have been, they have been restricted in their field, and they have been inconspicuous outside Congress. He has shaped legislation, and he goes into the cabinet equipped as few men could be for the duties of the particular Department to which he has been assigned. But we no [do] not know in what degree he may be qualified for general political counsel when sitting with his colleagues. He is in no broad sense a leader of his party.

Very few thoughtful men, I suppose, would maintain that Mr. Cleveland should have put some representative of the stalwart wing of his party among his advisers. All who cherish liberal views of reform must hope that the future of the party is in the hands of its other, its newer elements and must rejoice that the President has made up his body of counsellors from those sections of the party which seem, so far as we know the new men, to be represented. But with the conspicuous exception already mentioned, he has chosen from the rank and file of that division of his following, and not from among leaders at all. Mr. Josiah Quincy, the First Assistant Secretary of State, is a Democratic leader in the best sense of the term, and a very influential and important one, who has constantly, of recent months, been at Mr. Cleveland's elbow; but Mr. Gresham, his chief, of course is not. He was a leader the other day of the liberal wing of the other party; now, if he is to be classified at all, he is an independent. He carries great weight with those who, like himself, are becoming Democrats in the Northwest. He leads in opinion among those whose party ties are loose or loosening—leads very honorably, very ably, and with an enviable distinction—but he does not yet, at any rate, lead either a party or the section of a party. If he leads a section of a party it is a section of the party which has hitherto been opposed to Mr. Cleveland. Mr. Lamont has taken confidential part in the counsels of leaders, but he is not himself a leader. Mr. Morton has been prominent among Democratic campaign speakers in Nebraska, and has had such functions of leadership as force of character and of conviction give when publicly displayed; but there has of course been no place of national leadership hitherto for Nebraska Democrats. Messrs. Olney, Bissell and Smith have been quiet lawyers, leading only as men of local prominence must always lead when they hold and express pronounced views upon party questions. Mr. Cleveland's first cabinet was much more of the historical pattern than this one. It was in some sense a group of leaders.

It is not often enough noted that we have really never answered for ourselves clearly and with definite purpose the question, What *is* the Cabinet? Is it the President's cabinet, or are the heads of the executive departments meant by the spirit of our national institutions to be real party colleagues of the President, in council, chosen by him, indeed, but from among men of accredited political capacity, not from among the general body of the citizenship of the country? It is a question fundamental to our whole political development, and it is by no means to be answered from out the text of the Constitution simply. That Constitution is a vehicle of life. Its chief virtue is, that it is not too rigidly conceived. It leaves our life free to take its own courses of well considered custom, its own chosen turns of development. Presidents who are themselves of the stuff out of which real party leaders are made—men like Jackson and Lincoln and Cleveland—will of course dominate their cabinets, no matter what the principle of appointment; but headstrong men like Andrew Johnson will rule only to ruin; will goad parties into extreme and ill considered courses by the sheer exasperations of their obstinacy; and men who are not by natural constitution equipped for leadership will only make the more conspicuous, it may be the more disastrous, failures by seeking, in the choice of their advisers, to play a role beyond their talents. Our party leaders we can choose slowly, by the conservative processes of the survival of the fittest in Congress, by the exacting tests of command over public opinion. Our Presidents, experience has taught us, we must often choose hastily, by the unpremeditated compromises or the sudden impulses of huge popular conventions.

It is impossible, moreover, that the President should really decide all the issues of choice which come to the several executive departments. There are only twenty-four hours in the day for him, as for other men, and some of these he must, I suppose, devote to sleep. The departments are not executive bureaus merely: their chief officers are much more than a superior sort of secretaries to the President. Their functions are political, outside the cabinet as well as within it. They must decide many questions which bear directly upon the general policy of the Administration, as well as innumerable questions of routine detail, and must decide them independently of their colleagues and the President. It is only concerning the largest, broadest, most general matters of policy that they can consult the judgment of the cabinet as a whole, or the wishes of the President. The presidency is thus inevitably put, as it were, into the hands of a sort of commission, of which the President is only the directing head.

Not only so, but, inasmuch as, whether we wish it or not, the President is necessarily a party leader, *ex officio*, there ought to be some regular, open, responsible connection established between him and his party. He is not always, as we know, a real leader before he is chosen to his great office of leadership. It has several times happened that he was not even personally acquainted with the men by whom the policy of his party had been habitually determined before he was discovered by a popular convention. Once and again a President has come to Washington ignorant both of men and of measures. How is he to make the acquaintance of his party; how are they to learn his character and intentions? He must somehow get the confidence of the men in whom the party habitually places confidence and whom it will follow, or else he must consent to be quite impotent during his four years in everything but the mere routine of executive action.

I go a step further. It is necessary that the members of the cabinet should be recognized party leaders, not only because the President's day is as short as other men's, and many important and far-reaching decisions of policy must be left to them, but also because the literally constitutional position of the President, as an absolutely separate, self-sufficient part of the government, is a practically impossible position. No government can be administered with the highest efficiency unless there be close co-operation and an intimate mutual understanding between its Administration and its legislature. The real and conclusive test of excellency for all laws is their workability, and no legislature can intelligently apply that test unless it be in constant correspondence with the administrative branch of the government. Legislative proposals, too, are usually more apt to be well considered, feasible, business-like, when they come from the Administration, which is immediately in the presence of the practical conditions under which they must be carried out, in the presence, too, of the practical difficulties which create the need for such legislation, than when it comes from committees of the Houses themselves, committees which cannot co-operate for the construction of a consistent policy, and which are not sobered by the knowledge that they will be obliged to find practicable ways of putting their schemes into actual execution.

This is the argument, to which the country is becoming more and more inclined to listen, for the introduction of the members of the cabinet into the Houses; the argument for making it their duty to be present in Congress to give information and offer advice, their privilege to propose measures and take part in debate. Ours is the only country in the world of any consequence which does not in some direct way facilitate co-operation between its executive and its legislature; and it is only because unbounded material prosperity and unprecedented freedom from social disorder and discontent have made it easy to conduct our government, despite its disintegrated structure, that we have not yet become conscious of the pinch of disadvantage which must sooner or later result from the singular division of our government into groups of public servants looking askance at one another.

Sooner or later we must recognize in the cabinet the President's responsible party council, and must require our Presidents, not by hard and fast constitutional provision, but by the more flexible while equally imperative mandates of public opinion, operating through the medium of the Senate, to call to the chief places in the departments representative party men who have accredited themselves for such functions by long and honorable public service. We cannot be forever running the risks involved in the elevation of unknown men to the presidency. The present posture of affairs is altogether exceptional, and Mr. Cleveland is an altogether exceptional man, a real leader, but a leader created by circumstances which can hardly soon recur. We do not know many of the men who are in his cabinet because we do not yet know the new Democratic party which is now in process of formation. The men in that cabinet whom we do know we know as leaders in things which are the vital and operative causes of that reformation. The financial policy of the country is to be reformed; its new naval strength is to give us proper dignity and proper assurance of safety among the nations; the reform of the civil service is to be carried forward on the lines now, it is to be hoped, definitely established; the executive departments are to be conducted on business principles, with a view to making them as economical and as efficient as possible. New men have come to the front for the accomplishment of the new tasks; new regions of the country are turning toward the new party. Parties, whether they retain old names or not, are making ready for the new start which the rise of new interests has now for some time been commanding. The politics of the war time are to be forgotten, even by select men of the very generation which engaged in the stupendous struggle, and convictions made up, not of reminiscence, but of firm purpose for the future development of the country along normal lines of growth, are to be the controlling forces of politics, which shall come in with a new generation which lives for the future, not in the past. We like this cabinet well enough until the new movement shall have shown us who the real leaders are. Then parties must choose the men who really lead them for Presidents, and Presidents thus chosen must give us responsible party government by surrounding themselves with a cabinet council made up from among party men whom the people have known and have shown themselves disposed to trust.

The degree of separation now maintained between the executive and legislative branches of our government cannot long be preserved without very serious inconvenience resulting. Congress and the President now treat with one another almost like separate governments, so jealous is each of its prerogatives. The Houses find out only piecemeal and with difficulty what is going on at the other end of the avenue, in bureaus which have been created by statute. Members have been known to grow uneasy, and even indignant, if cabinet officers followed the debates from the galleries. Congress, consequently, often gropes very helplessly for lack of guidance which might be had almost for the asking, while the tasks of the departments languish or miscarry for lack of appreciative co-operation and support on the part of Congress. We risk every degree of friction and disharmony rather than hazard the independence of branches of the government which are helpless without each other. What we need is harmonious, consistent, responsible party government, instead of a wide dispersion of function and responsibility; and we can get it only by connecting the President as closely as may be with his party in Congress. The natural connecting link is the cabinet.

Printed in the New York *Review of Reviews*, vii (April 1893), 286-97.

From Cyrus Hall McCormick

My Dear Wilson: [Chicago] Mch. 18, 1893.

Your favor of the 15th, and telegram of the 17th, are received.[1] I have consulted the Executive Committee, and inasmuch as it is not convenient for us to have the dinner on the 23rd or 24th, or 30th or 31st inst. we will wait for you, and will ask how soon you can come to us after the 21st of April. Our fellows have determined that you are to be with us. Could you arrange for the 20th or 21st of April, or for the week following?[2]

As I shall have left town for a little while, please send your reply to this to Mr. John Maynard Harlan,[3] who is the Chairman of the Executive Committee, Ashland Block, Chicago.

Yours very sincerely,   Cyrus H. McCormick

TLS (C. H. McCormick Letterpress Books, WHi).
    [1] Wilson's letter and telegram are missing.
    [2] As C. H. McCormick to WW, April 14, 1893, reveals, Wilson agreed to speak on April 28.
    [3] Born Frankfort, Ky., Dec. 21, 1864, the son of Associate Justice John Marshall Harlan. A.B., College of New Jersey, 1884; LL.B., George Washington University, 1888. Practiced law in Chicago throughout most of his professional career. Alderman, Chicago, 1896-98; unsuccessful Republican mayoralty candidate, 1897 and 1905. Died March 23, 1934.

To Horace Elisha Scudder

My dear Mr. Scudder,   Princeton, New Jersey, 19 March, 1893.

'Tis a long time "after the fact," I am afraid you will think, to speak of your estimate of the two party platforms in the November *Atlantic*;[1] but I really have been hurried past all opportunities to write hitherto by pressing engagements of all sorts; and this, besides, is a cool distance from which to judge the article. I was looking over it again just now. It seems to me even more just and courageous than it seemed when it came out. It requires more courageous thinking to be just to two sides than to be just to only one; and, at this safe remove from the heat of the campaign, your "Two Programmes" seems to me a piece of work to be proud of. You are to be congratulated as an editor upon the circumstances that you were obliged to write it yourself.[2] As an author you should be condoled with because you could not sign your name and get the immediate credit.

You see your last letter is never so far away from me in time as to be forgotten; I write this about the November number to make connections in our correspondence—and get uttered what has so long been hanging on my pen waiting till the ink should begin to flow hence in your direction. The real business of this letter is, not to address you as an author I sincerely admire, but as a trustee of Williams College. I suppose that the election of Mr. Bliss Perry[3] to our faculty here creates a vacancy which you will wish to fill at once, and I write to ask if an opportunity might be offered me to urge a candidate. My brother in law, Mr. Stockton Axson, is occupying this year a (necessarily) temporary place in the English department of the University of Vermont, where he is doing work very similar, I judge, to that which Mr. Perry is doing at Williamstown—and doing it with marked success. This is his first year of teaching; but I think I could submit evidences of his worth which you would think of great value, even when submitted by his kinsman. His training was gotten partly at the Johns Hopkins, but principally under Winchester at Wesleyan—the best man, I am convinced, for his particular function in the country; and Winchester will give Axson the most cordial support as I have no doubt will also his present employers and colleagues.

If you encourage me to go on and speak of him more at length and more to the point—with proof and circumstances, I will be only too glad to do so; and I sincerely hope to be able to serve Williams in this matter.

With warmest regards,
            Cordially and faithfully yours,   Woodrow Wilson

P.S. I trust you will not dislike my little "Epoch," "Division and Reunion."   W.W.

TCL (RSB Coll., DLC).
¹ "The Two Programmes of 1892," *Atlantic Monthly*, LXX (Nov. 1892), 688-98.
² A reference to Scudder's invitation to Wilson to write the article, which Wilson had declined. See WW to H. E. Scudder, Aug. 11, 1892.
³ Born Williamstown, Mass., Nov. 25, 1860. A.B., Williams College, 1881; A.M., same institution, 1883. Studied at the Universities of Berlin and Strasbourg, 1886-88. Professor of English, Williams College, 1886-93. Professor of Oratory and Aesthetic Criticism, Princeton, 1893-99; Holmes Professor of Belles Lettres and English Language and Literature, Princeton, 1899-1900. Editor of the *Atlantic Monthly*, 1899-1909. Professor of English Literature, Harvard University, 1906-26; Francis Lee Higginson Professor of English Literature, Harvard, 1926-30. Editor of numerous literary works and anthologies and author of several volumes of fiction and of many scholarly works. Died Feb. 13, 1954. His autobiography, *And Gladly Teach* (Boston and New York, 1935), includes an intimate sketch of Wilson during the 1890's.

To John Irenaeus McCain¹

My dear Sir,   Princeton, New Jersey, 21 March, 1893.

I have been both very much interested and very much gratified by your kind letter of March 6.² I have once and again thought somewhat seriously of writing a history of the United States for school use, but other things have always drawn me away from the idea. After you have read my little volume on "Division and Reunion" will you not write to me again upon this matter? The point of view I occupy in that volume would of course be the the [*sic*] point of view I should occupy in anything else I might write on the same subject. I should be very much indebted to you if you would give me your candid opinion as to whether a school history embodying the same views would be acceptable in southern schools. That what I have written does full honor to the South, which I dearly love, and that it contains the historical truth, I am of course convinced; but some parts of the truth are not palateable, and I am in doubt as to what impression will be produced in the South by such writings.

    With sincerest thanks and regards,

             Faithfully Yours,   Woodrow Wilson

WWTLS (in possession of Isabel McCain Brown).
  1 Ph.D., College of New Jersey, 1892, and Professor of English Literature and Language, Erskine College.
  2 It is missing.

From Horace Elisha Scudder

My dear Wilson,   [Cambridge, Mass.] 21 March 1893

    It is always a pleasure to have a letter from you and your last has two or three delights hidden in it. I chuckle over the praise of a friend's article, for instance, and feel a glow of pride at discovering that you thought me capable of writing *The Two Programmes*,—which I didn't![1]

    Thank you for telling me about Axson. I remember an individual piece of writing that you sent me once[2] and I shall take pleasure in nominating him to Carter,[3] though from what he has said I suspect Carter has pretty nearly decided whom to name to the Trustees.

    I received yesterday your little book and anticipate great pleasure in digging into it. Perhaps I may even have some unlooked for day of leisure in which really to read it. How good Hart's own book was.

    Now that you have got your book out of the way, you may be swinging [?] your heels in the market place and wishing some one would come along. Well, here I come and bid you straightway review for me Rhodes's two volumes. Have you the book? If not I will send it to you, and I sincerely hope you will undertake the task. By the way did you read Jameson's admirable critique of Campbell in the Atlantic?[4]

    Are you coming this way again? If not, I shall have to skip over to Princeton some time [when] I am in New York. Don't your people ever have miscellaneous lectures? I have two, one The American Man of Letters which I gave lately at Brown at Jameson's instigation, and one on Whittier which I have given at Williams, Vassar, Wellesley & Cleveland. Much lecturing you see makes me over bold.   Ever Yours H. E. Scudder

ALS (Houghton Mifflin Letterpress Books, MH).
  1 The author was E. M. Shepard.
  2 It was probably Stockton Axson's story, "Thornton vs. Thornton," which Wilson sent to Robert Bridges on August 18, 1892.
  3 Franklin Carter, President of Williams College, 1881-1901.

4 John Franklin Jameson's review of Douglas Campbell, *The Puritans in Holland, England, and America* (2 vols., New York, 1892), in the *Atlantic Monthly*, LXX (Nov. 1892), 698-704.

From Colyer Meriwether[1]

Dear Prof. Wilson,   Baltimore, Md.   Mar. 23–1893.

Would you kindly mark out for me a short course of reading in English [government] for one year of your lectures here that I am not provided for? If you may remember I took notes for this year, and, for another year, I have as substitute "The State." It is for the remaining year that I now trouble you.

I spoke to you about this the last day you were at the University, and you advised me to write.

Hoping I do not inconvenience you too much,

I remain,   Yours truly,   C. Meriwether.

ALS (WP, DLC) with WWhw notation on env.: "Ans. 14 July, 1893." Att: WWhw reading list.
1 A graduate student in history and political science at The Johns Hopkins University.

To Horace Elisha Scudder

My dear Mr. Scudder,   Princeton, New Jersey, 27 March, 1893.

I am sincerely obliged to you for your letter of the 21st. It is a disappointment to me that there is no chance for Axson at Williams, but your letter made the disappointment as easy to bear as possible; particularly its intimation—which I will interpret as a promise—that you will come over to Princeton the next time you come this way. The Wednesdays and Thursdays of April I am to be engaged with a class in Constitutional law at the New York Law School;[1] but the rest of the time, including the summer months, I am to be at home, and we (Mrs. Wilson and I) cannot think of your coming without being impatient to have you come at once.

Yes, our people *do* have some "miscellaneous lectures," and, although I fear their programmes are full for this year, I could want no better news than that you are in the field and may be had another year. I will spread the information in the proper quarters.

I will review Rhodes for you with pleasure, provided you don't want the copy too soon. I am very tired just now and could not write freshly if I were obliged to write under pressure. I have the volumes, but have not yet had time to read them. How many words would you want—from 2300 to 3000, three to four pages?

Meantime, I again come to you unbidden with a piece of an entirely different kind. It goes to you either today or tomorrow by express. It is on "Political Sovereignty,"—you might call it "Popular Sovereignty," if you choose,—and I would rather get the constituency of the *Atlantic* to peruse it than the readers of any technical journal I know of,—if you can in conscience indulge me by publishing it.[2]

So you did *not* write the "Two Programmes"! Well, it would have been even better done if you had.

Ever faithfully and cordially yours,   Woodrow Wilson

TCL (RSB Coll., DLC).

[1] There is no explicit evidence in letters, in the New York newspapers, or in the catalogues and records of the New York Law School to reveal whether Wilson did in fact give these lectures. However, the *Daily Princetonian*, March 7, 1893, announced that Wilson would deliver them. Moreover, the *Princeton Press*, May 13, 1893, noted that he had just been "named as one of the lecturers on special subjects before the students of the New York Law School," and Wilson was listed as "Special Lecturer on Constitutional Law" in the catalogues of the Law School from 1893 through 1897. It seems a safe assumption, therefore, that he did go to New York and deliver ten lectures during April, and also that he more or less repeated those described in the Editorial Note, "Wilson's Lectures at the New York Law School," Vol. 7.

[2] Since most of the subsequent correspondence between Wilson and Scudder about this essay is missing, one can only conclude that Scudder either rejected it or (more likely) that Wilson, deciding soon afterward to include "Political Sovereignty" in a volume of essays (see WW to C. Scribner, May 16, 1893), asked Scudder to return it.

From Horace Elisha Scudder

My dear Wilson   [Cambridge, Mass.] 28 March 1893

Many thanks for your letter of 27 March and for the MS which I shall be sure to like better after reading it than before.

As for Rhodes, if I had say 3000 words, by April 10, I should like it, but I am entirely willing to wait till 8 May, and think you will prefer the later date: that means publication in the June number. . . .   Sincerely Yours   H. E. Scudder.

ALS (Houghton Mifflin Letterpress Books, MH).

From Joseph Leland Kennedy

Dear uncle: Batesville, Ark. 3/28/93

Having carefully read your article on "Clevelands Cabinet" in the "Review of Reviews," allow me to congratulate you on your first efforts as a philosophical & historical writer. You are coming out right along. I hope for you *much* greater success in the future.

Pressing business demands my immediate attention or would say more concerning you & your family.

Hoping you are all well I remain as ever your

Critical nephew—Joe Kennedy

P.S. Please answer right away & accept my congratulations. Love to my cousins & aunt. I am an an [*sic*] Arkansas hoosier and am out of gas, so good bye.   Joe

ALS (WP, DLC) with Joseph Kennedy's request, "Please send me a copy of your book entitled 'Division and Reunion,' " and WWhw notation, "Ans. 9 April '93," on env.

From the Minutes of the Princeton Faculty

5 5′ P.M., Wednesday, March 29, ''93.

. . . *Resolved,* That the question as to the method of Conducting Examinations under the principle of honor be referred to the Committee on the New Method of conducting Examinations[1] for consideration and report.

Professor Fine was added to the Committee.

[1] About the appointment and membership of this committee, of which Wilson was a member, see the Princeton Faculty Minutes printed at Jan. 25, 1893. For the committee's report and recommendation, see the Princeton Faculty Minutes printed at April 19, 1893.

To Albert Shaw

My dear Shaw,   Princeton, New Jersey,   31 March, 1893.

Please accept my sincere thanks for the check sent me for the cabinet article, and for your kind words of appreciation concerning the article itself.[1] Of course the check is all right: that is what I understood I should get, and is quite as much as the article is worth.

I am glad to think of you as off on a little vacation, and I hope it will bring you no end of refreshment.

With affectionate regards for you both (*videlicet*, Finley[2] and yourself),   Faithfully yours,   Woodrow Wilson

TCL (in possession of Virginia Shaw English).
[1] Shaw's letter is missing.
[2] Robert Johnston Finley, assistant editor of the New York *Review of Reviews*.

From Joseph Ruggles Wilson

My precious Woodrow—   N. York Ap 10/93

I was so sorry not to see you when you called. I had been *particularly* hungry for you and that is saying much—for when is not this hunger upon me? My hip (Sciatica) has hurt me very much of late, and I sometimes go out just to see what change of posture will do. It is better to-day. Last night Stockton was kind enough to call upon me; but as I had suffered more than usual with my leg during the evening I was constrained to go to bed;—for when I am thus resting there is no hurt—and so didn't see the dear boy whom I sincerely love, and to whom I was grateful because of his call.

I wish I knew whether you got the key I returned!—but presume you did.

I shall try to see you all a few days before going South to Gen Assly.[1]

Meanwhile you know my love to be unbounded

Your affc   Father

ALS (WP, DLC).
[1] The General Assembly of the southern Presbyterian Church met at the First Presbyterian Church, Macon, Georgia, May 18-28, 1893. Dr. Wilson was still the Stated Clerk.

A News Item

[April 10, 1893]

Professors Woodrow Wilson and Allan Marquand are members of the Alumni Association of Johns Hopkins, which has just been formed in New York City.[1]

Printed in the *Daily Princetonian*, April 10, 1893.
[1] On April 7, 1893, according to the *New York Times*, April 8, 1893. Wilson was apparently not elected an officer or a member of the committee to draft a constitution and by-laws.

The Nation's Review of *Division and Reunion*[1]

[April 13, 1893]

AN HISTORIAN'S FACTS.

Division and Reunion, 1829-1889. By Woodrow Wilson, Ph.D., LL.D. With five maps. Longmans, Green & Co. 1893. (Epochs of American History.)

We have here what the author calls "a sketch in broad outline—not so much a compact narrative as a rapid synopsis—of the larger features of public affairs in the crowded space of sixty years that stretches from the election of Andrew Jackson to the end of the first century of the Constitution." As might be expected from the learning and literary skill of the writer, he holds his subject well in hand, and, after a liberal allowance made for his point of view, he divides what seems to him the word of truth with a candor and a discrimination that are worthy of praise. In reviewing a period of "misunderstanding and of passion" he does not claim to have judged rightly in all cases as between parties. He claims only to have practised that impartiality of judgment which is a matter of the heart. This latter claim may be frankly conceded by those who feel constrained to dissent, as we do, from many of his historical appreciations. Where impartiality of judgment was difficult, he often holds the scales of justice with a steady hand. Where impartiality of judgment was easy, he seems to us to have sometimes been much less happy in summing up the judicial verdicts of history; and this because his point of view, as we conceive, sometimes subjects his observations to a species of obvious historical parallax, only the more misleading for being entirely unconscious. There must necessarily be a large angular variation in the position of events in American history, according as they are viewed from the South Carolina theory of the Constitution or the theory expounded by Madison and Webster. Mr. Wilson holds that the South Carolina theory of the Constitution was the only true theory, because it was the original theory that dated from the formation of the instrument.

The editor of this series informs us, we presume by way of explanation, that each author of the successive volumes "has kept his own point of view, and no pains have been taken to harmonize divergencies of judgment." This course undoubtedly has its advantages, and guarantees to each author that intellectual integrity which it is his right to assert and maintain, but it is a course which may easily lend itself to much confusion of ideas so far as the average reader is concerned. In a synopsis like this he naturally looks for some similarity of historical perspective where the larger features of our public affairs are delineated.

To such a reader it may easily seem that the *Proteus historicorum* has slightly abused his privileges when Mr. Wilson is allowed to teach in this volume that we must wholly discard the constitutional theory which Prof. Hart inculcated in the preceding volume of the series. Prof. Hart had told us, what we were quite ready to believe for reasons other than he gives, that the Constitution, at the time of its formation, was understood to be not a mere compact, but a permanent instrument of government for the whole people. He affirmed that the defects of the Confederation "had educated the American people to the point where they were willing to accept a permanent federal union." A nation without a national government seemed to him, as to the authors of the 'Federalist,' "an awful spectacle."

Mr. Wilson assumes in the volume before us that this whole *manière de voir* is entirely unhistorical and false. Mr. Hart had told us that a clear statement of the "compact" theory of government was put forward for the first time in the Kentucky and Virginia "Resolutions of '98." Mr. Wilson, on the contrary, holds that the "compact" theory was congenital with the Constitution, and that the famous reply of Webster to Hayne struck the chords of national sympathy with might in 1830, only because "the North was now beginning to insist on a national government," whereas the South, he adds, "was continuing to insist on the original understanding of the Constitution: that was all." He asserts that "it was for long found difficult to deny that a State could withdraw from the Federal arrangement, as she might have declined to enter it"; that Webster's epoch-marking speech, considered as an interpretation of the Constitution, "had been a prophecy rather than a statement of accomplished fact"; that it is because the Constitution was "the skeleton frame of a living organism" that the course of events in that organism came in the end "to nationalize the government once deemed confederate"; that while this process of change was going on in the social tissue and economic forces of both the North and the West, the South "had stood still," and, "standing still, she retained the old principles which had once been universal." And these, we are told, "are not lawyer's facts: they are historian's facts."

Our readers are well aware that at this late date in our annals we resolutely decline to discuss "lawyer's facts" concerning the true intendment of the Constitution, as ascertained by "construction construed" in the matter at issue. Not that we are quite prepared to say, with John Taylor of Caroline, that when "construction" gives right answers, "it ought to be laughed at for playing the fool," and that when it gives wrong answers, "it ought to be suspected of playing the knave." This compendious contempt of the Virginian exegete seems a little too insulting to deductive logic considered as an organon of discussion. It is enough for us that there is no end to the mere processes of legal dialectic, and that a few cold facts of history are often conclusive against a logomachy which has embroiled whole generations of men.

It is no more certain, it seems to us, that the Constitution was adopted than that it was adopted as the bond of a permanent Union. The idea that the Constitution could be adopted with a reservation of the right to withdraw from the Union, in case certain amendments were not secured, appears to have been started in the Massachusetts Convention of 1788, but it was speedily abandoned. The same idea was championed by a powerful minority in the Virginia Convention, but was formally voted down. Alexander Hamilton, in his despair of securing a majority for the pure and simple ratification of the Constitution by the New York Convention, wrote to ask Madison in 1788 if a State could ratify the instrument conditionally on the adoption of certain amendments, and therefore with a reserved right to withdraw in case those amendments were not adopted. Madison, as we all know, replied that "a conditional ratification did not make a State a member of the Union"; that "the Constitution required an adoption *in toto* and for ever"; and that "it had been so adopted by the other States." Nothwithstanding this explicit statement of Madison, a whole host of amendments, some conditional, some explanatory, and some recommendatory, were submitted to the New York Convention for discussion in its Committee of the Whole, but all conditional amendments, and the words "on condition" in the form of the ratification, were rejected. The Convention then resolved unanimously that a circular-letter should be sent to all the States as expressive of the views of New York. That circular-letter contains the following passage: "Our attachment to our sister States, and the confidence we repose in them, cannot be more forcibly demonstrated than by acceding to a government which many of us think very imperfect, *and devolving the power of determining whether that government shall be rendered perpetual in its present form,* or altered agreeably to our wishes and a minority of the States with whom we unite."

These "historian's facts" (we apologize to our readers for rehearsing them) would seem to be tolerably conclusive, unless they can be traversed by some "historian's facts" equally clear in an opposite direction and of even date with them. We have not been able to find any such, and, until they are pointed out, we purpose to persist in our repugnance to "lawyer's facts," whether based on the "Resolutions of '98," the South Carolina "Exposition" of 1828, the Nullification Ordinance of 1832, or the Secession Ordinance of 1860.

Coming to matters of opinion, we venture to express the conviction that Mr. Wilson has looked at his "historian's facts" through the wrong end of the telescope, and so has fallen into an inversion of ideas when he argues that it was the growing power and the altered social tissue of the North and the West which incubated and energized at the North and at the West a sense of nationalism never quickened at the South, because "the

South had stood still while the rest of the country had undergone profound changes," and, standing still, had retained, as Mr. Wilson says, "the old principles which had once been universal." It would have been better to say that it was the waning power and social insulation of the South which incited her to invent and to energize in the interest of slavery the whole latter-day theory of "Separate State Sovereignty." It is undoubtedly true that in the course of events the South was left in a painful state of political and economic isolation by reason of her adherence to slavery— the "peculiar institution" which generated in the bosom of Southern society the fact and the sense of "separateness" to which the author refers again and again. But so far is it from being true that there had been "nothing active on the part of the South" in sectionalizing the Union, it would rather seem more correct to say that she had the larger share in this process. "A mild anti-slavery sentiment, born of the philanthropic spirit, had existed in all parts of the country from the first," says Mr. Wilson. Elsewhere he comments on the effect of slavery in generating "a stubborn pride of class privilege, and a watchful jealousy of interference from any quarter, either with that privilege itself, or with any part of the life which environs and supports it." He shows how slavery, after the invention of the cotton-gin, came to seem "nothing less than the indispensable economic instrument of Southern society." He shows how the South "grew more and more self-conscious as the anti-slavery agitation proceeded" at the North; and that this self-consciousness acted both as cause and as effect, he admits when he says that the ruling class at the South had "more political power, and clearer notions of how it meant to use that power, than any other class in the country."

Now, it is to be observed, we think, that in proportion as this feeling of "separateness" from other sections of the country grew more and more intense at the South; in proportion as "its sense of dependence for the preservation of its character upon a single fateful institution grew more and more keen and apprehensive" (these words are Mr. Wilson's), precisely in that proportion did the Southern politicians proceed to generate novel pseudo-theories of constitutional construction, by way of a State-rights prophylaxis for the defence of the "peculiar institution." Hence their successive shifts in manœuvring for a defensive position according to the South Carolina tactics: first, that a State may provisionally nullify an act of Congress till its constitutionality shall be affirmed by three-fourths of the States; then, that each State may separately and alone nullify an act of Congress, in the exercise of its separate reserved rights; then, the theory of nullification as rendered express and organic in Calhoun's scheme of a Dual Executive, with a veto power vested in each head for the mutual countercheck of all legislation deemed by either inimical to the respective sections comprised in the political equilibrium; and, finally, the theory of separate State secession which was reduced to practice in 1860 and 1861. To speak of the South as "standing still" on such a *glissade,* or to speak of the South as having retained "the old principles which had once been universal," is to baffle criticism by dealing in contradictions which are self-destructive.

The style of Mr. Wilson's narrative, though sometimes careless, is always easy and flowing, but occasionally there are strange slips of the historian's pen, as when we read that Delaware cast eight electoral votes for Fillmore in the Presidential election of 1856, where of course Maryland was meant.[2]

Printed in the New York *Nation,* LVI (April 13, 1893), 278-79.
[1] A copy of this review was printed in the New York *Evening Post,* April 15, 1893.
[2] The author of this brilliant review, which forecast the thesis of Jesse T. Carpenter's *The South as a Conscious Minority, 1789-1861* (New York, 1930), was James Clarke Welling. See Daniel C. Haskell, compiler, *The Nation, Volumes 1-105, New York, 1865-1917, Indexes of Titles and Contributors* (2 vols., New York, 1951-53), II, 504. Welling, a graduate of the College of New Jersey, 1844, had a long and distinguished career in journalism and was President of Columbian College (now George Washington University) from 1871 until just before his death in 1894. He reviewed many historical works for *The Nation.* For Wilson's oblique commentary on Welling's review, see WW to EAW, Feb. 23, 1894.

From Cyrus Hall McCormick

My dear Wilson: [Chicago] April 14, 1893.

I am glad to know that you are to be with us on the 28th. I write to ask that you will come directly to my house and that you will inform me by what train you expect to arrive. I would like to make an appointment for you to speak to University School if you expect to arrive in time for that. The head master of the University School is E. C. Coulter, Princeton '85, and I think it would have a good effect for you to address the boys.

Yours sincerely,   Cyrus H. McCormick.

TCL (C. H. McCormick Papers, WHi).

The *Church Union*'s Review of *Division and Reunion*

[April 15, 1893]

Division and Reunion; 1829-1889. By Woodrow Wilson, Ph D. LL D., Prof. of Jurisprudence in Princeton University. With five maps. New York and London: Longmans, Green & Co. $1.25, cloth.

The author of this volume (the third and last in a series to be known as "Epochs of American History,"[)] although yet young, has a distinguished reputation both for his success as a brilliant writer and for the enthusiasm he awakens as a class-room instructor; so that now the name of "Woodrow Wilson" prefixed to a publication ensures for it a prompt reception in literary circles and a quick reading among students young and old. Many of our readers will recollect his "Congressional Government," which attracted and charmed so much attention seven or eight years ago, and also his later work, "The State," whose merits have had a wide appreciation. And this present volume, just issued by the Longmans, will add, we think, another degree to Dr. Wilson's already high rank as a rare scholar, a ripe thinker and an accomplished writer. It was a difficult and delicate task which was assigned to his pen. As the philosophy of history is more remote than the facts which it explains, so the preparation of a work in which this philosophy is meant to be uppermost is harder to compose satisfactorily to all than would be the mere recital of connected events. In our judgment, Prof. Wilson has given the very best account which has yet been written of those causes which led to our civil war, of those other causes which brought it to an end, and of that third class of causes which served to promote the reunion of the States after such a terrible severance. Never was there a more impartial estimate of men and of men's conduct. Never could there be a more graphic threefold picture of a country torn and bleeding by reason of intestine conflict; of this same country as previously conditioned by its colliding policies and opposing interests; and of the same, yet another country, emerging from the stormy sea which engulfed its past to gaze with cleansed and hopeful eyes upon the assured future of a stronger and statelier growth than had before been more than dreamed of. The book we are thus noticing is intended for a text-book in the more advanced institutes of education, and we are pleased to think of its being studied by the thousands of our youth who are, under God, to make the country what it is yet to become. The pages are marred by the necessity of dividing it into short sections for convenience of teacher and student, but the general reader will overlook this when once he gets fairly afloat upon the stream of instruction which winds so smoothly while flowing onward so irresistibly. The table of "contents" and the "index" are admirable specimens of analytical labor leaving nothing to be desired in the way of finger board at any point of the picturesque road.[1]

Clipping from the New York *Church Union*, xx (April 15, 1893), in WP, DLC.
[1] The style of this review strongly suggests that Joseph Ruggles Wilson, who was at this time a contributing editor of the *Church Union*, was its author.

A News Item

[April 17, 1893]

Prof. Woodrow Wilson, of Princeton, President Seth Low, of Columbia, and President Gates, of Amherst, have been asked to act as judges at the next Harvard-Yale debate.[1]

Printed in the *Daily Princetonian*, April 17, 1893.
[1] Wilson withdrew from this commitment at some point. The debate took place in New Haven on May 2, with Low, President Merrill E. Gates of Amherst, and Professor Richmond Mayo-Smith of Columbia as judges.

To Legh Wilber Reid[1]

My dear Mr. Reid,   Princeton, New Jersey, 18 April, 1893.

I have taken great pleasure in speaking to Prof. Rockwood in your favour, and think that I made some impression upon him. Indeed I found that I was even ahead of the letter from Mr. Gilman and Craig,[2] so that letter reached here, no doubt, with the way properly paved for it. Of course I knew absolutely nothing about your mathematical equipment, but I said all in general that you could desire. It would be a genuine pleasure to have you here.[3] We remember our afternoon together at Mrs. Bird's with the utmost satisfaction.

With much regard,

Sincerely Yours,   Woodrow Wilson

WWTLS (WP, DLC).
[1] A.B., the Johns Hopkins, 1889; graduate student in chemistry, same institution, 1892-93.
[2] President D. C. Gilman and Thomas Craig, Professor of Mathematics at the Johns Hopkins.
[3] Reid was appointed Instructor in Mathematics at Princeton in 1893.

To Charles William Kent

My dear Kent,   Princeton, New Jersey, 18 April, 1893.

It was a genuine pleasure to get your letter of the 13th., particularly as it brought the welcome news of your coming. I am truly delighted. Only one thing mars my satisfaction. I must start for Chicago, to meet an engagement,[1] on the afternoon of

Wednesday, April 26, the day after you promise to come, and I fear that I shall on that account see less of you than I otherwise might. You *can* stay more than twenty-four hours, can't you?— you must if you possibly can; and if that is possible could you not make your visit to Boston first and stop with me on the way *back*, so as to stay as much longer with me as your engagements will permit? If you cannot stay longer than twenty-four hours, come on the twenty-fifth or on your way back, as will best suit your plans already formed; but if the later time will allow you a longer stay, by all means choose it. I want just as much of you as I can get.

I heartily congratulate you, my dear fellow, on your election to a chair in the dear old University,[2] and I hope for you a long career of distinction in it. But these things are to be talked over, not written about when something so much better than a letter is at hand.

With most cordial regards,
Your sincere friend,   Woodrow Wilson

P.S. If your successor has not been chosen yet at Knoxville, I should like very much to interest you in an excellent candidate, my own brother in law, about whom I have just written to Dr. Dabney.[3]   W. W.

WWTLS (Tucker-Harrison-Smith Coll., ViU).
[1] The speech to the Princeton alumni of Chicago on April 28. See the news report printed at April 29, 1893.
[2] Kent had just been named Professor of English Literature, Rhetoric, and Belles Lettres at the University of Virginia.
[3] Charles William Dabney, President of the University of Tennessee.

An Announcement

[April 18, 1893]

COLLATERAL READING.

In addition to the books suggested for collateral reading in the various courses, as published last evening, the following works are recommended by Prof. Wilson: In Administration—Bryce's "American Commonwealth," Parts I., II. Trail's "Central Government" (in the "English Citizen Series"). Chalmers' "Local Government" (in the same series). In Constitutional Law—Dicey's "Law of the Constitution." Fisk's "Critical Period of American History." Johnston's "First Century of the Constitution" in the "New Princeton Review," pp. 175-190 of Vol. IV. Burgess' "Political Science and Constitutional Law," Part I., Book III.; Part II., Book I.

Printed in the *Daily Princetonian*, April 18, 1893.

From the Minutes of the Princeton Faculty

5 5′ P.M., Wednesday, April 19, 1893.

. . . The Committee appointed to consider the New Method of Conducting Examinations reported that the Committee deemed it unadvisable at present to make any changes in the method of conducting the Examinations or in the existing rules in reference to the pledge exacted in connection with the written Examinations.

The Report of the Committee was approved. The Method of conducting the Examinations in the Freshman Class was referred to the Committee on the Freshman Class.

Longmans, Green, & Company to Albert Bushnell Hart

Dear Sir,   New York, April 19, 1893

We are likely to send Wilson's "Division & Reunion" to press with a second edition almost at once & in answer to a letter addressed to the author asking for corrections he sends us the enclosed which we have forwarded to the printers with instructions to proceed.[1] Before ordering the book to press however we should like to know whether you have any other suggestions to make with regard to corrections. These Dr. Wilson sends are all easily made.   Yours very truly   Longmans Green & Co.

TCL (RSB Coll., DLC).
[1] Wilson's correction sheet is missing. However, his emendations for the new edition, written in longhand and shorthand on the margins of the pages, appear in the copy of *Division and Reunion* now in the possession of Robert Reidy Cullinane, Washington, D.C.

From Cyrus Hall McCormick

My Dear Friend: [Chicago] April 21st 1893

Your note of the 18th[1] is received on my return to the city this morning. I shall look for you on Thursday evening the 27th, and will make an arrangement with Coulter, the Principal of the University School for you to address the boys on Friday morning. It will be a pleasure to you, and will be of great interest to the boys. When President Elliott, of Harvard, was here, he made an address to them which produced a very favorable impression. A visit by Professors of Princeton to these schools keeps up the connection and reminds them of the progress of the institution.
                    Yours sincerely,   Cyrus H. McCormick

TLS (C. H. McCormick Letterpress Books, WHi).
[1] It is missing.

Cyrus Hall McCormick to Eugene Calvin Coulter

Dear Mr. Coulter: [Chicago] April 21st 1893

I have just received a note from Prof. Wilson, saying he arrives here Thursday evening, the 27th. He will be at liberty all of Friday morning, and we will come to school at any time you may suggest as most convenient.

Yours very truly,   Cyrus H. McCormick

TLS (C. H. McCormick Letterpress Books, WHi).

The London *Daily Chronicle*'s Review of *Division and Reunion*

[April 21, 1893]

THE GROWTH OF A GREAT STATE.

"Division and Reunion. 1829-1889." By Woodrow Wilson, Ph.D., LL.D. (London: Longmans, Green and Co.)

Mr. Woodrow Wilson has already made an honourable reputation for himself as a political thinker by his work on "Congressional Government," in which he insists on the vast and growing powers of the Speaker of the House of Representatives as the central fact in American politics. In the present little work, which is one of the Epochs of American History Series, Mr. Wilson considers the period of sixty years from the accession of General Jackson to the Presidency down to the defeat of Mr. Cleveland in 1889. Mr. Wilson says of his own book that "it is not so much a compact narrative as a rapid synopsis," and therefore we must, of course, expect to find some events passed rapidly over which might have deserved in a larger work a more extended treatment. But in the main this book is a most lucid and admirable account of two generations of American political progress. The Presidency of Jackson began a new era in the United States in many ways. Jackson was a rough, powerful soldier, a popular idol, and his election broke down the old tradition of filling the Presidential chair with scholarly gentlemen of the old school. Besides, Jackson believed in rewarding his friends and punishing his enemies, and to him is due the beginning of the "spoils" system in American politics. At the same time the suffrage began to be widened, and the old barriers of class distinction fell before the Democratic onset. The "caucus" with its "bosses" and their hold over the nominating conventions began to develop those tendencies which we now see fully grown

into fixed political habits. The railway system, the new indus-
trialism, European immigration, the growth of towns, the opening up of the West, Labour disputes, war on monopolies like the
United States Bank—all these great factors came into operation
about this time, thus converting the old simple agricultural States
of the early century into the vast complex nation we know now.

Mr. Woodrow Wilson has first brought out very clearly that the
United States at first were not only not democratic, but that the
Constitution was very carefully framed in the interests of money
and monopoly. The "glittering generalities" of the Declaration of
Independence found a strong counteractive in the conservative
legal mechanism which Hamilton devised for preventing the
people from having their own way. Although there came a vigorous Democratic outburst under Jefferson, yet in the main conservatism prevailed for the first forty years of the Republic's
existence: and this conservatism was aided by a revulsion against
revolutionary excesses in France. But with Jackson the rule of
the common people began; and fastidious observers will perhaps
add that the era of vulgarity began. Perhaps so, but at least there
was life in place of the prim decorum which had marked the
earlier period; and the new life showed itself in new and vigorous literary and religious as well as political developments. We
cannot have everything in this world; and it is better, perhaps,
to have vulgarity and life than gentility and death. In the second
place, Mr. Woodrow Wilson has shown with almost equal clearness the economic basis of the whole of American political controversy. Not only were the bank and tariff contest obviously
economic, but the slavery conflict was, except among the Abolitionist enthusiasts, essentially an economic conflict also, as
Cairnes had previously shown in that singularly lucid book, "The
Slave Power." Slavery prevented the South from sharing with the
North and West in the economic advantages of the new era of
railways and factories. Life in the South was organised on an
old-fashioned pre-scientific basis, and slavery did not pay. Hence
the frantic effects [efforts] to extend the sphere of its operations,
to make slave States of Kansas and Nebraska, to annex Cuba, &c.
Slavery must extend itself or die out, and if there had been no
Civil War, slavery would have perished all the same, provided the
Northerners could keep all the vast new territories closed to the
slave power.

And, in the third place, the author has also shown that the
merely legal forms of a Constitution can never stand in the way
of the permanent spirit and sense of the people. Much that
Jackson did would have horrified the founders of the Republic,

but he had the people behind him. The supreme instance of this, however, is Lincoln, whose policy all through was extra-constitutional. Though a Northener, Mr. Wilson is scrupulously fair to the Southern men, and he holds that the South had at least a strong case for their legal position until they began a direct onslaught on the Federal Power. On the other hand many of Lincoln's acts, such, *e.g.*, as his Emancipation Proclamation, had no legal authority whatsoever. Why then do we applaud and reverence Lincoln and condemn the South? Not on the mere superficial ground of vulgar success or failure, but because we see that the Southerners were wanting in insight into the true tendencies of their nation and age, and that men like Lee, however noble personally, were mere dreamers, while Lincoln was the embodiment of the national genius and temper. It is this penetration into the essence of American political history which makes Mr. Wilson such a safe guide. His chapter, too, on the Constitution and Government of the Confederate States is a good piece of work, which only a trained political thinker could have written. This history may be safely commended to English readers, who, as a rule, have but the vaguest notions about American politics, and who will learn a great deal from it. It is true that American history is lacking in the dramatic features which one finds in the history of Western Europe and of classical antiquity. If one is in search of the picturesque, American history does not afford it any more than the American Continent presents picturesque ruins. But if one understands with Professor Seeley that history is not the record of individuals but an intelligible account of the growth of States, then the reader ought to find interest in this modest but accurate and intelligent explanation of the growth of the greatest single State of modern times.

Printed in the London *Daily Chronicle*, April 21, 1893.

To Richard McIlwaine[1]

My dear Dr. McIlwaine,   Princeton, New Jersey, 23 April, 1893.

I take the liberty of addressing you upon a matter of business. I understand that the Professor of English at Hampden Sydney[2] has been called to fill the vacancy made in the faculty of the University of Tennessee by the election of my friend Kent to the new chair of English Literature in the University of Virginia; and I am very anxious to have you consider my brother-in-law, Stockton Axson, before choosing a new man for your own English department. I write now, not so much to present his name, as to ask your permission to present it more formally if you should feel disposed to consider it.

He is the grandson and namesake of the late Dr. I. S. K. Axson of Savannah. He has studied at the Johns Hopkins and with Professor Winchester and his colleagues at Wesleyan University, where there are much better advantages to be had in the study of English than at the Johns Hopkins, not only because Winchester, by reason of the rarest critical and lecturing powers, is one of the foremost men in the country, but also because they do not even attempt instruction in literature at Baltimore, confining themselves to what I cannot help regarding as a very narrow and unintelligent course in English philology. He has had what is, therefore, practically the best course in English in the country; and has the highest endorsements from his instructors. He is teaching this year in the University of Vermont, where he has had the most gratifying success, but where they cannot make room for him permanently because of arrangements made before he was engaged. He went simply to fill an *interim*. This is his first year of teaching.

I could myself give you the strongest assurances of the fine character and unus[u]al gifts and attainments of the man; but I should not ask you to consider him simply on my own recommendation. I would wish to present his formal credentials instead, if you will permit me to do so. I do not write at his request or with his knowledge, but entirely upon my own motion.

With much regard, and the hope that you have not forgotten me,   Very sincerely Yours,   Woodrow Wilson

WWTLS (WC, NjP).
    1 President of Hampden-Sydney College, 1883-1904.
    2 John Bell Henneman, Professor of English and History at Hampden-Sydney, 1889-93. Wilson had undoubtedly heard about Henneman's impending move to the University of Tennessee from C. W. Dabney or C. W. Kent.

From Joseph Ruggles Wilson

My precious son—   N. York, Ap. 25/93

I was glad to get your note of the 23d—although not at all grateful for its enclosed check[1] which I would immediately return if you had not written about it in such an imperative way as to cause me to believe that you would send it back to me; and so on indefinitely! Well, it will always be at your order when you shall want it, or more, or less.

I think you have made a good sale, and a wise one.[2] True, the part of the lot which you reserve is a little out of line with the best of property in that locality, yet it is good for building on if you should wish, or for selling,—one day—to advantage. Meanwhile you escape from a needless weight of debt—although you ought never to have regarded the $1,500 as a burden to make you uneasy. You well know that what is mine is yours to the fullest extent possible. This is an unwritten part of that law of love by which we are united so warmly, and by a tie that nothing can ever break—not even death I believe.

I have been very ill since you were here—the sciatic trouble having assumed its most acute form, and giving me such pain as I never felt—unless once—before. It put me to bed and into the doctor's hands. I am now up for the first time since Saturday (this is Tuesday)[.] The thing yielded to remedies, and has left me comparatively easy.

Thanking you an[d] dear Ellie for the love you bear a poor old fellow I am as ever, to you both, the loving

Father.

Jessie[3] has been to see me—twice—and was very affectionate—bringing me flowers, &c. She is a dear good girl, and very proud of a certain brace of cousins

ALS (WP, DLC).
  [1] Woodrow Wilson was paying back the $1,500 he had borrowed from his father for the purchase of a lot on Washington Street two years before. See JRW to WW, May 11, 1891, Vol. 7.
  [2] On April 19, 1893, Wilson had sold a two-hundred-foot frontage of his lot on the Prospect Avenue side to John Grier Hibben for $4,500. See the printed purchase agreement with handwritten entries, dated April 19, 1893 (WP, DLC). For a precise definition of the boundaries of the lot that Hibben bought, see "Description of Prof. J. G. Hibben's lot," by Walter B. Harris, civil engineer of Princeton, dated May 2, 1893 (WP, DLC), prepared, undoubtedly, before Wilson conveyed title to the lot to Hibben.
  [3] Probably Jessie Bones Brower.

From Horace Elisha Scudder

My dear Wilson   [Cambridge, Mass.] 27 April 1893

What do you say to adding the two new volumes of Sumner[1] and Morse's Lincoln[2] to your review? If you would like to take these and need more time I can give you another month, though if you do Rhodes alone I would prefer to keep to the time already named. Don't you think times have changed when the *Atlantic* asks a Southerner to review Lincoln and Sumner?

Yours ever   H. E. Scudder.

ALS (Houghton Mifflin Letterpress Books, MH).
  [1] Edward L. Pierce, *Memoir and Letters of Charles Sumner*, Vols. III and IV (Boston, 1893).
  [2] John T. Morse, Jr., *Abraham Lincoln*, "American Statesmen" series (Boston and New York, 1893).
  [3] Wilson's reply is missing, but he did review the two books in the review article printed at Aug. 1, 1893.

From William Henry Bartlett

Dear Sir: Worcester, Mass. Apr. 29, 1893

I write you at the request of several gentlemen residents of this city, some of whom served with distinction in the Union army and all of whom are deeply interested in all that pertains to the Civil War and the principles on which it was fought.

These gentlemen have read your work entitled, unfortunately, as they think, "Division and Reunion." To some of them your work seems to teach the doctrine of secession as legitimate and proper, and further that some of the Southern States did actually secede and by that act divided the United States into two distinct national entities. They hold this to be the drift of your argument and they quote your words on p. 212, "The South withdrew from the Union etc." in support of their interpretation. They contend that if this position be allowed, it follows that the States which passed ordinances of secession were during the war to all intents and purposes a foreign country and that the soldiers of the Union were only an army of conquest employed to subjugate a foreign foe. Such a doctrine they consider wrong in principle, dangerous in tendency and disparaging to the motives of the Union soldiers who fought not to form a "New Union" but to defend and preserve a Union which they believed and proved to be indissoluble.

These gentlemen think that if their understanding of your position is correct they ought not to let your statements go un-challenged especially in view of the fact that your work is in-tended for use in schools and colleges, and they have requested me, as one who has an interest in this question both as soldier and teacher to ask you if they have fairly and justly interpreted your position.

A reply as early as may suit your convenience will greatly oblige   Yours Very Truly   W H Bartlett,

Com'dr Post No. 10 G.A.R. and Prin. Chandler St. School, Wor-cester, Mass.

ALS (WP, DLC) with WWhw notation on env.: "Ans. 3 May, 1893" and WWT notation: "What is the matter with this machine?"

A Newspaper Report of an Alumni Meeting in Chicago

[April 29, 1893]

PRAISE OF OLD NASSAU.

REUNION OF PRINCETON GRADUATES.

It was Princeton's turn at the University club last evening. The proud sons of the old New England college resident in Chicago gathered in the large banquet hall to celebrate with feast, speech and song the praises of their alma mater. And this they did with loyal spirit and with hearty good cheer. They listened also to charming addresses by distinguished guests, each one of whom they cheered to the echo, following up the cheer with a Princeton tiger and rocket. They sang time and again with the vim of undergraduates at a mock funeral, but the song that stirred them most was the distinctive Princeton hymn, "Old Nassau."

> Tune every heart and every voice,
>> Bid every care withdraw;
> Let all with one accord rejoice
>> In praise of "Old Nassau."

. . . The banquet was served at a number of small tables so arranged that every person present sat facing or half facing the table at which sat the president and his guests. Tomaso's mandolin orchestra occupied the balcony and regaled the company with delightful music between the courses. Rev. Thomas C. Hall presided at the after-dinner exercises, and his little speeches introducing the speakers of the evening were charmingly graceful and witty. The first one he called on was Professor Wilson.[1] He told the assembled alumni that the professor was an "antiquity" of the class of '79, in which he himself graduated, but added that he was very modern and progressive in his scholarship. Professor Wilson made a speech in which he proved himself to be both a wit and a thinker, and when he cracked a joke of which a clergyman happened to be the kernel no one smiled more broadly over it than Rev. Mr. Hall. Professor Wilson said he felt very much at home. In some subtle manner which he could not explain he could always tell a Princeton crowd when he saw one, and he always had a good time when with a Princeton crowd. He then became serious and talked of the differences in character of state universities and private institutions like Yale and Harvard and Princeton. He said:

> In a state university you must act upon common lines, which represent the common sentiment and desire of the community with reference to educational questions. In an institution like

Princeton we can reach standards of our own without regard to universal lines of action on which the community is all agreed. We can experiment and reach new results. It is the same difference that there is between a private school and a public school. German and drawing and other so-called fads may be excluded from the public schools, but you can try all the fads you please in a private school. In a private college you have men of kindred spirit, met together in the formation of character, and thus Princeton and the other great private colleges turn out men with certain characteristics imbibed within their precincts. I believe in state universities and would like to see every state with one, but the differences I have pointed out are always apparent.

Professor Wilson then spoke of some of Princeton's distinguished characteristics, particularly her record and influence with respect to the subject of history. He claimed that for a distinctively American institution of learning the two things to be developed were the study of law and literature. These were inseparably linked together. Continuing, he said:

> You can learn more of the institutions of a free nation from its poetry than from the works of formal writers on laws and constitutions. We have ceased to be a properly political race because we do not go to the old fountains of inspiration. In order to rehabilitate ourselves we want to make the legal profession a learned profession again. Our lawyers, especially our young lawyers, have become a body of experts in a technical business. They used to go far back of their law books and seek in the literary treasures of the race for the spirit and circumstances that produced those laws. Literature and law are in every way interpretative of each other.

. . . "Old Nassau" again reverberated among the rafters, and at midnight the company broke up with rousing cheers for alma mater.

Printed in the *Chicago Herald*, April 29, 1893; some editorial headings omitted.
    [1] Wilson's notes for this address, headed "Chicago, 28 April," are on loose pages in WP, DLC.

From John Irenaeus McCain

Erskine College, Due West, S. C.

Dear Prof. Wilson: April 29, 1893.

I have read with much pleasure your volume on Division and Reunion; and, in accordance with your request, I write this letter to let you know how I think a school history written from the same standpoint would be received by the people of the South. It is my opinion that such a history would be heartily endorsed by the vast majority of the people. Some persons of the rather "unreconstructed" type might think that there ought to be a more decided leaning toward the Southern side. But it seems to me that the position you take in your recent volume is just to the South and just also to the North, and I think that thoughtful men generally would say so. I noticed one expression, I might say, that I think it would not be well to use in a school history. It is found on page 239, and reads, "And all for a belated principle of government, an outgrown economy." It sometimes happens that a work is objected to because of some single expression that might have been left out without any sacrifice of truth or without any yielding of an author's view.

I have told you briefly but candidly how I think a history from your standpoint would be received in the South, and I would say in conclusion that I should be delighted to see such a work appear. I hope you may see your way clear to write the book.

Yours very truly,   J. I. McCain

ALS (WP, DLC) with WWhw notation on env.: "Ans. 4 May, '93."

Kemp Plummer Battle's Review of *Division and Reunion*

[May 1893]

DIVISION AND REUNION. 1829-1889. By Woodrow Wilson, Ph.D., LL.D. 16-mo., pp. 345, $1.25. New York: *Longmans, Green & Co.*

This is the third and last volume of the Epoch of American History, edited by Dr. Albert Bushnell Hart. Its accomplished author maintains the high reputation acquired by his two previous works and makes us all the more proud that he is Southern born. His father is an eminent minister of the Presbyterian Church; born in Virginia; in charge for ten years of a church in Wilmington, North Carolina, and now professor of a college in Tennessee. Dr. Woodrow Wilson has spent his mature years mainly in Pennsylvania and New Jersey. We are glad to see that he has been successful in viewing all sides of the questions which arose in the epoch of which he writes with the eye of the philosophic seeker of truth. While in all probability he will not satisfy extremists North or South, he has come as near to the Right as any writer has done or, in our opinion, will be able to do. He refrains from impeaching the motives of public men. He assumes their honesty and endeavors to look at the political issues through their eyes. He sums up the arguments on both sides with the impartiality of an upright judge charging a jury. Take for example his conclusion as to the conduct of Georgia towards the Cherokees: "Those who would judge for themselves between Georgia and the Cherokees must resolve this point of law: If the power of the Federal Executive to negotiate treaties be added to the power of Congress to regulate commerce with the Indian tribes, do they together furnish a sanction for the erection of a permanent independent State within the territory of one of the members of the Union, and so override that other provision of the Constitution which declares that 'no new State shall be formed or erected within the jurisdiction of any other State' without the express consent of the Legislature of that State and of Congress. Judgment was passed upon the law of the case by the Supreme Court and Jackson should unquestionably have yielded obedience to that judgment; but the point of law is a nice one."

Again, take his conclusions as to the treatment of slaves: "Scarcely any generalization that could be formed would be true for the whole South, or even for all periods alike in any one section of it. Slavery showed at its worst where it was most seen by observers from the North—upon its edges." . . . "In the heart of the South conditions were different, were more normal. Domestic slaves were almost uniformly dealt with indulgently, even affectionately, by their masters." . . . "The negroes suffered most upon the larger properties, where they were under the sole direction of hired overseers." . . . "Books like Mrs. Stowe's 'Uncle Tom's Cabin,' which stirred the pity and deep indignation of Northern readers, certainly depicted possible cases of inhuman conduct towards slaves. Such cases there may have been; they may have been frequent, but they were in every sense exceptional, showing what the system could produce, rather than what it did produce as its characteristic spirit and method. For public opinion in the South, while it recognized the necessity for maintaining the discipline of subordination among the hosts of slaves, was as intolerant of the graver forms of cruelty as was the opinion of the best people in the North." . . . "Even in the ruder communities public opinion demanded that when negroes were sold families should be kept together, particularly mothers and their children."

We know that these statements are true as to North Carolina, and we venture the assertion with confidence that, judging from the reports of cruelty to wives and children by drunken husbands in the slums of great cities, there is as much physical suffering there as was inflicted by the worst of masters. Even such masters protected their dependents from cruelty to one another.

We regret that we have not space for more quotations from

this uncommonly strong, impartial, interesting book. Giving only enough facts to elucidate the matters discussed, it omits no important questions. It furnishes the reader clear-cut views of the right and the wrong of them all. It gives admirable pen-portraits of the great personages of the period with as much freedom from bias and as much pains to be just as if the author were delineating Pericles or Alcibiades, Sulla or Cæsar. Dr. Wilson has earned the gratitude of seekers after truth by his masterly production.[1]

Printed in the *North Carolina University Magazine*, New Series, XII (May 1893), 283-85.
[1] For Wilson's grateful comment, see WW to K. P. Battle, June 29, 1893.

From the Minutes of the Princeton Faculty

5 5′ P.M.   Wednesday, May 3, 1893

... The Committee on Discipline reported on the case of Mr. —— who had been negligent, intoxicated & disorderly. It was *Resolved* That Mr. —— of the Freshman Class be suspended until the end of the present term, on account both of disorderly conduct and persistent neglect of duty; that he be required to take a Tutor in all his studies during his suspension; and be required to present himself for Examination in June.[1]

[1] Hearings on this case, dated May 2, 1893, are recorded in the body of WWsh notes described in Princeton Faculty Minutes, Sept. 23, 1891, n. 1, Vol. 7.

To William Henry Bartlett

[Dear Sir,]   [Princeton, N. J., May 3, 1893]

This is the rule I have followed in my treatment of the question of secession. It does not seem to me possible successfully to deny that the Constitution was viewed differently at different times or that the view held of it in the South was a view very generally entertained throughout the states at the first. This is merely a question of fact. But it does not do to stop there. Let me, for the sake of brevity, put the matter thus. If the Constitution is a mere document it must be dealt with, by lawyers at any rate, as other documents are: It must be interpreted by the intentions and views of those who framed it. I do not think that the generation which saw the Constitution framed would have denied the theoretical right of secession (see, among other authorities, Schurz); and if we are to treat the Constitution as a mere legal document, I think that we must take this lawyer's view of it. But I do not think that a Constitution can be treated in that way (see Division and Reunion, p.   ). It is a vehicle of life. Looking at it from the statesman's point of view, we must see that, whereas the right of secession may have existed (theoretically) at the first, it presently ceased to exist by reason of the growth of national sentiment, which put into the Constitution the new life of the nation. It had been thus changed before the period of the Civil War arrived. Looked at from a third point of view, the moralist's, I think it must be conceded that the right of secession never did exist: It was bad political morals to fling out of the game so soon as it went against you.

I hold most decisively, therefore, that the right of secession did not exist at the time the South sought to exercise that right, whatever might have been the rights of a state in the first years of the century. I hold that a Government is what its people and its history make it and that our Government had been made national and indissoluble long before 1861; though there are many evidences that even the North had not fully realized that fact until the war came and the new national spirit asserted itself. It is in this way that I try to keep to the facts of the case. The same distinctions between fact and theory are to be kept steadily in mind in connection with the other question which you propound, namely did some of the states actually withdraw from the Union. In fact they obviously did; in theory, having no right to do so, they as obviously did not. The facts are plain enough. The principal southern states were independently governed for the greater part of the period covered by the war. Their governments were in actual separate operation. But this does not mean that the northern soldiers were fighting a foreign power. Their right existed in their conviction, in what seems to me their just conviction, that the South was wholly in the wrong. Our history had effected a fundamental change in our constituent law and the South was making a revolutionary attempt to turn back her development to its origins. Their separateness was a revolutionary separateness and the northern soldiers were preventing a fatal revolution. They need no further justification than that.

The legal theory of the whole matter, though not a little confused as it seems to me, and not a little marred by inconsistency, has been settled for us of course [by the Supreme Court's declaration][1] that the southern states were never legally out of the Union. Their matter-of-fact revolutionary separation from the Union for a time does not affect this theory at all. But the historian must narrate the facts as well as state the theories.

These, sir, are the considerations which guided my treatment of the whole matter in my late volume. I have no fear that you will either misunderstand or reject them as unsound. History must be written in this way, or not written at all.

[Sincerely yours,   Woodrow Wilson]

Transcript of WWshL (draft) (WP, DLC), with WWhw and WWsh heading "Was secession legitimate and proper? Did some of the States actually secede?"
¹ The words in brackets are the Editors'. The shorthand outlines were blotted out.

To John Irenaeus McCain

My dear Prof. McCain,   Princeton, New Jersey, 4 May, 1893.

I am sincerely obliged to you for your very kind letter of April 29. I need hardly say that its contents gratify me very deeply. I would rather win commendation for impartiality from men like yourself in the South than from any other quarter.

What you say about the possible effects of an unnecessary phrase or two I appreciate fully. It is perfectly true. In a school history such expressions could very well be omitted without any change at all of the essential point of view.

I certainly have the strongest inclination to attempt such a history, particularly after the encouragement you have given me. Whether I shall be able to do so in addition to the other work which I have promised myself to do remains to be seen. But I will certainly give the matter very serious consideration, with the purpose of undertaking it if possible.

With renewed thanks for your kindness,

Very sincerely Yours,   Woodrow Wilson

WWTLS (in possession of Charles R. McCain).

A News Report

[May 5, 1893]

PHILADELPHIAN MEETING.

Prof. Woodrow Wilson addressed the meeting of the Philadelphian Society held in Murray Hall yesterday evening. Taking as his theme the practical philosophy of life taught by the Bible, the speaker said that the righteous man should not be long-faced or morose, but joyful, diligent, fervent in spirit. We are to-day living in the light and we should seize every opportunity for doing our whole duty. Above all, let us not be frivolous, but serious in the proper sense, as on that depends our future success.

Printed in the *Daily Princetonian*, May 5, 1893.

An Announcement

[May 5, 1893]

Prof. Woodrow Wilson will conduct the services in Marquand Chapel on Sunday morning [May 7].

Printed in the *Daily Princetonian*, May 5, 1893.

Notes for a Chapel Talk

May 7, 1893.

ISAIAH, LXI.   Liberty.

Parellel Text: *Galatians*, V., 1., "Stand fast, therefore, in the liberty wherewith Christ hath made us free, and be not entangled again with the yoke of bondage." Where it stands without explanatory or argumentative context.
This chapter a sort of *Charter of Liberties*:
Jural Freedom: the right to make a choice;
Moral Freedom: choice of that which is good.
      A *likeness* between the two, *nevertheless*. A man comes under civil bondage when he chooses that which is unlawful, under moral bondage when he chooses that which is evil. "Sin is the transgression of the *law*."
Bondage of the *kite* and of the *sailing vessel*, held fast by an external force; freedom of the steamer, having an originative force in its own bowels.
Our *instinctive homage to the equable and elevated* in character, demeanor, utterance,—not the quick shot, but the crack shot. *The impotency of irregular force*. The absence of dignity from an acident.
Read the last verse of the chapter: the forces of nature producing unobstructed and after their own kind.
Freedom means the best order: the machine free that runs with perfect adjustment, without friction; the skein free that is without tangle; the man free whose powers are without impediment to their best development.
The highest freedom rightly conceived to be *self-government*, self-direction, a self-originated rectitude, a self-sustained order.

WWT MS. (WP, DLC).

To Richard McIlwaine

My dear Dr. McIlwaine,   Princeton, New Jersey, 9 May, 1893.

When I wrote to you I had not consulted my brother-in-law as to his becoming a candidate; but I forwarded your exceedingly kind reply to him, and I have no doubt that he will become a candidate. He was elected to his present place, as I believe I explained in my former letter, only to fill an *interim*, and had supposed that there was no room for either his promotion or retention; but they are apparently trying to make a place for him there, and he feels bound to defer to their wishes, at least for a few days, until they can canvass the possibilities. I will write at once for letters concerning him to Wesleyan, where he is best known; and he will forward, no doubt, testimonials from the authorities of the University of Vermont.

Meanwhile, let me give you some general preliminary account of him.

His Freshman year of college training he took at Davidson College, from which he withdrew, however, on account of his health. When ready to go on he took two years at the University of Georgia, in Athens, and then, at my advice, he went to Wesleyan University, Middletown, Conn., to take his Senior year with Prof. C. T. Winchester, unquestionably the best professor of English Literature in the country, in my opinion, and rapidly gaining recognition as such, as fast as his modesty will permit him to become known. Axson was already looking forward to teaching literature, and so took double work, under Winchester, whose confidence and admiration he immediately won. Despite double work in one department, he graduated with distinction, with very unusual distinction, in a very strong class.

After graduation he studied one year at the Johns Hopkins, and (because very justly dissatisfied with the character of the instruction there) another with Mr. Winchester again, and with Mr. [William Edward] Mead, the admirable philological instructor who had, meantime, been added to the Wesleyan faculty. Then he went to his present temporary post in the University of Vermont, as instructor in English.

Of his training in History and Political Science I suppose that I am the only person who can speak with any degree of authority, for such training as he has gotten from anyone but himself in these branches he got from me. English and American history he has studied with a keen appetite in connection with his study of English. I do not think that he would experience the least embarrassment in teaching them. And his aptitsde [aptitude] for political studies evinced in my class room at Wesleyan makes me equally confident that he could soon make himself at home there.

He will be twenty-six the first of next month. He is not the son of Mr. Randolph Axson, but of his brother, the Rev. S. E. Axson, for a great many years pastor in Rome, Georgia. He is a fellow of charming personality and manners, with whom everybody falls in love as promptly as his friends could desire. There is a certain very attractive distinction about his bearing, marking him a southern gentleman. He has, besides, found out now that teaching is his proper vocation (he doubted his talents at first for that function), and, his former self-distrust being measureably thrown off, makes his enthusiasm for his studies the more contagious. I think that I can say (so far as anyone can speak with confidence on so intimate a matter of private belief) that his religious views are perfectly straight and sound on every essential tenet of the Christian faith.

I shall ask Professors Winchester and Mead to write directly to you. Dr. Boggs[1] would probably be glad to make his contribution, if you should ask him.

With warmest regard,

Most sincerely Yours,   Woodrow Wilson

WWTLS (WC, NjP).
[1] William Ellison Boggs, Chancellor of the University of Georgia.

From Azel Washburn Hazen

My dear Dr Wilson: Middletown, Conn.   13 May 1893.

I cannot refrain from expressing the pleasure I felt in seeing even a poor likeness of you in the Review of Reviews.[1] It called up scores of happy memories. Then the clever piece of writing on the Cabinet I much enjoyed, also.

You may be indifferent to merely provincial fame, but I venture to send you a notice of your recent book, from the Hartford Courant of this morning.[2] It is supposed to be from the pen of Richard Burton.[3] I am hoping for the stimulus of reading the volume soon.

Our connections with Princeton are so many, that I frequently get enthusiastic words concerning yourself and your charming wife[.] Dr Bradley[4] you know is now in your old home here, but it is not the place it once was for me

Mrs Hazen joins me in love to Mrs. Wilson & yourself.

Believe me as ever

Affectionately yours,   A. W. Hazen

ALS (WP, DLC) with WWhw notation on env.: "Ans. 17 May/93." Enc.: clipping of a review of Division and Reunion from the Hartford Courant, May 13, 1893.
[1] Wilson's photograph by Pach Brothers was reproduced along with an unsigned review of Division and Reunion in the New York Review of Reviews, VII (April 1893), 364.

2 It was a glowing review which said, among other things, that *Division and Reunion* was the best book of the "Epochs of American History" series.

3 Poet and literary critic, at this time literary editor of the *Hartford Courant.*

4 Walter Parke Bradley, Associate Professor of Chemistry at Wesleyan University.

To Caleb Thomas Winchester

My dear friend,   Princeton, New Jersey, 13 May, 1893

It would have been difficult for you to make to me a more attractive proposition than this, to edit Burke for your series.[1] Anything you should ask me to do I should be inclined to do, simply because of my affection for you; but this particular thing tempts me in a peculiar degree. If I should claim any man as my master, that man would be Burke. I am this summer going to write a lecture on him,[2]—and why not an Introduction? All work put on a text of his would be labour of love. But must not a man decide what is to be his principal work, and set himself firmly to do that, being chary of taking out a year or fifteen months from his life for anything else. For the first time since I was at all fit to do systematic work I am now free to do it: lecture courses in shape and all *jobs promised to publishers* done and off my conscience. What I have planned to do in the field of systematic political exposition will take all my best energy and all the rest of my probable life. I fret and am uneasy till I get at it. And so I *must* decline.   [Most cordially Yours,   Woodrow Wilson]

AL (CtW); last page of letter missing.

1 Winchester and George Lyman Kittredge were editors of the Athenaeum Press Series, in English literature, published by Ginn and Company from 1890 to 1906.

2 Wilson's lecture on Burke is printed at Aug. 31, 1893.

To Charles Scribner

My dear Sir,   Princeton, New Jersey, 16 May, 1893.

Acting upon the suggestion of my friend, Robert Bridges, I take the liberty of sending you copies of five essays[1] which I hope you will find suitable for publication in a small volume.[2]

I have arranged and numbered the essays in what seems to me their most natural and most logical order, with a view to giving the collection a certain degree of unity. I think that, if made up into a volume, they might very well take the title of the first essay. The title page might read, "An Old Master, and Other Political Essays,"—'political' in order to avoid creating the impression that they are concerned with the old masters of quite another art!

I send the essays without any altering touches, in order that you may judge them at their worst as a *collection*. If you think them worthy of publishing together, I should like to make alterations in the detail of their treatment throughout: and in one of them, the last ("Responsible Government under the Constitution") some rather radical changes.[3]

With much regard,

Very sincerely Yours,   Woodrow Wilson

WWTLS (Charles Scribner's Sons Archives, NjP).

[1] Wilson sent reprints or tear sheets of "An Old Master," printed at Feb. 1, 1887, Vol. 5; "The Study of Politics," printed at Nov. 25, 1886, Vol. 5; "Character of Democracy in the United States," the first version of which is printed at May 10, 1889, Vol. 6; and "Responsible Government under the Constitution," printed at Feb. 10, 1886, Vol. 5. He also included a new draft of "Political Sovereignty," printed at Nov. 9, 1891, Vol. 7. This new draft is in WP, DLC, as are the reprints that he sent to Scribner.

That Wilson had earlier contemplated writing a new essay for the projected book (and abandoned the idea by the time that he wrote this letter) is suggested by the following fragment of a memorandum (WP, DLC):

'Political Fact'

Might not a chapter be written on *political fact*[,] what it is, and how to be discerned?

A writer [Irving Berdine Richman] in the *Atlantic Monthly* for August 1889, assumes, in an article entitled "Law and Political Fact in the United States," that the lodgment of sovereignty in the electors of the several states acting together as the law-making power of the Union (in accordance with the Austinian definition) is the single 'political fact' at the basis of our law, while tradition and opinion are not political facts because inconsistent with the idea of such a lodgment. Looked at from another point of view, his statement of the lodgment of sovereignty in the U. S. is not a fact at all, but only a necessary logical conclusion from the Austinian analysis: and the real facts are the tradition and opinion which he rejects. The only soil stiff enough to bear the weight of the huge (and now complicated) structure of law is the soil of *habit*. Which 'political fact' is to be [blank]

[2] Charles Scribner's Sons did publish the essays later in 1893 under Wilson's title, *An Old Master and Other Political Essays*.

[3] That Wilson made only minor changes in the other four essays can be seen by comparing the versions printed in *An Old Master* with those printed in this series or, again, by seeing Wilson's changes in the reprints which he later sent in as copy for the printer. However, he made very extensive changes in a new draft of "Responsible Government under the Constitution," even altering the title in *An Old Master* to "Government under the Constitution." His revised essay is printed at June 26, 1893, with a note about Wilson's copy.

To Charles William Kent

My dear Kent,   Princeton, New Jersey, 17 May, 1893.

I did not get a chance while you were here to tell you of Axson what you wanted to know in case Henneman should seek your advice about the filling of the Hampden-Sidney chair. Fortunately I can tell you what there is to tell without lenghty [lengthy] discourse, and so I will put it into this letter. I can make it very brief simply because I know my ground so well and can be so certain of my propositions that limiting explanations are not necessary.

In the first place, Axson is an exceptionally charming fellow. Anybody who knew the distinguishing marks of a southern gentleman would identify him as one at once. He seems to attract all sorts of people, and would certainly find the greatest ease in attaching young men to him. In the second place, he certainly possesses a very rare capacity of literary discrimination. He is author's kin unmistakably. His enthusiasm is catching; and yet it is not enthusiasm unbalanced by judgment. He has a very catholic capacity of critical judgment, seeming to experience a certain pleasure in correcting his own too partial preferences for particular authors. He regards literature and methods of teaching it in just the light in which we so delightfully agreed the other evening that it ought to be taught and studied. Nor does he lack philological training and accuracy. I can say in all candour that I do not know of any man whom it would so well pay Hampden-Sidney to take young and enjoy during the period when he is coming to full maturity under the influence of the best ideals. The very variety of the work to be done there would argue to the same purpose. They ought to have a man in his lithe youth. It is not necessary for me to say more to you, I feel sure; for you know that I mean every word, and mean it carefully. I have already given to Dr. McIlwaine a detailed account of Axson's training; and he will hear more about that from Winchester.

I cannot tell you, Charlie, how much Mrs. Wilson and I enjoyed your little visit to us. It did me a vast deal of good. I had forgotten how completely we were of one mind; I did not realize how closely we had kept together since those old University days when we started together. Your visit, consequently, gave me that most heartening of all assurances, the assurance of the company of a loved friend in respect of the things my interests and hopes are most centered upon.

Mrs. Wilson joins me in the very warmest regards.
Affectionately Yours,   Woodrow Wilson

P.S. Axson is now definitely a candidate for the H. S. chair.
W.W.

WWTLS (Tucker-Harrison-Smith Coll., ViU).

To William Ellison Boggs

My dear Dr Boggs,   Princeton, New Jersey, 17 May, 1893
I trust that you will not esteem it an unwarrantable liberty on my part if I address you on a matter affecting the University [of Georgia] without having been asked my advice.

I understand that the chair of English in the University is vacant, and I write to call your attention very earnestly to my brother-in-law, Mr. Stockton Axson, as a candidate for the vacancy. I believe that in so doing I am seeking to render the University a real service, for a man of rarer endowments or a more brilliant promise I do not know. I am pretty familiar, for various reasons, with the available academic supply in English (knowing very well, for example, and condemning very heartily the methods of training at the Johns Hopkins); and I can say with no little confidence that Mr. Axson seems to me surer of the higher kind of success than any other man I know of. He has had admirable training added to a quite exceptional natural capacity for the sort of work he has chosen.

He took his Senior year, by my advice, at Wesleyan University, where I was then teaching; for I knew his desire to become a professor of English and I was convinced that Prof. Winchester of Wesleyan (who has been kept from the enjoyment of a world-wide reputation only by his own extraordinary modesty) was the best teacher of English in the country. Axson took double work under him, and immediately won both his confidence and his admiration. In spite of his devotion of a large proportion of his time to English, however, Axson graduated among the very first men in a large and strong class (in June, 1890). Prof. Winchester pronounced him the most brilliant student he had ever had, being particularly struck by his mature powers as a writer and speaker, and his very singular penetration as a thinker.

After graduation he took a year of graduate study at the Johns Hopkins. The year was not satisfactory to him. He returned for a second year of graduate study at Middletown. Winchester had, in the meantime, been reinforced by the appointment of an admirable philologist to the Wesleyan faculty. Winchester's own teaching has always been exclusively in the field of literature. From Prof. Mead, the newly appointed philologist, Axson got what he had hoped to secure in Baltimore, thoroughly competent guidance in philological study.

I believe that it can be said that Axson thus obtained the most thorough and intelligent training obtainable in this country, little as is known of Wesleyan in the country at large.

This past academic year he has been instructor in English at the University of Vermont, where he has had both rhetorical work with the lower classes and advanced literary work with the Seniors. His success has been extraordinary. He does not mean to retain the place because the line of promotion is practically blocked completely and because he finds the climate intolerable;

but one of his friends in the faculty had to lock several of the students up in his own room in order to restrain them long enough from their project of petitioning the trustees of the University to remove the head of the English department and put Axson in his place to convince them of its folly and of the scandal it might create!

Mr. Axson is twenty-six years old; but remarkably mature for his years. I have no more satisfactory intellectual companion than he. He is a fellow of charming address, a real southern gentleman. He is the son of the Rev. S. E. Axson, who was for many years pastor of the Presbyterian church in Rome, Georgia,— and grandson of Dr. I. S. K. Axson, of the Independent Church of Savannah.

I trust you will pardon this very long letter. I have praised Axson in the strongest terms because I am sure of my ground, not relying wholly on my own judgment, and having the very concrete evidence of his very unusual success in Vermont. I really feel that I should be doing the University a real and permanent service if I could, in any degree, be instrumental in securing for him the vacant chair of English. I know that Prof. Winchester would (in his cautious New England way) be glad to say quite as much for him.

With much respect and warmest regards,
[Woodrow Wilson]

AL (WC, NjP); signature excised.

From Charles Scribner's Sons

Dear Sir,   [New York] May 18. [189]3

We have your letter of 16th inst. and the essays therein referred to have just come to hand. Mr. Scribner is at present absent from the city, but as soon as he returns we shall call the matter to his attention. Meantime pray accept our acknowledgments for your courtesy in sending the essays to us.

Very truly yours   Charles Scribner's Sons

ALS (Charles Scribner's Sons Archives, NjP).

From Annie Wilson Howe

My dearest Brother,   Columbia, S. C. May 20th/93

I think I wrote to Ellie that Wilson [Howe] would go to Poughkeepsie to take a course in the business college there. He will leave home on Thursday or Friday of next week—the twenty fifth or sixth—and if convenient to you and dear Ellie would like to spend a day with you on his way. He will go to Lawrenceville, and stay for two or three days. I cannot tell you how distressed I feel about his going this time. I feel as if he were going for *good*, and would never spend much of his time at home again. When a boy goes out from home, away from its influence and restraints his mothers heart is naturally full of anxiety and I feel especially anxious, because Wilson is so easily influenced by anyone he likes. Do give him some advice, dear, for me. He is eager to take the course at the school I mentioned, and will do well, I hope.

I am still somewhat under the weather—but better than I have been. I hope you are all well. I wish I could go with Wilson and stay until George comes back.

Dr. Green will spend a week with us before taking the girls home[1]—so I could not leave. I would like you to see Annie[2] and hear her talk. I will try and get a good picture of her for Wilson to take to you. Father looked very well when he left us for Macon. I hope he continues to improve.

In haste and warmest love to you both—& kisses for the babies
                    Your devoted sister   Annie.

ALS (WP, DLC).
    [1] About Dr. Green and his daughters, see George Howe, Jr., to WW, Nov. 5, 1890, n. 1; Annie W. Howe to WW, Nov. 17, 1890; and EAW to WW, April 5, 1892, n. 2, all in Vol. 7.
    [2] Her little daughter, now two years old.

From Joseph Ruggles Wilson

My precious son—   Macon, Ga., May 22/93
    Your dear good letter has done me a "heap" of good. I was quite sure you would write an "Assembly letter" as for so many years you have been so kind as to do.[1] And it is like gleams of sunlight in a murky air.

Of *course* I will do what I can for Stock, and do hope that the Athens chance will prove *the* one. I will write at once both to Boggs and McIlwaine[.] There is no telling though what little complication may prevent the right man from getting his right place.

I am somewhat expecting to go North almost immediately after the Assembly is dissolved[.] And if so I shall, with dearest Ellie's & your permission, go directly to Princeton, to remain for a few days. Meanwhile, please *retain* any letter which may come for me—especially one from Nebraska[2] that I have ordered sent to me at your address.

In haste and love. The haste might be described, but the love never could find words of portrayal—for you both—

Your affc   Father

ALS (WP, DLC).
[1] The only "Assembly" letter known to be extant is WW to JRW, May 23, 1877, Vol. 1, pp. 265-66.
[2] That is, concerning the Estate of Janet Woodrow Wilson. See M. R. Hopewell to WW, Oct. 25, 1889, Vol. 6.

From Mary C. Olden

My dear Prof Wilson,   East Orange [N.J.] May 24, 1893

I received the two checks, for $1800. and for $45., the one in payment of the principal of the mortgage, the other in payment of interest to July 1st next, also the form for a discharge of the mortgage, which Judge Stevens has executed. He is fully authorized to do anything of this kind, so you will find it lawfully done. Enclosed you will find the latter, also the Bond, which I hope you will receive safely and at the time you need them.[1]

Very sincerely yours   Mary C Olden

ALS (WP, DLC). Encs.: "Bond, Woodrow Wilson to Mary C. Olden" and printed mortgage form with handwritten entries, both dated June 26, 1891.
[1] Wilson had just discharged the indebtedness to Miss Olden incurred when he purchased the lot on Washington Street in 1891. For background, see JRW to WW, May 11, 1891, n. 2, Vol. 7.

From the Minutes of the Princeton Faculty

5 5' P.M., Wednesday, May 24th, 1893.

. . . An Invitation to the Faculty to attend the Decennial Commencement of the John C. Green School at Lawrenceville, N.J.,[1] May 30th was presented.

The Dean [James O. Murray] and Professors Shields & Wilson were appointed a Committee to represent the Faculty upon the occasion. . . .[2]

The following was adopted and ordered to be communicated to each Member of the Fac. & Examiner.

Resolved, That every Officer conducting an Examination should remain with his Class throughout the period of the Examination.[3]

[1] That is, the Lawrenceville School, heavily endowed by the trustees of the estate of John Cleve Green of New York.
[2] See the news report printed at June 3, 1893.
[3] This resolution was not intended to end the honor system (see, for example, the Princeton Faculty Minutes printed at June 9, 1893), but simply to settle the

much controverted question of whether professors should remain in their class-
rooms during examinations.

To Robert Bridges

My dear Robert,   Princeton, New Jersey, 25 May, 1893.

I think that your suggestion[1] that Mr. Howells, rather than Mr.
Stedman,[2] be invited to take part at the Whig meeting at Commencement is most happily conceived. I am delighted to acquiesce
in it; and I sincerely hope that you can secure Mr. Howells and
put it through. It ought certainly to make the success of the celebration secure.[3]

I hear golden opinionr [opinions] of your speech at the "Lit."
dinner[4] from everybody who heard it. I hope that you will come
as often as possible on such errands, with such messages.

I sent in the essays of which we were speaking to Mr. Scribner
rome [some] week or ten days ago.

Pardon the haste with which this has been run off on my
machine, and believe me, as ever,

Your affectionate friend,   Woodrow Wilson

WWTLS (WC, NjP).
  [1] Bridges's letter is missing.
  [2] William Dean Howells and Edmund Clarence Stedman, poet, critic, and
literary editor.
  [3] The minutes of the American Whig Society do not mention this affair, and
the brief notice of the annual meeting of the society on June 13, in the *Daily
Princetonian*, June 14, 1893, named neither the speakers nor the special guests.
  [4] The fifty-first anniversary of the *Nassau Literary Magazine* was celebrated
on May 15, 1893, by a dinner given to the retiring editorial board by the
incoming board. Bridges spoke in response to a toast to "The Writer."

The New Orleans *Picayune*'s Review of *Division and Reunion*

[May 28, 1893]

Division and Reunion. By Woodrow Wilson, Ph.D., LL.D. 16mo.;
pp. 326; cloth. $1 25. New York and London: Longmans,
Green & Co. New Orleans: Geo. F. Wharton.

The third and concluding volume of Epochs of American History, published by these publishers. It covers the time from 1829
to 1889, and makes slavery the turning point of the history. The
author, in his preface, suggests a fear that he may be unable
to handle the subject without prejudice, and presently justifies
the fear by manifesting the most violent partisan bias. The
ignorance that he displays of the real conditions of the slaves in
the south is simply amazing, and the pictures that he draws of

their miseries would be appalling if they were not ridiculous. Every one who knows anything about it understands that the slaves before '61 were far better off than the inhabitants of the slums and sweatshops of New York are to-day. The breaking up of the marriage relation among the slaves, which the author deplores, was nothing to compare with the looseness of that relation among the free negroes of to-day. Slavery had little to do with the secession, anyway. This volume is the least valuable and the most heavily written of the series.[1]

Printed in the New Orleans *Picayune*, May 28, 1893.
  [1] For Wilson's comment on reviews expressing this point of view, see WW to K. P. Battle, June 29, 1893.

To Caleb Thomas Winchester

My dear Winchester,   Princeton, New Jersey, 29 May, 1893

Such friends as you are raise beyond estimation the average of human happiness![1] I wish I knew how to tell you in words that would not seem extravagant what we think of your indefatigable kindness in helping Axson with the most desirable endorsements possible (without weariness by reason of the *number* of colleges he is an applicant for!). The Georgia place is really a very snug berth and we are pushing his candidacy by every means we know of,—Mrs. Wilson being the chairman of our campaign committee!

But what touches me quite as closely as even your extraordinary services in Axson's behalf is your indulgent estimate of my own capacities (e.g., as an editor of Burke). You must, I please myself by arguing, like me very much indeed to be so blinded to my limitations. One can not only forgive mistakes of this kind without number, but loves the man who makes them, and, with most outrageous inconsistency, conceives a high opinion of his judgment,—just because his heart is so warmed by the praise!

What I dread about that editorial work is, not the introduction—that would come easily and pleasantly enough: every man who has had Burke's music much in his ears wants to say—even to *print*—something about him—*but the notes*: the long search for disconnected historical points, a task peculiarly harassing to me—worse than an "Epoch." And Burke bristles with allusions that would call—*would cry out*—for annotation. It would be the death of me, as well as of all other kinds of work, were I to undertake it. The *prospectus* (very judiciously) makes much of the notes:

they *ought* to be a prominent feature of the editorial job—and I'm no scholar, Sir.

What do you expect to do this summer—besides going to Chicago?[2] We expect to stay here the vacation through—and we could imagine nothing more delightful than to have you and Mrs. Winchester visit us. Occasional letters are tantalizing: we want to *see* you and *talk* with you. There are all sorts of topics buzzing in my head which I would like to test the merits of by canvassing them with you. Friends who are really intellectually akin ought to have some clearing house system by which they could check off against each other. The tribe I professionally belong to (historians, economists, jurists,—what not!) are desperately dull fellows. They have no more *literature* in them than an ass has of beauty. They don't know anything, because they know only *one* thing; and I am terribly afraid of growing like them. I am not only not a scholar, but I don't want to be one. I love excursions and hate *incisions*—and I need you, for I know of nobody else half so satisfactory to a man in search of outlooks. I would court your friendship if only for selfish motives. As it is, I am, if you will let me say so,

Most affectionately Yours,   Woodrow Wilson

ALS (CtW).
   [1] Winchester's letter to which this was a reply is missing.
   [2] Perhaps Winchester had told Wilson that he was going to the World's Columbian Exposition.

To William Ellison Boggs, with Enclosure

My dear Dr Boggs,   Princeton, New Jersey, 29 May, 1893

I am deeply obliged to you for your very kind letter. Its cordiality and directness gave me a home feeling, as of the South, at once. I took the liberty of sending it at once to Mr. Axson, that he might get its suggestions in your own words. I can emphasize as much as you could wish his attractive and effective qualities as a speaker; and I have no doubt that he can and will do anything that may be necessary to acquaint himself with the methods of the best masters in elocution. (I enclose a formal statement)

His success as a teacher is all the more noteworthy and substantial because it seems so clearly a case of natural selection. He persisted in following his instincts in spite of the most seductive offers to do work of a different kind. A publishing house in Boston made him an offer of a (permanent) editorial appointment at a salary, to begin on, greater than the full professor's salaries in most colleges. The *Review of Reviews* has made repeated efforts to get him. He has made pecuniary sacrifices to become a finished scholar and an admirable teacher, for sheer love of understanding and imparting literature and language. This seems to me to constitute the strongest sort of argument in his favour.

Let me thank you again most warmly for your letter, and to add Mrs. Wilson's sincerest regards to my own.

Most sincerely and cordially Yours,   Woodrow Wilson

P.S. We have taken every legitimate means to commend Axson directly to the favourable attention of such of the Trustees as we knew or felt at liberty to approach.[1]   W. W.

ALS (WC, NjP).
[1] See WW to A. O. Bacon, June 2, 1893.

E N C L O S U R E

To William Ellison Boggs

Princeton, New Jersey, 29 May, 1893.

I desire to add to what I have had occasion to say already concerning Mr. Axson's fitness for the position he is seeking, a word or two about his unusual powers as a speaker. These have long attracted attention. At Wesleyan, where they pay more, and more intelligent, attention to elocutionary training than anywhere else that I know of, with admirable results, Mr. Axson, who had not received their training, won a commencement appointment,[1] a coveted honor, on his merits as a speaker, the commencement appointments being awarded on that basis. The musical qualities of his voice, and the grace of his action in speaking, particularly, won universal notice and praise, from the best judges. Eminence as a speaker was confidently predicted for him by such men as Professor Winchester.

These facts seem to me worth dwelling upon because, in my observation, success as a lecturer depends so much upon the possession of such powers. High gifts miscarry and are without effect upon the average class without them.

Very sincerely,   Woodrow Wilson

WWTLS (WC, NjP).
[1] Axson spoke at the Wesleyan commencement exercises on June 25, 1890, on the subject, "Character of the Statesman." See the Middletown, Conn., *Wesleyan Argus*, XXIII (June 28, 1890), 186.

Hermann Eduard von Holst's Review of *Division and Reunion*

[June 1893]

Division and Reunion: 1829-1889.—By WOODROW WILSON, Ph. D., LL. D. [Epochs of American History.] New York and London: Longmans, Green & Co., 1892, pp. xix, 326. Price $1.25.

Professor Wilson's task has been an uncommonly difficult one. If he had written a text-book it would have been no great feat to compress the history of the United States from the accession of Andrew Jackson to the end of Grover Cleveland's first presidency into 292 pages. To write a commendable treatise *about* the history of this period within such a compass would also not be an extraordinary achievement. What he has undertaken to do and succeeded in doing is, however, a very different thing. He relates *the* history of those seventy years, not merely stringing fact to fact, but weaving all the countless facts into a smooth-running narrative. The book really is a book—no piece and patchwork, but cut of whole cloth. The thoughtful reader's interest is never allowed to flag for a moment. Though the facts are marched up in close array, he never feels hurried. There are no details to confuse him. While he has but seldom to halt to listen to comments, he learns much more than the mere facts, for they are put forth in their relation of cause and effect with such lucidity that they are pregnant with all the suggestive force of an evolutionary process. The author is no votary of that exaggerated, nay, impossible *objectivität*, which virtually amounts to a denial of his right to hold any political or moral opinion as to the events and men he is treating of. But he has no thesis to prove. With unimpeachable honesty and undeviating singleness of purpose he strives—as Ranke puts it—"simply to say how it was." He does not write to please anybody, and therefore he will please all that are fair-minded enough to be able to understand, for to really understand is the best safeguard not only against injustice, but also against uncharitableness. While rigorously abstaining from didactic moralizing, he has succeeded, unquestionably more than fairly well, in presenting the facts in such a way that one cannot help understanding the great evolutionary process in its leading features. Therefore he will surely communicate to every reader also something of the glow of the broad and intense, but chaste and unobtrusive, patriotism pervading his book from the first to the last page. Though deserving much praise, Mr. Wilson can, however, not expect to run the gauntlet of criticism unscathed. Too few of the most prominent men have been deemed worthy of the honor of having a pen picture of their individuality drawn in a line or two. Such men as Chase, Sumner, Stanton, and even Jefferson Davis, fleet past our eyes as shadows without any substance. Men of the rank of Yancey, Toombs, H. Cobb, are not mentioned at all. For this reason, among many others, it seems to me that the book can be properly appreciated only by those who already have a comparatively thorough knowledge of the history of the United States. Some inaccuracies have crept in which might have been easily avoided. Thus we are told on p. 101: "The Whigs, too, were to have a majority of forty-seven in the House, and of seven in the senate," and, on p. 134, of the same congress: "In the next House the Whigs were to have a majority of twenty-five, and in the senate a majority of six." The wording of general statements will sometimes bear careful revision. Does it, for instance, quite tally to say (p. 209): "The South . . . knew . . . that it was morally impossible to preserve the Union any longer," and (p. 215): "Compromise was hoped for (*i.e.*, by the South), even confidently expected"? Or: if the protective system of the tariff of 1829 "notoriously bore with its whole [!] weight upon a single section" and "the other sections were exempt" (!) from its "burden," because they were not, like the South, purely agricultural, are, then, not necessarily to-day all the States that are not purely agricultural the victims of a strange delusion if they think that any part of the burden imposed by the McKinley tariff rests upon them? That opinions will differ as to what might justly be left untold goes without saying. Still the necessity of mentioning some things is too obvious to admit of any dispute. A correct conception of the history of the annexation of Texas cannot be conveyed without doing justice to the part played in it by Calhoun, who emphatically claimed to be its "real author" (*Works*, IV: 362, 363). Mr. Wilson does not even mention that he was Tyler's Secretary of State at the time. Nor has he a word to say about the constitutionality of annexation by joint resolution. Two other striking omissions are of a different character. Nothing is told of either Webster's 7th of March speech or Brook's [Brooks's] attempt upon Sumner. Apart from their consequences, both were by their symptomatic significance events of such magnitude that without any knowledge of them a correct understanding of the general situation is impossible. That they are left unnoticed I attribute to what is in my opinion the greatest defect of the book, and it is a very grave one. Professor Wilson does not duly appreciate the part played by the purely moral element in the irrepressible conflict.

Wherever this has been the originating, impelling, and formative force, the light is dim—one has more or less to guess and infer what one ought to be emphatically told—and sometimes, as in the case of John Brown, one gets a positively distorted view, because the most essential traits are almost absolutely ignored. The shrill and ever shriller commingling of Calhoun's "a good, a positive good," and the abolitionist's "the sum of all villainies," is, after all, the keynote of the sectional controversy, and in Mr. Wilson's pages it rings upon our ears but in a muffled tone and as from afar off. It is hardly distinguishable in his summing up of the cause the Confederacy is contending for: "A belated principle of government, an outgrown economy, an impossible purpose." I was at a loss to account for this striking feature of the book until I accidentally learned that Mr. Wilson is a Virginian (or North Carolinian?). That this was surprising news to me sufficiently proves that, in my opinion, he has not laid himself open to the charge of writing history in a partisan spirit. I, however, do think that the bias of his Southern blood asserts itself to some extent, and casts a film over his eyes in regard to some persons and questions. Whether and how far the view he holds of the original political nature of the Union under the constitution is due to the same reason is a question I do not feel entitled even to propound. Mr. Cabot Lodge (*Daniel Webster*, p. 176) has very strikingly proved that one need not be a Southerner to assert most apodeictically that for some forty years the opinions of the Southern States' Rights school were the absolutely uncontradicted creed of the whole American people. I have merely to state that Mr. Wilson substantially agrees with Mr. Lodge, and as an historian explicitly to record my dissent from them. In spite of all Mr. Wilson says on pp. 111, 112 of the "historian's facts," the North would stand in a truly awful predicament if it were true *and the whole truth* what these two gentlemen maintain. My hearty commendation of the book can go out to the world only accompanied by an emphatic protest.

H. von Holst

University of Chicago

Printed in the New York *Educational Review*, VI (June 1893), 87-90.

To Augustus Octavius Bacon

My dear Sir: [Princeton, N. J., c. June 2, 1893]

I am sincerely obliged to you for your courteous letter of May 31.[1] If I write again it is not because I would change, if I could, the altogether admirable attitude of judgment concerning the university which the letter discloses, but only because I thought it due to you to speak a word upon one of the points which the letter raises.

You intimate that, even if Mr. Axson should not be chosen for the full chair of English, it might be possible to secure a minor position for him in the university. I do not know how Mr. Axson would feel about that, for I have not written to him about it, but I fear that it would not be possible to get him for any but the full appointment. For he is in demand already. He has been offered a full chair in a large western university,[2] he is being sought for a full chair in a small southern college,[3] and efforts are being made to secure his promotion where he is, if the money can be had.[4] He is not seeking *a* position but *the* position now vacant at Athens,—not only because he wants to go south, but rather because he wants to go to the University of Georgia.

My own tastes drew me very strongly in the same direction that Mr. Axson's training has taken. I have consequently devoted not a little time and attention to the question of university instruction in English;[5] and I am convinced that, at this particular juncture, when the university world is in a stage of such rapid progress, it is not so much the length of experience that ought to be considered in the choice of professors as the kind of experience, added to the time and character of their training. Mr. Axson has reaped in his experience, so to say, the very ripest fruit of modern English scholarship and his success as a teacher is an earnest of the way in which he has reaped it. I do not know of any man who is obtainable whose experience is so exactly of the right sort.

But pardon me for writing so much. I have a strange ardor for this man, I so thoroughly believe in him.

Very sincerely yours,   Woodrow Wilson

Transcript of WWshLS (draft) (WP, DLC) with WWhw heading "2nd letter to Hon. A. O. Bacon."

[1] Both Wilson's letter and Bacon's reply of May 31, 1893, are missing.

[2] At the University of Kansas in 1892. WW to EAW, April 30, 1892, Vol. 7, suggests that Axson had been offered an instructorship.

[3] That is, Hampden-Sydney College. WW to C. W. Kent, June 29, 1893, reveals that Axson never had an offer from Hampden-Sydney.

[4] At the University of Vermont. The authorities did raise the money and keep Axson for 1893-94.

[5] See the Editorial Note, " 'Mere Literature.' "

To Albert Shaw

My dear Shaw,   Princeton, New Jersey,   2 June, 1893.

Your letters in re Axson were works of art; and we are most deeply obliged to you for them.[1] Mrs. Wilson, who is chairman of our campaign committee, pronounces them perfect. If I could get testimonials as warm as those Axson is getting, I think I should apply for a place somewhere myself, just for the pleasure of warming my heart at such letters.

I hope that your outing will carry you still further towards complete strength. I wish it might carry you all the way at once.

Mrs. Wilson joins me in the warmest regards,

Affectionately yours,   Woodrow Wilson

TCL (in possession of Virginia Shaw English).

[1] Shaw's letter to Wilson and his letters in support of Stockton Axson are all missing.

A News Report

[June 3, 1893]

FOUNDER'S DAY EXERCISES.

About three o'clock the School assembled and escorted the distinguished guests and the Alumni from the Foundation House to Memorial Hall. Here the exercises of the afternoon were opened by singing "March, March Onward, Soldiers True." At the close of this hymn a portion of the thirteenth chapter of Matthew was read and the School was led in prayer. When another hymn had been sung Dr. [William Henry] Green announced that, owing to an accident to his train, the Hon. W. C. P. Breckenridge [of Kentucky], who was to have delivered the commemoration address, would be unable to be present, and that, in his place, Prof. Woodrow Wilson, of Princeton, had kindly consented to deliver a brief address. Prof. Wilson's speech was full of interest and instruction, and was very much enjoyed by all present. At its conclusion, Dr. [Timothy] Dwight, Chancellor of Yale University, gave a brief talk. This, also, was very suggestive, and was highly appreciated.[1]

Printed in the Lawrenceville, N.J., *Lawrence*, XIII (June 3, 1893), 10.

[1] This ceremony was the final one in a series of decennial festivities held on May 28, 29, and 30, 1893. This account from the monthly of the Lawrenceville School is the most substantial contemporary report of the ceremony in which Wilson participated. For a detailed memoir of the occasion, see T. Dean Swift, "Recollections of Lawrenceville School and the Work of Dr. James Mackenzie" (MS. in the Library of the Lawrenceville School).

From the Minutes of the Princeton Faculty

5 5' P.M. Wednesday, June 7th, 1893.

. . . A case of copying in an Examination in the School of Science was referred to the Committee on the Method of Conducting Examinations upon the New System for investigation and report. A resolution in reference to putting students "on their honor" at the Entrance Examinations was presented and laid upon the table until the next meeting.

5 5' P.M., Friday, June 9th, 1893.

. . . Upon report and recommendation of the Committee on the New Plan of Conducting Examinations it was *Resolved*, That when a Professor has reason to believe that there has been cheating in his Examination he shall present the evidence at his disposal to the Class Presidents and such other students as they may see fit.

Ordered That a copy be sent by the Clerk to every Instructor. . . .

Upon recommendation of the Committee on Out-Door Sports it was *Resolved*, That the regulation which forbids members of the College Athletic Associations—Base-ball, Foot-ball, and Track-athletics—to participate in contests as representatives of other Athletic Associations be understood to apply to contests held during College vacations.

From Charles Scribner's Sons

Dear Sir.   [New York] June 12, [189]3

We shall be much pleased to undertake the publication of your "An Old Master, and Other Political Essays" assuming the whole cost of publishing[,] advertising, distributing &c and paying you a royalty of ten per cent. on the retail price of all copies sold, if these terms seem acceptable to you. We should hardly think the probable sale of so special a book would be such as to make them seem inadequate and we trust that we may hear from you speedily that we may put the work in hand,

Very truly yours   Charles Scribner's Sons

ALS (Charles Scribner's Sons Archives, NjP).

A Newspaper Report

'83 MEMORIAL.   [June 14, 1893]

The exercises in connection with the transfer of the class of '83's memorial to the college were held in the Library yesterday morning.

For the customary memorial on the occasion of a decennial reunion, the class of '83 has chosen to found a Library of Political Science and Jurisprudence. For this memorial they have given about one thousand volumes, and a substantial endowment for the increase of the collection. The books are in a separate alcove, above which is hung an iron-work tablet with the words "Political Science and Jurisprudence" in brass letters. Mr. J. Aspinwall Hodge of New York made the presentation speech. He said that no such instruction was given ten years ago, and it was with the hope that the volumes might be the germs of a Law School that they had been presented. President Patton accepted the gift, complimenting the class on their choice of a memorial which tends to subserve the best interests of the college rather than perpetuate the class. Professor Woodrow Wilson, '79, expressed his belief that a Law School could be established apart from the courts and offices, which would graduate jurists and not mere trained lawyers.

Printed in the *Daily Princetonian*, June 14, 1893.

EDITORIAL NOTE

WILSON AND THE CLASS OF 1883 LIBRARY OF POLITICAL
SCIENCE AND JURISPRUDENCE

In February 1893, it was announced that, as a memorial on the occasion of its tenth reunion, the Class of 1883 intended to present to Princeton a collection of books to form a Library of Political Science and Jurisprudence. The *Daily Princetonian* reported on February 28, "Several thousand dollars have been raised and it is expected that about one thousand volumes will be purchased at once, the remainder of the money to be kept for a permanent endowment." In an editorial a few days later, the *Princetonian* commented: "The lack of reference works in the department of political science and jurisprudence has been felt for a long time, without much hope of an appreciable addition. This class . . . could not have decided upon a gift which would have been more acceptable or upon one which would be a means of greater benefit to the college."[1] It is entirely possible that Wilson had suggested the gift, not only because the books would be used in

[1] *Daily Princetonian*, March 2, 1893.

his own courses, but also because he conceived of the collection as the foundation of the library for his School of Law at Princeton.[2]

While in Baltimore delivering his annual lectures at the Johns Hopkins, Wilson received several letters from Winthrop More Daniels concerning the gift, as well as one from the college librarian.[3] Wilson had evidently agreed to prepare a list of books that should be included in the collection. He wrote to Daniels on February 23: "I shall make up a short list here and leave the rest until my return to Princeton, for a final rush—if necessary by cable in the case of foreign books." The matter seems to have preyed on his mind in Baltimore, for in another letter to Daniels he added the postscript: "I almost wish '83 had done something else with their money!"[4]

However, Wilson's tentative bibliography was made up in due course. It consists of ten handwritten pages, headed "List for the '83 Gift,"[5] and contains 133 titles in abbreviated form, many of them partially in shorthand. The first three pages appear to be the "short list" compiled in Baltimore; the remaining items were evidently set down from time to time after Wilson had returned to Princeton in March.

The college library's accession books, now in the Princeton University Archives, enable one to trace fairly accurately the accumulation of volumes for the Class of 1883 gift. Of the items on Wilson's lists, eight already held by the library were transferred to the new collection, as is indicated by the stamped notice "Tr to '83" at the point where the original acquisition of the book was recorded. In addition, 115 other titles were transferred from accessions recorded between September 1890 and April 1893. There is no record of transfers of books acquired earlier than 1890, although some may have occurred. Moreover, there is no direct evidence that Wilson chose all the transferred titles, but it is highly possible that he did so in consultation with the college librarian.

On April 12, 1893, the first purchase is noted of a book intended expressly for the Library of Political Science and Jurisprudence, the source of the accession being given as "Class of '83." From that date until August 1893, sixty-eight titles from Wilson's lists were purchased, clearly identifiable as those he specified, although sometimes in a later edition or an American rather than a British one. During that period, and principally before the middle of June, 824 other books were also bought for the Class of 1883. (In computing this figure, back periodical volumes have been counted individually.) While there is no documentary evidence that Wilson was responsible for all these additional purchases, a great many of them (including some of Wilson's titles) arrived in batches from various American and British publishers, thus suggesting that he had recommended placing blanket orders with those publishers for all the volumes in the field in print. The transfers (123), the titles Wilson had specified (68), and the other purchases (824) totaled 1,015 volumes, thus ful-

[2] See the Editorial Note, "Wilson's Plans for a School of Law at Princeton," Vol. 7.
[3] WW to W. M. Daniels, Feb. 23, 1893.
[4] WW to W. M. Daniels, Feb. 27, 1893.
[5] WP, DLC.

filling the terms of the gift, which had provided for the immediate acquisition of "about one thousand volumes."

When the college reopened in September 1893, the collection, now arranged according to a system of classification devised by Wilson and Daniels, was combined with 2,000 other volumes in the same field that had been purchased on the Elizabeth Foundation.[6]

Purchases for the collection continued during the next few years, but on a much reduced scale. Forty-two more titles were acquired in the academic years 1894-95 and 1895-96, chiefly in continuing series. Only seven titles were bought for the Class of 1883 between June 1896 and September 1897, and it may be assumed that by this date the Library of Political Science and Jurisprudence was substantially complete.

In the bibliography that follows, Wilson's titles have been recast according to modern usage and rearranged alphabetically, and the citations refer to the editions that the library actually purchased. Those marked "tr" were transferred from the library's earlier holdings; those bearing an asterisk were bought for the class gift (sixty-eight from April through August 1893; one in April 1895). Of the remainder, thirty-six are now in the Princeton University Library, but no record has been found that they were purchased for or assigned to the Library of Political Science and Jurisprudence. Those that still carry the Elizabeth Foundation bookplate are marked "EF."

Generally speaking, the whole body of books for the Class of 1883 gift was of the same character as those on Wilson's lists. They included complete sets of some twenty scholarly legal journals, both British and American. The entire list of titles in the Library of Political Science and Jurisprudence is not printed below, since it would in large measure duplicate, among other things, the bibliography printed in "Wilson's Working Bibliography, 1883-90," in Volume 6, and in the Editorial Note, "Wilson's Working Bibliography on Law" in the present volume.

EF   Allen, John, *An Inquiry into the Rise and Growth of the Royal Prerogative in England*, new edn. by B. Thorpe (London, 1849).

      Amir 'Ali, Maulawi Saiyid, *Personal Law of the Mahommedans* . . . (London, 1880).

EF   Amos, Sheldon, *Fifty Years of the English Constitution, 1830-1880* (London, 1880).

      Amos, Sheldon, *A Systematic View of the Science of Jurisprudence* (London, 1872).

      Ancient Law and Institutes of England, printed under the direction of the Commissioners on the Public Records of the Kingdom (2 vols., London, 1840).

tr   Anson, Sir William Reynell, *The Law and Custom of the Constitution*, 2nd edn. (2 vols., Oxford, 1892).

tr   Anson, Sir William Reynell, *Principles of the English Law of Contract and of Agency in Its Relation to Contract*, 6th edn. (Oxford, 1891).

[6] *Daily Princetonian*, Sept. 21, 1893. The Elizabeth Foundation was an endowment for the library given by John Cleve Green in 1868 in memory of his mother, Elizabeth Van Cleve Green.

Anstey, Thomas Chisholm, *Guide to the History of the Laws and Constitutions of England* (London, 1845).

* Anstey, Thomas Chisholm, "On the Competence of Colonial Legislatures to Enact Laws in Derogation of Common Liability or Common Right," *Juridical Society Papers*, Vol. III (London, 1871), Part X.

Bar, Karl Ludwig von, *International Law: Private and Criminal*, trans. with notes by G. R. Gillespie (Boston, 1883).

Barclay, Sir Thomas, *The French Law of Bills of Exchange, Promissory Notes and Cheques* ... (London and Paris, 1884).

Béchard, Ferdinand, *De l'administration intérieure de la France* (2 vols., Paris, 1851).

Béchard, Ferdinand, *Droit municipal au moyen âge* (2 vols., Paris, 1861-62).

Béchard, Ferdinand, *Droit municipal dans les temps modernes: XVIe et XVIIe siècles* (Paris, 1866).

Bentham, Jeremy, *Works* (11 vols., Edinburgh and London, 1843).

Bigelow, Melville Madison, *History of Procedure in England from the Norman Conquest: The Norman Period, 1066-1204* (Boston, 1880).

Bigelow, Melville Madison, *Placita anglo-normannica: Law Cases from William I to Richard I, Preserved in Historical Records* (Boston, 1879).

Bisset, Andrew, *The History of the Struggle for Parliamentary Government in England* (2 vols., London, 1877).

Bluntschli, Johann Caspar, *Deutsches Staats-wörterbuch.* . . , unter Mitredaktion von Karl Brater (11 vols., Stuttgart and Leipzig, 1857-70).

* Bourinot, Sir John George, *A Manual of the Constitutional History of Canada, from the Earliest Period to the Year 1888* (Montreal, 1888).

* Bouvier, John, *A Law Dictionary, Adapted to the Constitution and Laws of the United States of America*, 15th edn., rev. and enl. by Francis Rawle (2 vols., Philadelphia, 1892).

* Bowyer, Sir George, *Commentaries on Universal Public Law* (London, 1854).

Bradford, Alden, *History of the Federal Government, for Fifty Years, from March, 1789, to March, 1839* (Boston, 1840).

tr Broom, Herbert, *Commentaries on the Common Law, Designed as Introductory to Its Study*, 8th edn., with W. F. A. Archibald and Herbert W. Greene (London, 1888).

* Broom, Herbert, *Constitutional Law Viewed in Relation to Common Law, and Exemplified by Cases*, 2nd edn., with George L. Denham (London, 1885).

* Broom, Herbert, *The Philosophy of Common Law: A Primer of Legal Principles*, 3rd edn., with John C. H. Flood (London, 1883).

Broom, Herbert, and Edward Alfred Hadley, *Commentaries on the Laws of England* (4 vols., London, 1869).

EF Brown, Archibald, *An Epitome and Analysis of Savigny's Treatise on Obligations in Roman Law* (London, 1872).

EF   Burlamaqui, Jean Jacques, *The Principles of Natural and Politic Law*, trans. by Thomas Nugent, 2nd rev. edn. (2 vols., London, 1763).

Campbell, John, Lord, *The Lives of the Chief Justices of England* (4 vols., New York, 1874).

Campbell, John, Lord, *The Lives of the Lord Chancellors and Keepers of the Great Seal of England, from the Earliest Times Till the Reign of Queen Victoria*, new edn., by John Allan Mallory (10 vols., New York, 1874).

Carter, James Coolidge, *The Provinces of the Written and the Unwritten Law* (New York and Albany, 1889).

Chambrun, Charles Adolphe de Pineton, Marquis de, *The Executive Power in the United States: A Study of Constitutional Law*, trans. by Mrs. Madeleine Vinton Dahlgren (Lancaster, Pa., 1874).

*   Chan-Toon, *The Nature and Value of Jurisprudence*, 2nd enl. edn. (London, 1889).

EF   Clark, Edwin Charles, *Early Roman Law: The Regal Period* (London, 1872).

*   Colquhoun, Sir Patrick MacChombaich de, "The Rise and Progress of the Roman Civil Law Before Justinian Historically Considered," *Juridical Society Papers*, Vol. I (London, 1858), Part XVII.

*   Colquhoun, Sir Patrick MacChombaich de, *Summary of the Roman Civil Law, Illustrated by Commentaries and Parallels from the Mosaic, Canon, Mohammedan, English, and Foreign Law* (4 vols., London, 1849-60).

Constant de Rebecque, Benjamin de, *Collection complète des ouvrages publiés sur le gouvernement représentatif et la constitution actuelle de la France, formant une espèce de cours de politique constitutionelle* (4 vols., Paris, 1818-20).

Constant de Rebecque, Benjamin de, *Cours de politique constitutionelle, ou Collection des ouvrages publiés sur le gouvernement représentatif*, 2nd edn. (2 vols., Paris, 1872).

EF   Cooley, Thomas McIntyre, *A Treatise on the Constitutional Limitations Which Rest upon the Legislative Power of the States of the American Union*, 4th edn. (Boston, 1878).

*   Cooley, Thomas McIntyre, *A Treatise on the Law of Taxation, Including the Law of Local Assessments . . .* , 2nd enl. edn. (Chicago, 1886).

*   Cox, Homersham, *The Institutions of the English Government* (London, 1863).

Creasy, Sir Edward Shepherd, *The Imperial and Colonial Constitutions of the Britannic Empire, Including Indian Institutions* (London, 1872).

*   Creasy, Sir Edward Shepherd, *The Rise and Progress of the English Constitution*, 15th edn. (London, 1886).

*   Dickinson, Reginald (compiler), *Summary of the Constitution and Procedure of Foreign Parliaments*, 2nd edn. (London, 1890).

tr   Digby, Sir Kenelm Edward, *An Introduction to the History of* the Law of Real Property, with Original Authorities, 4th edn. (Oxford, 1892).

* Dodd, Joseph, A History of Canon Law in Conjunction with Other Branches of Jurisprudence (London, 1884).

Duer, William Alexander, A Course of Lectures on the Constitutional Jurisprudence of the United States, 2nd rev. enl. edn. (Boston, 1856).

* Elton, Charles Isaac, Custom and Tenant-Right (London, 1882).

English Citizen Series:

* Craik, Sir Henry, The State in Its Relation to Education (London, 1884).

* Farrer, Thomas Henry, The State in Its Relation to Trade (London, 1883).

* Fowle, Thomas Welbank, The Poor Law (London, 1881).

* Jevons, William Stanley, The State in Relation to Labour (London, 1887).

* Maitland, Frederic William, Justice and Police (London, 1885).

* Pollock, Sir Frederick, The Land Laws, 2nd edn. (London, 1887).

* Walpole, Sir Spencer, The Electorate and the Legislature (London, 1881).

* Walpole, Sir Spencer, Foreign Relations (London, 1882).

* Ewell, Marshall Davis (ed.), Essentials of the Law, . . . for the Use of Students at Law (2 vols., Boston, 1889).

Ford, Paul Leicester (ed.), Pamphlets on the Constitution of the United States, Published During Its Discussion by the People, 1787-1788 (Brooklyn, N. Y., 1888).

* Forsyth, William, History of Trial by Jury, 2nd edn. by J. A. Morgan (New York, 1878).

* Forsyth, William, Hortensius: An Historical Essay on the Office and Duties of an Advocate, 3rd edn. (London, 1879).

* Fortescue, Sir John, The Governance of England, rev. text ed. by Charles Plummer (Oxford, 1885).

* Gaius, The Commentaries of Gaius and Rules of Ulpian, trans. and ed. by John Thomas Abdy and Bryan Walker, 3rd edn. (Cambridge, Eng., 1885).

* Gilbart, James William, The History, Principles and Practice of Banking, rev. edn. by A. S. Michie (2 vols., London, 1892).

* Gilbert, Sir Geoffrey, The History and Practice of the High Court of Chancery, ed. by Samuel Tyler (Washington, D. C., 1874).

Giraud, Charles Joseph Barthélemy, Essai sur l'histoire du droit français au moyen âge (2 vols., Paris, 1846).

tr Hale, Sir Matthew, The History of the Common Law of England and an Analysis of the Civil Part of the Law. . . , 6th edn. by Charles Runnington (London, 1820).

* Hare, John Innes Clark, American Constitutional Law (2 vols., Boston, 1889).

* Hare, John Innes Clark, and John William Wallace (eds.), American Leading Cases: Being Select Decisions of American Courts, in Several Departments of Law, 5th enl. edn. (2 vols., Philadelphia, 1871).

EF   Hearn, William Edward, *The Aryan Household, Its Structure and Its Development: An Introduction to Comparative Jurisprudence* (London, 1879).

EF   Hearn, William Edward, *The Government of England, Its Structure, and Its Development* (London, 1867).

Heron, Denis Caulfield, *An Introduction to the History of Jurisprudence* (London, 1860).

tr   Indermaur, John, *An Epitome of Leading Common Law Cases, with Some Short Notes Thereon . . .* , 7th edn. (London, 1891).

*   Indermaur, John, *A Manual of the Principles of Equity*, 2nd edn. (London, 1890).

tr   Indermaur, John, *Principles of the Common Law*, 6th edn. (London, 1891).

*   *Johns Hopkins University Studies in History and Political Science* (10 vols., Baltimore, 1883-92), and extra vols.:

*   Allinson, Edward Pease, and Boies Penrose, *Philadelphia 1681-1887: A History of Municipal Development* (Philadelphia, 1887).

*   Andrews, Charles McLean, *The Old English Manor* (Baltimore, 1892).

*   Blackmar, Frank Wilson, *Spanish Institutions of the Southwest* (Baltimore, 1891).

*   Brackett, Jeffrey Richardson, *The Negro in Maryland: A Study of the Institution of Slavery* (Baltimore, 1889).

*   Brown, George William, *Baltimore and the Nineteenth of April 1861: A Study of the War* (Baltimore, 1887).

*   Cohn, Morris M., *An Introduction to the Study of the Constitution* (Baltimore, 1892).

*   Howard, George Elliott, *An Introduction to the Local Constitutional History of the United States* (Baltimore, 1889).

*   Levermore, Charles Herbert, *The Republic of New Haven: A History of Municipal Evolution* (Baltimore, 1886).

*   Nitobe, Inazo Ota, *The Intercourse Between the United States and Japan: An Historical Sketch* (Baltimore, 1891).

*   Scaife, Walter Bell, *America: Its Geographical History, 1492-1892* (Baltimore, 1892).

*   Vincent, John Martin, *State and Federal Government in Switzerland* (Baltimore, 1891).

*   Willoughby, Westel Woodbury, *The Supreme Court of the United States: Its History and Influence in Our Constitutional System* (Baltimore, 1890).

*   *Juridical Society Papers* (3 vols., London, 1858-71).

Krüger, Paul, and Theodor Mommsen (eds.), *Corpus juris civilis: Editio stereotypa . . .* (2 vols., Berlin, 1872-77).

Laferrière, Louis-Firmin Julien, *Histoire du droit civil de Rome et du droit français* (6 vols., Paris, 1846-58).

*   Landon, Judson Stuart, *The Constitutional History and Government of the United States: A Series of Lectures* (Boston and New York, 1889).

*   Lawson, John Davison, *The Law of Usages and Customs, with Illustrative Cases* (San Francisco, 1887).

* Lawson, John Davison (ed.), *Leading Cases Simplified: A Collection of the Leading Cases in Equity and Constitutional Law* (San Francisco, 1892).

* Lewis, Hubert, *The Ancient Laws of Wales. . .* , ed. by J. E. Lloyd (London, 1892).

* Lindley, Nathaniel (trans. and ed.), *An Introduction to the Study of Jurisprudence: Being a Translation of the General Part of Thibaut's System des Pandekten Rechts* (Philadelphia, 1855).

* Mackeldey, Ferdinand, *Handbook of the Roman Law*, trans. and ed. by M. A. Dropsie, from the 14th German edn. (2 vols., Philadelphia, 1883).

EF Maitland, Frederic William (ed.), *Bracton's Note Book* (3 vols., London, 1887).

Marquardsen, Heinrich von (ed.), *Handbuch des oeffentlichen Rechts der Gegenwart, in Monographien* (4 vols., Freiburg i.B., 1883-[1906]).

Maurer, Georg Ludwig von, *Geschichte der Dorfverfassung in Deutschland* (2 vols., Erlangen, 1865-66).

Maurer, Georg Ludwig von, *Geschichte der Fronhöfe, der Bauernhöfe, und der Hofverfassung in Deutschland* (4 vols., Erlangen, 1862-63).

Maurer, Georg Ludwig von, *Geschichte der Markenverfassung in Deutschland* (Erlangen, 1856).

Maurer, Georg Ludwig von, *Geschichte der Städteverfassung in Deutschland* (4 vols., Erlangen, 1869-71).

Meier, Ludwig Arnold Ernst von, *Die Reform der Verwaltungsorganisation unter Stein und Hardenberg* (Leipzig, 1881).

EF Merrill, George, *Studies in Comparative Jurisprudence and the Conflict of Laws* (Boston, 1886).

* Monroe, James, *The People the Sovereigns*, ed. by Samuel L. Gouverneur (Philadelphia, 1867).

Moyle, John Baron (ed. and trans.), *Imperatoris Iustiniani Institutionum libri quattuor* (Oxford, 1883).

* Nasmith, David, *The Institutes of English Adjective Law (Procedure in Court)* . . . (London, 1879).

* Ordronaux, John, *Constitutional Legislation in the United States: Its Origin and Application* . . . (Philadelphia, 1891).

Palgrave, Sir Francis, *The Rise and Progress of the English Commonwealth: Anglo-Saxon Period* (2 vols., London, 1832).

* Pollock, Frederick, *Principles of Contract at Law and in Equity*, 2nd Amer. edn. from 4th Eng. edn. (Cincinnati, 1885).

* Pomeroy, John Norton, *An Introduction to the Constitutional Law of the United States*, 10th edn., rev. and enl. by Edmund H. Bennett (Boston and New York, 1888).

* Pomeroy, John Norton, *A Treatise on Equity Jurisprudence, as Administered in the United States of America* (3 vols., San Francisco, 1892).

* *The Presidential Counts: A Complete Official Record* . . . (New York, 1877).

* Ross, Denman Waldo, *The Early History of Land-holding Among the Germans* (Boston, 1883).

*   Salkowski, Karl, *Institutes and History of Roman Private Law*,
      trans. and ed. by E. E. Whitfield (London, 1886).

      Savigny, Friedrich Karl von, *Of the Vocation of Our Age for
      Legislation and Jurisprudence*, trans. by Abraham Hayward
      (London, 1831).

      Savigny, Friedrich Karl von, *Private International Law, and the
      Retrospective Operation of Statutes: A Treatise on the Con-
      flict of Laws*, trans. by William Guthrie, 2nd rev. edn. (Edin-
      burgh, 1880).

      Seebohm, Frederic, *The English Village Community* . . . (Lon-
      don, 1883).

      Simonde de Sismondi, Jean Charles Léonard, *Études sur les
      constitutions des peuples libres* (3 vols., Paris, 1836).

      Smith, Joshua Toulmin, *The Parish: Its Powers and Obligations
      at Law* . . . , 2nd edn. (London, 1857).

*   Smith, Josiah William, *A Manual of Equity Jurisprudence for
      Practitioners and Students* . . . , 14th edn. by J. Trustram
      (London, 1889).

*   Spence, George, *An Inquiry into the Origin of the Laws and
      Political Institutions of Modern Europe, Particularly of Those
      of England* (London, 1826).

*   Stephen, Henry John, *New Commentaries on the Laws of Eng-
      land*, 11th edn. by Archibald Brown (4 vols., London, 1890).

EF   Stephen, Sir James Fitzjames, *A Digest of the Law of Evidence*
      (Boston, 1877).

*   Stephen, James Kenneth, *International Law and International
      Relations* (London, 1884).

EF   Stirling, James Hutchison, *Lectures on the Philosophy of Law:
      Together with Whewell and Hegel, and Hegel and Mr. W. R.
      Smith* . . . (London, 1873).

*   Stokes, Whitley (ed.), *The Anglo-Indian Codes* (2 vols., Oxford,
      1887-88).

      Thibaudeau, Antoine-Claire, *Histoire des États généraux et des
      institutions représentatives en France* (Paris, 1843).

EF   Todd, Alpheus, *On Parliamentary Government in England* (2
      vols., London, 1867-69).

*   Tomkins, Frederick James, and Henry Diedrich Jencken, *A
      Compendium of the Modern Roman Law* . . . (London, 1870).

*   Warren, Samuel, *A Popular and Practical Introduction to Law
      Studies, and to Every Department of the Legal Profession*,
      3rd enl. edn. (2 vols., London, 1863).

tr   Wilson, Sir Roland Knyvet, *History of Modern English Law*
      (London, 1875).

From the Diary of Horace Elisha Scudder

Thursday 15 June [1893]

After much perplexity revised Woodrow Wilson's review of
Morse's Lincoln so as to get rid of the most objectionable feature[1]
and sent it to the Press. . . .

Bound diary (H. E. Scudder Papers, MH).
  1 Which Scudder explains in the letter that follows.

From Horace Elisha Scudder

My dear Wilson   [Cambridge, Mass.] 15 June 1893

I came back from a journey to Kansas, where I indulged in two Commencement addresses, a few days ago, to find your two letters and the article on my desk. I have read the paper[1] with great interest, but I will admit frankly with some perplexity. I respect the integrity of other men's work, and I should be slow to take exception with my less severe training, to any interpretation you might give to historical writing. Nevertheless, I doubt the absolute justice of your review of Morse, because I think you are demanding of him one kind of a book when he has chosen deliberately to write another. I do not think he set himself the task of writing a biography of Lincoln. The "Statesmen" books are studies in public service based upon biography, just as the "Men of Letters" both in the English & the American series are studies in literary history based upon biography.

After due reflection I have decided to revise your paper in the light of this. If it were professedly yours I should not do this, but return it to you. In my apprehension it is an *Atlantic* paper and therefore I have felt justified in making certain changes which I think keep your statements as written but modify the applicability to Morse's book. You will see proof and I shall be very glad if you find it possible further to touch up the paper.

What you say of Rhodes's point of view is so good that I re-enforced it by a brief sentence. Now I wish you would write a signed paper upon the qualities which should enter into a history of the United States of the period embraced in Rhodes's history. Perhaps you might be embarrassed by the fact of your own book, but I think I see a first rate essay.

Faithfully yours   H. E. Scudder.

ALS (Houghton Mifflin Letterpress Books, MH).
  1 Wilson's review of Rhodes's first two volumes, Morse's *Lincoln*, and Pierce's *Sumner*.

To Charles Scribner's Sons

My dear Sirs,   Princeton, New Jersey, 17th. June, 1893.

Your letter of June 12th. reached me just as I was on the eve of leaving home for a few days;[1] this must explain my delay in answering it.

It gives me pleasure to accept your proposal to publish my "Old Master, and Other Political Essays," upon the terms mentioned, in your letter of the above named date. If you will be kind enough to have the essays returned to me at an early date, I will undertake the revision of which I spoke in my letter at once. I can promise that the revision will occupy only a short time.

Very sincerely Yours,   Woodrow Wilson

WWTLS (Charles Scribner's Sons Archives, NjP).
 [1] He delivered "Democracy" as the Commencement Oration at Elmira College on June 14. See the news item printed at July 1, 1893.

To Horace Elisha Scudder

My dear Mr. Scudder,   Princeton, New Jersey, 17 June, 1893.

You did perfectly right to treat my review as you pleased. It *is* an *Atlantic* article and I have no jealousy of changes. I am only sorry I could not suit your taste in the writing. I approached both books with strong favourable prepossessions; but, as I read, these gave way to a deep disappointment. I even made the judgment I wrote much milder in its strictures than it would have been had it been a *signed* review. But it is wholly at your disposal,—even to return unused, if you prefer. All I can say of it is, that it is as carefully adjusted to right standards as I am capable of making it.

I am sorry I cannot write the article you suggest. I should be very sensitive to a charge of bad taste in writing it just now. At the risk of seeming a bit perverse, I send you, instead, a piece entitled "Mere Literature,"—a companion essay to that on "The Author Himself," which you were good enough to publish two years ago. I hope you will find this better than that.

Most cordially Yours,   Woodrow Wilson

ALS (WC, NjP).

EDITORIAL NOTE
"MERE LITERATURE"

Wilson's essay, "Mere Literature," printed below, was his most passionate protest against the trend, current in the 1880's and 1890's in the United States, principally at The Johns Hopkins University, toward the "scientific" study of literature through philology and textual criticism. "Mere Literature" was also one of Wilson's most eloquent pleas for studying literature because it was a prime vehicle of enduring western and Judeo-Christian traditions and values, and for a decent regard for good style and emphasis upon the "human element" in historical writing.

According to Lyman Pierson Powell, who was a graduate student at the Hopkins from 1890 to 1892, the writing of "Mere Literature" grew out of an incident that occurred while Wilson was giving his lectures on administration at the university in 1891. Powell later recalled that Stockton Axson, who was spending an unhappy year as a graduate student in the English Department,[1] told Wilson that the distinguished philologist, James Wilson Bright, had referred to some work as "mere literature." Wilson, Powell's account continues, stormed into the Bluntschli Library and said to Powell, "Mere literature—mere literature; I'll get even with him!"[2]

There is no reason to believe that Powell's story is apocryphal. However, all evidence indicates that Wilson wrote "Mere Literature" in 1893, not at white heat after the incident of 1891. Robert Bridges, in a letter to Wilson of September 20, 1891,[3] commenting on the latter's literary essay, "The Author Himself,"[4] said that Edward Livermore Burlingame, editor of *Scribner's Magazine*, who had earlier rejected several of Wilson's pieces, had liked the essay very much; and that he, Bridges, hoped that Wilson would send his next such article to *Scribner's*. Wilson replied on September 22, 1891, promising to let *Scribner's* have his next literary essay. If he had already written "Mere Literature," he surely would have sent it at once after receiving Bridges' letter.

The evidence indicates that the following is what happened:

Wilson did not forget Bright's slur against "mere literature." Moreover, his dislike of Bright and the Hopkins English Department was exacerbated when the university authorities did not yield to Wilson's strong plea that they appoint his friend, Caleb Thomas Winchester of Wesleyan, to the Donovan Chair of English Literature.[5] Wilson may well have written "Mere Literature" during the last two weeks of February 1893. Having completed the new notes for his administration lectures on February 15, he would have had plenty of time for such an exercise before he returned to Princeton in early March. In any event, Wilson almost certainly wrote "Mere Literature" between about February 15 and June 1, 1893. Joseph Ruggles Wilson's letter of July 6, 1893, reveals that at some time well before this date Woodrow Wilson had submitted the essay to *Scribner's*, as he had earlier promised Bridges he would do, and that Burlingame had rejected it. Wilson seized the opportunity afforded by the invitation in Scudder's letter of June 15, 1893, to submit "Mere Literature" to the *Atlantic Monthly*.

One finds persuasive corroboration of the conclusion that "Mere Literature" came from Wilson's pen in the early months of 1893 in certain letters that he wrote in the spring of that year. The sentence in Wilson's letter to August Octavius Bacon of June 2, 1893—"I have

[1] See, e.g., S. Axson to WW, Oct. 15, 1890, Vol. 7.
[2] Henry W. Bragdon, notes of an interview with Lyman P. Powell, March 26, 1940, MS. in the possession of Mr. Bragdon.
[3] Printed in Vol. 7.
[4] Printed at Dec. 7, 1887, Vol. 5.
[5] See, e.g., WW to D. C. Gilman, March 29 and April 16, 1891, and D. C. Gilman to WW, April 7, 1891, all in Vol. 7.

. . . devoted not a little time and attention to the question of university instruction in English"—might well have referred to the recently completed essay. The strong antipathy voiced in "Mere Literature" toward what Wilson condemned as pedantic philological study comes out in his letters, for example, to Richard McIlwaine of April 23, 1893, and to William Ellison Boggs of May 17, 1893. The exasperated comments in these and other letters make it perfectly clear that "Mere Literature" was a direct reply to and condemnation of Bright and his method. Furthermore, there is a strong echo of Wilson's strictures against pedantic historians who wrote without regard to style in his letter to Professor Winchester of May 29, 1893, in which he said that historians had no more literature in them than "an ass has of beauty."

No manuscript copy of "Mere Literature" has survived. The text as it first appeared in the *Atlantic Monthly* is printed at the date on which Wilson sent it to Scudder, on the assumption that it includes changes made just before Wilson mailed it.

A Literary Essay

[*c. June 17, 1893*]

"MERE LITERATURE."

A singular phrase this, "mere literature,"—the irreverent invention of a scientific age. Literature we know, but "mere" literature? We are not to read it as if it meant *sheer* literature, literature in the essence, stripped of all accidental or ephemeral elements, and left with nothing but its immortal charm and power. "Mere literature" is a serious sneer, conceived in all honesty by the scientific mind, which despises things which do not fall within the categories of demonstrable knowledge. It means *nothing but literature*, as who should say, "mere talk," "mere fabrication," "mere pastime." The scientist, with his head comfortably and excusably full of knowable things, takes nothing seriously and with his hat off except human knowledge. The creations of the human spirit are, from his point of view, incalculable vagaries, irresponsible phenomena, to be regarded only as play, and, for the mind's good, only as recreation,—to be used to while away the tedium of a railway journey, or to amuse a period of rest or convalescence; mere byplay, mere make-believe.

And so very whimsical things sometimes happen, because of this scientific and positivist spirit of the age, when the study of the literature of any language is made part of the curriculum of our colleges. The more delicate and subtle purposes of the study are put quite out of countenance, and literature is commanded to assume the phrases and the methods of science. It would be very painful if it should turn out that schools and universities were agencies of Philistinism; but there are some things which should prepare us for such a discovery. Our present plans for teaching everybody involve certain unpleasant things quite inevitably. It is obvious that you cannot have universal education without restricting your teaching to such things as can be universally understood. It is plain that you cannot impart "university methods" to thousands, or create "investigators" by the score, unless you confine your university education to matters which dull men can investigate, your laboratory training to tasks which mere plodding diligence and submissive patience can compass. Yet, if you do so limit and constrain what you teach, you thrust taste and insight and delicacy of perception out of the schools, exalt the obvious and the merely useful above the things which are only imaginatively or spiritually conceived, make education an affair of tasting and handling and smelling, and so create Philistia, that country in which they speak of "mere literature." I suppose that in Nirvana one would speak in like wise of "mere life."

The fear, at any rate, that such things may happen cannot fail to set us anxiously pondering certain questions about the systematic teaching of literature in our schools and colleges. How are we to impart classical writings to the children of the general public? "Beshrew the general public!" cries Mr. Birrell. "What in the name of the Bodleian has the general public got to do with literature?" Unfortunately, it has a great deal to do with it; for are we not complacently forcing the general public into our universities, and are we not arranging that all its sons be instructed how they may themselves master and teach our literature? You have nowadays, it is believed, only to heed the suggestions of pedagogics in order to know how to impart Burke or Browning, Dryden or Swift. There are certain practical difficulties, indeed; but there are ways of overcoming them. You must have strength so that you can handle with real mastery the firm fibre of these men; you must have a heart, moreover, to feel their warmth, an eye to see what they see, an imagination to keep them company, a pulse to experience their delights. But if you have none of these things, you may make shift to do without them. You may count the words they use, note the changes of phrase they make in successive revisions, put their rhythm into a scale of feet, run their allusions—particularly their female allusions—to cover, detect them in their previous reading. Or if none of these things please you, or you find the big authors difficult or dull, you may drag to light all the minor writers of their time, who are easy to understand. By setting an example in such methods you render great services in certain directions. You make the higher degrees of our universities available for the large number of respectable men who can count, and measure, and search diligently; and that may prove no small matter. You divert attention from thought, which is not always easy to get at, and fix attention upon language, as upon a curious mechanism, which can be perceived with the bodily eye, and which is worthy to be studied for its own sake, quite apart from anything it may mean. You encourage the examination of forms, grammatical and metrical, which can be quite accurately determined and quite exhaustively catalogued. You bring all the visible phenomena of writing to light and into ordered system. You go further, and show how to make careful literal identification of stories somewhere told ill and without art with the same stories told over again by the masters, well and with the transfiguring effect of genius. You thus broaden the area of science; for you rescue the concrete phenomena of the expression of thought—the necessary syllabification which accompanies it, the inevitable juxtaposition of words, the constant use of particles, the habitual display of roots, the inveterate repetition of names, the recurrent employment of meanings heard or read—from their confusion with the otherwise unclassifiable manifestations of what had hitherto been accepted, without critical examination, under the lump term "literature," simply for the pleasure and spiritual edification to be got from it.

An instructive differentiation ensues. In contrast with the orderly phenomena of speech and writing, which are amenable to scientific processes of examination and classification, and which take rank with the orderly successions of change in nature, we have what, for want of a more exact term, we call "mere literature,"—the literature which is not an expression of form, but an expression of spirit. This is a troublesome thing, and perhaps does not belong in well-conceived plans of universal instruction; for it offers many embarrassments to pedagogic method. It escapes all scientific categories. It is not pervious to research. It is too wayward to be brought under the discipline of exposition. It is an attribute of so many different substances at one and the same time that the consistent scientific man must needs put it forth from his company, as without responsible connections. By "mere literature" he means mere evanescent color, wanton trick of phrase, perverse departures from categorical statement,—something *all* personal equation, such stuff as dreams are made of.

We must not all, however, be impatient of this truant child of fancy. When the schools cast her out, she will stand in need of friendly succor, and we must train our spirits for the function.

We must be free-hearted in order to make her happy, for she will accept entertainment from no sober, prudent fellow who shall counsel her to mend her ways. She has always made light of hardship, and she has never loved or obeyed any save those of her own mind,—those who were indulgent to her humors, responsive to her ways of thought, attentive to her whims, content with her "mere" charms. She already has her small following of devotees, like all charming, capricious mistresses. There are some still who think that to know her is better than a liberal education.

There is but one way in which you can take mere literature as an education, and that is directly, at first hand. Almost any media except her own language and touch and tone are non-conducting. A descriptive catalogue of a collection of paintings is no substitute for the little areas of color and form themselves. You do not want to hear about a beautiful woman, simply,—how she was dressed, how she bore herself, how the fine color flowed sweetly here and there upon her cheeks, how her eyes burned and melted, how her voice thrilled through the ears of those about her. If you have ever seen a woman, these things but tantalize and hurt you, if you cannot see her. You want to be in her presence. You know that only your own eyes can give you direct knowledge of her. When once you have seen her, you know her in her habit as she lived; nothing but her presence contains her life. 'T is the same with the authentic products of literature. You can never get their beauty at second hand, or feel their power except by direct contact with them.

It is a strange and occult thing how this quality of "mere literature" enters into one book, and is absent from another; but no man who has once felt it can mistake it. I was reading the other day a book about Canada.[1] It is written in what the reviewers have pronounced to be an "admirable spirited style." By this I take them to mean that it is grammatical, orderly, and full of strong adjectives. But these reviewers would have known more about the style in which it is written if they had noted what happens on page 84. There a quotation from Burke occurs. "There is," says Burke, "but one healing, catholic principle of toleration which ought to find favor in this house. It is wanted not only in our colonies, but here. The thirsty earth of our own country is gasping and gaping and crying out for that healing shower from heaven. The noble lord has told you of the right of those people by treaty; but I consider the right of conquest so little, and the right of human nature so much, that the former has very little consideration with me. I look upon the people of Canada as

[1] The Editors have been unable to identify this book.

coming by the dispensation of God under the British government. I would have us govern it in the same manner as the all-wise disposition of Providence would govern it. We know he suffers the sun to shine upon the righteous and the unrighteous; and we ought to suffer all classes to enjoy equally the right of worshiping God according to the light he has been pleased to give them." Now, the peculiarity of such a passage as that is, that it needs no context. Its beauty seems almost independent of its subject matter. It comes on that eighty-fourth page like a burst of music in the midst of small talk,—a tone of sweet harmony heard amidst a rattle of phrases. The mild noise was unobjectionable enough until the music came. There is a breath and stir of life in those sentences of Burke's which is to be perceived in nothing else in that volume. Your pulses catch a quicker movement from them, and are stronger on their account.

It is so with all essential literature. It has a quality to move you, and you can never mistake it, if you have any blood in you. And it has also a power to instruct you which is as effective as it is subtle, and which no research or systematic method can ever rival. 'T is a sore pity if that power cannot be made available in the classroom. It is not merely that it quickens your thought and fills your imagination with the images that have illuminated the choicer minds of the race. It does indeed exercise the faculties in this wise, bringing them into the best atmosphere, and into the presence of the men of greatest charm and force; but it does a great deal more than that. It acquaints the mind, by direct contact, with the forces which really govern and modify the world from generation to generation. There is more of a nation's politics to be gotten out of its poetry than out of all its systematic writers upon public affairs and constitutions. Epics are better mirrors of manners than chronicles; dramas oftentimes let you into the secrets of statutes; orations stirred by a deep energy of emotion or resolution, passionate pamphlets that survive their mission because of the direct action of their style along permanent lines of thought, contain more history than parliamentary journals. It is not knowledge that moves the world, but ideals, convictions, the opinions or fancies that have been held or followed; and whoever studies humanity ought to study it alive, practice the vivisection of reading literature, and acquaint himself with something more than anatomies which are no longer in use by spirits.

There are some words of Thibaut, the great jurist, which have long seemed to me singularly penetrative of one of the secrets of the intellectual life. "I told him," he says,—he is speaking of an interview with Niebuhr,—"I told him that I owed my gayety and vigor, in great part, to my love for the classics of all ages, even those outside the domain of jurisprudence." Not only the gayety and vigor of his hale old age, surely, but also his insight into the meaning and purpose of laws and institutions. The jurist who does not love the classics of all ages is like a post-mortem doctor presiding at a birth, a maker of manikins prescribing for a disease of the blood, a student of masks setting up for a connoisseur in smiles and kisses. In narrating history, you are speaking of what was done by men; in discoursing of laws, you are seeking to show what courses of action and what manner of dealing with one another men have adopted. You can neither tell the story nor conceive the law till you know how the men you speak of regarded themselves and one another; and I know of no way of learning this but by reading the stories they have told of themselves, the songs they have sung, the heroic adventures they have conceived. I must know what, if anything, they revered; I must hear their sneers and gibes; must learn in what accents they spoke love within the family circle, with what grace they obeyed their superiors in station; how they conceived it politic to live, and wise to die; how they esteemed property, and what they deemed privilege; when they kept holiday, and why; when they were prone to resist oppression, and wherefore,—I must see things with their eyes, before I can comprehend their law books. Their jural relationships are not independent of their way of living, and their way of thinking is the mirror of their way of living.

It is doubtless due to the scientific spirit of the age that these plain, these immemorial truths are in danger of becoming obscured. Science, under the influence of the conception of evolution, devotes itself to the study of forms, of specific differences, of the manner in which the same principle of life manifests itself variously under the compulsions of changes of environment. It is thus that it has become "scientific" to set forth the manner in which man's nature submits to man's circumstances; scientific to disclose morbid moods, and the conditions which produce them; scientific to regard man, not as the centre or source of power, but as subject to power, a register of external forces instead of an originative soul, and character as a product of man's circumstances rather than a sign of man's mastery over circumstance. It is thus that it has become "scientific" to analyze language as itself a commanding element in man's life. The history of word roots, their modification under the influences of changes wrought in the vocal organs by habit or by climate, the laws of phonetic change to which they are obedient, and their persistence under all disguises of dialect, as if they were full of a self-originated life, a self-directed energy of influence, is united with the study of grammatical forms in the construction of scientific conceptions of the evolution and uses of human speech. The impression is created that literature is only the chosen vessel of these forms, disclosing to us their modification in use and structure from age to age. Such vitality as the masterpieces of genius possess comes to seem only a dramatization of the fortunes of words. Great writers construct for the adventures of language their appropriate epics. Or, if it be not the words themselves that are scrutinized, but the style of their use, that style becomes, instead of a fine essence of personality, a matter of cadence merely, or of grammatical and structural relationships. Science is the study of the forces of the world of matter, the adjustments, the apparatus, of the universe; and the scientific study of literature has likewise become a study of apparatus,—of the forms in which men utter thought, and the forces by which those forms have been and still are being modified, rather than of thought itself.

The essences of literature of course remain the same under all forms, and the true study of literature is the study of these essences,—a study, not of forms or of differences, but of likenesses, likenesses of spirit and intent under whatever varieties of method, running through all forms of speech like the same music along the chords of various instruments. There is a sense in which literature is independent of form, just as there is a sense in which music is independent of its instrument. It is my cherished belief that Apollo's pipe contained as much eloquent music as any modern orchestra. Some books live; many die: wherein is the secret of immortality? Not in beauty of form, nor even in force of passion. We might say of literature what Wordsworth said of poetry, the most easily immortal part of literature: it is "the impassioned expression which is in the countenance of all science; it is the breath of the finer spirit of all knowledge." Poetry has the easier immortality because it has the sweeter accent when it speaks, because its phrases linger in our ears to delight them, because its truths are also melodies. Prose has much to overcome,—its plainness of visage, its less musical accents, its homelier turns of phrase. But it also may contain the immortal essence of truth and seriousness and high thought. It too may clothe conviction with the beauty that must make it shine forever. Let a man but have beauty in his heart, and, believing something with his might, put it forth arrayed as he sees it, the lights and shadows falling upon it on his page as they fall upon it in his heart, and he may die assured that that beauty will not pass away out of the world.

Biographers have often been puzzled by the contrast between certain men as they lived and as they wrote. Schopenhauer's case is one of the most singular. A man of turbulent life, suffering himself to be cut to exasperation by the petty worries of his lot, he was nevertheless calm and wise when he wrote, as if the Muse had rebuked him. He wrote at a still elevation, where small and temporary things did not come to disturb. 'T is a pity that for some men this elevation is so far to seek. They lose permanency by not finding it. Could there be a deliberate regimen of life for the author, it is plain enough how he ought to live, not as seeking fame, but as deserving it.

"Fame, like a wayward girl, will still be coy
To those who woo her with too slavish knees;
But makes surrender to some thoughtless boy,
And dotes the more upon a heart at ease.

.   .   .   .

"Ye love-sick bards, repay her scorn with scorn;
Ye love-sick artists, madmen that ye are,
Make your best bow to her and bid adieu:
Then, if she likes it, she will follow you."[2]

It behooves all minor authors to realize the possibility of their being discovered some day, and exposed to the general scrutiny. They ought to live as if conscious of the risk. They ought to purge their hearts of everything that is not genuine and capable of lasting the world a century, at least, if need be. Mere literature is made of spirit. The difficulties of style are the artist's difficulties with his tools. The spirit that is in the eye, in the pose, in mien or gesture, the painter must find in his color box; as he must find also the spirit that nature displays upon the face of the fields or in the hidden places of the forest. The writer has less obvious means. Word and spirit do not easily consort. The language that the philologists set out before us with such curious erudition is of very little use as a vehicle for the essences of the human spirit. It is too sophisticated and self-conscious. What you need is, not a critical knowledge of language, but a quick feeling for it. You must recognize the affinities between your spirit and its idioms. You must immerse your phrase in your thought, your thought in your phrase, till each becomes saturated with the other. Then what you produce is as necessarily fit for permanency as if it were incarnated spirit.

2 From Keats's "Sonnet on Fame."

And you must produce in color, with the touch of imagination which lifts what you write away from the dull levels of mere exposition. Black-and-white sketches may serve some purposes of the artist, but very little of actual nature is in mere black-and-white. The imagination never works thus with satisfaction. Nothing is ever conceived completely when conceived so grayly, without suffusion of real light. The mind creates, as great Nature does, in colors, with deep chiaroscuro and burning lights. This is true not only of poetry and characteristically imaginative writing, but also of the writing which seeks nothing more than to penetrate the meaning of actual affairs,—the writing of the greatest historians and philosophers, the utterances of orators and of the great masters of political exposition. Their narratives, their analyses, their appeals, their conceptions of principle, are all dipped deep in the colors of the life they expound. Their minds respond only to realities, their eyes see only actual circumstance. Their sentences quiver and are quick with visions of human affairs,—how minds are bent or governed, how action is shaped or thwarted. The great "constructive" minds, as we call them, are of this sort. They "construct" by seeing what others have not imagination enough to see. They do not always know more, but they always realize more. Let the singular reconstruction of Roman history and institutions by Theodor Mommsen serve as an illustration. Safe men distrust this great master. They cannot find what he finds in the documents. They will draw you truncated figures of the antique Roman state, and tell you the limbs cannot be found, the features of the face have nowhere been unearthed. They will cite you fragments such as remain, and show you how far these can be pieced together toward the making of a complete description of private life and public function in those first times when the Roman commonwealth was young; but what the missing sentences were they can only weakly conjecture. Their eyes cannot descry those distant days with no other aids than these. Only the greatest are dissatisfied, and go on to paint that ancient life with the materials that will render it lifelike,—the materials of the constructive imagination. They have other sources of information. They see living men in the old documents. Give them but the torso, and they will supply head and limbs, bright and animate as they must have been. If Mommsen does not quite do that, another man, with Mommsen's eye and a touch more of color on his brush, might have done it,—may yet do it.

It is in this way that we get some glimpse of the only relations that scholarship bears to literature. Literature can do without exact scholarship, or any scholarship at all, though it may impoverish itself thereby; but scholarship cannot do without literature. It needs literature to float it, to set it current, to authenticate it to the race, to get it out of closets, and into the brains of men who stir abroad. It will adorn literature, no doubt; literature will be the richer for its presence; but it will not, it cannot, of itself create literature. Rich stuffs from the East do not create a king, nor costly trappings a conqueror. There is, indeed, a natural antagonism, let it be frankly said, between the standards of scholarship and the standards of literature. Exact scholarship values things in direct proportion as they are verifiable; but literature knows nothing of such tests. The truths which it seeks are the truths of self-expression. It is a thing of convictions, of insights, of what is felt and seen and heard and hoped for. Its meanings lurk behind nature, not in the facts of its phenomena. It speaks of things as the man who utters it saw them, not necessarily as God made them. The personality of the speaker runs throughout all the sentences of real literature. That personality may not be the personality of a poet: it may be only the personality of the penetrative seer. It may not have the atmosphere in which visions are seen, but only that in which men and affairs look keenly cut in outline, boldly massed in bulk, consummately grouped in detail, to the reader as to the writer. Sentences of perfectly clarified wisdom may be literature no less than stanzas of inspired song, or the intense utterances of impassioned feeling. The personality of the sunlight is in the keen lines of light that run along the edges of a sword no less than in the burning splendor of the rose or the radiant kindlings of a woman's eye. You may feel the power of one master of thought playing upon your brain as you may feel that of another playing upon your heart.

Scholarship gets into literature by becoming part of the originating individuality of a master of thought. No man is a master of thought without being also a master of its vehicle and instrument, style, that subtle medium of all its evasive effects of light and shade. Scholarship is material; it is not life. It becomes immortal only when it is worked upon by conviction, by schooled and chastened imagination, by thought that runs alive out of the inner fountains of individual insight and purpose. Colorless, or without suffusion of light from some source of light, it is dead, and will not twice be looked at; but made part of the life of a great mind, subordinated, absorbed, put forth with authentic stamp of currency on it, minted at some definite mint and bearing some sovereign image, it will even outlast the time when it shall have ceased to deserve the acceptance of scholars,—when it shall, in fact, have become "mere literature."

Scholarship is the realm of nicely adjusted opinion. It is the business of scholars to assess evidence and test conclusions, to discriminate values and reckon probabilities. Literature is the realm of conviction and of vision. Its points of view are as various as they are oftentimes unverifiable. It speaks individual faiths. Its groundwork is not erudition, but reflection and fancy. Your thoroughgoing scholar dare not reflect. To reflect is to let himself in on his material; whereas what he wants is to keep himself apart, and view his materials in an air that does not color or refract. To reflect is to throw an atmosphere about what is in your mind,—an atmosphere which holds all the colors of your life. Reflection summons all associations, and they throng and move so that they dominate the mind's stage at once. The plot is in their hands. Scholars, therefore, do not reflect; they label, group kind with kind, set forth in schemes, expound with dispassionate method. Their minds are not stages, but museums; nothing is done there, but very curious and valuable collections are kept there. If literature use scholarship, it is only to fill it with fancies or shape it to new standards, of which of itself it can know nothing.

True, there are books reckoned primarily books of science and of scholarship which have nevertheless won standing as literature: books of science such as Newton wrote, books of scholarship such as Gibbon's. But science was only the vestibule by which such a man as Newton entered the temple of nature, and the art he practiced was not the art of exposition, but the art of divination. He was not only a scientist, but also a seer; and we shall not lose sight of Newton because we value what he was more than what he knew. If we continue Gibbon in his fame, it will be for love of his art, not for worship of his scholarship. We some of us, nowadays, know the period of which he wrote better even than he did; but which one of us shall build so admirable a monument to ourselves, as artists, out of what we know? The scholar finds his immortality in the form he gives to his work. It is a hard saying, but the truth of it is inexorable: be an artist, or prepare for oblivion. You may write a chronicle, but you will not serve yourself thereby. You will only serve some fellow who shall come after you, possessing, what you did not have, an ear for the words you could not hit upon, an eye for the colors you could not see, a hand for the strokes you missed.

Real literature you can always distinguish by its form, and yet it is not possible to indicate the form it should have. It is easy to say that it should have a form suitable to its matter; but how suitable? Suitable to set the matter off, adorn, embellish it, or suitable simply to bring it directly, quick and potent, to the apprehension of the reader? This is the question of style, about which many masters have had many opinions; upon which you can make up no safe generalization from the practice of those who have unquestionably given to the matter of their thought immortal form, an accent or a countenance never to be forgotten. Who shall say how much of Burke's splendid and impressive imagery is part and stuff of his thought, or tell why even that part of Newman's prose which is devoid of ornament, stripped to its shining skin, and running bare and lithe and athletic to carry its tidings to men, should promise to enjoy as certain an immortality? Why should Lamb go so quaintly and elaborately to work upon his critical essays, taking care to perfume every sentence, if possible, with the fine savor of an old phrase, if the same business could be as effectively done in the plain and even cadences of Mr. Matthew Arnold's prose? Why should Gibbon be so formal, so stately, so elaborate, when he had before his eyes the example of great Tacitus, whose direct, sententious style had outlived so many hundred years the very language in which he wrote? In poetry, who shall measure the varieties of style lavished upon similar themes? The matter of vital thought is not separable from the thinker; its forms must suit his handling as well as fit his conception. Any style is author's stuff which is suitable to his purpose and his fancy. He may use rich fabrics with which to costume his thoughts, or he may use simple stone from which to sculpture them, and leave them bare. His only limits are those of art. He may not indulge a taste for the merely curious or fantastic. The quaint writers have quaint thoughts; their material is suitable. They do not merely satisfy themselves as virtuosi, with collections of odd phrases and obsolete meanings. They needed twisted woods to fit the eccentric patterns of their thought. The great writer has always dignity, restraint, propriety, adequateness; what time he loses these qualities he ceases to be great. His style neither creaks nor breaks under his passion, but carries the strain with unshaken strength. It is not trivial or mean, but speaks what small meanings fall in its way with simplicity, as conscious of their smallness. Its playfulness is within bounds, its laugh never bursting too boisterously into a guffaw. A great style always knows what it would be at, and does the thing appropriately, with the larger sort of taste.

This is the condemnation of tricks of phrase, devices to catch the attention, exaggerations and loud talk to hold it. No writer can afford to strive after effect, if his striving is to be apparent. For just and permanent effect is missed altogether, unless it be so completely attained as to seem like some touch of sunlight, perfect, natural, inevitable, wrought without effort and without deliberate purpose to be effective. Mere audacity of attempt can, of course, never win the wished-for result; and if the attempt be successful, it is not audacious. What we call audacity in a great writer has no touch of temerity, sauciness, or arrogance in it. It is simply high spirit, a dashing and splendid display of strength. Boldness is ridiculous unless it be impressive, and it can be impressive only when backed by solid forces of character and attainment. Your plebeian hack cannot afford the showy paces; only the full-blooded Arabian has the sinew and proportion to lend them perfect grace and propriety. The art of letters eschews the bizarre as rigidly as does every other fine art. It mixes its colors with brains, and is obedient to great Nature's sane standards of right adjustment in all that it attempts.

You can make no catalogue of these features of great writing; there is no science of literature. Literature in its essence is mere spirit, and you must experience it rather than analyze it too formally. It is the door to nature and to ourselves. It opens our hearts to receive the experiences of great men and the conceptions of great races. It awakens us to the significance of action and to the singular power of mental habit. It airs our souls in the wide atmosphere of contemplation. "In these bad days, when it is thought more educationally useful to know the principle of the common pump than Keats's Ode on a Grecian Urn," as Mr. Birrell says, we cannot afford to let one single precious sentence of "mere literature" go by us unread or unpraised. If this free people to which we belong is to keep its fine spirit, its perfect temper amidst affairs, its high courage in the face of difficulties, its wise temperateness and wide-eyed hope, it must continue to drink deep and often from the old wells of English undefiled, quaff the keen tonic of its best ideals, keep its blood warm with all the great utterances of exalted purpose and pure principle of which its matchless literature is full. The great spirits of the past must command us in the tasks of the future. Mere literature will keep us pure and keep us strong. Even though it puzzle or altogether escape scientific method, it may keep our horizon clear for us, and our eyes glad to look bravely forth upon the world.

Woodrow Wilson.

Printed in the *Atlantic Monthly*, LXXII (Dec. 1893), 820-28.

To Albert Bushnell Hart

My dear Hart,   Princeton, New Jersey, 19 June, 1893.

All my correspondents have had of late to await the close of our college year, such is the rush of examination work at the end; but now the embargo is raised.

I have noted the corrections contained in the letters you were kind enough to forward to me. Those tabulated on one of the sheets you enclosed were my own, I suppose you know. Are the publishers going to afford another opportunity soon for corrections? I am noting these simply, not sending them to Longmans.

I do not see the Educational Review, and so have not seen von Holst's notice of my book.[1] The Longmans have sent me almost everything else, with great kindness.[2] I am still rather sick of the little volume, and read the reviews from a sort of sense of duty merely. Some day I may come to regard the thing with less dis-relish.

With warm regard,

Sincerely Yours,   Woodrow Wilson

TCL (RSB Coll., DLC).
   [1] It is printed at June 1, 1893.
   [2] The reviews that Longmans sent him are still in the Wilson Papers, Library of Congress, many of them in their original envelopes.

To Charles Scribner's Sons

My dear Sirs,   Princeton, New Jersey, 26 June, 1893.

I return the copy of "An Old Master and Other Political Essays" by Adams Express today revised and ready for the press, together with a very brief Prefatory Note.

The *New Princeton Review* was bought (what remained of it), you will remember, by Messrs. Ginn & Co. I wrote to them about a week ago to ask permission to publish the first and second of these essays. I have not heard from them yet, but take it for granted that their consent will not be withheld. The proprietors of the *Atlantic* sent their consent at once.

Very sincerely Yours,   Woodrow Wilson

WWTLS (Charles Scribner's Sons Archives, NjP).

A Political Essay

[c. *June 26, 1893*]
GOVERNMENT UNDER THE CONSTITUTION[1]

It is by no means wholly to our advantage that our constitutional law is contained in definitive written documents. The fact that it is thus formulated and rendered fixed and definite has seriously misled us, it is to be feared, as to the true function and efficacy of constitutional law. That law is not made more valid by being written, but only more explicit; it is not rendered more sacred, but only more definite and secure. Written constitutions are simply more or less successful generalizations of political experience. Their tone of authority does not at all alter the historical realities and imperative practical conditions of government. They determine forms, utter distinct purposes, set the powers of the State in definite hierarchy; but they do not make the forms they originate workable, or the purposes they utter feasible. All that must depend upon the men who become governors and upon the people over whom they are set in authority. Laws can have no other life than that which is given them by the men who administer and the men who obey them. Constitutional law affords no exception to the rule. The Constitution of the United States, happily, was framed by exceptional men thoroughly schooled in the realities of government. It consists, accordingly, not of principles newly invented, to be put into operation by means of devices originated for the occasion, but of sound pieces of tested experience. It has served its purpose beneficently, not because it was written, but because it has proved itself accordant in every essential part with tried principles of government—principles tested by the race for whose use it was intended, and therefore already embedded in their lives and practices. Its strength will be found, upon analysis, to lie in its definiteness and in its power to restrain rather than in any unusual excellence of its energetic parts. For the right operation of these it has had to depend, like other constitutions, upon the virtue and discretion of the people and their ministers. "The public powers are carefully defined; the mode in which they are to be exercised is fixed; and the amplest securities are taken that none of the more important constitutional arrangements shall be altered without every guarantee of caution and every opportunity for deliberation. . . . It would seem that,

[1] The copy of this essay that Wilson sent to the printer consists of tear sheets of "Responsible Government under the Constitution" (about which see WW to C. Scribner, May 16, 1893, ns. 1 and 3), to which Wilson added a long, new typed introduction and on which he made additions and changes by hand and typewriter.

by a wise constitution, democracy may be made nearly as calm as water in a great artificial reservoir."[2]

We possess, therefore, not a more suitable constitution than other countries, but a constitution which is perfectly definite and which is preserved by very formidable difficulties of amendment against inconsiderate change. The difference between our own case and that of Great Britain upon which we have most reason to congratulate ourselves is that here public opinion has definite *criteria* for its conservatism; whereas in England it has only shifting and uncertain precedent. In both countries there is the same respect for law. But there is not in England the same certainty as to what the law of the constitution is. We have a fundamental law which is written, and which in its main points is read by all alike in a single accepted sense. There is no more quarrel about its main intent than there is in England about the meaning of Magna Charta. Much of the British constitution, on the contrary, has not the support of even a common statute. It may, in respect of many vital parts of it, be interpreted or understood in half a dozen different ways, *and amended by the prevalent understanding*. We are not more free than the English; we are only more secure.

The definiteness of our Constitution, nevertheless, apart from its outline of structural arrangements and of the division of functions among the several departments of the government, is negative rather than affirmative. Its very enumeration of the powers of Congress is but a means of indicating very plainly what Congress can *not* do. It is significant that one of the most important and most highly esteemed of the many legal commentaries on our government should be entitled 'Constitutional Limitations.' In expounding the restrictions imposed by fundamental law upon state and federal action, Judge Cooley is allowed to have laid bare the most essential parts of our constitutional system. It was a prime necessity in so complex a structure that bounds should be set to authority. The 'may-nots' and the 'shall-nots' of our constitutions, consequently, give them their distinctive form and character. The strength which preserves the system is the strength of self-restraint.

And yet here again it must be understood that mere definiteness of legal provision has no saving efficacy of its own. These distinct lines run between power and power will not of their own virtue maintain themselves. It is not in having such a constitution but in obeying it that our advantage lies. The vitality

[2] Sir Henry Maine: Popular Government (Am. ed.), pp. 110, 111. [This and the following notes by WW. They have been numbered.]

of such provisions consists wholly in the fact that they receive our acquiescence. They rest upon the legal conscience, upon what Mr. Grote would have called the 'constitutional morality,' of our race. They are efficient because we are above all things law-abiding. The prohibitions of the law do not assert themselves as taskmasters set over us by some external power. They are of our own devising. We are self-restrained.

This legal conscience manifestly constitutes the only guarantee, for example, of the division of powers between the state and federal governments, that chief arrangement of our constitutional system. The integrity of the powers possessed by the States has from the first depended solely upon the conservatism of the federal courts. State functions have certainly not decayed; but they have been preserved, not by virtue of any forces of self-defence of their own, but because the national government has been vouchsafed the grace of self-restraint. What curtailment their province might suffer has been illustrated in several notable cases in which the Supreme Court of the United States has confirmed to the general government extensive powers of punishing state judicial and executive officers for disobedience to state laws. Although the federal courts have generally held Congress back from aggressions upon the States, they have nevertheless once and again countenanced serious encroachments upon state powers; and their occasional laxity of principle on such points is sufficiently significant of the fact that there is no *balance* between the state and federal governments, but only the safeguard of a customary 'constitutional morality' on the part of the federal courts. The actual encroachments upon state rights which those courts have permitted, under the pressure of strong political interests at critical periods, were not, however, needed to prove the potential supremacy of the federal government. They only showed how that potential supremacy would on occasion become actual supremacy. There is no guarantee but that of conscience that justice will be accorded a suitor when his adversary is both court and opposing litigant. So strong is the instinct of those who administer our governments to keep within the sanction of the law, that even when the last three amendments to the Constitution were being forced upon the southern states by means which were revolutionary the outward forms of the Constitution were observed. It was none the less obvious, however, with what sovereign impunity the national government might act in stripping those forms of their genuineness. As there are times of sorrow or of peril which try men's souls and lay bare the inner secrets of their characters, so there are times of revolution which act as fire in burning away all but the basic elements of constitutions. It is then, too, that dormant powers awake which are not afterward readily lulled to sleep again.

Such was certainly the effect of the civil war upon the Constitution of the Union. The implying of powers, once cautious, is now become bold and confident. In the discussions now going forward with reference to federal regulation of great corporations, and with reference to federal aid to education, there are scores of writers and speakers who tacitly assume the power of the federal government to act in such matters, for one that urges a constitutional objection. Constitutional objections, before the war habitual, have, it would seem, permanently lost their prominence.

The whole energy of origination under our system rests with Congress. It stands at the front of all government among us; it is the single affirmative voice in national policy. First or last, it determines what is to be done. The President, indeed, appoints officers and negotiates treaties, but he does so subject to the 'yes' of the Senate. Congress organizes the executive departments, organizes the army, organizes the navy. It audits, approves, and pays expenses. It conceives and directs all comprehensive policy. All else is negation. The President says 'no' in his vetoes; the Supreme Court says 'no' in its restraining decisions. And it is as much the law of public opinion as the law of the Constitution that restrains the action of Congress.

It is the habit both of English and American writers to speak of the constitution of Great Britain as if it were 'writ in water,' because nothing but the will of Parliament stands between it and revolutionary change. But is there nothing back of the will of Parliament? Parliament dare not go faster than the public thought. There are vast barriers of conservative public opinion to be overrun before a ruinous speed in revolutionary change can be attained. In the last analysis, our own Constitution has no better safeguard. We have, as I have already pointed out, the salient advantage of knowing just what the standards of our Constitution are. They are formulated in a written code, wherein all men may look and read; whereas many of the designs of the British system are to be sought only in a cloud-land of varying individual readings of affairs. From the constitutional student's point of view, there are, for instance, as many different Houses of Lords as there are writers upon the historical functions of that upper chamber. But the public opinion of Great Britain is no more a juggler of precedents than is the public opinion of this country. Perhaps the absence of a written constitution makes it even less a fancier of logical refinements. The arrangements of the British constitution have, for all their theoretical instability, a very firm and definite standing in the political habit of Englishmen: and the greatest of those arrangements can be done away with only by the extraordinary force of conscious revolution.

It is wholesome to observe how much of our own institutions rests upon the same basis, upon no other foundations than those that are laid in the opinions of the people. It is within the undoubted constitutional power of Congress, for example, to overwhelm the opposition of the Supreme Court upon any question by increasing the number of justices and refusing to confirm any appointments to the new places which do not promise to change the opinion of the court. Once, at least, it was believed that a plan of this sort had been carried deliberately into effect. But we do not think of such a violation of the spirit of the Constitution as possible, simply because we share and contribute to that public opinion which makes such outrages upon constitutional morality impossible by standing ready to curse them. There is a close analogy between this virtual inviolability of the Supreme Court and the integrity hitherto vouchsafed to the English House of Lords. There may be an indefinite creation of peers at any time that a strong ministry chooses to give the sovereign its imperative advice in favor of such a course. It was, doubtless, fear of the final impression that would be made upon public opinion by action so extraordinary, as much as the timely yielding of the Lords upon the question at issue, that held the ministry back from such a measure, on one notable occasion. Hitherto that ancient upper chamber has had in this regard the same protection that shields our federal judiciary.

It is not essentially a different case as between Congress and the Executive. Here, too, at the very centre of the Constitution, Congress stands almost supreme, restrained by public opinion rather than by law. What with the covetous admiration of the presidency recently manifested by some alarmed theorists in England, and the renewed prestige lately given that office by the prominence of the question of civil service reform, it is just now particularly difficult to apply political facts to an analysis of the President's power. But a clear conception of his real position is for that very reason all the more desirable. While he is a dominant figure in politics would seem to be the best time to scrutinize and understand him.

It is clearly misleading to use the ascendant influence of the President in effecting the objects of civil service reform as an illustration of the constitutional size and weight of his office.

The principal part in making administration pure, business-like, and efficient must always, under any conceivable system of government, be taken by the executive. It was certainly taken by the executive in England thirty years ago; and that much in opposition to the will of Parliament. The prominence of our President in administrative reform furnishes no sufficient ground for attributing a singularity of executive influence to the government of this country.

In estimating the actual powers of the President it is no doubt best to begin, as almost all writers in England and America now habitually begin, with a comparison between the executives of the two kindred countries. Whilst Mr. Bagehot has done more than any other thinker to clear up the facts of English constitutional practice, he has also, there is reason to believe, done something toward obscuring those facts. Everybody, for instance, has accepted as wholly true his description of the ministry of the Crown as merely an executive committee of the House of Commons; and yet that description is only partially true. An English cabinet represents, not the Commons only, but also the Crown. Indeed, it is itself 'the Crown.' All executive prerogatives are prerogatives which it is within the discretion of the cabinet itself to make free use of. The fact that it is generally the disposition of ministers to defer to the opinion of Parliament in the use of the prerogative, does not make that use the less a privilege strictly beyond the sphere of direct parliamentary control, to be exercised independently of its sanction, even secretly on occasion, when ministers see their way clear to serving the state thereby. "The ministry of the day," says a perspicacious expounder of the English system,[3] "appears in Parliament, on the one hand, as personating the Crown in the legitimate exercise of its recognized prerogatives; and on the other hand, as the mere agent of Parliament itself, in the discharge of the executive and administrative functions of government cast upon them by law." Within the province of the prerogative "lie the stirring topics of foreign negotiations, the management of the army and navy, public finance, and, in some important respects, colonial administration." Very recent English history furnishes abundant and striking evidence of the vitality of the prerogative in these fields in the hands of the gentlemen who "personate the Crown" in Parliament. "No subject has been more eagerly discussed of late," declares Mr. Amos (page 187), "than that of the province of Parliament in respect of the making of treaties and the declaration of

[3] Mr. Sheldon Amos: Fifty Years of the English Constitution, page 338.

war. No prerogative of the Crown is more undisputed than that of taking the initiative in all negotiations with foreign governments, conducting them throughout, and finally completing them by the signature and ratification of a treaty. . . . It is a bare fact that during the progress of the British diplomatic movements which terminated in the Treaty of Berlin of 1878, or more properly in the Afghan war of that year,"–including the secret treaty by which Turkey ceded Cyprus to England, and England assumed the protectorate of Asia Minor,–"Parliament never had an opportunity of expressing its mind on any one of the important and complicated engagements to which the country was being committed, or upon the policy of the war upon the northwest frontier of India. The subjects were, indeed, over and over again discussed in Parliament, but always subsequent to irreparable action having been taken by the government" (page 188). Had Mr. Amos lived to take his narrative of constitutional affairs beyond 1880, he would have had equally significant instances of ministerial initiative to adduce in the cases of Egypt and Burmah.

The unfortunate campaign in the Soudan was the direct outcome of the purchase of the Suez Canal shares by the British government in 1875. The result of that purchase was that "England became pledged in a wholly new and peculiar way to the support of the existing Turkish and Egyptian dominion in Egypt; that large English political interests were rendered subservient to the decisions of local tribunals in a foreign country; and that English diplomatic and political action in Egypt, and indeed in Europe, was trammelled, or at least indirectly influenced, by a narrow commercial interest which could not but weigh, however slightly, upon the apparent purity and simplicity of the motives of the English government." And yet the binding engagements which involved all this were entered into "despite the absence of all assistance from, or consent of, Parliament."[4] Such exercises of the prerogatives of the Crown receive additional weight from "the almost recognized right of evolving an army of almost any size from the Indian seed-plot, of using reserve forces without communication to Parliament in advance, and of obtaining large votes of credit for prospective military operations of an indefinite character, the nature of which Parliament is allowed only dimly to surmise" (page 392). The latest evidence of the "almost recognized" character of such rights was the war preparations made by England against Russia in 1885. If to such powers of committing the country irrevocably to far-reaching for-

[4] Amos, page 384.

eign policies, of inviting or precipitating war, and of using Indian troops without embarrassment from the trammels of the Mutiny Act, there be added the great discretionary functions involved in the administration of colonial affairs, some measure may be obtained of the power wielded by ministers, not as the mere agents of Parliament, but as personating the Crown. Such is in England the independence of action possible to the executive.

As compared with this, the power of the President is insignificant. Of course, as everybody says, he is more powerful than the sovereign of Great Britain. If relative personal power were the principle of etiquette, Mr. Cleveland would certainly not have to lift his hat to the Queen, because the Queen is not the English executive. The prerogatives of the Crown are still much greater than the prerogatives of the presidency; they are exercised, however, not by the wearer of the crown, but by the ministry of the Crown.

As Sir Henry Maine rightly says, the framers of our Constitution, consciously or unconsciously, made the President's office like the King's office under the English constitution of their time,—the constitution, namely, of George III., who chose his advisers with or without the assent of Parliament. They took care, however, to pare down the model where it seemed out of measure with the exercise of the people's liberty. They allowed the President to choose his ministers freely, as George then seemed to have established his right to do; but they made the confirmation of the Senate a necessary condition to his appointments. They vested in him the right of negotiating treaties with foreign governments; but he was not to sign and ratify treaties until he had obtained the sanction of the Senate. That oversight of executive action which Parliament had not yet had the spirit or the inclination to exert, and which it had forfeited its independence by not exerting, was forever secured to our federal upper chamber by the fundamental law. The conditions of mutual confidence and co-operation between executive and legislature now existing in England had not then been developed, and consequently could not be reproduced in this country. The posture and disposition of mutual wariness which were found existing there were made constitutional here by express written provision. In short, the transitional relations of the Crown and Parliament of that day were crystallized in our Constitution, such guarantees of executive good faith and legislative participation in the weightier determinations of government as were lacking in the model being sedulously added in the copy.

The really subordinate position of the presidency is hidden from view partly by that dignity which is imparted to the office by its conspicuous place at the front of a great government, and its security and definiteness of tenure; partly by the independence apparently secured to it by its erection into an entirely distinct and separate 'branch' of the government; and partly by those circumstances of our history which have thrust our Presidents forward, during one or two notable periods, as real originators of policy and leaders in affairs. The President has never been powerful, however, except at such times as he has had Congress at his back. While the new government was a-making—and principally because it was a-making—Washington and his secretaries were looked to by Congress for guidance; and during the presidencies of several of Washington's immediate successors the continued prominence of questions of foreign policy and of financial management kept the officers of the government in a position of semi-leadership. Jackson was masterful with or without right. He entered upon his presidency as he entered upon his campaign in Florida, without asking too curiously for constitutional warrant for what he was to undertake. In the settlement of the southern question Congress went for a time on all-fours with the President. He was powerful because Congress was acquiescent.

But such cases prove rather the usefulness than the strength of the presidency. Congress has, at several very grave crises in national affairs, been seasonably supplied with an energetic leader or agent in the person of the President. At other times, when Congress was in earnest in pushing views not shared by the President, our executives have either been overwhelmed, as Johnson was, or have had to decline upon much humbler services. Their negotiations with foreign governments are as likely to be disapproved as approved; their budgets are cut down like a younger son's portion; their appointments are censured and their administrations criticized without chance for a counter-hearing. They create nothing. Their veto is neither revisory nor corrective. It is merely obstructive. It is, as I have said, a simple blunt negation, oftentimes necessarily spoken without discrimination against a good bill because of a single bad clause in it. In such a contest between origination and negation origination must always win, or government must stand still.

In England the veto of the Crown has not passed out of use, as is commonly said. It has simply changed its form. It does not exist as an imperative, obstructive 'No,' uttered by the sovereign. It has passed over into the privilege of the ministers to throw their party weight, reinforced by their power to dissolve Parliament, against measures of which they disapprove. It is a much-tempered instrument, but for that reason all the more flexible and useful. The old, blunt, antagonistic veto is no longer needed. It is needed here, however, to preserve the presidency from the insignificance of merely administrative functions. Since executive and legislature cannot come into relations of mutual confidence and co-operation, the former must be put in a position to maintain a creditable competition for consideration and dignity.

A clear-headed, methodical, unimaginative President like Mr. Cleveland unaffectedly recognizes the fact that all creating, originating power rests with Congress, and that he can do no more than direct the details of such projects as he finds commended by its legislation. The suggestions of his message he acknowledges to be merely suggestions, which must depend upon public opinion for their weight. If Congress does not regard them, it must reckon with the people, not with him. It is his duty to tell Congress what he thinks concerning the pending questions of the day; it is not his duty to assume any responsibility for the effect produced on Congressmen.

The English have transformed their Crown into a Ministry, and in doing so have recognized both the supremacy of Parliament and the rôle of leadership in legislation properly belonging to a responsible executive. The result has been that they have kept a strong executive without abating either the power or the independence of the representative chamber in respect of its legislative function. We, on the contrary, have left our executive separate, as the Constitution made it; chiefly, it is to be suspected, because the explicit and confident gifts of function contained in that positive instrument have blinded us by their very positiveness to the real subordination of the executive resulting from such a separation. We have supposed that our President was great because his powers were specific, and that our Congress was not supreme because it could not lay its hands directly upon his office and turn him out. In fact, neither the dignity and power of the executive nor the importance of Congress is served by the arrangement. Being held off from authoritative suggestion in legislation, the President becomes, under ordinary circumstances, merely a ministerial officer; whilst Congress, on its part, deprived of such leadership, becomes a legislative mass meeting instead of a responsible co-operating member of a well-organized government. Being under the spell of the Constitution, we have been unable to see the facts which written documents can neither establish nor change.

Singularly enough, there is sharp opposition to the introduction into Congress of any such leadership on the part of the executive as the Ministers of the Crown enjoy in Parliament, on the ground of the increase of power which would accrue as a result to the legislature. It is said that such a change would, by centring party and personal responsibility in Congress, give too great a prominence to legislation; would make Congress the object of too excited an interest on the part of the people. Legislation in Parliament, instead of being piecemeal, tessellated work, such as is made up in Congress of the various fragments contributed by the standing committees, is, under each ministry, a continuous, consistent, coherent whole; and, instead of bearing the sanction of both national parties, is the peculiar policy of only one of them. It is thought that, if such coherence of plan, definiteness and continuity of aim, and sanction of party were to be given the work of Congress, the resulting concentration of popular interest and opinion would carry Congress over all the barriers of the Constitution to an undisputed throne of illimitable power. In short, the potential supremacy of Congress is thought to be kept within bounds, not by the constitutional power of the executive and the judiciary, its co-ordinate branches, but by the intrinsic dullness and confusion of its own proceedings. It cannot make itself interesting enough to be great.

But this is a two-edged argument, which one must needs handle with great caution. It is evidently calculated to destroy every argument constructed on the assumption that it is written laws which are effective to the salvation of our constitutional arrangements; for it is itself constructed on the opposite assumption, that it is the state of popular interest in the nation which balances the forces of the government. It would, too, serve with equal efficacy against any scheme whatever for reforming the present methods of legislation in Congress, with which almost everybody is dissatisfied. Any reform which should tend to give to national legislation that uniform, open, intelligent, and responsible character which it now lacks, would also create that popular interest in the proceedings of Congress which, it is said, would unhinge the Constitution. Democracy is so delicate a form of government that it must break down if given too great facility or efficacy of operation. No one body of men must be suffered to utter the voice of the people, lest that voice become, through it, directly supreme.

The fact of the overtopping power of Congress, however, remains. The houses create all governmental policy, with that wide latitude of 'political discretion' in the choice of means which the Supreme Court unstintingly accords them. Congress has often come into conflict with the Supreme Court by attempting to extend the province of the federal government as against the States; but it has seldom, I believe, been brought effectually to book for any alleged exercise of powers as against its directly competing branch, the executive. Having by constitutional grant the last word as to foreign relations, the control of the finances, and even the oversight of executive appointments, Congress exercises what powers of direction and management it pleases, as fulfilling, not as straining, the Constitution. Government lives in the origination, not in the defeat, of measures of government. The President obstructs by means of his 'No'; the houses govern by means of their 'Yes.' He has killed some policies that are dead; they have given birth to all policies that are alive.

But the measures born in Congress have no common lineage. They have not even a traceable kinship. They are fathered by a score or two of unrelated standing committees: and Congress stands godfather to them all, without discrimination. Congress, in effect, parcels out its great powers amongst groups of its members, and so confuses its plans and obscures all responsibility. It is a leading complaint of Sir Henry Maine's against the system in England, which is just under his nose, that it confers the preliminary shaping and the initiation of all legislation upon the cabinet, a body which deliberates and resolves in strict secrecy,—and so reminds him, remotely enough, of the Spartan Ephors and the Venetian Council of Ten. He commends, by contrast, that constitution (our own, which he sees at a great distance) which reserves to the legislature itself the origination and drafting of its measures. It is hard for us, who have this commended constitution under our noses, to perceive wherein we have the advantage. British legislation is for the most part originated and shaped by a single committee, acting in secret, whose proposals, when produced, are eagerly debated and freely judged by the sovereign legislative body. Our legislation is framed and initiated by a great many committees, deliberating in secret, whose proposals are seldom debated and only perfunctorily judged by the sovereign legislative body. It is impossible to mistake the position and privileges of the British cabinet, so great and conspicuous and much discussed are they. They simplify the whole British system for men's comprehension by merely standing at the centre of it. But our own system is simple only in appearance. It is easy to see that our legislature and executive are separate, and that the legislature matures its own measures by means of committees of its own members. But it may readily escape superficial observation that our legislature, instead of being served, is ruled by its committees; that those committees prepare their measures in private; that their number renders their privacy a secure secrecy, by making them too many to be watched, and individually too insignificant to be worth watching; that their division of prerogatives results in a loss, through diffusion, of all actual responsibility; and that their co-ordination leads to such a competition among them for the attention of their respective houses that legislation is rushed, when it is not paralyzed.

It is thus that, whilst all real power is in the hands of Congress, that power is often thrown out of gear and its exercise brought almost to a standstill. The competition of the committees is the clog. Their reports stand in the way of each other, and so the complaint is warranted that Congress can get nothing done. Interests which press for attention in the nation are reported upon by the appropriate committee, perhaps, but the report gets pushed to the wall. Or they are not reported upon. They are brought to the notice of Congress, but they go to a committee which is unfavorable. The progress of legislation depends both upon the fortunes of competing reports and upon the opinions held by particular committees.

The same system of committee government prevails in our state legislatures, and has led to some notable results, which have recently been pointed out in a pamphlet entitled *American Constitutions*, contributed to the Johns Hopkins series of Studies in History and Political Science by Mr. Horace Davis. In the state legislatures, as in Congress, the origination and control of legislation by standing committees has led to haphazard, incoherent, irresponsible law-making, and to a universal difficulty about getting anything done. The result has been that state legislatures have been falling into disrepute in all quarters. They are despised and mistrusted, and many States have revised their constitutions in order to curtail legislative powers and limit the number and length of legislative sessions. There is in some States an apparent inclination to allow legislators barely time enough to provide moneys for the maintenance of the governments. In some instances necessary powers have been transferred from the legislatures to the courts; in others to the governors. The intent of all such changes is manifest. It is thought safer to entrust power to a law court, performing definite functions under clear laws and in accordance with strict judicial standards, or to a single conspicuous magistrate, who can be watched and cannot escape responsibility for his official acts, than to entrust it to a numerous body which burrows toward its ends in committee-rooms, getting its light through lobbies; and which has a thousand devices for juggling away responsibility, as well as scores of antagonisms wherewith to paralyze itself.

Like fear and distrust have often been felt and expressed of late years concerning Congress, for like reasons. But so far no attempt has been made to restrict either the powers or the time of Congress. Amendments to the Constitution are difficult almost to the point of impossibility, and the few definite schemes now-adays put forward for a revision of the Constitution involve extensions rather than limitations of the powers of Congress. The fact is that, though often quite as exasperating to sober public opinion as any state legislature, Congress is neither so much distrusted nor so deserving of distrust. Its high place and vast sphere in the government of the nation cause its members to be more carefully chosen, and its proceedings to be more closely watched, and frequently controlled by criticism. The whole country has its eyes on Congress, and Congress is aware of the fact. It has both the will and the incentive to be judicious and patriotic. Newspaper editors have constantly to be saying to their readers, 'Look what our state legislators are doing'; they seldom have to urge, 'Look what Congress is doing.' It cannot, indeed, be watched easily, or to much advantage. It requires a distinct effort to watch it. It has no dramatic contests of party leaders to attract notice. Its methods are so much after the fashion of the game of hide-and-seek that the eye of the ordinary man is quite baffled in trying to understand or follow them, if he try only at leisure moments. But, at the same time, the interests handled by Congress are so vast that at least the newspapers and the business men, if no others, must watch its legislation as best they may. However hard it may be to observe, it is too influential in great affairs to make it safe for the country to give over trying to observe it.

But though Congress may always be watched, and so in a measure controlled, despite its clandestine and confusing methods, those methods must tend to increase the distrust with which Congress is widely regarded; and distrust cannot but enervate, belittle, and corrupt this will-centre of the Constitution. The question is not merely, How shall the methods of Congress be clarified and its ways made purposeful and responsible? There is this greater question at stake: How shall the essential arrangements of the Constitution be preserved? Congress is the purposing, designing, aggressive power of the national government. Disturbing and demoralizing influences in the organism, if there be any, come out from its restless energies. Damaging encroachments upon ground forbidden to the Federal government generally originate in measures of its planning. So long as it continues to be governed by unrelated standing committees, and to take its resolves in accordance with no clear plan, no single, definite purpose, so long as what it does continues to be neither evident nor interesting, so long must all its exertions of power be invidious; so long must its competition with the executive or the judiciary seem merely jealous and always underhand; so long must it remain virtually impossible to control it through public opinion. As well ask the stranger in the gallery of the New York Stock Exchange to judge of the proceedings on the floor. As well ask a man who has not time to read all the newspapers in the Union to judge of passing sentiment in all parts of the country. Congress in its composition is the country in miniature. It realizes Hobbes's definition of liberty as political power divided into small fragments. The standing committees typify the individuals of the nation. Congress is better fitted for counsel than the voters simply because its members are less than four hundred instead of more than ten millions.

It has been impossible to carry out the programme of the Constitution; and, without careful reform, the national legislature will even more dangerously approach the perilous model of a mass meeting. There are several ways in which Congress can be so integrated as to impart to its proceedings system and party responsibility. That may be done by entrusting the preparation and initiation of legislation to a single committee in each house, composed of the leading men of the majority in that house. Such a change would not necessarily affect the present precedents as to the relations between the executive and the legislature. They might still stand stiffly apart. Congress would be integrated and invigorated, however, though the whole system of the government would not be. To integrate that, some common meeting-ground of public consultation must be provided for the executive and the houses. That can be accomplished only by the admission to Congress, in whatever capacity,—whether simply to answer proper questions and to engage in debate, or with the full privileges of membership,—of official representatives of the executive who understand the administration and are interested and able to defend it. Let the tenure of ministers have what disconnection from legislative responsibility may seem necessary to the preservation of the equality of House and Senate, and the separation of administration from legislation; light would at least be thrown upon administration; it would be given the same advantages of public suggestion and unhampered self-defence that Congress, its competitor, has; and Congress would be constrained to apply system and party responsibility to its proceedings.

The establishment in the United States of what is known as 'ministerial responsibility' would unquestionably involve some important changes in our constitutional system. I am strongly of the opinion that such changes would not be too great a price to pay for the advantages secured us by such a government. Ministerial responsibility supplies the only conditions which have yet proved efficacious, in the political experience of the world, for vesting recognized leadership in men chosen for their abilities by a natural selection of debate in a sovereign assembly of whose contests the whole country is witness. Such survival of the ablest in debate seems the only process available for selecting leaders under a popular government. The mere fact that such a contest proceeds with such a result is the strongest possible incentive to men of first-rate powers to enter legislative service; and popular governments, more than any other governments, need leaders so placed that, by direct contact with both the legislative and the executive departments of the government, they shall see the problems of government at first hand; and so trained that they shall at the same time be, not mere administrators, but also men of tact and eloquence, fitted to persuade masses of men and to draw about themselves a loyal following.

If we borrowed ministerial responsibility from England, we should, too, unquestionably enjoy an infinite advantage over the English in the use of it. We should sacrifice by its adoption none of that great benefit and security which our federal system derives from a clear enumeration of powers and an inflexible difficulty of amendment. If anything would be definite under cabinet government, responsibility would be definite; and, unless I am totally mistaken in my estimate of the legal conscience of the people of this country,—which seems to me to be the heart of our whole system,—definite responsibility will establish rather than shake those arrangements of our Constitution which are really our own, and to which our national pride properly attaches, namely, the distant division of powers between the state and federal governments, the slow and solemn formalities of constitutional change, and the interpretive functions of the federal courts. If we are really attached to these principles, the concentration of responsibility in government will doubly insure their preservation. If we are not, they are in danger of destruction in any case.

But we cannot have ministerial responsibility in its fulness under the Constitution as it stands. The most that we can have is distinct legislative responsibility, with or without any connection of co-operation or of mutual confidence between the executive and Congress. To have so much would be an immense gain. Changes made to this end would leave the federal system still an unwieldy mechanism of counteracting forces, still without unity or flexibility; but we should at least have made the very great advance of fastening upon Congress an even more positive form of accountability than now rests upon the President and the courts. Questions of vast importance and infinite delicacy have constantly to be dealt with by Congress; and there is an evident tendency to widen the range of those questions. The grave social and economic problems now thrusting themselves forward, as the result of the tremendous growth and concentration of our population, and the consequent sharp competition for the means of livelihood, indicate that our system is already aging, and that any clumsiness, looseness, or irresponsibility in governmental action must prove a source of grave and increasing peril. There are already commercial heats and political distempers in our body politic which warn of an early necessity for carefully prescribed physic. Under such circumstances, some measure of legislative reform is clearly indispensable. We cannot afford to put up any longer with such legislation as we may happen upon. We must look and plan ahead. We must have legislation which has been definitely forecast in party programmes and explicitly sanctioned by the public voice. Instead of the present arrangements for compromise, piecemeal legislation, we must have coherent plans from recognized party leaders, and means for holding those leaders to a faithful execution of their plans in clear-cut Acts of Congress.

Printed in *An Old Master and Other Political Essays* (New York, 1893), pp. 141-81.

From Horace Elisha Scudder

My dear Wilson   [Cambridge, Mass.] 28 June 1893

I am very glad to find that in doing carpentry on your piece I did not seriously damage the foundation. Since receiving your proof and your kind letter I have read "Mere Literature" and am delighted with it. It is another good instrument in an orchestra which keeps playing the same rousing air. I recognize notes in it of an address which I gave at a big Normal School in Kansas two or three weeks ago!

Yours sincerely   H. E. Scudder.

ALS (Houghton Mifflin Letterpress Books, MH).

To Hermann Eduard von Holst

My dear Sir,   Princeton, New Jersey, 29 June, 1893

Your very generous appreciation of my little volume, "Division and Reunion," in the June number of the *Educational Review*, seems to me to demand a word of thanks. It is exceedingly gratifying to me that you should deem the book, slight as it is, worthy of such warm praise. I of course tried to do as thorough and honest a piece of work as possible; but I have been even more keenly aware of its defects than any of my critics can have been. I by no means solved to my own satisfaction the many problems of treatment created for me by the narrow scale to which I was restricted.

What you yourself say about the absence of *men* from my narrative is certainly most just. I simply have not yet attained to sufficient literary skill to be able to bring them into so brief an account of affairs, looked at on the large scale, in a fashion vivid enough to render them *alive* to the reader, without using more space for personal detail than was at my disposal. I did not see *how* to remedy the defect, in short.

Whether I saw some things and some men with southern eyes or not, I of course cannot tell. It may be that you are right about that. I can only say that I was not *conscious* of any such prepossession. I think the southern case an arguable case, and I thought I could see southern motives as, perhaps, other writers had not seen them. I am convinced, moreover, than [that] only a minority in the South deemed slavery "a good, a positive good," and that only a minority in the North were ready to pronounce it "the sum of all villainies." A wide acquaintance with elderly men in the South is the basis of this conviction, on the one hand, and the slowness and difficulty with which the war was made directly and avowedly a war against slavery, instead of simply "for the Union," on the other.

As for the point in controversy concerning the nature of the Constitution, I of course realize the responsibility of holding the views I do. It seems to me impossible to treat a written Constitution as you would treat any other document. A Constitution must hold (contain) *the prevalent opinion*, and its contents must change with national purpose. It does not seem to me to follow at all, therefore, that, because the southern view was the original view of the Constitution, the North must be pronounced to have stood "in a truly awful predicament" at the bar of history for what was begun in 1861. *I think the North was wholly right then*, and that the South paid the inevitable penalty for lagging behind the national development, stopping the normal growth of the national constitution. Otherwise we must come to this (quite intolerable) practical conclusion, that lawyers and historians—at length antiquarians—are to determine what the course of national affairs shall be, binding up new situations, new exigencies, in old conceptions produced by old conditions. And, if the content of the Constitution remains always the same, what is there for patriotism to strive for? Advance will always involve revolution.

But pardon me—I did not mean to write a controversial letter, but only to express my very warm appreciation of the generous terms in which you have spoken of my little "Epoch."

Believe me, with highest respect and esteem,

Most sincerely Yours,   Woodrow Wilson

ALS (von Holst Papers, ICU).

To Charles William Kent

My dear Charlie,   Princeton, New Jersey, 29 June, 1893.

I have been waiting till the end of term time, when all my examination papers should be read and I could possess my soul in leisure, to write you a letter that should be something more than the mere note which seems to be all that a fellow can find time for while classes are to be lectured to.

I cannot tell you how much I appreciated you[r] last letter; and especially the evidence of your trust in my judgment shown by your action with respect to Axson's candidacy at Hampden Sidney. That matter turned out very singularly. There was such a row in the college where my brother is teaching when it was learned that he was not to return next year that the President actually bestirred himself so vigourourly [vigourously] as to obtain money enough to offer him a full appointment for next year. He felt obliged, since it was necessary (or that made it so) to decide at once, to accept this bird in hand, rather than risk the Virginia bird in the bush; and so he accepted and withdrew from his candidacy for the chair at Hampden Sidney. I was sorry, for I want very much to see him in the South, but of course he acted prudently, and therefore wisely.

Are you going to Chicago,—or perhaps I should ask, *When* are you going to Chicago? I have been once, for a very brief visit at the time of the opening,[1] but I may have to go again to read a paper at one of the "Congresses" which are to vex the spirits of the learned; and it would be an immense satisfaction to see you there. If I go, it will be the last week in July.[2]

For the rest, I expect to spend the vacation as quietly as possible, indulging in the luxury of reading whole books instead of browsing throughout whole libraries. I mean to write a little; but only what I please, as a mental recreation, and not as a task. I expect that most of my reading and most of my writing too will be in the field which is yours rather than mine. Reading in "mere literature" is, for me, not only *re*creation but *cre*ation as well. It stimulates and enriches my mind as no amount of formal study can. It is both tonic and food. And this is all the more the case because I do not enjoy it alone. Mrs. Wilson is in all senses my literary partner, and I must say in justice to her that she furnishes more of the capital than I do. I enjoy the business with her as it would be impossible for me to enjoy it alone, as I am sure you will readily believe. Mrs. Wilson was particularly delighted with your little visit to us because she discovered in you a kindred spirit. For me the discovery had been made long since.

I hope that when you see Heath [Dabney] you will urge him to write to me. It is a great privation to me to be cut off from him; and I trust he can forgive me "Division and Reunion"! As for yourself, do not fail to keep me informed as to what you are doing and thinking. It will not satisfy me to hear *of* you; I must hear *from* you. Will you deem it impertinent in an old friend, Charlie, to wonder whether you are contemplating doing that best of things that a literary man particularly can do, namely, get married? That would seem a natural corollary to your appointmen to a berth in which you will wish to spend your life.

　　With most cordial regards from us both,

　　　　　Affectionately Yours,　Woodrow Wilson

WWTLS (Tucker-Harrison-Smith Coll., ViU).

1 Of the World's Columbian Exposition, when he went to Chicago to address the Princeton alumni of that city on April 28, 1893.

2 As forthcoming letters and documents will reveal, Wilson did go to the Exposition to deliver the address printed at July 26, 1893.

To Kemp Plummer Battle[1]

My dear Sir,　　　　　Princeton, New Jersey, 29 June, 1893

I take the liberty of writing to thank you most warmly for your exceedingly kind notice of my little volume, "Division and Reunion," in the N. C. *University Magazine*.[2] I should have written sooner had I not been held fast in the toils of class work until just the other day.

Warm praise such as you give the little book is peculiarly acceptable to me as coming from the South. I tried earnestly, even—for I may say so without a touch of exaggeration—with travail of spirit, to write a *just* account of the great controversy and I was especially anxious that the people of the South, whom I love, should acknowledge it just. Such praise as yours, therefore, coming from a southerner who is recognized as a most competent judge, heartens me, I can assure you, as nothing else could. Some bitter things have been said about the book in the South[3] (doubtless a great deal more than I have seen) but it has been welcomed, too, in such quarters and with so much openness of mind and generosity of judgment as to make me esteem myself a most fortunate man. Allow me once more to express my very cordial appreciation of your review.

Most sincerely Yours,   Woodrow Wilson

ALS (Battle Family Papers, NcU).
  [1] President of the University of North Carolina, 1876-91; Professor of History, 1891-1907; and author of *History of the University of North Carolina* (2 vols., Raleigh, N. C., 1907-12).
  [2] It is printed at May 1, 1893.
  [3] He was undoubtedly referring, *inter alia*, to the review printed at May 28, 1893.

To Charles Scribner's Sons

My dear Sirs,   Princeton, New Jersey, 30 June, 1893.

I enclose Messrs. Ginn & Co's consent to the publication of the essays which appeared in the *New Princeton Review*. Of course I could not manage, if I would, the elaborate advertisement they suggest. I think that what I have said in the Prefatory Note sufficiently covers the comity of the case.

Trusting that you do not consider it beyond an author's province to suggest the form in which his book is to appear, I venture to say that the form given to Augustin Birrell's essays[1] (though I fear that it is rather expensive for a volume which will doubtless have only a limited sale) would be most acceptable to my taste for "An Old Master," and might, I should think, beguile even such book lovers as are not in the habit of reading in the field of politics into making this book also one of their friends,

Very sincerely Yours,   Woodrow Wilson

WWTLS (Charles Scribner's Sons Archives, NjP). Enc. missing.
  [1] Scribner's had just published a handsome new two-volume edition of Birrell's classic, *Obiter Dicta*. The New York publisher followed Wilson's suggestion. *An Old Master*, though slightly larger than the Birrell volumes, was fully as handsome.

A News Report of a Commencement Oration at Elmira College

[July 1893]

COMMENCEMENT.

. . . Commencement day [June 14] dawned bright and clear— the sun beamed down upon us in all his glory, not with scorching rays but with the soft mild warmth of a perfect June day. Had the class of '93 itself had control of the weather it could not have ordered a more delightful day on which to celebrate the completion of a four years' course in college. . . .

We were extremely fortunate in securing for our orator Prof. Woodrow Wilson, Ph. D., LL. D., of Princeton, who, though still young, has attained a foremost place among the professors of one of our leading American colleges and has also won for himself no small reputation as a writer. The subject of his address was "Democracy," and in the developement of his theme he displayed much ability and deep research. The address is given in full in another part of this number of *The Sibyl*.[1] . . .

Printed in the Elmira, N. Y., *Sibyl*, xx (July 1893), 171-72.
[1] Pp. 174-94. The address is printed, along with an Editorial Note, at its composition date, Dec. 5, 1891, Vol. 7.

To Charles Scribner's Sons

My dear Sirs,   Princeton, New Jersey, 3 July, 1893.

Knowing that you may have proof to send me during the Summer, if it should be your purpose to put my essays through the press at once, I send you my address for the coming few weeks. It will be as below from July 5th. to July 24th. After the latter date it will be Princeton again.[1]

Very truly Yours,   Woodrow Wilson

WOODROW WILSON
Care Mrs. S. S. Topping,
Sagaponock (Sagg)
Near Bridgehampton,
Long Island.

WWTLS (Charles Scribner's Sons Archives, NjP).
[1] Actually, the Wilsons remained at Sagaponack until August 1.

To Albert Bushnell Hart

My dear Hart,   Princeton, New Jersey, 3 July, 1893.

Thank you for your letter of June 26. I will gladly make a list of corrections for the Longmans for the next edition. I can forward it any time on a couple of days' notice.

I congratulate you on your opportunity to spend a year abroad. I hope it will be a year full of benefit to you in every way. Would that I could hope to see you there; but I cannot. I can only bid you God-speed. Mrs Wilson joins me in warm regards to Mrs. Hart and yourself.

Most sincerely Yours,   Woodrow Wilson

TCL (RSB Coll., DLC).

From Joseph Ruggles Wilson

My precious son—   Saratoga Springs, N. Y. July 6 1893

Your letter of the 3d inst. prepares me to think that you are all very miserable at the sea-shore. I certainly would be with such March-y weather as we are having. But I do hope that better things await the dear family than my fears are ready to conjure up. As to our dear Ellie's trip to Chicago—I am sure she would enjoy it, every hour, where there is so much for an intelligent person to see, because knowing *how* to see. For my own part I have no desire to go—for with my mind's eye I can see nothing but the jostling snatching *crowd* of Dicks, Toms and Harrys. Wasn't I at Philadelphia during the "Centennial"?[1]—and if what was experienced there was the small green tree, what must be the fate of the poor wretch who gets hold of the big dry one? All the same if I shall hear of a desirable party whose purpose is to be unhappy for a given space of days, the fact will be at once communicated to those whom I love and—pity.

You say nothing touching Stock's fate at Athens—whether he was elected, and then—what. I am really anxious to learn the facts in this singular case of needless recommendations.

The Scribners!—I can see their ears from here, so asininely prodigious are they! The "Atlantic" knows a good thing when it sees it. What were Scribners' objections?[2] The *real* one was that the essay was too good for pages which have wofully degenerated within a year or so, and which has I presume a class of readers now that demands literary swill only.

The waters here have done me a 'heap' of good I believe; and I shall remain for a few weeks longer. The big hotels—including this one [the Congress Hall]—are still almost empty. Here there may be 50 or 60. The fare is first rate however[.] The companionship is limited to a few old chaps and chapesses who are agreeable enough in their routine way. I have a bright room, and although time hangs heavy at hours of the day, I am not any more solitary than has been usual with me.

Please write and tell me how you fare, at some of the mercies of old ocean. Love to *"all."*

Your affectionate   Father.

ALS (WP, DLC).
 1 He visited the Philadelphia Exposition with Woodrow Wilson. See Wilson's diary entries for September 7 and 8, 1876, Vol. 1, p. 190.
2 He refers to Woodrow Wilson's essay, "Mere Literature," which Scudder of the *Atlantic Monthly* had just accepted. It is printed at June 17, 1893.

Marginal Note

John Beattie Crozier, *Civilization and Progress* (London and New York, 1892). P. 129:

Notwithstanding the preponderance of the lower instincts of our nature, and their tendency to overpower the higher sentiments, each man has within him an ideal of right and justice, to which in his heart of hearts he does homage, and which he longs to see realised in the world. And although he habitually falls below this ideal in his own life and character, it nevertheless serves as the guage and standard by which he measures his neighbour. It differs, of course, in different ages and nations, and in different stages of civilization and culture, but for persons living at the same time, in the same community, it is practically the same. Held thus in common by many minds, it takes form and embodiment, not only in that code of public law which regulates the civil and commercial intercourse of a people, but also in that unwritten code which takes cognisance of those social misdemeanours which lie beyond the reach of positive law. In this way it becomes the public conscience—the organ of right and justice, before which all bow, and to which all appeal. Now it is by the pressure put on the moral nature of the *individual* by this *public* conscience—this public sentiment—that the triumph of justice is secured. It is this public conscience

Transcript of WW Shorthand Comment
[c. July 12, 1893[1]]

The reason is obvious. When we act individually our passions overcome our sense of right; but the passions of the community are not engaged as ours are: they judge as we should judge: their sense of right is not overborne. Every man is in a minority when he acts: there is a huge disengaged conscience ready to assess his actions.

which restrains men when they are tempted to push their own interests to the detriment of their fellows.

1 Wilson's reading date at the end of this volume, in the Wilson Library, DLC.

From George Howe, Jr.

Dear Woodrow   Columbia, S. C., July 15 1893

Margaret suffers either from enlarged tonsils or some form of catarrh. It may be nasal or post nasal. You had better consult a specialist. Any directions I might give might also fall short of the mark. I think you will find Dr. Clarence Rice at #115 East 18th St. [New York]. (If he has changed his address the directory will show.) Dr. Rice is master of the subject, and will probably be reasonable. I do not know Dr. Simpson.[1] When you see the Dr. you can write me and I can then help you out.

Wilson has been sick, laid up for 4 days in his room. He is out again and at work. George goes to Chicago in a week or ten days. I wish I knew someone there that could help him out in seeing the wonders. He will go with two or three boys from here. Annie & the baby will go mountainwards about the same time. The heat is driving them away. I will have to tough it out at home this year. Annie joins me in a great deal of love to you all

Yrs affly   Geo Howe

Did you receive my letter, (written about May),[2] asking about scholarships at Princeton, and concerning the result of treatment of Mrs Brown's ear? I have heard nothing from you

ALS (WP, DLC) with WWhw notation on env.: "Ans 22 July '93."
  1 Probably Dr. William Kelly Simpson, a distinguished physician and surgeon then practicing in New York. He became Professor of Laryngology at the College of Physicians and Surgeons in 1904.
  2 George Howe, Jr., to WW, March 11, 1893.

From Frederick Jackson Turner

My dear Wilson: Chicago University July 16, 1893.

I received your letter[1] while in the final agonies of getting out a belated paper for the Am. Hist. Association[2] and since I have been here I have not found opportunity to write you as I wish to. I go home in a day or so and will write you fully then. Let me say now simply that I am delighted to learn that you contemplate a history of the United States. I believe no one is so well qualified to do for us what Green did for England, and I shall be glad to be of any service.[3] I am one of the enthusiasts over your *Division and Reunion*[.] In style it is your most attractive work, and in treatment judicial. Some of the chapters are destined to live with the classics of our literature and history. I will write you in detail later, but will only say just now in criticism of your book that I think you hold the doctrine of survival of state sovereignty in too absolute a form. Admitting the dominant particularism in 1790, it is yet true that the South (and the South is *complex* in respect to the doctrine) intensified, systematized, and modified the doctrine to suit her changing economic conditions. The south did remain behind the procession of American advance, but she did not remain *preserved* by the ice of slavery like a Siberian mammoth. She changed greatly. I will write you what I mean soon, and will send you a copy of my syllabus on colonization,[4] and my paper before the Am. Hist. Assoc.

With warm regards, yours   Frederick J. Turner

ALS (WP, DLC).
   [1] It is missing.
   [2] Turner refers to his paper, "The Significance of the Frontier in American History," delivered at a special meeting of the American Historical Association at the World's Columbian Exposition on July 12, 1893.
   [3] This is the first reference in the documents to what would, after several metamorphoses, become Wilson's five-volume *History of the American People*. Obviously, Wilson in his missing letter had told Turner that he contemplated writing a history of the American people modeled after John Richard Green's *Short History of the English People*. For a description of Wilson's early work on what he first called "A Short History of the United States," see the following Editorial Note, "Wilson's 'Short History of the United States.'"
   [4] *The Colonization of North America from the Earliest Times to 1763: Syllabus of a Course of Six Lectures*, University of Wisconsin Extension Department Syllabus, No. 12 (Madison, Wisc., 1893).

EDITORIAL NOTE
WILSON'S "SHORT HISTORY OF THE UNITED STATES"

The letter from Frederick Jackson Turner just printed provides the first definite evidence that Wilson was, as Turner put it, contemplating writing a general history of the United States. Wilson spent much of his spare time during the next nine years composing this history and commented on his progress frequently in letters. Although his various versions of chapters and the final product, *A History of the American People*, published in 1902, will not be printed in this series, his progress in research and writing will be described in Editorial Notes from time to time. This Editorial Note covers the first phase of his work, between 1893 and 1895.

It is altogether possible that Wilson had passed well beyond the stage of contemplation by the time that he told Turner about his projected history. He had found his title, "A Short History of the United States," composed the first two chapters in longhand (the first without a title, the second entitled "The Virginia Company"), and made typed copies of these chapters by November 22, 1893, for he affixed this date to the end of the second typed chapter.[1] Since Wilson was preoccupied with other writings during August and September, and very intensively with class work between September and November of 1893, it seems highly probable that he had at least begun the composition of the first longhand chapter by the time he divulged his plans for the book to Turner.

Wilson made typed copies of the first two chapters in November in part no doubt because he was eager to have something in hand as a basis for negotiations with publishers. At any rate, he did approach one firm before he had done much work beyond the first two chapters. As his letter to Robert Bridges of April 22, 1894, reveals, Wilson had told his friend about his history and asked him to talk to Charles Scribner about it. Wilson's letter also reveals that he planned to discuss the book with editors at the Century Company.

Wilson described the nature and scope of his history, as well as his special plans for it, in a letter to Scribner on May 11, 1894. It would, he wrote, occupy him for several years, for he was taking this work "very seriously indeed" and wanted to "perfect its form by the most careful study." However, he was not ready to consider publication in book form, for he wanted to carve from his manuscript "some twenty-four historical essays for publication throughout a couple of years in a magazine" so that the work might be "subjected to the test of exposure to the air, and to the scrutiny of critics." There was, Wilson went on, an additional advantage to serialization. He planned a heavily illustrated history, and spreading its parts over two years would afford the time for the selection of illustrations "which would themselves be vehicles of history."

Between November 1893 and the summer of 1894, Wilson completed in longhand one more chapter, "New Netherland and New Plymouth," to which he later added the composition date of August 30, 1894. Two further chapters, "New England, New Netherland and Maryland, 1628-1649" and "The Province of Maryland," were composed before October 25, 1894. He wrote this date at the end of the handwritten version of "The Province of Maryland." A sixth chapter, "The Expansion of New England," was completed by December 22, 1894.

In a letter to Turner on December 10, 1894, Wilson reported that he was about halfway through the period to 1755 and expressed the hope that he would complete that phase before commencement. He fell far short of this goal, for only one additional chapter, "The Civil Wars and the Commonwealth," was composed before June 1895. Although undated, it seems to have been written between mid-December and his annual trip to The Johns Hopkins University to lecture on administration.

Wilson returned to Princeton from Baltimore on March 1, 1895, and soon afterward made a new typescript, 511 pages in length, of his work thus far, incorporating a number of stylistic changes as he typed. More than two years were to pass before he resumed work on the history. As documents to be printed in Volume 9 will reveal, he and Ellen Wilson became deeply involved in the spring of 1895

[1] All references in this Editorial Note are to manuscripts, notes, etc., in WP, DLC.

in plans for building their first house. Moreover, articles and addresses were consuming a good share of his free time. However, the receipt of a letter from Henry M. Alden, editor of *Harper's Magazine*, in late June was the crucial event that caused Wilson to turn aside from his "Short History of the United States." In a letter dated June 28, 1895, Alden asked Wilson to write six essays on George Washington and offered $300 for each article. Wilson jumped at the opportunity. Not only would the $1,800 go far toward easing the burden of building his house, but the experience of writing a life of Washington would fit in well with his plans for the "Short History." Moreover, *Harper's* might well prove to be the very vehicle for the serialization of the history that he had earlier sought in *Scribner's* and the *Century Magazine*.

In writing the first seven chapters of the "Short History," Wilson's method seems to have been to immerse himself in the printed sources, general histories, and monographs of the period, and then to write each chapter by referring directly to the works that he had read. The research notes that he may have taken for these first chapters are few in number. Many of them are on small sheets, about 100 in number, which contain brief outlines of events, chronologies, memoranda on incidents, and some analytical comments on periods. There is in the Wilson Papers also a packet of cards containing similar notes, several of which bear handwritten headings such as "guide," "sub-guide," and "analysis" or outline.

To Albert Shaw

My dear Shaw,   Sagaponack, Long Island, 18 July, 1893

Your letter[1] did *not* reach me promptly, having to be forwarded to this remote end of Long Island,—so I write to the Office. Alas! I *cannot* comply with your request—it's flatly impossible,—for the most distressing, because most discreditable, reason that I do not know *what* Congress ought to do. I have not really studied the existing situation; and I am not entitled to an opinion. In brief, I am estopped *by ignorance*, and there's no immediate remedy. I only know that the Sherman law,[2] which ought never to have been passed, ought immediately to be repealed.

About the other matter of your letter,[3] however, I can write with both knowledge and enthusiasm. I know what it is to love—and to be loved—if ever a man did. I know what marriage does for a man,—for his mind and heart, as well as for his mere domestic comfort and his digestion: and I can say that the best thing I could wish for a man I wanted to see happy would be his marriage to the right woman. I want *you* to be happy and I feel every confidence that you have chosen the right woman—I like her very name—and I rejoice, my dear fellow, from the bottom of my heart that you have won her. Mrs. Wilson—though she has not, I must say, gained half as much by marriage as I have—rejoices with me, and sends her warmest congratulations. The best of it is, that you are not as happy now as you will be. For the thing grows and grows, gets deeper and deeper into the heart, indefinitely, so far as I know.

As ever,   Affectionately Yours,   Woodrow Wilson

ALS (in possession of Albert Shaw, Jr.).
¹ It is missing.
² That is, the Sherman Silver Purchase Act.
³ Shaw's recent engagement to Elizabeth L. Bacon of Reading, Pa. They were married on September 5, 1893, as WW to A. Shaw, Aug. 7, 1893, reveals.

From Ellen Axson Wilson, with Enclosure

My darling,   Sagaponack [N.Y.] July 24 [1893]

A telegram has just arrived which I hasten to send you hoping it may reach you in time for you to avail yourself of the invitation. The enclosed receipt also arrived today and is your only mail.

I scribble this in great haste in order if possible to get it off at six—havn't time for a letter. We are all well. It is so *very* cool here that I am hoping it is also cool inland, and that you are having a comfortable journey. How I hope the cool wave will last a week!

Take care of yourself, my precious one, and remember that I *love* you with all my heart, soul and mind.

Your little wife,   Eileen

ALS (WP, DLC). Encs.: C. H. McCormick to WW, tel. dated July 24, 1893, printed below; and a receipt, dated July 22, 1893, for a room deposit of $2, given by the "Department of World's Fair Accommodations" of the University of Chicago.

E N C L O S U R E

From Cyrus Hall McCormick

Chicago Ill   July 24 1893

Just learned you coming educational congress.¹ Come direct our house   Cyrus H McCormick

Hw tel. (WP, DLC).
¹ See "An Address at the World's Columbian Exposition," printed at July 26, 1893, n. 1.

To Ellen Axson Wilson

My own Eileen,   321 Huron St.,[1] Chicago, Ill., 25 July [1893]

I saw the Fair this afternoon—I did, indeed—no inconsiderable part of it, and the Midway Plaisance[2] to boot. Our train got in earlier than I thought and I had some five hours to give to the business. And, oh, wasn't I tired when I got through: if I had not had the past two weeks of exercise as preliminary training, I should have been utterly exhausted. As it is, I am rested already, after a good dinner and a good *sit* this evening, with a number of people sufficient to relieve me of the necessity to talk much. I am so glad, for your sake, as well as my own, that I am staying here with Cyrus. For now you will *know* that I am most delightfully comfortable,—most delightfully taken care of. I only wish you could have known sooner. Perhaps you did. Cyrus telegraphed to me: perhaps they forwarded the telegram to Sagaponack?

I think I saw enough of the Fair this afternoon to know where to linger during the few afternoons that remain available. I rushed through the Art Building, for example, and know that it is the American exhibit I want to look at in detail. But I wont *write* about the Fair; you will see that for yourself—and we can *talk* about that.

What I cannot postpone speaking of is yourself,—a theme which presses upon me more imperatively even, if possible, while I am away from you than while I am with you,—and you will bear me witness I often speak of it when we are together! When I am with you I am afraid I get just a little bit *used* to your loveliness and attractiveness, take them for granted, enjoy them as if they were to be *expected* in one's wife,—so spoiled of fortune am I! But when I am away from you what impresses me is the contrast that other people—other women, other *men*,—present to my incomparable Nellie,—so gentle, "simple, affecting," so wise and so sweet in her wisdom, so winning and yet so unconscious of charm. What I don't like about other people is, their obtrusive difference from her. And they carry it off with such a fine air,—as if *that* was to be charming. You are like nobody but yourself, my jewel, my solitaire. And to think that, in a world full of different people, I should have *found* you, is to go far toward esteeming myself a genius, or else the star I was born under the luckiest in all the heavens. I am still too fagged to tell you just what you are, my vocabulary can't meet the demand at present. Suffice it to say, that, in every sense of the word you are all the world to me. I'll try to write again tomorrow; but possibly I cannot. Whether I do or not, I shall love you consciously, gloryingly every minute of the day; for in every breath I draw I am

Your own   Woodrow

ALS (WP, DLC).
  1 The home address of Cyrus H. McCormick.
  2 The Midway Plaisance was the amusement area of the World's Columbian Exposition and included everything from reproductions of foreign villages to the world's first Ferris wheel.

From Ellen Axson Wilson

My own darling,   Sagaponack [N.Y.], July 25 [1893].

I did not write this morning as I intended because just at the time I should have done so I found it would be best to take Jessie to the beach today and let her have her long-promised bath,—Mrs. Simpson offering to take charge of her;—so that business occupied the rest of the morning. Jessie surprised us by not being in the least afraid, she took the waves boldly and apparently had what Janet calls an "elegant" time. But she has seemed quite fatigued this afternoon,—though otherwise well.

This act of daring on Jessie's part is really the only *event* that has occurred since you left. We still have lovely weather and are enjoying everything extremely. I still go to the beach at the old hour; yesterday I had it absolutely to myself and it was *beautiful*. This afternoon alas, I had to share it with Mrs. Simpson. Would that she were not quite so anxious to prevent my feeling lonely! She came upstairs last night and was with me 'till very late— telling me 'all about Sallie'!

I am still working green doylies and still reading "Past and Present[.]"[1] So you see your imagination will have little indeed to do to realize us! By the way we stopped "Past and Present" just before coming to two very good chapters. You must read them. One is on the characteristic subject of "Plugson of Undershot" (!) and another on the still more characteristic one of "Labour."

By the way, we have had another sensation since you left; the German wash-woman has run away from her husband with another man. She is forty-nine and the man is quite young. She took her little girl with her. She also took two hundred dollars— *they say*—which she had borrowed chiefly from the Cases to bring out a cousin from Germany. But surely the amount is exaggerated!

Speaking of the Cases Miss F. has just been giving us a treat in the way of singing—such sweet German songs! Apparently she has not been embittered against that nation by her above-mentioned experience!

I have received letters today for you and Father and Stock and Ed [Axson] and *Mr. Daniels*[2] (as Prof. of Pol. Economy) and not *one* for myself! Nothing at all interesting for you,—only boys wanting advice, &c.

But it grows late and I must say 'good-night':—ah! if you could only *hear* me say it—and a few other things! How strange and lonely it seems to be here without you, dear heart!—yet not so lonely as it might be because I still feel close—so close to you in spirit! Though we *cannot* hear each other speak—

"Our hearts ever answer in tune & in time love
As octave to octave & rhyme unto rhyme, love."
Believe me, dearest, from the depths of that heart
Your own   Eileen.

ALS (WP, DLC).
  [1] Carlyle's volume.
  [2] They are all missing.

An Address at the World's Columbian Exposition[1]

[[*July 26, 1893*]]

Should an Antecedent Liberal Education Be Required of Students in Law, Medicine, and Theology?

We shall, I think, escape entanglements if we note at the very outset the twofold aspect of the subject. It may be discussed (1) from the point of view of the individual who is seeking profes-

[1] Wilson delivered this address on July 26 before one of the "congresses" of the International Congress of Education, organized by the Columbian Exposition and held under the auspices of the National Educational Association of the United States from July 25 through July 28, 1893. Arrangements for the session at which he spoke were made by Professors Nicholas Murray Butler of Columbia College and Andrew F. West of Princeton. The invitation to Wilson was presumably made orally by West (near the end of June, as Wilson's letter to C. W. Kent of June 29, 1893, suggests), hence the absence of any letter of invitation in the Wilson Papers.

The affair on July 26 was the first session of the Congress of Higher Education. The chairman, President Gilman of the Johns Hopkins, made the opening address and was followed by President Martin Kellogg of the University of California, who read a paper entitled "How Far Is It Desirable That Universities Should Be of One Type?" Next was read a translation of a paper, "The Division of Labor in the University," by Professor Giuseppe Allievo of the University of Turin. Wilson then read a letter from Professor James Barr Ames of the Harvard Law School, at the conclusion of which he began his own paper, printed here.

A brief discussion followed each paper. President Gilman, Melvil Dewey, the noted librarian, President James Hutchins Baker of the University of Colorado, President Henry Turner Eddy of the Rose Polytechnic Institute of Terre Haute, and Professor J. Imelmann of the Joachimsthal Gymnasium of Berlin commented on Wilson's address.

See International Congress of Education, *Proceedings*, pp. 5, 87-176, and Rossiter Johnson (ed.), *A History of the World's Columbian Exposition* (4 vols., Chicago, 1897-98), IV, 1-14, 179-220. The Chicago newspapers carried only brief accounts of the session on July 26.

DR. WOODROW WILSON.

*The first known cartoon of Wilson, which appeared
in the* Chicago Herald *on July 27, 1893*

sional instruction as a means of gaining a livelihood, or (2) from
the point of view of society itself, which must wish to be well
served by its professional classes. The community will doubtless
be inclined to demand more education than the individual will be
willing to tarry for before entering on the practice of his profession. To which shall we give greater weight, the self-interest
of the individual or the self-interest of the community? The community, if it be wise, will be anxious to see practical knowledge
advanced all along the line; will wish the physician to be something more than an empiric, capable himself of sure-footed search
for the origins and determining conditions of disease; will desire
to find in the preacher something larger and more generous in
temper and endowment than dogmatism—even the liberal spirit
of a serious and withal practical philosophy; will look for dignified parts of learning in the lawyer, something better than practical shrewdness and successful chicane, a capacity to rise at
need to the point of view of the jurist, as if aware of the great
and permanent principles of large-eyed justice. The average individual, on the other hand, will be eager to make his way as
rapidly as possible to business; and when once business engagements begin to press upon him, his thought will adjust itself to
them. If the habit of carrying special cases up into the region of
general principles—where alone the real light of discovery burns—
be not formed during the period of preparation, it will hardly
come afterward, when the special cases crowd fast and the general principles remain remote. Only the pastor has any leisure
then for the higher sort of study, and even he is not likely to
begin it then if he has never known before what it is and what
it may do for him. The old women, and the young, will prevent
his becoming studious if he be not already a confirmed student,
safe in "his pensive citadel."

An antecedent liberal education, it must of course be admitted,
does not necessarily disclose general principles; is too often so
*il*liberal in its survey of subjects as to leave upon the mind no
trace of the generalizing habit. But usually it is liberal, at any
rate, in being general; and, without a survey of the field of knowledge, a various view of the interests of the mind, it is hard to see
how a man is to discern *the relations of things*, upon the perception of which all just thought must rest. It is something simply
to have traversed many fields of thought, to have seen where they
lie, and how surrounded, with what coasts, what natural, what
"scientific" boundaries. It is something to have made "the grand
tour," even under indifferent tutors; something to have had a
Wanderjahr, if only to see the world of men and things. A man

who has not had an antecedent liberal education can certainly never get a subsequent equivalent; and, without it, he must remain shut in by a narrow horizon, imagining the confines of knowledge to lie very close about him on every side. Such is the "practical" physician, lawyer, or preacher who now rides us like the Old Man of the Sea, monarch of his little isle of expert knowledge until we can drug and dislodge him.

The world woke once, in that notable fifteenth century, to find itself standing in the clear dawn of the New Learning, and the light which then came has never since been taken away. But we have played tricks with it; we have defracted it, distinguishing the lines of its spectrum with an extreme nicety exceeding that of the Rowland grating, and so have brought upon ourselves a New Ignorance. In our desire to differentiate its rays we have forgotten to know the sun in its entirety—its power to illuminate, to quicken and expand. Knowledge has lost its synthesis, and lies with its colors torn apart, dissolved. That New Learning, which saw knowledge whole, shattered the feudal system of society; this New Ignorance, which likes knowledge piecemeal and in weak solution, has created a feudal system of learning. There is no common mastery, but everywhere separate baronies of knowledge, where a few strong men rule and many ignorant men are held vassals—men ignorant of the freedom of more perfect, more liberal knowledge. We need a freer constitution of learning. Its present constitution only makes it certain that we shall have disorder and wasteful war. To come to the matter immediately in hand, see to how many subjects the student of medicine must turn if he would master his single practical art. It is impossible he should understand the physical life of man without understanding the physical life of the universe. He may not wisely stop short of the widest ranges of biology. And yet the physical life of man is made distinctive, after all, by his singular mental life. He may imagine himself into distemper and disease, and the physician will lose trace of causes of great moment to his own art if he know nothing of the laws of the mind—of physiological psychology not only, but of pure psychology too. He cannot get this range of knowledge in the medical school; he must get it from an antecedent liberal education; and it will be sheer misfortune for him, even as a practical man, if that antecedent training bring him not out upon a plane of knowledge, a vantage ground of outlook and command, higher even and more invigorating than these special fields of science. The student of theology, it will be admitted, is but a poor pretender if no serious survey of other subjects precede and accompany his direct preparation for the ministry. He, of all men, must understand mankind if he is to lead them into better ways of living and to a death of hope. And how can he understand modern society without a knowledge of the scientific standards and conceptions that condition all modern thought? How can he understand any society without knowing aught of philosophy or politics or economy? He will never reach any motive unless he learn to read men and their life.

The student of law, too: what can he know but the forms and the tricks of the law if he know nothing of the law's rootage in society, the principles of its origin and development; how it springs out of material and social conditions which it is the special task of economy and political science to elucidate, out of elements which run centuries deep into the history of nations? No mere technical training can ever make a first-rate lawyer. Observe, I do not say jurist—that, of course. I say that no first-rate lawyer can be made by merely technical training, no lawyer of mastery and real resource. General principles learned *memoriter* are as useless for mastery as precedents learned *memoriter*. No man shall command them who does not know whence they came, and what like occasions must be made to yield new principles alike to bar and bench. Such is the practitioner who is armed *cap-a-pie*, to be feared by every opponent in the mere matter of winning cases. How shall a man who knows nothing of history, of economics, or of political science ever know more than the technical rules of the law, which must for him be rules dead, inflexible, final?

All this is plain enough, at least to every liberally educated man, and to every one who considers first of all the good of the community and the advancement of the professions. But immediate self-interest, haste to get at the pecuniary rewards of his profession, to make a supporting business of it, will make the individual indifferent to these larger considerations. He is willing to leave the higher reaches of his calling to those who have time to seek them. The physician is content to be a successful empiric, and learn useful practical lessons from his daily experience. The minister is satisfied if he please his congregation by agreeable sermons and still more agreeable pastoral visits. The lawyer does not aspire to be more than an expert in a technical business. As many will go without a "liberal education" as the community will permit to do so. Public opinion does not act imperatively in the matter, because not all of the public, at any rate here in the United States, has made up its mind that a general training need precede professional training. Some communities even seem inclined to boast of their "born" preachers, and their lawyers who have gained admission to the bar after only six weeks' study. There is among us a somewhat general skepticism as to the efficacy of college instruction, and a very widely diffused belief in the sufficiency of natural endowments. And, of course, no one will claim that the colleges give a man all, or even any considerable part, of what he should have by way of equipment for one of the learned professions. All that we can say is that the colleges can give him the point of view, the outlook and the habit of mind, of the scholar; that, without an "antecedent liberal education," not one man in a thousand will have the studies he ought to undertake so much as suggested to him. His little world will be flat, not round, shut in by an encompassing sea, bounded by the near horizon. A professional man ought to have a liberal education, if only to make him aware of his limitations, careful not to blunder into fields of which he knows that he is ignorant.

The practical side of this question is certainly a very serious one in this country. That there should be an almost absolute freedom of occupation is a belief very intimately and tenaciously connected with the democratic theory of government, and our legislators are very slow to lay many restrictions upon it. Our colleges and universities, and our law and medical and theological schools have seldom endowment enough to render them independent of popular demands and standards. They are wholly independent, however, of each other, and cannot be constrained to accept any common scheme or standard. Even if the public had made up its mind very definitely on this subject, no means are at hand to facilitate concerted action. Reform must come piecemeal, and by example; not all at once and by authority. The remedy for the present state of affairs in this country seems to me to lie in resolute independent experiment by individual institutions. Let leading universities and colleges that have or can get money enough to make them free to act without too much regard to outside criticism, first erect professional schools upon a new model of scholarship, and then close the doors of those schools to all who have not a first-rate college training. It would not take the country long to find out that the best practical lawyers and doctors and preachers came out from those schools—and the rest would be discredited. I believe that no medical or law or theological school ought to be a separate institution. It ought to be both organically and in situation part of a university, a university big and real enough to dominate it. It ought to be permeated with the university atmosphere; it ought to employ university methods; it ought itself to exemplify the liberal spirit of learning. It would do little good to the professions to send only college graduates to many of our separate professional schools. They would find nothing but empiricism there. To nothing there would their college training seem applicable. It is useless, too, to try to reform these separate schools as they stand. Build a university over them and extend the university faculty into them, and they may be made to your mind; but do not dream of making them like universities in spirit, method, thoroughness in any other way. When universities put students trained in chemistry, biology, and psychology into their own medical schools; students drilled in history, in economics, in philosophy, and in the natural history of society into their law schools; students informed in the various thought of the age and read in the literature of all ages into their schools of theology, the country will begin to be filled with real lawyers, capable physicians, powerful preachers once more, and these great professions will once again deserve the name of learned professions.

The separation of general and special training is an acute symptom of the disease of specialization by which we are now so sorely afflicted. Our professional men are lamed and hampered by that partial knowledge which is the most dangerous form of ignorance. I would no more employ a physician unacquainted with the general field of science than I would employ an oculist who was ignorant of the general field of medicine. Knowledge is trustworthy only when it is balanced and complete. This is the reason why the whole of the question we are now considering is a university question. Knowledge must be kept together; our professional schools must be university schools. Our faculties must make knowledge whole. The liberal education that our professional men get must not only be antecedent to their technical training; it must also be concurrent with it.

No more serious mistake was ever made than the divorce of technical or practical education from theoretical, as if principles could be made use of and applied without being understood. It is, indeed, true that a locomotive driver may handle his engine with dexterity and safety without being either a machinist or an engineer, but the body of knowledge of which the physician or the lawyer or the preacher makes practical application is no machine. It is a body of *thought*; it does not stand alone; it is not even true except in its proper relations to other thought. To handle it requires not only skill, but insight also—a trained perception of relative values, a quick capacity for sifting and assessing evidence. As liberal an education as possible is needed for such functions, if only to open the eyes and accustom the faculties to a nice manipulation of thought. The empiric is the natural enemy of society, and it is imperative that everything should be done—everything risked—to get rid of him. Nothing sobers and reforms him like a (genuine) liberal education.

Printed in International Congress of Education, *Proceedings* (New York, 1894), pp. 112-17.

From Ellen Axson Wilson

My own darling,　　　　　　　　　　Sagaponack [N.Y.] July 26/93

Will you be surprised when I say that I have been glad you were *not* here for the last few hours! We have broken our record at last in the matter of fine weather and have been having a violent thunderstorm (now over)—a house or barn in Wainscot was struck and burnt up before our eyes. It was something of an adventure to go over to tea,—indeed Mrs. Simpson had David hitch up and *drive* Sallie over! Mrs. Topping very kindly sent our children's supper over without my asking. So no day is without its sensation!

As regards yesterday's sensation it was as I supposed about the money. Miss Case says it was *two* dollars—not two hundred that the woman got from her!

The older brother of the terror—who by the way was *not* returned to our table—has just come from Chicago. He seems to be a nice boy but is looking *dreadfully* because he had a sun-stroke while there,—was ill three days and lost fifteen pounds. It makes me feel uneasy, my precious one, to hear such things; but I know you will be very, very careful if only for my sake. In the meantime it will do no harm to record this case for a warning.

I have been getting acquainted with the party in this house;— was greatly surprised to discover the manner of person Mrs. Cameron was. I had fancied she was rather silly; on the contrary she has a great deal of sense and a vast deal of ability of the executive kind; but such *aggressive* egotism and selfishness I don't think I ever saw in anyone,—except perhaps Miss Graham.[1] Mrs. Snow is just what I fancied—rather foolish but very amiable. It is decidedly amusing to sit by and watch the clash of words when Mrs. Simpson & Mrs. C. come in contact. When egoist meets egoist then comes the tug of war. But Mrs. C. is a very Lancelot in that sort of tilt and invariably rides down her adversary. Mrs. S. in consequence hates her with an exceeding bitter hatred. She confides to me that she never met anyone before who had "such an effect" on her!—and I can well believe it.

No mail today for you or me—nor even for Mr. Daniels!

I have just finished "Past and Present" and after all it has left a very good taste in the mouth. There were many fine passages and some very suggestive ones in this last part. However, though his indignation still glowed, it was really hopeful in tone,—very far indeed from being a "gospel of despair."

But this is already too long a letter wherewith to tease a sight-seer so I will say "good-night." Do you know, darling, that, incredible as it is, my love is still *increasing* all the time! One would have thought I had reached the limit of my powers in that direction long ago. But no, I am distinctly conscious that I love you more than when I last wrote letters to you—that somehow I have grown *closer* to to [sic] you in this last year,—and happier in my love. I feel, as it were, more completely *in touch* with you. Indeed so perfect has the union grown that I scarcely seem to myself separated from you even with half the continent between us. I am so vividly *conscious* of you that it seems sometimes as though you must be present at my side. Woodrow my own, my love, I am sure that I am the happiest woman in the world—that *no* other is so blessed!

Believe me, darling, now and forever

All quite well.   Your own   Eileen

ALS (WP, DLC).
¹ Mary Graham of Middletown, Conn., who had been graduated with double honors from Wesleyan in 1889 at the age of twenty-seven. A member of Phi Beta Kappa, she had won the John D. Weeks Prize in political economy (see WW to J. F. Jameson, June 12, 1889, n. 1, Vol. 6). In 1893 Miss Graham was a Ph.D. candidate in economics at Yale. For the Wilsons' later characterizations of her, see WW to EAW, Feb. 21, 1895, and EAW to WW, Feb. 22, 1895, both in Vol. 9.

To Ellen Axson Wilson

My own darling,   [Chicago] Saturday [July 29, 1893].

I am sure you understand why I have not written; and yet I do not believe that anybody who is not here can imagine the rush. I am perfectly well, perfectly comfortable, and have had a jolly good time. This evening I go to Madison;¹ Monday afternoon I start for N. Y.

I have sent to the University for your letters, but none had come. I am uneasy, but suppose it means nothing to be alarmed at. Your sweet face fairly haunts me: I love you more and more passionately every moment of my life, it seems to me,—I want to get back to you, for all the good time I'm having, more than I ever did before!   Your own   Woodrow

ALS (WP, DLC).
¹ To visit Frederick Jackson Turner. For one of the reasons for his visit, see WW to C. T. Winchester, Aug. 17, 1893.

A Review Article[1]

[August 1893]

ANTI-SLAVERY HISTORY AND BIOGRAPHY.

The time has come for some one to write the classical biography of Abraham Lincoln. All the essential materials for such a life are now in our possession. Memoirs and Reminiscences without number have given us to the full the singular flavor of Mr. Lincoln's personality: a close friend has left us an authoritative account of his life; his secretaries have overwhelmed us with ten volumes of particulars concerning it; and Mr. Herndon, his partner in the practice of the law, has disclosed it to us with a frankness little short of brutal. We know the man as those who were imaginative saw him, and we know him also as those who could not penetrate beneath the mere external features of his life would have us believe him to have been. All the evidence being in, it is eminently desirable that some master of the art of biography should sum it up, sift, assess it, and picture for us the man Lincoln as he was.

If Mr. Morse has not done what we hoped and ventured to expect,[2] the reasons why he has not are obvious. He has attempted a bit of scientific painting, and not a portraiture to the life. The book is a criticism, consequently, rather than an appreciation. It unquestionably adds, and adds a great deal, to our command of the materials out of which a real and definitive Life of Lincoln is to be extracted; but it adds very little, if anything, to our knowledge of Lincoln himself. We are advanced several stages nearer a correct apprehension of the facts of that singular life by reason of this careful book, but it may be doubted whether we are any nearer to Lincoln.

This result is not due entirely, however, to the colorless scientific method which Mr. Morse endeavors to maintain. It is due also to the plan of the book. The series in which it appears carries by its title the assumption, not of biographic study, but of an inquiry into the public relations of the persons dealt with, the part which they played in the great political drama of their day. Mr. Morse is concerned with the statesmanship of Lincoln, and with his personality only so far as this accounts for individual notes in the story. Only one hundred and sixty of the seven hundred and forty-five pages of his volumes are given to the consideration of

---

[1] Scudder wrote the portion of this article reviewing *Division and Reunion*. The following notes are in the text and have been renumbered.

[2] *Abraham Lincoln*. (American Statesmen Series.) By John T. Morse, Jr. In two volumes. Boston and New York: Houghton, Mifflin & Co. 1893.

the fifty years of Mr. Lincoln's life which preceded his election to the presidency, and these are devoted largely to his political career; the rest of the two volumes is given up to a narrative of the events of the five years which ensued. The reason for this is, of course, that those five years were of incalculably more consequence than the preceding five decades, in their transcendent importance both as respects the destinies of the country and the opportunity which they afforded for the display of Mr. Lincoln's character. During those years he stood forth one of the most conspicuous figures in the world's history, for he held steadily in his hand the destinies of a great nation. They were not simply the dramatic culmination of his own life; they were also one of the chief points of dramatic culmination in the history of the United States, and even of the world. If length of life is to be reckoned by intensity, there was unquestionably more of Mr. Lincoln's life in those five years than in the preceding fifty: and in these years he was not a mere political orator, as before; he was a statesman, having to put his political principles into action, to translate his theories into momentous practice. Our keen regret is that, in leading up to this great period, Mr. Morse has not given us a more penetrating study of those American forces which shaped Lincoln in his youth and obscure manhood. History underlies statecraft, and there is as much history in those forces as in the events which furnished scope for Lincoln's great powers amidst the tumults and storms of war. Even the very broad scale Mr. Morse has allowed himself for the consideration of the events of Mr. Lincoln's presidency is not broad enough for the purpose; he is obliged to refer to more history than he tells; and if Mr. Lincoln remains somewhat dim and shadowy the while, it is because we did not know him well before the stage became so crowded. If we could have mastered his character and made it real to our thought before this rush of momentous history came upon him and upon us, the outlines of his part would remain clear-cut and prominent throughout. As it is, we note him only when our attention is called to him.

This explains the inadequacy of the book as a personal biography. Mr. Lincoln can be known only by a close and prolonged scrutiny of his life before he became President. The years of his presidency were not years to form, but rather years to test character. The strain was too great to harden and perfect any sinew but that which was already tough and firmly knit. There is something of the quality and method of the analytical novelist in Mr. Morse's manner of dealing with his subject. He frequently pauses to explain and analyze Mr. Lincoln; modestly, indeed, and without the novelist's confidence that he thoroughly understands the workings of his singular hero's mind, since he did not create him, but still with the novelist's art of making the character distinct by description rather than by action. And yet these descriptions of the man are confessedly incomplete. Like most modern historians, Mr. Morse uniformly suspects and rejects, if he can, every explanation that is extraordinary, and insists upon believing that some quite commonplace explanation exists, if it could but be discovered; though he very often admits a failure to discover it, and rather helplessly suggests that we must feel convinced both of its existence and of its sufficiency without knowing what it is. He is subtly disquieted, nevertheless, by the consciousness, which every one must have in studying Lincoln, that the more ordinary and within easy view of reason you seek to make the life of this strange man, the more extraordinary it becomes, and the more inexplicable. Mr. Morse is keenly alive to the desirability of avoiding the foolish habit of most biographers, of beckoning their great men impatiently on to their greatness, wondering the while and fretting at their laggardliness and blindness to the destiny in store; and yet he himself gives frequent evidence of having his eye on the future always rather than directly on the present, in dealing with Lincoln's years of preparation. He is himself irritated by the narrowness of the life Lincoln so long led, and hurries over it as merely preliminary to his narrative.

And yet the real Lincoln was alive in 1850 quite as much as in 1860. Mr. Morse presents the key to the whole matter on pages 31-34 of his first volume: "The preëminently striking feature in Lincoln's nature," visible in the early days scarcely less than in the later, "was the extraordinary degree to which he always seemed to be in close and sympathetic touch with the people; that is to say, the people in the mass wherein he was embedded, the social body amid which he dwelt, which pressed upon him on all sides, which for him formed 'the public.' First this group or body was only the population of the frontier settlement; then it widened to include the State of Illinois; then it expanded to the population of the entire North." But it strikes us that he hardly sees the full value of the solution; he only marvels at the rapidity of the transition from the public of Illinois to the public of the Union, on Lincoln's part, without loss of head or flaw of complete insight and sympathy, and leaves the capacity a sign and wonder rather than an explanation. The fact would seem to be that there was no sudden broadening of view, no marvel of an instantly widened vision. Lincoln's capacity to understand and

persuade men was indeed marvelous in its perfection, its in-
errancy, but in kind it was no new wonder. And in Illinois, in
Lincoln's day, there was every opportunity for an eye like Lincoln's to see the thought and spirit of the whole country. The
youth of the State was coincident in time with his own youth,
and Illinois grew to maturity as rapidly as Lincoln did. The Western frontier population was, moreover, an intensely political population. It felt the very keenest throbs of the nation's life, for the
nation's energy was directed westward. The West was not separate from the East: its communities were every day receiving
fresh members from the East, and fresh impulse of direct suggestion; their blood flowed to them directly from the veins of the
older communities. Elements separated in the East, moreover,
were united in the West, which displayed to the eye a sort of
epitome of the more active and permanent forces of the national
life. In such communities as these Lincoln mixed daily with men
of all types and from every quarter of the country. With them
he discussed neighborhood politics, the politics of the State, the
politics of the nation, now more and more centring in Western
questions. He went twice down the Mississippi to its mouth, and
his eyes, so accustomed to look directly, point-blank, upon men
and affairs, saw characteristic regions of the South. He worked
his way slowly and sagaciously, with the larger sort of sagacity,
into the active business of state politics, he sat twice in the legislature and for one term in Congress; his singularly sensitive mind
open all the time to every aspect, especially every human aspect,
of what was going on about him. All the while, too, he was
canvassing, piece by piece, every item of politics, familiarly
around the stove, more formally upon the stump, in direct contact always with the ordinary views of ordinary men. He was
reading, too, as nobody else of those around him read, seeking a
complete mastery over speech with the conscious purpose to prevail in its use; deriving zest from the study of mathematical
proof, amusement in clean and naked statements of truth. It was
all irregularly done, but it was strenuously done, and done
throughout with the same instinct and with a steady access of
facility and power. There was no sudden leap for this man, any
more than for other men, from crudeness to finished power,
from an understanding of the people of Illinois to an understanding of the people of the United States. He came to his great
national task with a capacity trained to an equality with its magnitude. You could not then set a pace in learning and perceiving
that was too hard for him.

If we have dwelt upon the possibilities contained in such a

study, it is because every fresh presentation of Lincoln makes us more eager for that characterization of the man which shall not indeed detach him from his times, but which shall build up the figure with such truthfulness and skill as shall justify the unique position which he holds in history. For the rest, Mr. Morse's contribution is marked by such full knowledge, calm judgment, and eminent fairness that after we have regretted the neutral tints in which the chief figure is drawn, we can thank the writer heartily for an able historical study.

Both the plan and the subject of Mr. Pierce's volumes[3] are very different. They complete his monumental Memoir of Charles Sumner in the style of which the earlier volumes gave promise. They do not attempt a portrait of the man; a portrait extended throughout four octavo volumes would of course be no portrait at all. They are a careful and elaborate recital of all the events, both great and small, of Mr. Sumner's interesting and eventful life; full of long extracts from his speeches and addresses; full of his letters, both formal and familiar, and of letters written to him by others. They are not an historian's work, but teem with such materials as historians are most grateful for; such materials as furnish minutely elaborated pictures of men, of situations in affairs, of places and social conditions, and bring the imagination into direct contact with persons and times now passed away. This Memoir, with due allowance made for the prepossessions of the devoted biographer, unquestionably gives us Charles Sumner as he was, a man of high tastes and refined sensibilities; meant for the profession of the scholar, but forced by exceptional times and causes into public stations for which he had a decided distaste, into public functions for which he had little real capacity or fitness of temperament. Mr. Sumner was by nature a philanthropist. His capacity for affairs was a capacity for understanding them in their larger aspects rather than for conducting them in detail. Immediate hot contact with practical politics sometimes destroyed his self-possession, as it is so apt to do in the case of all men of fervid moral temperament. He now and again suffered himself to be goaded into utterances which were wholly unbecoming his elevated genius. He often spoke like an apostle, too, when the occasion required that he should speak like a statesman. Powers meant, perhaps, for mankind were given up to an agitation. His life had dignity, had largeness, had even, in the broader conception of events, a generous measure of success; but one cannot suppress a regret, after reading Mr. Pierce's

[3] *Memoir and Letters of Charles Sumner.* By Edward L. Pierce. Volumes III. and IV. 1845-1874. Boston: Roberts Brothers. 1893.

worthy memorial, that such a man should have been denied to some quiet time, when his powers could have worked the gentler works of amity and peace.

So far, such materials of our history as this great biography affords have proved more interesting and enlightening than the formal histories that have been constructed out of them. Biographies, especially when they are full of letters, as this one is, are at least pervaded by the flavor of the personality of the men whose lives they recount. But the historian introduces what individualities he will, distributes flavor to his taste, reconceives the story, recasts it, colors it to his own eye. And it must be said that we have not been very fortunate in our later historians of the antislavery struggle. Elevated as are the character and purpose of Mr. Schouler, it is impossible to convey right impressions in his swashbuckler style. Mr. Rhodes has been hardly more successful. It is unpleasant, it even seems ungrateful, to set less than full value on his painstaking volumes.[4] They are studiously conceived, they are full of a pleasing candor, they try diligently to tell the whole story, their purpose is just and their manner unpretentious. But for all that, if the balance be wisely cast, they must be pronounced not to be what a history of the period they cover ought to be. Nothing short of catholicity of sympathy, a most delicate and discriminating appreciation of opposite points of view, and a rare literary skill in nicely modulated statement is required by the historian of the time since 1850; and Mr. Rhodes does not, if the truth may be candidly put, possess these elements of success. This is not harsh criticism; it is simply the inevitable conclusion of the critic.

His attitude towards the South is of course the crucial test of the whole matter. He declares, with his usual candor, at the outset of his chapter on slavery, that what he shall have to say "can only be a commentary on the sententious expression of Clay: 'Slavery is a curse to the master, and a wrong to the slave.'" He has already avowed, in a previous passage, the belief that only "the historian whose sympathies are with the antislavery cause of 1850" "can most truly write the story" of the ways in which that cause was advanced. Accordingly, his volumes become a superior sort of anti-slavery pamphlet, and, by reason of the extreme exaggeration of his emphasis of the national life and feeling, the features of the story are thrown hopelessly, almost grotesquely, out of proportion. There was space enough in these two large volumes, surely, to tell the history of the whole country

---

[4] *History of the United States from the Compromise of 1850.* By James Ford Rhodes. Volumes I. and II. 1850-1860. New York: Harper & Brothers. 1893.

during the ten years they cover, stirring times as those were; but Mr. Rhodes's view is confined to the Northern States, and, within the Northern States, almost exclusively to the anti-slavery struggle. All other matters, even all other features of national legislation, not only fall into the background, but practically pass out of view altogether. No one now needs to be persuaded that slavery ought to have been extirpated, the country rendered homogeneous and safely united both in spirit and in interest; and yet those who believe in the necessary and indissoluble nature of the Union, before the war as since, can hardly be satisfied with Mr. Rhodes's treatment. He quietly dissolves the Union from the outset of his narrative. The South is throughout, for him, a foreign country, whose condition and sentiments he learns piecemeal and at intervals from travelers. It is a region from which many rumors come to him; he speculates and concludes concerning it, but he has no authentic knowledge or direct realization of it himself. His Union is not to be preserved so much as created by the suppression of slavery.

That the whole matter of the condition of the South and the character of slavery is foreign to his apprehension is shown most sharply in his deliberate estimate of the slave system. He sets forth the evils of slavery in black catalogue, and then he turns suddenly about and smilingly recites the brighter and more benignant features of the institution. The two passages are simply contradictory; and he is either unconscious of the fact, or quite helpless in the presence of it. He makes no attempt at a consistent assessment of the thing as it was when seen whole and in its normal aspects. This is the result in part, perhaps, of the leisurely spaces of the narrative, and in part, no doubt, of the false canons of modern historical writing. Both long histories and modern canons prompt the historian to set forth his material rather than to digest it, to give grounds for a conclusion rather than the conclusion itself.

But such methods, such temptations, when yielded to, simply rob history of all significance or right to be. Mr. Rhodes ought to have realized for himself, and ought to have written the history of the whole country. Even during the decade 1850-1860 that history by no means narrows itself to a history of the Northern States and the anti-slavery struggle. The forces that were to win in the deadly contest coming on were gathering head in the North, and the South was approaching the end of her belated régime. But the historian who confines his view to these things merely skims the surface; he by no means penetrates to the real life of the times. There was much genuine community of view between North and South in those days. The South was rashly forfeiting the confidence of those who nevertheless held her general principles of politics as stanchly as she did; but the Republican party, fast as it gathered strength, was the party of a minority even at the very threshold of the war. There was a real and abiding basis for the Union in spite of slavery; and if there had been no persistently open question concerning the extension of slavery, its mere continued existence in the Southern States would never have been a question at all,—at any rate never a question capable of affecting the vitality of the Union. The history of the anti-slavery propaganda, therefore, is not, taken apart, the history either of the affairs or of the thought of the country. Its affairs had a deeper guiding principle, its thought an infinitely profounder complexity, than one would dream of in reading these pages. The very term which most comprehensively characterizes the war which followed, the war for the Union, is a protest against a more limited conception of the principles involved in the contest.

The truth is that Mr. Rhodes has no insight, at least into complex characters, taking men either individually or in the mass. His delineations of character and appraisements of motive in public men give even a painful evidence of the fact. No historian of real insight could for a moment accept his portrait of Calhoun, or of Douglas, or of Seward, or of Sumner. The historian needs nothing less than the insight of the best novelists into character and the grounds of action. Mr. Rhodes gives us only very singular and whimsical sketches of the outsides of men. The same man is now one thing, and again quite another, according as his acts are approved or disapproved. Seward is a politician when he is wrong, a statesman when he is right. Douglas is a time-server when he proposes the repeal of the Missouri Compromise; yet he suddenly becomes unselfish and disinterested at the very moment when he might, by trimming, reap the identical advantage he is supposed to have played for in that legislation. The author's descriptions of the personal appearance and outward fortunes of his characters are equally capricious and oddly proportioned, reminding one sometimes of the dear old lady who described an intellectual friend who had impressed her very deeply as "having a great mind and shaggy eyebrows"! Lincoln, "like Socrates, was odd in personal appearance, though with a different grotesqueness of exterior. And to Lincoln, as to Socrates, were denied the felicity of domestic life and the pleasures of a quiet home." Could Mr. Rhodes find no homely man whose wife was uncongenial who was at the same time in other respects more like Lincoln than Socrates was? Such comparisons are not even like Banks, "sagacious in appearance."

These, it will be perceived, are not mere literary defects. They betoken a real obtuseness of vision. Mr. Rhodes's method is crude and with the flat hand rather than refined and discriminating. It never penetrates to any interior meaning, nor to the real centre of any complex situation. His soft-spoken judgment of John Brown, his tendency to speak of "the South" in a lump, his sometimes credulous entertainment of rumors, of which his pages are often as full as Washington itself, are evidences of this that will occur to any one who has read the book. The writing is not dogmatic in terms, one feels, only because the author is aware that it is "bad form" to be dogmatic; for it is strongly dogmatic in spirit.

However much one deplores these grave defects of the book, and however radical he must pronounce them to be, he cannot quit its perusal without a kindly feeling for the author. It is so honest a piece of work. It is elaborate,—unduly, inartistically elaborate, indeed,—giving symptoms everywhere of that demoralizing disease known as "materials-in-the-footnotes"; but its elaborateness is unmistakably the result of a painstaking examination of the sources. If the colors of the narrative are not successfully blended, they are at least not pale or neutral in tint, but the strong and definite colors of conviction. It is a pleasure to see the period so studiously canvassed, so frankly discussed. There are vigor, honesty, and knowledge throughout; and so full a setting forth of the matter for judgment will contribute in a very important degree, it may be hoped, to the formation of right views. Where there is no concealment the truth may be expected eventually to emerge.

An old member of one of our historical societies used to say, some years ago, that he didn't know but the time had about come when we might tell the truth concerning Great Britain and the Revolution. Dr. Woodrow Wilson[5] evidently thinks the time has come when the country is ready to hear the truth about the South and the war. We believe that he is right. The generation which participated in the final struggle has largely passed away. It has contributed much toward bringing on the better era in the historical treatment of the conflict by the good work it has done in the impartial discussion of its military history. In this field it was easier to bring the views of the opposing parties into re-

---

[5] *Division and Reunion.* 1829-1889. (Epochs of American History.) By Woodrow Wilson, Ph. D., LL. D., Professor of Jurisprudence in Princeton University. New York and London: Longmans, Green & Co. 1893.

conciliation. But that participants in the political history of the time should come to agreement about its events and questions was not to be expected. Unquestionably, our civil war is not exempt from the fate of all other civil wars,—that the ultimate judgment of mankind upon it is something different from that held at the time by either of the parties engaged. But for this judicial and intermediate view we look rather to the new generation, which can more easily acquire that sympathy with both sides which is the indispensable condition of just narration. This new generation Dr. Wilson fully represents. Such a temper is a primary qualification toward writing the history of the period of sectional division and reunion in the United States. The resulting view of the conflict is one which we believe will commend itself more and more, especially to the newer generation. We may quote as typical Professor Wilson's words regarding secession: "The legal theory upon which this startling and extraordinary series of steps was taken was one which would hardly have been questioned in the early years of the government, whatever resistance might then have been offered to its practical execution. It was for long found difficult to deny that a State could withdraw from the federal arrangement, as she might have declined to enter it. But constitutions are not mere legal documents: they are the skeleton frames of a living organism; and in this case the course of events had nationalized the government once deemed confederate. Twenty States had been added to the original thirteen. . . . These are not lawyer's facts: they are historian's facts. There had been nothing but a dim realization of them till the war came and awoke the national spirit into full consciousness. They have no bearing upon the legal intent of the Constitution as a document, to be interpreted by the intention of its framers; but they have everything to do with the Constitution as a vehicle of life. The South had not changed her ideas from the first, because she had not changed her condition. She had not experienced, except in a very slight degree, the economic forces which had created the great northwest and nationalized the rest of the country, for they had been shut out from her life by slavery. . . . She had stood still while the rest of the country had undergone profound changes; and, standing still, she retained the old principles which had once been universal."

In other words, Professor Wilson refuses to engage in the old debate upon the ground originally occupied by the disputants, but leads us away to another position, from which both sides of the shield can easily be seen. From the strictly legal point of view, that which was the Constitution in 1789 was the Constitution in

1830 and in 1860; and what it was, was to be discovered by in-spection of the document in the light of the remarks of those who originated it. In the old debate, each party argued from this as-sumption, and claimed the victory on this battle-ground. In Web-ster's great speech, the best remembered portion is the im-passioned appeal to the sentiment of nationality with which he closed; but the bulk of the argument is upon the documentary evidence as to the original meaning of the Constitution. Taken upon this ground, the Southern chieftains were in reality difficult to assail. While we should not wish to assent to the proposition that the extreme state-rights theory would hardly have been ques-tioned in the early years of the government (for the writings of the fathers give an uncertain sound), the weight of evidence seems on the whole to be with those who think the doctrine of state sovereignty to have been the doctrine held, consciously or unconsciously, by most instructed persons at the time when the Constitution was formed. But the legal point of view is not the only one from which a constitution can be considered. There is another,—that of the historian, regardful of development; of the practical statesman or humbler man of affairs, to whom it seems obvious that the growth of a nation to adult maturity should cause, and sufficiently justify, a fortification of its vertebræ. Hence arose, by 1861, another theory of the Constitution, equally valid with the other, and, as the event proved, vastly more potent, but quite irreconcilable therewith. It is one of the chief merits of Dr. Wilson's little book that he has perceived not only the irre-concilable quality of the two, but the real validity of each, its genuine title to respect.

We have lingered long upon those portions of the book which deal with the great crisis toward which the thirty preceding years of the period were leading us, and from which the thirty succeed-ing years have but slowly, painfully, and in some respects im-perfectly extricated us. These are the parts of the book which will most arouse discussion, and in regard to which the author's lucid mind and liberal spirit will have their most ample chance to exert a beneficent influence on those who may use his volume for reading or as a textbook. Yet, after all, the slavery conflict was, in its relation to the logical development of American democracy, only an episode, though a gigantic one, and Dr. Wilson is careful not to give it undue prominence in his narrative, nor to neglect for its sake the record of that development. We could ask for a student of Mr. Rhodes's History, for example, no better prepara-tion than would follow upon a careful reading of Dr. Wilson's volume. Considered as a general history of the United States from 1829 to 1889, his book is marked by excellent sense of proportion, extensive knowledge, impartiality of judgment, unusual power of summarizing, and an acute political sense. Few writers can more vividly set forth the views of parties. Indeed, we should be inclined to say that the book is stronger in its exposition of the development of political thought than in any other department of the narrative; certainly stronger here than in regard to the development of external institutions, the anatomy of government. Yet here it is only fair to remember how little has been done to elucidate the history of our governmental institutions during the present century. What do we know about the history of the nominating convention, for instance? Have we not left it to be described by M. Ostrogorski and Mr. Bryce? And the writer of the small book upon a long period, however zealous he may be in research, is to a great extent limited by the existence or absence of larger or more special treatises.

Though Dr. Wilson's book is mainly a history of our political development, he has a manifest desire to consider the history of our civilization, at least in so far as it illustrates our political history. In his remarks on such topics one notes the influence of the writings of the late Professor Alexander Johnston. One notes, too, an appreciation of the fact, which we hope will be increasingly perceived by our historians, that at many points in our history subsequent to the Treaty of Ghent there have been intimate connections between the movements of public thought in Europe and those in America. In spite of our political separateness since 1815, more is common in the nineteenth-century history of the two continents than is usually imagined.

If one compares Dr. Wilson's book with the two which have preceded it in the same series, some results of the comparative want of predecessors are apparent. There is not the same evidence of compression forced upon the writer by the presence of a vast body of facts already long recognized as of necessity to be included in a history of the time. The narrative is easier, the style more fluid. It may be that the book will not be so easy to use as a textbook as Dr. Hart's admirable volume, but it will be more enjoyed as reading. As regards arrangement, the author has intentionally dealt somewhat more fully with the years of Jackson and Van Buren's administrations, as constituting a formative period the understanding of which is in an especial degree necessary to that which follows. Particularly interesting and important is the short chapter on the constitution and government of the Confederate States. Dr. Wilson rightly remarks that, "stupendous as was the war struggle from every point of view, its deepest and most extraordinary qualities are revealed only when it is viewed from the side of the Southern Confederacy." He therefore gives an instructive account of the constitution of the Confederate States, of their resources, army, and finances, and of the character of the government, the symptoms of opposition, and the final collapse.

Save for a number of annoying misprints in the references, the volume has the same excellence in respect to bibliographical aids which characterized its predecessors in the series.

Printed in the *Atlantic Monthly*, LXXII (Aug. 1893), 268-77.

From Walter Hines Page

The Forum, Union Square, New York
My dear Mr. Wilson: August the first, Eighteen, Ninety-three

The time is come, I think, when the truth ought to be set forth about the Mining Camp and Ranch States—set forth from the point-of-view, not of the mere statistician or politician, but of the student of our Institutions. We made States out of these settlements, by statistics: so many square miles, so many people, such a rate of increase, an output of products of such and such value; and we made them States really of course for political reasons but we justified their manufacture (it was an out-and-out manufacture of States) by statistics and the ever delusive percentages of things mechanically measurable.

Now in the old times when States grew—when communities by the development of society and politics and all the fundamental institutions naturally ripened into States—there was a public consciousness of what a State is. It was a growth; it was a community that had reached a definite stage in its development and by its character had got ready for statehood. This idea used to come out even when new States were made alternately by the Slave Power and the Free-Soil Power. But after the war, the public lost that organic and institutional notion of a State, and the statistical notion was substituted. Isn't this true?

If it is, the time is opportune to make an examination of the Mining-Camp and Ranch States by the light of this old-time idea. We should see then the more clearly how we mortgaged our national character for a pile of silver. Therein, too, lies an explanation, in great measure, of the coming of Money-Bags into the Senate.[1]

———

Now will you not do me the kindness and (this is much more

important) do the country the service to write such an article for the October number of *The Forum*?[2] That number we put to press very soon after September the first.

I have no carpenter's rule in my office, and no space-rate. If you will remember that *The Forum* is neither bulky nor rich, I shall ask that you take as much space as you like and that you will yourself fix your *honorarium*.

I sincerely hope for your consent. Of one thing I can assure you: scrappy as *The Forum* is, it has the best audience in America.

I should feel greatly pleased if you would come to see me when you are in town.

Very Sincerely Yours,   Walter H: Page

ALS (WP, DLC).

[1] Page was of course writing this letter just before the convening of the special session of Congress called by President Cleveland to repeal the Sherman Silver Purchase Act. Page, as a strong supporter of Cleveland, was eager to join in the eastern attack against the so-called "silver senators," that is, the senators who represented mining states and had large personal interests in silver mines. Among these in 1893 were Henry Moore Teller of Colorado and William Morris Stewart and John Percival Jones of Nevada. The most famous of the "silver senators," George Hearst of California, had died in 1891.

[2] Wilson's reply is missing, but in it he declined Page's request.

From Charles Scribner's Sons

Dear Sir,   [New York] Aug 2, [189]3

We like to make as little prominent as may properly be the fact that the substance of a book has appeared in print before, and beg to suggest that instead of your "Prefatory Note" you make some simple expression of acknowledgment to the editors of the Atlantic & N. Princeton Review in a line or two, or three—which we may place with ⁎⁎⁎ at the end of the Contents. If Mrs. Van Rensselaer's "Art Out of Doors"[1] is accessible it will illustrate our preference. (At the same time do not understand that *any* acknowledgment is *due* a magazine, which has only *serial* rights in its publication). Of course we mention this merely in the interests of the book, as we conceive them, and not because of a wish to impose our preferences upon you in a matter of taste.[2]   Very truly yours   Charles Scribner's Sons

ALS (Letterpress Books, Charles Scribner's Sons Archives, NjP).

[1] Mariana Griswold Van Rensselaer, *Art Out-of-Doors. Hints on Good Taste in Gardening* (New York, 1893).

[2] As WW to Charles Scribner's Sons, Aug. 3 and 4, 1893, and the "Contents" page of *An Old Master* make clear, Wilson readily acceded to this suggestion.

Two Letters to Charles Scribner's Sons

My dear Sirs,   Princeton, New Jersey, 3 August, 1893.

Your letter of August 2nd. reached me this morning. I think your suggestion as to the form of acknowledgment of the previous publication of the substance of my essays an excellent one. I have not a copy of Mrs. Van Rennselaer's "Art Out-of-Doors" at hand, so that I cannot see the form of acknowledgment employed in it; but I hope that you will formulate a similar note for me. I should prefer that some acknowledgment be made to the *Atlantic*, and *New Princeton*, but I am really indifferent what form it may take. I shall be content to see it in proof.

Very sincerely Yours,   Woodrow Wilson

My dear Sirs,   Princeton, New Jersey, 4 August, 1893.

The printer's proofs of "An Old Master" came last evening after I had written and posted my letter to you. I return them this morning, corrected. I have stricken out the Prefatory Note, and will still ask that a note such as you suggest be appended to the table of contents.

I hope that you will intimate to the printer quite strongly the propriety, not to say necessity, of following my punctuation, of following the copy in all respects. He has taken singular liberties with it in some respects.

Very sincerely Yours,   Woodrow Wilson

WWTLS (Charles Scribner's Sons Archives, NjP).

To Albert Shaw

My dear Shaw,   Princeton, New Jersey,   7 August, 1893.

I was in Chicago when your last letter[1] reached Sagaponack. We are all at home again now, to receive visits from our southern relatives.

You may be sure that, unless something imperative, now unforeseen, occurs to prevent, I will attend that wedding, in which I am deeply interested, on the 5th of September. I am glad to know that it is to be so soon. Your plans for a wedding journey are certainly most attractive. I know that you will have such a time as to make you forget that you ever meditated a breakdown.

Mrs. Wilson joins me in warmest regards,

Affectionately yours,   Woodrow Wilson

TCL (in possession of Virginia Shaw English).
[1] Shaw's letter is missing.

From Adrian Hoffman Joline

My Dear Sir: New York Aug 10, 1893.

I am reading, with great interest and very sincere appreciation your book "Division and Reunion, 1829-1889" which any student and lover of American political history must read with interest and appreciation. It is in no carping or criticising spirit that I venture to make an inquiry.

On page 92, referring to Van Buren, you say: "He did not lead, or constitute, a party as Jackson did, and he deliberately emphasized his subordination by explicit public pledges *that he would in all respects follow carefully in Jackson's footsteps.*"

I confess that I am an admirer of Van Buren. I regard him as a great and unappreciated American statesman[.] I have had favorable opportunities of making a study of him. I have in my hands and under my eye his autobiography—never published—and his private correspondence. He was a remarkable man and the present generation wholly fails to accord to him the reputation he justly deserves.

Tradition has ascribed to him a subordination to Jackson which he did not have—any more than Chase or Stanton had to Lincoln—even less.

The fable about his following in Jackson's footsteps is familiar. In Bartlett's Familiar Quotations will be found (p. 364) the words "I shall tread in the footsteps of my illustrious predecessor. Martin Van Buren, Inaugural Address, March 4, 1837."

But Martin Van Buren, in his inaugural address, never said any such thing.

He *did* say this:

"The practice of my predecessors imposes on me an obligation I cheerfully fulfil, to accompany the first and solemn act of my public trust with an avowal of the principles that will guide me in performing it, and an expression of my feelings on assuming a charge so responsible and vast. In imitating their example, I tread in the footsteps of illustrious men."

And, at the close of his address: "In receiving from the people the sacred trust since confided to my illustrious predecessor, and which he has discharged so faithfully and so well, I know that I cannot expect to perform the arduous task with equal ability and success."

I fail to find in Mr. Van Buren's papers anything which binds him "to follow carefully in Jackson's footsteps." I know that it is common report that he said something of that sort. Can you refer to anything which literally sustains such an assertion?

Yours very truly   Adrian H Joline

ALS (WP, DLC).

To Horace Elisha Scudder, with Enclosure

My dear Mr. Scudder,   Princeton, New Jersey, 14 August, 1893

The temper of Mr. Rhodes's letter is certainly exemplary, and I admire him for it.[1] I should admire him more, however, if he had not written at all; and I must say that his defence shows him am [an] amiable goose. I wish we could have done with histories written by men whose training and associations have fitted them for something else. It's delicious to have a comparison between Lincoln and Socrates justified by the brilliant conversation of "General J. D. Cox,"—and nobody can doubt for a moment that the Shakespearean method of delineating character is superior to the consistency of treatment to be attained by occupying "the point of view of the philippic or the panegyric"! Here are the sentences about Socrates, you remember: "Lincoln, like Socrates, was odd in his personal appearance, though with a different grotesqueness of exterior. And to Lincoln, as to Socrates, were denied the felicity of domestic life and the pleasures of a quiet home." In these respects he equally resembled Dr. Johnson, or my neighbour, the irritable professor. But Mr. Rhodes is a good fellow; and I hope you will give him my History of the United States to review when it comes out.

I was startled to see a notice of my little "Division and Reunion" put in with what I had myself written;[2] but I should like to thank my critic very heartily for his all too generous appreciation of the wee volume,—and to tell him he under-did the "buts."

Most sincerely Yours,   Woodrow Wilson

ALS (de Coppet Coll., NjP).
[1] Scudder's letter to which this was a reply is missing.
[2] See the review article printed at Aug. 1, 1893.

ENCLOSURE

James Ford Rhodes to Horace Elisha Scudder

Dear Mr. Scudder,   Rye Beach, N. H. Aug. 4, 1893

I should be either more or less than human if I were elated over the criticism of my history in the current Atlantic but as the writer gives me credit for honesty and industry, which are conceded to be essential qualities in an historian, I can forgive him for laying stress on certain defects, hoping with continued study and thought to overcome at least some of them. Of crudity from a literary point of view I am conscious. My friends however tell me that my second volume is an improvement on the first and I hope the third will show a further betterment.

I am amused at your writer making merry over the comparison of Lincoln to Socrates. This was suggested to me by a writer in The Nation whom I afterwards found to be General J. D. Cox. I feel quite sure that if you could have heard him last week in really brilliant conversational discourse elaborate and extend the parallel, you would have acknowledged its justice and effectiveness.

Touching the inconsistencies of the characterizations, I was struck with that myself and gave much thought to the subject, arriving at the conclusion that it was not I who was inconsistent but the men themselves. On a careful examination and a comparison of my practical experience of men with a study of the development of character as Shakespeare delineates it, this matter ceased to trouble me, for I felt convinced than [that] all estimate of the men, by making their actions consistent from the point of view of the philippic or the panegyric would be untrue to life. That I have dealt justly with Seward and Douglas, several of their contemporaries, men of judgment, have assured me, and the nature of the criticisms I have had from both their friends and detractors confirm me in this opinion.

With regard to the point that the slavery question is too prominent, it is curious that some of my critics compare me unfavorably with Von Holst because I have not made it prominent enough. I have written a supplemental chapter on the decade of 1850-60, which will be the first of Vol III and with that complement, I am ready to stand by the historical accuracy of my picture. From the influence of my early political training and from a revolt at certain anti-slavery histories, which, being the product of men of one idea, seemed to suppress the facts that told for the other side, I started out with a preconceived notion of the decade, something such as your writer obviously has, but a careful study of the contemporary evidence brought me to the result you see.

Conscious of many defects for the work projected, I have now arrived at the point of being grateful for honest criticism, no matter how hard it hits. When I make a careful revision of Vols I and II, the Atlantic article shall again have my careful consideration and if with mature reflection, I shall see that I have been wrong in many respects or even on the central topic, I believe that I shall have the candor to own it.

Very truly yours,   James Ford Rhodes.

ALS (H. E. Scudder Papers, MH).

To Caleb Thomas Winchester

My dear Winchester,   Princeton, New Jersey, 17 August, 1893

I am ashamed that I should have suffered a number of jobs connected with our home coming to postpone my writing to you about the matter I took in hand for you. I went up to Madison and saw Turner, as I promised. I put the Burke, and the Webster, at him as persuasively as ever I could: I even urged him to the utmost of my influence over him; but he was stubbornly unwilling, and would not even consider the matter beyond the time of my visit. He is both doubtful of his own fitness for such a job and shy of letting himself out for a specific service to a publisher. I am afraid there's no arguing with him any farther.[1]

And now, as you know, I am at my wit's ends as to what to advise you to do,—unless you act upon my suggestion (which really seems the only feasible one) about securing some young Englishman, by taking counsel with some omniscient like Lang.[2]

At the risk of seeming to rub a difficult matter into you, I am going to suggest that you call the attention of your editor (when you catch him) to the advantage of comparing the published versions of Burke's speeches in the Hastings trial with the official *verbatim* reports (See Craik's History of English Literature,—Scribner & Armstrong ed.–II., p. 329, note), for the sake of getting specimens of his extemporaneous, *unrevised* style.

We have been home a couple of weeks—long enough to feel like going away again to escape the rather trying weather that has set in of late. But we are not likely to stir again now until the Sherman law is repealed. I hope you are going—or have been—to Chicago. Having seen it this time in its full glory, I am ready to advise you more strongly than ever by no means to miss it.

Mrs Wilson joins me in warmest regards to both Mrs. Winchester and yourself. My visit to Middletown was truly delightful and I shan't soon forget it.

As ever   Most cordially Yours,   Woodrow Wilson

ALS (CtW).
    [1] As this letter will soon reveal, Wilson, during a visit to Winchester in Middletown before his trip to Chicago, had promised to go to Madison from Chicago to try to persuade Frederick Jackson Turner to edit one of the volumes in Winchester's and Kittredge's Athenaeum Press Series, about which see WW to C. T. Winchester, May 13, 1893, n. 1.

[2] Andrew Lang, journalist, poet, and scholar. He did not edit a volume in the series.

From Franklin William Hooper[1]

My dear Sir: Walpole, N. H. Aug 17th 1893.

Your letter selecting the dates for your lectures was received just as I was leaving Chicago.[2] I take my first opportunity after a ten days tour to reply.

We will consider that the dates for your lectures are fixed in accordance with your wishes, viz.–Nov. 16, 23 Dec 7 14, 21, 28. If by any chance Thanksgiving day should be appointed for Nov. 23rd instead of Nov 30th it would be necessary to have the second lecture occur on Nov. 30th in place of Nov 23rd

I shall be glad to receive from you at your convenience between this and Aug. 24th the exact wording of the general subject of your course of lectures together with the titles of the individual lectures and such brief description of the purposes of the course and your method of treatment of the subject as will enable me to present the course in an attractive form in our forthcoming prospectus and announcement.[3]

Very respectfully yours   Franklin W. Hooper

ALS (WP, DLC) with WWhw notation on env.: "Ans. 21 Aug. '93."
  [1] Director of the Brooklyn Institute of Arts and Sciences.
  [2] Hooper's and Wilson's earlier correspondence about a series of lectures by Wilson at the Brooklyn Institute in 1893 is missing.
  [3] Wilson gave his lectures on the dates that Hooper proposed. See the Editorial Note, "Wilson's Lectures at the Brooklyn Institute of Arts and Sciences."

EDITORIAL NOTE
WILSON'S FIRST LECTURE ON BURKE

Wilson's rather offhand remark in his letter to his wife of January 31, 1894–"Friday evening I [will] read my 'Burke' before the Historical Seminary"; the record in the Hopkins Historical Seminary Minutes of February 15, 1894, to the effect that Wilson had presented such a paper before the Seminary on February 2; and brief notices of this address in the Baltimore *American* and Baltimore *Sun* on February 3, 1894, are the first pieces of conclusive evidence that Wilson had written a lecture on Edmund Burke. The account of his second delivery of the lecture–at Princeton, before an undergraduate organization called the Monday Night Club–in the *Daily Princetonian* of October 9, 1894 (to be printed in Volume 9), furnishes the first outline of the contents of the lecture. But this is all that the *direct* evidence tells us, for Wilson apparently did not give the lecture again, and no manuscript copy of it seems to have survived.[1]

  [1] The only manuscript related to the lecture that survives is a four-page WWhw MS. (WP, DLC) entitled *"Quotations."*

However, the circumstantial evidence is so abundant and revealing that we can come very close, perhaps within a week, to the date on which Wilson completed the lecture.

Wilson's casual reference to "my 'Burke'" in his letter to Ellen indicates that she was well acquainted with it—in other words, that he had composed the lecture and read it to her some time before the end of January 1894.

However, we can be more precise than to say that Wilson wrote the Burke lecture in late 1893 or very early 1894. His letter to Caleb T. Winchester of May 13, 1893, makes it clear both that he had not yet written the lecture and that he planned to write it during the coming summer. His letter to Winchester of August 17 reveals that he was at this very time deeply immersed in Burkeian sources, biographies, and related works. A more important clue is the reading date of "8/28/93" near the end of Burke's speech on conciliation with America in the edition of Burke's works upon which Wilson was relying as his major source and about which more will be said later in this Editorial Note.

It is barely possible that Wilson wrote the lecture at some time during the last three and a half months of 1893. On the other hand, it does not seem probable that he could have found an opportunity for such an exercise during term, especially since he was spending most of his free time during the autumn on his "Short History of the United States."[2] The absence in the documents of any indications of other activity during August suggests that Wilson devoted his time to Burke after his return from the World's Columbian Exposition in Chicago; and we conclude that he completed the Burke lecture in the last week of August. This conclusion is supported by the fact that there are clear echoes of what we shall see was the Burke lecture in Wilson's strictures against French libertarian philosophy in "A Calendar of Great Americans," printed at September 15, 1893. And all the evidence suggests that he composed "A Calendar of Great Americans" around the middle of September.

However all this may have been, the evidence leaves no doubt that Wilson composed the Burke lecture at least between late August 1893 and late January 1894. Having said this, we still face the equally important and more baffling task of finding the text of the lecture.

We have concluded that the text of that lecture was embodied in the essay, "The Interpreter of English Liberty," published for the first time in Wilson's *Mere Literature and Other Essays* in 1896. We have also concluded that it is possible to extract the lecture from the essay, and that, in fact, is what we have tried to do in reproducing the text that follows this Editorial Note.

A comparison of the text of the lecture printed below with that of the essay in *Mere Literature* will at once reveal those portions of the latter that were discarded because they were deemed to have been added at a later date. There is considerable evidence as to how and when Wilson transformed, or tried to transform, the lecture into the essay, and it was this evidence that guided us in establishing the text of the former.

The indispensable clue was the outline of Wilson's address, "Burke:

[2] See the Editorial Note, "Wilson's 'Short History of the United States.'"

The Man and His Times," in the *Daily Princetonian*, cited earlier. It reveals beyond cavil that in his lecture Wilson used large portions of what was later published in *Mere Literature*. On October 29, 1895, he prepared a long outline and partial draft of a lecture on Burke[3] for delivery, in 1895-96, in a series on "Great Leaders of Political Thought" under the auspices of the American Society for the Extension of University Teaching. For this lecture, Wilson adopted the title "Burke, the Interpreter of English Liberty." The outline and partial draft dated October 29, 1895, naturally drew heavily from the lecture, "Burke" or "Burke: The Man and His Times," for biographical data and quotations. However, the partial draft of "Burke, the Interpreter of English Liberty" included the gist of what would later become the two opening paragraphs—about the coming of Burke and Goldsmith to England—of the essay in *Mere Literature*. The report in the *Daily Princetonian* indicates that Wilson began his lecture with the sentence "There is no man anywhere to be found in the annals of Parliament. . . ." Thus the two opening paragraphs in the essay in *Mere Literature* were almost certainly later additions based upon the University Extension lecture.

In April 1896, Wilson submitted to Houghton Mifflin the copy for the volume that this firm soon published under the title of *Mere Literature and Other Essays*. Although Wilson's letter accompanying the copy is missing, it is reasonable to assume that he submitted tearsheets of seven articles that had already been published in magazines: " 'Mere Literature,' " "The Author Himself," "On an Author's Choice of Company," "A Literary Politician," "The Truth of the Matter," "A Calendar of Great Americans," and "The Course of American History."

Horace E. Scudder, replying for Houghton Mifflin on April 25, 1896,[4] said that the firm would be happy to publish the book. However, Scudder went on, it would be undersized, and he wondered whether Wilson did not have another essay "to increase the volume a little."

Wilson's reply is missing, but this, undoubtedly, is what he did: Taking the typescript of his lecture, "Burke: The Man and His Times," he changed the title to "Interpreter of English Liberty," added, in the form of typed inserts, the two new opening paragraphs and the other sections which the Editors have deleted from the text below; and made a few minor emendations, two of which are signaled in the notes appended to the lecture as reproduced.

There is strong internal evidence that this was the time when Wilson added the deleted portions. In all the additions of 1896 (including the two new opening paragraphs), he used contractions like "t'was" and "t'would." Never before had he resorted to these particular literary affectations. Use of these contractions is almost positive proof that the portions in which they appear were the additions that Wilson made to his typescript just before he sent it to Houghton Mifflin.

Further evidence tends to confirm this argument. First, we have to rule out the possibility that the copy that Wilson sent to Houghton

---

[3] WWhw and WWT MS. with heading "1729) IV. *Burke. The Interpreter of English Liberty* (1797" (WP, DLC).
[4] Printed in Vol. 9.

Mifflin was a typescript of his University Extension lecture. It is of course possible that he did write or type a full text of this lecture, but no manuscript of it exists. In any event, such a manuscript, if it was based upon Wilson's partial draft of October 29, 1895, would have been so different from the essay in *Mere Literature* as to disqualify it from being the text of that essay. Second, the lecture, "Burke: The Man and His Times," as printed below, follows very closely the outline in the *Daily Princetonian*. Third, and most convincing, the essay in *Mere Literature* is not really an essay at all like the others in the volume. It is in fact a hortatory speech, written for delivery and intended to stir emotions and ideas through the spoken word, and Wilson's few additions, obviously made in haste, did not succeed in transforming a lecture into an essay.

Wilson himself gives the clue to the significance of the date of composition and of the contents of his Burke lecture in the following sentence in his letter to Winchester of May 13, 1893: "If I should claim any man as my master, that man would be Burke." New words, these, for Woodrow Wilson! His master, after whom he had self-consciously and frankly modeled himself, hitherto had been Walter Bagehot, the English essayist, literary critic, and political commentator. As late as October 1891, we find Winchester echoing Wilson's long-held sentiments of attachment: "There is your ideal and model—Walter Bagehot."[5]
Wilson's avowal of a change of masters signaled a very important shift in his own political thought and concerns. To state the matter in its essence, under the impact of the Populist upheaval and the national crisis that was developing by the summer of 1893 in the wake of the Panic of that year, Wilson turned to Burke to find political principles to guide the nation through the storm.
One has to avoid the temptation to exaggerate at this point. Wilson's political thought was a continuing stream that expanded as it was fed by new tributaries. Burke's own thought had long been one of these tributaries. Wilson had read Burke and his biography at least since his freshman year at Princeton. For example, he had included an excerpt from Burke's speech on conciliation with America and a long biographical sketch of Burke in his "Index Rerum" in 1876.[6] He had read John Morley's biography of Burke in 1878. He had purchased the latest edition of Burke's *Works*[7] in early 1883; and his reading dates in these volumes reveal that he ranged widely if selectively through them at this time. He returned to Burke from time to time. For example, he quoted from Burke four times in *Congressional Government* and in that book referred to him as "learned in the profoundest principles of statecraft." During the years following the publication of *Congressional Government*, Wilson was unconsciously absorbing some of Burke's basic political principles. They were reflected most clearly, perhaps, first in "The Modern Demo-

[5] C. T. Winchester to WW, Oct 24, 1891, Vol. 7. There is also the following statement in WW to C. F. Beach, Jr., March 3, 1891, *ibid.*: "For me he [Bagehot] has a great and enduring fascination."
[6] Printed in Vol. 1, pp. 87-88, 94-98.
[7] *The Works of the Right Honorable Edmund Burke*, 6th-7th edn. (12 vols., Boston, 1880-81). This set is still in the Wilson Library, DLC.

cratic State" of December 1885, in that treatise's emphasis upon the organic nature of society and its assertion that self-government and democracy could develop only through the long and disciplined training of peoples. Evidences of Burke's continuing influence are scattered among Wilson's writings between 1885 and 1893—for example, in his essay on political sovereignty of November 1891, with its emphatic rejection of Dicey's theory of positive law.

What occurred in 1893, and what is dramatically revealed in the Burke lecture, was a change in the emphasis and direction of Wilson's political thought. Before 1893, he had counted himself a disciple of Bagehot because he shared Bagehot's interest, among other things, in hard-headed analysis of political institutions and the machinery of government. Although he had been considerably influenced by Burke's political thought, Wilson, in his confidence in the inevitability of progress and the onward march of democracy (most notably revealed in his essays and lectures, "The Modern Democratic State," "Leaders of Men," and "Democracy"), had not shared Burke's concern about the demonic and destructive forces allegedly inherent in majoritarian democracy.

The significant portions of the Burke lecture were not the biographical section or the discussions of Burke and the American Revolution, reform of the English government, and reform of the government of India. The significant portion of the lecture was Wilson's discussion of Burke and the French Revolution. In this we can see Wilson's own reactions to the social, economic, and political upheaval of 1893. After reading lessons from the Burkeian scriptures, Wilson proceeds to preach his own sermon to the American people: On all sides there are loud demands for change, but to innovate is not necessarily to reform. There must be progressive, constructive change, but such reform has to be expedient, that is, prudent because based upon tradition and consonant with prevailing majority habit. Adoption of utopian theories as guides to public policy can only lead to disaster, as had happened in France. America in the 1890's, like England a century before, has to be made immune to the "radically evil and corrupting" libertarian theories that had found their fullest application in the French Revolution. The state exists primarily to establish justice, not to maintain liberty. Above all, order is the absolutely indispensable prerequisite of progress.

The reader will hear numerous echoes of this sermon in the speeches and writings that follow in this volume and many beyond it, particularly in Wilson's lecture, "Political Liberty," the fullest text of which is printed at December 20, 1894, Volume 9. In this and other lectures and essays between 1894 and 1896, we find repeated warnings against popular excesses and doctrinaire socialism and new emphasis on order and obedience and on expediency as the only safe guide to public policy.

However, it is important to repeat that the Burke lecture reflected a new emphasis or direction, not a fundamental change, in Wilson's political thought. He did not abandon his belief in democracy, even majoritarian democracy, Moreover, he did not deny that the nation was in crisis and needed far-reaching reform. On the contrary, he was as much alarmed by the failure of political and legal leadership to act responsibly as he was about the dangers of popular excesses. He even admitted that at times revolutions were necessary.

What Wilson was saying in the Burke lecture, and what he would repeat in speeches and essays to be printed in this volume and the next, was simply that Burke was eternally right in marking out the only road to lasting change of political institutions and programs, with or without revolution, and that the American people would do well to heed the master's advice.

The text of the Burke lecture is reproduced below without annotation of Wilson's quotations and references, except for the poetical passage at the end, because such annotation would for the most part be an exercise in documenting the obvious. Wilson drew his extracts from Burke's writings and speeches from the edition of his *Works* cited above. For biographical information, he mined John Morley's *Burke* (New York, 1879); he also drew information from various encyclopedias and perhaps from some of the memoirs and biographies about Burke and his times in print by 1893.

A Lecture

[c. Aug. 31, 1893]

Edmund Burke: The Man and His Times

There is no man anywhere to be found in the annals of Parliament who seems more thoroughly to belong to England than does Edmund Burke, indubitable Irishman though he was. His words, now that they have cast off their brogue, ring out the authentic voice of the best political thought of the English race.[1] "If any man ask me," he cries, "what a free government is, I answer, that, for any practical purpose, it is what the people think so,— and that they, and not I, are the natural, lawful, and competent judges of the matter." "Abstract liberty, like other mere abstractions, is not to be found. Liberty adheres in some sensible object; and every nation has formed to itself some favorite point, which by way of eminence becomes the criterion of their happiness." These sentences, taken from his writings on American affairs, might serve as a sort of motto of the practical spirit of our race in affairs of government. Look further, and you shall see how his imagination presently illuminates and suffuses his maxims of practical sagacity with a fine blaze of insight, a keen glow of feeling, in which you recognize that other masterful quality of the race, its intense and elevated conviction. "My hold on the colonies," he declares, "is in the close affection which grows from

[1] In his address, Wilson seems to have substituted for this sentence the following one: "Burke was a mouthpiece for English politics, and England may well forgive Ireland for all the trouble she has given if by so doing she might gain a few such men as Burke." From the newspaper report of the address printed at Oct. 9, 1894, Vol. 9.

common names, from kindred blood, from similar privileges, and equal protection. These are the ties which, though light as air, are as strong as links of iron. Let the colonies always keep the idea of their civil rights associated with your government,—they will cling and grapple to you, and no force under heaven will be of power to tear them from their allegiance. But let it once be understood that your government may be one thing and their privileges another, that these two things may exist without any mutual relation,—and the cement is gone, the cohesion is loosened, and everything hastens to decay and dissolution. So long as you have the wisdom to keep the sovereign power of this country as the sanctuary of liberty, the sacred temple consecrated to our common faith, wherever the chosen race and sons of England worship freedom, they will turn their faces towards you." "We cannot, I fear," he says proudly of the colonies, "we cannot falsify the pedigree of this fierce people, and persuade them that they are not sprung from a nation in whose veins the blood of freedom circulates. The language in which they would hear you tell them this tale would detect the imposition; your speech would betray you. An Englishman is the unfittest person on earth to argue another Englishman into slavery." Does not your blood stir at these passages? And is it not because, besides loving what is nobly written, you feel that every word strikes towards the heart of the things that have made your blood what it has proved to be in the history of our race?

These passages, it should be remembered, are taken from a speech in Parliament and from a letter written by Burke to his constituents in Bristol. He had no thought to make them permanent sentences of political philosophy. They were meant only to serve an immediate purpose in the advancement of contemporaneous policy. They were framed for the circumstances of the time. They speak out spontaneously amidst matter of the moment: and they could be matched everywhere throughout his pamphlets and public utterances. No other similar productions that I know of have this singular, and as it were inevitable, quality of permanency. They have emerged from the mass of political writings put forth in their time with their freshness untouched, their significance unobscured, their splendid vigor unabated. It is this that we marvel at, that they should remain modern and timely, purged of every element and seed of decay. The man who could do this must needs arrest our attention and challenge our inquiry. We wish to account for him as we should wish to penetrate the secrets of the human spirit and know the springs of genius.

Of the public life of Burke we know all that we could wish. He became so prominent a figure in the great affairs of his day that even the casual observer cannot fail to discern the main facts of his career; while the close student can follow him year by year through every step of his service. But his private life was withdrawn from general scrutiny in an unusual degree. He manifested always a marked reserve about his individual and domestic affairs, deliberately, it would seem, shielding them from impertinent inquiry. He loved the privacy of life in a great city, where one may escape notice in the crowd and enjoy a grateful "freedom from remark and petty censure." "Though I have the honor to represent Bristol," he said to Boswell, "I should not like to live there; I should be obliged to be *so much upon my good behavior*. In London a man may live in splendid society at one time, and in frugal retirement at another, without animadversion. There, and there alone, a man's house is truly his *castle,* in which he can be in perfect safety from intrusion whenever he pleases. I never shall forget how well this was expressed to me one day by Mr. Meynell: 'The chief advantage of London,' he said, 'is, that a man is always *so near his burrow*.'" Burke took to his burrow often enough to pique our curiosity sorely.

Just where Burke got his generous constitution and predisposition to enlightened ways of thinking it is not easy to see. Certainly Richard Burke, his brother, the only other member of the family whose character we discern distinctly, had a quite opposite bent. The father was a steady Dublin attorney, a Protestant, and a man, so far as we know, of solid but not brilliant parts. The mother had been a Miss Nagle, of a Roman Catholic family, which had multiplied exceedingly in County Cork. Of the home and its life we know singularly little. We are told that many children were born to the good attorney, but we hear of only four of them that grew to maturity, Garret, Edmund, Richard, and a sister best known to Edmund's biographers as Mrs. French. Edmund, the second son, was born on the twelfth of January, 1729, in the second year of the reign of George II., Robert Walpole being chief minister of the Crown. How he fared or what sort of lad he was for the first twelve years of his life we have no idea. We only know that in the year 1741, being then twelve years old, he was sent with his brothers Garret and Richard to the school of one Abraham Shackleton, a most capable and exemplary Quaker, at Ballytore, County Kildare, to get, in some two years' time, what he himself always accounted the best part of his education. The character of the good master at Ballytore told upon the sensitive boy, who all his life through had an eye for such elevation and calm force of quiet rectitude as are to be seen in the best Quakers; and with Richard Shackleton, the master's son, he formed a friendship from which no vicissitude of his subsequent career ever loosened his heart a whit. All his life long the ardent, imaginative statesman, deeply stirred as he was by the momentous agitation of affairs,—swept away as he was from other friends,—retained his love for the grave, retired, almost austere, but generous and constant man who had been his favorite schoolfellow. It is but another evidence of his unfailing regard for whatever was steady, genuine, and open to the day in character and conduct.

At fourteen he left Ballytore and was entered at Trinity College, Dublin. Those were days when youths went to college tender, before they had become too tough to take impressions readily. But Burke, even at that callow age, cannot be said to have been teachable. He learned a vast deal, indeed, but he did not learn much of it from his nominal masters at Trinity. Apparently Master Shackleton, at Ballytore, had enabled him to find his own mind. His four years at college were years of wide and eager reading, but not years of systematic and disciplinary study. With singular, if not exemplary, self-confidence, he took his education into his own hands. He got at the heart of books through their spirit, it would seem, rather than through their grammar. He sought them out for what they could yield him in thought, rather than for what they could yield him in the way of exact scholarship. That this boy should have had such an appetite for the world's literature, old and new, need not surprise us. Other lads before and since have found big libraries all too small for them. What should arrest our attention is, the law of mind disclosed in the habits of such lads: the quick and various curiosity of original minds, and particularly of imaginative minds. They long for matter to expand themselves upon: they will climb any dizzy height from which an exciting prospect is promised: it is their joy by some means to see the world of men and affairs. Burke set out as a boy to see the world that is contained in books; and in his journeyings he met a man after his own heart in Cicero, the copious orator and versatile man of affairs,—the only man at all like Burke for richness, expansiveness, and variety of mind in all the ancient world. Cicero he conned as his master and model. And then, having had his fill for the time of discursive study and having completed also his four years of routine, he was graduated, taking his degree in the spring of 1748.

His father had entered him as a student at the Middle Temple in 1747, meaning that he should seek the prizes of his profession in England rather than in the little world at home; but he did not take up his residence in London until 1750, by which time he had attained his majority. What he did with the intervening two years, his biographers do not at all know, and it is idle to speculate, being confident, as we must, that he quite certainly did whatever he pleased. He did the same when he went up to London to live his terms at the Temple. "The law," he declared to Parliament more than twenty years afterwards, "is, in my opinion, one of the first and noblest of human sciences,—a science which does more to quicken and invigorate the understanding than all other kinds of learning put together; but it is not apt, except in persons very happily born, to open and to liberalize the mind exactly in the same proportion"; and, although himself a person "very happily born" in respect of all natural powers, he felt that the life of a lawyer would inevitably confine his roving mind within intolerably narrow limits. He learned the law, as he learned everything else, with an eye to discovering its points of contact with affairs, its intimate connections with the structure and functions of human society; and, studying it thus, he made his way to so many of its secrets, won so firm a mastery of its central principles, as always to command the respect and even the admiration of lawyers. But the good attorney in Dublin was sorely disappointed. This was not what he had wanted. The son in whom he had centred his hopes preferred the life of the town to systematic study in his chambers; wrote for the papers instead of devoting himself to the special profession he had been sent to master. "Of his leisure time," said the "Annual Register" just after his death, "of his leisure time much was spent in the company of Mrs. Woffington, a celebrated actress, whose conversation was not less sought by men of wit and genius than by men of pleasure."

We know very little about the life of Burke for the ten years, 1750-60, his first ten years in England,—except that he did *not* diligently apply himsely [himself] to his nominal business, the study of the law; and between the years 1752 and 1757 his biographers can show hardly one authentic trace of his real life. They know neither his whereabouts nor his employments. Only one scrap of his correspondence remains from those years to give us any hint of the time. Even Richard Shackleton, his invariable confidant and bosom friend, hears never a word from him during that period, and is told afterwards only that his correspondent has been "sometimes in London, sometimes in remote parts of the country, sometimes in France," and will "shortly, please God, be in America." He disappears a poor law student, under suspicion of his father for systematic neglect of duty; when he reappears he is married to the daughter of a worthy physician and is author of two philosophical works which are attracting a great deal of attention. We have reason to believe that, in the mean time, he did as much writing as they would take for the booksellers; we know that he frequented the London theatres and several of the innumerable debating clubs with which nether London abounded, whetting his faculties, it is said, upon those of a certain redoubtable baker. He haunted the galleries and lobbies of the House of Commons. His health showed signs of breaking, and Dr. Nugent took him from his lodgings in the Temple to his own house and allowed him to fall in love with his daughter. Partly for the sake of his health, perhaps, but more particularly, no doubt, for the sake of satisfying an eager mind and a restless habit, he wandered off to "remote parts of the country" and to France, with one William Burke for company, a man either related to him or not related to him, he did not himself know which. In 1755, a long-suffering patience at length exhausted, his father shut the home treasury against him; and then he published two philosophical works and married Miss Nugent.

The two books which he gave the world in 1756 were "A Vindication of Natural Society," a satirical piece in the manner of Bolingbroke, and "A Philosophical Inquiry into the Origin of Our Ideas of the Sublime and Beautiful," which he had begun when he was nineteen and had since reconsidered and revised. Bolingbroke, not finding revealed religion to his taste, had written a "Vindication of Natural Religion" which his vigorous and elevated style and skillful dialectic had done much to make plausible. Burke put forth his "Vindication of Natural Society" as a posthumous work of the late noble lord, and so skillfully veiled the satirical character of the imitation as wholly to deceive some very grave critics, who thought they could discern Bolingbroke's flavor upon the tasting. For the style, too, they took to be unmistakably Bolingbroke's own. It had all his grandeur and air of distinction: it had his vocabulary and formal outline of phrase. The imitation was perfect. And yet if you will scrutinize it, the style is not Bolingbroke's, except in a trick or two, but Burke's. It seems Bolingbroke's rather because it is cold and without Burke's usual moral fervor than because it is rich and majestic and various. There is no great formal difference between Burke's style and Bolingbroke's: but there is a great moral and intellectual difference. When Burke is not in earnest there is perhaps no important difference at all. And in the "Vindication of Natural Society" Burke is not in earnest. The book is not, indeed, a parody, and its satirical quality is much too covert to make it a successful satire. Much that Burke urges against civil society he could urge in good faith, and his mind works soberly upon it. It is only the main thesis that he does not seriously mean. The rest he might have meant as Bolingbroke would have meant it.

The essay on The Sublime and Beautiful, though much admired by so great a master as Lessing, has not worn very well as philosophy. It is full, however, of acute and interesting observations, and is adorned in parts with touches of rich color put on with the authentic strokes of a master. We preserve it, perhaps, only because Burke wrote it; and yet when we read it we feel inclined to pronounce it worth keeping for its own sake.

Both these essays were apprentice work. Burke was trying his hand. They make us the more curious about the conditions of what must have been a notable apprenticeship. Young Burke must have gone to school to the world in a way worth knowing. But we cannot know, and that's the end on 't. Probably even William Burke, Edmund's companion, could give us no very satisfactory account of the matter. The explanation lay in what he thought and not in what he did as he knocked about the world.

The company Burke kept was as singular as his talents, though scarcely so eminent. *We* speak of "Burke," but the London of his day spoke of "the Burkes," meaning William, who may or may not have been Edmund's kinsman, Edmund himself, and Richard, Edmund's younger brother, who had followed him to London to become, to say truth, an adventurer emphatically not of the elevated sort. Edmund was destined to become the leader of England's thought in more than one great matter of policy, and has remained a master among all who think profoundly upon public affairs; but William was for long the leader and master of "the Burkes." He was English born; had been in Westminster School; and had probably just come out from Christ Church, Oxford, when he became the companion of Edmund's wanderings. He was a man of intellect and literary power enough to be deemed the possible author of the "Letters of Junius"; he was born moreover with an eye for the ways of the world, and could push his own fortunes with an unhesitating hand. It was he who first got public office, and it was he who formed the influential connections which got Edmund into Parliament. He himself entered the House at the same time, and remained there, a useful party member, for some eight years. He made those from whom he sought favors dislike him for his audacity in demanding the utmost, and more than the utmost, that he could possibly hope to get; but he seems to have made those whom he served love him with a very earnest attachment. He was self-seeking; but he was capable of generosity, to the point of self-sacrifice even, when he wished to help his friend. He early formed a partnership with Richard Burke in immense stock-jobbing speculations in the securities of the East India Company; but he also formed a literary partnership with Edmund in the preparation of a sketch of the European settlements in America, and made himself respected as a strong party writer in various pamphlets on questions of the day. He could unite the two brothers by speculating with the one and thinking with the other.

Such were "the Burkes." Edmund's home was always the home also of the other two, whenever they wished to make it so; the strongest personal affection, avowed always by Edmund with his characteristic generous warmth, bound the three men together; their purses they had in common. Edmund was not expected, apparently, to take part in the speculations which held William and Richard together; something held him aloof to which they consented,—some natural separateness of mind and character which they evidently accepted and respected. There can hardly be said to have been any aloofness of *disposition* on Edmund's part. There is something in an Irishman,—even in an Irishman who holds himself to the strictest code of upright conduct,—which forbids his acting as moral censor upon others. He can love a man none the less for generous and manly qualities because that man does what he himself would not do. Burke, moreover, had an easy standard all his life about accepting money favors. He seems to have felt somehow that his intense and whole-hearted devotion to his friends justified gifts and forgiven loans of money from them. He shared the prosperity of his kinsmen without compunction, using what he got most liberally for the assistance of others; and when their fortunes came to a sudden ruin, he helped them with what he had. We ought long ago to have learned that the purest motives and the most elevated standards of conduct may go along with a singular laxness of moral detail in some men; and that such characters will often constrain us to love them to the point of justifying everything that they ever did. Edmund Burke's close union with William and Richard does not present the least obstacle to our admiration for the noble qualities of mind and heart which he so conspicuously possessed, or make us for a moment doubt the thorough disinterestedness of his great career.

Burke's marriage was a very happy one. Mrs. Burke's thoroughly sweet temperament acted as a very grateful and potent charm to soothe her husband's mind when shaken by the agitations of public affairs; her quiet capacity for domestic manage-

ment relieved him of many small cares which might have added
to his burdens. Her affection satisfied his ardent nature. He
speaks of her in his will as "my entirely beloved and incomparable wife," and every glimpse we get of their home life confirms
the estimate. After his marriage the most serious part of his intellectual life begins; the commanding passion of his mind is
disclosed. He turns away from philosophical amusements to public affairs. In 1757 appeared "An Account of the European Settlements in America," which William Burke had doubtless written, but which Edmund had almost certainly radically revised;
and Edmund himself published the first part of "An Abridgment
of the History of England" which he never completed. In 1758,
he proposed to Dodsley, the publisher, a yearly volume, to be
known as the "Annual Register," which should chronicle and discuss the affairs of England and the Continent. It was the period
of the Seven Years' War, which meant for England a sharp and
glorious contest with France for the possession of America. Burke
was willing to write the annals of the critical year 1758 for a
hundred pounds; and so, in 1759, the first volume of the "Annual Register" appeared; and the plan then so wisely conceived
has yielded its annual volume to the present day. Burke never
acknowledged his connection with this great work,—he never publicly recognized anything he had done upon contract for the publishers,—but it is quite certain that for very many years his was
the presiding and planning mind in the production of the "Register." For the first few years of its life he probably wrote the
whole of the record of events with his own hand. It was a more
useful apprenticeship than that in philosophy. It gave him an
intimate acquaintance with affairs which must have served as a
direct preparation for the great contributions he was destined to
make to the mind and policy of the Whig party.

But this, even in addition to other hack work for the booksellers, did not keep Burke out of pecuniary straits. He sought,
but failed to get, an appointment as consul at Madrid, using the
interest of Dr. Markham, William's master at Westminster
School; and then he engaged himself as a sort of private secretary or literary attendant to William Gerard Hamilton, whom he
served, apparently to the almost entire exclusion of all other
employments, for some four years, going with him for a season
to Ireland, where Hamilton for a time held the appointment of
Secretary to the Lord Lieutenant. Hamilton is described by one
of Burke's friends as "a sullen, vain, proud, selfish, cankered-
hearted, envious reptile," and Mr. Morley says that there is "not
a word too many nor too strong in the description." At any rate,

Woodrow Wilson as photographed by Pach Brothers in 1893

The Dean's House in the 1890's

Old Dickinson Hall, where Wilson lectured as a professor and which was destroyed by fire in 1920

Frederick Jackson Turner

Albert Bushnell Hart

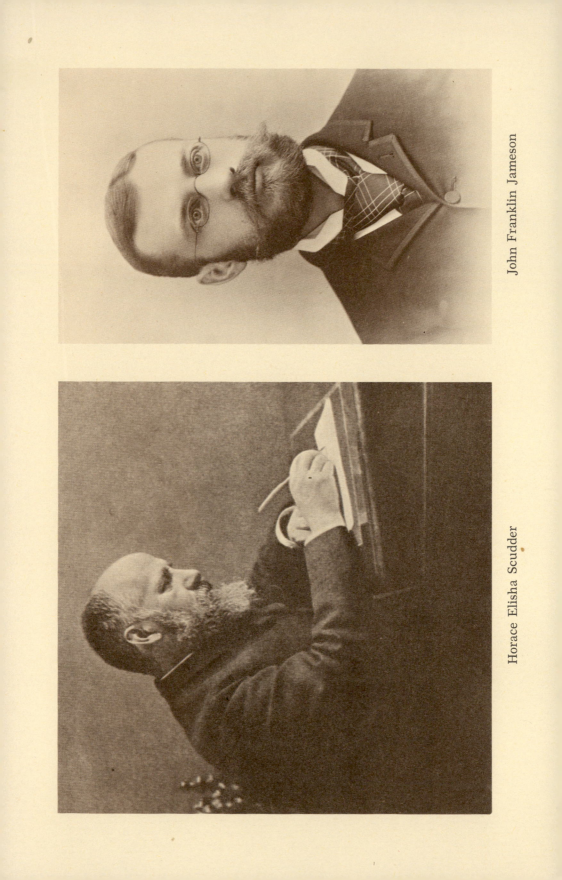

John Franklin Jameson

Horace Elisha Scudder

Winthrop More Daniels

Charles William Kent

prejudices could be nursed in security; when old opin-

ion was safe against disturbance; when discussion must

be ill-informed and dogmatic, ~~and purpose illiberal.~~

The whole people, moreover, were self-absorbed, their

entire energies consumed in the dull, prosaic ~~daily~~ tasks

imposed upon them by their incomplete civilization.

Everything was both doing and to be done. There was no

store of things accomplished, and there must needs be

haste in progress. ~~Not many manufactures had been devel-~~

A great change had come about in the commercial

~~oped, comparatively little agricultural produce was sent~~

condition of the country. The exports and imports were about

~~abroad. Exports there were indeed, but the imports~~

the same in value as thirty years earlier; and their growth,

~~and~~ neither ~~of these~~ bore any ~~direct proportion to the~~

Prices had been much reduced, so

increase of population. ~~war carried with it in fact~~

that the same values included larger quantities: her,

~~use of crops in Europe created prices in trans-Atlantic~~

besides the fluctuations in agricultural export, re-

~~markets which greatly tempted to exportation, exporta-~~

sulting from variations in the European demand, the country

~~tion of course took place, even for a year or two~~

exported less per capita, because they bought less;

~~greatly stimulated as for example, in 1807. But pres-~~

and they bought less because they were more

~~ently it would fall to its old level again.~~ The total

manufacturing more at home. more less

value of the imports of 1829 ~~was no greater~~ than the

total value of those of 1799. Manufactures ~~too~~ had

? ?
Manufactures
and Commerce

A page from Wilson's typescript of *Division and Reunion*,
showing one of A. B. Hart's editorial changes
(which, incidentally, Wilson rejected)

Burke's proud spirit presently revolted from further service, and he threw up a pension of three hundred pounds which Hamilton had obtained for him rather than retain any connection with the man, or remain under any sort of obligation to him. In the mean time, however, his relations with Hamilton had put him in the way of meeting many public men of weight and influence, and he had gotten his first direct introduction to the world of affairs.

It was 1764 when he shook himself free from this connection. 1764 is a year to be marked in English literary annals. It was in the spring of that year that that most celebrated of literary clubs was formed at the Turk's Head Tavern, Gerrard Street, Soho, by notable good company: Dr. Johnson, Garrick, Sir Joshua Reynolds, Goldsmith, Sheridan, Gibbon, Dr. Barnard, Beauclerk, Langton,—we know them all; for has not Boswell given us the freedom of the Club and made us delighted participants in its conversations and diversions? Into this company Burke was taken at once. His writings had immediately attracted the attention of such men as these, and had promptly procured him an introduction into literary society. His powers told nowhere more brilliantly than in conversation. "It is when you come close to a man in conversation," said Dr. Johnson, "that you discover what his real abilities are. To make a speech in an assembly is a sort of knack. Now I honor Thurlow; Thurlow is a fine fellow, he fairly puts his mind to yours." There can be no disputing the dictum of the greatest master of conversation: and the admirer of Burke must be willing to accept it, at any rate for the nonce, for Johnson admitted that Burke invariably put him on his mettle. "That fellow," he exclaimed, "calls forth all my powers!" "Burke's talk," he said, "is the ebullition of his mind; he does not talk from a desire of distinction, but because his mind is full; he is never humdrum, never unwilling to talk, nor in haste to leave off." The redoubtable doctor loved a worthy antagonist in the great game of conversation, and he always gave Burke his ungrudging admiration. When he lay dying, Burke visited his bedside, and, finding Johnson very weak, anxiously expressed the hope that his presence cost him no inconvenience. "I must be in a wretched state indeed," cried the great-hearted old man, "when your company would not be a delight to me." It was short work for Burke to get the admiration of the company at the Turk's Head. But he did much more than that: he won their devoted affection. Goldsmith said that Burke wound his way into a subject like a serpent; but he made his way straight into the hearts of his friends. His powers are all of a piece: his heart is inextricably mixed up with his mind: his opinions are immediately

transmuted into convictions: he does not talk for distinction, because he does not use his mind for the mere intellectual pleasure
of it, but because he also deeply feels what he thinks. He speaks
without calculation, almost impulsively.

That is the reason why we can be so sure of the essential purity
of his nature from the character of his writings. They are not
purely intellectual productions: there is no page of abstract reasoning to be found in Burke. His mind works upon concrete objects, and he speaks always with a certain passion, as if his
affections were involved. He is irritated by opposition, because
opposition in the field of affairs, in which his mind operates,
touches some interest that is dear to him. Noble generalizations,
it is true, everywhere broaden his matter: there is no more philosophical writer in English in the field of politics than Burke. But
look, and you shall see that his generalizations are never derived
from abstract premises. The reasoning is upon familiar matter
of to-day. He is simply taking questions of the moment to the
light, holding them up to be seen where great principles of conduct may shine upon them from the general experience of the
race. He is not constructing systems of thought, but simply
stripping thought of its accidental features. He is even deeply impatient of abstractions in political reasoning, so passionately is he
devoted to what is practicable, and fit for wise men to do. To
know such a man is to experience all the warmer forces of the
mind, to feel the generous and cheering heat of character; and
all noble natures will love such a man, because of kinship of
quality. All noble natures that came close to Burke did love him
and cherish their knowledge of him. They loaned him money
without stint, and then forgave him the loans, as if it were a
privilege to help him, and no way unnatural that he should never
return what he received, finding his spirit made for fraternal,
not for commercial relations.

It is pleasing, as it is also a little touching, to see how his
companions thus freely accorded to Burke the immunities and
prerogatives of a prince amongst them. No one failed to perceive
how large and imperial he was, alike in natural gifts and in the
wonderful range of his varied acquirements. Sir James Mackintosh, though he very earnestly combated some of Burke's views,
intensely admired his greatness. He declared that Gibbon "might
have been taken from a corner of Burke's mind without ever
being missed." "A wit said of Gibbon's 'Autobiography' that he did
not know the difference between himself and the Roman Empire.
He has narrated his 'progressions from London to Buriton and
from Buriton to London' in the same monotonous, majestic

periods that he recorded the fall of states and empires." And we certainly feel a sense of incongruity: the two subjects, we perceive, are hardly commensurable. Perhaps in Burke's case we should have felt differently,—we *do* feel differently. In that extraordinary "Letter to a Noble Lord," in which he defends his pension so proudly against the animadversions of the Duke of Bedford, how magnificently he speaks of his services to the country; how proud and majestic a piece of autobiography it is! How insignificant does the ancient house of Bedford seem, with all its long generations, as compared with this single and now lonely man, without distinguished ancestry or hope of posterity! He speaks grandly about himself, as about everything; and yet I see no disparity between the subject and the manner!

Outside the small circle of those who knew and loved him, his generation did not wholly perceive this. There seemed a touch of pretension in this proud tone taken by a man who had never held high office or exercised great power. He had made great speeches, indeed, no one denied that; he had written great party pamphlets,—that everybody knew; his had been the intellectual force within the group of Whigs that followed Lord Rockingham,— that, too, the world in general perceived and acknowledged; and when he died, England knew the man who had gone to be a great man. But, for all that, his tone must, in his generation, have seemed disproportioned to the part he had played. His great authority is over us rather than over the men of his own day.

Burke had the thoughts of a great statesman, and uttered them with unapproachable nobility; but he never wielded the power of a great statesman. He was kept always in the background in active politics, in minor posts, and employed upon subordinate functions. This would be a singular circumstance, if there were any novelty in it; but the practice of keeping men of insignificant birth out of the great offices was a practice which had "broadened down from precedent to precedent" until it had become too strong for even Burke to breast or stem. Perhaps, too, there were faults of temper which rendered Burke unfit to exercise authority in directing the details, and determining the practical measures, of public policy:—but we shall look into that presently.

In July, 1765, the Marquis of Rockingham became prime minister of England, and Burke became his private secretary. He owed his introduction to Lord Rockingham, as usual, to the good offices of William Burke, who seems to have found means of knowing everybody it was to the interest of "the Burkes" to know. A more fortunate connection could hardly have been made. Lord Rockingham, though not a man of original powers, was a man of the greatest simplicity and nobleness of character, and, like most upright men, knew how to trust other men. He gave Burke immediate proof of his manly qualities. The scheming old Duke of Newcastle, who ought to have been a connoisseur in low men, mistook Burke for one. Shocked that this obscurely born and unknown fellow should be accorded confidential relations by Lord Rockingham, he hurried to his lordship with an assortment of hastily selected slanders against Burke. His real name, he reported, was O'Bourke; he was an Irish adventurer without character, and a rank Papist to boot; it would ruin the administration to have such a man connected with the First Lord of the Treasury. Rockingham, with great good sense and frankness, took the whole matter at once to Burke; was entirely satisfied by Burke's denials; and admitted him immediately to intimate relations of warm personal friendship which only death broke off. William Burke obtained for himself an Undersecretaryship of State and arranged with Lord Verney, at that time his partner in East India speculations, that two of his lordship's parliamentary boroughs should be put at his and Edmund's disposal. Edmund Burke, accordingly, entered Parliament for the borough of Wendover on the 14th of January, 1766, at the age of thirty-seven, and in the first vigor of his powers.

"Now we who know Burke," announced Dr. Johnson, "know that he will be one of the first men in the country." Burke promptly fulfilled the prediction. He made a speech before he had been in the House two weeks; a speech that made him at once a marked man. His health was now firmly established; he had a commanding physique; his figure was tall and muscular, and his bearing full of a dignity which had a touch almost of haughtiness in it. Although his action was angular and awkward, his extraordinary richness and fluency of utterance drew the attention away from what he was doing to what he was saying. His voice was harsh, and did not harmonize with the melodious measures in which his words poured forth; but it was of unusual compass, and carried in it a sense of confidence and power. His utterance was too rapid, his thought bore him too impulsively forward, but the pregnant matter he spoke "filled the town with wonder." The House was excited by new sensations. Members were astonished to recognize a broad philosophy of politics running through this ardent man's speeches. They felt the refreshment of the wide outlook he gave them, and were conscious of catching glimpses of excellent matter for reflection at every turn of his hurrying thought. They wearied of it, indeed, after a while: the pace was too hard for most of his hearers, and they finally gave over following him when the novelty and first excitement of the exercise had worn off. He too easily lost sight of his audience in his search for principles, and they resented his neglect of them, his indifference to their tastes. They felt his lofty style of reasoning as a sort of rebuke, and deemed his discursive wisdom out of place amidst their own thoughts of imperative personal and party interest. He had, before very long, to accustom himself, therefore, to speak to an empty House and subsequent generations. His opponents never, indeed, managed to feel quite easy under his attacks: his arrows sought out their weak places to the quick, and they winced even when they coughed or seemed indifferent; but they comforted themselves with the thought that the orator was also tedious and irritating to his own friends, teasing them too with keen rebukes and vexatious admonitions. The high and wise sort of speaking must always cause uneasiness in a political assembly. The more equal and balanced it is, the more must both parties be threatened with reproof.

I would not be understood as saying that Burke's speeches were impartial. They were not. He had preferences which amounted to prejudices. He was always an intense party man. But then he was a party man with a difference. He believed that the interests of England were bound up with the fortunes of the Rockingham Whigs; but he did not separate the interests of his party and the interests of his country. He cherished party connections because he conceived them to be absolutely necessary for effective public service. "Where men are not acquainted with each other's principles," he said, "nor experienced in each other's talents, nor at all practiced in their mutual habitudes or dispositions by joint efforts in business; no personal confidence, no friendship, no common interest, subsisting among them; it is evidently impossible that they can act a public part with uniformity, perseverance, or efficacy. In a connection, the most inconsiderable man, by adding to the weight of the whole, has his value, and his use; out of it, the greatest talents are wholly unserviceable to the public." "When bad men combine, the good must associate." "It is not enough in a situation of trust in the commonwealth, that a man means well to his country; it is not enough that in his single person he never did an evil act, but always voted according to his conscience, and even harangued against every design which he apprehended to be prejudicial to the interests of his country. . . . Duty demands and requires, that what is right should not only be made known, but made prevalent; that what is evil should not only be detected, but defeated. When the public man omits to put himself in a situation of doing his duty with effect, it is an omission that frustrates the purposes of his trust almost as much as if he had formally betrayed it." Burke believed the Rockingham Whigs to be a combination of good men, and he felt that he ought to sacrifice something to keep himself in their connection. He regarded them as men who "believed private honor to be the foundation of public trust; that friendship was no mean step towards patriotism; that he who, in the common intercourse of life, showed he regarded somebody besides himself, when he came to act in a public situation, might probably consult some other interest than his own." He admitted that such confederacies had often "a narrow, bigoted, and proscriptive spirit"; "but, where duty renders a critical situation a necessary one," he said, "it is our business to keep free from the evils attendant upon it; and not to fly from the situation itself. If a fortress is seated in an unwholesome air, an officer of the garrison is obliged to be attentive to his health, but he must not desert his station." "A party," he declared, "is a body of men united for promoting by their joint endeavors the national interest upon some particular principle in which they are all agreed." "Men thinking freely, will," he very well knew, "in particular instances, think differently. But still as the greater part of the measures which arise in the course of public business are related to, or dependent on, some great, *leading, general principles in government*, a man must be peculiarly unfortunate in the choice of his political company, if he does not agree with them at least nine times in ten. If he does not concur in these general principles upon which the party is founded; and which necessarily draw on a concurrence in their application, he ought from the beginning to have chosen some other, more conformable to his opinions. When the question is in its nature doubtful, or not very material, the modesty which becomes an individual, and that partiality which becomes a well-chosen friendship, will frequently bring on an acquiescence in the general sentiment. Thus the disagreement will naturally be rare; it will be only enough to indulge freedom, without violating concord, or disturbing arrangement."

Certainly there were no party prizes for Burke. During much the greater part of his career the party to which he adhered was in opposition; and even when in office it had only small favors for him. Even his best friends advised against his appointment to any of the great offices of state, deeming him too intemperate and unpractical. And yet the intensity of his devotion to his party never abated a jot. Assuredly there was never a less selfish allegiance. His devotion was for the principles of his party, as he conceived and constructed them. It was a moral and intellectual devotion. He had embarked all his spirit's fortunes in the enterprise. Faults he unquestionably had, which seemed very grave. He was passionate sometimes beyond all bounds: he seriously frightened cautious and practical men by his haste and vehemence in pressing his views for acceptance. He was capable of falling, upon occasion, into a very frenzy of excitement in the midst of debate, when he would often shock moderate men by the ungoverned license of his language. But his friends were as much to blame for these outbreaks as he was. They cut him to the quick by the way in which they criticised and misunderstood him. His heart was maddened by the pain of their neglect of his just claims to their confidence. They seemed often to use him without trusting him, and their slights were intolerable to his proud spirit. Practically, and upon a narrow scale of expediency, they may have been right: perhaps he was *not* circumspect enough to be made a responsible head of administration. Unquestionably, too, they loved him and meant him no unkindness. But it was none the less tragical to treat such a man in such a fashion. They may possibly have temporarily served their country by denying to Burke full public acknowledgment of his great services; but they cruelly wounded a great spirit, and they hardly served mankind.

They did Burke an injustice, moreover. They greatly underrated his practical powers. In such offices as he was permitted to hold he showed in actual administration the same extraordinary mastery of masses of detail which was the foundation of his unapproachable mastery of general principles in his thinking. His thought was always immersed in matter, and concrete detail did not confuse him when he touched it any more than it did when he meditated upon it. Immediate contact with affairs always steadied his judgment. He was habitually temperate in the conduct of business. It was only in speech and when debating matters that stirred the depths of his nature that he gave way to uncalculating fervor. He was intemperate in his emotions, but seldom in his actions. He could, and did, write calm state papers in the very midst and heat of parliamentary affairs that subjected him to the fiercest excitements. He was eminently capable of counsel as well as of invective.

He served his party in no servile fashion, for all he adhered to it with such devotion. He sacrificed his intellectual independence as little as his personality in taking intimate part in its counsels. He gave it principles, indeed, quite as often as he accepted principles from it. In the final efforts of his life, when he engaged every faculty of his mind in the contest that he waged with such magnificent wrath against the French revolutionary spirit, he gave tone to all English thought, and direction to many of the graver issues of international policy. Rejected oftentimes by his party, he has at length been accepted by the world.

His habitual identification with opposition rather than with the government gave him a certain advantage. It relaxed party discipline and indulged his independence. It gave leave, too, to the better efforts of his genius: for in opposition it is principles that tell, and Burke was first and last a master of principles. Government is a matter of practical detail, as well as of general measures; but the criticism of government very naturally becomes a matter of the application of general principles, as standards rather than as practical means of policy.

Four questions absorbed the energies of Burke's life and must always be associated with his fame. These were, the American war for independence; administrative reform in the English home government; reform in the government of India; and the profound political agitations which attended the French Revolution. Other questions he studied, deeply pondered, and greatly illuminated, but upon these four he expended the full strength of his magnificent powers. There is in his treatment of these subjects a singular consistency, a very admirable simplicity of standard. It has been said, and it is true, that Burke had no system of political philosophy. He was afraid of abstract system in political thought, for he perceived that questions of government are moral questions, and that questions of morals cannot always be squared with the rules of logic, but run through as many ranges of variety as the circumstances of life itself. "Man acts from adequate motives relative to his interest," he said, "and not on metaphysical speculations. Aristotle, the great master of reasoning, cautions us, and with great weight and propriety, against this species of delusive geometrical accuracy in moral arguments, as the most fallacious of all sophistry." And yet Burke unquestionably had a very definite and determinable system of thought, which was none the less a system for being based upon concrete, and not upon abstract premises. It is said by some writers (even by so eminent a writer as Buckle) that in his later years Burke's mind lost its balance and that he reasoned as if he were insane; and the proof assigned is, that he, a man who loved liberty, violently condemned, not the terrors only,—that of course,—but the very principles of the French Revolution. But to reason thus is to convict one's self of an utter lack of comprehension of Burke's mind and motives: as a very brief examination of his course upon the four great questions I have mentioned will show.

From first to last Burke's thought is conservative. Let his attitude with regard to America serve as an example. He took his stand, as everybody knows, with the colonies, against the mother country; but his object was not revolutionary. He did not deny the legal right of England to tax the colonies (*we* no longer deny it ourselves), but he wished to preserve the empire, and he saw that to insist upon the right of taxation would be irrevocably to break up the empire, when dealing with such a people as the Americans. He pointed out the strong and increasing numbers of the colonists, their high spirit in enterprise, their jealous love of liberty, and the indulgence England had hitherto accorded them in the matter of self-government, permitting them in effect to become an independent people in respect of all their internal affairs; and he declared the result matter for just pride. "Whilst we follow them among the tumbling mountains of ice, and behold them penetrating into the deepest frozen recesses of Hudson's Bay and Davis's Straits," he exclaimed, in a famous passage of his incomparable speech on Conciliation with America, "whilst we are looking for them beneath the arctic circle, we hear that they have pierced into the opposite region of polar cold, that they are at the antipodes, and engaged under the frozen serpent of the South. Falkland Island, which seemed too remote and romantic an object for the grasp of national ambition, is but a stage and resting place in the progress of their victorious industry. Nor is the equinoctial heat more discouraging to them than the accumulated winter of both the poles. We know that whilst some of them draw the line and strike the harpoon on the coast of Africa, others run the longitude, and pursue their gigantic game along the coast of Brazil. No sea but what is vexed by their fisheries. No climate that is not witness to their toils. Neither the perseverance of Holland, nor the activity of France, nor the dexterous and firm sagacity of English enterprise, ever carried this most perilous mode of hardy industry to the extent to which it has been pushed by this recent people,—a people who are still, as it were, but in the gristle, and not yet hardened into the bone of manhood. When I contemplate these things,—when I know that the colonies in general owe little or nothing to any care of ours, and that they are not squeezed into this happy form by the constraints of watchful and suspicious government, but that, through a wise and salutary neglect, a generous nature has been suffered to take her own way to perfection,—when I reflect upon these effects, when I see how profitable they have been to us, I feel all the pride of power sink, and all the presumption in the wisdom of human contrivances melt and die away within me,—my rigor relents,—I pardon something to the spirit of liberty."

"I think it necessary," he insisted, "to consider distinctly the true nature and the peculiar circumstances of the object we have before us: because, after all our struggle, whether we will or not, we must govern America according to that nature and those circumstances, and not according to our own imaginations, not according to abstract ideas of right, by no means according to mere general theories of government, the resort to which appears to me, in our present situation, no better than arrant trifling." To attempt to force such a people would be a course of idle folly. Force, he declared, would not only be an odious "but a feeble instrument, for preserving a people so numerous, so active, so growing, so spirited as this, in a profitable and subordinate connection with" England.

"First, Sir," he cried, "permit me to observe, that the use of force alone is but *temporary*. It may subdue for a moment; but it does not remove the necessity of subduing again: and a nation is not governed which is perpetually to be conquered.

"My next objection is its *uncertainty*. Terror is not always the effect of force, and an armament is not a victory. If you do not succeed, you are without resource: for, conciliation failing, force remains; but, force failing, no further hope of reconciliation is left. Power and authority are sometimes bought by kindness; but they can never be begged as alms by an impoverished and defeated violence.

"A further objection to force is, that you *impair the object* by your very endeavors to preserve it. The thing you fought for is not the thing you recover, but depreciated, sunk, wasted, and consumed in the contest. Nothing less will content me than *whole America*. I do not choose to consume its strength along with our own; for in all parts it is the British strength I consume. . . . Let me add, that I do not choose wholly to break the American spirit; because it is the spirit that has made the country.

"Lastly, we have no sort of *experience* in favor of force as an instrument in the rule of our colonies. Their growth and their utility has been owing to methods altogether different. Our ancient indulgence has been said to be pursued to a fault. It may be so; but we know, if feeling is evidence, that our fault was more tolerable than our attempt to mend it, and our sin far more salutary than our penitence."

"Obedience is what makes government," "freedom, and not

servitude, is the cure of anarchy," and you cannot insist upon one rule of obedience for Englishmen in America while you jealously maintain another for Englishmen in England. "For, in order to prove that the Americans have no right to their liberties, we are every day endeavoring to subvert the maxims which preserve the whole spirit of our own. To prove that the Americans ought not to be free, we are obliged to depreciate the value of freedom itself; and we never seem to gain a paltry advantage over them in debate, without attacking some of those principles, or deriding some of those feelings, for which our ancestors have shed their blood." "The question with me is, not whether you have a right to render your people miserable, but whether it is not your interest to make them happy. It is not what a lawyer tells me I *may* do, but what humanity, reason, and justice tell me I *ought* to do. . . . Such is steadfastly my opinion of the absolute necessity of keeping up the concord of this empire by a unity of spirit, though in a diversity of operations, that, if I were sure that the colonists had, at their leaving this country, sealed a regular compact of servitude, that they had solemnly abjured all the rights of citizens, that they had made a vow to renounce all ideas of liberty for them and their posterity to all generations, yet I should hold myself obliged to conform to the temper I found universally prevalent in my own day, and to govern two million of men, impatient of servitude, on the principles of freedom. I am not determining a point of law; I am restoring tranquillity: and the general character and situation of a people must determine what sort of government is fitted for them. That point nothing else can or ought to determine." "All government, indeed every human benefit and enjoyment, every virtue and every prudent act, is founded on compromise and barter. We balance inconveniences; we give and take; we remit some rights, that we may enjoy others; and we choose rather to be happy citizens than subtle disputants." "Magnanimity in politics is not seldom the truest wisdom; and a great empire and little minds go ill together."

Here you have the whole spirit of the man, and in part a view of his eminently practical system of thought. The view is completed when you advance with him to other subjects of policy. He pressed with all his energy for radical reforms in administration, but he earnestly opposed every change that might touch the structure of the constitution itself. He sought to secure the integrity of Parliament, not by changing the system of representation, but by cutting out all roots of corruption. He pressed forward with the most ardent in all plans of just reform, but he held back with the most conservative from all propositions of radical change. "To innovate is not to reform," he declared, and there is "a marked distinction between change and reformation. The former alters the substance of the objects themselves, and gets rid of all their essential good as well as of all the accidental evil annexed to them. Change is novelty; and whether it is to operate any one of the effects of reformation at all, or whether it may not contradict the very principle upon which reformation is desired, cannot certainly be known beforehand. Reform is not a change in the substance or in the primary modification of the object, but a direct application of a remedy to the grievance complained of. So far as that is removed, all is sure. It stops there; and if it fails, the substance which underwent the operation, at the very worst, is but where it was." This is the governing motive of his immense labors to accomplish radical economical reform in the administration of the government. He was not seeking economy merely; to husband the resources of the country was no more than a means to an end, and that end was, to preserve the constitution in its purity. He believed that Parliament was not truly representative of the people because so many placemen found seats in it, and because so many members who might have been independent were bought by the too abundant favors of the Court. Cleanse Parliament of this corruption, and it would be restored to something like its pristine excellence as an instrument of liberty.

He dreaded to see the franchise extended and the House of Commons radically made over in its constitution. It had never been intended to be merely the people's House. It had been intended to hold all the elements of the state that were not to be found in the House of Lords or the Court. He conceived it to be the essential object of the constitution to establish a balanced and just intercourse between the several forces of an ancient society, and it was well that that balance should be preserved even in the House of Commons, rather than give perilous sweep to a single set of interests. "These opposed and conflicting interests," he said to his French correspondent, "which you considered as so great a blemish in your old and in our present Constitution, interpose a salutary check to all precipitate resolutions. They render deliberation a matter, not of choice, but of necessity; they make all change a subject of *compromise*, which naturally begets moderation; they produce *temperaments*, preventing the sore evil of harsh, crude, unqualified reformations, and rendering all the headlong exertions of arbitrary power, in the few or in the many, forever impracticable. Through that diversity of members and interests, general liberty had as many securities as there are separate views in the several orders; whilst by pressing down the whole by the weight of a real monarchy, the separate parts would have been prevented from warping and starting from their allotted places." "*We* wish," he said, "to derive all we possess *as an inheritance from our forefathers.* Upon that body and stock of experience we have taken care not to inoculate any scion alien to the nature of the original plant." "This idea of a liberal descent inspires us with a sense of habitual native dignity, which prevents that upstart insolence almost inevitably adhering to and disgracing those who are the first acquirers of any distinction. By this means our liberty becomes a noble freedom. It carries an imposing and majestic aspect. It has a pedigree and illustrating ancestors. It has its bearings and its ensigns armorial. It has its gallery of portraits, its monumental inscriptions, its records, evidences, and titles. We procure reverence to our civil institutions on the principle upon which Nature teaches us to revere individual men: on account of their age, and on account of those from whom they are descended."

"When the useful parts of an old establishment are kept, and what is superadded is to be fitted to what is retained, a vigorous mind, steady, persevering attention, various powers of comparison and combination, and the resources of an understanding fruitful in expedients are to be exercised; they are to be exercised in a continued conflict with the combined force of opposite vices, with the obstinacy that rejects all improvement, and the levity that is fatigued and disgusted with everything of which it is in possession. . . . Political arrangement, as it is a work for social ends, is to be only wrought by social means. There mind must conspire with mind. Time is required to produce that union of minds which alone can produce all the good we aim at. Our patience will achieve more than our force. If I might venture to appeal to what is so much out of fashion in Paris,—I mean to experience,—I should tell you that in my course I have known, and, according to my measure, have coöperated with great men; and I have never yet seen any plan which has not been mended by the observations of those who were much inferior in understanding to the person who took the lead in the business. By a slow, but well sustained progress, the effect of each step is watched; the good or ill success of the first gives light to us in the second; and so, from light to light, we are conducted with safety, through the whole series. . . . We are enabled to unite into a consistent whole the various anomalies and contending principles that are found in the minds and affairs of men. From hence arises, not an excellence in simplicity, but one far superior, an excellence in composition. Where the great interests of mankind are concerned through a long succession of generations, that succession ought to be admitted into some share in the counsels which are so deeply to affect them."

It is not possible to escape deep conviction of the wisdom of these reflections. They penetrate to the heart of all practicable methods of reform. Burke was doubtless too timid, and in practical judgment often mistaken. Measures which in reality would operate only as salutary and needed reformations he feared because of the element of change that was in them. He erred when he supposed that progress can in all its stages be made without changes which seem to go even to the substance. But, right or wrong, his philosophy did not come to him of a sudden and only at the end of his life, when he found France desolated and England threatened with madness for love of revolutionary principles of change. It is the key to his thought everywhere, and through all his life.

It is the key (which many of his critics have never found) to his position with regard to the revolution in France. He was roused to that fierce energy of opposition in which so many have thought that they detected madness, not so much because of his deep disgust to see brutal and ignorant men madly despoil an ancient and honorable monarchy, as because he saw the spirit of these men cross the Channel and find lodgment in England, even among statesmen like Fox, who had been his own close friends and companions in thought and policy; not so much because he loved France as because he feared for England. For England he had Shakespeare's love:

> "That fortress built by nature for herself
> *Against infection and the hand of war;*
> That happy breed of men, that little world,
> That precious stone set in the silver sea,
> Which serves it in the office of a wall,
> Or as a moat defensive to a house,
> *Against the envy of less happier lands;*
> That blessed plot, that earth, that realm, that England."

'T was[2] to keep out infection and to preserve such precious stores of manly tradition as had made that little world "the envy of less happier lands" that Burke sounded so effectually that extraordinary alarm against the revolutionary spirit that was racking France from throne to cottage. Let us admit, if you will, that

2 Wilson apparently substituted the contraction " 't was" for "it was" in 1896.

with reference to France herself he was mistaken. Let us say that when he admired the institutions which she was then sweeping away he was yielding to sentiment, and imagining France as perfect as the beauty of the sweet queen he had seen in her radiant youth. Let us concede that he did not understand the condition of France, and therefore did not see how inevitable that terrible revolution was: that in this case, too, the wages of sin was death. He was not defending France, if you look to the bottom of it; he was defending England:—and the things he hated are truly hateful. He hated the French revolutionary philosophy and deemed it unfit for free men. And that philosophy is in fact radically evil and corrupting. No state can ever be conducted on its principles. For it holds that government is a matter of contract and deliberate arrangement, whereas in fact it is an institute of habit, bound together by innumerable threads of association, scarcely one of which has been deliberately placed. It holds that the object of government is liberty, whereas the true object of government is justice; not the advantage of one class, even though that class constitute the majority, but right equity in the adjustment of the interests of all classes. It assumes that government can be made over at will, but assumes it without the slightest historical foundation. For governments have never been successfully and permanently changed except by slow modification operating from generation to generation. It contradicted every principle that had been so laboriously brought to light in the slow stages of the growth of liberty in the only land in which liberty had then grown to great proportions. The history of England is a continuous thesis against revolution; and Burke would have been no true Englishman, had he not roused himself, even fanatically, if there were need, to keep such puerile doctrine out.

If you think his fierceness was madness, look how he conducted the trial against Warren Hastings during those same years: with what patience, with what steadiness in business, with what temper, with what sane and balanced attention to detail, with what statesmanlike purpose! Note, likewise, that his thesis is the same in the one undertaking as in the other. He was applying the same principles to the case of France and to the case of India that he had applied to the case of the colonies. He meant to save the empire, not by changing its constitution, as was the method in France, and so shaking every foundation in order to dislodge an abuse, but by administering it uprightly and in a liberal spirit. He was persuaded "that government was a practical thing, made for the happiness of mankind, and not to furnish out a spectacle of uniformity to gratify the schemes of visionary politicians. Our business," he said, "was to rule, not to wrangle; and it would be a poor compensation that we had triumphed in a dispute, whilst we had lost an empire." The monarchy must be saved and the constitution vindicated by keeping the empire pure in all parts, even in the remotest provinces. Hastings must be crushed in order that the world might know that no English governor could afford to be unjust. Good government, like all virtue, he deemed to be a practical habit of conduct, and not a matter of constitutional structure. It is a great ideal, a thoroughly English ideal; and it constitutes the leading thought of all Burke's career.

In short, as I began by saying, this man, an Irishman, speaks the best English thought upon the essential questions of politics. He is thoroughly, characteristically, and to the bottom English in all his thinking. He is more liberal than Englishmen in his treatment of Irish questions, of course; for he understands them, as no Englishman of his generation did. But for all that he remains the chief spokesman for England in the utterance of the fundamental ideals which have governed the action of Englishmen in politics. "All the ancient, honest, juridical principles and institutions of England," such was his idea, "are so many clogs to check and retard the headlong course of violence and oppression. They were invented for this one good purpose, that what was not *just* should not be *convenient*." This is fundamental English doctrine. English liberty has consisted in making it unpleasant for those who were unjust, and thus getting them in the habit of being just for the sake of a *modus vivendi*. Burke is the apostle of the great English gospel of Expediency.

The politics of English-speaking peoples has never been speculative; it has always been profoundly practical and utilitarian. Speculative politics treats men and situations as they are supposed to be; practical politics treats them (upon no general plan, but in detail) as they are found to be at the moment of actual contact. With reference to America Burke argues: No matter what your legal right in the case, it is not *expedient* to treat America as you propose: a numerous and spirited people like the colonists will not submit; and your experiment will cost you your colonies. In the case of administrative reform, again, it is the higher sort of expediency he urges: If you wish to keep your government from revolution, keep it from corruption, and by making it pure render it permanent. To the French he says, It is not *expedient* to destroy thus recklessly these ancient parts of your constitution. How will you replace them? How will you conduct affairs at all after you shall have deprived yourselves of all balance and of all old counsel? It is both better and easier to reform than to tear down and reconstruct.

This is unquestionably the message of Englishmen to the world, and Burke utters it with incomparable eloquence. A man of sensitive imagination and elevated moral sense, of a wide knowledge and capacity for affairs, he stood in the midst of the English nation speaking its moral judgments upon affairs, its character in political action, its purposes of freedom, equity, wide and equal progress. It is the immortal charm of his speech and manner that gives permanence to his works. Though his life was devoted to affairs with a constant and unalterable passion, the radical features of Burke's mind were literary. He was a man of books, without being under the dominance of what others had written. He got knowledge out of books and the abundance of matter his mind craved to work its constructive and imaginative effects upon. It is singular how devoid of all direct references to books his writings are. The materials of his thought never reappear in the same form in which he obtained them. They have been smelted and recoined. They have come under the drill and inspiration of a great constructive mind, have caught life and taken structure from it. Burke is not literary because he takes from books, but because he makes books, transmuting what he writes upon into literature. It is this inevitable literary quality, this sure mastery of style, that mark the man, as much as his thought itself. He is a master in the use of the great style. Every sentence, too, is steeped in the colors of an extraordinary imagination. The movement takes your breath and quickens your pulses. The glow and power of the matter rejuvenate your faculties.

And yet the thought, too, is quite as imperishable as its incomparable vehicle.

> "The deepest, plainest, highest, clearest pen;
> The voice most echoed by consenting men;
> The soul which answered best to all well said
> By others, and which most requital made;
> Tuned to the highest key of ancient Rome,
> Returning all her music with his own;
> In whom, with nature, study claimed a part,
> And yet who to himself owed all his art."[3]

Extracted from "The Interpreter of English Liberty," in *Mere Literature and Other Essays* (Boston and New York, 1896), pp. 104-60.

[3] From an anonymous sonnet in *Jonsonus Virbius: or, the Memorie of Ben: Johnson Revived by the Friends of the Muses* (London, 1638).

Frederic Bancroft's Review of *Division and Reunion*

[September 1893]

Division and Reunion, 1829-1889. By Woodrow Wilson. (Epochs of American History.)¹ New York and London, Longmans, Green & Co., 1893.—12mo, xix, 326 pp., five maps.

As a rule the writing of an abridged history is a very difficult and almost thankless task. In the little volume before us Professor Wilson aims to give "a sketch in broad outline," "a rapid synopsis . . . of the larger features of public affairs" during the seventy [*sic*] years, 1829-1889. He has endeavored to write a brief but systematic narrative that would interest the general reader, instruct and direct the student and aid the teacher. A carefully selected list of about fifty books of reference is given at the beginning, and at the head of each of the five parts into which the work is divided, extensive references are furnished under the subdivisions of "bibliographies," "historical maps," "general accounts," "special histories" and "contemporary accounts." The five historical maps that accompany the volume are so clear and instructive as to make the work valuable to every one who takes any interest in United States history. The classifications, the grouping of subjects and the titles of chapters and sections are peculiarly clever and helpful.

The author has given the first third of his volume to the treatment of the period which was under the direct influence of General Jackson. Professor Wilson's insight into the tendencies of the times, the impulses of Jackson's nature, and into the effect which both had upon the contemporary political life, and especially the vivid manner in which all are characterized, indicate historical talent of an extraordinary quality. It is not so much in any originality of idea as in his frequently brilliant precision of expression. No one has ever said so much about this epoch in so few words as is expressed in the following sentences, taken almost at random:

He (Jackson) impersonated the agencies which were to nationalize the government. Those agencies may be summarily indicated in two words, "the West." They were agencies of ardor and muscle, without sensibility or caution. (Page 25.)

Jackson's election was the people's revolution; and he brought the people to Washington with him. (Page 27.)

Jackson certainly embodied the spirit of the new democratic doctrines. His presidency was a time of riot and of industrial revolt, of

¹ Bancroft used both square brackets and parentheses in his review. His brackets have been changed to parentheses.

brawling turbulence in many quarters, and of disregard for law; and it has been said that the mob took its cue from the example of arbitrary temperament set it by the president. (Page 115.)

It is with all the more regret, therefore, that we find the author compelled to crowd the last fifty years of his whole period into the procrustean measure of two hundred pages. At times he shows evidence of being ill at ease under his limitation; and the narrative in places becomes dogmatic, indistinct or abridged into inaccuracies. It will not suffice, with historical scholars, to assume that every threat of secession prior to Nullification was a sober exposition of the general interpretation of the constitution at the time. Nor will the average reader think the historian very clear and consistent in these sentences:

> The ground which Webster took, in short, was new ground; that which Hayne occupied, old ground. . . . The right upon which Hayne insisted, indeed, was not the right of his state to secede from the Union, but the singular right to declare a law of the United States null and void by act of her own legislature and remain in the Union while denying the validity of its statutes. There were many public men, even in South Carolina, who held such claims to be ridiculous. (Page 47.)

The author's reasoning on the subject of the sectionalization of the Union is nothing less than amazing. Taking von Holst's striking sentence: "The Union was not broken up because sectional parties had been formed, but sectional parties were formed because the Union had actually become sectionalized," he proceeds:

> There had been nothing active on the part of the South in this progress. She had stood still while the rest of the country had undergone profound changes; and, standing still, she retained the old principles which had once been universal. (Page 212).

The startling ellipsis here both of thought and of fact is probably due to the author's making a generalization while bearing in mind merely the economic conditions of the two sections; for surely no scholar would venture to make deliberately the assertion that there was no change in the principles on which the South acted in 1820, 1850 and 1861. In fact, because the economic development of the South was no match for that of the North, she had to enlarge her political principles almost in exact proportion to Northern economic superiority.

There are many indications that the volume was written with a view to brilliancy in style and arrangement rather than to a complete mastery and sober presentation of all the facts. The author's statement (page 112) that by 1837 no Northern states except Connecticut, New Jersey and Ohio retained any property restriction upon manhood suffrage, overlooks the fact that the New York constitution of 1821 and 1846 disfranchised all men of color not possessed of a freehold estate of the value of $250. A less excusable error is the assertion that the Peace Congress of 1861 was "made up of delegates from all but the seceding states" (page 214); whereas neither Michigan, Wisconsin, Minnesota, California nor Oregon was represented there. We are also told that the processes of presidential reconstruction were complete in the autumn of 1865 "in every state except Texas" (page 259). The author might have learned from Johnson's message of December 18, 1865 (McPherson, *Reconstruction*, p. 67) that Florida also was still in a transition state.

Notwithstanding these and other mistakes, and in spite of an overwrought style and many almost bewildering refinements of adjectives and phrases, it is impossible to criticize the little volume without reluctance. The sincerity and uncommon ability which Professor Wilson shows are worthy a much more elaborate work. In fact, it seems to me that only in such an undertaking will he be able to do his talent full justice and perform his entire duty toward American history.

FREDERIC BANCROFT.

Printed in the *Political Science Quarterly*, VIII (Sept. 1893), 533-35.

A Book Review

[*c. Sept. 5, 1893*]

MR. GOLDWIN SMITH'S "VIEWS" ON
OUR POLITICAL HISTORY.

Mr. Goldwin Smith has just published a volume[1] on the political history of the United States which is noteworthy for many reasons. It is a very brief book, in which the history of some four hundred years is indicated in broad and dashing strokes; but it is hardly singular on that account, for Mr. Goldwin Smith is known to be nothing if not bold. It is doubtless noteworthy that in an age when scholarly criticism so solemnly demands histories altogether made up of statements of fact and quite void of the offence of comment we should be given a history nearly all comment, striding with seven-league boots from period to period, with almost no detailed or carefully wrought statements of fact.

[1] Goldwin Smith, *The United States: An Outline of Political History, 1492-1871* (New York, 1893). [Eds.' note]

And yet it is neither its daring brevity nor its confident comment that makes the book worth looking at a moment, but the extraordinary nature of the views which fill its pages. It was quite unexpected that such things as Mr. Smith says in this volume should be spoken so confidently just at this stage of the study of our history. We have here what may turn out to be the last, as well as the most trenchant, statement of certain leading conceptions concerning the history of the United States which are now undergoing criticism so sharp and decisive that they will hardly survive another generation.

Mr. Smith, it is true, is not an American; there are evidences of that fact on every page. When he speaks of "our point of view," it is clear that he does not mean the American, but the British point of view; and from that point of view familiar matters often look oddly enough to the American reader. But it is singular how native views and [are] acquired, how English prepossessions and instruction received from American writers, are mingled, even if they are not fused, in this queerly compounded volume. There is, first of all, the quality which we recognize as Mr. Smith's own, belonging to the man rather than to the race; then there is the quality, not of mercy, which we know to be a national, not a personal, attribute; and, last of all, there is the color of the American books which Mr. Smith has read. The personal quality, to be quite frank, is cynical and impracticable; the national trait appears whenever either the theory or the practice of the Revolution is under review; the tone and method of the old books predominate when the subject is the development of the nation and its institutions.

It is, doubtless, Mr. Smith's own temperament which renders the tone of the book disagreeable. He writes as if he were irritated, with an air of belligerency and a readiness to attack; and one is repelled even by a true judgment if it be sourly uttered. Examples fill the book. No one can justly object to hear Charles James Fox condemned for his follies or for the tricks of party policy to which he stooped; but when Mr. Smith speaks of him as "a debauchee in politics as in private life, whose reckless violence and revolting displays of sympathy with the Americans" made the king's course consonant with the honor of the country, we can only stare and feel uneasy to hear a historian speak so violently. It is not necessary to admire Samuel Adams and Patrick Henry over much to feel the injustice of the sneers with which Mr. Smith speaks of them, as men neither pure nor sincere, who turned to the trade of agitation because they failed in everything else. He cannot understand coarse-grained and strenuous men, filled with an ardor none the less wholesome because incapable of a nice discrimination. He goes through our history looking for modern English gentlemen; he naturally finds very few, for the young nation is struggling to make conquest of a continent, not to acquire a temperate and cultivated judgment; and the men whom he does find are for the most part not to his taste.

Equally significant of personal temperament are the passages in which Mr. Smith stops passionately to deplore the whole course of events. The most noticeable of these is the passage on pages seventy-three and seventy-four beginning, "Woe to them by whom the offence came." He is speaking of the Revolution. "Woe," he cries, "to the arbit[r]ary and bigoted king"; woe to Grenville; woe above all to Charles Townshend; woe to Lord North; "woe even to Lord Mansfield"; woe to the Parliament, to the Tory squires and the Tory parsons; woe to the pamphleteers of prerogative! "But woe also to the agitators of Boston," to the preachers of Boston, "to contraband traders if there were any"; "woe to all on either side who under the influence of passion, interest, or selfish ambition fomented the quarrel which rent asunder the English race." The passage is longer than that in which he says all that he has to say of the entire colonial history of New York. Amen, let us say, with deepest unction. Woe indeed to all who may be reckoned responsible for bringing strife and hatred into the great English family! But is our indignation profitable: does it elucidate the history? Mr. Smith himself says that separation was inevitable; he would also doubtless admit that human nature likewise is inevitable, and that the whole course of events was what was to have been expected under the circumstances. It is too late now to be contemptuous or indignant about the matter. Nor does it contribute to a just understanding either, as Mr. Smith's initial thesis itself demonstrates.

That thesis is, that a radically false relation existed between the colonies and the mother country from the beginning. "The English colony unhappily," he says, "was a dependency, and when it grew strong enough to spurn dependence there was a bond to be broken which was not likely to be broken without violence and a breach of affection." The whole difficulty he believes to have been, that the colonists "deemed themselves still liegemen of a sovereign on the other side of the Atlantic." And yet it could not have been otherwise in that age and generation. This unnatural relation, if we are to deem it such, was the characteristic flower of the time. The establishment of colonies was but a part of the schemes of empire which everywhere filled the minds of monarchs and statesmen in that age of keen rivalry among the nations to draw to themselves the commerce and the riches of the world. Colonies were means of trade and of territorial aggrandizement; and that they were so was the logical and inevitable outcome of the centuries that had gone before. It is idle, as it is also unphilosophical, to wish that it had been otherwise. Unnatural though the relation between colony and motherland may have been, moreover, the colonists for long earnestly desired to maintain it and exhibited a passionate pride in holding their place as Englishmen.

The real difficulty was, that the relationship was new, and that there was no common understanding of its real nature. England did not regard the colonists in the same light in which they regarded themselves. In their own view they were simply Englishmen away from England; while in the view of the merchants and politicians in England they were dependents, directly subject in all things to the authority of the Crown. The policy of England, moreover, had not been consistent with her theory, and did not remain consistent with itself. For generations together, until indeed the colonies had grown into power and self-consciousness as free English communities, their dependence upon the mother country had not been insisted upon, except in matters of strictly imperial policy; and in these matters the colonists could yield without any intolerable sense of injustice. During all that time they were treated most generously. So long as they paid the expenses of their own governments they were defended by English ships and English troops, paid out of the English treasury, as an English county would have been. Then, after being thus nursed and indulged in independence, and when, under this "wise and salutary neglect," they had grown into a people capable of united self-defence in support of common principles and accepted precedents, the principles and precedents which seemed most surely settled were of a sudden rejected and reversed.

It is wholesome, though it is not new, to hear the English side of the question urged. American writers some time since began to admit the technical legal right of the English government in the matter of taxing the colonies, and the entire fallaciousness of the claim to representation in Parliament made by the colonial agitators. They always have admitted that the tax on tea was a small matter, and no very substantial grievance in itself. Every reputable American writer, too, now speaks with shame of the unjust and brutal treatment of the colonial 'Tories.' It was shameful that they should be mobbed and despoiled because they stood manfully to principles of loyalty and allegiance only yesterday universal, and refused to be turned about by a sudden revulsion of feeling and a temporary grievance. But that, which is much, is all that just history can say. Mr. Smith pushes his English view of the matter much beyond this point of calm judgment. He quotes the words which, on the eve of the civil war in England, Sir William Waller the Parliamentarian, wrote to Sir Ralph Hopton the Royalist: "My affections to you are so unchangeable that hostility itself cannot violate my friendship to your person, but I must be true to the cause wherein I serve. . . . We are both on the stage and we must act the parts that are assigned to us in this tragedy. Let us do it in a way of honor, and without personal animosities"; and Mr. Smith's comment is, "Such was the spirit of men mournfully obeying in a great cause the inevitable call of civil war. There was little of it on either side in the American Revolution." Was there much of it on either side in the Parliamentary wars; and are we writing homilies or are we writing history?

Mr. Smith cannot see any greatness in the cause of the American revolutionists; for he denies that there was any adequate provocation for revolution in the Stamp Act, and believes the American leaders to have been guilty of rash and contumacious folly in bringing on so dreadful a contest upon so small an issue. "It is true," he concedes, "that in the case of the tea duty, as in that of Hampden's assessment to ship money, what was to be considered was the principle, not the amount." But the principle, he urges, was not the same in the two cases. Ship money was illegal; the stamp duty was not. The impositions which Hampden resisted were parts of a plan and system of tyranny; but the stamp tax was nothing more than a most impolitic piece of lawful legislation.

True enough, let us say; but the point was not one of law, and taxes of this kind unresisted would assuredly have proved but the beginnings of a system. The American grievance was not that it was unlawful to tax them, though they may loosely have called it unlawful, but that it was intolerable, a part, a too practical part, of that false conception of the relationship between colony and mother country which Mr. Smith so strongly condemns, and which English policy had hitherto refrained from insisting upon. The historian is bound, if he would be just, to deal with the humors of men as the wise statesman would. He should reckon with them, not quarrel with them. The colonists had oftentimes protested against having their money spent by any one but themselves, and they had always hitherto been suffered to spend it as their own representative bodies willed. This was the only representation they really wanted. When Grenville proposed to tax them by act of Parliament he was proposing to do what is as intolerable to Englishmen as the violation of law itself, the violation, namely, of precedent. A situation was created over which courts had no jurisdiction, indeed, but which must go into the forum of conscience and policy. In that forum the Americans had the strongest possible claims to redress. The relation of nominal dependence had subsisted only upon sufferance with these mettlesome people with their "fierce spirit of liberty," and they could suffer it no longer the moment it threatened to become real instead of merely nominal.

The claim to representation, though it may have had no legal basis, had a very substantial historical foundation. The American demand was, that the colonists be allowed to act through their representatives, whether in Parliament or in America, as they had always done hitherto, according to a principle lying deeper in the English constitution, as they conceived, than even the privileges of Parliament or the powers of the Crown. If this was in effect a claim to independence, that is why a war for right so suddenly became a war for separation. There had been virtual separation in matters of this kind all along; if it could not remain virtual, it must be made real. That was the revolution; and it is vain to cry "Woe!" The direful spirit of civil war did all the rest, that was not just but bitter and shameful. The cause itself was great, if the spirit of English liberty is great; and Mr. Smith differs from the greatest English historians, not only, but also from most informed and liberal Englishmen of our day in not perceiving that it was really the authentic spirit of English liberty that moved in the Revolution. No other outcome was conceivable, except by us who sit at this cool distance.

For what his book contains as the result of his reading our own historians Mr. Smith is hardly to be held responsible, except that, sketching in outline, he seems to exaggerate what he copies. He gives us that view of our development which might very appropriately be entitled The Expansion of New England. It is singular how crude and baseless this familiar view seems when stated absolutely and without qualification, as the writer of an outline finds himself obliged to state it. Our own writers, giving details, seem also to imply limitations: what they do not tell us in so many words that we got from New England we feel at liberty to regard as having come from some other source. There was a time when it did not seem possible to write the history of the United States in any other way. It was delightfully simple. There were, at most, but two sets of forces to be reckoned with, the one set proceeding from New England, the other, which was in the long run to be discredited, from the South; and the permutations and combinations of these could be worked out at leisure. This is the way Mr. Smith puts it: The southern settlements "were colonies of the same mother country as New England, but widely different from her in religious, social, and political character, destined presently to be joined to her in an ill-starred union, then to come to an inevitable rupture with the confederation of which she was the soul, and after a desperate struggle to be subjugated and reannexed." It will be noted that in this view of the matter, not only the great middle States, which have made their own rich and characteristic contributions to the institutions and spirit of the country, but also the whole West, with its great populations so thoroughly its own, are accounted but parts and projections of New England. If it were true, it would be marvellous, a most signal manifestation of a mysterious Providence!

This simplified method of writing history has had some very remarkable, though quite logical, results. The most remarkable is the most recent, Mr. Douglas Campbell's two volumes on the Puritan in Holland and New England. Mr. Campbell maintains that a great deal of what we regard as Puritan in our institutions was really Dutch in its origin, and had been learned or absorbed by the Puritans while they were exiles in Holland. Our history has thus shown a singular tendency to revert to origins, and make origins do service as an explanation of development, instead of moving forward through the great processes of modification which have really constituted the only part of our history that is distinctively our own. Why would it not be better still, if this is the truly scientific method of writing history, to go back of New England to the counties and neighborhoods of the old country from which the Puritans came out to America, and view American civilization as the expansion of Suffolk, Norfolk, and Essex? "The history of New England," we have already been told, "begins in an obscure Lincolnshire village."

But, after all, very little of it began there. The seventeenth century brought all sorts and conditions of men to the Atlantic coasts of America. From Yorkshire to the Land's End, England contributed her populations. Scotchmen came, too, fortunately, and Swedes, and a great colony of Dutchmen. There were whole commonwealths of Catholics and Church of England men, as well as Dissenters of every cast and description. The variety was complete while the settlements still clung to the seashore. When the great westward migration began everything was modified. Then there came a mixture and fusion of these and of many other elements. Beyond the mountains, not only new settlements, but a new nation sprang up. Of all this Mr. Smith drops scarcely a hint, though the dramatic quality of the process would unquestionably be to his taste. We are forced to conclude that he got no hint of it from his authorities. The history of the United States is very far from being a history of origins. It is just the opposite: it is a history of developments. You have not described the manufacture of steel when you have discussed the qualities of pig iron. This great continent, then wild and silent, received European populations, European manners and faiths, European purposes, into its forests, and, finding they meant to stay, proceeded to work its will upon them. They took on a new character, and submitted to a new process of growth. Our continental life is a radically different thing from our life in the old settlements. Every element of the old life that penetrated the continent at all has been digested and has become an element of new life. It is this transformation that constitutes our history.

In order to understand the development of the United States, indeed, we have even to make a new reckoning of the original elements. In talking of the New England and of the Southern forces in our life, we have dismissed the Middle States from the reckoning under the impression that they were only a region in which New England and the South shaded off to a middle neutral line lying, no doubt, somewhere in Pennsylvania. As a matter of fact, if we are determined to be partial in our view and to pick out a single set of influences to be traced through the later intricacies of our history, the Middle States have rather more claim to our choice than either New England or the South. Throughout the eighteenth century, at any rate, the middle colonies were more distinctively American in constitution and character than either their northeastern or their southern neighbors. They had that mixture of populations, that variety of structure, that materialistic and progressive way of looking at things, which have been the really characteristic marks of American development. New England and the South were for a long time, in temper at any rate, like detached pieces of England, though of different and contrasted parts of England. Their statesmen presided over the formation of the Confederation and the Union with a conservatism and regard for precedent of which the Middle States were inclined to be not a little impatient. Then the conservative populations of New England and the South and the mixed population of the Middle States, along with many bands of settlers from foreign lands, crossed the mountains and met on the western prairies. The New Englander, gone into the West, the Southerner, gone out of the South, found himself dominated by conditions much less familiar to him, it is safe to say, than to his new comrades from New York, Pennsylvania, and New Jersey. He had emigrated into a new atmosphere as well as into a new land; found himself becoming a westerner and a distinctively American man.

The formative period of American history has had no geographical limitations. It did not end in colonial times or on the Atlantic coast. It has not ended yet; nor will it end until we cease to have frontier communities and a young political life just accommodating itself to fixed institutions. Our heritage is much, our origin deeply significant, but most significant of all is the way in which we have traded with the estate we received at the first. That part of our history, therefore, which is most truly national is the history of the West. Almost all the critical issues of our politics have been made up beyond the mountains, beginning with the Louisiana purchase, which neither New England nor the South would ever have insisted upon on its own account, and ending, if the civil war be taken as the culmination, with that greatest question of all, the extension of slavery. Mr. Smith, following our own historians, talks as if the slavery question had been an issue of morals simply, made up between the New England conscience and the South. It was a question made up, in fact, between the South and the West. It was the men whom Lincoln represented, and not the anti-slavery societies, that pushed the question to a settlement. The New England conscience would have worked *in vacuo* if there had been no territories and no intense and expanding western life.

It is this making of the nation in the great central basins of the continent that an outline history should principally exhibit. It lends itself willingly to broad treatment in rough body colors. But one must have the taste and temper for it. He can do nothing with it if the rough and ready western man hopelessly repels him. The typical Americans have all been western men, with the exception of Washington. Washington had not had much of European culture. He had got his experience and his notions of what ought to be done for the country from actual contact with the wilderness, and actual life on the western frontier. He conceived the expansion of the country much more liberally than others of his generation, and looked confidently forward to many a great national enterprise which even yet we have not had the spirit to undertake. The qualities that made him a great commander and a great president were qualities which would have made him an equally great frontiersman. You cannot imagine Hamilton or Madison, or Livingston, or John Adams, or the Pinckneys living tolerably on the frontier. They are not Americans in the sense in which Clay and Jackson and Lincoln were Americans.

We may wish that the typical Americans of the past had had more knowledge, a more cultivated appreciation of the value of what was old and established, a juster view of foreign nations and foreign politics; that they had been more like Webster and less like Jackson; and we may hope that the typical American of the future will be wiser and better poised. But in the mean time the past is to be understood and estimated as the facts stand, and only a thoroughly sympathetic comprehension of these men who have actually been the typical Americans will enable us to effect that purpose. The fact that Clay rather than Webster, Jackson and not John Quincy Adams, represented the forces which were really predominant and distinctively American in our development is commentary enough on any theory that makes either of the peculiar sections of the Atlantic seaboard the principal or only theatre of American history. Mr. Smith stares and shudders in Jackson's presence, and looks upon Clay very much as one would regard an uninstructed child.

With regard to the central legal question of our history, as to the right of secession and the constitutional character of the war for the Union, Mr. Smith occupies a position which is certainly altogether his own. He cuts the knot instead of untying it. "The Constitution was on this point," he holds, "a Delphic oracle." The struggle for the Union was not a civil war in any proper sense of the term since it "was not a struggle between two parties for the same land, but between two communities, territorially separate, for the land of one of them which the other had taken arms to reannex." The legal question is in his view hardly material, no theory being necessary to explain the falling asunder, or to justify the separation, if it could have been accomplished, of two communities so radically antagonistic and incompatible in temper, life, and purpose as New England and the South,–the two "communities" he has in mind. It is the mere fact of the situation that arrests his attention. Like most foreigners, he is not impressed by the fine spun legal niceties of the constitutional question, for he is accustomed to a constitution which moves with circumstance and national policy. It is an excellent point of observation for American readers to be led to once and again, if only to see how things clear up when viewed from it, and how much of a constitution is obedient, whether it be written or unwritten, to the course of events. But, after all, to look at it so is to miss a very essential feature of American history. Americans have never waived a point of law. We have always been a law-regarding and litigious race. Accustomed to put our institutions into written statements and then argue every point of interpretation as if it were a condition precedent to development, we have, so to say, gotten the legal lines and constitutional anatomy of our government indelibly worked into our consciousness; and neither side could have fought the battles of the war of 1861-65 until they had satisfied themselves that they had a legal right to do so. That they both thought themselves in the right proves what subtle litigants they were. But to waive the point of law is to skim the surface of the history.

It is this sense for law that has given to the whole development of the nation its cohesion. It is because of this that our great community while it has spread has not fallen to pieces. The sentiments of the war time were steeped in legal conceptions. The surviving soldiers of that war would feel with keen shame that they had fought unrighteously if they could not still feel that they had fought for law, not to make a right but to preserve one,–not to "reannex," but to keep, the South. It is this strong conscience and instinct for law, indeed, which has rendered our written constitutions valid and serviceable as sound vehicles of the national life. Those constitutions are not causes, but results,–results of inbred character and of a desire for distinct coherence in respect of every step of construction in the development of institutions.

I must say that I am affected by this volume of Mr. Goldwin Smith's very much as Walter Bagehot was affected by Mr. Canning. "He was a man of elegant gifts, of easy fluency, capable of embellishing anything, with a nice wit, gliding swiftly over the most delicate topics; passing from topic to topic like the *raconteur* of the dinner table, touching easily on them all, letting them go as easily; confusing you as to whether he knows nothing, or knows everything." I cannot but feel that its views have not been carefully enough considered; above all, that they have not been carefully enough fused and rendered consistent. It is singularly, almost perversely, wrong in some places; it is singularly able and in the right in other places. Mr. Smith has a very penetrative insight into some matters and some characters; but if he cannot do a thing in a flash he cannot do it at all. He cannot wait on the slowness of his thought, for none of his thought is slow. He is not careful that his views and conclusions should be scrupulously and patiently wrought. Even where the pages shine with an unmistakable brilliancy they are bright with a hard glitter that is metallic and cold. The book is rather a strong pamphlet containing views than a real history containing dispassionate and well considered truth.   WOODROW WILSON.

Printed in the New York *Forum*, XVI (Dec. 1893), 489-99.

To Ellen Axson Wilson

My own darling,   Princeton, 6 Sept., 1893

Your telegram[1] reached me to-day and was a great comfort. I suppose my little queen is actually at the Fair by this time. I am *so* glad to think of it, for I know what you are seeing and how much it must delight you. It's a great deal better than seeing it myself—only I wish I could *see you seeing it*.

We are doing famously, my sweet one. I am all the time where the children can get at me, and I at them, and I know exactly what they are doing every hour of the day. It's not a bore, either, but a pleasure. It does not worry me, for I am not *trying* to do anything else—and there is nothing else that I have to do or want to do at present.

This afternoon is fixed for "the party," which is to take place at 4:15—for we hope to see Ed. back by that time. Mr. Bryant[2] is going to arrange the hours of exercise so that Ed. can get off every day on the 2 o'clock train and reach home by four. "The neighbours" are to come in, of course, and we are going to have a jolly time. It is after three as I write.

Mrs. Brown[3] came over (before your telegram arrived) to see if I had heard of your safe arrival and, so soon as the news came I went over and told her and we rejoiced together.

Oh, my darling, take care of yourself. I hardly dare trust myself even yet to write "a real love letter"—my heart is *too* full of being   Your own   Woodrow

ALS (WC, NjP).

¹ It is missing.

² A speech therapist, probably connected with the Philadelphia Institute, who had been working with Edward Axson to cure his stammering.

³ Susan Dod (Mrs. David) Brown, a wealthy widow of 65 Stockton Street. Albert B. Dod and David Brown Halls, dormitories at Princeton, named for her brother and husband and built in 1890 and 1891, respectively, were evidences of her generosity. She gave half the funds for the construction of the Second Presbyterian Church in Princeton and, among numerous other good works, built the Mary Dod Brown Chapel and founded the David Brown Professorship of the English Bible at Lincoln University. She was born in Mendham, N.J., on February 1, 1812, and died in Princeton on October 10, 1902.

From Ellen Axson Wilson

Hotel Holland [Chicago]
My own darling,　　　　　　Thursday morn. [Sept. 7, 1893]

As I telegraphed we¹ arrived quite safe and well,—are having glorious weather—bright and cool,—and are having a glorious time! We saw the "Court of Honour" the first time late in the afternoon from a launch. Oh how wonderful! words fail me indeed. The whole sail was enchantment! I should like to spend the whole time doing that. I shall spend most of today sitting still looking at it (the Court of Honour) for I woke up in the night & found myself unwell! I am feeling perfectly comfortable but of course shall be very careful.

Dr. Shorey² called last evening & is going to meet us at three on the grounds and spend the rest of the afternoon & evening with us,—getting our dinner in Germany! I have a quite comfortable little room & the other two have a splendid big one facing the lake & commanding a view of the fair. I expect I shall have to share it with Alice when Minnie goes, though I should prefer my small one alone.

The station was not on Van Buren St. after all. We got almost hopelessly lost hunting for our hotel & did not reach it until half past ten, when we all had bad headaches from fatigue & want of food. Breakfast, a bath & a pill cured Alice & myself, however, but poor Minnie had to go to bed with hers. Alice & I left her at two to see if she could sleep it off & she joined us at five & we stayed there till eight. We did not try to "do" any of the main buildings yesterday—saw the "Woman's exhibit[,]" the "Loan collection" & the Cal. exhibit,—where we went for our lunch. We had dinner on the roof of the Woman's building—and oh! how grand the view was, with all the lights ablaze, the dazzling buildings and the shining water.

Pray excuse this shocking scrawl. Of course I write in haste & Minnie's pen "won't work." Oh, my precious darlings how I want to see you all! How I *love* you all!—how I *love you* especially. My heart fairly melts within me at thought of you my love, my love! Love to all[—]a hundred kisses for my little treasures! Do they miss me at all? Ah how I miss them! I was *wretched* with home-sickness on the journey. Goodbye dear love.

Your own   Eileen

ALS (WC, NjP).
 [1] That is, Ellen, her two cousins, Alice Hoyt Truehart and Mary Eloise Hoyt, and a Miss Gould.
 [2] Paul Shorey, an old friend from Bryn Mawr days, who had recently gone to the University of Chicago as Professor of Greek.

To Ellen Axson Wilson

My own darling,   Thursday Princeton, 7 Sept., 1893

Still we thrive as much as you could wish,—for I'm sure you don't want us not to miss you. That's something beyond praying for,—and there's a sort of sweet pain in it after all. To miss you is to realize our love for you, and if ever there was a woman whom it was sweet to love—glorious to love—you are she. We don't *talk* about you much—that would not be prudent, but we *all* act as if something serious were the matter. Stock and Florence[1] exclaim at the *loneliness* of the situation as often and with as much feeling as I do, though I suspect that I have some private meditations which are wholly my own. What they are "I'll tell you bye and bye." In the meantime know that you are deeply beloved by this *household*.

"The party" went off famously. Two little tables (the childrens' and the one from our room) were placed on the back piazza. At one,—the old ladies' table,—sat Margaret, Rebecca, and Eleanor; at the other, Nellie, boy, Mildred, and Jessie.[2] We had ice-cream, cake, and candy. I helped the cream, at the old ladies' table. After the "things" were eaten,—and while I was off on my ride,—the crowd played every game known to any of them. It was a perfect success throughout!

In the evening I called at the Purves's and was told that Boy had announced that he meant to marry Jessie when he grew up; but had said that he might have to wait until you and I were out of the way, because "the old man might object."

I find that I'm getting much more intimately acquainted with the children. Nellie now comes to me, as she would come to you, with all sorts of odd little confidences and singular narratives which delight me. It somehow touches me deeply to be both father and mother to the sweet little chicks. I am really enjoying my maternal functions very keenly—odd as I feel.

I forward a letter which I suppose is from Mrs. Candler.[3]

Stock's friend Graham[4] turned up here day before yesterday. We could not "keep" him, but he has taken lunch with us.

There's no other news.

I love you, darling, with an intensity and a longing little short of terrible, tender as the passion is of being

Your own   Woodrow.

ALS (WC, NjP).

[1] Florence Stevens Hoyt of Rome, Georgia, Ellen's first cousin, who was visiting the Wilsons.

[2] The children just mentioned were Margaret Wilson, Rebekah Purves, Elinor Purves, Eleanor (Nellie) Wilson, William Marot Purves (the first Purves boy after three girls), Mildred Purves, and Jessie Wilson. The parents of the Purves children were the Rev. Dr. and Mrs. George Tybout Purves of 73 Stockton Street. Dr. Purves was Professor of New Testament Literature and Exegesis at the Seminary.

[3] As EAW to WW, September 10, 1893, reveals, this letter was from Ellen's girlhood friend, Janie Porter Chandler. It is missing.

[4] Probably James Chandler Graham, Stockton's classmate at Wesleyan.

From Ellen Axson Wilson

My own darling,   Chicago, Sept. 8/93

Will you excuse pencil. I am saving that precious commodity time by writing at the table while waiting for breakfast.

The perfect weather continues & I am feeling *perfectly* well. I had *such* a lovely time yesterday. I spent the morning among the pictures chiefly! After lunch Dr. Shorey joined us, & as I was not able to climb about with them I took a chair & was trundled about the main building looking chiefly at the lovely china. I had a *delightful* time. (The chairs by the way are only fifty cents an hour now. I had one two hours.[)] Then I enjoyed the court of honour for awhile, after which the others joined me & we had dinner. *Then the illuminations*!! Ah, what bliss! You can't imagine how nice Dr. Shorey was, much *too* nice indeed for he actually *would* hire *chairs* & take us down the Midway Plaisance, late in the evening "to stir the Bohemian" in us. Of course he dined us too at the Casino, and he seemed so "sincerely happy" to do it all. He actually wants to repeat the pleasure another evening!

Your *sweet* letter came last night,[1]—how the mere hand-writing stirred my heart-strings! What a narrow escape you had, dearest! It frightens me to think of it. Take care of yourself my precious one. Kiss the little darlings for me a score of times. Oh how I *love* you all. My Woodrow, my treasure how I love *you*.

Your own   Eileen

Love to the boys & Florence.

ALS (WC, NjP).
¹ Probably written September 5. It is missing.

To Ellen Axson Wilson

My own darling,   Princeton, Friday, 8 Sept., '93

I was writing to Charlie Kent this morning, wishing him success in a certain undertaking, and one passage from what I wrote I think you would like to read. "My sympathy is the more eager and the more profound because I *know* what felicity I am wishing you when I wish you success. My own sweet partner has been the making of my heart not only, but of my mind, too, quickening it where it was sluggish, waking it where it had slept,—supplementing it on all sides. I *must* have wide sympathies with such a mind as hers,—with no vice or necessity of specialization to spoil or narrow it,—so close neighbour to my own. Any success I may have of the truly literary kind will be more than half due to my intimacy with her. God speed you, my dear fellow, in making sure of the same sort of aid and comfort!"¹ For fear such a quotation should betray me into writing the passionate love letter my indiscreet heart is longing to pour forth, I'll quote you another passage from the same epistle—to get your *intellectual* sympathy. "Our *sane* literature, Charlie, must, I am convinced, so far as this country produces it, for a long time come from the South. The more of the *spirit*, of the *ideal*, you can put into your students the more eminent your services to the country. The New England genius, never catholic, has produced its characteristic fruits and is stale. The South is catholic, expansive, full of heart and imagination, and must take us in charge and give us a literature that will smack true to all palates!" Do you agree with that—or do you not?

The mails have not yet had time to bring me anything from you, darling, but I am hoping for a card to-night. How I do long to write you a love letter:—we are getting on so smoothly there's nothing else to write:—but the only way I can manage this time, my pet, is by suppressing my intense yearning and longing for you. It would become intolerable if I were to indulge it even a little. It is not, of course, the *duties* I have while you are gone that make my impatience for your return so extreme and intemperate: I am getting quite fond of *them*, quite domesticated. I wrote a letter—a careful letter to Winchester²—this morning with Jessie standing by and overlooking my writing, without getting the least bit worried or even threatened with nervousness! What do you think of *that* for a change of life? What oppresses me is this fact of "home" without the home-maker. But, bless me, I make as much home as I can—think about nothing and nobody in particular, and get along famously.

I shall feel very badly, dear, if you start home before Wednesday afternoon. Don't let yourself forget that.

Nellie's cold is well: we are comfortable, and we are happy—all that you could wish, in your absence, for

Your own   Woodrow

ALS (WC, NjP).

¹ Both Wilson's letter and Kent's letter, to which Wilson's was a reply, are missing. Evidently Kent had complained of the life of a bachelor and told Wilson that he intended to court, or had begun to court, Eleanor Smith Miles, daughter of Professor Francis H. Smith of the University of Virginia and widow of Fielding D. Miles. Kent and Wilson had known Mrs. Miles well during their student days at the university. She married Kent on June 4, 1895.

² It is missing.

From Ellen Axson Wilson

My dearest Woodrow,   Chicago Sept 9 [1893]

Your second most welcome letter came duly to hand yesterday. Am so glad you are getting on so well. We did not go to the fair yesterday morning on account of Minnie. She left at 1.16—sick & rather miserable, poor girl! We are anxious to hear from her—it is a six hours journey to Indianapolis. We spent the afternoon in the Midway Plaisance & the evening on the Court of Honour & in a launch. Had, of course, a charming time. The glorious weather still continues. We were very late in rising this morning so please excuse haste. With a heart full of love to all my dear ones, I am as ever   Yours   E. A. W.

API (WC, NjP).

To Ellen Axson Wilson

My own darling,   Saturday. Princeton, 9 Sept., 1893

I am rejoicing in your first letter, which came this morning, and was devoured more eagerly than if it had been bread from Eden. I had been waiting for it as a convalescent waits for health. Indeed I have been in a sort of convalescence ever since I was stricken by your departure, and now that I am in communication with you once more my strength will return apace. Oh, how sweet these words of love are in this precious letter—and how happy I am over my love's delight with the Fair! I should have regretted it, and have been unhappy about it, the rest of my life, I'm sure, if *you*—with your incomparable taste and zest for what is artistic and beautiful,—had not seen this exposition, the most artistic and beautiful the world has ever seen. I am glad all day long with thought of your delight. It's *too* bad, oh, it's too bad, that you should be unwell so inopportunely! But I rely on your promise of care; and, after all, one can sit still and see the *best* of the show. Come back, darling, with your eyes *full* of the things you have seen, and let me see whether they *can* look any brighter, any *deeper*, with glad lights, than I have seen them when my love was in her warmest, gladdest moods. Nothing (except love only) so fills these eyes with inexpressible beauty as thoughts that satisfy the charming mind that looks forth through them. My dear love's silence would sometimes come near to kill me if these sweet eyes did not hold such a wealth of meaning for me. Oh, Nellie, my love, my queen!

We are getting on nicely, as usual, with an occasional stomach-ache or other transient ailment, but with so [no] trouble worth mentioning. I am already so habituated to my new functions that they go off with the most perfect naturalness. I am not spoiling the servants a bit. They willingly do everything there is to do, and I don't interfere: I only keep an eye on everything. Maggie and Mary[1] unite in bathing the children in the afternoon and in putting them to bed at night—are indeed joint nurses; and I have no trouble at all. Nothing is absorbed except my thoughts.

Willie Hoyt[2] arrived yesterday, just after I had finished my letter to you. I expected a delicate chap, but not a prim one, a southern, not a New England, boy. Imagine cousin Mary[3] at her gauntest in physique and transformed in manner into a New England old maid of the traditional (and Wilkins) type,[4] and you have this singular, precise, and nasal lad. We may be able to "limber" him up, but at present he is as stiff as aluminum, and as light, though, I fear, not as strong! Poor chap, I wish we could get life into him somehow,—and food, for of this profane thing he will take almost none at all. He's not the least of an incumbrance. The children have taken possession of him, and keep him employed!

My sweetheart, we love you—we miss you! My passion for you is simply inexpressible. You are in all things all the world to

Your own   Woodrow

ALS (WC, NjP).

1 Maggie Foley and Mary Foley, who may have been related but lived at separate residences.

2 William Dana Hoyt, born in 1880, son of Dr. William Dearing Hoyt of Rome, Georgia, and Ellen's first cousin.

3 Probably Mary ("Minnie") Hoyt, Willie's sister.

⁴ The type portrayed by the prolific New England novelist, Mary Eleanor Wilkins, who later wrote under her married name, Mary Eleanor Wilkins Freeman.

From Ellen Axson Wilson

My own darling,   Chicago, Sept. 10. [1893]

Your *charming* letter telling about the "party" &c. came duly to hand yesterday morning together with Janie's. The latter contained quite a surprise, by the way:—she will have a baby,—about the 1st of Dec.!—after all these years!¹ I am *very* glad for her, though it *has* kept her from coming east and going to the fair; which is a great pity. The wonderful weather continues,—was there ever such good fortune. I enjoyed yesterday more than any day yet I think. I was quite sick the night before & early in the morning;— vomiting & dirrhoea, (how *do* you spell that?) So I took brandy & lay still 'till half past eleven. Then, feeling well again, we started out, and as I was on milk diet I decided I could afford to spend most of the day in a chair. I had it *four* hours,—two dollars worth. It was *so* delightful to enjoy all the beautiful things without the draw-back of fatigue. We thoroughly inspected the "Horticultural," the "Agricultural," the "Mining," the forestry & the Anthropological exhibits, also the Convent of La Rabida. The display of plants & fruits was *beautiful*. I am so bored with Georgia,—you would not know there was such a state in the union. No building & no exhibit in any of these houses, though she might have made such a fine show in all. I have not had the *slightest touch* of the afore-mentioned trouble since yesterday morning. Indeed am feeling *particularly* well now,—and was last night. The evening was *glorious*! We spent it as usual on the Court of Honour. We have fallen so into the spirit of the place & time that we never think of needing an escort but stay every night till nine o'clock as a matter of course. The lights and crowds are a perfect protection. Last night there were beautiful fire-works besides the usual splendid electric display.

But enough of the fair. It will keep until my return. Speaking of that I have had a little disappointment. Miss Gould told me two days ago that she was afraid she would have to go Monday night as her college opened on Wed. You can't think how my heart leaped with delight at the thought of getting home so soon. Fair or no Fair I was charmed with the idea. But now she has heard from her friend the professor of classics, who begs her to wait here for her until Wed. night and she "will be responsible for her tardiness." So I will probably have to stay until Wed. night too.

Since writing the above we have been consulting together, and I *think* I can get off on *Tuesday* night. Some friends of Miss Gould's are coming to the Windermere on Tuesday & she can—& I think would *like*,—to spend the night there with them. So if they come I will leave Tuesday night, unless something unforeseen happens. As well as I can make out from the schedule a train leaves here Tuesday night 9.30 and reaches New York at 7.40 Thursday morning. That will enable me if we reach N. Y. on time to take the 8.30 to Princeton,—otherwise the *eleven*[.] I will write a postal tomorrow after I have made enquiries and can be more definite. What is bothering me is how to get this huge valise across New York!

We think we will go today to the Court of Honour just to "loaf and invite our souls." It will be pleasant, we think, to go when there is nothing to do,—or to look at except the grand total. So as Miss Gould is waiting for me I must close.

Just think, love, only four more days & I will be *at home*!—in my darling's arms! Oh I will be the happiest girl in the world then. Sweetheart, you can't imagine how constantly my thoughts play about you here as well as everywhere else. *Nothing* makes me forget you for the shortest time. Indeed everything manages to get itself *associated* with *you* in the strangest manner! It is especially so with the Court of Honour; one would suppose I thought you had *made* it (!) so inextricably are thoughts of you blended with all my memories of it. In short, darling, I *love* you with all my heart & soul & mind. And ah how I love & long for my babies! Make them all kiss each other for Mama. Give my dearest love to the dear boys & Florence. Now and always

Your own   Eileen

I am *almost* sure to start on Tuesday night, so if tomorrow's postal should be delayed you may look for me anyhow on Thursday morning.

ALS (WP, DLC).
  1 She had married Samuel Chandler in 1884.

Two Letters to Ellen Axson Wilson

My own darling,   Princeton, Sunday, 10 Sept., '93

Your letters no sooner begin to come than Sunday intervenes to cut us off again. This letter will, I suppose, reach you some time on Tuesday. To-morrow's can not get to you till Wednesday

[September 13], the day on which you are to start for home. This letter and another, then,—after that, only to wait for the inexpressible joy in store for me on Friday, when, God willing, my treasure, my queen shall be in my arms again! Ah, Ellie, my matchless darling, for what,—for what that is sweet and precious, —do I not wait when I wait for you! You seem to me to contain, in your sweet person and your sweet nature, everything that is worth living for in the world,—besides duty. Duty is worth living for, no *man* could think otherwise; but there is often no *joy* in living for it. Everything connected with living for you is *full* of joy, if only it can be combined with living *with* you. I suppose there is *duty*, too, in living for you; but the duty never comes to the surface, so deep buried is it beneath the gladness that quickens every thought and every act that has you for its object. Nellie told the whole secret to-day. I said "Nen, *why* do you want mama to come back?" and she said, in that quick, sweet way of hers, "To *love* her!" That's the whole matter. To live with you is to love you: to live *for* you is to love you. Not only the sentiment but the life also is delightful because of its object. You call forth devotion very much as a keen air calls forth quick and active and joyous exercise, and the devotion is rewarded just as the exercise is, by a quickening of the whole nature. To love you is a liberal education, gotten without pains! If you could see me *now* and then see me after you get back! But you never see me except in your presence! Not that I am blue,—my love for you is too strong for that. Doubtless, too, I am *more* philosophical when you are away,—more given to sedate and equable thought,—less careless and more thoughtful,—more like a professor and the father of a family, less like a boy,—not less inclined to laugh, but less apt to laugh thoughtlessly, as a mere utterance of heart. You serve me as a sort of perpetual source of youth. The sort of love I have for you has no age: it is as much a young man's love as a mature man's. It is at once the pledge of youth and of manhood. You got it fresh and you keep it fresh. You are the companion of all my growth, whether of mind or of heart, and I associate you with all my ages. I loved you (oh, how passionately!) long before I ever saw you, for you are my ideal. You have been with me, in my desires, ever since I was a boy; you know and keep me close company as a man; you are all that I *would* be, brought into my life and kept constantly at hand, to excite my enthusiasm, to kindle my heart into a constant blaze of joy, a constant warmth of sweet life:—you are my queen, and I am   Your own   Woodrow

My own darling,   Princeton, Monday, 11 Sept., '93

This is my last letter: somehow that fact lightens my heart. I hope it is not selfish to feel so. I am unaffectedly willing that you should stay another week at the Fair, if you wish; but since you *are* coming home, it lifts a load of loneliness off my heart to think that I shall see you so soon. 'Tis an odd sort of loneliness, —not sad, for we are *all* perfectly well and are getting on without the least bit of trouble, and I love to think of you at the Fair—I don't *want* you back yet. My spirits are excellent, and my days very happy. But—as I have often expressed it before—my feeling is one of *suspended animation*, as if I were just existing provisionally, to begin my real *life* again when you come back. It is a singular sort of state to be in: placid enough, easy to maintain a very pleasant sort of content in,—quite as good a state as I was in while I was a bachelor, except that *then* I did not *know*, but only imagined, what I needed and was missing. When I was a bachelor I did not know what *full life* was; now I do know, and this state seems singular, empty, provisional. I love to live, but I can endure to exist. You, my love, taught me what it was to live: you drew me out to the height of all my powers—and are still constantly drawing me out. You not only *gave* me full life, but are constantly *giving* it to me. Bless you, my sweet, sweet wife, my Eileen. How I honour and admire and *love* you! You are so *reliable*, whatever a fellow may want,—whether sense, or sensibility, or imagination, or mere joy and *fun*! To possess you is to possess all resources!

You are so sensible, darling, in the way you are taking the Fair,—to judge by these sweet little letters,—not trying to "do" the huge affair, but only to enjoy it equably and without extreme fatigue. It makes me love you all the more to see you do so. But then everything makes me love you more! Stock and I sat in the dusk last evening in the most delightful discourse about you. He admires you—your "wonderful" critical faculty, your illuminating sense, your sweet womanliness and sterling strength of character—as much as he should—as much as he loves you. I enjoyed what he said more than fine wine. He said just what he ought to have said,—just what is true,—and said it with warm enthusiasm. And *I*—said more than I ever said to any one else about you, spoke of you as I never ventured to speak of you to anybody but yourself! You may imagine how I enjoyed the conversation! It helped me to dream about you. I saw your face in my dreams last night illuminated with the sweet colour and life that come into it when you are most interested and excited in the discussion of some favourite subject—saw it, in short *almost* at its best. Its *very* best and most beautiful expression you have been generous enough to reserve for my arms! Oh, my love, my life, you are coming back to me, to   Your own   Woodrow

ALS (WC, NjP).

EDITORIAL NOTE
"A CALENDAR OF GREAT AMERICANS"

The idea for "A Calendar of Great Americans" was conceived in the fertile brain of Walter Page, editor of the *Forum*, and the catalyst was Wilson's review of Goldwin Smith's *The United States*, printed at September 5, 1893. Page, excited by Wilson's characterization (in his review) of the Middle Colonies and the West as the cradles of true American nationality, proposed an essay on this theme. These facts we know from Wilson's letter to Lyman P. Powell of February 8, 1894.

Allowing for an ordinary lapse of time between submission of copy and its publication, we assume that Wilson sent this review to Page early in September. The absence in the Wilson Papers of a letter from Page about the proposed essay suggests that the editor went at once to Princeton after reading the review and persuaded Wilson, then and there, to write the essay. There is a hint that Page dealt with the matter in this fashion in the following portion of Wilson's later letter to his wife from Baltimore of January 31, 1894: "I am sorry that I missed Page's visit: my curiosity is piqued to know what he can be anxious enough to talk over with me to come all the way to Princeton for the interview. Doubtless he wants to cajole me into doing some big piece of work for the *Forum*, and I shall be saved the embarrassment of refusing him to his face."

The composition dates of September 5 and September 15, 1893, have been ascribed to the review and the essay, respectively, on the assumption, *inter alia*, that Wilson wrote both pieces before the beginning of the autumn term at Princeton. In any event, we can be reasonably certain that they were written soon after the Burke lecture printed at August 31, 1893, so striking is the relation between certain themes in the Burke lecture and in the review and essay.

An Historical Essay   *[c. Sept. 15, 1893]*

A CALENDAR OF GREAT AMERICANS.

Before a calendar of great Americans can be made out, a valid canon of Americanism must first be established. Not every great man born and bred in America was a great "American." Some of the notable men born among us were simply great Englishmen; others had in all the habits of their thought and life the strong flavor of a peculiar region, and were great New Englanders or great Southerners; other, masters in the fields of science or of pure thought, showed nothing either distinctively national or characteristically provincial, and were simply great men; while a few displayed odd cross-strains of blood or breeding. The great Englishmen bred in America, like Hamilton and Madison; the great provincials, like John Adams and Calhoun; the authors of such thought as might have been native to any clime, like Asa Gray and Emerson; and the men of mixed breed, like Jefferson and Benton,—must be excluded from our present list. We must pick out men who have created or exemplified a distinctively American standard and type of greatness.

To make such a selection is not to create an artificial standard of greatness, or to claim that greatness is in any case hallowed or exalted merely because it is American. It is simply to recognize a peculiar stamp of character, a special make-up of mind and faculties, as the specific product of our national life, not displacing or eclipsing talents of a different kind, but supplementing them, and so adding to the world's variety. There is an American type of man, and those who have exhibited this type with a certain unmistakable distinction and perfection have been great "Americans." It has required the utmost variety of character and energy to establish a great nation, with a polity at once free and firm, upon this continent, and no sound type of manliness could have been dispensed with in the effort. We could no more have done without our great Englishmen, to keep the past steadily in mind and make every change conservative of principle, than we could have done without the men whose whole impulse was forward, whose whole genius was for origination, natural masters of the art of subduing a wilderness.

Certainly one of the greatest figures in our history is the figure of Alexander Hamilton. American historians, though compelled always to admire him, often in spite of themselves, have been inclined, like the mass of men in his own day, to look at him askance. They hint, when they do not plainly say, that he was not "American." He rejected, if he did not despise, democratic principles; advocated a government as strong, almost, as a monarchy; and defended the government which was actually set up, like the skilled advocate he was, only because it was the strongest that could be had under the circumstances. He believed in authority, and he had no faith in the aggregate wisdom of masses of men. He had, it is true, that deep and passionate love of liberty, and that steadfast purpose in the maintenance of it, that mark the best Englishmen everywhere; but his ideas of government stuck fast in the old-world polities, and his statesmanship was of Europe rather than of America. And yet the genius and the steadfast spirit of this man were absolutely indispensable to us. No one less masterful, no one less resolute than he to drill the minority, if necessary, to have their way against the majority, could have done the great work of organization by which he established the national credit, and with the national credit the national government itself. A pliant, popular, optimistic man would have failed utterly in the task. A great radical mind in his place would have brought disaster upon us: only a great conservative genius could have succeeded. It is safe to say that, without men of Hamilton's cast of mind, building the past into the future with a deep passion for order and old wisdom, our national life would have miscarried at the very first. This tried English talent for conservation gave to our fibre at the very outset the stiffness of maturity.

James Madison, too, we may be said to have inherited. His invaluable gifts of counsel were of the sort so happily imparted to us with our English blood at the first planting of the States which formed the Union. A grave and prudent man, and yet brave withal when new counsel was to be taken, he stands at the beginning of our national history, even in his young manhood, as he faced and led the constitutional convention, a type of the slow and thoughtful English genius for affairs. He held old and tested convictions of the uses of liberty; he was competently read in the history of government; processes of revolution were in his thought no more than processes of adaptation: exigencies were to be met by modification, not by experiment. His reasonable spirit runs through all the proceedings of the great convention that gave us the Constitution, and that noble instrument seems the product of character like his. For all it is so American in its content, it is in its method a thoroughly English production, so full is it of old principles, so conservative of experience, so carefully compounded of compromises, of concessions made and accepted. Such men are of a stock so fine as to need no titles to make it noble, and yet so old and so distinguished as actually to bear the chief titles of English liberty. Madison came of the long line of English constitutional statesmen.

There is a type of genius which closely approaches this in character, but which is, nevertheless, distinctively American. It is to be seen in John Marshall and in Daniel Webster. In these men a new set of ideas find expression, ideas which all the world has received as American. Webster was not an English but an American constitutional statesman. For the English statesman constitutional issues are issues of policy rather than issues of law. He constantly handles questions of change: his constitution is always a-making. He must at every turn construct, and he is deemed conservative if only his rule be consistency and continuity with the past. He will search diligently for precedent, but he is content if the precedent contain only a germ of the policy he proposes. His standards are set him, not by law, but by opinion: his constitution is an ideal of cautious and orderly change. Its fixed element is the conception of political liberty: a conception which, though steeped in history, must ever be added to and altered by social change. The American constitutional statesman, on the contrary, constructs policies like a lawyer. The standard with which he must square his conduct is set him by a document upon whose definite sentences the whole structure of the government directly rests. That document, moreover, is the concrete embodiment of a peculiar theory of government. That theory is, that definitive laws, selected by a power outside the government, are the structural iron of the entire fabric of politics, and that nothing which cannot be constructed upon this stiff framework is a safe or legitimate part of policy. Law is, in his conception, creative of States, and they live only by such permissions as they can extract from it. The functions of the judge and the functions of the man of affairs have, therefore, been very closely related in our history, and John Marshall, scarcely less than Daniel Webster, was a constitutional statesman. With all Madison's conservative temper and wide-eyed prudence in counsel, the subject-matter of thought for both of these men was not English liberty or the experience of men everywhere in self-government, but the meaning stored up in the explicit sentences of a written fundamental law. They taught men the new—the American—art of extracting life out of the letter, not of statutes merely (that art was not new), but of statute-built institutions and documented governments: the art of saturating politics with law without grossly discoloring law with politics. Other nations have had written constitutions, but no other nation has ever filled a written constitution with this singularly compounded content, of a sound legal conscience and a strong national purpose. It would have been easy to deal with our Constitution like subtle dialecticians; but Webster and Marshall did much more and much better than that. They viewed the fundamental law as a great organic product, a vehicle of life as well as a charter of authority; in disclosing its life they did not damage its tissue; and in thus expanding the law without impairing its structure or authority they made great contributions alike to statesmanship and to jurisprudence. Our notable literature of decision and commentary in the field of constitutional law is America's distinctive contribution to the history and the science of law. John Marshall wrought out much of its substance; Webster diffused its great body of principles throughout national policy, mediating between the law and affairs. The figures of the two men must hold the eye of the world as the figures of two great national representatives, as the figures of two great Americans.

The representative national greatness and function of these men appear more clearly still when they are contrasted with men like John Adams and John C. Calhoun, whose greatness was not national. John Adams represented one element of our national character, and represented it nobly, with a singular dignity and greatness. He was an eminent Puritan statesman, and the Puritan ingredient has colored all our national life. We have gotten strength and persistency and some part of our steady moral purpose from it. But in the quick growth and exuberant expansion of the nation it has been only one element among many. The Puritan blood has mixed with many another strain. The stiff Puritan character has been mellowed by many a transfusion of gentler and more hopeful elements. So soon as the Adams fashion of man became more narrow, intense, acidulous, intractable, according to the tendencies of its nature, in the person of John Quincy Adams, it lost the sympathy, lost even the tolerance, of the country, and the national choice took its reckless leap from a Puritan President to Andrew Jackson, a man cast in the rough original pattern of American life at the heart of the continent. John Adams had not himself been a very acceptable President. He had none of the national optimism, and could not understand those who did have it. He had none of the characteristic adaptability of the delocalized American, and was just a bit ridiculous in his stiffness at the Court of St. James, for all he was so honorable and so imposing. His type—be it said without disrespect—was provincial. Unmistakably a great man, his greatness was of the commonwealth, not of the empire.

Calhoun, too, was a great provincial. Although a giant, he had no heart to use his great strength for national purposes. In his youth, it is true, he did catch some of the generous ardor for national enterprise which filled the air in his day; and all his life through, with a truly pathetic earnestness, he retained his affection for his first ideal. But when the rights and interests of his section were made to appear incompatible with a liberal and boldly constructive interpretation of the Constitution, he fell out of national counsels and devoted all the strength of his extraordinary mind to holding the nation's thought and power back within the strait limits of a literal construction of the law. In powers of reasoning his mind deserves to rank with Webster's and Marshall's: he handled questions of law like a master, as they did. He had, moreover, a keen insight into the essential principles and character of liberty. His thought moved eloquently along some of the oldest and safest lines of English thought in the field of government. He made substantive contributions to the permanent philosophy of politics. His reasoning has been discredited, not so much because it was not theoretically sound within its limits, as because its practical outcome was a negation which embarrassed the whole movement of national affairs. He would have held the nation still, in an old equipoise, at one time normal enough, but impossible to maintain. Webster and Marshall gave leave to the energy of change inherent in all the national life, making law a rule, but not an interdict; a living guide, but not a blind and rigid discipline: but Calhoun sought to fix law as a barrier across the path of policy, commanding the life of the nation to stand still. The strength displayed in the effort, the intellectual power and address, abundantly entitle him to be called great; but his purpose was not national. It regarded but a section of the country, and marked him—again be it said with all respect—a great provincial.

Jefferson was not a thorough American because of the strain of French philosophy that permeated and weakened all his thought. Benton was altogether American so far as the natural strain of his blood was concerned, but he had encumbered his natural parts and inclinations with a mass of undigested and shapeless learning. Bred in the West, where everything was new, he had filled his head with the thought of books (evidently very poor books) which exhibited the ideals of communities in which everything was old. He thought of the Roman Senate when he sat in the Senate of the United States. He paraded classical figures whenever he spoke, upon a stage where both their costume and their action seemed grotesque. A pedantic frontiersman, he was a living and a pompous antinomy. Meant by nature to be an American, he spoiled the plan by applying a most unsuitable gloss of shallow and irrelevant learning. Jefferson was of course an almost immeasurably greater man than Benton, but he was un-American in somewhat the same way. He brought a foreign product of thought to a market where no natural or wholesome demand for it could exist. There were not two incompatible parts to him, as in Benton's case: he was a philosophical radical by nature as well as by acquirement; his reading and his temperament went suitably together. The man is homogeneous throughout. The American shows in him very plainly, too, notwithstanding the strong and inherent dash of what was foreign in his make-up. He was a natural leader and manager of men, not because he was imperative or masterful, but because of a native shrewdness, tact, and sagacity, an inborn art and aptness for combination, such as no Frenchman ever displayed in the management of common men. Jefferson had just a touch of rusticity about him, besides; and it was not pretence on his part or merely a love of power that made him democratic. His indiscriminate hospitality, his almost passionate love for the simple equality of country life, his steady devotion to what he deemed to be the cause of the people, all mark him a genuine democrat, a nature native to America. It is his speculative philosophy that is exotic, and that runs like a false and artificial note through all his thought. It was un-American in being abstract, sentimental, rationalistic, rather than practical. That he held it sincerely need not be doubted; but the more sincerely he accepted it so much the more thoroughly was he un-American. His writings lack hard and practical sense. Liberty, among us, is not a sentiment, indeed, but a product of experience; its derivation is not rationalistic, but practical. It is a hard-headed spirit of independence, not the conclusion of a syllogism. The very aërated quality of Jefferson's principles gives them an air of insincerity, which attaches to them rather because they do not suit the climate of the country and the practical aspect of affairs than because they do not suit the character of Jefferson's mind and the atmosphere of abstract philosophy. It is because both they and the philosophical system of which they form a part do seem suitable to his mind and character, that we must pronounce him, though a great man, not a great American.

It is by the frank consideration of such concrete cases that we can construct, both negatively and affirmatively, our canons of Americanism. The American spirit is something more than the old, the immemorial Saxon spirit of liberty from which it sprang. It has been bred by the conditions attending the great task which we have all the century been carrying forward: the task, at once material and ideal, of subduing a wilderness and covering all the wide stretches of a vast continent with a single free and stable polity. It is, accordingly, above all things, a hopeful and confident spirit. It is progressive, optimistically progressive, and ambitious of objects of national scope and advantage. It is unpedantic, unprovincial, unspeculative, unfastidious; regardful of law, but as using it, not as being used by it or dominated by any formalism whatever; in a sense unrefined, because full of rude force; but prompted by large and generous motives, and often as tolerant as it is resolute. No one man, unless it be Lincoln, has ever proved big or various enough to embody this active and full-hearted spirit in all its qualities; and the men who have been too narrow or too speculative or too pedantic to represent it have, nevertheless, added to the strong and stirring variety of our national life, making it fuller and richer in motive and energy; but its several aspects are none the less noteworthy as they separately appear in different men.

One of the first men to exhibit this American spirit with an unmistakable touch of greatness and distinction was Benjamin Franklin. It was characteristic of America that this self-made man should become a philosopher, a founder of philosophical societies, an authoritative man of science; that his philosophy of life should be so homely and so practical in its maxims, and uttered with so shrewd a wit; that one region should be his birthplace and another his home; that he should favor effective political union among the colonies from the first, and should play a sage and active part in the establishment of national independence and the planning of national organization; and that he should represent his countrymen abroad. They could have had no spokesman who represented more sides of their character. Franklin was a sort of multiple American. He was versatile without lacking solidity; he was a practical statesman without ceasing to be a sagacious philosopher. He came of the people, and was democratic; but he had raised himself out of the general mass of unnamed men, and so stood for the democratic law, not of equality, but of self-selection in endeavor. One can feel sure that Franklin would have succeeded in any part of the national life that it might have fallen to his lot to take part in. He will stand the final and characteristic test of Americanism: he would unquestionably have made a successful frontiersman, capable at once of wielding the axe and of administering justice from the fallen trunk.

Washington hardly seems an American, as most of his biographers depict him. He is too colorless, too cold, too prudent. He seems more like a wise and dispassionate Mr. Alworthy, advising a nation as he would a parish, than like a man building states and marshalling a nation in a wilderness. But the real Washington was as thoroughly an American as Jackson or Lincoln. What we take for lack of passion in him was but the reserve and self-mastery natural to a man of his class and breeding in Virginia. He was no parlor politician, either. He had seen the frontier, and far beyond it where the French forts lay. He knew the rough life of the country as few other men could. His thoughts did not live at Mount Vernon. He knew difficulty as intimately and faced it always with as quiet a mastery as William the Silent. This calm, straightforward, high-spirited man, making charts of the western country, noting the natural land and water routes into the heart of the continent, marking how the French power lay, conceiving the policy which should dispossess it, and the engineering achievements which should make the utmost resources of the land our own; counselling Braddock how to enter the forest, but not deserting him because he would not take advice; planning step by step, by patient correspondence with influential men everywhere, the meetings, conferences, common resolves which were finally to bring the great constitutional convention together; planning, too, always for the country as well as for Virginia; and presiding at last over the establishment and organization of the government of the Union: he certainly—the most suitable instrument of the national life at every moment of crisis—is a great American. Those noble words which he uttered amidst the first doubtings of the constitutional convention might serve as a motto for the best efforts of liberty wherever free men strive: "Let us raise a standard to which the wise and honest can repair; the event is in the hand of God."

In Henry Clay we have an American of a most authentic pattern. There was no man of his generation who represented more of America than he did. The singular, almost irresistible attraction he had for men of every class and every temperament came, not from the arts of the politician, but from the instant sympathy established between him and every fellow countryman of his. He does not seem to have exercised the same fascination upon foreigners. They felt toward him as some New Englanders did: he seemed to them plausible merely, too indiscriminately open and cordial to be sincere,—a bit of a charlatan. No man who really takes the trouble to understand Henry Clay, or who has quick enough parts to sympathize with him, can deem him false. It is the odd combination of two different elements in him that makes him seem irregular and inconstant. His nature was of the West, blown through with quick winds of ardor and aggression, a bit reckless and defiant; but his art was of the East, ready with soft and placating phrases, reminiscent of old and reverenced ideals, thoughtful of compromise and accommodation. He had all the address of the trained and sophisticated politician, bred in an old and sensitive society; but his purposes ran free of cautious restraints, and his real ideals were those of the somewhat bumptious Americanism which was pushing the frontier forward in the West, which believed itself capable of doing anything it might put its hand to, despised conventional restraints, and followed a vague but resplendent "manifest destiny" with lusty hurrahs. His purposes were sincere, even if often crude and uninstructed; it was only because the subtle arts of politics seemed inconsistent with the direct dash and bold spirit of the man that they sat upon him like an insincerity. He thoroughly, and by mere unconscious sympathy, represented the double America of his day, made up of a West which hurried and gave bold strokes, and of an East which held back, fearing the pace, thoughtful and mindful of the instructive past. The one part had to be served without offending the other: and that was Clay's mediatorial function.

Andrew Jackson was altogether of the West. Of his sincerity nobody has ever had any real doubt; and his Americanism is now at any rate equally unimpeachable. He was like Clay with the social imagination of the orator, and the art and sophistication of the eastern politician, left out. He came into our national politics like a cyclone from off the Western prairies. Americans of the present day perceptibly shudder at the very recollection of Jackson. He seems to them a great Vandal, playing fast and loose alike with institutions and with tested and established policy, debauching politics like a modern spoilsman. But whether we would accept him as a type of ourselves or not, the men of his own day accepted him with enthusiasm. He did not need to be explained to them. They crowded to his standard like men free at last, after long and tedious restraint, to make their own choice, follow their own man. There can be no mistaking the spontaneity of the thoroughgoing support he received. He was the new type of energy and self-confidence bred by life outside the States that had been colonies. It was a terrible energy, threatening sheer destruction to many a carefully wrought arrangement handed on to us from the past; it was a perilous self-confidence, founded in sheer strength rather than in wisdom. The government did not pass through the throes of that signal awakening of the new national spirit without serious rack and damage. But it was no disease. It was only an incautious, abounding, madcap strength that proved so dangerous in its readiness for every rash endeavor. It was necessary that the West should be let into the play: it was even necessary that she should assert her right to the leading rôle. It was done without good taste, but that does not condemn it. We have no doubt refined and schooled the hoyden influences of that crude time, and they are vastly safer now than then, when they first came bounding in; but they mightily stirred and enriched our blood from the first. Now that we have thoroughly suffered this Jackson change, and it is over, we are ready to recognize it as quite as radically American as anything in all our history.

Lincoln, nevertheless, rather than Jackson, was the supreme American of our history. In Clay, East and West were mixed without being fused or harmonized: he seems like two men. In Jackson there was not even a mixture; he was all of a piece, and altogether unacceptable to some parts of the country,—a frontier statesman. But in Lincoln the elements were combined and harmonized. The most singular thing about the wonderful career of the man is the way in which he steadily grew into a national stature. He began an amorphous, unlicked cub, bred in the rudest of human lairs; but, as he grew, everything formed, informed, transformed him. The process was slow but unbroken. He was not fit to be President until he actually became President. He was fit then because, learning everything as he went, he had found out how much there was to learn, and had still an infinite capacity for learning. The quiet voices of sentiment and the murmurs of resolution that went whispering through the land, his ear always caught, when others could hear nothing but their own words. He never ceased to be a common man: that was his source of strength. But he was a common man with genius, a genius for things American, for insight into the common thought, for mastery of the fundamental things of politics that inhere in human nature and cast hardly more than their shadows on constitutions, for the practical niceties of affairs, for judging men and assessing arguments. Jackson had no social imagination: no unfamiliar community made any impression on him. His whole fibre stiffened young, and nothing afterward could modify or even deeply affect it. But Lincoln was always a-making; he would have died unfinished if the terrible storms of the war had not stung him to learn in those four years what no other twenty could have taught him. And, as he stands there in his complete manhood, at the most perilous helm in Christendom, what a marvellous composite figure he is! The whole country is summed up in him: the rude Western strength, tempered with shrewdness and a broad and humane wit; the Eastern conservatism, regardful of law and devoted to fixed standards of duty. He even understood the South, as no other Northern man of his generation did. He respected, because he comprehended, though he could not hold, its view of the Constitution; he appreciated the inexorable compulsions of its past in respect of slavery; he would have secured it once more, and speedily if possible, in its right to self-government, when the fight was fought out. To the Eastern politicians he seemed like an accident; but to history he must seem like a providence.

Grant was Lincoln's suitable instrument, a great American general, the appropriate product of West Point. A Western man, he had no thought of commonwealths politically separate, and was instinctively for the Union; a man of the common people, he deemed himself always an instrument, never a master, and did his work, though ruthlessly, without malice: a sturdy, hard-willed taciturn man, a sort of Lincoln the Silent in thought and spirit. He does not appeal to the imagination very deeply; there is a sort of common greatness about him, great gifts combined singularly with a great mediocrity; but such peculiarities seem to make him all the more American,—national in spirit, thoroughgoing in method, masterful in purpose.

And yet it is no contradiction to say that Robert E. Lee also was a great American. He fought on the opposite side, but he fought in the same spirit, and for a principle which is in a sense scarcely less American than the principle of Union. He represented the idea of the inherent—the essential—separateness of self-government. This was not the principle of secession: that principle involved the separate right of the several self-governing units of the federal system to judge of national questions themselves independently, and as a check upon the federal government,—to adjudge the very objects of the Union. Lee did not believe in secession, but he did believe in the local rootage of all government. This is at bottom, no doubt, an English idea; but it has had a characteristic American development. It is the reverse side of the shield which bears upon it the devices of the Union, a side too much overlooked and obscured since the war. It conceives the individual State a community united by the most intimate associations, the first home and foster-mother of every man born into the citizenship of the nation. Lee considered himself a member of one of these great families; he could not conceive of the nation apart from the State: above all, he could not live in the nation divorced from his neighbors. His own community must decide his political destiny and duty.

This was also the spirit of Patrick Henry and of Sam Houston,—men much alike in the cardinal principle of their natures. Patrick Henry resisted the formation of the Union only because he feared to disturb the local rootage of self-government, to disperse power so widely that neighbors could not control it. It was not a disloyal or a separatist spirit, but only a jealous spirit of liberty. Sam Houston, too, deemed the character a community should give itself so great a matter that the community, once made, ought itself to judge of the national associations most conducive to its liberty and progress. Without liberty of this intensive character there could have been no vital national liberty; and Sam Houston, Patrick Henry, and Robert E. Lee are none the less great Americans because they represented only one cardinal principle of the national life. Self-government has its intrinsic antinomies as well as its harmonies.

Among men of letters Lowell is doubtless most typically American, though Curtis must find an eligible place in the list. Lowell was self-conscious, though the truest greatness is not; he was a trifle too "smart," besides, and there is no "smartness" in great literature. But both the self-consciousness and the smartness must be admitted to be American; and Lowell was so versatile, so urbane, of so large a spirit, and so admirable in the scope of his sympathies, that he must certainly go on the calendar.

There need be no fear that we shall be obliged to stop with Lowell in literature, or with any of the men who have been named in the field of achievement. We shall not in the future have to take one type of Americanism at a time. The frontier is gone: it has reached the Pacific. The country grows rapidly homogeneous. With the same pace it grows various, and multiform in all its life. The man of the simple or local type cannot any longer deal in the great manner with any national problem. The great men of our future must be of the composite type of greatness: sound-hearted, hopeful, confident of the validity of liberty, tenacious of the deeper principles of American institutions, but with the old rashness schooled and sobered, and instinct tempered by instruction. They must be wise with an adult, not with an adolescent wisdom. Some day we shall be of one mind, our ideals fixed, our purposes harmonized, our nationality complete and consentaneous: then will come our great literature and our greatest men.

WOODROW WILSON.

Printed in the New York *Forum*, xvi (Feb. 1894), 715-27.

From Frederick Jackson Turner

Dear Professor Wilson: Madison, Wis Sept. 16, 1893

I send you this circular because I know you are interested in western ideals. The *kind* of growth promoted by the "limestone region" about Columbia is fully indicated by the circular.

Yours cordially   Fredr. J. Turner

ALS (WP, DLC). Enc.: Richard Henry Jesse, *The University of the State of Missouri* (Columbia, Mo., [1893]), printed circular.

EDITORIAL NOTE
WILSON'S TEACHING AT PRINCETON AND THE
JOHNS HOPKINS, 1893-97

During the autumn term of the academic year 1893-94, Wilson gave his junior and senior elective, outlines of jurisprudence, to 182 students[1] and used the notes described in Volume 7.[2] In the same term, he gave his annual advanced course, the history of law, to twenty-nine seniors, using the notes referred to in the Editorial Note, "Wilson's Teaching at Princeton, 1892-93."

In the copy for the Princeton catalogue for 1893-94, which he sent to the printer probably in early December 1893, Wilson announced that during the spring term in 1894 he would offer the two courses scheduled in the catalogue of the year before—international public law and administration. He did repeat the former, with 112 students enrolled, and he used the body of lecture notes described at March 8, 1892, Volume 7. However, as the news item from the *Daily Princetonian*, January 23, 1894, reveals, Wilson announced to his classes on January 22 that he would substitute a course in the history of English common law for the one in administration during the coming spring term. (The change, actually, was permanent.) Fifty seniors were enrolled in the new course in the spring of 1894.

Wilson's Course in the History of English Common Law

Wilson had announced a course in the history of English common law for 1891-92 in the program that he laid out in the Princeton *Catalogue* for 1890-91.[3] However, lack of time to prepare the new course had caused him to abandon it and to substitute one in administration, for which he had ample notes for lectures, in 1892.

There is some doubt about whether it was Wilson or his students who originated the idea of inaugurating the course in the history of English common law in 1894. The most reasonable explanation seems to be that Wilson, while giving his history of law course for the second time in 1893-94, realized more vividly than ever before that that course covered only Continental law; and that, since he was already giving an advanced course in American constitutional law, the one great gap in his pre-legal program was lack of coverage of the basis of American law, English common law. Hence his decision to drop the marginal course on administration and to develop the new one. However, the comment in Wilson's letter from Baltimore to his wife of January 27, 1894, about "that course on the Common Law

[1] This and the following figures on enrollments in Wilson's courses in 1893-94 are taken from President Patton's report to the Board of Trustees on February 8, 1894. "Minutes of the College of New Jersey, Vol. VII, February 10, 1887-February 8, 1894," bound ledger book (University Archives, NjP). This was the only time that Patton made such a report.

[2] See the Editorial Note, "Wilson's Teaching at Princeton, 1891-92," and the description of the jurisprudence notes printed at Sept. 26, 1891, both in Vol. 7.

[3] See the Editorial Note, "Wilson's Teaching at Princeton, 1890-91," Vol. 7.

which I have promised the Seniors when I get back," raises at least the possibility that the students in the history of law course themselves suggested that Wilson carry the story of the development of European law from the Continent to England. In any event—and it is probable that Wilson simply had his announcement of January 22 in mind when he referred to his promise to his seniors—he clearly intended his new course as a sequel to his general history of law and as a background for his course in American constitutional law.

Wilson's letter to his wife of January 27, 1894, also signals the beginning of his intensive reading and research in the subject matter of his new course. With notes for his administration lectures at the Hopkins already in hand, he had much free time during the next five or six weeks. Since he did not begin to write up the notes for his lectures on English common law until after his return to Princeton, and since he barely managed to stay ahead of his class to the end of the spring term, it is obvious that Wilson did most of his reading and research for these lectures while in Baltimore. He seems also to have prepared at this time the several outlines of his lectures and the outline of the major periods in the history of English law that survive in his Papers in the Library of Congress.

A clear idea of the scope of the course, including its expansion by notes prepared in 1898 and 1900, may be obtained from the description of his lecture notes printed at March 6, 1894. The notes for his introductory lecture, printed at March 6, 1894, and the final examination printed at May 14, 1894, give a good conspectus of the course in its first year. Some idea of the level of the lectures may be obtained from the notes on the parts and genesis of English law printed at April 2, 1894.

Characteristically, Wilson annotated his notes on English common law very carefully. Since only one substantive and well-annotated section is printed in this series, the following bibliography of Wilson's major sources and authorities (including those used for notes for additional lectures in 1898 and 1900) is offered in order to show the range of Wilson's reading in the field. The references to specific editions of certain volumes and of particular volumes come from Wilson's notes.

[Adams, Henry, et al.] Essays in Anglo-Saxon Law (Boston, 1876).
Blackstone, William, Commentaries on the Laws of England (4 vols., various edns.), Vols. II and III.
Boutmy, Émile Gaston, The English Constitution (London and New York, 1891). Used as the textbook in the course in 1894.
Broom, Herbert, Commentaries on the Common Law, 8th edn. (London, 1888).
Brunner, Heinrich, The Sources of the Law of England (Edinburgh, 1888).
Digby, Kenelm Edward, An Introduction to the History of the Law of Real Property, 4th edn. (Oxford, 1892).
Freeman, Edward Augustus, The History of the Norman Conquest of England, Its Causes and Its Results (6 vols., Oxford, 1869-79), Vol. V.
Green, John Richard, A Short History of the English People (New York, 1876).

Hale, Matthew, *The History of the Common Law of England*, 6th edn. (London, 1820).

Hare, John Innes Clark, *The Law of Contracts* (Boston, 1887).

Holmes, Oliver Wendell, Jr., *The Common Law* (Boston, 1881).

Maitland, Frederic William, "The Materials for English Legal History," *Political Science Quarterly*, iv (Sept. and Dec. 1889), 496-518, 628-47. Wilson seems to have relied upon these articles as guides, particularly to fugitive items such as Ernest D. Glasson, *Histoire du droit et des institutions politiques, civiles et judiciaires de l'Angleterre* . . . (6 vols., Paris, 1882-83), which Wilson cited incorrectly.

Pollock, Frederick, *Essays in Jurisprudence and Ethics* (London, 1882).

Pollock, Frederick, and Frederic William Maitland, *The History of English Law Before the Time of Edward I* (2 vols., Cambridge, 1895).

Pollock, Frederick, *The Land Laws* (London, 1883).

Stubbs, William, *Select Charters and Other Illustrations of English Constitutional History* . . . (Oxford, 1874).

Traill, Henry Duff (ed.), *Social England: A Record of the Progress of the People* . . . (6 vols., London, 1894-98), Vol. I. Wilson used Maitland's chapters on old English law, English law under the Normans and Angevins, and the growth of jurisprudence in the thirteenth century.

During the autumn term of the next academic year, 1894-95, Wilson offered his junior and senior elective, general public law, and his senior elective, the history of law. He very considerably recast earlier versions of the notes for both courses. Printed in their entirety, both at September 22, 1894, Volume 9, these notes not only give a comprehensive view of the content and level of Wilson's lectures but, because of their extensive annotation, also show very clearly the scope and depth of his reading and research in these two fields.

In the spring term of 1895, Wilson offered what he now called "The Development of English Common Law: the genesis, growth, character, and general principles of English law."[4] He also gave his junior and senior elective, American constitutional law. Wilson had, actually, rewritten the notes for the lectures in this course the year before, and they are printed in their entirety in this volume at their first composition date, March 2, 1894.

The complete notes for Wilson's second three-year cycle of lectures on administration at The Johns Hopkins University have been printed, along with Editorial Notes about them, in Volumes 6, 7, and 8. Wilson returned to Baltimore during the academic years 1893-96 to repeat his three-year cycle. He began a third cycle in 1897 but terminated his lectureship at the Hopkins in that year.

At Princeton, Wilson followed the program of alternating courses described above until 1897-98. Various documents in this and the next volumes—announcements, reading assignments, examinations, newspaper reports, etc.—will be printed to illustrate his classroom work until 1897.

[4] *Catalogue of the College of New Jersey at Princeton . . . 1894-95* (Princeton, N.J., n.d.), p. 42.

From Eugene Bouton[1]

Dear Sir: Bridgeport, Conn., Sept. 20, 1893.

In "The State," p. 503, Sec. 928, you say that "in the Connecticut legislature of that time the senate represented the towns, as the confederate units of the state, while the house represented the people directly. Even Connecticut has now abandoned this arrangement, &c."

The Connecticut constitution of 1776, continuing the charter of 1662, was enacted by "the Governor, and Council, and House of Representatives, in General Court assembled," so that it seems *technically* incorrect to speak of the senate.

The charter of 1662, p. 253 U. S. Charters and Constitutions, speaks of "One Governor, One Deputy-Governor, and Twelve Assistants, to be from time to time constituted, elected and chosen out of the Freemen of the said Company." It later, on same page, says, "the Assistants, and Freemen of the said Company, or such of them (not exceeding Two Persons from each Place, Town, or City) who shall be from Time to Time thereunto elected or deputed by the major Part of the Freemen of the respective Towns, Cities, and Places for which they shall be elected or deputed," &c.

It seems to me, therefore, that you have alleged of the house what is true of the senate and *vice versa*. I think the matter of town representation in Connecticut is still essentially the same as it was in those days.

My excuse for this suggestion is that I have occasion to set forth the same matter. If I am wrong, I shall be glad to be corrected. Trusting that this will be received in the same spirit in which it is written,[2] I am

Sincerely yours,   Eugene Bouton.

ALS (WP, DLC).
[1] Superintendent of Schools in Bridgeport, 1890-93.
[2] Wilson's reply is printed at Oct. 28, 1893.

From Wilson's Minutes of the Discipline Committee

Discipline Comm   Faculty Room   20 Sept., '93, Noon.
Hazing:[1]
———:[2]

Went out to tower[3] about one-half past seven and heard noise up by the tower; heard the freshmen say oh oh oh. Being moonlight I was seen. I managed to catch one; the rest disappeared in the corn field. ———, '96. Took the freshmen from a drugstore, where the freshmen were buying ink. Must have been right after supper.

Mr. ——

One night went down to Mrs. King's,[4] and asked for Mr. —— '97. Had not known him before; have no excuse for calling on him. Had heard that this man had a revolver, and we went to see if he would use it.

Had nothing to do with climbing up on the roof. But the first part of testimony is true. Denies being under the influence of liquor at Mr. Vanderbilt's.[5] Roomed at Vanderbilt's himself, this year. Admits that the hazers are his companions, among others. Admits that he was put out of Mr. Vanderbilt's because men were making a noise in his room. That was the reason he left Vanderbilt's. A freshman came in on this occasion; the fellows simply asked the man what he was doing. This freshman came up the steps and was called into the room by the fellows. This '97 man was ——. Admits that he was with the crowd which stood outside when a man climbed up to freshman's room at Mrs. King's. But this was not the same night. It was —— who was summoned to light up by the man on the roof.

Resolved Be directed to return home to await the action of the faculty in the case.

——: Admits that he was down at the tower, but says that it was merely as a spectator. Went down to the tower to see if anything was going on.

Resolved that he be directed to return home to await the action of the faculty in his case.

——.

At Mrs. King's on Saturday night midnight, Mr. —— and others came: tried to get in; said they were juniors and wanted to see a freshman with regard to tutors. Door shut. Then came around at 12 o'clock, night, climbed up on the porch. "Freshman light up and don't make any noise." The freshman did not do it, but went into the next room and locked himself in. —— rooms in University Hall.[6]

These same men came to the house of the Vanderbilts, acting as if under the influence of liquor.

Transcript of WWsh in body of notes described in n. 1 to the extract from the Princeton Faculty Minutes, Sept. 23, 1891, Vol. 7.

[1] These hearings signal the outbreak of an epidemic of hazing of freshmen by sophomores which prompted Dean James O. Murray to make a special report about the disturbances to the trustees on November 9, 1893, and the trustees to give their formal approval to the action taken by the Dean and the Discipline Committee against "the crime of hazing." "Minutes of the College of New Jersey,

Vol. VII, February 10, 1887-February 8, 1894," bound ledger book (University Archives, NjP). Wilson's typed and handwritten summaries of the evidence in these cases and most of those that follow in the documents through October 13, 1893, are in the Trustees' Papers, University Archives, NjP.

2 Hearings of the Discipline Committee, as well as that body's reports to the faculty, are printed with the names of culprits omitted because of the confidential nature of these records.

3 A water tower on what are now the grounds of the Graduate College of Princeton University.

4 Mrs. M. M. King, who kept a rooming house at 76 University Place.

5 Probably George O. Vanderbilt of 36 University Place.

6 Formerly the University Hotel, at the corner of University Place and Nassau Street.

From the Minutes of the Princeton Faculty

3 P.M., Wednesday, Sep. 20th, 1893.

The College was opened in the Chapel with the reading of the Scriptures, an address and prayer by the President, after which the Faculty met & the minutes of the meetings held in the vacation were read and approved. . . .

The Dean reported that Messrs. —— & —— of the Sophomore Class had been directed by the Committee on Discipline to return home for participating in hazing. . . .

From Wilson's Minutes of the Discipline Committee

Discipline Comm   Fac. room 22 Sept. '93

Case of ——, *'96*

Last night at about 8 o'clock saw a crowd of students crossing the tennis court. Walked out after them. Got out past Mr. German's [?] farm, heard them starting to haze. Could not approach in moonlight. Made the freshmen dance and whistle; made them sing we are jolly sophomores, we are freaks of freshmen. Then let two go: guying them until they got away. Had still another man left, doing something. Then made him run. "If we catch you again." I ran out and caught this fellow. The rest got away. Had freshmen out there between ½ and ¾ of an hour. "You do so and so: damn it don't stop until we tell you to. Don't bow: say yes sir."

—— (examined): deposition.

A slight number of the fellows, about 8, on the corner of Nassau and Chambers Streets. I met these fellows with three freshmen. Went with them down Bayard Avenue. I stayed with them the rest of the performance. One of the fellows (there were four I did not know) had nothing to do with the hazing. I think that he had the least to do with it of the rest. Seven or 8 sophomores. Knew about half of these. Taken with one of these men into a lot. Went with the others over the lot. The freshmen were made to sing, dance, etc. I was abreast of the freshman when I was caught.

Pleads that his father has Bright's Disease: the physicians warn against excitement. Afraid that if he were informed suddenly of this it might make him worse.

Discipline Comm. Fac. room 22 Sept. '93

Case of —— (Rush at freshman class-meeting 22 Sept., 1893.)

Warned the sophomores: "Now gentlemen, those freshmen have their meeting in there, and if you touch any of them you will be dealt with." Most of them then went away; only about 25 or 30 waited. He was keeping them back. —— knocked one of them down with his fist, while the man was running.

——. Leggett[1] saw [him] hit several men. I saw him later hitting the class men down Nassau Street. I told him that he must stop. Then he stopped and went home. Was active in keeping the class together after the rush.

——. Saw him hit a fellow. Hit with his fist.

Leggett examined: Saw him on the road to main street pushing a freshman several times. It was not hitting but pushing. Some 50 yards from the chapel where the meeting took place. Saw him pushing men back from coming out of the chapel.

—— '96 (examined) Heard what Dr. Patton said.[2] Denies striking him with his fist. Put his foot out, probably pushed the man with his hand. The freshman was a heavy man and fell forward quite heavily. The freshman was struggling towards him and I tripped him up. Did not strike the man at all. Was right at the 15 yards towards Dickinson Hall, next to the Library. After the affair went over to Nassau Street eating club. Had his back towards chapel door. The freshmen were made to run towards Dickinson Hall. Topley[3] was standing between him and the chapel where he could see very well what happened.

——, '96, was examined. Did not hear the President in the morning at the chapel, or hear Topley when he was ordering to disperse.

——, '96, heard the President. Was at the old chapel most of the time of the meeting—at the windows most of the time.

[1] William Leggett, a college night watchman.
[2] A warning against hazing, delivered apparently in an address in Murray Hall on the evening of September 21, or perhaps in an address to the student body not reported in the *Daily Princetonian*, Sept. 22, 1893.
[3] John W. Topley, a college proctor.

Topley spoke to him once, calling him by name, saying "That's enough of that." I was down on my knees at the time scuffling with somebody. Did not hear Topley say anything, not being near the door of the chapel at any time. Denies *intentionally* striking a blow of any kind. Topley says the blow was backhand—that was possible. I was in a crowd that was violently struggling; was down on the ground several times. This was because I was standing off to right-hand side of the walk. The crowd struck me and knocked me down; grappled once a man of his own class. Couldn't see with whom he came underhand. Went down in same direction that the freshmen went; went down with the general crowd; went to Chambers Street, where his club is. Supposes he was in crowd once (a small number of sophomores) of perhaps 25 men who formed in sort of crowd. Right on place when the calls of '96 this way were given. Constituted part of such groups as did form. He was with that part of the class that kept together.

Did not know men who were shipped last year for this offense. Understood the purpose of the President's remarks.

Transcript of WWsh in body of notes described in n. 1 to the extract from the Princeton Faculty Minutes, Sept. 23, 1891, Vol. 7.

From the Minutes of the Princeton Faculty

12 5 P.M., Saturday, September 23, 1893.
. . . The Committee on Discipline reported that Messrs. ——— (Sc. Sci) and ——— of the Sophomore Class had been directed to return home for participation in hazing. Also Mr. ——— of the Sophomore Class.

4 5' P.M. Wednesday, Oct. 4th, 1893
. . . The Dean reported in reference to recent cases of hazing, that the Committee on Discipline had ascertained the names of seven (7) persons who had been engaged in them and that their cases were undergoing investigation. . . .

From Wilson's Minutes of the Discipline Committee

Discipline Comm.   Faculty Room 5 Oct., 1893
Canal (———) Cases.
    Written statement read.
    ——— led the procession to which the written statement refers. ——— immediately behind ———, kicking him and otherwise abusing him.

——, —— [home address]. 21 Chambers Street. The eating club Mrs. Hamilton's.[1] Met him; the other freshman being a friend of mine. I went with —— in front. Followed with him, more or less: asked him if he did not mean to be fresh; pulled him around, asked him questions concerning his freshness. "Don't you think you are fresh[?]" He had to learn not to be. "My own language was a little off-color." Might have been both profane and obscene. Admits using language that he would not choose to say in the presence of the committee.

He had heard that there was going to be hazing: and wanted to be in on it; met the crowd with ——, told them not to hurt him much because he was a friend and was also on the track team.

40 men, anyway, in the crowd. Heard it generally talked about that this man had been very fresh and was to be hazed. There was a general understanding or rumor that this business was up. Heard it 3 or 4 days before that the man was to be taken out. Do not remember when the particular evening was fixed. It was before supper at any rate. Some time Sunday afternoon or Monday. Has no exact recollection of time.

The crowd was all friends of his. Had held him only a part of the time. Pulled body around, might have put sand on his face to rub the smile off. —— was kicked: I did it once with the flat of my foot. Had no say as to the direction taken. Some understood that he was to be taken from the varsity grounds: supposed that he would be taken down to the canal. The crowd was given a regular meeting place, at the corner as stated. The crowd not so large at the corner as at the canal.

At the canal we tackled him as if in football. No one put him in the canal. Told him to put his head in the canal: this only once. He was walked out about 5 yards when he jumped in. Some of the crowd started to run around after ——. He was held by the legs while he lay upon his stomach. He was given no push at all. His face was probably under water. It is said that —— was being hazed by another squad behind the —— squad. Heard rumors beforehand that others (freshmen) were to be there. No fun to take a man who is not fresh.

It was said that if the sophomores had not taken this man out that night the juniors and seniors would have done so.

My father is living. The Dean here read the laws of the college to Mr. ——. Had not read the laws. Did not know that it was necessary.

Sent home to await the action of the Faculty.

[1] Ida Hamilton, who ran an eating club at 21 Chambers Street.

——, '97 —— [home address]. Heard at the supper table (Mrs Lavake's)[2] that he was going to be taken out. Had been hearing sophomores talking about it for some time. Did go along and did shove him and kick him once. Went down as far as the canal, staying until he jumped in. Had no motive. Heard about the affair on Sunday, by some upperclassmen. That night those upperclassmen tried to get —— out of his room, in order that the sophomores might get at him. I did not know this fact at the time—heard it later in the evening. He was made to sing some songs, somebody tackled him and threw him down. Did not know what further was contemplated.

Saw Mr. —— but had nothing to do with that case. Saw ——'s head put into the canal. 4 or 5 fellows held him by the feet; he was carried towards the canal; they put his face down.

At the canal there must have been 50 men; at least 20 or 30 (upperclassmen among them, 4 or 5 perhaps—juniors, no senior class) The additional men came from various directions: generally understood the men went down to see it. No others in the establishment that night.

One freshman brought to my club the early part of the night before; he was made to act as a waiter. 6 or 7 men went with me from my club to the corner.

Knows of several juniors who have been egging the sophomores on to these sort of things. The rough fellows among the juniors.

Sent home to await the action of the Faculty.

——, —— [home town] '97. Eats at the Athletic Club with Mr. ——. Was behind accompanying the crowd that went with him. Was in the rear of the crowd all the time and just heard what went on. Understood the purpose of the proceeding. Had heard the general talk about the affair. Heard the talk that afternoon. Suggested by senior and junior classes, because of ——'s action. When he followed ——, he knew what would probably happen. Did not understand that going with the crowd would be considered hazing. Did not see —— after he was taken—did not see what was done at the canal—was fully 50 feet from him. I left the canal immediately after he swam the canal; went up to Brown Hall to Mr. ——'s room; spent about 5 minutes there. Went there with one other person. Then went to my own room, —— [address]. Saw —— in the middle of the crowd. Was told what was done to Mr. —— after he left. Thought it was a

---

[2] Juliet Stratton (Mrs. Thomas William) Lavake, who ran a boarding house at 148 Nassau Street.

good thing to do to him. Went down ready and willing to see what was done. Knew that —— expected to be hazed: asked some of the men to protect him (——). He went off with about 6 fellows from the club. Walked fast after him, after looking for his hat in the club house. Saw one junior and all the rest I saw were sophomores. The crowd at the canal was greater than that at the corner of the streets.

Sent home to await the action of the Faculty.

——, '96, —— [home town]. —— made no remark: started out behind ——. I said "Boys do not take this boy because he comes from the training table." I was told to shut up. First met by a few fellows; then reached the big crowd. Went over and talked with the bridge master. Talking to the bridge master when —— was being dealt with; only knew from report what was done to him. I was there after the crowd went up to the college. Went to the canal (1) because sorry to see —— carried off; I had told him what to say if he was molested. (2) Went to see the bridge keeper. Did not see anything else after the big crowd was reached. I was on the right hand side to the rear of the center, —— being some distance in front. —— was just behind ——. Discussed with other boys how to face up with ——. Entirely out of sympathy with the effort to haze ——. Did not know that —— was in the crowd until the crowd had gotten some distance down the road. Knew that —— was to be hazed very soon. Do not approve of any hazing that is violent. Did not leave the club house with Mr. ——. "Said nothing to me at all about protecting him that night." —— was selected because he struck a sophomore (——'s roommate) at the fire lighted by the fresh near Brown Hall.

——, '96, —— [home town].—Saturday afternoon after the football game, all the balls were taken in. I got a ball to kick. —— got the ball; I said "Please give that to me." He said "You have a terrible lot of nerve." I had never seen —— before (I had a broken collar bone) I was told afterwards that it was ——. I said to —— "As soon as my collar bone gets well I'll lick that fellow." Went to see Mr. —— once Saturday night to tell him that I would whip him. Mr. —— '96 was with me. Sunday night I was at the class prayer meeting; then went over to hear Dr. Purves. Went over to Dr. Macdonald.[3] Saw a crowd then starting to get —— out. Did not join it but went to my room.

[3] The Rev. Dr. George T. Purves, who preached at the evening service in the First Presbyterian Church on October 1, 1893; and Dr. Arthur Kendrick Macdonald, 11 University Place.

Understood Sunday night that —— was to be hazed the next night if possible. Next night at 5 o'clock, I went down and kicked the football. Lost my cap on the field: found it had been taken by —— '97. Stayed there until after 6 o'clock. Dressed in the field house. It was then only 7 o'clock. Then went over to the club house to find my cap. Came out and saw a crowd of sophomores right in front of Ivy Hall—4 or 5 men—who said they were waiting for ——. —— came out and I waited there. I said I was not going to have anything to do with hazing—was not within 20 feet of ——. Went down to the canal, not nearer than 20 feet, I saw them hazing him: I saw that once he fell down, on the way to the canal. At the bridge I stopped and saw nothing from then on. I had no reason for stopping. Was satisfied with seeing that he was hazed. Saw that he must have been hit.

Waited there ½ hour: the crowd was dispersed up and down the canal: waiting to hear from the crowd. After I heard the result, came back and went directly to room (——). In 10 or 15 [minutes] afterwards went down to the pool room. Walked around some, around about. Went to ——'s room in Reunion. Stayed there to eat. Then went to my own room.

I was 30 feet away from —— when he was seized. Stood in the field until they got some distance past; until some sophomores joined me and then went on. Kept carefully at a distance because —— had misled me and he was going to have a fight with me upon perfectly equal terms.

If I had seen the proctor I would have run. Board at Mrs. Hamilton's with ——. The club have had freshmen in to wait on them.

—— was accompanied by only one man, I think. Men were waiting for —— in every direction. Heard this from other men. Saw Mr. —— in the crowd; knew that he was to be hazed; was present when —— was hazed. He was hazed near the bridge—nearer than ——.

Same action.

——, —— [home address]. I was at the meeting of the scrub after the training table. I met the crowd; they passed me (in the same direction) as I went out. I was walking slow because of injury. I kept up with them and joined about the 3rd of 3 or 4 crowds. Saw Mr. —— possibly 30 or 40 feet. On the way to the canal saw the crowd pushing and surging and that's all. When I got to the canal, we (the —— party) stood and debated what to do with ——. I told the fellows I did not want to see him hazed. One of the men asked me to say that he was not hazed. I did not want to say anything more. There was no need to interfere. Did not see anything that I disapproved of. Approved of all that I saw except one thing: he was pushed down a bank against a wire fence. I heard that he was made to run on all fours: I was walking on toward the bridge. Went on; stopped; —— came up and walked up Canal Street with them. Knew that he was in an unlawful proceeding.

Faculty Room.   *Discipline Comm.*   7 October, 1893.

Resolved that —— be dismissed from college and that the faculty recommend to the trustees that —— be expelled from college. *Carried.*

Resolved that —— be finally dismissed from college. *Carried.*

Resolved that in the case of ——, his mother be informed that he cannot return to college. *Carried.*

Discipline Comm.   Faculty Room 9 Oct., 1893.

——, —— [home town]—Have been in Princeton up until Thursday night. Had to go down to get a suit. I came over from the dressing room with —— that afternoon. At the scrub meeting was beside ——. During the meeting asked if I would walk up with him. I promised to call to him; I was with ——. I called him and we started out together, we two. The crowd we met said "Here he is." They wanted to take him over. I said "Hold on, I promised to walk up with him." I was taken by the arms; and offered little resistance. ["]You had your fling last year; let him go on.["] Found out how many were going down, 4 or 5 of us followed the big crowd. Could not see the crowd, it was so far out.

Stood at the canal talking and doing nothing else. A small group of personal friends. Went to see the hazing, but did not want to be mixed with the affair at all. Understood that I was doing an illegal thing.

Told them that they could do what they pleased with —— except to chuck him in the canal. Understood that the threat was that he was to be thrown into the canal. First heard of the purpose that Monday. Did not hear [it] over Sunday. Have been attending mathematics class (sees Professor Rockwood). Once again this last week. Was not quite decided to get back until about a week after the term opened.

Said the above (about not putting —— in the canal) to men who were moving backwards and forwards between my crowd and the crowd that was hazing him.

Had talked with —— before supper about swimming canals. I knew then that he was going to be hazed.

Coming from the club house, we two were together; may have been some coming out behind; do not remember.

Do not remember that the crowd that first met us consisted of only 4 or 5 sophomores; there was suddenly a huge number of fellows. He was pulled back a considerable distance by those who seized him. I heard him say "——, ——!" I thought if there was to be a small crowd I would take him through. It was my sincere purpose at first to defend him.

Sent home to await the action of the Faculty.

Resolved that in the case of ——, his father be informed that he cannot return to the college.

Adjourned Meeting, 10 Oct. '93, same place

Resolved that —— be suspended until the 16th of January, 1894. Passed.

Resolved that Messrs —— and —— be suspended until the first of March, 1894, prepared for examination. Passed.

Chapel cases:

Resolved that Mr. ——'s suspension be continued until the first of November. Passed.

Resolved that Mr. —— be suspended until Thanksgiving. Passed.

Resolved that Mr. —— be suspended until the 16th of January, 1894. Passed.

Resolved that Mr. —— be dismissed from the college. Passed.

Transcripts of WWsh in body of notes described in n. 1 to the extract from the Princeton Faculty Minutes, Sept. 23, 1891, Vol. 7.

From the Minutes of the Princeton Faculty

4 5′ P.M., Wednesday, Oct. 11th, 1893.

... The Dean reported the action of the Committee on Discipline on the recent cases of hazing. Upon recommendation of the Committee It was Resolved That Mr. —— of the Sophomore Class ('96) be suspended from College until January 16th, 1894 for participation in hazing. In the cases of others guilty of the same offence but in varying degrees, in like manner it was Resolved that Mr. ——, of the Sophomore Class (Sc. Sci. '96), be dismissed from College.

Resolved That Mr. ——, of the Sophomore Class ('96), be suspended until November 1st.

Resolved That Mr. ——, of the Sophomore Class ('96), be suspended until Thanksgiving.

Resolved That Mr. ——, of the Sophomore Class ('96), be dismissed from College, and that the Faculty recommend to the Board of Trustees that he be expelled.

Resolved That Mr. ——, of the Freshman Class ('97. & Formerly of 1896 in Sc. Sci.), be finally dismissed from College.

Resolved That in the case of Mr. —— of the Freshman Class ('97 & formerly of 1896), his mother be informed that he cannot return to College.

Resolved That in the case of Mr. —— of the Sophomore Class ('96, Sc. Sci. & formerly of 1895 Sc. Sci.), his Father be informed that he cannot return to College.

Resolved That Messrs. —— and ——, of the Sophomore Class ('96), be suspended until March 1st, 1894, and be required to be ready upon their return for examination.

Resolved That Mr. ——, of the Sophomore Class ('96), be suspended until January 16th, 1894. . . .

A Report of the Committee on Special and Delinquent Students

Princeton, October 11th 1893.

The Committee on Special and Delinquent Students[1] respectfully reports to the Faculty that they have again examined the case of Mr. ——, who was dropped at the close of the last academic year.

The first review of the case was made when the June reports were completed. It then appeared that Mr. —— was dropped for the third time, and the Committee was accordingly of opinion that he ought to be withdrawn from college. In view of representations from Mr. ——'s father and from other quarters the case was again reviewed at the opening of college in September in order to show such leniency as could properly be allowed. The Committee arrived at a recommendation, which was approved by the Dean and afterwards by the President and adopted by a formal vote of the Faculty. That recommendation, thus adopted, allowed Mr. —— to go on with the Junior class, but declined his request to go on with his own class, and recited the facts in the case as follows:

"Mr. —— has been a student in this college for three years. During all that time he has been very irregular in his attendance

---

[1] This was a new standing committee of the faculty, appointed in the latter part of the spring term of 1893. In 1893-94, West was chairman and Daniels was secretary. Wilson became chairman in the following year.

on college exercises and very low in his scholarship. He has not passed the examinations of any term unconditioned. At the end of his Freshman year he failed to pass and would have been dropped, had not the Faculty exercised clemency in his case. At the end of the first term of Sophomore year he failed again; but, after promises of amendment and full warning as to the danger of his course, was given another trial. He has now failed for the third time. A case of such aggravated and persistent disregard of college duties rarely comes to the Faculty's notice."

Since then it has been urged in Mr. ——'s behalf that the validity of one of his June "conditions" was doubtful. This point had been previously raised and considered. It was clearly shown that neither the regularity nor the justice of the "condition" could be impugned. In this, the third review of the case, this point has been re-examined and the whole record searched again, Dr —— and his son, as well as others interested in his behalf, having been invited to meet with the Committee.

There are no facts in the case, which have not been considered previously[.] The only feature of note is Mr. ——'s petition to be allowed to pursue Senior studies as a Special Student, deferring his degree until his Junior deficiencies are made up, instead of going into the Junior class as required by the Faculty. The Committee cannot favor granting such a request. To do so would be to send into the studies of the Senior class a student whom we know to be unprepared and who would accordingly be likely once more to fail. It would also in our opinion destroy the moral effect of the discipline Mr. —— has incurred, and do marked injustice to other students, who, though less culpable than Mr. ——, have been dropped and required to repeat the year in which they failed, notwithstanding the fact that several of them petitioned to be made Special Students. It would reverse the policy of the college regarding special courses, which under the rule are not to be offered to those who fail in the regular course,—a rule of great value and one which this Committee has invariably observed,— a rule, moreover, which we feel should at least not be broken in a case of continued disregard of college duty.

The Committee feels that requiring Mr. —— to repeat the Junior year is a sufficiently mild penalty, and that the value of even this penalty depends on Mr. ——'s appearing in the exercises of the Junior class. If a student may go on with the studies of the Senior class after having failed successively in Freshman, Sophomore and Junior years, we feel there is little use in trying to maintain a standard of scholarship. If, moreover, when required to go back a class, a student may, by becoming a Special, really continue with his former class and thus have all the advantage of his old position, except that he defers his degree, it becomes very difficult to drop any student. And if this is done for Mr. —— alone, or for others only because it is first done for him, our discipline is thereby exposed to the charges of injustice and favoritism.

The Committee is therefore constrained to recommend that Mr. —— be required to join the Junior class at once or withdraw from college.[2]

Committee $\left\{\begin{array}{l}\text{Andrew F. West}\\\text{Woodrow Wilson,}\\\text{J. H. Westcott}\\\text{H. B. Fine}\\\text{W. M. Daniels}\end{array}\right.$

Hw MS. (WP, DLC).
[2] The faculty approved this recommendation at its meeting on October 11, 1893. The student chose to join the junior class, but did not receive his degree until 1896.

To Robert Bridges

My dear Bob,   Princeton, 12 Oct., 1893

Thank you sincerely for your letter.[1] I thought it not improper, between old friends, to let you discover the dedication of my "Old Master";[2] you have discovered it, and you have written about it in a way that goes to my heart—as so many of the things you have *done* for me have. I love and honour you, Bob, with a depth of feeling which I like to acknowledge. The dedication was made to please myself, by associating my name with yours. That you take pleasure in it is so [to] my clear, delightful gain.

As ever,   Affectionately Yours,   Woodrow Wilson

ALS (WC, NjP).
[1] It is missing.
[2] The dedication reads: "To Robert Bridges with hearty acknowledgment of long and tried friendship."

From Wilson's Minutes of the Discipline Committee

Discipline Comm.   Faculty Room 13 Oct., 1893 5 P.M.
Disorder in Chinaman's Shop, near Anderson's Shoe-Shop.

Last night Mr. —— ('95) and —— went into this shop,[1] about 9 or 9½. It was a mistake on Mr. ——'s part, as to the shop. The Chinaman denied having the laundry and the Chinaman called Mr. —— a son of a bitch. —— struck him and knocked him down. Acknowledges that he had taken 2 or 3 glasses of punch last night. But he was not drunk. The Chinamen are very fiery fellows, refusing to give the clothes. —— had no part in the affair at all. Both taken before the magistrate this morning and bound over in $200 bail. There was a town fellow in there at the same time.

Mr. ——'s case re-opened: Mr. —— exam.

Denies being intoxicated in his room: it was someone else, he says. Claims that Mrs. Vanderbilt[2] overcharged him. Claims that Mrs. Vanderbilt knew who it was that was sick from drinking on the night in question. Had not taken anything himself at all that night. The man who was sick was drinking in the room. Two fellows came up; one had a flask of wine. I had some lemons and some sugar, and they made lemonade and put the wine in it. I drank a little of this mixture. This was not the night of the hazing in his room. There was no drinking in his room on the night of the hazing. The drinking of the lemonade was some nights before the affair of the hazing. Denies being intoxicated at any time in Mrs. Vanderbilt's house. The vomiting out of the window was the night that the lemonade was taken. It must have been about 11 or 11:30 in the evening.

During the hazing sat in my room, asked the fellows some questions, but did not make him sing obscene songs. No one did that in my room. No such songs were sung. I wrote to every fellow concerned, and none of them could understand it. Have been looking for —— this afternoon but could not find him.

I intended to ask the man if he had a revolver or asking him if he was going to use it: this was my purpose when I went to Mrs. King's.[3] Does not know what he would have done if the men had resented these questions.

Remembers no singing on the night when the lemonade was taken. He went to the door when Mrs. Vanderbilt came, at the time of the vomiting, and Mrs. Vanderbilt must have known that I was not the man who vomited.

Mr. Vanderbilt came to the door on the night of the hazing, and said I wish your friends would leave the house. Same night —— was in my room, when outside the house, "I joined my friends in calling up to —— to come out, telling him that it would be best for him to come and have it out." When I returned that night; found the door bolted inside; went around to the side door, but that was locked. I then went away and slept elsewhere. Was told the next day to leave the house.

Mr. —— suspects that these charges are brought against him

because he refused to pay all that she charged for his room there.

Offers to prove every statement he has made. Sorry he was not warned. That night at Mrs. King's Mr. —— warned me and advised me to stop, and I had nothing further to do with it.

Transcript of WWsh in body of notes described in n. 1 to the extract from the Princeton Faculty Minutes, Sept. 23, 1891, Vol. 7.
1 Probably Sing Lee's laundry, at 140 Nassau Street.
2 Probably Mrs. George O. Vanderbilt of 36 University Place.
3 Mrs. M. M. King of 76 University Place.

To Azel Washburn Hazen

My dear Friend,   Princeton, New Jersey, 17 October, 1893

Alas! it is not possible.[1] I wish I *could* say 'Yes'; nobody, I am sure, could enjoy more than I should, being with you and taking part in the services you have planned.[2] But *all* my college work here comes on Mondays and Tuesdays: our work is so bunched here that to take one day from it is to take a great deal, and we make it a point of honour not to "cut." To be absent on a Monday, in short, would be a simple dereliction of duty, and I *must* decline,—you would not wish me to do otherwise.

That I shall be with you in spirit I need not tell you. Quite apart from my very deep interest in the church itself, and even affection for it, anything that engages your interest must, out of sympathy, engage mine.

This is a Tuesday and I must stop with these few lines: I write now rather than keep you waiting for a reply—yesterday I could not write even a line. But it does not take many words to carry a great burden of affection. Mrs. Wilson and I do not find that separation makes any difference or causes any abatement in our warm regard for you both. She sends her love.

Affectionately Your Friend,   Woodrow Wilson

ALS (in possession of Frances Hazen Bulkeley).
1 Hazen's letter to which this was a reply is missing.
2 To be held in the North, or First, Congregational Church of Middletown, Conn., of which Hazen was the pastor and the Wilsons were still members.

From the Minutes of the Princeton Faculty

4 5′ P.M., Wednesday, Oct. 18th, 1893.

. . . Upon the report of the Committee on Discipline it was Resolved That Mr. —— of the Sophomore Class ('96), for participation in hazing, be suspended from College until March 1st, 1894. . . .

The subject of the Foot-Ball Game between Yale and Princeton in New York on Thanksgiving Day was discussed[1] and, The Dean and Professors Wilson and Fine were appointed a Committee to report in reference to arrangements for the Game.[2] . . .

[1] This discussion was set off by fear that there would be a repetition of the rioting and disorders that had accompanied football games between Princeton and Yale in New York City in recent years.

[2] The committee's report is printed at Nov. 1, 1893.

A News Item

[Oct. 19, 1893]

FALL HANDICAP GAMES.

The annual handicap games of the Princeton Track Athletic Association, were held yesterday afternoon. Although but one record was broken, that of the Freshman 440 yards, which was lowered by one second, the games on the whole were very good. The light weight cane spree was especially good; the contestants being compelled to compete in two rounds. . . .

The officials of the day were: Referee, Prof. Woodrow Wilson; Judges, Max Farrand '92, P. Vredenburgh '92, Irving Brokaw '93. . . .

Printed in the *Daily Princetonian*, Oct. 19, 1893.

The Boston *Beacon*'s Review of *An Old Master*

[Oct. 21, 1893]

POLITICAL ESSAYS BY WOODROW WILSON.

How agreeable the study of political topics may be made under the guidance of an intelligent thinker and an accomplished writer is once more practically demonstrated in *An Old Master and Other Political Essays*, by Professor Woodrow Wilson, who holds the chair of jurisprudence in Princeton University (Charles Scribner's Sons, 12mo, pp. 181, $1.00). The first essay, giving its title to the volume, is a remarkably instructive appreciation of Adam Smith as a lecturer, in which art he was indeed "an old master." Following this is a thoughtful discussion of methods in "The Study of Politics," wherein the closet philosopher is relegated to his proper position as a theorist, and the truth insisted upon that a practical knowledge of details is essential, but that these details are only raw material to be put into related form. The economist, says Professor Wilson, must be a literary artist and bring his discoveries home to the imagination. The science of politics, he declares, is the science of the life of man in society.

"Nothing which elucidates that life ought to be reckoned foreign to its art, and no picture of that life can perish out of literature. Ripe scholarship in history and jurisprudence is not more indispensable to the student of politics than are a constructive imagination and a poet's eye for the detail of human incident. The heart of his task is insight and interpretation. . . . His materials are often of the most illusive sort, the problems which he has to solve are always of the most confounding magnitude and variety." Professor Wilson has an admirable essay on "Political Sovereignty," thoroughly logical in reasoning and lucid in form. His exposition of the organic quality of the law-making power is excellent. The key-note of the next essay, that on "Character of Democracy in the United States," is the insistence on the need of deference to leadership if we are to have a compact and enduring national life. In discussing "Government Under the Constitution" Professor Wilson suggests the advisability of fastening upon Congress a more positive form of accountability that now rests upon the President and the federal courts. Instead of the present arrangement of compromise, piecemeal legislation, we must have, according to Professor Wilson, coherent plans from recognized party leaders and means for holding these leaders to a faithful execution of their declared purposes. The book is readable from beginning to end, for it is written in clear-cut English, and is graceful, yet forcible, in expression. It ought to have a decidedly stimulative effect on political thought; and in guiding the student of politics to a rightful understanding of the dignity and importance of the subject, as well as in inculcating correct methods, its educational value is indisputable.

Printed in the Boston *Beacon*, Oct. 21, 1893.

From the Minutes of the Princeton Faculty

4 5′ P.M., Wednesday, Oct. 25th, 1893.
. . . The Committee in reference to the arrangements for the Foot-Ball Game on Thanksgiving Day presented a report and resolutions which were made the order of the day with the Dean's business Nov 1st. . . .

To Eugene Bouton

My dear Sir,   Princeton, New Jersey, 28 October, 1893.
    Let me thank you very sincerely for your letter of September 20th. I take such corrections as acts of genuine kindness. I have

not replied sooner because, when your letter came I was ill, and since recovering I have had heavy arrears of work to make way with.

As for the matter in question, you are certainly right. My attention has been called to it before; and I think that you will find a more accurate statement of the same thing in the sentence which passes from p. 473 to p. 474,—at least if you have the later edition of the book. I neglected to alter at that revision the passage you so kindly cite. I shall mark it for correction the next time the plates are altered. I am sincerely obliged to you for your letter.   Very truly Yours,   Woodrow Wilson

WWTLS (WC, NjP).

From George Platt Brett[1]

Dear Sir: New York, Oct. 30, 1893

For several years past we have felt the desirability of having on our list some book which could be used as a text-book or as a book of reference for the young students or indeed for the ordinary citizen of this country relative to his rights and duties. We have felt perhaps that with our mixed population there could be no more important part of education than that destined to fit the boy or young man for his duties when he should be ready to exercise the franchise and thus bear a part in the government of the country.

To a certain extent this want has been felt in England also, more especially since the recent extension of the franchise but it can hardly be as important a matter there as in this country where, as we have said before, so many different nationalities are found in our higher and lower educational institutions.

To meet this need on the other side our London house has prepared a little book which they call "The English Citizen: His Life and Duties,"[2] a copy of which we are taking the liberty of sending to you by even mail herewith.

It has been suggested to us that you might not be unwilling to prepare for us a somewhat similar book for the United States on American lines that would answer the same purpose in this country and we venture to request that you will kindly take the matter into consideration writing us at your convenience as to the possibility of your doing something of the kind for us.

We shall be happy to arrange with you for the book either on a royalty basis, or what in the success of the book itself would prove a more profitable arrangement to you, i.e. the half profit plan, or if you preferred we should be glad to entertain the proposal to pay you a certain sum for the production of such a work if you found it possible with your numerous duties to entertain the idea.

Trusting that at any rate we may be favored with a reply from you indicating the feasibility of the plan from your standpoint,[3]

We are,   Yours very truly,   Macmillan & Co:

Dictated by Mr. Brett.

TLS (WP, DLC).
[1] Resident partner of the American branch of Macmillan & Company of London.
[2] Charles Henry Wyatt, *The English Citizen: His Life and Duty. A Book for Continuation Schools* (London, 1893).
[3] Wilson's reply is missing, but in it he undoubtedly declined Brett's invitation, explaining that he had agreed to write a similar book for D. C. Heath & Company. About this projected book, see the Editorial Notes, "Wilson's Plan for a Textbook in Civil Government," Vol. 5, and "Wilson's Elementary Textbook in American Government," Vol. 6.

From the Minutes of the Princeton Faculty

4 5′ P.M., Wednesday, Nov. 1st, 1893

The faculty met. The Report and Resolutions of the Committee in reference to the Foot Ball Game in New York on Thanksgiving Day were then taken up (V.p. 491), considered and adopted and are as follows.

Report adopted and action taken.

The Faculty, having considered fully the subject of the evils connected of late years with the Foot-Ball Game in New York on Thanksgiving Day, desire to put on record the following minute.

1. They cordially approve the action of the Foot-ball management in requesting the Municipal Authorities of New York City to arrest any Princeton Students who may be found guilty of disorderly conduct.[1]

They recognize, however, the necessity of further steps, in view of the disorders attending the game and the injury thereby inflicted on the College and therefore

2. They appeal to the Alumni of the College to exert their influence in every way possible, to redeem the game from these objectionable features.

3. They would also express the wish that the President should address the College on the subject, setting forth the convictions of the Faculty as to the immoralities alleged to be attendant on the game.[2]

Finally the Faculty is constrained to inform all concerned,

that, should the efforts named above prove ineffectual in reforming these evils, they must at once take into consideraton the question of forbidding the Game on that day in New York City.

Upon the recommendation of the same Committee the Faculty adopted the following

Resolutions in reference to the Thanksgiving Recess: Resolved, That the Thanksgiving Recess shall begin on Wednesday, November 29th, at noon, and end on Thursday, November 30th, at twelve, midnight;

That all students who do not previously present through the Registrar, written requests from their parents that they be allowed to remain at home until Friday morning, December 1st, shall be required to register by twelve, midnight, Thursday, Nov. 30th;

That all students who present the written requests aforesaid shall be permitted to register by twelve, noon, Friday, December 1st; only the absences actually incurred by them on that day being recorded against them; and

That the penalty for failure to register within the time named shall be the forfeiture of the whole gratuity for the ensuing quarter.[3]

[1] This action went unreported in the *Daily Princetonian*.

[2] If President Patton ever made such an address, it was not reported in the *Daily Princetonian*.

[3] This report was printed in the *Daily Princetonian*, November 3, 1893. However, news of the faculty's action must have been circulated on the campus on November 1 and 2, for the student body met in mass meeting on November 3 and adopted a resolution which, after explaining that most of the "shameful" disorders that had accompanied the Princeton-Yale games had been the work of persons unconnected with the college, promised that Princeton students would engage in "no disorder nor breach of the public peace or decorum in any form." *Daily Princetonian*, Nov. 3, 1893.

Princeton defeated Yale 6 to 0 in a bitterly contested game played at Manhattan Field in New York on November 30. "The gentlemanly conduct of all Princeton men while in New York during the last few days was commendable," the *Daily Princetonian* editorialized in its issue of December 2, 1893. "The college to a man disapproves of any unseemly behavior, realizing that it reflects great discredit, not only upon the men themselves but upon the college. They have shown that even in time of victory, when they are more than ever inclined to give way to their feelings, they can conduct themselves in a manner above reproach. This fact, as far as Princeton is concerned, goes a great way toward insuring us the Thanksgiving day games of future years."

EDITORIAL NOTE
WILSON'S LECTURES AT THE BROOKLYN INSTITUTE OF ARTS AND SCIENCES

The Brooklyn Institute of Arts and Sciences was an outgrowth of the Brooklyn Apprentices' Library Association, chartered in 1824, and its successor, the Brooklyn Institute, founded in 1843. The Brooklyn Institute was reorganized in 1890 as the Brooklyn Institute of Arts and Sciences, with Franklin William Hooper (connected with the old Institute since 1888) as director. By 1893 the Institute was well established as the center of the cultural life of the borough. Among other things, it offered a series of public lectures and extension courses, held usually in the lecture rooms of the Brooklyn Y.M.C.A. and the Brooklyn Art Association.

In response to Hooper's invitation,[1] Wilson gave a course of six lectures on "The Character of the Constitutional Government of the United States" on November 16, November 23, December 7, December 14, December 21, and December 28, 1893. If Wilson prepared a syllabus that was printed, it has not survived. The reports of the Institute and of the New York, Brooklyn, and Princeton newspapers tell us merely that he gave his lectures on schedule. Hence Wilson's notes for these lectures, printed below in a body, yield the only significant available evidence of the coverage of the course.

As for the notes themselves, readers familiar with this series will very quickly recognize that the lectures on constitutional government, written constitutions, the theory and practice of the American government, the organization and powers of Congress, and the functions of the courts were mainly digests of Wilson's lectures on these subjects at the New York Law School and in his course on American constitutional government at Princeton.[2] However, the lecture on political liberty was substantially new, the only explicit harbinger of it having been the talk or sermon that Wilson delivered in Marquand Chapel at Princeton on May 7, 1893.[3] Wilson gave his lecture, "Political Liberty," many times later. The fullest text of it is printed at December 20, 1894, Volume 9.

[1] See F. W. Hooper to WW, Aug. 17, 1893.
[2] See the Editorial Notes, "Wilson's Lectures at the New York Law School" and "Wilson's Teaching at Princeton, 1890-91," both in Vol. 7.
[3] The notes for this talk are printed at May 7, 1893.

Notes for Lectures at the Brooklyn Institute of Arts and Sciences

[c. Nov. 15-Dec. 27, 1893]

I.

WHAT IS CONSTITUTIONAL GOV'T?

Vitality and New Importance of the Subject. Is there relaxation? *Our specialized idea* of a constitution.

What is a constitution, and *where and how* did the idea arise of a separate and distinct body of constitutional law? A POWER OUTSIDE THE GOVERNMENT.

England's a test case: What can Parliament change?
"The Eng. constitution has no real existence."—*de Tocqueville.*

The State vs. the GOVERNMENT. Origination of the first, outside constitutional, or other positive, law.

Written constitutions make the existence of the State more explicit, but not more real.

A *constitutional State*, a self-conscious, adult, self-directed State.

Elements: A *law-making body representative* of the State, not of the government. To direct and control the Gov't.

An *Administration subject* to the laws.

A *Judiciary secured* against corrupt or other improper influences.

A *more or less careful and complete formulation* of the rights of individuals as against the government.

Federal constitutional law transitional? A vehicle for the unification of habit and law. For the national sentiment and purpose.

Our own constitutional law a complex of historical pieces, to be interpreted by the logic of history, as Marshall interpreted it.

II.

POLITICAL LIBERTY.

Liberty, a word of enthusiasm,—adventure,—heroism,—romance. A word *also of license and folly*, stained with bloodshed and crime.

Enjoyment of Liberty vs. Speculation about it: the nations which have had it, and those which have desired it.

Institutions vs. Natural Rights. The nations which have enjoyed liberty have found it in institutions: by practice, not by analysis.

Absence of speculation, abundance of hard-headed practice *in English politics*.

Liberty is of Order and Union, not of Separation or contest. It is an antimony, not of Society, but of rigid and arbitrary authority, of an unchecked and arbitrary choice of Order by the Government: restraint by friction. *It is restraint by adjustment* and coöperation.

Can a man do without Society? He is free in nothing in which he is alone.

The State is neither a mere necessity nor a mere convenience, but *an abiding natural relationship*; the invariable and normal embodiment and expression of *a higher form of life than the individual*: of *that common life which gives leave to the individual life*, and opportunity for completeness:

makes it possible; makes it full and complete: *makes it spiritual*.

The State directly conditions both the existence and the competence of the individual:

Authenticates his personality and status;

Economic guardian (post, telegraph, coin, weights, etc.).

Spiritual god parent (Education, suppression of vice).

Health (Sanitation, licensing physicians, etc.).

Means of knowledge underlying reform (Statistics)

Liberty is a systematic balance between private right and public power: between assistance and interference.

It is such an adjustment as will give individual spirit *free play*, as a contribution to the general variety of force: not in separation, but *in coöperation*. A man is free in nothing in which he is alone,—helpless.

Ruskin—"*How false is the conception*, how frantic the pursuit, of that treacherous phantom which men call Liberty! There is no such thing in the universe. There never can be. The stars have it not; the earth has it not; the sea has it not; and we men have the mockery and semblance of it only for our heaviest punishment.

The enthusiast would reply that by liberty he meant *the Law of Liberty*. Then why use the single and misunderstood word? If by liberty you mean chastisement of the passions, discipline of the intellect, subjection of the will; if you mean the fear of inflicting, the shame of committing, a wrong; if you mean respect for all who are in authority, and consideration for all who are in dependence; veneration for the good, mercy to the evil, sympathy with the weak; if you mean watchfulness over all thoughts, temperance in all pleasures, perseverance in all toils; if you mean, in a word, *that Service* which is defined in the liturgy of the English church to be *perfect Freedom*, why do you name this by the same word by which the luxurious mean license, and the reckless mean change; by which the rogue means rapine, and the fool, equality; by which the proud mean anarchy, and the malignant mean violence? Call it by any name rather than this, but its best and truest is, *Obedience*.

Obedience is, indeed, *founded on a kind of freedom*, else it would become mere subjugation, but that freedom is only granted that obedience may be more perfect; and thus, while a measure of license is necessary to exhibit the individual energies of things, the fairness and pleasantness and perfection of them all consist in their restraint. *Compare a river* that has burst its banks with one that is bound by them, *and the clouds that are scattered* over the face of the whole heaven with those that are marshalled into ranks and orders by its winds. So that though restraint, utter and unrelaxing, can never be comely, this is not because it is in itself an evil, but only because, when too great, it overpowers the nature of the thing restrained, and so counteracts the other laws of which that nature is itself composed. And *the balance wherein consists the fairness of creation* is between the laws of life and being in the things governed and the laws of general sway in which they are subjected; and the suspension or infringement of either kind of law, or, literally, disorder, is equivalent to, and synonymous with, disease; while the increase of both honour and beauty is habitually on the side of *restraint* (or the action of superior law) *rather than of character* (or the action of inherent law). The noblest word in the catalogue of social virtue is 'Loyalty,' and the sweetest which men have learned in the pastures of the wilderness is 'Fold.'

Nor is this all; but we may observe, that *exactly in proportion to the majesty of things in the scale of being* is the completeness of their obedience to the laws that are set over them. *Gravitation* is less quietly, less instantly obeyed by a grain of dust than by the sun and moon; and *the ocean* falls and flows under influences which the lake and river do not recognize. So also in estimating the dignity of any action or occupation of men, there is perhaps no better test than the question, '*are its laws strait*'? For their severity will probably be commensurate with the greatness of the numbers whose labours it concentrates or whose interest it concerns."

> *Ruskin*: "*Seven Lamps of Architecture*": the "Lamp of Obedience."

History and character of English Bills of Rights, and, derivatively, of our own:

> *Negative and practical*: meant, not to keep the hands of gov't off, but simply *to prevent irregular and arbitrary exercises of power.*

> *The difference between liberty and despotism* is a difference simply *in the kind, spirit, and degree of obedience.*

Constitution of Government vs. Constitution of Liberty: Organization vs. Delimitation of sphere, accommodation of elements.

Differences: (1) *In Age*. Ancient constitutions distributed power but did not recognize rights.

(2) *In Character*: organization vs. restraint.

(3) *In Source*: Liberty proceeds necessarily from a power outside government: gov't may give itself organization.

(4) *In Necessary Distinctness*.

Legal aspects of Socialism: Socialistic schemes reverse the historical order of development, strengthening and consolidating government in order to realize Liberty. Never done so in the past.

A *"constitutional government,"* not one which has a constitution merely, of course; but *one which is restrained in some systematic way by the recognition of Liberty*.

CAN a man, then, *"do what he will with his own?"*

"Slight those who say, amidst their sickly healths,
Thou livest by rule. What doth not so but man?
Houses are built by rule and Commonwealths.
Entice the trusty sun, if that you can,
From his ecliptic line; beckon the sky.
Who lives by rule, then, keeps good company.

"Who keeps no guard upon himself is slack,
And rots to nothing at the next great thaw;
Man is a shop of rules: a well-truss'd pack
Whose every parcel underwrites a law.
Lose not thyself, nor give thy humours way;
God gave them to thee under lock and key."

George Herbert.[1]

III.

WRITTEN CONSTITUTION
NATURE, ORIGIN, AND SIGNIFICANCE OF OUR OWN.

Review: "Constitution of Government" *vs*. "Const. of Liberty."

Have we really deemed soberly of the nature of our written constitutions?

Two theories: (1) *Phenomenal*, of something unprecedented, the product of a peculiar and original national genius.

(2) *The opposite*: a mere business creation: the government of the U. S. put on a par with the Penn. R. R. Co.

History, the sovereign corrective of theory:

The Derivation of the original state constitutions:

Source: the will of the king.

---

1 From George Herbert, "The Church Porch" in *The Temple*. [Eds.' note]

Legal Character: Corporations, though public corporations, with high governmental functions.

The colonial legislatures non-sovereign: A non-sovereign law-making body: "First, the existence of laws affecting its constitution which such body must obey and cannot change; hence, secondly, the formation of a marked distinction between ordinary laws and fundamental laws; and, lastly, the existence of some person or persons, judicial or otherwise, having authority to pass upon the validity or constitutionality of laws passed by such law-making body."

Transition to statehood: No longer corporations, but possessing constitutions modelled upon the charters and giv[ing] their legislatures the same non-sovereign charcater.

N. B. Arrangements of local government not created, but taken for granted, recognized.

Principles of Reconstruction: Not essential change, but simply practical adaptations of colonial institutions.

Derivation of the Federal Constitution. Here, also, we have growth, though a very rapid growth.

Previous arrangements:

The Continental Congress (1774-1781) A consulting, advisory, coöperative body, without any regular constitution, but accumulating, so long as the war lasted, the sort of authority which was inevitable under the circumstances.

Articles of Confederation: Made previous arrangements, which had been tacit and habitual, formal and explicit.

Maryland and the Northwest Territory. The Ordinance of 1787. *Reconstitution on the part of the States* meanwhile, making provision in some cases for the regular appointment of delegates to Congress.

Method of considering and effecting a Change:

1785, Md. and Va. at Washington's house.

1786, Sept., five States at Annapolis.

1787, The Constitutional Convention.

All of this extra-constitutional.

The making of the Constitution: Derivation of its various provisions from the several state constitutions

Revolutionary Method of Adoption: "Nor shall any alteration at any time hereafter be made in any of them, unless such alteration be agreed to in a Congress of the United States, and be afterwards confirmed by the Legislatures of every State," Art. XIII.

A Fresh Creation: If revolutionary in origin, the new government was a fresh creation, not an amendment of the Articles. It must therefore have had, if not a different, at least a separate legal character. The States for themselves, and not as members of the Confederation, acceded to it, and it was regard[ed] at the time as a compact, a fresh compact.

Conclusions: Our definition of a constitutional gov't again: a gov't watched and restrained in the interests of liberty: the freest relations (or the best adjusted) between man and man. Our consts. vehicles of experience, with a certain amount of the old ideas about corporations still clinging. In reality consts. of liberty in all their parts—meant to effect the adjustments wh. we deem favourable to liberty.

[IV.]

THEORY AND PRACTICE
IN THE ORGANIZATION OF OUR GOVERNMENT

The Theory I refer to is the theory of *Checks and Balances.*

Our allegiance to Montesquieu, though we began by understanding him amiss (*See Madison*). *Montesquieu meant*, "not that these departments ought to have no partial agency in, or no control over the acts of each other. His meaning can amount to no more than this, that when the whole power of one department is exercised by the same hands which possess the whole power of another department, the fundamental principles of a free constitution are subverted." —*Madison in the Federalist*, No. XLVII.

The "Law State," at once cause and effect, our habit as lawyers.

Small attention given in this country to *"Administration,"* because *our history has emphasized the "constitutional" questions*, the questions of control.

Legislation vs. Administration—Independence of Will *vs.* Subordination: Origination *vs.* Discretion.

The Field of Administration—Effective means for practical ends. *What is feasible? Government in contact with the life of the State*, its whole front resting along the line drawn between state interference and *Laissez faire.*

Division of Functions vs. Division of Organs.

Theoretical Basis of the Division of Functions:

Legislation vs. Adjudication: A rule of law vs. determination of a concrete legal relationship.

Adjudication vs. Administration: A logical process vs. the carrying out of the conclusion.

Legislation vs. Administration: Delimitation of Rights and Duties vs. Regulation of state business.

Actual Division of Functions. ☞ (See class notes).[2] ☜

Action and Reaction of Law-making and Administration: Through Administration the State makes test of its own powers and of the public needs; of the suitability and efficiency of law. Law a summing up of the past; Administration always in contact with the present.

General Conclusion: The *argument for a division of Functions* sim[ilar to] an argument for convenience, in the highest sense of the term. The object: *Not checks and balances, but organic differentiation,* diffusion of vitality and access of vigour.

V.

ORGANIZATION AND POWERS OF CONGRESS.

Significance of Methods of Business,—Parliamentary Law a very important *part of Constitutional Law,*—of which we must widen and liberalize our conception.

The House of Representatives and the Senate:

Why "courtesy" in the one and not in the other?

The Senate a remaining *fragment of the old Confederation,* with some reminiscence of the the [*sic*] awful dignity of plenopotentiary representatives of States.

The question of popular election to the Senate, its historical and and constitutional bearings.

What does the House of Representatives *represent*? The "sovereignty of the People"?

The Committees and *the disintegration of Business.*

Less disintegration *in the Senate, because* more debate, more consideration by the whole body.

The question of "closure" in the Senate.

The De-nationalization of Business, by reason, not so much of the committee organization as of what that represents, the *incoherence of the House;*—and in the Senate (Silver). This the more *serious because—*

The Powers of Congress are distinctively national

Contrasted with the powers of the States:

Compare 12 English questions: Catholic emancipation, parl. reform, abolition of slavery, amendment of poor laws, munici-

---

[2] Here Wilson probably refers to his notes for his course on American constitutional law.

pal reform, *corn law repeal*, admission of Jews to Parl., Irish church, Irish land laws, national education, the ballot, the reform of the criminal law.

Division of Functions again: What part of our Gov't is national? Proper relations between that part and Congress.

Need of Re-integration.—Govt. no longer easy, even for us.

Dec. 20, 1893

VI.

THE COURTS UNDER A CONSTITUTIONAL GOVERNMENT.

The constitutional Powers of our courts the most conspicuous, and most novel feature of our system, *in foreign eyes.*

> *But it is* not a piece of construction at all: it is *merely a piece of inference. No gift* of this function in the Const. *It is the arrangement* from which the inference is made that is novel:

Separation of Constituent and Law-making Functions peculiar to us, among independent States. Found also in *the British colonies. By no means necessary* to a written constitution, or invariable.

> Improbable, indeed, because of inherent weakness of Judiciary.

General English Principle: Parliament itself subject to the laws unless it repeal them. (Stockdale vs. Hansard).

> *The Commons supreme only since* they became constituent (1688). *Burke*: "The House of Commons was supposed originally to be no part of the standing government of this country. It was considered as a control, issuing immediately from the people, and speedily to be resolved into the mass from whence it arose. In this respect it was in the higher part of government what juries are in the lower."
>
> *History of the Legislative power* of Parliament: *Taxes— Petition—Bill—Constitution.*

Strictly Normal and *strictly Legal* Nature of the Function:

1. May fall to *a court of any grade;*
2. *Must be necessary* to the determination of the case;
3. Question must be *raised by a party in interest;*
4. *No other ground of invalidation* except inconsistency with the Constitution;
5. *Must be Plain Conflict.*

How Far Are Other Departments Bound? To the extent of their legal conscience and political responsibility. ☞ (*Lincoln*).

Bluntschli's Objections:
   Met by attitude of courts
                        (1) Toward legislature (*McC. vs. Md.*).
                        (2)   " Exec. (*Decatur vs. Paulding*).

Bibliography.

A. V. Dicey, "The Law of the (English) Constitution." Macmillan.
Walter Bagehot, "The English Constitution." Appleton.
Jas. Bryce, "The American Commonwealth," Part I. Macmillan.
Woodrow Wilson, "Congressional Government." Houghton, Mifflin & Co., Boston.
Woodrow Wilson, "An Old Master and Other Political Essays," Essay III, on "Political Sovereignty." Scribners.
J. W. Burgess, "Political Science and Comparative Constitutional Law," Part I., Book III., and Part II. Ginn & Co.
The Federalist.
C. Ellis Stevens, "Sources of the Constitution of the United States." Macmillan.
Brinton Coxe, "Judicial Power and Constitutional Legislation." Phila., Kay & Brother.

WWT MSS. with WWhw and WWsh additions (WP, DLC).

To Robert Bridges

My dear Bobby,   Princeton, 21 Nov., 1893.

   I was out of town, lecturing, when your note[1] reached me, and ever since I got back I have been unspeakably busy with every sort of affair that can reach a man in this small town. I am coming to the dinner,[2] notwithstanding the fact that I shall have to cut a lecture to do so; and I will be delighted to come to your quarters. I shall enjoy myself all the way through on that programme.[3]

   In haste, and with much love,
                        Affectionately Yours,   Woodrow Wilson

ALS (WC, NjP).
   [1] It is missing.
   [2] He referred to a meeting of the Princeton Club of New York, at the Brunswick Hotel, on November 23.
   [3] Because he did not have to give a speech.

From the Minutes of the Princeton Faculty

4 5' P.M., Wednesday, Dec. 13, 1893

. . . The case of a Student reported for the plagiarism of an Essay was referred to the Committee on Discipline and Prof. Hunt.[1] . . .

[1] See the Princeton Faculty Minutes printed at Jan. 3, 1894, for the action taken in this case.

Two News Items

[Dec. 14, 1893]

TEAM DINNER.

The dinner given to the Princeton Foot-ball team by the management of the Princeton Inn, which was held last evening in the main dining hall of the Inn, was a decided success. . . .

Mr. J. MacN. Thompson, '94, acted as toast-master and the following graduates responded to toasts during the evening: J. W. Alexander '60, A. H. Joline '70, Prof. W. Wilson '79, A. H. Scribner '81, H. F. Osborn '77, P. W. Miller '79, H. B. Thompson '77, C. C. Cuyler '79, Tracy Harris '86, Alex. Moffat '84, G. K. Edwards '89, T. McCarter '88; also T. G. Trenchard '95 and Trainer McMaster.[1] . . .

Printed in the *Daily Princetonian*, Dec. 14, 1893.
[1] John McMasters.

[Dec. 18, 1893]

JOINT MEETING OF THE GRADUATE ADVISORY
AND EXECUTIVE COMMITTEE.

An important joint meeting of the Graduate Advisory and Executive Committees [of the University Athletic Association][1] was held last Saturday afternoon at the Princeton Inn. The members present were Chairman C. C. Cuyler, Prof. Woodrow Wilson and Messrs. P. W. Miller, Tracy Harris, and Max Farrand of the Graduate Advisory, and Humphrey, Perkins, McIlwain, Mackenzie, Swain, Bissell, and Huntington of the Executive Committee.[2] An elaborate lunch was served to the members before the meeting was called. Reports were made by the graduate treasurer, Mr. Cuyler, and by the treasurers of the baseball and track athletic associations. Steps were also taken for the immediate improvement of the cage,[3] so as to allow the baseball team to go into practice in good season. Mr. Miller, on behalf of the Philadelphia alumni, offered a cup, valued at $250.00 to be competed for in Princeton by the schools of Philadelphia. The contest is to be one in track athletics, and the cup will be presented to the school winning it three times successively. This offer was accepted by the committees with thanks, and the track athletic association was instructed to enter into correspondence with the schools on the subject. The absence of the football members handicapped the committees, as no appropriations could be made without a correct estimate of the surplus of that association. The meeting adjourned until January 13th, 1894.

Printed in the *Daily Princetonian*, Dec. 18, 1893.
  [1] About which, see J. L. Williams to WW, Sept. 25, 1891, Vol. 7. Wilson had been elected to the Graduate Advisory Committee on September 24, 1891.
  [2] Theodore Friend Humphrey, Thomas Jefferson Perkins, Charles Howard McIlwain, Charles Stevens Mackenzie, James Ramsey Swain, and John Livingston Bissell, all of the Class of 1894, and Theodore Sollace Huntington, '95.
  [3] The Field House on the University Athletic Grounds.

To Charles Scribner's Sons

My dear Sirs,   Princeton, New Jersey, 19 December, 1893

I take pleasure in returning one copy of the memorandum of agreement concerning "An Old Master" &c., signed as you request.[1]

Very truly Yours,   Woodrow Wilson

ALS (Charles Scribner's Sons Archives, NjP).
  [1] Wilson's copy of this contract, dated October 10, 1893—the date of publication of *An Old Master*—is in WP, DLC. The contract embodied the terms offered in Charles Scribner's Sons to WW, June 12, 1893.

To Albert Shaw

My dear Shaw,   Princeton, New Jersey, 20 December 1893.

The trouble with me is, that I have saddled myself with as many engagements as a city man, and can never say certainly what else I can do, or when I can do it.

I appreciate your kind note of the 9th,[1] ever so much; and I shall certainly manage to see you soon, by hook or by crook. I wish I could promise as much for Mrs. Wilson, who is as anxious to meet Mrs. Shaw as even you could wish; but, alas, a mother of young children has no time of her own,—at any rate, no time away from home. Let us hope for the best, however; nothing ought to be impossible when we are so near each other.

We wish you a most happy Christmas; I have little doubt that it will be the happiest of your life, so far.

Faithfully yours,   Woodrow Wilson.

TCL (in possession of Virginia Shaw English).
    [1] It is missing.

From Frederick Jackson Turner

My dear Wilson: Madison, Wisconsin, December 20, 1893.

Since your letter[1] reached me I have been beset with so many cares—the illness of my wife, extension lectures, etc.,—that I have not found opportunity to reply.

The lucid and effective statement which you make, in the Forum,[2] of the importance of the Middle Region, and the West, and the doctrine of American *development*, in contrast with Germanic *germs*, is very gratifying. It cannot fail to help to a more rational study of our history. I am glad that you think I have helped you to some of these ideas, for I have many intellectual debts to repay to you. The main point is to bring about the right view in these questions, and your article will fix attention upon the subject.

I am a convert to the utility of a style!

"An Old Master" etc., is delightful reading—a plea for Woodrow Wilsons in the professorial chair! Heartily as I assent to this essay, I cannot so entirely agree with your essay on sovereignty; though you put your thesis deftly, and I may reach your conclusions as an acquired taste!

With holiday greetings,
          Very truly yours   Frederick J. Turner

ALS (WP, DLC).
    [1] It is missing.
    [2] Wilson's review of Godwin Smith's *The United States*, printed at Sept. 5, 1893.

From John Calvin Metcalf[1]

Dear Sir: Murfreesboro, Tenn., Dec. 25, 1893.

I hope you will pardon the interruption,—but I cannot refrain from writing a few lines to thank you heartily for your excellent article in the December *Atlantic* on "Mere Literature."[2] Your words are full of a kind of inspiration to all who possess a deep love for the true and the beautiful in literature; who feel the spirit that makes for culture in any production in which the deeper energies of the soul have been enlisted.

I thank you earnestly for this blast against Philistinism, for this protest against the materializing tendencies which are so powerful in this age, an age whose genius has but little kinship with what may be called divine inshinings.

And so I believe your words will help others like myself who love "mere literature," and who think, as Joubert[3] has suggested, that it is better to have an inward sense of life and fruitfulness than to be concerned chiefly about temporal glory—such a concern as is manifested in a disdainful, utilitarian attitude.

Gratefully yours,   J. C. Metcalf.

ALS (WP, DLC) with WWhw notation on env.: "Ans. 2 Jany, '94."
[1] Professor of Ancient Languages at Soule College, Murfreesboro, Tenn.
[2] Printed at June 17, 1893.
[3] Joseph Joubert (1754-1824), French moralist and literary critic.

From the Minutes of the Princeton Faculty

5 5' P.M., Wednesday, Jany 3, 1894

. . . Upon recommendation of the Committee of Discipline, Mr. —— of the Sophomore Class, who had been guilty of plagiarism in connection with an Essay and who had admitted his guilt, was suspended from College until the end of the present Term. . . .

The New York *Nation*'s Review of *An Old Master*

[Jan. 4, 1894]

An Old Master, and Other Political Essays. By Woodrow Wilson. Professor of Jurisprudence in Princeton University. Charles Scribner's Sons. 1893.

Prof. Woodrow Wilson gives us, in a small volume, five essays, four of which have already appeared in the pages of the *Atlantic* and *New Princeton Review*. The first of these lends its name to the volume, 'An Old Master,' and the Old Master is Adam Smith. This essay is a most appreciative and agreeable study of a great, brave, modest man, whose simplicity and unassuming reticence in his daily intercourse with his fellow-men seem strangely at variance with his boldness—his almost audacity—of conception and design whenever he took his pen in his hand. At this day, when Adam Smith is little more than a name, though still a respected and renowned name, this sketch is most acceptable.

On other subjects, "The Study of Politics," "Political Sovereignty," "Character of Democracy in the United States," "Government under the Constitution," Prof. Wilson writes with a facile pen—a too facile pen, many people may think, for there are subjects that demand a cautious pen which will record only guarded utterances. Prof. Wilson talks with his pen: it runs in a clear, fluent, unhesitating manner, and it throws off unguarded expressions as if they came in the warmth of animated conversation. It is an easy thing for him to write that "the English have transformed their Crown into a Ministry," and "have kept a strong executive without abating either the power or the independence of the representative chamber," while we, *being under the spell of the Constitution*, have been unable to see the facts which written documents can neither establish nor change"; or that "the old, blunt, antagonistic veto is no longer needed" in England, yet "is needed here, however, to preserve the Presidency from the insignificance of merely administrative functions"; that the veto is "neither revisory nor corrective"; that it "is merely obstructive," "a simple blunt negation." But such seed, planted in the minds of many who will accept his conclusions as superior to their own knowledge, may bear very undesirable fruit.

Prof. Wilson knows, though many of his readers do not know, that the veto of the Crown has been obsolete for more than two centuries, and that there is no power that can revise or disapprove an act of Parliament. Yet he says:

> "In England the veto of the Crown has not passed out of use, as is commonly said. It has simply changed its form. It does not exist as an imperative, obstructive 'No' uttered by the sovereign. It has passed over into the privilege of the ministers to throw their party weight, reinforced by their power to dissolve Parliament, against measures of which they disapprove. It is a much-tempered instrument, but for that reason all the more flexible and useful."

Now, "the privilege of the ministers to throw their party weight"—whatever that may mean—"reinforced by their power to dissolve Parliament, against measures of which they disapprove," has not one element of the veto power. That the Opposition can frame a political measure and carry it through Parliament against the will of the existing Government is an impossibility. There never was a case where a ministry dissolved Parliament to prevent the passage of a bill of which they disapproved. The veto power is a supervision of legislative action lodged in some one who is outside of the law-making or (if it be preferred) the bill-making machinery of government; and a disapproval by the President is not "a simple, blunt negation," "merely obstructive," for the very plain reasons that the President is required to set forth his objections for the consideration of Congress, and if those objections are not deemed well taken, Congress can immediately pass the bill over the veto, the only restriction being that there must be a decisive majority in favor of the measure. A prime minister, on the contrary, is neither a President nor a King, but a person who is an integral part of the legislative machinery, and who has undertaken to carry on the government agreeably to the will of Parliament. When he fails to do so, the bargain is at an end, and out he goes. Such were the agreed terms of his employment. Occasionally he may say to Parliament, "You employed me to carry through this and that measure, or to manage the government on such and such lines of policy, and I have done so and am willing to continue to do so—it is not I, but you who have broken the compact; I appeal to the country"; and then, as the representative of the sovereign, he dissolves Parliament and orders a general election.

This "flexible and useful" veto power of an English ministry, which appears so superior to our own in the eyes of persons who are not "under the spell of the Constitution," then amounts to this: If the legislative power is not of the premier's way of thinking, he can influence and bully and intimidate members by threatening them with the pains and penalties of a new election; if, notwithstanding his threats, a sufficient number stand firmly by their convictions and refuse to pass one of his measures of which they disapprove, he can smash the existing government, legislative and executive, and plunge the country into the turmoil of one of our Presidential elections. That any intelligent person, American or English, can characterize such a *quasi* revolution, constitutional though it be, which may be precipitated on a country at any moment and by the will of one man, as "flexible and useful," and that he can regard it as superior to the quiet and orderly proceeding of the American veto, would be inconceivable if it were not in print. Such comments on constitutional systems will not affect the judgment of any man who has given the matter thoughtful attention, but they form most unfortunate seed to be sown in the minds of young American citizens.

Printed in the New York *Nation*, LVIII (Jan. 4, 1894), 18.

An Announcement

[Jan. 5, 1894]

Sunday, Jan. 7 . . .

5 P.M.—Services in Marquand Chapel. Conducted by Prof. Woodrow Wilson.

Printed in the *Daily Princetonian*, Jan. 5, 1894.

Recommended Reading in Jurisprudence and the History of Law

[Jan. 9, 1894]

COLLATERAL READING

A list of the books recommended for collateral reading by Professor Woodrow Wilson for his Junior and Senior Elective in Jurisprudence, and for his Senior Elective in History of Law, and the passages especially mentioned for reading, are given below:[1]

JURISPRUDENCE:

Puchta, "Outlines of Jurisprudence," chap. III.

Clark, Prof. E. C., "Practical Jurisprudence," on the meaning of "Law," and its origins.

Merkel, A., "Elemente der Allgemeinen Rechtslehve" (in Holtzendorff's Encyklopädie der Richtswissenschaft), and "Juristiche Encyclopädie."

Maine, "Ancient Law," chap. X.

Austin, "Lectures on Jurisprudence," *passim* on topics of the course.

Markby, Sir Wm, "Elements of Law."

HISTORY OF LAW:

Leist, B. W., "Altarisches Jus Civile."

Maine, "Early Law and Custom," chaps. II.-IV., and VI. "Early History of Institutions," chaps. III., IX., and X.

Ihering, R. V., "Geist des römischen Rechts," an original system of self-help.

Holmes, O. W., Jr., "The Common Law," chaps. I., II., VII. "Essays in Anglo-Saxon Law," pp. 183 and following.

Sohm, "Institutes of Roman Law," Part I. and pp. 163-179, 278-354.

Muirhead, "Roman Law," in Encyclopaedia Britannica.

Bruns, C. G., "Geschichte und Quellen des römischen Rechts" (in Holtzendorff's Encyklopädie), pp. 176-183.

Turner, Sam'l E., "The Germanic Constitution."

Sohm, "Die deutsche Rechtrenwickelung," in Grüntent's Zeitschrift.

Brunner, H., "Überblick über die Geschichte der Französischen, Normannischen, und Englischen Rechtsquellen" (in Holtzendorff).

Stephen, Sir Jas., "Lectures on the History of France," Lecture IX.

Printed in the *Daily Princetonian*, Jan. 9, 1894.
[1] The *Princetonian*'s occasional German misspellings have been retained. "Grüntent" should read "Grünhut."

To Lyon Gardiner Tyler[1]

My dear Sir   Princeton, 9 Jan'y, 1894

It will be entirely satisfactory to me to receive vol. I.[2] in book form, and the delay will not be an inconvenience. I am sincerely obliged to you for your kindness in writing.[3] I shall await the coming of the journal with genuine interest.

Cordially Yours   Woodrow Wilson

ALS (Tyler Family Papers, ViW).
[1] President of the College of William and Mary and proprietor and editor of the *William and Mary College Quarterly Historical Magazine.*
[2] Of the *William and Mary College Quarterly Historical Magazine.*
[3] Tyler's letter is missing.

To Herbert Baxter Adams

My dear Dr. Adams,   Princeton, 11 Jan'y, 1894

You may expect me to be ready to begin on a Thursday,[1] as usual, the 25th of January, at such hour as you may appoint. I expect to reach Baltimore on the evening of Wednesday, the 24th. I hope these plans are what you had anticipated, and will suit your convenience. I hear glowing accounts of the Dept. from Gresham and Stevenson.[2]

Hoping that you are quite well, with warm regards,

Cordially Yours,   Woodrow Wilson

ALS (H. B. Adams Papers, MdBJ).
[1] That is, to begin his annual course in administration at the Johns Hopkins.
[2] Le Roy Gresham, College of New Jersey, '92, at this time a graduate student in history at the Hopkins, and Robert Alston Stevenson, '92, a graduate student in economics.

A News Report

[Jan. 15, 1894]

MEETING OF THE GRADUATE ADVISORY
AND EXECUTIVE COMMITTEES.

An important meeting of the Graduate Advisory and Executive Committees of the Athletic Association was held at the Princeton Inn on Saturday afternoon. The members present were Chairman C. C. Cuyler, Prof. Woodrow Wilson, Messrs. Tracy Harris, Phillippus W. Miller, and Max Farrand of the Graduate Advisory, and Messrs. Humphrey, Thompson, McIlwain, Perkins, Mackenzie, Swain, Munn, Bissell, and Huntington of the Executive Committee.[1] Lunch was served to the members before the meeting.

Rapid progress on the improvements in the drainage of the cage was reported. The Advisory Coaching Committee announced the appointment of Mr. J. B. Fine[2] as head coach in football next season. On their recommendation a motion was passed to the effect that the joint committee authorize the expenditure through Mr. Fine of money only for travelling expenses and board bills of such coachers as are invited, and for such times only, as they are asked for. A partial report of the football treasurer was made, showing approximate net receipts for the season of $8,500.

Mr. Farrand handed in his resignation from the Graduate Advisory Committee, to be acted upon at the next meeting of the Executive Committee.

The next matter considered was a change which involves the reconstruction of almost the entire constitution of the Athletic Association. It provides for an officer to be known as the General Athletic Treasurer, who is to take charge of all accounts and moneys handled by the various associations. He is to receive a fixed salary for his services, and shall not be pursuing a regular course for a degree in college. He is to be appointed annually by the Executive Committee, subject to the ratification of the Graduate Advisory Committee. He is also to have charge of the training table, athletic grounds, buildings, and grand-stand, and to perform all duties heretofore appertaining to the office of University Treasurer. This latter office is to be entirely abolished, and those heretofore known as Treasurers will be styled Managers of the various associations. The creation of this office will relieve the undergradustes [undergraduates] of much of the routine work at present connected with the athletic offices, and will at the same time provide for a more systematic and business-like supervision of the finances of the athletic associations. The enormous sums of money handled by them have made necessary the adoption of some such plan.

The following amendment to the constitution, providing for this new office, will be brought before the college at some date in the near future for ratification:

GENERAL ATHLETIC TREASURER.

Article I,

There shall be an officer of this association known as the General Athletic Treasurer, who shall hold office for one year, beginning July 1st.

Article II.

He shall be appointed annually by the unanimous vote of the Executive Committee at their January meeting, subject to the ratification of the Graduate Advisory Committee at their next meeting thereafter.

Article III.

He shall not be pursuing a regular course for a degree in the college.

Article IV.

He shall be provided with an office and shall have regular office hours, the rental of said office to be paid out of the funds of the Athletic Association.

Article V.

He shall receive a fixed salary, the amount of which shall be determined by the Graduate Advisory and Executive Committees, to be paid quarterly by the Graduate Treasurer.

Article VI.

The duties of this office shall be as follows:

(a) To receive gate receipts, guarantees, and other moneys from the respective managers, keeping separate accounts of such receipts with the various associations.

(b) To turn over to the Managers of the Football, Baseball, and Track Athletic Associations for travelling expenses, such amounts as may be approved by the Presidents of the respective associations; and to receive from the various managers, not later than forty-eight hours after the return of the teams to Princeton, an itemized report of the disbursement of these moneys.

(c) To receive and settle all outstanding bills against the Associations, subject always to the counter-signature of the proper President or Manager.

(d) To procure and pay the proper servants and attendants for the University Athletic Club House, and to act as purveyor for the different teams as they may be at the Training Table, settling the bills therefor. By and with the advice and consent of the Graduate Advisory and Executive Committees, he may employ a steward.

(e) To have a general supervision of the University Athletic Field and buildings, to see to and defray the expense of all necessary repairs and alterations of the same, obtaining authority from the Executive Committee for any expenditure of over ($100) one hundred dollars.

(f) To have special charge of the Grand Stand.

Article VII.

He shall make detailed reports at the three regular meetings of the Graduate Advisory and Executive Committees, the same to be printed in the *Daily Princetonian.*

Article VIII.

His accounts shall be audited by an expert accountant previous to each report, and shall be open for inspection at all times.

Article IX.

After the close of each Athletic season, he shall reserve moneys sufficient to meet all liabilities of the associations, and furthermore, amounts sufficient to start the coming season with. All moneys in the treasury, over and above these amounts, he shall pay to the Graduate Treasurer to be invested by him for the general athletic interests of the college, subject to the approval of the Graduate Advisory and Executive Committees.

Article X.

He shall be under bond or bonds to the amount of ten thousand dollars ($10,000.00), the sufficiency of his security to be determined by the Graduate Advisory and Executive Committees. Any necessary expenditure incurred in securing bonds shall be met by the Association.

Printed in the *Daily Princetonian*, Jan. 15, 1894.
  1 The members of the Executive Committee not heretofore identified were James MacNaughton Thompson, '94, and Edward Munn, '95.
  2 John Burchard Fine, Headmaster of the Princeton Preparatory School, 1888-1929; Director of Athletics, Princeton University, 1903-1909.

From Cyrus Hall McCormick

My Dear Wilson: [Chicago] Jany. 17, 1894.

Will you give me your judgment upon a personal matter which is of considerable interest to me? I am now collecting the data for a biography of my father. The arrangement of this into authentic and readable form will be quite a task, but its value will be permanent, and the book will have, I am sure, great general interest aside from its character as a biography, inasmuch as it must deal with the agricultural development of this country in connection with the invention and development of the reaping machine.

I have in mind two eminent men, either of whom would probably be well qualified to undertake such a work, but I have not decided which would be able to handle the subject with the greatest success.

The first is your warm friend, *Dr. Albert S. Shaw*: I lunched with him at the invitation of Robert Bridges some weeks since, and was delighted to find in him a man of quick perception, clear insight, bright mind and forceful presentation of his subjects. I have no doubt that, busy as he is, he could, in his spare hours during two years, gather the material into a volume, but I am not sure whether he has time to go as carefully and ploddingly into all the details as would be necessary to anyone who expects to make this an authentic record.

The other name which I have in mind is that of *Prof. Judson*,[1] of the University of Chicago. His nearness to us is a great argument in his favor. He would perhaps be more painstaking, more systematic, go more into detail than Dr. Shaw, but would probably not have the brilliancy nor the general attractiveness of style as would Dr. Shaw. Furthermore, Prof. Judson has not, I believe, much mechanical instinct, and this would be an important requirement in the treatment of a subject of this character involving patent questions &c &c

As between these two men, whose name would you prefer to have on the title page of so important a contribution to American history? And I ask you, in giving me this opinion, to lay aside your personal feelings of friendship for Dr. Shaw.

The biography would necessarily touch upon and deal with

1. The agricultural standing of the United States prior to 1831 (the year of my father's invention) and the development since that time.

2. The part which the reaping machine has played in all this, as compared with the railroad, the steam engine, the printing press, the telegraph, telephone and other great improvements.

3. The mechanical steps of progress from the original machine down to the present more complicated, but more useful structure.

4. The consideration of my father's claims as the pioneer in this art and the inventor of the first successful reaper. This would involve a careful investigation of records, and the sifting of many unwarrantable attacks which have been made upon my father by jealous and disappointed competitors from the days of his early achievements until the present time.

5. The economic value of the reaping machine, as developed by all other countries patterning after the American type of machine.

Which of the gentlemen I have named would have the best all around ability to deal with these complex and many sided questions? Which of their names would carry most weight after the volume was issued? Which of them would be most painstaking in studying up the details and searching the records?

I must say in this connection that I have employed a young man who is now at work collecting and searching among old records for data, and we have already secured a large amount of material, so that the first work of plowing up has already been done.

Your reply may be as brief as possible, to save your time, but I have put the various points at some length before you, and will ask you to regard this as *entirely confidential*, for with either of these men it would seem that no one could make a mistake.

Yours sincerely,   Cyrus H. McCormick

TLS (C. H. McCormick Letterpress Books, WHi).
¹ Harry Pratt Judson, at this time Professor of Political Science and Dean of the Faculties of Arts, Literature, and Science at the University of Chicago. President of the University of Chicago, 1907-23.

From John Adams Wilson¹

Dear Woodrow: Franklin, Pa. Jan. 17th. 1894

When in New York during Thanksgiving week I met Mrs. Frank Hickox of Cleveland and during our talk I happened to speak of Princeton when she astonished me by saying "John you have a cousin at Princeton: Woodrow Wilson is your Uncle Joseph's son." Supposing of course I should meet you at the game did not take special pains to run you down. I felt when I met you that there was something which drew me towards you, but it never struck me that one of our blood should have become so well known in letters as you have, and I did not attempt to trace a relationship.

My father was Edwin C. Wilson, one of the famous set of triplets.² There are three boys of the family living, Alexander who is in the Pension Bureau at Washington; Henry M., who makes his home here at Franklin and myself, who as you may learn from this letter head, tries to make a living out of oil.³ Please let me hear from you soon. Tell me all about your family: where uncle is living, and if you cannot make it to get to Franklin sometime. I have made a promise to put in a week or two with the Princeton Base Ball Nine this Spring, but cannot say if I will be able to make my promise good. I am very anxious that our team this Summer, should become a good batting team and to that end

I am willing to put myself out a little. There is no good reason why we should not make as good a showing on the Diamond as we did on the "Gridiron."

Tell your father that both Henry and myself, would be glad to see him at any time he can get to see us, and would be happy to have him make a long stay. Am about to start on a flying trip to St Louis and expect to return Saturday. With best wishes for you and yours I am

Affectionately yours   Jno. A. Wilson

TLS (WP, DLC) with WWhw notation on env.: "Ans. 21 Jan'y, '94."

[1] First cousin of Woodrow Wilson, born Franklin, Pa., Sept. 24, 1851. After attending the Lawrenceville School and Washington and Jefferson College, he entered the College of New Jersey as a junior in 1871. Completed the requirements for the A.B. degree in 1873, but the degree was not conferred until 1904. Admitted to the Pennsylvania bar in December 1873, he practiced law in San Jose, Cal., and Butler, Pa. Abandoned law to enter the oil business as a broker. Active in sports as an undergraduate, he maintained a lifelong interest in Princeton athletics. Died June 6, 1923.

[2] The triplets, born in 1820, were Henry Clay Wilson, Edwin Clinton Wilson, and Margaretta Wilson.

[3] His firm was the Galena Oil Works, Limited, "Manufacturers of the Celebrated Galena Engine, Car, Coach & Machinery Oils."

A News Item

[Jan. 20, 1894]

NEW YORK ALUMNI DINNER

The annual dinner of the New York Alumni was held at the Hotel Brunswick last night. The large dining room was beautifully decorated with orange and black and the National colors. On the mantel was a stuffed tiger.

Adrian H. Joline '70, president of the club, occupied the chair. On his right and left were J. W. Alexander '69 ['60] and W. B. Hornblower '71, the former presidents; Parke Godwin '34, ex-Judge Henry E. Howland, of Yale; George G. De Witt, of Columbia; Austen G. Fox, of Harvard, and Professor Woodrow Wilson, who represented Princeton University in the absence of President Patton, and who responded to the toast "Alma Mater."

Mr. Joline made a very pleasing address of welcome, and introduced the following speakers:

Dr. Woodrow Wilson, "Princeton University";[1] Parke Godwin, LL.D., '34, "The Alumni"; Austen G. Fox, "Harvard"; Hon. Henry E. Howland, "Yale"; George G. De Witt, Esq., "Columbia."

Mr. James W. Alexander, in behalf of the New York Alumni, tendered the members of the football team with loving cups of solid silver and the substitutes with silver match boxes. . . .

Printed in the *Princeton Press*, Jan. 20, 1894.

1 EAW to WW, Feb. 6, 1894, reveals that Wilson spoke on "the football question."

To Cyrus Hall McCormick

Princeton, New Jersey,

My dear McCormick,   22 January, 1894

Your letter of the 17th came during my absence from home for a day or two last week.

I could answer your question with much more assured judgment if I knew Prof. Judson better. As it is, I know him only by report through common friends. I have read almost nothing that he has written. I cannot, therefore, make any real comparison between him and Shaw. I can, however, and will with pleasure, give you my candid opinion of the latter.

The way in which you formulate the matter makes it easy to give succinct answers. I should judge that Shaw "would have the best all-round ability to deal with the complex and many sided questions" that would be involved. He has a really extraordinary acquaintance with those conditions of growth and development, particularly of the western country, that would bear upon the matter of the biography. I should expect his name, too, to carry much more weight than Judson's. As for the painstaking care in the study of details and the examination of records, no one would know better than Shaw what was pertinent and what was needed; but I know the extraordinary drain, both as regards time and energy, to which he is subjected in his regular work, and I cannot see how he could possibly spare either time or strength (or judgment, either, for that matter) for the careful detail and elaboration that would be involved. I should take it for granted that in this respect Prof. Judson was in a much better position to accomplish what you wish.

This is my candid judgment.

With warmest regards, both to Mrs. McCormick and yourself,— and delightful recollections of your generous hospitality,

Cordially Yours,   Woodrow Wilson

ALS (C. H. McCormick Papers, WHi).

A News Item

[Jan. 23, 1894]

PROFESSOR WILSON'S COURSES.

Professor Wilson announced to his classes yesterday that, instead of the course in Administration, senior elective for next term, he will substitute a course in English Common Law. This course, he stated, is not to be considered a professional law course, but is rather a history of the development of the Common Law in its main outlines and a study of its fundamental principles. Technicalities will be entered into only when needed as illustrations. According to his custom, Prof. Wilson will be absent during the first part of the term, while lecturing at Johns Hopkins. Those who elect the course will be expected to be prepared to take a written recitation on Monday, March 5th, on the text-book used, namely, "The English Constitution," by Emile Boutney [Boutmy]. The book is published by Macmillan, and it is recommended that orders for them be sent immediately.

The text-book to be used in the Junior and Senior elective in International Law is "Treatise on International Law," by Wm. E. Hall. A written recitation on Parts I and II of this book will also be held on Mar. 5th, in the afternoon.

Printed in the *Daily Princetonian*, Jan. 23, 1894.

To Ellen Axson Wilson

906 McCulloh St.,[1] Balto.,

My own darling,   Thursday, 25 Jan'y, '94

It is just twenty-four hours since I left you—it seems a week at least: my heart is already tired with the *strain* there is upon it. My first lecture comes this afternoon. All morning I was busy with formal calls on the President, Dr. Adams, and others about the University. But I got settled in my room—all unpacked and stowed away, as I knew *you* would have done—last night before I went to bed. Now for the conning of my task and the last touches of preparation for the lecture.

I have no ink yet, you see; but I know you will not mind this scribble.

My room is large, light; and in every way comfortable,—even pretty in many of its appointments, and as if meant for human habitation.

This is my first love message. There are two parts of every period of absence from home when I can't bear to write: the very beginning and the very end—when I have just been with you, and when I am just about to be with you. Then all my love seems a *cry*—I can't *think* about you and speak calmly to you—I can only *yearn* for you and keep myself from desperate impatience! Oh, my love! my life!

I am perfectly well. Love to all.

Your own   Woodrow

ALS (WP, DLC).
  [1] The new street number of Mary Jane Ashton's boarding house, where Wilson
was staying again.

George Stevenson Patton to Robert Newton Willson

Dear Sir—   [Princeton, N.J.] January 25 1894

Dr Patton begs to thank you for your kind invitation just received to address the "Contemporary Club"[1] on the subject of Football.[2] It would give him great pleasure to do so but the demands upon his time are such that it is impossible for him to leave home at this season of the year. He has referred your letter to Prof Wilson. With the hope that Prof Wilson will be able to do what Dr Patton regrets that he is unable to do,

Very truly yours   George S. Patton

ALS (Patton Letterpress Books, University Archives, NjP).
  [1] The Contemporary Club of Philadelphia, of which the Woodrow Wilsons had been members in 1887-88. About this organization, see WW to Sophia Royce Williams, Feb. 2, 1888, n. 1, Vol. 5. In 1894, R. N. Willson was on the executive committee of the Contemporary Club. He was president in 1896-97.
  [2] The Contemporary Club was organizing a symposium on college football, then the subject of much controversy on account of the abuses and dangers of the game. Wilson participated in the symposium on February 13, 1894. See the news report printed at Feb. 14, 1894.

From George Stevenson Patton

Dear Prof Wilson   [Princeton, N.J.] January 25 [1894]

The enclosed letter explains itself.[1] Father is unable to accept the invitation and according to request I refer the matter to you with father's sincere hope that you will be able to go. I have written Mr Willson to that effect.

Sincerely and respectfully   George S. Patton

ALS (Patton Letterpress Books, University Archives, NjP).
  [1] Willson's letter to President Patton, which Ellen enclosed in her letter to Woodrow of January 25, 1894, is missing.

From Ellen Axson Wilson

My darling   Princeton, Jan. 25/94

Your telegram[1] came duly to hand & was most welcome;—what a comfort it is to be able to re-establish communication so promptly! I have sent the opera-glasses—hope they will reach you safely. We are all well and I am "doing as well as could be expected" considering how recently I have lost you and how many weeks stretch before me ere I can find you again. Fortunately this has been a very fine exhilerating day. I hope you have had as good a one in which to make your start. I really had a delightful time at the Frothinghams,[2] and the old gentleman was inspired by my enthusiasm to give me *five* beauties! I protested vigorously but he *would* do it;—he "so seldom found anyone so appreciative"! They are all splendid line engravings, early impressions, some by Raphael Morghen[3] one of the greatest engravers that ever lived and others by an almost equally famous pupil of his. There is a Correggio, a beautiful Christ by Carlo Dolci; one of Raphael's Madonnas with a most beautiful Child; a magnificent large group, a "Burial of Christ" by Andrea Del Sarto, and another, perhaps the most beautiful of all, by a Rennaissance artist whose name was unfamiliar to me. (I have already forgotten it again.) It is one of the lovliest Madonnas I ever saw. Don't you know I feel rich! I am trying to decide whether to have them framed now or not. With their wide "mounts" they would require pretty large frames; but on the other hand we have no portfolio or other convenience for taking proper care of them unframed. What do you advise? They have not come home yet; he offered to send them.

There has been no mail of consequence except the enclosed,— which is a bore!—is it not? I was tempted to save you the trouble of replying by myself telling Dr. Patton that you couldn't go! I don't know why they should try to put everything off on you.

Give my love—and the children's—to the ladies.[4]

I love you, dear, with a love beyond all power of words to express, and I am always and altogether,

Your own   Eileen

ALS (WC, NjP). Enc. missing.

[1] It is missing.

[2] Mr. and Mrs. Arthur Lincoln Frothingham of Hodge Ave., parents of the Professor of Archaeology and the History of Art at Princeton, Arthur L. Frothingham, Jr.

[3] Raffaello Morghen. Born in Naples in 1758, he was trained by his father and Giovanni Volpato, whom he assisted in engraving the paintings of Raphael in the Vatican. Morghen moved to Florence and engraved many masterpieces of that city. He died in 1833.

[4] That is, Mary Jane Ashton and her sister, Hannah.

From Cyrus Hall McCormick

My Dear Wilson: [Chicago] Jany. 26, 1894.

I thank you for your note of Jany. 22nd, which seems to be much in the line of my own thought on the subject of the best person to whom to commit so important a matter as the biography referred to.[1]

I hope to be in Princeton next week, and will take pleasure in seeing you and Mrs. Wilson.

Yours sincerely,   Cyrus H. McCormick

TLS (C. H. McCormick Letterpress Books, WHi).
1 McCormick apparently failed to find a biographer of his father at this time. The first full-scale biography was Herbert Newton Casson's *Cyrus Hall Mc-Cormick, His Life and Work* (Chicago, 1909).

To Ellen Axson Wilson

My own darling,   Balto., 26 January, 1894

I don't know how much of a letter I can write yet,—it is still so short a time since I was in your arms: the look I left in your eyes is still so vividly before me; that I must not write anything that would make me more desperate still, with loneliness and longing.

It was absurd in me to ask for the opera glasses in a telegram, but it was sweet of you to send them so promptly; they came this morning while I was at breakfast. I did not wait for them, how-ever, to go to the theatre: my country soul was too eager for that. I borrowed Miss Ashton's glasses and went last night to see that pantomime, "L'Infant Prodigue," which you no doubt remember seeing described and praised while it was in New York—a whole play with never a word spoken![1] I[t] was immensely clever: but I found it a great strain on my *eyes*, and *only* clever: I should not care particularly to see it again.

I met Mr. Victor Smith and Edgeworth[2] on the street yesterday —and Charley Mitchell on the street car. I have not seen any oth-ers of my friends yet, outside the university circle. I am thinking of calling on Mrs Bird this evening,—instead of going to the "Eco-nomic Seminary."

My first lecture went off as well as usual. This first part of the course is always a nervous, trying business for me. I never enjoy *beginning*. Oh, my darling, how desperately do I long for you at every turn, at every moment; how entirely, how intensely, I am

Your own   Woodrow

Unmeasured love for Marga, Jessie, Nellie,—and great lots for the boys.[3] I'm *so* sorry I did not see George at the last moment! I've thought of it ever since. (Don't forget to take him to Dr. Hins-dale)[4]   Your W.

ALS (WC, NjP).
1 It was being presented that week at the Lyceum Theatre by a touring com-pany of French actors.
2 Victor Smith, son-in-law of Mrs. William Edgeworth Bird, and his son, Edgeworth Smith. The Smiths lived with Mrs. Bird.

[3] Edward William Axson and George Howe III, both freshmen at Princeton and living with the Wilsons at 48 Steadman Street.
[4] To the Rev. Dr. Horace Graham Hinsdale, pastor of the First Presbyterian Church of Princeton, 1877-95, to arrange about George's joining the church.

From Ellen Axson Wilson

My darling,   [Princeton, N.J.] Friday [Jan. 26, 1894]

It is bedtime & I must try and content myself with a very short note. Helen[1] and the boys have been "cutting up" all the evening in the room and of course writing was out of the question. It is odd that I can read with complete absorption no matter what people are doing about me, but I cannot write a word except where it is quiet.

Helen appeared just before lunch with Mr. Brown[2] who lunched —or rather dined with us—(it is Friday you know) after which they both went over to Lawrenceville. There was a fine combination of rain and snow falling at the time, but they had Guinns[3] close carriage & I hope the child got no harm. George is much better though his face is not yet quite restored to its usual fine proportions.

There has been no mail for you today; somehow there is never much for you when you are absent—it is odd. I shall get some stamped envelopes for enclosures so that you may know them from my valuable missives.

Your first note came today, darling and was so sweet & oh *so* welcome! How glad I am that you have a bright and cheerful room. Ah, love, if I were only there with *you* it would seem to me the brightest room in the world! But I will be good and not utter vain wishes. With all my heart

Your own   Eileen

ALS (WC, NjP).
[1] Wilson's first cousin, Helen Woodrow Bones, who was a boarding student at Evelyn College in Princeton.
[2] Probably Irving S. Brown of 82 Bayard Avenue.
[3] William Guinn, who ran a hack service.

Two Letters to Ellen Axson Wilson

My own darling,   Baltimore, 27 January, 1894

Your first letter came this morning and has been a genuine blessing to me, with its sweet cheerful tone and its enthusiasm because of Mr. Frothingham's generous gift of the engravings. I am so glad—and so much obliged to him for giving my darling so much pleasure. I think, dear, it would be only common prudence to have them framed. I don't see how else—in a house full of mice—we could keep them:—and of course we want to *enjoy* them as well as keep them. How delightful it was in Mr. Frothingham to treat you so generously in the very matter in which you are capable of enjoying yourself most. I shall like him better than ever for doing it.

I went last night to see Mrs. Bird and Mrs. [Victor] Smith[1]— and spent most of the evening there. Mrs. Bird has had an attack of the grippe, poor lady, and has not yet quite recovered from it. She had already retired when I reached the house about eight o'clock; but she actually got up and dressed to see me! That, certainly, was a sincere compliment,—wasn't it? She was almost as bright as ever—and Mrs. Smith was much more animated and interesting than usual. I go to-morrow, Sunday, to take dinner with them. To-night I think I shall go to the Symphony concert at the Peabody Institute. You see I am doing a little spreeing before settling down to the preparation of that course on the Common Law which I have promised the Seniors when I get back.

I am afraid I shall have to go to Phila. as the President requests. It will not be hard to make a (serious) speech about football, and to do so in such company will be very much more important for the college than an alumni dinner speech. Our constituency in Phila. is larger and more influential than in any other place except New York, and it is "in a state of mind" about football. The President *ought* to have gone; but, if he will not, somebody else must go—and I am chosen, not by him, but by the people from whom this invitation comes. It will be a close shave in time, after a four o'clock lecture; but I must attempt it.

Ah, sweetheart, this dear letter of yours has made me temporarily worse—it comes so directly from you—the very handwriting seems to render me more keenly alive to our separation! I love you, oh so passionately—I long for you, oh, so intolerably. I am so intensely and with so deep a tenderness and devotion,

Your own   Woodrow

906, dear, not 909.

ALS (WC, NjP).
  [1] Saida Bird Smith.

My darling   Balto. 27 January [1894], again.

I took the square of fine cashmir to the Decorative Art Society's[1] rooms this afternoon (after writing to you) to be stamped, and got into trouble. The lady there wants to know if you want it stamped only on one—the 'upper'—corner, folded thus or on all the corners. She also wants to know whether you mean to *bind* it, or want the edges *scolloped* (for embroidered edges, I suppose)[.] You will have to answer these questions before the good work can go on   Yours in haste and ignorance   Woodrow

ALS (WP, DLC).
¹ An art institute.

From Ellen Axson Wilson

My darling,   Princeton, Jan. 28/94

We had visitors until late last evening so I did not try to write as I knew I would gain nothing by doing so,—that the letter written today would reach you as soon.

Mr. Richardson came first to report about his wife;—afterwards Mr. Harper & Mr. Howard.¹ I was very glad Mr. Harper happened upon one of Helen's nights. Mrs. Richardson is at the Sand Hills² and delightfully situated he says; "thanks to you" (!) he was pleased to add. The Arnolds³ put them on the right track and she seems to be in a really ideal place,—a Mrs. Heard's,⁴—with beautiful surroundings, delicious fare and extremely nice people about her. Mr. Richardson saw Boudre⁵ who is going to call; so you will not have to write him.

By the way, the enclosed blank came yesterday.⁶ I don't know how to fill it out so I will sign my name and send it on to you to finish up and forward. Did any "blank" come in the Eagle & Phoenix case?⁷ You forgot to show me their letter and I have no idea what is required of me in the matter; so please sir, give me instructions.

Your receipt came from the Equitable—no other mail of any consequence except the "Journal"⁸ for the book-binder,—which I sent him,—and a note from Prof. Baldwin asking you to meet Prof. [Josiah] Royce⁹ at luncheon on Friday. I answered it, but perhaps you had better acknowledge it too.

Mr. Daniels very kindly wrote asking to take Helen & myself to the Club concert¹⁰ on Tuesday night;—it is the Beethoven Quartette. Miss McIlvaine¹¹ proved gracious for once, so we are going. Am so sorry you will miss it; for once I find myself looking forward with keen pleasure to a musical event, having heard so much of these concerts.

One other little matter,—since you left I have planned changes in that white flannel which make it *very* desirable that the skirt should be ripped from the band *before* it is cleaned, so that it may "do up" smoothly.¹² Won't you ask Miss Jane or "Miss Han"¹³ to rip it for me? it will not take them ten minutes.

We are all *quite* well. Georges jaw is all right; his lower lip is swollen a little which makes him look oddly like *Josie*. We had Friday night a rather heavy and very beautiful snow-storm, and yesterday and today have been perfect days. Ed rode the children a good deal on their sled yesterday, to their great joy. Jessie's latest exploit is learning yesterday all of Tennyson's "Brook" by heart. One of her speeches caused a laugh at Ed's expense. She says "Ed, what *are* you doing in the world!" meaning nothing more invidious than "what in the world are you doing."

I find like you, darling, that it is not quite safe yet to let my thoughts dwell much on certain things, so I will not try to tell you how much I miss you. I am glad that the duty of "not dwelling on things" does not involve the impossible task of trying to banish thoughts of *you*, for to *live* and to think of you are one and the same thing. But I can elect to think not so much of what I have temporarily lost, as of what I have gained forever in you,—of your constant presence in my life. If I could only tell you all that means to me! how you have quickened and broadened that life—have furnished, it would seem, the motive power, and all the joy in living. Ah my love, my pride, my delight, my *hero* you are in very truth *all the world* to

Your little wife, Eileen

ALS (WC, NjP). Enc. missing.

1 Ernest Cushing Richardson, College Librarian; George McLean Harper, Assistant Professor of French and Instructor in Romance Languages; and William Guild Howard, Instructor in German.

2 The resort section of Augusta, Ga.

3 Mr. and Mrs. Richard J. Arnold, of 31 Nassau Street.

4 Anna (Mrs. Richard Willis) Heard, widow of a Confederate soldier, who took in guests at her home, "Three Oaks," on Hickman Road in Augusta. She later married J. Rice Smith.

5 Bowdre Phinizy, '92, of Augusta.

6 WW to EAW, Jan. 29, 1894, goes into considerable detail about this matter. Ellen was referring to a proxy sent by Hugh M. Comer, president and co-receiver of the Central Railroad and Banking Company of Georgia. The Central had been in receivership since early 1892 and was to be sold under foreclosure on September 1, 1894. The Central had been leasing the track and equipment of the South-Western Railroad since 1869, and, as Wilson's letter to Ellen of January 28, 1894, explains, was now seeking to gain complete control of the solvent South-Western in order to bolster its own sinking fortunes. Ellen owned thirteen shares of stock in the South-Western.

7 This, apparently, was another proxy fight between the Eagle and Phenix cotton mills of Columbus, Ga. Contemporary evidence about the controversy is missing, but the Eagle and Phenix Mills were incorporated as a single company in 1898.

8 One of the scholarly journals to which Wilson subscribed at this time.

9 Josiah Royce of Harvard was visiting Princeton at the invitation of the Monday Night Club, an organization of seniors and graduate students. He was staying with James Mark Baldwin, Stuart Professor of Experimental Psychology.

10 A concert by an informal musical group of Princetonians to be held at Evelyn College. The local newspapers did not report on this affair.

11 Either Alice or Elizabeth McIlvaine, co-principals of Evelyn College.

12 Wilson had taken one or more of Ellen's dresses to Baltimore for dry cleaning.

13 That is, Hannah Ashton.

To Ellen Axson Wilson

My own darling,   Baltimore, 28 January, 1894

I am going to begin this letter before going to Mrs. Bird's, but I'm afraid that I shall have to finish it after I come back. It is already nearly time for church (I am going to hear Mr. Babcock) —so late was I in getting up.[1]

Let me begin with two matters I am afraid I should forget if I did not put them first. Wont you please tell me the name of the gentleman who sent me "Was Davis a Traitor?"[2] I ought to call on him as soon as possible. His name is in the book, if you cannot find it in your memory. I should like his initials, too.

Will you not get for me a copy of the prescription for my eye wash? My eyes are stinging me a great deal. Probably you could mail me the "pipette" at the same time, and so save the expense of getting another. I think perhaps my eyes are sympathizing with the rest of my head. I have caught a not very severe "face cold"— as Mr. Hinton[3] would call it—and that naturally 'goes for' one's eyes. Just now my head is throbbing with the quinine I took last night (though it was only four grains): you will please attribute to that any absurdities this letter may contain. I *am* taking good care of myself,—so you need not be anxious.

I thought I remembered what it was like to be without you, my Eileen—but I did not,—I had forgotten. I suppose no one *can* remember *detailed* pain: and it is the detail of this pain that makes it so terrible. Those little nameless, half remembered acts of friendship and of love (*you* can recall the words exactly enough to make them a *quotation*) with which you surround me when I am at home, but which then seem to make no separate impression on me, now come crowding back into my heart to emphasize my present deprivation. Your sweet love is my *atmosphere* when I am at home: without it, I seem to lack breath,—the heart seems gone out of me. No wonder Mrs. Bird said to me to-day "Whenever I see you I feel as if Nellie ought to be, *must* be, somewhere around." I hope I *do* suggest your influence! Surely I must: you have supplied me, directly or indirectly, with so much of both the substance and the form of my talk: you have formed me to so much of what I am. I should love myself very much more if I could feel that I *had* caught and embodied some part of your sweet *personality*. Mrs. Bird and Mrs. Smith both speak of you with genuine affection, my darling: they mourn your absence, I am sure, unaffectedly. We may rejoice, I think, in having won in them very staunch friends. Mrs. Bird is far from well of her cold; but she was very interesting, and the dinner was certainly excellent. By the way, we had a good deal of a talk about the Central and Southwestern roads—too much even to summarize in a letter —even if I understood her account of it (full of personal details, as it was) well enough to summarize it. The Central's case is hopeless; the Southwestern may come all right if it can be cut loose from the Central—and a committee of the S. W. directors, appointed at a meeting of the stockholders to accomplish the separation, are trying to get all the proxies they can. One of these Directors is Dr. John S. Baxter, Mrs. Bird's brother, President of the S. W. I am going to write to him to-night to send you a blank form for the appointment of a proxy. When it comes, please fill it out, dear, with his name as proxy, sign it, and send it to him immediately—addressed simply, Dr. John S. Baxter, Macon, Georgia. The decisive meeting comes on February 10th, Mrs. Bird thinks. The three directors appointed to take proxies are Dr. Baxter, Mr. Tom Gresham[4] here, and Mr. Raoul,[5] in New York. For the Central there seems no hope at all. It is completely overwhelmed with debt, and it wants to hold on to and ruin the Southwestern. You will have no difficulty in making out the proxies, and they do not have to be attested. But if you *should* be puzzled, get Mrs. [Eliza] Ricketts to direct you.[6] If it is necessary for you to state the number of your shares, they are in the tin box, you know.

And, now, enough business for the nonce. I must torture myself a few minutes before closing with a thought or two sent directly home to you. Oh, my sweet intimate, my precious confidante, how sweet it is to pour my heart out to you without reserve —to know that the little woman, the beautiful, the ideal little woman by whom it seems better worth while to be understood than by anybody else in the world, does understand me, and thinks it worth while to understand me! Your tenderness for me and belief in me I live on. They seem to *constitute* me in every effort I make. I depend upon them for inspiration and for confidence in what I undertake. You are my *life*, and I am, in heart and equipment too, Your own Woodrow

Love unbounded to the babies, and unstinted to the boys.

ALS (WC, NjP).

1 Wilson was going to attend the Brown Memorial Presbyterian Church, the Rev. Dr. Maltbie Davenport Babcock, pastor.

2 The sender was Thomas B. Mackall, as EAW to WW, Feb. 1, 1894, reveals. The book was Albert Taylor Bledsoe, *Is Davis a Traitor, or, Was Secession a Constitutional Right Previous to the War of 1861?* (Baltimore, 1866). The copy in the Wilson Library, DLC, is inscribed: "For Profr. Woodrow Wilson With the Compliments of Thos. B. Mackall. Baltimore Md. April 1, 1893."

3 Probably Charles Howard Hinton, Instructor in Mathematics at Princeton.

4 Thomas Baxter Gresham, lawyer of Baltimore, formerly of Macon, and brother of Mary or Minnie Gresham Machen.

5 William G. Raoul.

6 "As she [Mrs. Ricketts] had some money that she invested shrewdly, mother accepted her advice about her own modest financial affairs." Eleanor Wilson McAdoo, *The Woodrow Wilsons* (New York, 1937), p. 48.

From Ellen Axson Wilson

My darling,   [Princeton, N.J.] Monday [Jan. 29, 1894]

I regret to say that I have yielded to the temptation of "finishing" something!—and that it is now a quarter past ten! I do repent me now that it is too late, for letter-time has sped and I must send you a hurried scrawl. But I am flushed with triumph all the same, for the thing finished is a *stunning* new evening gown—black silk and lace—which I have achieved at the total cost of 30cts! It is both picturesque, "stylish" and becoming,—I think you will like it.

I am *so* sorry dear about the eyes and the cold. Am distressed that I cannot enclose the prescription tonight. But it has been raining horizontally and terrifically all day & I hated to send Ed out in it again after your letter came. But I will be sure to send it tomorrow. Will also try to find out if Davis was a traitor (!) Wish I knew what the book looks like,—whether a pamphlet or a bound volume. I had the greatest hunt this morning for something containing the address of the "Forum," so that I might telegraph Mr. Page in answer to enclosed.[1] I never found it, but Ed thought it was on "Union Square" so we put that rather vague address.

We are all well. George has seen Mr. Hinsdale and will meet the session Saturday.[2] He received today two most beautiful pictures of Annie.[3] Tell Sister A. to send ours to you that you may see them at once. Tell her we must have *both*; we have sent her a whole gallery of ours, you know.

I overheard the following remark from Jessie as she was undressing. "Isabel,[4] do you know what I wish I was?" "No." "A poet!"

I shall not try, dearest, to answer tonight this sweet Sunday letter—not with my pen at least—my heart makes constant answer true, & in every beat of it feels itself to be altogether,

                                        Your own   Eileen

ALS (WC, NjP).
  1 It is missing, but see WW to EAW, Jan. 31, 1894.
  2 George Howe III was admitted to the membership of the First Presbyterian Church on February 3, 1894. "Minutes of the First Presbyterian Church, Princeton, New Jersey, June 4, 1892-April 4, 1908," p. 26, bound ledger book, Speer Library, Princeton Theological Seminary.
  3 His sister, then not quite three years old.
  4 A nursemaid.

Two Letters to Ellen Axson Wilson

My own darling,   Baltimore, Monday, 29 Jan'y, 1894

Your little note of Friday night reached me this morning. What 'surcease of sorrow' a few words from your [you] bring, my sweet, sweet love. It seems to me to be a comfort just to sit with one of your letters in my hand and look at it. I seem to feel the sentiments with which it was written and so to be filled with some winning influence. You are certainly my good genius, darling. Every influence that proceeds from you seems to make me at once better and stronger. Bless you for a sweet conjurer!

I went to hear Jere Witherspoon[1] at Dr. Leftwich's church last night, and oh, *what* a jejune sermon. There was absolutely nothing in it—nothing even in the delivery—that *any* one else might not have done just as well. But I introduced myself to him afterwards, and was pleasantly amused by his thoroughly southern manners.

I am going to write Mrs. Brown a note, to say good-bye. I feel very badly about not going over to see her before I came away. Do go over and soften it some way.

My cold is a trifle better.

I love you with a overmastering love, my Eileen, and am altogether   Your own   Woodrow

[1] The Rev. Dr. Jere Witherspoon, formerly pastor of the First Presbyterian Church of Nashville, had just succeeded the Rev. Dr. James Turner Leftwich as pastor of the First Presbyterian Church of Baltimore.

My own darling,   Baltimore, 29 & 30 January, '94

I am extremely glad that you allowed me to intercept this proxy to Mr. Comer. It illustrates what I told you in my Sunday letter. There is a great struggle in progress. The Central is straining every nerve to obtain a majority of proxies to vote the Southwestern back into its own hands, and so divest all its naturally rich earnings into the bottomless depth of its own (the Central's) liabilities. The men most immediately interested in the Southwestern, on their part, are striving, though not by direct appeals like this of Mr. Comer's, to get enough votes to get their road out of the clutches of the Central. We must go in with the latter party, of course. If they succeed, they are positively assured of abundant financial aid in New York to put the road on a paying basis again within a couple of years. I've changed the proxy to the form it ought to have to go to Dr. Baxter. If the blank from Dr. Baxter comes in time to be gotten back to Macon before the 8th of February, fill it out as this is filled out. If it does not come in good season, send this altered one—and don't delay either of them for my inspection. Every few shares count for *something*. That Lawton-Alexander crowd has played a rascally game. They prevented Raoul's election (as you remember uncle Randolph told us) in order,—it now appears,—to sell out to the Richmond Terminal Co., and enable *some*body to make four or five millions.[1] Alexander may have been duped, but he was certainly the instrument of the transfer. Comer *seems* to be of the same connection.

The Eagle and Phenix blank is in an envelope on my desk, at the left hand end. It is like this blank from Savannah and you can fill it out very easily without assistance. But the letter accompanying it no more explains the object of the meeting than Mr. Comer's circular letter does. Besides, we concluded that nothing could be done about the matter because we knew no one in Columbus whom you could appoint your proxy. Perhaps Mr.—the father of the boy at the Rectory[2]—I can't think of his name—Mr. *Harold* is interested and would act for you. You might get his son to send the proxy for you at a venture. He could give you his father's initials.

Unfortunately, for once I was prompt and had sent your skirt to the cleaner some hours before your letter came. But I will rush down to the place as soon as possible and try to have it ripped from the band. I may *possibly* not be too late—I *hope* so. It is night now or I should go at once. Your letter reached me at dark—the dress went down right after breakfast. I will go down to-morrow morning early.

Has no letter come from North Carolina?[3] A N. C. man told me he had seen an announcement in the Durham paper that I was going to deliver my "celebrated lecture on Democracy."

The alumni dinner here is to be held Thursday evening next, February 1st. The President, it seems, is not coming (he *is* a rum President, to be sure!) and I, as usual, must make the speech for the college![4] I am getting very tired of this. It *may* be an honour; but it *looks* very much like being made a convenience of.

This is the second part of this letter, dear: I've been down to the cleaner's. The skirt was already in process, but they said it was not too late to have what you wished done, and they agreed to do it themselves: so I have no doubt it will be all right.

Your sweet letters are such a comfort to me, darling: they are so full of the little happenings and sayings of my dear home,—where *you* are, and the precious words of endearment with which they close make their way somehow into my life. I am conscious of them all day. They make all my tasks light and full of pleasure

—as when you come into my study and kiss me as I sit at my desk. It is odd how this attachment of yours to me seems part of the force of my mind. I think and write with a different *flavour* because of it. It is the source of the imaginative colour that has come into my writing of late years. My own personality is expanded, enriched, made bright and attractive by the transfusion of *your* personality—the sweetest I ever knew; richer with the colours of heart and mind which make the perfect woman, keen to perceive and appreciate whatever a man can, and yet "a Spirit still, and bright with something of angelic light." I should be nothing without you. I should never have come within hailing distance of literature, if I had married anyone else. Women like Miss [Henrietta] Ricketts have a touch too much of *cleverness*. In you the same powers exist in a different atmosphere. Your mind burns with such a soft and warming flame, sacrifices nothing to brilliancy: gives as *much* light, but a so much *sweeter* light, as if it burned always for the sake of others. Perhaps if you *knew* your power it would be spoiled. Ah, darling, I trust it is not wrong to worship you as I do. You are the presiding genius of both my mind and heart—and in that fact consists the happiness and the strength of   Your own   Woodrow

The cold is a great deal better, sweetheart.
Love to all.

ALS (WC, NjP).
¹ Alexander R. Lawton, former Confederate general and prominent in the postwar politics and business life of Georgia, was an old friend of Ellen's from Savannah. His law firm had been the chief counsel for the Central Railroad of Georgia. Edward P. Alexander, a former Confederate brigadier, was a businessman and planter of Augusta. The "Lawton-Alexander crowd" had ousted William G. Raoul as president of the Central of Georgia in 1887 and elected Alexander in his stead. Then, in the following year, they had sold for $12,000,000 the entire capital stock of the Central of Georgia to the Richmond and West Point Terminal Railway and Warehouse Company, which was the holding company for the numerous railroads that later became the Southern Railway System.
² William Elliott Harrold of Americus, Ga., a freshman in the School of Science, who roomed at the Episcopal rectory on Stockton Street. His father was W. B. Harrold.
³ See WW to EAW, Feb. 6, 1894, n. 2.
⁴ See F. L. Patton to WW, Jan. 30, 1894.

From Francis Landey Patton

My dear Professor Wilson: [Princeton, N.J.] Jany 30 94

Your kind letter to George¹ I have seen & I write now to say that I am glad you will go to the Contemporary Club & that I must rely on you also to do the kind service again which you did so well in New York; by speaking in my place at the dinner in Baltimore.

I am sorry to miss the dinner in Baltimore: but the Phila. dinner also occurs on Feb 1st[.] I am bound by a prior engagement to attend it   Very faithfully yours   Francis L Patton

ALS (Patton Letterpress Books, University Archives, NjP).
  ¹ His son, George Stevenson Patton. Wilson's letter is missing.

From Ellen Axson Wilson

[Princeton, N. J.]
My darling,   Wednesday Morning [Jan. 31, 1894].

We reached home at half past eleven or later last night, and I was so "dead tired" I couldn't write. I scribble a hasty note now to catch my usual mail. Will try to make up with a long letter tonight.

We had a delightful time last night and the concert was exqui*site*! How I wished for you! Mr. Daniels brought a carriage and also, sent in the morning *three dozen* of the lovliest roses!— extravagant fellow! Helen met all the young (!) professors & seemed to have a very good time! She looked lovely in black & yellow with beautiful yellow roses at her waist.

We are all well. How I *hope* you are the same!—and that the eyes are better. I sent the pipette &c. yesterday. And now goodbye for a few hours darling. With a heart brimming over with love for my dearest I am as ever,   Your own   Eileen.

ALS (WP, DLC).

To Ellen Axson Wilson

My own darling,   Baltimore, 31 January, 1894

This letter from Longmans makes it necessary for me to have one more thing from home.¹ My copy of the Epoch (in the first, the smaller, form of binding) contains all my notes for the correction of the text. Will you not get Ed. or George to do it up at once and send it to me by mail?

I am sorry that I missed Page's visit: my curiosity is piqued to know what he can be anxious enough to talk over with me to come all the way to Princeton for the interview. Doubtless he wants to cajole me into doing some big piece of work for the *Forum*, and I shall be saved the embarrassment of refusing him to his face.

By-the-way, dear, that book, "Was Davis a Traitor" is a rather rusty black book, old-fashioned looking and thin (by reason of want and neglect?) and is in the third book case from the door— I *think*.

What about the cashmire that is to be stamped, sweetheart? Did you not receive my letter containing questions about it asked me at the Decorative Art Society's rooms? You have not answered them yet.

I don't know how I can approve a gown which made you sit up too late—and neglect me (!); but it was certainly a triumph to make it for 30¢—and anything that you design as well as make must always be pretty and tasteful, my sweet little artist.

The rest of the week is rather full of engagements for me. This evening I go to see Daisy Woods[2] married. I don't know whether there is a reception after the ceremony in the church or not. If there is, I am not invited. To-morrow evening I go to the alumni dinner and speak for Dr. Patton and the college—as serious a speech as possible on foot-ball, in rehearsal of what I shall say in Philadelphia. Friday evening I read my 'Burke' before the Historical Seminary[3]—then adjourn and attend a Y.M.C.A. reception at Levering Hall. Saturday evening I think I shall have to relieve the strain by going to see Lillian Russell in "Princess Nicotine"![4] I've never seen the wanton minx; and, though she is no longer as beautiful as she once was, she is said to *sing* beautifully still.

I am so glad you are going to the Club concert, darling—or, rather, that you have gone. I *hope* you enjoyed it.

What an interesting saying, that of Jessie's, bless her heart! I hope she may have her wish and be a poet! *You* are a *mute* poet (perversely mute) and I might have been a poet, if I could have married you when I was a boy:—why may not our most gifted child be a poet?

I love you, my precious pet, beyond all words even of poetry and am in every beat of my heart

Your own   Woodrow

ALS (WC, NjP).

1 It is missing.

2 Elizabeth Fuller Woods, sister of Wilson's classmate, Dr. Hiram Woods, married Richard Henley Woodward in the Eutaw Place Baptist Church on January 31. There was no reception after the ceremony.

3 See the Editorial Note, "Wilson's First Lecture on Burke," and the Minutes of the Seminary of Historical and Political Science, Feb. 15, 1894.

4 This comic opera by Charles A. Byrne, Louis Harrison, and William W. Furst was playing at Ford's Grand Comic Opera in Baltimore. For Wilson's comment on Lillian Russell and the opera, see WW to EAW, Feb. 4, 1894.

From Ellen Axson Wilson

My darling,   Princeton, Jan. 31/94.

It is indeed fortunate that I sent the Comer blank to you! I realized that as soon as I received your Sunday letter;—mine con-

taining the blank having just gone before it came. How lucky
you heard about it all from Mrs. Bird, for if it is such a close
shave our thirteen shares may "count." I signed today the Eagle
& Phenix blank & sent it to Uncle Randolph asking him to put in
any name he chose—or to tear it up if he pleased! I am so sorry
to have given you all that extra trouble about the dress! I had no
idea you would have taken it down so soon. About the shawl.
I want it arranged for a rather narrow hem feather-stitched with
the blue, a bunch of flowers tied with ribbons (embroidered) in
the upper corner, & a few loose flowers straggling towards the
front;—no embroidery on the under part.

No, nothing has come from N. C. How very odd! I am sorry
there is another Alumni speech in prospect. It is a *shame* that
you should have it all to do; what a "roi faineant" is ours! It seems
they are in a good deal of trouble about George,[1] who, Mrs. Brown
told me today, has catarrh of the stomach. I was struck Sunday
by the poor fellow's wretched, *wizened* appearance. He seems to
be shrivelling away. That is a dreadful disease; it is what Papa
was supposed to have.

We have heard from Stockton at last. He was quite ill,—laid
up,—with the grip just after leaving here; is improving now but
still very unwell. I feel quite unhappy about him. Burlington
must disagree with him. If you hear of anything that might be
to his advantage while there please make a note of it. I cannot
help thinking that the University Extension work[2] for a year
or two might be to the advantage of his health. Would you mind
making a few inquiries to see if he *could* make a living out of it
next winter if he would?

And I may as well exhaust my budget of commissions at once,—
will you, when you get time, write to [D. C.] Heath for those speci-
men books,—geographies, arithmetics, histories and spelling books,
—primary? Margaret will soon be eight, you know, and I feel that
I must be thinking about more systematic instruction. They are
so funny! M. was telling a terrible dream she had had;—a "bull
cow" had eaten them all up. "But a wolf is the worst," objected
Jessie. "I don't care" said Margaret indignantly, ["]I *dreamt* a
bull cow! I can't tell a lie!" This was a delicious day & they had
a happy time on their sleds again, & were filled with wild delight
over a snow man that Ed made for them.

A curious thing happened today. A whole barrel of *ale* was
brought up from the freight office, distinctly marked "W. Wilson."
Hogarty said it was from Phila. What can it mean?[3] The freight—
43 cts—was not prepaid. They left it here, but promised to make
further inquiries.

Miss Ricketts & I had arranged to spend the afternoon at the Art Gallery[4]–started soon after two–but it was so cold there we could only stay a hour or less. We had a *very* good time while we were there. Mr. Clarke[5] has a few good things; one splendid and very famous one–a Madonna by Dainan-Bouvret.(?)[6] I have seen many engravings of it. It is *beautiful*.

How can I thank you, dearest, for the sweet things you say in today's letter! How happy it makes me that you think such things of me even when I feel with a heart-ache how sadly unworthy I am of it all! Surely so long as you love me like that I can never be anything but happy whatever betide. And oh, darling, you do not know with what deep, intense, and constant happiness I dwell in your love and upon it. It seems sometimes almost too wonderful and perfect to be true that I should be blessed with *such* love from such an one as you. Sometimes I wonder for an instant as I used to do when I was a queer little child, if I shall wake up some day and find that I only "dreamed it in a dream." Ah my love, my joy, I can never, never tell you how passionately I love you in return! I too "trust it is not wrong to worship you as I do." I had as well question if it be wrong to *breathe*; both are inevitable if I am to *live* at all, for I am in every breath altogether   Your own   Eileen.

ALS (WC, NjP).
¹ "They" referred to President and Mrs. Patton. George was their son, George Stevenson Patton.
² About the American Society for the Extension of University Teaching, see G. Henderson to WW, May 18, 1891, n. 1, Vol. 7; about Stockton Axson's future connection with the Society, see L. P. Powell to WW, Feb. 18, 1894, n. 2.
³ The mystery of the barrel of ale will be cleared up in future correspondence. "Hogarty" was Joseph Hogarty of the freight office of the Pennsylvania Railroad.
⁴ The College's Museum of Historic Art, then in process of construction.
⁵ Thomas Shields Clarke, '82, a sculptor, painter, and collector who was living temporarily in Princeton and had put his collection on exhibit in the Art Museum.
⁶ Ellen garbled the name of the French painter under whom Clarke had studied, Pascal Adolphe Jean Dagnan-Bouveret.

To Ellen Axson Wilson

My own darling   Baltimore, 1 February, 1894

Mr. Page, of the *Forum*, turned up here, but, as I did not see him alone, I do not know whether he had anything special to say to me or not. Dr. H. B. Adams, H. C. Adams (who is also lecturing here now),[1] Page, and I dined together last evening at the University Club–and our party did not break up until nearly midnight. We had a *very* interesting and very jolly time. I feel that I know H. C. Adams and Page much better than I should have been able to know them within the same space of time under any other circumstances.

We had our dinner just after I had seen Daisy Woods married. The marriage was very pretty; Frank Woods, the bride's brother, performed the ceremony with real dignity and refined feeling; and *Kate* Woods, who was her sister's only attendant, looked perfectly stunning in her white and blue dress. There was no reception afterwards, for the couple left on an early train for their trip "to the North" (which sounds quite southern, doesn't it?).

So you found the music at the Club concert "exquisite," did you, dear? I am so glad. I never had any doubt that your apparent lack of a taste for music was due to your having heard only inferior performers for the most part. A love for genuine, delicately modulated music is certainly a necessary part of your nature. I've been sure of that from the first. Your make-up and your tastes are the very negation of everything that is crude or unrefined. Have I not suffered the keen rebuke of that fact on more than one occasion? You always make me think either of some simple and noble poem or else of some exquisite harmony, and it has always seemed to me that some sweet and elevated harmony would best express your delightful personality—which I so adore—which purifies me as music and poetry do—making my bondage sure as   Your own   Woodrow

ALS (WC, NjP).
    [1] Henry Carter Adams, the noted economist of the University of Michigan, gave a course of twenty lectures on problems of transportation at the Johns Hopkins in January and February 1894.

From Ellen Axson Wilson

My own darling,   [Princeton, N. J.] Thursday [Feb. 1, 1894]

Mr. & Mrs. Waldo[1] have been making a long visit and it is now after ten so I must try to write a short letter; especially as I am rather tired, as I have been sewing pretty hard. It is funny what an "ignis fatuus" the hope of ever "getting through with my sewing" is! As soon as I finish the *last* of the "fall" sewing I find that the *first* of it is worn out & is to do again! I am now putting new sleeves in the children's dresses, renovating the bottoms of my skirts &c. &c. As soon as I finish all this it will be high time to begin the "spring" sewing,—and so it is an endless "merry-go-round"!

I sent the book—the Epoch—today. The name of the person who sent you the "Davis" is "Thos. B. Mackall"[.] The author is Albert T. Bledsoe. Your only mail today except this from Columbia

College[2] concerns Prof. Royce [—] invitations to hear him at the Philosophical Club and to see him at Prof. Marquand's—who gives him a reception.[3]

We are all quite well. I hope you, dearest, are the same. I fear you are overworking; you seem to be in a perfect rush of *hard* engagements! But I really must not run over this third page to-night. How hard it is to leave any part of a sheet to you unfilled even in a daily letter! Ah my darling, my Woodrow, I love you *love you love you*! How happy it makes me to think that one week of your stay is gone—that at any rate not *more* than a whole month is left. With dearest love   Your own   Eileen.

ALS (WC, NjP).
  [1] Mr. and Mrs. Frank Waldo, of 95 Mercer Street.
  [2] It is missing.
  [3] About the Philosophical Club, see n. 1 to the address, "Political Sovereignty," printed at Nov. 9, 1891, Vol. 7. Royce spoke to the Philosophical Club at Dr. McCosh's on the evening of February 2, on knowledge of externality, social consciousness, and faculties of imitation. Professor Allan Marquand's reception was held at 4:30 that afternoon.

A News Report of a Meeting of the Maryland Alumni

[Feb. 2, 1894]

THE TIGER RAMPANT.

Nearly a hundred old and young Princeton men, some with white beards and others with no beards at all, but all graduates of the New Jersey college, assembled in the parlors of the Lyceum Theatre last night to attend the ninth annual reunion and banquet of the Princeton Alumni Association of Maryland. . . .

There were present as guests of the association Woodrow Wilson, '79, professor of political economy at Princeton and representing the university; J. Stanley Addicks,[1] representing the Philadelphia alumni; J. B. Noel Wyatt,[2] representing Harvard; Dr. Bernard C. Steiner,[3] representing Yale, and Leroy Gresham, representing the Johns Hopkins University.

After the good things which Caterer Harris had furnished had been dealt with, President J. Edwin Michael[4] called upon Professor Wilson to answer to the toast, "Princeton University." Professor Wilson devoted most of his time to the place of athletics, particularly foot-ball, in the college curriculum. He said, in part:

"My principal reason for being here is to express the good feeling existing between those at old Nassau and those who have left its sacred walls. Princeton is noted in the wide world for three things—foot-ball, baseball and collegiate instruction. I suppose the first of these is what you want to hear about. Maryland is a bad place to come to to talk foot-ball, for, as usual, the captain of the team is a Marylander.[5] In the criticisms of foot-ball lots has been said that is true and more that is untrue. The religious press declares the game to be dangerous because of the 'masse plays.' Now, I don't believe the men who write these critiques know what masse plays are. The men who were killed last year playing foot-ball were not killed in masse plays, but in open plays. Most of the casualties occurred in England, where masse plays are unknown. Foot-ball is a manly game, and the present proposition is to reform it—to make it more manly. Those who say, 'let the faculties reform it,' seem to think the faculties are foot-ball experts. That suggestion is humorous. The only real difficulty apparent is in the character of the players. We at Princeton are perfectly satisfied with all of our men from that standpoint. They know the changes they want, and they want them as badly as any one. These men are manly enough to modify the game as much as it needs modifying. The parent class is not being trampled upon, either, as some of the editorials of which I have spoken would lead one to suppose. Out of forty-two parents whose consent was asked for their sons to play foot-ball at Princeton last year forty consented. The other two men were not allowed to play. I believe in college athletics. Athletics are a safety-valve for animal spirits, and if these don't have a safety-valve, they mix kindly with other spirits. If the men don't play foot-ball they will play less legitimate games. As soon as the students of the college take the subject of athletics in their own hands and draw the boundary lines then will that college be the [out]standing college of the future." . . .

Printed in the Baltimore *Sun*, Feb. 2, 1894; some editorial headings omitted.
    [1] William H. Addicks, '74, corporation lawyer of Philadelphia. The reporter undoubtedly mistook his name, as William H. Addicks is the only Princeton graduate of this surname listed in the alumni catalogues.
    [2] James Bosley Noel Wyatt, Harvard, '70, an architect of Baltimore.
    [3] Bernard Christian Steiner, Yale, '88, at this time Librarian of the Enoch Pratt Free Library in Baltimore.
    [4] Dr. Jacob Edwin Michael, '71, Professor of Obstetrics, University of Maryland Medical School.
    [5] Thomas Gawthrop Trenchard, '95, captain in 1893 and 1894.

To Ellen Axson Wilson

My own darling,   Baltimore, 2 Feb'y, 1894

    I shall be obliged to confine myself to a little note to-day, for I am greatly pressed for time.
    I am glad to report that the chagrin of New York[1] was not repeated last night. I think I can say that my speech was a de-

cided success. It *seemed* to provoke considerable enthusiasm. Consequently, after it was over, I enjoyed myself very much.

My cold grows steadily better, though slowly because I have had to exert myself and use my voice so much of late. My eyes are very much better—so long as I can keep out of tobacco smoke.

Thank you, darling, for that long, sweet letter written on Wednesday. Your letters are like scraps of home to me—like detached pieces of you,—and as long as I linger over them,—*in* them,—I am happy. What a blessed solace they are, and how could I do without them! Ah, my darling, how my heart breaks with the longing to look into your eyes, feel your arms about me, your quick breath, and your eager caresses, hold you close to me and pour into your ears all the passionate love with which my heart—here where I cannot have you—is fairly oppressed, intolerably burdened. I am so *proud* of your love,—so exalted by it, and yet *away* from you it is such an exquisite pain to be

Your own   Woodrow

ALS (WC, NjP).

[1] A reference to his speech at the annual dinner of the Princeton alumni of New York on January 19, 1894. See EAW to WW, Feb. 6, 1894, for a different report.

From Ellen Axson Wilson

My darling,   Princeton, Feb. 2/94

I am perfectly at my wits ends as to what to do about this miserable proxy business. I have been to Mrs. Ricketts and she can't help me. The blank from Macon came tonight & with it this enclosed circular.[1] You see what the note says. Our shares have *not* been withdrawn from the "Mercantile Trust Co"![2] I find their certificate in the box but not securities of course. And the meeting is on the *eigth*. How can we get them in time? Mrs. Ricketts says the only way is for me to go to New York tomorrow & get them. She says that anyhow I ought by no means to let the certificates get out of my hands until I get the securities, because I would have nothing to show for them. But she thought that thirteen shares could not possibly make any great difference in the issue, and that it would not be worth the trouble & expense of a trip to New York to get them. So at first she advised me *not* to go,— and afterwards rather advised me to go, because you seemed to think it important! So there is my quandary! And since I left Mrs. R. I have remembered that it is practically impossible for me to go to New York tomorrow because I have promised Isabel that she may go to Phila. & she has made all her arrangements.

I fear those shares are doomed to remain voiceless. I shall send the proxy to Mr. Baxter tonight, anyhow, and write to the Trust Co. about it. But I don't suppose I will accomplish anything.

Your Equitable policy came tonight with enclosed note.[3]

Isn't it good that the Wilson Bill[4] has passed. I am *so* disappointed that you were not there to see the great scene & hear the great speech,—of Wilson's! It seems to have been *splendid*! I meant to have read it tonight but these "proxies & things" have interfered. With a heart as full as it can possibly hold of love & devotion I am, darling,   Your little wife   Eileen

Worse & worse! I can't even find the address of the "Mercantile Trust." It is not on these papers. I must simply send my note to New York.

I console myself with thinking that the Baxter side can't think 13 shares *very* important, or would they not have applied for my proxy? I suppose they have lists of the stockholders.

ALS (NjP). Enc.: J. S. Baxter, R. T. Wilson, and W. G. Raoul to the stockholders of the South-Western Railroad, printed letter dated Dec. 18, 1893.

[1] This communication, listed as an enclosure, informed the stockholders that the signators were a committee organized to cooperate with the board of directors of the South-Western Railroad in the board's efforts to protect their interests. It further advised that the annual meeting of the stockholders, to be held in Macon on February 8, 1894, would be one of crucial importance and urged full attendance or the giving of proxies to Baxter.

[2] A postscript to the circular from Baxter, Wilson, and Raoul said that the shares of the South-Western Railroad had been deposited with the Mercantile Trust Company of New York and had to be withdrawn "in order to give the owner the power of voting them or obtain power of Attorney from the Trust Company."

[3] This enclosure is missing.

[4] The Cleveland administration's bill for substantial tariff reductions, introduced on December 19, 1893, by Representative William Lyne Wilson of West Virginia, chairman of the Ways and Means Committee, was adopted by the House of Representatives on February 1, 1894, by a vote of 204 to 140. Just before the vote, Wilson spoke in defense of the bill with wit and eloquence, evoking frequent applause from his colleagues.

To Ellen Axson Wilson

My own darling,   Baltimore, 4 February, 1894

I am *so* sorry that you have had so much trouble about those proxies. I had no idea that the fact of our shares being in the Trust Co.'s vaults would make any difference. I supposed that was a mere deposit, and that the Co. had no rights of attorney after the breakdown of that first scheme of reorganization. To tell the truth, I had forgotten the shares were in New York. Perhaps, since you have sent Dr. Baxter the proxy, you had better go to New York, for a pleasure trip, on Tuesday or Wednesday and get the poor shares, so that when they are voted, on Thursday, it may be rightfully. But don't part with your certificate of deposit until you get your shares.

Can't you make a trip to New York do instead of most of your Spring sewing, darling? Can you not buy most of what will be needed? Surely you can. The mere mention of a season's sewing makes me desperately anxious and uneasy. Remember that you are under bonds to take care of yourself for my sake, and that you must do anything rather than undergo extreme fatigue or bring back that muscular trouble in your legs by the use of the sewing machine!

I wrote to Heath yesterday, my pet, about the books you want, and hope that he will be as prompt in sending them as I have been slow in asking for them. In that case, he would have to send them by telegraph, wouldn't he?

Indeed I will make inquiries about the University Extension work for Stockton. There is no one here who could tell me anything authentic; but I will write to Philadelphia and see what can be learned by letter. Poor boy! It is indeed pathetical that he should be so burdened by ill health. I am beyond measure distressed.

I received a letter from dear father[1] the other day which went much beyond the hint contained in that earlier letter about his distaste for the household on 22nd St.[2] He says that he has been a long time in discovering the thorough uncongeniality of his present "environment," but that he has found it out at last, and is impatient to get away! He deplores the fact that it is not yet time to start for the Assembly[3]—"too early to go to Columbia." I have written urging him to go to you,—and establish himself in our house, as we have so often and so earnestly urged him to do. You second the invitation, don't you, sweetheart? My heart bleeds to think of his desolateness and homelessness! He loves you, and I believe you love him. I would do anything in my power to make his last years bright and full of love, and I know you want to help me.

I am very grateful for this quiet, restful Sabbath, and this sweet leisure of communion with my darling, after the rush and strain of last week. It was all of a piece, and I was as much occupied yesterday as on previous days—though part of the occupation was voluntary. I spent the afternoon at the theatre—my first indulgence this week—just to get all the work and the rush of engagements out of my head,—and then I hurried away to a reception at Dr. James Carey Thomas's—where were the Dean-President,[4] Miss Gwinn,[5] *et id omne genus.* The evening was consumed by letter writing—answers to the stupid letters you have been enclosing me of late. My letter to you I saved for to-day when I could have leisure to enjoy the sweet intercourse, and *realize* you as I wrote— since it would make no difference in the frequency with which you would hear from me.

The reception was "the usual thing," the company for the most part academic and professional, Miss Gwinn as affected a nincumpoop as ever (bah!),—but Miss Thomas, the Dean-President, astonishingly cordial, asking most particularly after you, sending you her love—or something like it (I don't suppose she *has* any *love*!)—telling me of complimentary things she had heard about me, &c. &c. 'Tis a mad world, my masters! Mrs. Worthington[6] was very genuine, almost affectionate,—and I am to take tea with her and Tom. this evening.

By-the-way, did we meet a Mrs. [George] Small (16 Mt. Vernon Place) while you were here? A Mrs. Small sent me a note last night asking me to dine with her, and her nephew, Legh Reid, next Tuesday. I accepted quite in the dark.

Lillian Russell, whom I saw at the matinee yesterday was a great disappointment. She may have been a beauty once, of the voluptuous sort; but she is not now, the painted and bedizzened creature. She ought at any rate to devise means of excluding opera glasses from the house when she appears. But the opera itself, the singing, the scenery, and the dancing, were pretty enough, and I was sufficiently amused. Several of the chorus girls, at least, if not the *prima donna*, were beauties, and I rested my eyes with them.

Ah, sweetheart, if only I had *you*, it seems to me I should need no other rest than your tones and your caresses would give me,— no other recreation than your company would afford me. For some reason, I have thought of you more intensely, it seems to me, the three times I've been to the theatre here this time, than anywhere else. I wonder why it is? It is certainly not the sight of the vulgar love-making that goes on on the stage that makes me think of you. Neither is it simply that I am in a holiday humour and can have no *complete* enjoyment or relaxation without you (though that, no doubt, is a substantial part of the explanation). Perhaps it is, that when I see an image of life on the stage and look upon other women's faces there as they seem to be at home or abroad in the midst of the world, the meaning of my own relations in life, whether by contrast or suggestion, is brought vividly home to me,—the meaning of one woman's life to me. I am made somehow conscious of the springs of resolution and action within myself—and go away from the place (no matter how empty, frivolous, or imperfect the play may have been, or how vulgar the actors) awed and delighted by thoughts of the real life I am myself in the midst of. I remember having felt the same way, to some extent, when at the theatre *with* you:—it is only more vivid when I am alone. It was most powerful the evening I went to that terrible play of Oscar Wilde's in New York.[7] I was *overwhelmed* with tenderness for you, my pure and perfect little wife. I am always on such occasions fairly *intoxicated* with thoughts of the sweet simplicity of our lives: with your genuiness—with the quiet and love of our home—with the privilege of high thinking and plain living—with the delight of being simply and always your lover and husband and close companion, not a pretence or an artificiality or a breach of privacy in all our life. How unspeakably precious a thing it is, this life that is all our own, in which we are *sure* that we know and trust and help one another. It elevates me so to *know* that my marriage has made me a *nobler* man—and it elevates *you* in my honour and love beyond all measure. It is *this* that compels me to *worship* my darling—this knowledge, so intimate, so incontestable, of her power to bless and purify and idealize life for those who love her. It is this that makes her my queen!

Oh, Eileen, when these raptures come surging in upon my heart, I cry out in my haunted loneliness (for I am fairly haunted by your image and every delightful thought of you)—I cry out for some tone of your voice, a touch of your lips, a caress,—*some* escape from this mere longing! And yet it is not a *mere* longing, after all; for every kiss or caress or sweet word you ever gave me seems stored up as a fund of life in me. I trade on it at the same time that I hoard it—and so keep myself from despair. But seven lectures are past, love—that is *almost* a third, isn't it? And then—then will come the end of exile for

Your own   Woodrow

ALS (WC, NjP).
  [1] It is missing.
  [2] That is, the one kept by Dr. Wilson's friend, Elizabeth Bartlett Grannis.
  [3] The General Assembly of the southern Presbyterian Church was to meet in the Moore Memorial Church in Nashville on May 17, 1894.
  [4] Martha Carey Thomas, whom the Board of Trustees of Bryn Mawr College, on November 17, 1893, had elected to succeed James E. Rhoads as President. Her tenure was to begin on August 31, 1894. For many years she combined the positions of President and Dean.
  [5] Mary Gwinn, Associate Professor of English at Bryn Mawr.
  [6] Mrs. Thomas K. Worthington, whose husband was Wilson's friend from his graduate student days at the Hopkins.
  [7] "Lady Windermere's Fan," which Wilson saw at Palmer's Theatre in New York at some time during its run there between February 6 and April 15, 1893.

From Ellen Axson Wilson

My darling,   [Princeton, N.J.] Sunday Feb 4/94

I did not *mean* to omit my last night's letter—though I do not know that it makes much difference as it would have reached you at the same time with this. But it was one of my dead sleepy evenings,—after getting the children bathed and put to bed—Isabel being in New York you know,—I sat down to rest a minute before writing, and immediately went fast asleep, only rousing myself with the greatest difficulty at ten o'clock! So there was an end of letter-writing.

It has been snowing and sleeting all day and Helen I suppose did not venture out,—at least she did not turn up here. Ed & I went to the first church with George. There was no service of admission.[1] Their names were merely "read out," and there was no solemnity or impressiveness about it. I shouldn't think an individual church would be allowed to make such a radical change in the service as that.

I am so glad dear that the dinner and the speech were successful. And of course you can give that same speech in Washington if you must go there.[2] There is still no word from North Carolina; what will you do about it? And what must *I* do about this *ale*! There is still no light on it. It is a barrel of bottled ale; ought it to be unpacked and taken care of in any particular way?

There is to be a large reception at the Conover's[3] tomorrow afternoon, I am to help receive. Also Miss Ricketts & Mrs. Louis.[4] Oh for my pearls and diamond! How did you succeed in arranging that matter? Mr. [Bliss] Perry is to lecture to the "Tourist Club"[5] on Tuesday afternoon on the later poems of Tennyson. I accepted an invitation to attend, only remembering afterwards my employment society.[6] Am *so* disappointed that I can't hear him! Mr. Frothingham has offered to have a little "class" to study engravings &c. It is to consist of Miss[7] and myself and three or four others to be selected by us. Isn't that pleasant? I believe that is all the news—except the sad item that the old tree opposite with its beautiful crimson vine—the wood robin's tree,—was uprooted by the storm Monday night. Isn't that a sad loss?

How happy it make[s] me, darling, to feel that we are really making some appreciable progress towards the end of this dreary separation. There are only three more Sundays now; isn't that good? I am not unhappy, dear, but I have always the strangest feeling when you are away as if life itself had stopped for the time; and I was merely waiting for things to begin again. I feel so helpless somehow—so impotent—when my love can make no adequate demonstration of itself, but is nine parts unsatisfied yearning. Oh my Woodrow, my treasure, when I *do* get you back again take care of yourself! You will be in danger of death from suffocation! But there are other letters I simply *must* write to-night and there is not much time left, for Miss Ricketts and her brother[8] have been making quite a long visit; so I must say good-night, dear love,—we are all quite well.

With all my heart,   Your little wife,   Eileen.

ALS (WC, NjP) with WWhw sums on envelope.
[1] That is, when George Howe was publicly received into the membership of the church.
[2] She refers to an invitation to Wilson to speak at a meeting of the Washington Princeton alumni, which she enclosed in this letter and which is missing.
[3] Francis Stevens Conover and his wife, Helen Field Conover, who lived in "Avalon" at 59 Bayard Avenue.
[4] Mrs. Edwin Seelye Lewis of 22 Stockton Street, whose husband was Instructor in Romance Languages at the college.
[5] This must have been an ephemeral organization, as the local sources are entirely silent about it.
[6] The only clue as to the name of this organization was its listing in the Princeton city directories of the 1890's as the W.E.P.C. of 32 Nassau Street. The initials probably stood for "Women's Employment Provident Charity."
[7] Ellen omitted the name, but she meant Miss Ricketts, as EAW to WW, Feb. 7, 1894, reveals.
[8] Miss Ricketts had three brothers: Palmer Chamberlaine, Jr., Thomas Getty Ricketts, M.D., and Louis Davidson Ricketts.

To Ellen Axson Wilson

My own darling,   Baltimore, 5 February, 1894

That Washington alumni dinner, the invitation to which you sent me, is set for the same evening as the meeting of the Contemporary Club in Philadelphia, at which I am to defend foot-ball,—so that I had to decline. I hope this gets me past all risks of further after dinner speaking this season!

I spent a very pleasant evening with Tom. Worthington last night—principally with Tom., for Mrs. Worthington went up-stairs to the children after tea. Our conversation led naturally, almost inevitably, to a disclosure of my plan for a history of the United States, which we discussed at some length; and Tom was kind enough to say that there was no one in the country fitted as I was by gifts, training, and temperament for the task,—that I could take my time, and not fear that any one would anticipate me either in the conception or the execution of such a work. I know that this will establish Tom. in your esteem, as it did in mine, as a man of uncommon judgment and discernment! You can see why I enjoyed the evening!

The Worthington children—two boys (the oldest and the youngest) and a girl—are *beautiful*, nothing less, and as charming and straightforward in manner as ideal children should be. They quite took my admiration by storm.

I am in a very pleasant mood just now about my lectures—though it may be only this bright and bracing weather that makes me so. They seem to be "taking" as well as I could wish,—with a very sober class.

Ah, my darling, how everything accrues to your advantage,—if being loved is such! When I am in *glad* spirits, it but makes me love you the more, as my chief source of joy; and when I am *sad*, it but makes me love you the more, for you are my chief solace. In *any* mood, my intensest thoughts and desires and grati-fications are centred in you, my Eileen, my queen—and every *up* and every *down* makes me so much more

Your own   Woodrow

ALS (WC, NjP).

From Ellen Axson Wilson

My own darling,   [Princeton, N.J.] Monday [Feb. 5, 1894]

I have being [been] sitting here I know not how long dreaming over that precious letter of yours that came today, and if you were here I suppose you would ask me just to tell you what I had been thinking! But in very truth the three hours of standing and talking at the [Conovers'] reception have left me with no vocabulary and no thoughts that could be forced into words. I have been merely *resting* in your letter—enjoying it and myself. Indeed dearest it is a letter to be laid away forever and aye in my heart of hearts. Ah how I thank God for the sweet "quiet and love" of this home life of ours—for all its fine simplicity,—sincerity and sweet in-timacies. How I thank Him for *you*, my darling—noble man,—perfect husband that you are!—my own *true* love—so absolutely *all* that a woman could desire the man to be to whom she gives her heart and life!—"framed in the prodigality of nature." How can you wonder that I am filled with a very passion of love and enthusiasm in thinking of my peerless one?—and almost shamed too with the greatness of the blessing, with the wonder of it that all this should be mine. Ah, dear heart, you idealize me in a way that often can but frighten me, but one thing at least you cannot over-estimate and that is my great love.

With all my heart I hope that dear Father will do as you beg and come to us "to stay." I need no[t] tell you how glad I should be if he could be content and happy with us—if I could do anything to make him so. Shall I write and beg him to come *now*—before your return—or would it be best for me not to betray consciousness in that way of what he said in his last to you? Can we not find some occupation here for him—a suburban church—or a lecture-ship—one hour a week,—say,—compensation nominal, since they profess great poverty—at the Seminary. That would both help to anchor him and to make him happy again. I am sure, dear, from study of the "Report" that Mr. Baxter sent that to go to N. Y. about those bonds at this late date would be quite useless. If the Trust Co. means to vote them on either side its proxy has been already sent. I wrote, following the indications in the "Report," asking them to send a proxy for mine to Mr. Baxter. I had hoped to hear from them tonight.

I enclose the only letters received today.[1] Mr. MacCoun's[2] refers to sample pages of European History Charts.

We are all well and we all love you—I more than tongue can tell. As ever,   Your little wife,   Eileen.

ALS (WC, NjP).
    [1] They are missing.
    [2] Townsend MacCoun, distinguished geographer and cartographer.

To Ellen Axson Wilson

My own darling,   Baltimore, 6 February, 1894

This wish for your pearl and diamond pin in your last letter gives my conscience alarm. Did you instruct me to do whatever was possible about it at once and *send* you the pin back,—or else something in its place,—and have I forgotten in assuming that you would wait till my return? I have done nothing in the matter yet; but I will see to it now as soon as possible.

I went last night to see Sol. Smith Russell in his new play, "April Weather."[1] It is not so good as either "Peaceful Valley" or "A Poor Relation," but *he* was most enjoyable.

I have heard from North Carolina at last.[2] They "gladly" accept my terms, and I am to choose some date in March on which to lecture; for they cannot use a Saturday night for the purpose, as they should be obliged to do if I went from here.[3]

If that barrel contains *bottled* ale, dear, it will not be necessary to do anything with it so long as it remains cool weather. I believe that all that is necessary is, to keep it in a cool place,— though I know nothing about keeping ale!

I am so glad that there are receptions and entertainments for my darling to go to while I am gone: I *hope* she enjoys them,— and that she will enjoy the "class" with Mr. Frothingham too. You and Miss—who?—sweetheart, are to form and extend the membership of the class. You said "Miss" but left out the *name* in your hurry. Miss Frothingham?

To-night I dine with Legh Reid and his aunt, Mrs. Mary G. Small. She lives quite near Mrs. Bird's on Mt. Vernon Place.

When you get me back you'll smother me, will you, my sweet little lover? And what will I be doing all the while—simply submitting to be smothered? Do you think you can stand the innumerable kisses and the passionate embraces you will *receive*? Are you prepared for the storm of love making with which you will be assailed? You [Do] you not know by experience to what lengths and extravagancies of demonstration demonstrativeness on your part hurries your intemperate lover—and are you prepared to take the risks?

Oh, sweetheart, sweetheart, my precious, precious darling!— what a terrible longing it brings into my heart—how it makes all my pulses start, while my heart itself seems to stand still, when I think of having you in my arms again—of being in *your* arms again—touching your lips,—hearing you *say* you love me—seeing the burning light in your eyes as we are strained close in each others' embraces! If I were to allow myself to think of it much, I simply *could not stay here*!   Your own   Woodrow

ALS (WP, DLC).
    1 Sol Smith Russell appeared in "April Weather," by Clyde Fitch, at the Lyceum Theatre in Baltimore on February 5, 6, 7, 8, and 10, 1894.
    2 This letter—a lecture invitation from Trinity College in Durham, N. C.–is missing.
    3 An account of Wilson's lecture is printed at March 23, 1894.

Two Letters from Ellen Axson Wilson

My own darling,   [Princeton, N.J.] Tuesday Feb. 6/94

I am extremely glad that you are going to escape *one* Alumni speech;—sometimes these conflicting engagements serve a good purpose;—though I have been bored to a degree today because of one that was not so fortunate. Mr. Perry lectured today to the ladies,—and I had to be at the Employment Society! The hour was the same. I met everyone going to it and you can guess how I envied them. I met several afterwards and they all said it was *splendid*; he recited a great deal and,—they all said,—better than anyone they had ever heard. The subject was Tennyson's later poems.

Your hundred dollars came from the Forum today;[1] also, a day or two ago, ten dollars from Houghton and Mifflin. Shall I send you the checks—or what? They are at present in the tin box. There are also several *bills* on hand, Strawbridge, Wanamaker & the milkman. Shall I write checks for them? For Strawbridges ($10.00) I suppose I *must*. And by the way, I have forgotten on what days the servants' wages are due!

I am glad you had a pleasant time at the Worthingtons; but he is a friend of such a *spasmodic* sort that even these pleasant and appreciative words of his fail to put me in a *perfectly* good humour with him.

By the way, I received tonight an invitation for us,—you and me—to dine at the Garretts[2] on Saturday. Whence arrives this honour! Am rather sorry not to go, should like to see the house. A lot of blank invitations to the Contemporary Club came today;[3] shall I send them for you to anybody? Is Mrs. Wilson a member of the Club?

I am so happy, dear, that the lecture work is going well and pleasantly. And I am sure that if you are feeling comfortably about them they must be very good indeed. Only think! after all your chagrin about your New York speech the fame of it reached even to Burlington! Stockton in a letter to Ed said he had heard how good it was,—especially how well you spoke on the football question,—and he wished he could have heard it.

But as usual I was very tired after my work as "saleslady," & really spent the evening loafing and reading; it is now late and I must stop. By the way, I was glad to hear from Mrs. Young[4] that Daisy Woods married extremely well. And oh, I forgot to say that a letter from the "Trust Co." directly contradicts the statements in the "Report" and says that my proxy is perfectly good! So like "John T." I don't know "where I am at!" When are you going to Washington? And when are you going down—or *up*—the James?—be sure, dear, not to give up that trip.[5]

We are all quite well,—having glorious weather too.

I love you Woodrow my darling,—my husband with *all* my heart—"with all the smiles, tears, breath of all my life,"—I am in every thought. Your own Eileen

[1] For "A Calendar of Great Americans," which appeared in the February issue of the New York *Forum* and which is printed at Sept. 15, 1893.

[2] Alice Dickinson Whitridge Garrett of Baltimore, widow of Thomas Harrison Garrett, '68, who was renting the large house at 3 Stockton Street, on the northeastern corner of Stockton and Bayard Avenue, while her three sons—John Work Garrett, '95, Horatio Whitridge Garrett, '95, and Robert Garrett, '97—were in college.

[3] From Mrs. Robert N. Willson.

[4] Wife of Charles Augustus Young, Professor of Astronomy.

[5] Woodrow and Ellen obviously had talked about this matter before the former went to Baltimore.

My darling,   [Princeton, N. J., c. Feb. 6, 1894]

I *did* mean for you to *bring* my pendant,[1] but I am having such constant need of it that I wish you would send it instead. Indeed I should *like* it for Saturday night when I am to dine with the Garretts after all—but that is probably impossible, & of course it is of no great importance.   Lovingly,   Ellie

ALS (WC, NjP).
    [1] That is, when he returned after his stay in Baltimore. Wilson had taken the pendant to have it repaired.

To Ellen Axson Wilson

My own darling   Baltimore, 7 February, 1894

Father is going at once to Columbia: he starts to-day. In a short note received this morning,[1] he says, "I have broken finally with this household"! I wonder how the break came and upon what issue. Perhaps he only means *broken finally away*. I am *so* sorry he did not go to Princeton. I suppose he *has* no plans yet for any considerable time ahead: but I should so much like to know what he even *vaguely* intends. The breach with "that household" is something to be profoundly grateful for: I rejoice over it from the bottom of my heart. It was nothing less than a tragedy to see so fine a mind, and so elevated, under such influences, under the spell of all the namby-pamby thought of the day.[2] I believe his spirits will rise as he realizes his emancipation and returns to his normal frame of thought.

Ah, my Eileen, how my heart leaps as I read the sweet sentences of this letter in which you have been 'dreaming' over my letter of Sunday! How shall I ever repay you for such love writing as this! I could hardly see the lines for the rush of tears to my eyes. Oh, that you should love me so, and *regard* me so! Such a letter almost seems to bring you into my arms, and ever since I read it my longing seems to have increased. I seem to myself nowadays to do nothing, anyhow, when I am not engaged upon my books, but dream of you, having you in my arms and speaking directly into your sweet eyes the secrets of my heart. Such thoughts simply carry me away, into the home where all my happiness is, in your keeping, the home with "all its fine simplicity, sincerity, and sweet intimacies"—to use your own perfect words. I do not "idealize" you, darling; I simply *realize* you. It is perhaps good for me to be separated from you in this way— just long enough not to *kill*. It enables me to reckon up just what it is I gain by union with you. All the *light* goes out of my life when you are not in it at every turn, and all the *ease* of living.

I find myself craving excitement, as if I lacked vitality and were conscious of a need of stimulation. I never feel so at home. There my life seems always full—at the flood, while here it is at the ebb. And so I long for you as I suppose a highlander longs for the breath of the mountains, or a ranchman for the scope of the plains. I long for your *voice*, your touch, your glance of comprehension and sympathy; for your *counsel*, your comment, your *self*, till I realize in my extremity that it is my very life to be

Your own   Woodrow.

ALS (WC, NjP).
  [1] It is missing.
  [2] Wilson was undoubtedly referring to Mrs. Grannis's various crusades on behalf of moral purity, the sanctity of the American home, and sterilization of mental defectives and habitual criminals.

From Ellen Axson Wilson

My darling,   [Princeton, N.J.] Wednesday [Feb. 7, 1894]

I seem destined of late not to begin writing until bedtime. Mrs. Ricketts called late this afternoon and stayed until *seven*; we hurried through dinner, and I was still busy in the nursery when young Wisner[1] called. He left only long enough ago for me to write two necessary notes, and now it is after ten & I can scarcely see straight I'm so sleepy.

One of the notes was to *Miss Ladd*![2] She wrote begging us both to stay with her when you go to speak before the [Contemporary] Club. I told her I would write you at once; but I thought you had already accepted another invitation. When you write her be sure to say something about "the boy";—she is *wild* over it!

Then I had to write Helen to send her an invitation to go with me to a reception at Mrs. Fine's tomorrow.

Mrs. Garrett wrote back at once this morning begging me to dine with her anyhow and giving a very odd reason. She "doesn't know the Princeton people well and wants me to help her"—and she doesn't know *me* by sight! However it is kind in her to want me.

It is Miss Ricketts who is "running" the Frothingham class. The others are to be Mrs. Tilton,[3] Mrs. Conover, Miss Shields[4] & Mrs. Baldwin,[5]—the last by Mr. Frothingham's request. I love you,—*love* you my darling as much as you want me to and I am altogether & in every way   Your little wife,   Eileen.

We are all well. The children are out a good deal these bright days & I think are beginning to have a better colour. The boys have heard from one "exam,"—the classical. They each remain in their old division.

ALS (WC, NjP).
    1 Charles Wesley Wisner, Jr., '96.
    2 Carolyn Ladd Hall, M.D., whose husband, Lyman Beecher Hall, was Professor of Chemistry at Haverford College. "Miss Ladd" had been in charge of the gymnasium at Bryn Mawr College when the Wilsons were there.
    3 Mrs. J. R. Tilton, 86 Stockton Street.
    4 Helen, daughter of Professor Shields, of "Morven."
    5 Wife of Professor James Mark Baldwin.

To Ellen Axson Wilson

My own darling,   Baltimore, 8 February, 1894

    I am afraid that you will be very angry with me about the pin. I allowed the gentleman at Welsh's to persuade me that it could be fixed. There could be no mistaking his sincerity when he said that the pearls should never have come off; that if properly fixed there was no reason in the world why they should not be perfectly secure; that he would have the two that are off put on properly and the rest tested, to see that they are rightly secured; and I gave him leave. It is, in my taste, *so much* prettier than any other within our reach that I saw, that I was the more ready to try it again. But now I am, of course, very unhappy about it; for I think I see your face as you read this and nothing cuts me to the quick like your displeasure. Forgive me, pet, if I have erred in judgment. The pin is promised for to-morrow, and I will make a desperate effort to get it off in time to reach you Saturday afternoon.
    You had better pay Strawbridge's bill at once, as you say, but leave all that you can till the first of the next quarter. After the rent is payed and that premium on my life policy we are going to be very short of cash, as it is, in March. Send the checks to me, please, dear, to be endorsed, so that I may send them back to be deposited.
    Maggie's wages are due to-morrow, the 9th, Isabel's on the 17th.
    No, dear, there is no one to whom I care to have any of the Contemporary Club cards sent. I don't want any more than I can't help to hear me speak, ever—and I shall certainly never *invite* anybody to come to hear me. I presume Mrs. Wilson is a member.
    I am *so* sorry about your missing Perry's Tennyson lecture, darling; you have so few treats or pleasures that it seems specially hard that you should have to miss any. I am glad, therefore, that you are to go to Mrs. Garrett's after all. It's odd she should have invited me at all. Two of her sons attend my classes, and *they* at any rate must have known I was not in Princeton. She doubtless

did not think; and my darling must enjoy the occasion for both of us. I forgot to tell you how I fared at Mrs. Small's. The company was very pleasant indeed, and the dinner most elegant, and I enjoyed myself, in a mild way, very well; but Mrs. Small proved rather a conventional, artificial person (who did not always trouble herself to listen to one's remarks) and I cannot count her a great addition to my acquaintance. Legh Reid told me he had seen you at the Nassau Club concert, and oh, how I envied him that recent sight of my darling!

I don't know whether I shall get as far as the James river after all, and I have quite definitely made up my mind not to go to Washington. All sorts of little engagements, as well as work on my Princeton lectures, press upon me and steal my leisure, at the same time that my purse is in some way emptied of its contents.

Oh, what comfort those little words, "we are all quite well," in your letters bring to me. I am *so* anxious about you all the whole time: it is so hard to keep calm and believe you all safe,—though, no doubt, as a matter of fact, you are just as safe when I am away as when I am at home.

I am a very lonely fellow, my darling, to-day. Sometimes our separation tells upon me sadly,—and this is one of the times. The chief cause is *myself*. I feel often that the only real *claim* I have upon all my happiness is your love for me. My love for you, though the vivifying principle of my whole life, is not pure or disinterested enough to constitute a *right* to you. I am so often prompted to write to you in a strain that would inevitably offend your taste that I feel stung to the heart because of my inability to reach the standard you so unconsciously set me. The very fact that I have to cool and restrain my phrases when my heart is full of *you*, proves that I am not worthy of you, and I feel ready to go out and *mortify* myself in some way, in order to get the devil out of me, and make myself acceptable to you.

But I ought not to be *telling* you these things. It is sheer weakness to do so. I ought to master myself and say nothing about it. And I *should* do so (I hope) were it not for my morbid fear that you will not know just who it is—how weak and un-ideal—you are lavishing such sweet love upon,—a largess of precious comfort and stimulation and inspiration that would render *any* man rich and blessed beyond all reckoning. Oh my precious, my *precious* wife, my Eileen! Your own Woodrow

ALS (WC, NjP).

From Ellen Axson Wilson

My darling,   [Princeton, N.J.] Thursday [Feb. 8, 1894]

I sent you a package of those invitations last night; and I should have written that I had already sent them to Uncle Tom and Aunt Saidie.[1] There are still four here, if you want any more.

It is a perfectly delicious day,—like spring, or like *winter* in Savannah. I think I *must* try to get out this morning. The children are in high feather, they can stay out so constantly. They have just finished their lesson and are getting ready to go. They have just announced that Margaret is an "attorney[,]" Nellie a "sheriff" and Jessie a "bailiff"!—novel characters for a *fairy* tale, but which did never the less make their appearance in the latest.

The boys are wild about getting rooms at the college next year! Their friend Graham[2] has put them up to it. He wants them to get a suite in Brown if they can and the three share it together.[3] It would cost each of them they say only $30.00 a year. Of course it would be more fun for them, and not at all bad for us, especially if father is with us. But I told Ed I did not see how it was possible for him since his income is practically nothing a year. And of course there would be big bills for coal and gas too.

I hope my darling is still feeling bright and gay. Ah, my dear, how gay I would feel if you were with me here this sweet morning! With what indescribable yearning my heart turns toward you my husband—my joy—how absolutely I am,

Your own   Eileen.

ALS (WC, NjP).
  [1] The Rev. Dr. and Mrs. Thomas Alexander Hoyt of Philadelphia.
  [2] Harry James Graham, '97.
  [3] These plans did not materialize. Edward Axson and George Howe continued to live with the Wilsons.

To Lyman Pierson Powell[1]

My dear Powell,   Baltimore 8 February, 1894

Thank you most cordially for your letter.[2] Such appreciation does me good. It heartens me not a little. Such an article as "A Calendar of Great Americans"[3] it would never have occurred to my home-keeping mind to write. It was done at the suggestion of the editor of the *Forum*, being suggested to his theme-seeking mind by some hints contained in my review of Goldwin Smith's book.[4] [Theodore] Roosevelt and others are to write on the same theme,—whether in criticism of my views or not I do not know. I am sincerely glad that you like so thoroughly both the substance and the form of what I said.

Do you know whether there would be room and a livelihood for a man like Axson as a University Extension lecturer on English literature next winter? The climate at Bloomington [Burlington] disagrees with him so persistently and so wretchedly that I am anxious to get him away; and I know he thrives as a nomad. He has never said a word to me about it; but, if there is likely to be an opening for him, I want to urge it upon him. Your judgment would assist me very much. I feel sure I could guarantee his quality and style.   Most sincerely Yours,   Woodrow Wilson

ALS (WP, DLC).
1 Born Farmington, Del., Sept. 21, 1866. A.B., the Johns Hopkins, 1890; graduate student in history, the Johns Hopkins, 1890-92; graduate student, University of Wisconsin, 1892-93; graduated from the Philadelphia Divinity School, 1897. University Extension lecturer, 1893-95. Ordained deacon in the Protestant Episcopal Church, 1897, priest in 1898. Held various pastorates between 1897 and 1935; also Professor of Business Ethics, New York University, 1912-13, and president of Hobart College and William Smith College, 1913-18. Prolific author. Died Feb. 10, 1946.
2 It is missing.
3 Printed at Sept. 15, 1893.
4 Printed at Sept. 5, 1893.

To Ellen Axson Wilson

My own darling,   Baltimore, 9 February, 1894

The enclosed letter from Mr. Heath explains itself.[1] He is certainly most kind; and I have replied to him that I would send you his letter and ask you to write yourself as to what you would like him to do. Miss [Charlotte] Martins, at the Library, could give you the latest catalogues of the firms he alludes to, and you could judge which books would be best worth examining.

I have written to "Miss Ladd"; but you did not tell me her name or address. I wrote simply 'Mrs. Professor Hall, Haverford College.' I hope it will reach her: I've no doubt it will.

My darling, your being so extremely sleepy every night can mean only one thing, that you are overworking yourself in some way. It always does mean that, and I am made wretchedly anxious by it. I have noticed a suspicious absence from your letters of all mention of sewing, and other work, recently, and I know what it means. Oh, Ellie, my darling, take care. If you are doing what is imprudent, you are risking a heart-break for me. I implore you not to do anything you would not do, were I there. And, as for letters to me, you *must not write any* when you are so overcome by fatigue. You must simply write 'tired out: all well,' and let that do. I shall not complain, I promise you. I only want—I only *need*—to know that nothing has gone wrong. But, oh, darling, don't *get* so tired, as you love me,—as you *pity* me here in my worrying loneliness!

For all I am so troubled about this, however, darling, I'm not so blue as I was when I wrote yesterday. I never feel worthy of your love; but some days I feel surer than others that I can love you worthily. I know that I can say that I *never* have any thoughts about you that are not penetrated through and through with a love at once passionate, with a passion of the *soul*, and ideal, with an ideality that raises me quite above myself,—whatever *form* may be *foremost* and *seem* dominant in my expression of love for you at the moment. *My heart always approaches you with reverence*: you are my queen and my tenderly revenced [reverenced] wife, no matter what my mood or my passion. I never had a *vulgar* thought about you in my life. There is always a halo, a sweet something in my heart, which exalts you above all other women in my eyes, and makes me touch you always as if I were touching your *spirit* as well as your body. Oh, that I could express what it is in my heart to say to you, darling, and forever exalt and purify all our love-making by the words: oh, for just one inspiration of perfect expression—one perfect syllable of love that might linger in your thought for all the space of our life together!—one utterance that would keep my heart from *breaking* with its fulness and its impotency to speak!

I'm a foolish fellow, after all, I am afraid, to try so desperately to say what is—what *must* be, lying so deep in my life as it does,— wholly inexpressible. You *know* that I love you: I am really not trying to satisfy you, but to relieve myself,—to get some of the *burden* of my great love for you off my heart,—to let the great yearning out with a cry. But there is no articulate cry that can be made its vehicle and I shall only tear my heart strings by the effort. It's much better to take the old solace, and let my thoughts enjoy *you*, instead of striving to express *themselves*. There is so much to enjoy in you and the pleasure is so keen. I can let my thoughts run back to the time when you only excited dreams in me, and then let them rejoice in all the delightful realization of those dreams. You are such a delicious combination of sweetheart and wife. It is just as *romantic* to love you now as it was to love you when you seemed unattainable and were just my ideal of what I *wanted* but might never get. It is such an exquisite pleasure to see in your lovely eyes all that I saw then: and, added, another wonder and charm that unspeakably enhances that which I saw there from the first. Surely no other man ever found in his wife so exactly what he saw in his sweetheart, or ever had added to his anticipations so many discoveries of treasure in the mind and heart of the woman of his devotion. It does not make any difference what you think yourself, my darling. What I have found I have found: the woman that makes me supremely happy. I never feel so bouyant as when I can manage to think of you without thinking of myself.

Ah, sweetheart, how my heart smites me as I read this sweet, gay little note of yours written yesterday morning, in which, out of your own high spirits, you hope that I am "still feeling bright and gay" for I know that that wretched blue letter of mine reached you yesterday, and I know only too well how it would check my darling's flow of spirits. How I wish it had never been written. I have no right to send you a letter like that when you need cheer. Well, my treasure, my spirits have come back now. It was only the black reaction of conscience because I had been to a low theatre the night before—and that is so unworthy of you. I don't quite *respect* myself to-day; but your love revives me, and makes me happy in spite of myself. I think I can promise no more offences and no more letters of that kind. Forgive me and love me and all will be well with   Your own   Woodrow

ALS (WC, NjP).
    ¹ It is missing.

From Ellen Axson Wilson

My darling,   [Princeton, N.J.] Friday, Feb. 9 [1894].

I am so sorry to find that my dear one is not in so good spirits as when he last wrote! It is very naughty and morbid in you to talk about not being good enough for me; and you must not think about *yourself at all,* sir, if you cannot think more sensible things! You yourself destroy the force of your own remarks merely by explaining that you are careful to let me know just who and what you are! Then by your own confession I do really *know* you, —and you would not deny that I also know myself. And knowing thus the two of us it is my most profound conviction that you are a great deal *too* good for me,—or would be if love had to justify itself by any such balance of qualities. And it is not the partiality of love but mere common sense that makes me think so. I *could* not feel otherwise except on the principle of "compounding for sins that I'm inclined to, by damning those I have no mind to." Look down on you!—why I—petty contemptible little soul that I am, had as well,—and *better*—look down on David, the man after God's own heart. For did not *he* being "greatly tempted greatly *fall.*" Yet when I think of the *full measure* of his manhood, the nobility and the *essential* purity and tenderness, the unselfishness, and the sweetness and heroism combined, and add to all the profound depths of his spiritual nature and experience I could indeed laugh myself to scorn. No one knows better than I how far I am from being a woman after God's own heart. Ah darling I have no words to says [say] how I love and honour and admire you—what precious "largess of comfort and stimulation and inspiration" I gather from *your* love, my dear one!—As ever

Your own   Eileen.

ALS (WC, NjP).

Two Letters to Ellen Axson Wilson

My own darling,   Baltimore, 10-11 Feb'y, 1894

As I write, no doubt, you sit at dinner, in your pink gown,— I hope also in your necklace and pendant,—in all your sweet beauty, and talk to some man whom I envy the privilege of sitting by you as deeply as ever I envied any man anything! How lovely you look I know only too well for my present peace of mind. How you talk I am reminded every day, by contrast, as I meet the women of this town. How it would refresh me to hear, if only for a short half hour, your sweet, straightforward exercise of *mind* and womanly feeling! I walked the whole length of the crowded part of Charles St. several times this afternoon (remembering only one errand at a time and being obliged to return twice) and saw more pretty women than I could count, some of them beautiful and full of youth and grace. I looked into each pretty face as long as I dared in decency, and, without exception, *as long as I wanted to*. They were not faces to live with. They had none of them that *depth* of beauty, of ineffable sweetness, and of grave thoughtfulness that my darling's face has,—has in so striking and eminent a degree that from my first sight of it it took me captive, and I knew that I had found in a little country church a face that one might look for in vain the world over.[1] Even those that were sweetest,—and they were not all sophisticated city faces, set before a glass of fashion, but some exquisitely naive and womanly sweet—even those that showed an artless tenderness lacked in that finest, clearest depth of all, the depth of *thoughtfulness*. When a man wanted, not solace merely, but wanted to be interested and beguiled with talk,—if he were intellectual, these girls would fail him: he would have to go to his club. But *you*, my matchless darling, shine and are glorified so by comparison. It is a delight to walk among these pretty creatures and think of you. There is a captivating variety and play of beauty in your face like none I ever saw: beauty of colour and of form, but that is just a vehicle for the rest,—the beauty of sweetness and womanly tenderness, and the beauty of thoughtfulness: eyes full of a deep speculation, animated with a quiet ardour of interest in everything that people ought to see or read or think about. And your talk, not jejune and conventional,—not a series of attempts to say what you are expected to say, or to be eternally bright or eternally 'knowing'; but coming from your real mind, genuine and full of colour, with all your mind's own freshness and feeling —oh, what would I not give for never so little of its charm and refreshment now, in my loneliness: what would I not give to sit by you at dinner!

I don't mean that I am blue, sweetheart. I am not. I am lonely, of course—who would not be who had once had you in his life and then been obliged to do without you for a while? But I am not unhappy—who could be who might expect to go back to you within less than three weeks (the 12th lecture was delivered yesterday!). It makes me very happy—very, very happy—to think of you and dwell upon all the sweet charms that make you so dear to me. For am I not to *go back home*,—not only to sit by you at dinner and hear your voice, but to take you in my arms, and press my kisses upon your lips, and hold you to me till all your warm blood, quick with eager love, seems to enter my own veins, and all this cruel separation seems wiped out and forgotten in the unspeakable joy of having my little wife again all to myself! I verily believe, sweetheart—my queen!—that 'wife' is the sweetest word in the language. Certainly it is, when it is applied to you.

But, dear me! my heart beats too fast with the pace it's going. I must force it a little away from you,—if only for a little while, until it can get breath!

I dined last night (Friday) with the Wilson's (John Wilson's[2] family). The father[3] is a genuine Scotchman, an elder in Mr. Babcock's church, and a man, evidently, of sterling character and intelligence. One of his brothers, now dead, graduated at Princeton Seminary, and was a Presbyterian minister. He prizes some very old copies of the Catechism and Baxter's "Saints' Rest."[4] The mother was ill with the grippe, and so I did not see her; but I saw one of John's sisters (the other is away at school), who is a pleasant and very attractive looking girl. There were four other ladies present, whose names, as usual, are to me "as if they were not," besides Mr. and Mrs. Babcock—with both of whom I made fast progress in friendship, I think. She is full of sense and womanliness, and otherwise attractive, besides, with no mean claims to be called pretty. She said, by-the-way, in the simplest, most un-canting way possible, that 'she had no children *here*'; but she wanted to talk about mine. Mr. Babcock and I capped each others' stories all through the dinner, keeping the table in a roar—and Mrs. Babcock listened to his stories almost as well as you listen to mine. What is one to expect? I was the only one of the five men present (there was a Mr. Curtis[5] there, a Yale man, who seems to be one of Mr. Babcock's chief helpers in some of the church work) the only one,—for I can include the ladies, too,— who was in evening dress! For a little I felt as I did at Charlie Mitchell's last year—except that *this* crowd was—quite unlike that.

I dine with Mitchell, by-the-way, tomorrow (Sunday) to meet his new pastor.[6] Mr. Ball died in June.[7]

After accepting Charlie's invitation, I had invitations for the same day and hour from Mrs. Bird, [E.R.L.] Gould, Dr. Griffen,[8] and Mrs. Babcock! I am promised to Mrs. Bird for a week from to-morrow.

All sorts of people have been speaking of my "Mere Literature" and my "Calendar"—one sort of the one and another sort of the other. They both seem to have gone to the respective right spots of various persons, and you can imagine how much I am gratified.

Sunday

I went down to the Post Office this morning, to fetch your Friday letter, darling; and it brings me back to you—the first theme of this letter—with a rush. I pass over its argument about myself to its argument about you. How *dare* you call yourself a "petty, contemptible little soul"! My darling! Do you suppose that I know nobody but you—and have I ever given you good reason to believe that I was blinded to the qualities of those I love? I know you scarcely less than I know myself—and if ever there was a big-souled woman in the world, framed to love and to be loved, quick and catholic in all good thought, with the fine breath of tolerance and piety about all her moods, you are the woman,—a queen and a virgin in your disposition and in all your thought. That is the deliberate verdict alike of my mind and of my heart. My letter must indeed have cut you to the quick with some form of mortification to have moved you to such a morbid and despondent utterance,—and I pray God to forgive me for having been the cause of sorrow to you in such a way. Pray with me, my little wife, that I may be less subject to temptation. All my passions are upon so terrible a scale of power. But all my *good* impulses, everything *ideal* in all my nature turns to you for its perfect satisfaction—

and I will not have you speak so of yourself. It makes me almost angry—almost as if some one else had spoken the slander. My precious, my matchless little wife! Oh, how I rejoice in you! With what a singular delight—and how unlike any other in its intensity —does my thought dwell upon you, and all that you have been and will be (God being merciful) in my life. It exalts me; it keeps me young; it gives me spirit in all that I do; it makes me unspeakably happy!   Your own   Woodrow

ALS (WC, NjP).
  ¹ A reference to his sight of Ellen in the Rome, Georgia, Presbyterian Church on April 8, 1883. See the Editorial Note, "Wilson's Introduction to Ellen Axson," Vol. 2, pp. 333-35.
  ² John Glover Wilson, '92.
  ³ John Wilson, a coal merchant of Baltimore.
  ⁴ The famous Puritan tract, Richard Baxter, *The Saints Everlasting Rest*, first published in London in 1650.
  ⁵ George L. Curtis, Yale, '78, Stated Supply in the Park Presbyterian Church of Baltimore.
  ⁶ The Rev. Charles H. Caton, pastor of the Associate Reformed Presbyterian Church of Baltimore.
  ⁷ The Rev. Wayland D. Ball, Caton's predecessor.
  ⁸ Edward Herrick Griffin, Professor of the History of Philosophy and Dean of the College Faculty at The Johns Hopkins University.

My sweet Eileen,   [Baltimore] Sunday, again, 11th/94
    Just a few lines more, while I wait for the hour to go out to dinner. That letter I fetched from the post office this morning has moved me singularly, and I cannot sit still here without opening my heart *in words* to my little wife. I cannot read your letters as I read your face, but,—whether because of my own mood of tenderness or not, I cannot tell,—this letter disturbs me. Its tone has the intense quiet of endured pain. I read it hastily first, in a breath, a page at a time; and then, after I reached my room I read it again and again, sentence by sentence; and each time it made the same impression on me,—of a tender heart wounded and arguing itself out of pain. The tears come to my eyes every time I read it,—tears mixed of love, yearning, and self-reproach. My longing is,—not to justify myself—that would be both insincere and ineffectual,—but to speak some word so *burdened* with love and pure devotion as to carry solace and cheer to my darling. How shall I tell you my love, Eileen, and the purity of my devotion to you? What words are there that are a substitute for what I could tell you if I could only look in your eyes, and you would let me kiss you and do for you little services of love? There are no substitutes for what lovers can make each other understand when they can look each into the other's eyes. But I know that if my darling could realize just what is the nature and the strength of

the love for her with which my heart is so full this morning, she would rejoice in it, and forget every pain I may have caused her; and I hope that, *somehow*, a sense of it may be conveyed to her,— a sense of its joy, its elevation, its overpowering tenderness, its intense ardour of upright devotion, its enthronement of the one woman who seems to me framed to take all a man's allegiance. You are in my heart, Eileen, vested with a gracious presidency over all that I am. I am so proud to *own* (to other people, when I can without vulgarity) my allegiance to you as the central principle of my life. It makes me so *glad*, to be in love with you. It gives such bouyancy to my spirits to know whom I live for. I am happy *now*, darling, as I write, with the consciousness of the kind of love I have to offer you. I'm not ashamed of a *thought* of it—and I should be willing to see it weighed against any other the world ever contained. This I give for that precious love you grant me,—more precious than can be reckoned—the inspiration and support of   Your own   Woodrow

ALS (WP, DLC).

From Ellen Axson Wilson

My own darling,   Princeton Feb 11/94

The dinner last night made it necessary for me to postpone my Sat. letter again & send it in the same envelope with my Sunday one! The pin, by the way, came in good time yesterday; I am *so* much obliged to you for attending to it so promptly. Of course you were right to yield when the man insisted so that he could secure the pearls; indeed I do not see what else you *could* have done, you could not *make* him take it back.

The dinner was a grand affair indeed; there were eighteen at table—the Sloanes, Fines, Wikoffs & Lewis', Miss Frothingham, two lady guests & two boys of the house & Messrs. Marquand, Harper & McKay.[1] It was a pink & green dinner. I should think there was about fifty dollars worth of flowers! The table was really gorgeous, and the dinner to match. They had for one thing terrapin—Baltimore style,—something that I have had quite a curiosity to taste. Mrs. Garrett is really very agreeable,—perfectly unaffected. I sat near her,—only Mr. Sloane between, Dr. Wikoff, who carried me out, on the other side. We four talked together most of the time, so that I was sufficiently entertained without having to exert myself very strenuously. But Mr. Sloane is really disgusting with ladies,—his flattery is so fulsome and so artificial.

There is a party on hand for this week too. Friday night at the

Paxton's.[2] Suppose I will go,—but you can't imagine how strange it feels, dear, to be going out without you! It is really a dreary experience. I took Helen to a little reception at the Fines on Thursday & enjoyed much meeting Mr. Reid and hearing of you and that you were looking *very* well. He was enthusiastic about the dinner which you damn with faint praise.[3] He says "you know it *must* have been a brilliant occasion with two such men as Mr. Wilson and Mr. Remsen[4] there![")

I am also desired to go out to the ball at Lawrenceville as Helen's chaperone!—but I dare say "Miss Bessie" will relieve me of that necessity—and *not* by going herself either. Lefoy[5] has been over this afternoon with young Reynolds[6] from *Rome*—the latter on the above-mentioned errand. He is a perfect guy—long, lank sandy hair &c. and Helen is naturally not very enthusiastic over the affair. Charlie Wisner was at dinner; so we had quite a Lawrenceville crowd here.

I heard a sad piece of Rome news from this boy,—Mr. Goetchius younger son, a fine bright fellow, a student at Davidson was killed by a fall.[7] The banisters gave way with him and he fell three floors,—was dreadfully mangled but lingered some days. Also the son of an old friend of ours there, a fellow younger than Stockton, has become violently insane,—apparently from dissipation—and is at Milledgeville. Sad things have been happening in our Princeton circle too. Mr. Magie's mother[8] is paralysed down the whole of one side,—is speechless and quite low. It was her 6oth birthday, she had just been saying gayly at the breakfast table, "I feel very much alive for an old lady of sixty!"—and then the blow came. But worse still—Mr. Humphrey's father[9] has committed suicide! Isn't that terrible? The cause was business troubles combined with depression resulting from the grip. But I feel rather conscience-stricken to be writing you all these horrors.

I received a very nice letter from Mr. Heath and a big package of books,—*very* nice books. I had already written him before your letter came. I am glad of the names and suggestions in this letter you enclose, but do you think we need trouble *him* any further about it now? I very much dislike to write again asking for books outside his list. I have given M. one of the books, about the habits of insects and J. one about birds, and they are both perfectly fascinated. Jessie's is called "Our Saturday Bird Class"; she says, —"I tell you one of those little girls was bright, she looked *terrible* hard at the birds."

Miss Ladd gave no other address than Haverford, & I have no idea as to her husband's initials. But I daresay it is all right. Aunt

Saidie also wrote begging us to stay with them. They will be at the Club.

I assure you, dear, I am not over-working *at all*. Indeed we have had so many delicious days that I have been tempted out much oftener than usual,—have actually made errands to go out. Yesterday I went to the Library and read for an hour or more! I have sewed on the machine,—oh!—*very* little since you left; and I feel absolutely well. The children are looking very well again too I think, and as pretty as ever. They havn't had a touch of cold, or anything, since you left.

Mr. Kent's inauguration address[10] came yesterday, would you like me to send it you? Why don't you see if he can't run over and see you while there. How I wish you could go to the U. of Va. for a short trip! I *hope* you won't give up the James River plan! Can't you regard it as a *business* trip?

I met Mr. Perry at the Fines and told him how excessively disappointed I was;—and do you know, he has offered to do it all over for me! Isn't that *lovely*! I think we will have them to dinner again when you come back and have a treat all to ourselves.

I had such a strangely vivid dream, not *about* you but *of* you the night before last, my darling! You were simply *with* me, here —in my arms—in the closest of embraces. I never had such an experience before. It woke me up, alas! and I could not sleep again for a long time. I was so glad because of that brief visit from you, —so sad that you were gone again so soon. Somehow I cannot quite get over it. I have been more impatient of this long separation,—more eager for your presence ever since. It is like the first day of your absence when I have not yet schooled my heart to patience. Oh, love, that heart yearns for you with a passionate longing that will not be controlled,—but which is so intense that I hardly dare yield to it. Oh my darling, my darling *how* I love you! Oh for the "great heart word" that would tell you how entirely, passionately, tenderly, devotedly, I am

Your own   Eileen

ALS (WC, NjP).

1 All hitherto identified in this series. "McKay" was Leroy Wiley McCay, Professor of Chemistry.

2 The Rev. Dr. and Mrs. William Miller Paxton of 20 Steadman Street.

3 She refers to the dinner of the Princeton Alumni Association of Maryland on February 1.

4 Ira Remsen, Professor of Chemistry at the John Hopkins.

5 Lefoy Brower, son of Abraham T. H. Brower, then at Lawrenceville.

6 Hughes Turnley Reynolds, Lawrenceville, '94.

7 William Andrews Goetchius, son of the Rev. Dr. George Thomas Goetchius, pastor of the First Presbyterian Church of Rome, Georgia, who died on January 5, 1894, after falling in Old Chambers Building.

8 Sarah Baldwin (Mrs. William Jay) Magie, of Elizabeth, N.J., wife of the Princeton trustee and Associate Justice of the New Jersey Supreme Court.

9 A. Willard Humphreys of New York, whose son, Willard Cunningham Humphreys, was an Instructor in Latin at Princeton.

10 Charles William Kent, *Literature and Life: Being the Lecture Delivered upon the Inauguration of the Work of the Linden-Kent Memorial School of English Literature in the University of Virginia* (Richmond, 1894).

From Ferdinand Larnaude[1]

*Revue du Droit Public et de la Science
Politique en France et à l'Etranger*

Monsieur et chèr collègue   Paris, le 12 Fév. 1894

Je ne saurais vous remercier trop vivement de l'excellent acceuil que vous voulez bien faire à ma proposition et des voeux que vous formez pour mon entreprise. La France manquait d'un organe de ce genre. Ma seule ambition est d'ouvrir la voie où d'autres pourront s'engager.

Je comprends que vos occupations ne vous permettent pas de me promettre un concours bien actif. Si peu que vous me donniez je m'en déclarai satisfait. Ce sera dèjà une force pour la Revue nouvelle de compter parmi ses collaborateurs l'auteur de "Congressional government."

Veuillez agréer M' et chèr collègue l'assurance de mes meilleurs sentiments   F. Larnaude

Votre adhésion ne m'étant arrivée que pendant l'impression du premier numéro votre nom, à mon très grand regret, ne pourra, cette fois, figurer parmi ceux des collaborateurs de la Revue.[2]

ALS (WP, DLC).

1 Professor of General Public Law of the Faculty of Law of Paris and Director of the *Revue*.

2 Wilson apparently did not find time to contribute to the *Revue*, and his name was never listed as an editor or collaborator.

To Ellen Axson Wilson

My own darling,   Baltimore, 12 Feb'y, 1894

This afternoon I deliver my thirteenth lecture, *and so pass the middle point of the course*. Isn't that satisfactory? And think what a hole this week will make in the reckoning, carrying me through No. 17 of the total twenty-five of the course. *Week after next* I come home! How much that means for me I need not try to tell you. I thought of you so much and so intensely yesterday, my Eileen, that it was all I could do to refrain from writing you a *third* letter while I was waiting for supper! Why was it? Were you thinking also—almost as never before—of *me*, so that there was some subtle influence of concentrated emotion playing between us? I hope so, since you did not have anything to reproach yourself with, as I *did*, and could indulge in the luxury of loving me in spite of all my faults—the luxury of forgiveness.

I took dinner with Charlie Mitchell yesterday, as *per* programme, but did not meet the new pastor. He could not come. The only other guest was Hiram Woods, and the time passed off most agreeably with familiar talk. I heard Mr. Babcock twice yesterday; and both times with great pleasure. Though not at his best, it was all very vital and striking.

To-night I go to a meeting of the "Archeological Club"[1] (whatever that may be) at Mr. and Mrs. White's. Mr. Francis White is Treasurer of the Hopkins Board of Trustees. I expect to be decorously bored for about two hours. I shall try to while away the time of the papers (for I suppose there will be papers) by thinking of you, calculating the number of hours before I can hope to see you, estimating how many kisses you will let me give you the day of my home-coming, dreaming of your eyes and your sweet voice and your precious words of endearment;—and then, afterwards, how shall I manage to talk about the things that have been 'presented' in the papers? I shall have to fall back on 'general observations,' for I can't think of listening when there are such delightful things to think about that I can have all to myself.

I have spent the morning 'looking up' the football controversy in the magazines, in preparation for to-morrow evening in Phila.

I am in excellent spirits again to-day, my pet: a fellow who is as much and as sweetly loved as I am by a glorious little woman whom he can adore as the most lovely of her kind cannot long remain in the blues. He must forget to loathe himself in the joy and exaltation of loving her.   Your own   Woodrow

ALS (WC, NjP).
[1] An informal group, not listed in the Baltimore city directory or mentioned in the catalogues or President's Reports of the Johns Hopkins.

From Ellen Axson Wilson

My darling,   [Princeton, N.J.] Monday, Feb. 12 [1894]

I feel as though the "clan Wilson" were possessing the land. I have just finished writing to Mrs. Wilson of Phila. & Dr. Wilson of Trenton,[1]—now comes *Prof.* Wilson's turn!

Wasn't Mrs. Wilson's note a pleasant, cordial one? I fear the other Wilson letter I forwarded this morning,—the one from Josie was not so pleasant reading,—I really hated to send it to you, he speaks so unjustly and ungenerously of you and father.[2] What influence does he suppose you could have in newspaper offices!

If he had no family you might get Mr. Shaw or Finley to help him to some chance to "begin at the bottom" in New York. But that seems utterly out of the question with a "family man," for I have always understood that on those big dailies they are scarcely suffered to exist for the first few years. It seems to me that as a *married* man his chances to rise in the world would be much better in "business";—and certainly better in the South than the North. I think I will write to Stock and ask him if he ever spoke to Howell[3] about Josie as I asked,—and he promised—he would do.

I had a note from Stock this morning—he says he is a good deal improved,—but!—I think I will enclose it. Poor fellow,—I am not very happy about him these days,—yet this letter *is* a good many tones brighter than the last.

Ed is again first division in everything, & Mr. Mildner[4] informed him privately that he was also "first group" in German. George made first division in German too;—third in Math. & fourth in Classics as before. Sixteen boys dropped from the first in Math., and one came up from the sixth to the first! Ed has been having a sort of relapse into stammering here lately which is troubling me not a little. It may be the strain of examinations, and yet he has seemed perfectly serene through it & hasn't done a particle of cramming.

How I enjoyed that sweet, *sweet*, tender letter that came this morning, darling! Words fail me to say with what a full heart I read it. The second note—sweet as it is—has disturbed me as much as mine did you (!)—for I cannot think what I could have said that could have given you cause for "self-reproach,"—have made you think that *you* had "wounded" me. My precious, *perfect* lover and husband! how *could* that be! Of course I was distressed when I wrote at the deep depression evident in yours; but it is quite inconceivable that I could have found anything that would wound me personally in it; that would indeed have been "morbid" beyond belief. But I *don't* think it morbid, sir, to consider myself a poor little creature! I have *always* thought that. But if you don't like the fact mentioned I promise not to refer to it again!

But whatever else I am, dear, I am also the happiest girl in the world because I *know* that "I love my love and my love loves me."

With *all* my heart & soul & strength

Your own   Eileen

ALS (WC, NjP). Enc.: S. Axson to EAW, Feb. 10, 1894, ALS (WP, DLC).
1 Dr. Penrose J. Wilson, dentist, of 29 Prospect Street.
2 It is missing.
3 Albert Howell, son of Evan Park Howell of the Atlanta *Constitution*.
4 Ernst Otto Wilhelm Mildner, Assistant Professor of German.

To Ellen Axson Wilson

My own darling   Baltimore, 13 February, 1894

This precious Sunday letter of yours is one I shall not soon forget. All the sad news it contains cannot,—so selfish am I,—lessen the effect of the last part, in which you tell me of your and the children's perfect health, assure me that you are not over-working, but going out to take the air; and then, last of all, with a sweetness and modesty which is surely inimitable, tell me of that dream which waked you and over which you rejoiced, as over an actual visit from me. You may imagine the effect of that revelation upon me, and of the passionate words of love that accompanied it. And yet I doubt if you *can* imagine, after all, the effect it actually *did* produce. It not only brought a flood of tender gratefulness into my heart, but it brought a burst of tears into my eyes. I know how much,—and just *what*,—it means, *such* a revelation of your love for me. I know my darling so well—these delicate sentences, so beautiful in their simplicity and sincerity, are so eloquent of her character—I am so conscious of the exquisite quality of the combination of delicacy and ardour running through all her relations to me, so deeply affected by the privileged relation I bear her as her husband and confidant and by the ideals of wifehood which her sweet character has made part of my thought and life,—that a confidence like this comes to me as, somehow, the dearest token of her love, and I am in a way overcome by it. Does it increase *your* impatience of the separation, darling, *my* Eileen? Pity *me* for the desperate impatience with which I am filled by it! Are we to go on this way, love, I wonder, becoming more and more ardent lovers the older we get and the longer we live together? Oh, I *hope* so—I believe so. Let's don't think of the *separation* any more, my sweetheart-wife! Let's think always of the home coming,—which God grant us! Let's think of the joys we shall have when I am back again,—of the sweet, intoxicating zest of being together again—for another eleven months. Probably we can't *tell* each other of the full measure of our happiness and love even then, *in words*; but there will be so many other ways of telling,—if only by the catching of the breath, that will be beyond all eloquence! When I think of that time, of the sweet hours we shall spend together, and even of the hours I shall spend alone in my study with the consciousness *that you are within call*;—nothing will relieve me but a song—I feel all the joy and blitheness of a boy and all the strong ardours of a man when I realize what it means to be

                         Your own   Woodrow

ALS (WC, NjP).

From Ellen Axson Wilson

My own darling,   [Princeton, N. J.] Tuesday, [Feb. 13, 1894]

It is rather tantalizing to think that my dear one is so much nearer me tonight,—and still so far! and that he must turn back again tomorrow. Still the time is half gone and that is a great thing. Ah how quickly my heart beats to even think now of the end,—or rather the sweet *beginning* of better things.

We have had a heavy snow-storm and quite a gale last night; today was pleasant however and I enjoyed my walk to the [employment] society. Have come back pretty tired though so must make my letter rather short.

You must have had an interesting time at John Wilson's. I should like to have been there. By the way, if you have time I would be glad if you would call on Mrs. Green.[1] And will you please take her the children's photographs; I promised them to her a year ago. Tell her my other lot ran out before I had finished sending to the friends who had not seen the children.

The children are very happy over *pop-corn* just now. Something we read reminded [me] that this was one childish rapture they had never experienced. So I got the corn & a "popper," & I wish you could have seen their pretty excitement. When it was finished I told them to "run get some salt to eat with it," whereupon followed fresh shrieks of wonder & rapture;—"do you *eat* it!" It seems they had supposed the popping to be an end in itself.

Their other most vivid interest just now is "jogerfy"; I got out my old "manual" & have been giving them oral lessons combined with reading from "Parley's" History.[2] They study the maps & pictures half the day. I am also trying to teach them a wee bit about spelling—and finding it rather hard work! They have had three valentines each today & of course are in raptures. One set was from Balt. Do you know who sent them? We are all quite well and happy—at least I am as happy as I can be in my darling's absence, for my heart does fairly ache with longing for you my love.

Always & altogether,   Your own   Eileen

ALS (WC, NjP).

1 Aminta Green, widow of Charles Green.

2 Samuel Griswold Goodrich, *Peter Parley's Universal History on the Basis of Geography* (New York and Chicago, 1866).

A Newspaper Report

[Feb. 14, 1894]

FOOT BALL.
OUGHT THE GAME TO BE ENCOURAGED?

The galleries of the Art Club last evening were filled by an audience which included such well-known citizens as Dr. H. C. Wood, Robert C. Ogden, John B. Garrett, George C. Thomas, Edward Shippen, Dr. W. W. Keen, Professor [Edmund J.] James and Dr. A. P. Brubaker, with their lady friends, gathered in midwinter to hear a discussion of the subject, "Ought the Game of Foot Ball to be Encouraged."

The meeting was held under the auspices of the Contemporary Club, and Dr. Harrison Allen, who presided, in a few preliminary remarks introduced Professor Woodrow Wilson, of Princeton University, who took the affirmative side of the subject. It had been twenty years, he said, since he had taken that side of the question.

"I assume," he said, "that you regard this as a college question, and certainly there can be no doubt that the best foot ball men in the country are college men. But there is a sense in which it is not a college game, because the whole country plays it, and the question is whether it shall be the game for the country. We have, to my knowledge, young ladies in seminaries who play the game, but they may not want to have that fact known.

"The question has two sides to it. Are we going to encourage the game for the sake of others, and are we going to encourage it for the sake of the game itself? It seems to me unquestioned that anything which the colleges can control they should continue to control in the future for the sake of the athletics of this country, because you will observe that it is only by a leadership of gentlemen that this thing can be kept manly and clean. Notwithstanding the fact that the game of cricket has become popular in England it is nevertheless a gentlemen's game. They set the standard. The question therefore is, are manly influences and gentlemanly influences to control foot ball and preside over it? I think I can show you that college men can play ball better than others, and therefore they can maintain their leadership, and it will win as it has in the past, in the leadership of the most manly crowd."

Then taking up the other side of the question—shall the game be encouraged for the sake of the game itself, he said: "I must bear a most unhesitating affirmative, because I believe it develops more moral qualities than any other game of athletics. Ordinary athletics produce valuable qualities—precision, decision, presence of mind and endurance. No man can be a successful athlete without these four qualities.

"This game produces two other qualities not common to all athletics, that of co-operation, or action with others, and self-subordination. These are things to be encouraged, and they unquestionably come from the game of foot ball. In foot ball I have been close enough to it to understand all its developments.

"The opposition to foot ball comes from those colleges in which foot ball has not been successfully organized. I don't mean colleges that have not won. They have not succeeded [not] because they did not have manly men, but because they did not have the sort of organization to produce a good plan which wins in foot ball. This game can only be successfully played by undergraduates, because the men associated with that game have come to that conclusion themselves.

"Why is it that Harvard don't win in foot ball? President Eliot says they don't play well because of the elective system of studies, and I think he is practically right. The elective man is never subject to discipline. Let me assure you that the years in which Princeton was defeated were the years when she had not sense enough to win—or, in other words, the men organizing didn't have the qualities of generalship.

"Now comes a serious question, Does not the encouragement of foot ball decrease studiousness? Let us turn the question about and ask, Will the increase of foot ball discourage studiousness? You say it withdraws the attention of the student from his studies. It is the undergraduates that are going to play foot ball. I believe it ought to be the object of college faculties to forbid graduates to play foot ball, as they are now in that field of life where they must specialize themselves."

Continuing his remarks, Professor Wilson held that foot ball contests should be played only in the large cities. He had heard the game called a "prize fight" and a "bull fight," but it was because the men who played were in their athletic suits. The only reason they did not appear in evening dress was because it was inconvenient, and as to the large gate receipts, the players did not share in them as the money was devoted to keeping grounds in order, maintaining an organization, etc.

Professor Burt G. Wilder,[1] of Cornell University, took the "No," or negative side of the question, and said that he played foot ball 40 years ago, but it was 18 years since, after a most careful consideration of his own experience and observation of what was going on in his own University and in others, that he had come to the conclusion that there should be no inter-collegiate athletic contests whatever. He had hoped to hear Professor Wilson discuss the difference between foot ball as it is and as it might be.

He believed that the student of an American University was worthy of being told that he should lay aside all kinds of competition which pertain to athletic sports when he ceases to be a boy and begins to be a man. If it is true, he said, that college men are the best foot ball players it is because the young men of the colleges are the power of the land. If foot ball be so noble a game, if it be a game which has such possibilities for the training of youth, why then does an ex-foot ball captain, under his own name, state that an umpire in the shape of a perfect sport should be employed to keep the young men in order?

Professor Wilder believed that it was possible to have the game so modified as to become the best out-door cold weather exercise for vigorous young men, who like personal contact with their fellow men. He was in favor of a game rid of its present undesirable features. The surest way, he said, to do away with foot ball would be to compel every student in a University to play unless asked by his parents to be excused.

Professor Wilder also spoke of the extravagance, betting and general tendency towards a sporting habit which he said were engendered by the game, and, in conclusion, referred at some length to the disorders which he claimed followed in the footsteps of the game.

Printed in the Philadelphia *Public Ledger*, Feb. 14, 1894; some editorial headings omitted.
[1] Burt Green Wilder, Professor of Physiology, Vertebrate Zoology, and Neurology at Cornell University.

To Ellen Axson Wilson

My own darling,   Baltimore, 14 February, 1894

You will expect me to send you a Valentine to-day, won't you? I wish I could send you lines of my own; but I adopt these:

> "When I think on the happy days
> I spent wi' you, my dearie;
> And now what lands between us lie,
> How can I but be eerie!

How slow ye move, ye heavy hours,
As ye were wae and weary!
It was na sae ye glinted by
When I was wi' my dearie."[1]

"Love not me for comely grace
For pleasing eye or face,
Nor for any outward part,
No, nor for my constant heart,—
  For those may fail, or turn to ill,
    So thou and I shall sever
Keep therefore a true woman's eye,
And love me still, but know not why—
    So hast thou the same reason still
      To doat upon me ever!"[2]

"Bid me to live, and I will live
  Thy Protestant to be:
Or bid me love, and I will give
  A loving heart to thee

"Bid me to weep, and I will weep
  While I have eyes to see:
And having none yet I will keep
  A heart to weep for thee.

"Bid me despair, and I'll despair,
  Under that cypress tree:
Or bid me die, and I will dare
  E'en Death, to die for thee

"Thou art my life, my love, my heart,
  The very eyes of me,
And hast command of every part,
  To live and die for thee."[3]

So little love poetry is at once impassioned and natural enough to suit my love for *you*, Eileen. Oh, if I were only a poet, what a love poem,—what a *volume* of love poems I could write, for every lover and husband to speak his heart with—that might serve a man as some of the sonnets from the Portuguese may serve a woman!

Ah, me, how cruel R. R. schedules are! I eagerly studied them to yield me a sight of you this morning, but they would not. By leaving Phila. at 6:50 this morning I could have reached Princeton by 8:30; but I should have had to come away again in three quarters of an hour—and I did not dare try the experiment. It would have torn my heart more than it would have healed it— and this place would have been rendered *intolerable*. I dare not trust myself with you until I can stay: I know by the way I *trembled* from head to foot as I examined the time tables.

The speech-making came off very well,—the other men could not speak,[4] fortunately,—and every body was extremely cordial. The enclosed report[5] leaves out the greater part of my speech, but what it does give it gives very well.

I am very tired, as you may imagine; but I am very well. Aunt Sadie and uncle Tom. were not at the Club; but I saw Mr. and Mrs. Hall, and the Wilsons [Willsons].

Ah, my darling, my heartache for you increases every day. My treasure, my matchless, my indispensable darling: what would I do for joy if I were not   Your own   Woodrow.

ALS (WC, NjP).
  [1] From Robert Burns, "How Lang and Dreary Is the Night."
  [2] Anon., in John Wilbye, *The Second Set of Madrigals* . . . , ed. by George William Budd (London, 1846).
  [3] From Robert Herrick, "Hesperides. To Anthea, Who May Command Him Anything."
  [4] Wilson presumably meant that Wilder and Dr. Allen were poor speakers.
  [5] It is missing.

From Ellen Axson Wilson

My darling,   Princeton, Feb. 14/94

Mr. Reid has been spending the evening again,—has just left and it is bedtime! Moreover I have had the carpet taken up in my room today & put down again and am a little tired in consequence. Thirdly it is a bitter night and the house stubbornly refuses to be anything but cold. I fear that the sum total of these unpropitious facts is that I must confine myself to the merest hurried line tonight,—especially if I am to get it mailed by Ed.

We all very well still,—or to be perfectly exact I have just taken today a little "face cold" but mean to sleep it off tonight. It is nothing.

I am sorry that I cannot answer the *sweet* letter that came today;—my *heart* answers, dear, as you would wish to every word. I love you, Woodrow, with all my heart,—love you as much as you want me to,—am in *every way*,

                                              Your own   Eileen.

ALS (WC, NjP).

From the Minutes of the Seminary of Historical and Political Science of the Johns Hopkins University

Bluntschli Library, February 15, 1894.

The Historical Seminary held its regular meeting on the evening of February 15, Dr. Adams in the chair. . . .

At a public meeting of the Seminary on the evening of February 2, 1894, Professor Woodrow Wilson, of Princeton, N. J., read a paper on "Edmund Burke." The meeting adjourned at 9.30 to give members an opportunity to attend the Y.M.C.A. reception in Levering Hall.

G. F. Youmans, Secretary.

Typed entry, bound ledger book (MdBJ).

To Ellen Axson Wilson

My own darling,   Baltimore, 15 February, 1894

Your letters, these days, are so bright and cheery in their tone; bless you for a dear normal, light-hearted little woman, with a good conscience and an equable digestion! It does me good to read these wholesome epistles. I am so apt to be shaken in spirit by all sorts of influences, from all sorts of quarters; and you act on me like a quieting voice, with your fine sanity. Not that I am particularly shaken just now from any quarter: this is only general encomium on your disposition as shown in these letters, which I read over and over again so often that all sorts of sentences from them are continually running in my head,—making the best music I know.

My lecture of to-day is already off my hands (No. 16), for Henry C. Adams has finished his course and vacated the nine o'clock morning hour, and I have moved into his place. The new arrangement went into effect this morning. The afternoon hour was extremely inconvenient. Now that it is out of the way, I can make some calls.

While I think of it, dear: you have not sent me those checks, to be endorsed and sent back for deposit. They ought not to wait any longer.

Dear Josie's letter did hurt a little, but not so much as you seem to have feared that it would. I think I understand what he means, and the spirit, not of bitterness, in which he writes. He is father all over,—*minus* the literary and parliamentary art of expression. His *core* is as right and sound as possible. I think I can straighten him out with a letter easily enough. Poor fellow:

how my heart aches about it all, and how it hurts me that I cannot help him, and must even seem to throw cold water on his hopes of advancement! I shall write him to-night.

Stock's letter distresses me, too, but principally by its note of calm endurance,—not because it is itself discouraging. The *facts* are hopeful, even if the *mood* is not. I have written about the University Extension business, but no reply has come as yet.

Has your class in engravings gotten to work yet? I am so eager to know *all* that my darling does, to share as much of her life as it is possible to share through letters, that I find myself wondering about all her engagements. I shall deliver my last lecture *two weeks from to-day* and can reach home that same evening, love! When this letter reaches you there will be one day *less* in the reckoning! Every one of these lonely nights, when my heart almost breaks for you, really brings me ever so much nearer my sweet Eileen! When I think of that I can go to sleep—and dream!   Your own   Woodrow

ALS (WC, NjP).

From Ellen Axson Wilson

Princeton, Feb. 15/94.

Many thanks, my darling, for the charming valentines. Together they make a perfect little posy, as sweet as sweet can be. You have made a very fortunate raid on the fair old garden of verse. They make a brave show together and the pretty little *field* flower you have found to send with them does them no discredit. It is a lovely little blossom, and the breath of it went straight to my heart.

How that heart beat at the thought that I might have seen you yesterday! I feel my breath come quicker even now at the suggestion. Yet I think you were quite right in not attempting it. Ah well, it is only two weeks now,—it *is* on the 1st of March that you come,—is it not?

I wish you could have seen Princeton this morning; it was transformed into fairyland,—every twig of every tree covered with ice and the sun making one glory of it all;—you know the wonderful effect. I could not stay in the house, but wandered for two hours all over Princeton;—made an errand to the college &c.

The errand was to order one or two of the books that Mr. Heath mentioned—especially the one with the formidable title "The seven little girls,"—&c. &c. And, by the way, where have you secreted all the historical atlases? There was a small Labberton and a large ditto[1] and an old classical atlas of mine! But they are all missing.

The children are so funny. We were reading about the ancient Persians today & I told them how their young men were taught "to ride to shoot & to speak the truth." That seemed to strike their fancy amazingly; they all three marched about for half an hour shouting at the tops of their voices "to ride to shoot and to speak the truth!" Once Jessie stopped to enquire "and *did* they *all* speak the truth?" By way of illustrating the subject I read some verses of Tom Moore's—"Who has not heard of the vale of Cashmere?" &c.—rather nice lines & not too "flowery" for the climate described; but before I had finished Jessie interrupted me with,—"don't read that,—read Shakspere"! How is that for six years! We are all well except that Nellie has a little cold,—owing I suppose to the trying changes of weather. I have thrown mine off almost entirely.

I am *so* glad the speech went off well. Goodnight, my dear one,—I love I love you,—"Thou art the very eyes of me,"—and I am as ever   Your own   Eileen

ALS (WC, NjP).
    [1] Robert Henlopen Labberton's *Historical Atlas 3800 B.C. to 1886 A.D.* (New York, 1889) and *New Historical Atlas and General History* (New York, 1886).

To Ellen Axson Wilson

My own darling,   Baltimore, 16 February, 1894

Nothing happens to me now. Since I got back from Philadelphia my experience has been as uneventful as possible. I spend my energies, for the most part, reading examination papers!

I did make two calls yesterday, upon Mrs. Small and Mrs. Tom. Worthington, but that has been my only excitement. I spent most of last evening answering Josie's letter—to the length of eight pages!—which seems long for anything but a love letter!

I am very well, and serene, with a sort of *dogged* serenity,—the serenity which waits but does not *think*.

We, too, have been having bitter weather—some of it almost the worst I ever saw for its combination of trying elements. To-day is bright but intensely cold—and the cold hurled about by a boisterous wind. I feel like keeping within doors.

And yet, my stint of examination papers being gotten through with, I do not like to sit still in my room. It is too lonely to sit without you, when there is no imperative labour to be performed. I should infallibly grow sad were I to linger where I *must* think of the way I am living, here without you: it is too pathetic. My life seems so *grey* without you: I am impatient to be out of the room, seeking excitement and diversion. It is *tiresome* to be without you: there is no *relaxation* possible, no way in which I can *rest* my heart or expand it or clear it of all taint of dissatisfaction, without you. It seems to clear my eyes to look at you; it seems to freshen my faculties to talk to you; to reinvigorate and also to soothe my nerves to touch you; to fill me with youth and careless joy to kiss and caress you. I go to you as men in fables go to springs or throw themselves upon the earth, to regain my normal powers and get the serene and joyous strength that conquers without effort. Oh, how I love you and long for you, my Eileen. Five weeks will certainly be the limit of my endurance!   Your own   Woodrow

ALS (WC, NjP).

Two Letters from Ellen Axson Wilson

My darling,   [Princeton, N. J.] Friday [Feb. 16, 1894]

I have been just going to write every moment throughout the evening; but Nellie has been 'cutting up' so that there was no chance even to begin,—and now it is too late for more than a line. I don't think she is ill at all,—she doesn't seem feverish & coughs but little, but her nose is entirely stopped up—and you know how that affects her. She & Margaret each had a tremendous tantrum,—of course at the same time—this evening; and Nell is still threatening to begin again. Fortunately Maggie was in and helped me through. I will certainly send those checks tomorrow, dear; they are put away so carefully that I won't do it tonight.

Jessie has a very little cold,—the rest are quite well. I hope my darling is quite free from cold now.

Mr. Magie's mother is to be buried tomorrow. Someone has bought Mrs. Ricketts house![1]—it is said for $2600. I believe that is all the news.

Oh yes there is one more item—we had a Georgia broiled chicken for tea! The chicken cost 15 cts & the express on it was 5 cts. In New York they are selling now at 75 cts a lb. Uncle Will[2] kindly wrote to me about them. I didn't think it worth while to send,—cheap as they were—while you were away; but Mrs. Ricketts wanted some very much, so I sent. The express on 20 was $1.15. How I wish you were here! I would feast you daily on mayonnaise & young chicken. It will doubtless be cold enough for more after your return. But my wits are surely woolgathering tonight! the idea of spending these few precious minutes talking about *poultry*!

Goodnight my *dear* love. It is time I were dreaming of you.

Your own   Eileen.

---

1 This must have been an inaccurate report, as Mrs. Ricketts was living in her house at 80 Stockton Street the next year.

2 William D. Hoyt of Rome, Ga.

My darling,   [Princeton, N. J.] Saturday, [Feb. 17, 1894]

Just a hasty line enclosing the checks!

Nellie seems a good deal better this morning. She had a pretty good night in spite of her bad beginning. Jessie's cold seems almost gone. We have splendid clear cold weather now. I hope it is better there too, and that you will find something to amuse you out of doors. What good plays have you had? And what of the people in the house? You have been ominously silent about them. No more *Mr. Turners* I suppose![1] Does young Stevenson (?) stay there? Jesse Williams[2] had gotten a tale from him of how the men at Miss Ashton's ingratiated themselves with her. He said they stood in great awe of her but could always "get around" her by praising you! "Woodrow Wilson is certainly the finest man I ever saw;—may I have some more fire" &c. &c., is the way the tale went!

I feel simply furious this morning because of Peckham's defeat.[3] Oh what a disgrace to the Senate and the country! And was there ever such a contemptible hypocrite as Henry C Lodge; he voted against him, forsooth, on high moral grounds; because he disapproved of the *Administration methods* in working for him! It makes my blood boil!

I write in desperate haste so as to get the 2.30 mail.

With *best* love & devotion   Your own   Eileen

ALS (WC, NjP).

1 That is, no more bright and lively students like Frederick Jackson Turner.

2 Jesse Lynch Williams, '92, then living with his family at 90 Canal (now Alexander) Street.

3 The Senate, on February 16, 1894, rejected President Cleveland's nomination of Wheeler H. Peckham, president of the New York Bar Association, to the Supreme Court. Peckham's rejection was a victory for David B. Hill, leader of the New York State Democratic organization, who rallied so many Republicans and Democrats that the nominee did not receive even a majority approval. Cleveland and Hill were old enemies, and in this case Cleveland had again defied Hill, for Peckham was an open enemy of the Senator. Although Lodge referred to the administration's methods as one reason for voting against Peckham, the Massachusetts Senator was not averse to supporting Hill in order to exacerbate controversy within the Democratic party and to humiliate the President.

To Ellen Axson Wilson

My own darling,   Baltimore, 18 February, 1894

I had a caller until after ten o'clock last night, and so did not get my *Saturday start* on my Sunday letter. The caller was one of the men in the house,—a very interesting fellow,—a capital listener! and I poured out talk upon him until he must have been dazed. It is not because they are commonplace, but because I have seen very little of them, that I have said nothing of the people in the house,—or, rather, in the houses. While there is no Turner among them, the *average* of culture and intelligence is noticeably above previous years—with the exception, of course, of those first years when Shaw and Levermore, and Shinn, and Wright were all here together. I have been delighted to find two scientists,—a chemist and a mathematician,—who have an uncommon acquaintance with the best things that have been said and written, and as keen an appreciation, apparently, of literary form as the better students of literature. Yes, Stevenson is here—and a very bright and enjoyable fellow he is—a characteristic Princeton product. My meals are made very pleasant indeed by the conversation at table,—and I have nothing but praise for the company.

I can't imagine what has become of the atlases, dear. I thought that one of them was either on top of the book-case in my study that stands by the glass door or with the statistical atlas on top of the manuscript drawers; and I am quite sure that you will find the larger Labberton on some lower shelf of one of the book cases, filling the space between some book and the end of the shelf, and so behind the moulding of the outer edge of the side of the case. It is possible that you will find one in one of the closets where we have stored pamphlets in one of the back rooms.

I return the checks, endorsed. In this condition they are as good as money. You had better have Ed. deposit them at once, making out the proper deposit slips, &c. He understands perfectly how to do it.

I called on Mrs. Green yesterday afternoon and gave her the children's pictures. She seems very well,—and was in every way her usual self. She sent a great deal of love to you and the babies —as everybody does who knows you at all. I am not half as popular without you as with you, my charming little wife.

To-day, at two, I take my second Sunday dinner with Mrs. Bird. I have had about six invitations each Sunday for the last three weeks, for dinner! I'm very glad to have Mrs. Bird get her invitation in first.

There have been *no* plays here that I cared to go to, except those I have spoken of. Cocquelin, the French player, was here for two nights; but seats were very expensive and very difficult to get, and the play was wholly in French.[1] I did not go. Alexander Salvini (Thomaso's son) was here too,—in romantic drama (Dumas, &c.), and, hearing no very flattering account of him, I did not go.[2]

What charming stories you tell about the children, and our sweet little Jessie's sayings. If all my heart were not absorbed pining for their sweet mother, how I should pine for them! When I am separated from *you*, that pain swallows up all other pains, —and the children seem only part of *you*. But, if I could separate them from you in my thought, I should be profoundly unhappy without them—the sweet little sprites! I am *so* sorry to hear of the colds! I do hope you have all thrown them off entirely. Yes, my cold is gone. Mrs. Green remarked upon how well I was looking; and I certainly feel quite well.

And *now*, sweetheart, we can say '*next week*': I come home *next week*—and before the week is much more than half over! Only *one* more Sunday! Oh, it is too good to be true, almost. It makes my heart beat furiously to think of it—to think of seeing, of *having* you again, my blessed little wife! What a privilege it is to go back to you, and all your sweet endearments. It fairly intoxicates me to know that *such* a little wife,—the sweetest and most fascinating in all the world, the most delightful woman I ever knew or saw,—will not only be glad, but beside herself with joy and excitement to welcome me home, and to her arms once more! It all seems so strange. I feel so undeservedly rich to have the devotion,—the *romantic* devotion,—of such a woman so lavished upon me. I am so grateful, darling. I do not accept your love selfishly, as if I had a right to expect it; but as one takes a free gift made up of all that he craves but could never hope to earn. *No* man could *earn* such love as yours, with its infinite *detail* of delight and satisfaction. It is the nature of such lovely women as you to give with an incredible generosity; and I feel about it now exactly as I did when I was so agonizingly trying to get you. I knew there was nothing I could urge: that it was altogether a question of where you would be pleased to bestow: and the only thing I have ever given you is such love as it would have been niggardly to withhold—the absolute admiration and devotion of my whole heart. It is so far short of the truth to say that your love *satisfies* me. It fills me with an unspeakable delight and elation,—as if I had found a treasure and fountain of youth such as no other man can ever possess. It is thus, my Eileen, my beloved and adored little wife, that your love holds and thrills

Your own   Woodrow

ALS (WC, NjP).

¹ The great French actor, Benoît Constant Coquelin, and an all-French company appeared in three performances at the Lyceum Theatre on February 12 and 13, 1894.

² Salvini and his touring company appeared in three plays at Ford's Theatre during the week of February 12-17, 1894.

From Ellen Axson Wilson

My own darling,   Princeton, Feb. 18/94

One of the first things I thought of when I awoke this morning was that 'now I can say he will be back next week!' There is great comfort in that, it seems a long step forward. I begin to feel with you that five weeks is really the limit of endurance. And just think, it might have been—it used to be *six*! What an escape!

This has been such an exquisite spring day again, how I longed for you to enjoy it with me. I hope you have the sweet weather at least to enjoy.

The children seem almost free from cold again.

Margaret today was asking me something about the Greeks. I told her among other things that they wrote "the lovliest poetry in the world," whereupon *Nellie* standing by enquired incredulous-ly,—"lovlier than Shakspere?"

The boys report that Mr. Perry gave them a very good talk in chapel this afternoon on the subject of Paul's companions in work and travel,—Silas, Barnabas, &c. I am always so glad to hear of another layman who will perform that function; the influence of it is so fine on the boys. I wonder why Mr. [John Howell] West-cott, who teaches Bible classes &c., never does.

I took Helen there to a freshman tea yesterday afternoon; both the boys backed out, Ed because of his stammering & George be-cause he had to go to a "practice." They have gotten up an or-chestra and he is the drummer, & very much interested. They have engaged an instructor from Trenton and have taken one lesson.

Just here I was interrupted by Mr. Harper who spent the eve-ning. Now I must make haste to close if I want this mailed to-night. Our "lessons" by the way, with Mr. Frothingham begin to-morrow.

Goodnight, my dear love. I wonder if you realize how constantly I am thinking of you,—my thought seems always hovering about you,—cannot make long flights, must be ever near "that nest which it may drop into at will." Ah well, it is not long now before I will be with my darling not in thought alone! As ever—

Your own   Eileen.

ALS (WC, NjP).

From Lyman Pierson Powell

My dear Professor Wilson,   Boston, Feb. 18, 1894.

I am sure you will not think me unappreciative of your kindly letter because I am so tardy in replying. I have been working every wakeful hour on the Pilgrimage of 1894,[1] but have every day thought of your remarks about Axson and have written Dr. E. J. James about him. On my return to Phila. in three or four days, he and I will talk it all over, and shall, I trust, have something attractive to offer Axson. I have for a year had my eye on him as a possible extension lecturer. All I hear of him leads me to think he would be a very valuable man in this work. I am truly glad to hear you speak so frankly and so favorably about him. Were my time not so fully employed here I should run up to see him. Do you not think he would come to Phila. some time to look over the field and catch the spirit of things? But I will write you more fully on my return.[2]

I know you will be glad to hear that the Pilgrimage now promises to be more attractive even than I dared hope in my *Review of Reviews* article[3]—and that was prophecy. What think you of such cicerones in Boston as T. W. Higginson, E. E. Hale, Justin Winsor, Horace E. Scudder, E. D. Mead, and perhaps John Fiske! If you are in Baltimore on Wednesday and Thursday of this week I hope to hunt you out about lunch time so I may tell you over the luncheon about my plans and have your suggestions. Did I tell you about my plan for a volume on "Historic Towns"—a souvenir volume of the Pilgrimage?[4] Higginson, Williams, Sanborn, Mabie, Roosevelt will be among the contributors. One good publishing house is already clamoring for it and another is on the point of bidding.   Yours sincerely   Lyman P. Powell

I leave Boston tomorrow. Since the Pilgrimage is to follow Washington's Itinerary I want of course a *great* chapter on *Washington* the man. Whom shall I ask to write it? and to give the Pilgrims an address on him? I know whom I want, but I fear to ask him. He is such a busy man.[5]

ALS (WP, DLC).
[1] Powell was an enthusiastic organizer of pilgrimages to historic sites and

areas. He planned the "Pilgrimage of 1894" in connection with the summer institute of the American Society for the Extension of University Teaching. Commemorating Washington's assumption of command of the Continental Army, the pilgrimage was to begin in Philadelphia and wend its way through New England and back to New York. The "pilgrims" were to be addressed by prominent persons at each historic shrine.

[2] Axson did serve as staff lecturer—on nineteenth-century English literature—of the Society from 1894 to 1896.

[3] "The Renaissance of the Historical Pilgrimage," New York *Review of Reviews*, VIII (Oct. 1893), 411-20.

[4] Powell eventually produced four such volumes, all published by G. P. Putnam's Sons of New York: *Historic Towns of New England* (1898), *Historic Towns of the Middle States* (1899), *Historic Towns of the Southern States* (1900), and *Historic Towns of the Western States* (1901). Thomas Wentworth Higginson contributed "Boston" and Franklin Benjamin Sanborn "Concord" to the volume on New England. Talcott Williams wrote "Philadelphia" and Hamilton Wright Mabie "Tarrytown-on-Hudson" in the volume on the Middle States. Theodore Roosevelt was not among the contributors.

[5] He was of course referring to Wilson himself.

To Ellen Axson Wilson

My own darling,   Baltimore, 19 February, 1894

The dinner yesterday at Mrs. Bird's passed off most delightfully, of course, with all sorts of entertaining talk. I make them speak of you as often as possible, because they always do so with the warmest and the most discriminating praise, and it makes me glow with pride and delight to hear them. I admire you so intensely and so *discriminatingly* myself. Before I left, Miss [Edith] Duer[1] came in. Did I speak of her before, in telling of the meeting of the Archeological Club? I took her out to supper after the reading of the papers that evening and have seldom enjoyed any woman's talk more than I did hers: it was at once thoroughly intellectual and thoroughly feminine,—not so playful and amusing as Miss Ricketts', but quite as spirited and valid. I find she has quite a reputation for remarkable parts, and she is also very attractive in person. I was very glad indeed, as you may imagine, to meet her again at Mrs. Bird's. Since I met her (for I instinctively compare every woman with *you*) I have been trying to formulate the difference between your talk and the talk of women like Miss Duer which makes yours so much more attractive and satisfying than theirs,—for, if I had the choice, I would not change from yours to theirs even for the sake of variety. Even while I was talking to Miss Duer, conscious of being both entertained and delighted, I was trying to make the analysis, for I was conscious also of wishing that I was talking to you instead. I could not make it out then: I wish I could now—*for you*: it would interpret some of my devotion to you. Mrs. Bird helped me a little yesterday when she said (to Miss Duer) that you seemed to her a sort of embodiment of the poetry of which you are so fond. You are not different from other brilliant women because you lack anything they have, but because you have qualities which they lack. Your talk seems to be brilliant, *not deliberately* (theirs always has an element of deliberation in it) but *spontaneously* and as if (to speak paradoxically) by a sort of *natural accident*—as if out of the natural happenings of your mind. And so, from the very first time I ever heard you talk freely, your happy sayings have made me *love* you, admire your *nature* as well as your mind. These other women delight me as men do,—only with a certain added delicacy and charm. But your mind is so undived [undivided] a part of you that one can't know *it* without loving *you*. A spiritual beauty goes along with the intellectual—making a combination which fairly enslaves me, and makes me, mind and soul,

Your own   Woodrow

ALS (WC, NjP).
   [1] Who wrote to Wilson on June 10, 1902, recalling her earlier acquaintance with him. Miss Duer was not listed in the Baltimore city directories or social registers of this period.

From Ellen Axson Wilson

My darling,   [Princeton, N.J.] Monday [Feb. 19, 1894]

   The checks have just come safely to hand and shall be deposited immediately. I forward in another envelope all your letters,—there have been very few lately,—except one begging for an autograph, which with its stamped envelope may await your arrival. Your directions enabled me to find the "Labberton" directly and the children seem to find it very entertaining. We have just been studying the Macedonian supremacy, and of course, with great satisfaction to the children, reading Dryden where "he sings Darius great and good,—by too severe a fate,—fallen fallen fallen, fallen,—fallen from his high estate & weltering in his blood"![1] Jessie didn't even ask for Shakspere.
   You ask about my engagements,—that which looms largest at present is one with the dentist tomorrow morning at Trenton.[2] There is also Mr. Frothingham this afternoon, & Mr. Mildner on Lessing Friday afternoon before the Tourist Club. There is nothing else exciting. The party last week I of course did not go to because of Nellie's cold. Speaking of the dentist let me beg you to have your teeth examined while you have such a good opportunity. It is a terrible bore to have to go out of town for it. How I wish I could take the children in to Dr. Smith.[3] I shall have to take them *all* over to Trenton. And please, dear, get the tooth brushes and tooth-paste when you go. Have you gotten my things from the cleaners? Could they do the white ruffles nicely?

Nellie is still improving, Jessie well. I am struggling with a heavy cold in the head which makes me feel stupid to a degree. But Mrs. Hageman[4] is at the Ricketts & I am to run over and see her this morning so I must close. I wish I could write as sweet an *answer* to this sweet letter, darling, but I can't, it seems; the fault isn't with my heart but my head. Like the school-children "I know the answer but I can't express it,"—but the substance of it is all is that "there is none like him—none," and that I love him more than tongue can tell.   Your own   Eileen.

ALS (WP, DLC).
  [1] From "Alexander's Feast."
  [2] Dr. Wilson.
  [3] Probably a dentist in New York.
  [4] Probably Mary D. Hageman of 83 Mercer Street, widow of John Frelinghuysen Hageman.

To Ellen Axson Wilson

My own darling,   Baltimore, 20 February, 1894

I know that you will be delighted to learn that our friends were entirely successful at the Macon meeting in severing the connection between the Central and the Southwestern, and in reorganizing the latter to their minds. A new board of directors was chosen, Gen. Lawton and the rest of the hostile crowd being left out, and the Raoul group instated in their places. If they can make arrangements now with the Central for the use of their own (the Southwestern's) rolling stock, every wheel of which the Central has appropriated, they hope to pay dividends within a year. If they must go to the enormous expense of equipping the road with engines and cars, they can get the money, but dividends on the stock cannot be expected until after about two years and a half. But the paying basis will, they promise, certainly come again.

Yes, dear, I have gotten the things back from the cleaner's long ago; but I can't tell whether the ruffles are nicely done or not. They *said* they could do them nicely. I am right, I suppose, in understanding that I was to *bring*, not send, the things to you? I can send them as well as not, if you want them.

It distresses me beyond measure to hear of your "heavy cold in the head." Nothing depresses me quite so quickly as news that you are not well. May God keep you, my darling, from getting worse! And this is the week, too, when a cold is most dangerous, and when it is necessary that you should be most minutely careful. Do not neglect any precaution, I *beg* of you.

I am overwhelmed just now with making calls and meeting small and uninteresting engagements. This is the period of my visit here when I could almost find it in my heart to wish that I did not know anybody in the place, socially. There are so *many* people who *bore* me intolerably,—who are not even good listeners, even when I feel like talking to them!

I have made arrangements to deliver *two* lectures to-morrow,— one in the morning and one in the afternoon,—so as not to lose the 22nd., Washington's birthday, and that will enable me to finish my course (Providence permitting) on the 28th, and reach home the same day—whereby we are brought twenty-four hours nearer one another. That is a substantial gain, isn't it,—even if I do have to impose upon the good nature of my class to obtain it! They show all the interest in my lectures I could reasonably expect; but I am sadly weary of the business,—and only one thing can rest me —to go home to the little wife I love beyond all the world.

Your own   Woodrow

ALS (WC, NjP).

From Ellen Axson Wilson

My own darling,   [Princeton, N.J.] Tuesday [Feb. 20, 1894]

I left the house this morning at quarter of eight & got back at quarter past two,—had just time to read your *sweet* letter & take a hasty lunch before rushing to the employment society, from which I returned at dark. Result—I am now a total wreck!—have a large-sized tooth-ache & a head-ache to match; so I won't try to write a letter but only a hasty line & then hie me to my little bed. I have—or had—*ten* fillings to be renewed! I think I will send the bill to *Los Angeles*! That tale of Miss Calhoun's appealed very strongly to me today!—*Who is* Miss (or is it *Mrs.*?) Calhoun? She writes as if she had known you always.[1] What a *very* queer letter it was! Mr. Powell's was pleasant, was it not? There is also today a statement from Heath to the effect that he owes you $67.00 for the past six months.

My cold is better today. Nellie is all right, but Jessie is coughing; it is not serious though. We had a delightful time at Mr. Frothingham's looking at his pictures. They are magnificent. But we didn't get much information from him, so Miss Ricketts, Mrs. Conover & I are going to read up a little on the subject together, —will probably begin Friday.

What delicious praise you lavish on me, my darling! It is indeed one of the great mysteries of love that you should think thus of me. But I must not forget how you dislike to be contradicted in these matters,—I will enter no fresh protests. Goodnight my darling—I love oh I *love* you—I *want* you! If I could suddenly see you here now I feel as though I would almost die for joy.

Your devoted little wife,   Eileen.

ALS (WP, DLC) with WWhw notation on envelope: "Jas(?) Masson (Mobile) Look up for Mrs. Smith."
  [1] Her letter is missing, but see WW to EAW, February 24, 1894.

To Ellen Axson Wilson

My own darling,   Baltimore, 21 February, 1894

I have been writing steadily for two hours and a half, on an intercalated lecture[1] and several imperatively necessary 'society' notes, and I am afraid my hand can go neither very well nor very far. As before, the last week proves to be fullest of engagements of all kinds and I have to slip in the writing I must do at such times as I *can*, and in such amounts as I may.

I went yesterday afternoon, taking Mrs. Bird, to hear Mr. George Grossmith, a professional "entertainer" from England,— and really it was delightful. The man is an actor of considerable repute on t'other side, having 'created,' in unbroken succession, the principal male parts in each of Gilbert and Sullivan's comic operas and achieved a very great popularity. But now he is back in his original occupation. With songs and humourous sketches of himself and the rest of the world he keeps you for two hours enjoying both him and yourself.[2] *Him*, because he is genuinely cultivated and humourous, your*self*, because you can laugh heartily without feeling that you are laughing at mere buffoonery or at anything that is vulgar. Your taste and judgment approve. Really it is remarkable, and I wished for you with all my heart,—this time *for your sake*. All the rest of the time it is *for my own sake*.

Last night I dined with the Worthington's again, and met some very interesting people (I am rejoiced to find that my friends are beginning to deem it suitable to have me meet people with something to say), but interesting in rather too complex a fashion to be described by a tired fellow in a short and hasty letter. I will reserve them to talk about,—for soon we can talk, after five more letters! Don't neglect to write me a letter on next Monday, miss, even if I am to come back on Wednesday. I shall need a letter on Tuesday of next week as much as I needed it on Tuesday of this week!

To-night I go out beyond the 'Boundary' to take dinner with the Vincents[3] (you remember the place); to-morrow is Commemoration Day, with all its goings-on, &c. &c.,—thus runs the

world away with a man's time and energies. I shall return to
Princeton as to a peaceful haven. It contains the sweetest home
and the best cheer, the best hospitality and the most interesting
and engaging person I can find anywhere. I go back to *renew*
myself, and to learn what real 'converse' is once more. Ah, darling,
the shortening of the distance between us makes my heart pant
the more violently as if "winning near the goal." One week from
to-day—one week from this hour—I shall (God willing) be on my
way to my queen, my Eileen!   Your own   Woodrow

ALS (WC, NjP).
   1 It was a lecture dated Feb. 21, 1894, and entitled "VII (continued) The
Administration and the Courts." It is included in the body of lecture notes printed
at Jan. 26, 1891, Vol. 7.
   2 Grossmith appeared at Lehmann's Hall on February 19 and 20. The Baltimore *Sun*, Feb. 20, 1894, described his show as "mainly a burlesque of American
ways," adding that it "kept the audience in a hilarious mood throughout the
evening."
   3 The John Martin Vincents, who lived at 604 Lenox Street. At this time,
Vincent was an Associate in History at the Hopkins.

From Ellen Axson Wilson

My own darling,   [Princeton, N. J.] Wednesday [Feb. 21, 1894]

   I have just escaped with difficulty from three insatiable children clamouring for "more poetry," and again more. "More about
the *Arab*" is their specific cry tonight! though I had already given
them half a dozen poems on the subject, covering that gentleman's views regarding his sweetheart, his horse, his palm-tree,
& things in general.[1]
   That reminds me of the books I ordered for them. The "Seven
little sisters" &c. seems rather good,—somewhat idealized sketches
of the life of variously *tinted* little girls in seven remote regions
of the world. But the History that I ordered—"Montgomery's"—
is not what I wanted, but a U. S. history.[2] I too rashly jumped to
the conclusion that it was a general history. It is very unsatisfactory to order books without having seen them. I wonder if they
havn't primary general histories in that large book-store on Baltimore St. that you could examine a little for me. "Parleys" is really
not satisfactory. It doesn't give much of anything except trifling
anecdotes,—doubtless apocryphal. One wants a book that will give
in simple, clear outline a panoramic view of the larger movements of history and also vivid little pictures of the life, character,
ideals, general environment of each nation. By the way I am finding the vols. of the "Century"[3] quite a treasure in furnishing historical and geographical illustrations. One can find pictures there
of almost every place and people if one tries.

My cold is *much* better, dear; there is really *no* cause for concern about it. Jessie was again a little hoarse last night but seems better today.

No, dear, I do not want the things until you come. By the way the *ale* was called for today. It belonged to a student named W. W. Wilson.[4]

I am very glad indeed that the "Southwestern" is looking up. Surely the "Central" will not have the cheek to steal all their rolling stock!—unless indeed for them all is lost—*including* honour!

But after all the best news in your letter is that you are coming home Wednesday! It is *grand* to have twenty-hour hours thus disposed of with one stroke of the pen; and to think that it is only a week before you will actually be here! I am *so* happy to think how happy I *shall* be! And yet it makes my heart leap and throb so violently that I hardly dare let it dwell *too* long on that homecoming. I dont want to have a reaction and die of "heart-failure" before you get here! Ah, *how* I love you! I can hardly *bear* to love you so much. In the words of the Bedouin song just read to the children,—

> "I love thee,—I love but thee
> 'Till the sun grows cold,
> And the stars are old,
> And the leaves of the judgment book unfold."

And neither does that say how entirely I am

Your own   Eileen.

ALS (WC, NjP).

[1] She was reading them poems by Bayard Taylor, including his "Bedouin Song."

[2] Probably David Henry Montgomery, *The Beginner's American History* (Boston, 1892).

[3] That is, *The Century Illustrated Monthly Magazine*, more commonly known as the New York *Century Magazine*. The Wilson Library, DLC, contains all issues from November 1886 through October 1907.

[4] Walker Winfield Wilson, '97, of Clarion, Pa.

To Ellen Axson Wilson

My own darling,   Baltimore, 22 February, 1894

The exercises of the morning[1] were very interesting, but they were very long and have left me little time in which to write before the outgoing of the mail which usually carries my letters to my love. We had two addresses, one by Prof. Bloomfield,[2]—an excellent, an admirable exposition of the true function of comparative philology (for when such men represent it, it is just what they represent it to be),—the other by Mendenhall,[3] of the

Coast and Geodetic Survey, on systems of exact measurement, inferior to Bloomfield's both in form and substance, but very good indeed, and not too long.

At four o'clock I am to go calling—on *whom* I do not know,—with Mrs. Bird. Hence the too narrow space of time into wh. this poor letter is squeezed.

I am so much distressed at the thought of what you must have suffered on Tuesday, my sweet love. It tears my heart to think of you in pain. I like to think, by contrast, of what you are going to *enjoy* with Miss Ricketts and Mrs. Conover. Those are just the two women with whom, I think, you can enjoy most, and I am so deeply rejoiced to learn that you are to read together. My darling is made for that sort of thing and has had all too little of it.

Ah, darling, the shortening of our separation from weeks to days so increases my impatience that I am fairly ashamed of myself. The charm of your *presence* seems to take hold on my imagination and torment it with longing. To think of making love to you *directly*,—no medium of words and phrases needed, but only the direct language of kiss and glance and embrace,—ah, how it makes me despise this poor medium of writing, in which there is so much comfort when nothing better is *near*, either in the past or in the future. I love you passionately, extravagantly, with an unspeakable desire for your sweet voice and face. I am over-whelmed with love for you.   Your own   Woodrow

ALS (WC, NjP).
[1] The Founders' Day exercises at the university.
[2] Maurice Bloomfield, Professor of Sanskrit and Comparative Philology at the Hopkins.
[3] Thomas Corwin Mendenhall, Superintendent of the United States Coast and Geodetic Survey, 1889-94.

From Ellen Axson Wilson

My own darling,   [Princeton, N.J.] Thursday [Feb. 22, 1894].

I have been 'celebrating' very assiduously today and in consequence am excessively tired now,—am afraid I shan't get much of a letter written. I had no idea of going to the games this afternoon,[1] but Miss McIlvaine[2] would not allow Helen to go without a chaperone even with her own cousins; so I was obliged to come to the rescue. We were there from two until after five. But it was quite interesting, even exciting. There were contests in jumping, wrestling, &c., & the exhibition of the gymnastic team. We had never seen wrestling before and found it *terribly* exciting. The "middle weight" match became accidentally a class contest because the two men who won the places in the preliminary trial were Poe (97)[3] & a sophomore. After a long & exciting struggle Poe won. The freshmen won everything they tried for,—Garrett (97)[4] the high jump;—another was first in vaulting, &c.[5]

What *very* good fun Mr. Grossmith must have been! I am so glad you heard him. By the way what is Edgeworth Smith doing? —any more wonderful entertainments musical & otherwise?

My cold is still improving. Jessie seems almost well again— and Nellie too.

I am sorry to send this empty scrawl but I am really "dead tired"—have no words or ideas,—so I must content me, dear, to "love you only in silence with my soul." *Always* and *altogether*,

Your own   Eileen.

ALS (WC, NjP).
  [1] The Indoor Games of the Track Athletic Association and Exhibition by the Gymnastic Team, held in the College Gymnasium as part of the Washington's Birthday program.
  [2] Either Miss Alice McIlvaine or Miss Elizabeth McIlvaine, co-principals of Evelyn College.
  [3] Neilson Poe, '97.
  [4] Robert Garrett, '97.
  [5] Albert Clinton Tyler, '97.

An Editorial in *The Nation*

[Feb. 22, 1894]

The question whether the game of football ought to be encouraged was discussed in Philadelphia last week by two college professors—Woodrow Wilson of Princeton, who took the affirmative, and Burt G. Wilder of Cornell, in the negative. Prof. Wilson made the familiar plea that the game develops moral qualities, but Prof. Wilder met this very neatly when he asked, "If football be so noble a game—if it be a game which has such possibilities for the training of youth—why then does an ex-football captain, under his own name, state that an umpire in the shape of a perfect sport should be employed to keep the young men in order?" We think the defenders of the game as now played would do well to omit the "moral-qualities" argument. It is really a little too much.

Printed in the New York *Nation*, LVIII (Feb. 22, 1894), 131.

To Ellen Axson Wilson

My own darling,   Baltimore, 23 February, 1894

The two calls I made yesterday afternoon with Mrs. Bird were interesting enough to bear recording,—particularly the first, on

Mrs. Dawson,[1] a close friend of Mrs. Bird's and really a rewarding person to meet, full of good judgments of men and books and of the better sort of learning which becomes a woman. I wish you could know her, my darling. I crave all good things, and especially all stimulating friendships, for you. The other call was on a Mrs. Lord who has a son in Princeton,[2]—a nice, enthusiastic little person, though of Society and by no means an author of good sayings. After the calls, I stayed to tea with Mrs. Bird and spent part of the evening—and I go there next Sunday again! When I spoke to Mrs. Small the other evening about Col. Richard Malcolm Johnston, she said, "Oh, you mean Mrs. Bird's Col. Johnston"! I think I shall become known here as 'Mrs. Bird's Mr. Wilson'! She takes me around and shows me off. She fairly put me through my paces before Mrs. Dawson, making me repeat 'what I said to her the other day about Andrew Lang,' &c. &c! I felt quite like a prize horse at a fair! The descriptions she gives of you would lead you, if you could but hear them, to deem my praises dim and colourless by comparison. Her command of superlatives is beyond belief. I feel, after being with her, that I am stepping out of an *aurora borealis* into the common, unprismatic light.

To-night I go to a dinner at Mrs. Machen's[3] given specially for me, and, so far as I can understand it, offered in gratitude for your extraordinary graciousness and kindness in inviting Arthur[4] to Princeton! You certainly made a hit there, madam. I shall no doubt enjoy myself at the dinner a hundred *per cent.* more than poor shy Arthur would have enjoyed a visit to Princeton. I had three (no four) several invitations for this evening, and yet Friday is an unlucky day.

Dear little Nellie's letter[5] pleased me so much that it *touched* me. I send an answer by the same mail with this. I am *so* much relieved to hear that your cold is decidedly better. Have you recovered from the shock of the dentist's operations, too?

This week's *Nation* pays its compliments to me, as usual, you notice.

Two more letters, Eileen (Saturday-Sunday and Monday) and then I come myself, to bring the biggest love message you ever received! But I must bring it all. I can't trust letters any more, when I am so keenly conscious how soon you will be in my arms again. It would break my heart *now* to strain after an expression *in words* of the great love that makes me

Your own   Woodrow

ALS (WC, NjP).

  [1] Probably Mrs. William H. Dawson of 1731 Bolton Street.

  [2] Frances Elizabeth Waterhouse (Mrs. Charles King) Lord, of 1034 North Calvert Street. Her son was John Waterhouse Lord, '95.

[3] Wilson's old friend, Mary, or Minnie (Mrs. Arthur Webster), Machen.
[4] Mrs. Machen's son.
[5] It is missing.

From Ellen Axson Wilson

My own darling,　　　　　　[Princeton, N. J.] Friday [Feb. 23, 1894]

Helen is with us tonight & Flemming & Inch[1] are coming to call. I have just gotten away from the children and am expecting to hear the bell ring every minute,—not very favourable conditions for letter-writing! Am sorry I couldn't write *today*, but I was very much occupied with a sewing girl this morning, and this afternoon I went to Mr. Mildners lecture,—which with the extracts was nearly two hours long. It was very entertaining, chiefly by reason of Mr. Mildner's own personality, which revealed itself in delightful & amusing fashion. The lecture itself was only a very rambling sketch of Lessing's life,—wholly without any vital criticism of his work. He began by stating that Luther & Lessing were the two greatest Germans—their two great apostles of truth, but he really gave us no evidence worth mentioning in establishment of that proposition.

We are all better,—my cold has almost left me. And just think, dear, only five more nights,—and it used to be five weeks! that is progress indeed.

> "Thou comest! all is said without a word.
> I sit beneath thy looks as children do
> In the noon-sun, with souls that tremble through
> Their happy eyelids from an unaverred
> Yet prodigal inward joy."[2]

With *all my heart*　　　　　　　　　Your own　　Eileen.

ALS (WC, NjP).

[1] Robert Alexander Inch, '95, and James Ralston Flemming, '95, Wilson's first cousin twice-removed, son of Ella Ralston Flemming, identified in WW to EAW, March 18, 1889, Vol. 6.
[2] Elizabeth Barrett Browning, *Sonnets from the Portuguese*, XXXI.

From Wilbur Fisk Gordy[1]

Dear Prof. Wilson,　　　　　　Hartford, Conn., Feb. 24, 1894.

It was my pleasure this week to entertain an old friend, Mr. Lyman Powell. In our conversation about history your name was mentioned, and we both enthused warmly over your work in that field. I remarked that I had often been at the point of writing to thank you for your help and inspiration but was afraid to intrude by so doing. He encouraged me to throw aside my scruples and hence this letter.

I have just read "A Calendar of Great Americans" which is, in some respects, the best piece of work you have done, if I may be so frank. I especially like your paragraph on Lincoln. In delicate insight and nice discrimination it is equal to anything I have seen on the martyr-statesman. You there show a rare power of condensing in small space volumes of suggestion.

May I also refer with emphatic approval to the judicious statements you make of R. E. Lee. I wish you would write a magazine article on his place in history. You could say some wise things of this distinguished man that would appeal to the sober common sense of the American people. I have a warm admiration for him as a man and general. I believe he was as patriotic as Lincoln. His point of view was different but his loyalty to the Union as he understood it was as true as gold. Is it too early for such things to be said by one whose words would carry much weight? Is not the centripetal idea likely to gain rapidly unless offset by influences calling attention to State Rights? Centralization is one of the lurking dangers to our institutions, I fear.

Pardon me, Prof. Wilson, I could not resist the temptation of saying these things.

Very sincerely yours,   W. F. Gordy.

ALS (WP, DLC).
¹ Supervising principal of public schools in Hartford and author of many school books on American history.

To Ellen Axson Wilson

My own darling,   Baltimore, 24 & 25 Feb'y, 1894

The dinner last (Friday) night at Mrs. Machen's passed off most delightfully. The company consisted of Mrs. Bird, Mr. and Mrs. Harry Reid,¹ Mr. and Mrs. Remsen, and Mr. and Mrs. Green.² (Of the last named more anon. Mr. Green is the man from Wells College who came here *instead of Winchester!*). The feature of the evening, for me, was meeting Mrs. Harry Reid,—by far the most charming woman I've met here, Miss Duer not excepted. For, with all her brilliancy, Miss Duer did not have a tithe of Mrs. Reid's charm,—so bright, so whimsical, so sweet, so pretty! How I should like to see you two together,—as Mrs. Bird said! She is not at all *intense*, neither is she a bit 'advanced,' except in the power to think and to see. She engages one's affections at the same time that she captivates his mind. She seemed (I must say, even at the risk of alarming you) to take as much of a fancy to me as I took to her. This morning she sent her husband around with a note begging me to dine with them 'any evening I would name.' *This* evening was literally the only one left that was not spoken for by somebody else,—and so I am to go this evening. What would I not give to take you with me,—not for protection, madam, but for your own delight and mine. Your charm, with its deep and sweet seriousness, without intensity, its unpremeditated art, its constant fine mixture of qualities, as if your whole nature were as deep and sincere and eloquent as your matchless eyes,—*your* charm, which is so much greater than hers that, while she delights me, you enslave me, is also so different from hers that it would make an excellent foil,—and I believe that after fifteen minutes talk you would love one another 'for good and aye.'

Sunday morning—

Well the evening was a delightful one. Mrs. Reid had actually, notwithstanding the short notice, gotten together a company to meet me, *not* Mr. and Mrs. Remsen this time,—I'm tired meeting them,—but Mr. and Mrs. Victor Smith, Dr. and Mrs. Thomas (Zoe Carey),[3] and Mrs. [James] Gittings, Mrs. Reid's mother. We really had a most jolly little party. I felt perfectly at home, talked long and delightedly with Mrs. Reid,—who wears well,—and behaved myself with a reasonable degree, I hope, of dignity, affability, and propriety (ahem!). Oh, sweetheart, if *you* were only here and could be always with me, I could have some very good times once and again.

Never mind! *one more letter*, and then I am coming myself! Oh, how my heart beats when I think of it, how my mind *pants* for your companionship, as if it could not *think* normally without you! I love you, I admire you, I long for you more entirely, more passionately, more *intolerably* every day, and next Wednesday (God willing) I shall be the happiest man in the world! But I must not dwell on you and thoughts of the home-coming! If I do, I shall *cut* the three lectures remaining—and all my other engagements, too—and take the next train.

My remaining engagements are these: to-day at two I go to dinner with Mrs. Bird; to-night I take tea with Mr. and Mrs. Emmott;[4] to-morrow at two I have a conference (!) on legal education with a member of the Committee appointed by the national Bar Association to consider that subject;[5] to-morrow evening I take tea (missing my dinner altogether!) with Mrs. Green; and Tuesday evening I dine with the Babcocks. In the meantime I must crowd in eight or ten calls. Do you wonder that I have no time to study? I shall have to work for dear life on my lectures when I get home!

Take care of yourself in this savage weather, my precious one! Stevenson went up to Princeton to spend the 22nd and came back last night. He reports the cold there terrible, as indeed it has been here, too, for the past forty-eight hours. I hope *some* of the rooms in the house are warm. I do so dread hearing that you and the children have renewed your colds!

I keep very well indeed, though, being out every night keeps me from getting as much sleep as I am used to in our dear quiet home.

I have not answered that extraordinary letter from California yet. I never heard of Martha Calhoun, and cannot imagine who she can be. Her extreme separatist views would lead one to infer that she is of *the* Calhoun blood; but her "dear Dr. Holmes" would not. I shall cogitate my reply till I get home. I can't be elaborate enough for her in the midst of my rush here.

My darling, I *must* talk about you just a minute before I close, to run off to dinner at No. 22.[6] My heart is so full of you that I must let it overflow a little, to save it from damage. You fill my life with your sweet influence, my incomparable little wife. I can talk to other women because I know you—and I like to enjoy you through them. I never have such satisfying thoughts of you as while I am talking to them, and realizing your fuller variety, your sweeter naturalness, your more perfect companionableness. I love you with every faculty I have, and if I could *not* come back to you what a desperate thing it would be to be so passionately and wholly   Your own   Woodrow

The enclosed is the plate card from Mrs. Machen's dinner

ALS (WC, NjP).

[1] Harry Fielding Reid and Edith Gittings Reid. At this time Reid was Professor of Physics at the Case School of Applied Science in Cleveland. After serving as Lecturer at the Hopkins from 1894 to 1896 and as Associate Professor of Physical Geology at the University of Chicago from 1895 to 1896, he settled at the Hopkins and taught geological physics and geography there until his retirement in 1930. Edith Gittings Reid belonged to a prominent Baltimore family. She soon became a correspondent of Wilson and recorded her friendship with him in *Woodrow Wilson, The Caricature, the Myth and the Man* (New York, 1934). It should perhaps be noted that her memory of her first meeting and early friendship with Wilson, in pages 32-41 of her book, was clearly erroneous.

[2] Herbert Eveleth Greene, Collegiate Professor of English at the Johns Hopkins, and his wife, Harriet Chase Greene.

[3] Henry M. Thomas, M.D., and his wife Josephine ("Zoe") Carey Thomas. Henry Thomas, a brother of Martha Carey Thomas of Bryn Mawr College, was soon to begin a long career at the Johns Hopkins Medical School.

[4] Professor and Mrs. George Henry Emmott. Emmott was Professor of Roman Law and Comparative Jurisprudence at the Hopkins.

[5] Probably George M. Sharp of Baltimore, a member of the American Bar Association's Committee on Legal Education and Admission to the Bar. The committee was planning a portion of the 1894 meeting, and Sharp undoubtedly

asked Wilson to give the paper on the legal education of undergraduates printed at August 23, 1894.

 6 That is, Mrs. Bird's house at 22 East Mt. Vernon Place.

From Ellen Axson Wilson

My own darling, [Princeton, N.J.] Sunday [Feb. 25, 1894].

I have just gotten away from the children after a quite *long* reading, offered in atonement for having had to neglect them all day. Mr. Harper, called on Helen last Sunday & missed her, so I invited him to dine today,—and we had a *very* pleasant time. He had just left with Helen to escort her to Evelyn, (what fun if it should prove as eventful a walk as ours from East Rome!) when Miss Ricketts came in and stayed until tea-time. We had a cosy nice little talk by our little wood fire.

We are having the coldest weather of the winter—thermometer actually below zero; but it is clear and bright and with the aid of the wood fire we have been very comfortable. Mrs. Lewis came in yesterday & "spent the morning," southern style. I was glad to have had the fire made for Helen for otherwise she would have been frozen out. She is very attractive & I enjoyed her 'visit.'

But I am rather thwarted in my efforts to "make the most" of my sewing girl. She is to give me six days beginning last Thursday. I was away all day Thursday 'celebrating,' Friday afternoon there was the lecture, Sat. morn. Mrs. Lewis, & Sat. aft. the West-cotts who made a long visit,—spent entirely romping with the children! Tomorrow I must go to a lunch party at Mrs. Fine's, Tuesday morning read with Miss Ricketts & Mrs. Conover, & Tuesday aft. go to the Employment Soc. There is also a reception at the Frothingham's that aft., which of course I won't attend. So you see I am by no means overworking;—fortunately the girl is doing her share of the work both well and rapidly, and is giving me a great "lift" with my spring sewing.

What a nice gay little letter this is of yesterday's, dear! I am so glad that you are not only *receiving* attentions but *enjoying* them! that you are meeting such very attractive people. Did you meet a Miss Louise Dawson of Ga.,—presumably a daughter of the lady you mention? Mrs. Lewis was extravagant in praise of her beauty and brilliance. I have no doubt you *are* known in "society circles" there as Mrs. Birds Mr. Wilson! Funny,—isn't it?

Was interrupted here by a long call from Mr. Daniels. It is now ten & I must be closing. Only to think darling that there are but three more nights! And tomorrow I can say, "he is coming the day after tomorrow!" You have not told me yet at what *hour* you arrive, by the way. It is time to begin counting the *hours*. Oh how hungry I am for a sight of that dear face. It has been sweet to *think* of it—of you—day and night and all the time, but it becomes constantly less satisfying as the end draws near. "I will not have my thoughts instead of thee,—who art dearer, better." I crave

> "the deep joy to see and hear thee
> And breathe within thy shadow a new air,
> But not to *think* of thee—because too near thee."[1]

Ah *how I love you* my darling. I wonder if even you—"oh liberal and princely giver,"—know how much because, you see, not only your gift of *love* but of *worth* has been so princely; if ever there was a true prince among men it is you. How I *glory* in you! my precious possession!—a masterpiece over every detail of which I linger in rapturous admiration, trying to decide whether its greatness consists most in the nobility and largeness of its conception[,] the balance and harmony of its parts or the beauty of the execution.

Perhaps the harmony—the proportion—is the most wonderful part of it, after all,—the way in which you unite into one *perfect* whole *all* good gifts of heart and head. There are about you just the qualities which by analogy make a great epic or drama. We small people can only hope *at best* to make of ourselves a little lyric! But I must stop *at once* if this is to be mailed. Always & altogether   Your own   Eileen

ALS (WP, DLC) with WWhw notation on envelope: "Chas. D. Hazen to A. W. Hazen."
[1] From Elizabeth Barrett Browning's *Sonnets from the Portuguese*, XXIX.

To Ellen Axson Wilson

My own darling,   Baltimore, 26 Feb'y, 1894

I use a pencil to-day because I've been out to lecture in this dreadful weather and must sit by the register and dry my feet. I cannot write on my lap unless I use a pencil and a pad.

Have you, too, had this extraordinary storm? I have a vague fear that with you it has been like the blizzard of 1887 [1888]. Perhaps you will not get this letter much sooner than you get me. I hope I shall not find you all ill when I get home.

Mrs. Bird invited Miss Duer to meet me at dinner yesterday and I had a most interesting time, more interesting even than usual. This afternoon, in spite of the weather, I must make as many calls as possible.

I cannot *write*, darling—I am consumed—*rattled*—by an overwhelming impatience. Day after to-morrow (*to-morrow*, when you get this!) I am coming home *to be with you*, and the thought makes my heart leap beyond control,—throws my thoughts into a perfect turmoil of wild pleasure. I can't do *anything* that involves sitting still. I can only love you and long for you beyond all measure! I am quite well.   Your own   Woodrow

ALS (WC, NjP).

From Ellen Axson Wilson

My own darling,   [Princeton, N.J.] Monday [Feb. 26, 1894].

I fear this my last letter is doomed to be a very poor apology for one for I am so *sleepy* I can scarcely hold my pen! Was at Mrs. Fines from one to four & since have been very busy about my sewing. We have been having almost a blizzard all day,—the snow & wind together were overwhelming, but of course I rode & it was rather good fun to be out in it. Mrs. Fine was as exasperating as usual. The other guests were Mrs. Lewis, Mrs. Perry & Mrs. Baldwin. Mrs. Hibben was sick & couldn't come. Do you know Mrs. Fine is actually going abroad with her brother & Jack,[1] leaving Mr. F & the baby[2] at home, to stay eight months or more! At first she frankly described it as a pleasure trip & nothing more; but afterwards, apparently seeing in our faces the sentiments we were too polite to express, she saw fit to concoct another reason;—she is going in order that the four year old Jack may acquire the French language! She says (as usual) that it is Mr. Fine's scheme; "he is insisting on her going." If she were my wife I should also "insist" on her never coming back. A thoroughly selfish woman like that is really a monstrosity.

Dear, very sad and startling news has come from Clarksville.[3] On Friday Kate had little *twin* girls both of whom died the same day. The one lived an hour the other a day. It was due to the fact that they were seven months babies. Kate, I am glad to add is doing well. What a touching experience for the poor young things to have passed through. I am *so* sorry for them.

We have none of us renewed our colds,—they are very slight indeed.

I am *so* glad you have been having such good times, dear. You seem to have become *the* social lion. Arn't you afraid home will seem dull after it all? Will the love and devotion and admiration of one little woman take the place of all that? Certainly all of them together could not adore you as I do or love you with the infinite tenderness & passion of

Your little wife   Eileen

I enclose this nice letter to atone a little for the stupidity of mine![4] Now to sleep & dream,—and then to wake and think "It is *tomorrow!*" Oh! How *can* I wait so long!

ALS (WC, NjP).
1 Her son, John Fine, born June 20, 1889.
2 Susan Breese Packard Fine, born August 11, 1892.
3 The letter conveying this news is missing.
4 Probably W. F. Gordy to WW, Feb. 24, 1894.

To Ellen Axson Wilson

My darling,   [Baltimore, Feb. 27, 1894]

I expect,—with what sensations you know,—to reach Princeton at 4:30, the house about a quarter of 5.

                              Your own   Woodrow

ALS (WP, DLC).

A News Item

                                               [March 2, 1894]

Prof. Woodrow Wilson has returned and will meet his classes next week according to schedule. The Senior examination will be held on Monday as announced. The examination in International Law will be postponed.

Printed in the *Daily Princetonian*, March 2, 1894.

Notes for Lectures in American Constitutional Law

                              [March 2-May 10, 1894]
                              Course of 1894

I. *Constitutional Law.*
The Constitution as a Political Instrument.

The Two Aspects of the Constitution:
   (1) *Political,* What sort of a government, with what natural and what politic relations of parts and powers?
   "The law-maker can enumerate in a text the rights of the great political powers, regulate their organization up to a certain point, determine the exterior forms of their action; *he is powerless to control* the exact position of authority which each shall possess. That is a question which can be decided only by the relative strength of the several powers. Constitutional usages only establish the result of the struggle

which inevitably arises between them." *Dupriez*, "Les Ministres dans les principaux pays d'Europe et d'Amérique."[1]

(2) *Administrative*, With what methods and prescribed modes and limitations of action?

The first, the statesman's point of view, the lawyer's only incidentally. *The second, the lawyer's* point of view.

But the former point of view *must often be taken by the lawyer*, because *a constitution* is *a vehicle of life*, not a mere document. It affects the living organs of the national life as well as the rights of individuals. *And yet* the lawyer must take this point of view *like a lawyer*, in order to make—

The Lawyer's Analysis of the Character of the Government, as it is to be Found, *e.g., in the Decisions of the Supreme Court* of the United States: This analysis may be pieced together as follows:

Fricker: "Das in bestimmten Raume für das Recht organisirte Volk."[2]

1. A State consists of a body of people, more or less closely organized, within a territory *either permanently or temporarily occupied.*

"The people in whatever territory dwelling, either temporarily or permanently, and whether organized under a regular government, or united by looser or less definite ties, constitute the state. This is undoubtedly the fundamental idea upon which the constitutions of our own country are established." *Chase, J.*, in *Texas vs. White*, 7 Wall., 720, *quoting Paterson, J.*, in *Penhallow vs. Doane's Administrators*, 3 Dallas, 93.

2. *The people*, who, aggregately, as a body politic, constitute the State, *are sovereign*, and make sovereign choice of their constitutional principles.

"*The power* existing in every body politic is *an absolute despotism*; in constituting the government, it distributes that power as it pleases, and in the quantity it pleases, and imposes what checks it pleases upon its public functionaries" Johnson, J., in Livingston vs. Moore, 7 Peters, 546. This opinion affected the division of powers, and particularly the exercise of certain judicial powers by the legislature of Pa.

3. *Yet Sovereignty may be divided*, and there may be two soveriegn bodies politic within the same territory.

"The powers of the general government and of the state, although both exist and are exercised within the same terri-

---

[1] Wilson is translating a passage from Léon Dupriez, *Les Ministres dans les principaux pays d'Europe et d'Amérique*, 2nd edn. (2 vols., Paris, 1892-93). [Eds.' note]

[2] The Editors have been unable to locate this phrase in the works of Karl Viktor Fricker. [Eds.' note]

torial limits, are yet separate and distinct sovereignties, acting separately and independently of each other, within their respective spheres." *Ableman vs. Booth*, 62 U. S., 506. (21 How.)—*Taney*, 516.

"For all national purposes embraced by the federal constitution, the states and the citizens thereof are one, united under the same sovereign authority, and governed by the same laws; in all other respects the states are necessarily foreign and independent." *Washington, J.,* (rather incidentally) in *Buckner vs. Finley*, 2 Peters., 590. See also *Dodge vs. Woolsey*, 18 How., 350.

The government of the Union is "a government of the people. In form and in substance it emanates from them. Its powers are granted by them, and are to be exercised directly on them, and for their benefit." This government, "though limited in its powers, is supreme within its sphere of action. This would seem to result necessarily from its nature." *Marshall, C. J.,* in *McCulloch vs. Maryland*, 4 Wh., 405 (1819).

The prerogative powers of the king, acting as *parens patriae*, "remain with the States." Taney, C. J., in Fontain vs. Ravenel, 17 How., 395.

4. *The sovereign people*, moreover, *are bound* in all their choices *by the "great first principles of the social compact"*—which was the court's way of expressing its idea of the essential principles of justice and order.

"An act of legislature contrary to the great first principles of the social compact cannot be considered a rightful exercise of legislative authority." "The genius, the nature, and the spirit of our state governments, amount to prohibitions of such acts of legislation." *Chase, J.,* in *Calder vs. Bull*, 3 Dal., 388. (*Instances cited*: a law punishing a citizen for an innocent action, destroying lawful private contracts or making a man a judge in his own case). *The legislature of Conn.* had passed an act setting aside the decisiin [decision] of a court of probate, reopening the case, and granting a right of appeal for six months after the new decision. This action the court upheld; the above, therefore, an *obiter dictum*.

5. *The people* are *themselves bound* and limited in action *by the constitutions* which they have set up.

"The Constitution of the United States is supreme over the people of the United States, aggregately and in their separate sovereignties, because they have excluded themselves from any direct or immediate agency in making amendments to it, and have directed that amendments be made representatively for them." *Dodge vs. Woolsey*, 18 How., 547

Here we have a sovereign of his own motion *creating a regency* through which he must always act, and at the same time *very narrowly limiting himself* in respect of any subsequent changes in the character or exercise of this regency.

6. *The people should seldom indulge in so great an exertion of their power* as is involved in constitution making.

"The people have an original right to establish, for their future government, such principles as, in their opinion, shall most conduce to their own happiness. . . . The exercise of this original right is a very great exertion; nor can it, nor ought it, to be frequently repeated." *Marshall* in *Marbury vs. Madison*, 1 Cr., 176.

7. *Undeliberate usage* also may make up a part of the constitution made by the people.

Usage "must be a part of the constitution of Connecticut, and we are bound to consider it as such, unless it be inconsistent with the constitution of the United States." *Paterson, J., Calder vs. Bull*, 5 Dal., 395.

Certain powers like that of *eminent domain*, also, and certain *prerogatives of the king* of England, accrue to the governments thus established, *by necessary inference from historical circumstance or the essential nature of gov't.*

"Eminent domain belongs to every independent government. It is an incident of sovereignty, and requires no constitutional recognition." *109 U.S.*, 513.

"In the construction of the constitution we must look to the history of the times, and examine the state of things existing when it was framed and adopted, to ascertain the old law, the mischief, and the remedy." *Rhode Island vs. Mass.*, 12 Peters, 657.

Legal Tender Cases.

"The Constitution, establishing a frame of government, declaring fundamental principles, and creating a national sovereignty, and intended to endure for ages and to be adapted to the various crises of human affairs, is not to be interpreted with the strictness of a private contract." *Justice Marshall* insisted that it was a constitution. "The power, as incident to the power of borrowing money and issuing bills or notes of the government for money borrowed, of impressing upon those bills or notes the quality of being a legal tender for the payment of private debts, was a power universally understood to belong to sovereignty, in Europe and America, at the time of the framing and adoption of the

Constitution of the United States[.".] "The Congress, as the legislature of a sovereign nation, being expressly empowered by the Constitution to lay and collect taxes, to pay the debts and provide for the common defence and general welfare of the United States, and to borrow money on the credit of the United States, and to coin money and regulate the value thereof and of foreign coins; and being clearly authorized, as incident to the exercise of those great powers, to emit bills of credit, to charter national banks, and to provide a national currency for the whole people, in the form of coin, treasury notes and national bank bills; *and the power to make the notes of the government a legal tender in payment of private debts being one of the powers belonging to sovereignty in other civilized nations*, and *not expressly withheld* from Congress by the Constitutions; *we are irresistably impelled* to the conclusion that the impressing upon the treasury notes of the United States the quality of being a legal tender in the payment of private debts is an appropriate means, conducive and plainly adapted to the execution of undoubted powers of Congress, consistent with the spirit and letter of the Constituteon, and therefore, within the meaning of that instrument, 'necessary and proper' for carrying into execution the powers vested by the Constitution in the government of the United States." *Gray*, J., in *Juilliard vs. Greenman*, 110 U. S., 439, 447-450. THEREFORE,

8. *The powers of the government* created by the people *may grow* indefinitely within the limits of *inference* from either

   (a) *Specific provisions* of the constitutions themselves, or

   (b) *The exercise of like sovereign powers by governments of a similar range of functions* elsewhere.

All of which, being interpreted, *means*:

   I. *That*, however constituted, *government has certain essential characteristics*, a certain necessary nature and range of powers; and

   II. *That the assent of the people*, more or less consciously given, more or less deliberately, carefully, and explicitly formulated, *is necessary* in the conduct of, *at any rate, free institutions*.

The resulting necessity that the *constitutional lawyer be a jurist*, not a mere pleader; that he be *ready to suggest principles drawn*, not out of narrow precedent, but *out of essential principle*.

Re-cast, 2 March, '94.

II. *Constitutional Law.*
The Constitution as an Administrative Instrument.

Preliminary note *on text-books.*

> *Best of the larger books,* "American Constitutional Law," by J. I. *Clark Hare.* 2 vols., Boston, Little, Brown, & Co., 1889.

> *Next in size, and perhaps in excellence,* "An Introduction to the Constitutional Law of the United States," by *John Norton Pomeroy,* (10th. edition, E. H. Bennett), Boston, Houghton, M., & Co., 1888.

> *Smallest, but of the best,* "The General Principles of Constitutional Law in the United States of America," by *Thomas M., Cooley,* Bost., L. B., & Co.

The Constitution not meant to embody a theory, but to serve as *an Instrument, a Frame, of Government.* The uses of the building inferred from its structure and arrangement.

Administration the predominant feature of this, as it must be of every federal, Constitution. (*The constitution of the German Empire* even more prolific in administrative detail than our own, particularly with regard to the collection and administration of the imperial revenues).

> *Every lawyer should regard it* as his *Manual of Jurisdictions,* his main key to process and authority. Here he will find, with some degree of explicitness, *the way in which the government should be conducted*: his clients' rights and the proper resort for remedies.

> *E.G., as to Jurisdictions*: The Constitution having made distribution of the powers of government among the several federal organs, "neither the Legislative nor the Executive branches can constitutionally assign to the Judicial any duties, but such as are properly judicial, and to be performed in a judicial manner." I.e., *the constitution takes precedence of statutes as a manual of jurisdictions.* (See *note to Heyburn's Case,* 2 Dal., 409)

> *Again,* it is to be read as other manuals would be, and *not with subtlety.* "When the fundamental law has not limited, either in terms or by necessary implication, the general powers conferred upon the legislature, we cannot declare a limitation under the notion of having discovered something in *the spirit* of the constitution which is not even mentioned in the instrument." *People vs. Fisher,* 24 Wend., 220.

In order to realize the administrative character of the Constitution, let us *go through its provisions* with an eye to this point.

The state constitutions afford *even more striking* examples: They designate *election districts*, e.g., determine the *apportionment of representatives*, provide for the *keeping of the public records, prescribe the duties* alike of the governor and the principal executive officers of the State in considerable detail, *regulate* the conduct of *elections*, limit the *debt-contracting powers of local authorities*, and prescribe the period of the payment of their debts, determine *the organization of local government* and the powers of local officers, prescribe much of the *detail of legislative procedure* (like reference to committees, etc.), sometimes even go into the detail of the way in wh. the *public printing* shall be contracted for, and *stationery* supplied for the use of the legislature!

The most remarkable example among the cases, furnished *from the Iowa courts*: The *constitution of Iowa directed* that amendments to the constitution originating with the Legislature should pass two separate Assemblies (i.e., two Assemblies chosen at different elections), and then be adopted by a vote of the people. *Moreover*, "Under article X., section 1, of the Constitution of Iowa, it is necessary that the several houses of the General Assembly which first proposes an amendment to the Constitution, *cause* the same to be *entered at length upon their respective journals, with the yeas and nays* taken thereon. It is not necessary that the proposed amendment be enrolled, or signed by the presiding officers of the several houses, or by the governor; but where, as in this case, the proposed amendment was so enrolled and signed, and also entered at length, in *substantial compliance* with the Constitution, upon *the journal* of the Senate, that journal is the primary and *best evidence* of the proposed amendment, as agreed to by the Senate, . . . while the roll is, at best, but secondary evidence thereof; and *the parol testimony of members* of the Senate is *not admissible* to contradict the Senate journal as to the language of the proposed amendment, as agreed to by the Senate."

"Where an amendment to the Constitution proposed by the Eighteenth General Assembly, was not entered at length upon the journal of the House, as required by . . . the Constitution; and where it appeared from the journal of the Senate . . . that the amendment agreed to by the Senate was *different in language and substance*, from that agreed to, and submitted to the vote of the electors, by the Nineteenth General Assembly; *held*, that the amendment so submitted to the electors did not become a part of the Constitution, *notwithstanding it was approved by a large majority of the electors." Koehler and Lange vs. Hill*, 60 Iowa, 543, 544, four out of five justices concurring.

See Cooley, "Constitutional Limitations," Chap. VI.; *Jones vs. Hutchinson*, 43 Ala., 721; *People vs. Commissioners of Highways*, 54 N. Y., 276; *Walnut vs. Wade*, 103 U. S., 683 (the word 'Illinois' dropped out of a statute,—immaterial).

Ours a government of Explicit Powers, and of *explicit Limitations* of power (i.e., an explicit balance of powers.)

The lawyer's business is, to see that the law is interpreted and enforced in all strictness and fidelity.

Explicit, administrative character of our "Bill of Rights."

☞ *Read Amendments* III. to VIII., inclusive.

The Constitution should be reverenced as *the solemn Covenant of a People.*

9 March, 1894

III. *Constitutional Law.*
Function of the Courts under a Constitutional Government.

This function of the courts, to determine the constitutional validity of the acts of the other Departments of the Government, *affects the Constitution as an administrative instrument*, a frame of government, *almost exclusively.*

The constitutional powers of our courts the most conspicuous feature of our system *in foreign eyes*, and the most novel, but *erroneously* supposed to be an invention.

See Art. III. & Art. VI., 2.

I. *An Inference, not a piece of construction* at all, though *a necessary inference.* The inference elaborately established in *Marbury v. Madison*, (1803) 1 Cr., 176 ff. *No grant of the kind* in the Constitution. It is an inference (*an administrative inference*) from *the fact* that the *Constitution* is a *permanent* and (so far as Congress and the Executive are concerned) an *unalterable part of the "supreme law of the land."*

The only radical difference between our government and other governments is, that we have kept the law-making and the *constituent functions* separate in our constitutional procedure. This same arrangement is *found in the British colonies* with the same result. Not necessary in a written constitution, nor invariable. *Improbable*, indeed, *because of the inherent weakness of the Judiciary.*

A General English Principle: Parliament itself cannot disregard law without coming face to face with the courts.

and in Eng. before 1688.

Stockdale vs. Hansard, 9 Adolph & El., 1: "The House of Commons by ordering a report to be printed, cannot legalize the publication of libelous matter." *It can set law aside only by repeal.*

Parliament can set fundamental law aside now (e.g., invade the field of the king's prerogative) only because (*since 1688*) it has been a *constituent* as well as a law-making *authority*. "*The House of Commons* was supposed *originally* to be no part of the standing government of this country. It was considered as a control, issuing immediately from the people, and speedily to be resolved into the mass from whence it arose. In this respect it was in the higher part of government what juries are in the lower." Should the House cease to represent the people, "by this want of sympathy they would cease to be a House of Commons."—*Burke*.[3]

II. *Strictly normal and strictly legal* nature of the function.
   1. *May devolve upon a court of any grade* (though some decline the function through modesty).
   2. *Must be necessary to the determination* of the case, and *not obiter dictum.*

"While courts cannot shun the discussion of constitutional questions when fairly presented, they will not go out of their way to find such topics. *They will not seek to draw in such weighty matters collaterally*, nor on trivial occasions. It is both more proper and more respectful to a co-ordinate department, to discuss constitutional questions only where that is the very *lis mota*. Thus presented and determined, the decision carries a weight with it to which no extra-judicial disquisition is entitled." *Hoover vs. Wood*, 9 Ind., 287.
   3. *The Question must be raised by a Party in Interest.*

When an act "is alleged to be void, on the ground that it exceeds the just limits of legislative power, and thus injuriously affects the rights of others, it is to be deemed void *only in respect to those particulars, and as against those persons, whose rights are thus affected. Prima facie*, and upon the face of the act itself, nothing will generally appear to show that the act is not valid; and it is only when some person attempts to resist its operation and calls in the aid of the judicial power, to pronounce it void, as to him, his property, or his rights, that the objection of unconstitutionality can

3 From Burke's *Thoughts on the Cause of the Present Discontents*. [Eds.' note]

be presented and sustained. Respect for the Legislature, therefore, concurs with *well established principles of law*, in the conclusion, that *such act is not void, but voidable only*; and it follows as a necessary legal inference from this position, that this ground of avoidance can be taken advantage of, by those only who have a right to question the validity of the act, and not by strangers. . . . *To this extent only* are courts of justice called on to interpret. *Wellington, Petitioner*, 16 Pick. (Mass.), 96.

4. *No other ground of invalidation* except inconsistency with the letter or the plain inferential meaning of the Constitution. *I.e., not a political*, but *a purely legal question*.

Argued, that the legislature of New York had no power to erect any other local courts than those provided for in the constitution of the State, which "makes express provision for all the courts of justice which it permits to be established in the State."

Held, that it could erect no courts of the same jurisdiction as those provided for in the constitution, but that it "can provide such agencies for the administration of the law and the maintenance of public order as it shall judge suitable, where no prohibition, expressly made or necessarily implied, is found in the constitution." *Denio*, C. J., in *Sill vs. Corning*, 15 N. Y., 299, 300.

☞ *Not on the ground*, e.g., of the statute's being against public policy, or induced by *fraud*, or,—etc. (Yazoo Land Grants, Fletcher v. Peck, 6 Cr., 87; 2 Pet. 328).

5. *Must be plain conflict.*

"The question, whether a law be void for its repugnancy to the Constitution, is, at all times a question of much delicacy, which ought seldom, if ever, to be decided in the affirmative, in a doubtful case. The court, when impelled by duty to render such a judgment, would be unworthy of its station, could it be unmindful of the solemn obligations which that station imposes. But it is *not on slight implication or vague conjecture*, that the legislature is to be pronounced to have transcended its powers, and its acts to be considered as void. The opposition between the constitution and the law should be such that the judge feels *a clear and strong conviction* of their incompatibility with each other." *Marshall* in *Fletcher vs. Peck*, 6 Cranch, 128.

III. *Of What Nature, exactly, are these powers*, then?
    Necessary to do *some very careful thinking* here.

Differentiate Legislation and *Adjudication*:

Legislation is the binding enactment of a rule of law, the *establishment of an abstract legal principle*.

Adjudication, on the other hand, is the binding determination of *a concrete legal relationship*, the determination, recognition, or denial of *a specific claim*: the setting up of *a concrete judgment. It has nothing to do with criticism* of the abstact [abstract] nature, the timeliness, or the wisdom of the general principle enacted. *Differentiate Administration and Adjudication*:

An *action* vs. a *logical process*.

Administration is the actual carrying into effect of the purposes and judgments of the State; and *Adjudication furnishes to Administration a process and a concrete application*.

Adjudication is by its very nature *law in operation, policy given* its legal, not its political effect and *application to individuals*. The point of view of courts is always, the rights and interests of the individual; not the motive and policy of government. *They are intermediaries, not agents of originative power*.

At the same time, it is true that the courts are *in possession of the past* to the exclusion of the legislature. "*A legislative act cannot declare what the law was, but only what it shall be*." Head-note, *Ogden vs. Blackledge*, 2 Cr. 272. *Does Adjudication make law?*

Yes: to a certain extent and in a certain sense: *Legitimately* when by the exercise of strong reason, building the laws and their inferences together into a consistent and equitable system; *but Illigitimately when by the exercise of strong will*, simply. The exercise of independent choice belongs, not to the courts, but to the Legislature.

"*A great part of the law made by judges consists of strong decisions*, and as one strong decision is a precedent for another a little stronger, the law at last on some matters becomes such a nuisance, that equity intervenes or an act of parliament must be passed to sweep the whole away." (*C. J. Earle*, quoted in *Brinton Coxe's* "Judicial Power and Unconstitutional Legislation," 1893, p. 40.)

In cases like Juilliard vs. Greenman and the "*original package case*," (Leisy vs. Hardin, 133 H. S., 100.) *who is to do the sweeping away?*

III [IV]. *How far are the Legislature and the Executive bound* by decisions of the federal courts on the constitutionality of legislation or of administrative acts?

Only to the extent of their legal conscience and political responsibility.

"*The decisions* of even our higher courts are accepted as *final only in relation to the particular cases* with which they happen to deal, and their judgments do not impose compulsory limitations upon the action of any other department." *Ordronaux*, "Constitutional Legislation," p. 420.[4]

16 March, 1894

IV. *Constitutional Law.*
The Courts and the Legislature.

The Place of the Legislature in every system of government depends wholly upon historical (i.e., constitutional) circumstances and arrangements.

"I consider it a sound political proposition," says *Justice Patterson* in *Cooper vs. Telfair,* 4 Dal., 19, "that *wherever the legislative power of a government is undefined, it includes the judicial and executive attributes.*"

Necessary Presidency (Sovereignty) *of the Legislative Power:*

(1) *In the very nature of the case,* since it has free choice of policy, equips the administration, holds the purse, determines all rights and duties in the premises.

(2) *In the opinion of the Supreme Court:* "The executive power is vested in a President, and as far as his powers are derived from the Constitution, he is beyond the reach of any other department, except in the mode prescribed by the Constitution through the impeaching power. But it by no means follows that every officer in every branch of that department is under the exclusive direction of the President. . . . There are certain political duties imposed upon many officers in the executive department the discharge of which is under the direction of the President. But *it would be an alarming doctrine that Congress cannot impose upon any executive officer any duty* that they may think proper, which is not repugnant to any rights secured and protected by the Constitution; and in such cases the duty and responsibility grow out of and are *subject to the control of the law,* and not to the direction of the President. And this is em-

Case of the establishment of the Treasury Dept.

---

[4] John Ordronaux, *Constitutional Legislation in the United States: Its Origin, and Application to the Relative Powers of Congress and of State Legislatures* (Philadelphia, 1891). [Eds.' note]

phatically the case where the duty enjoined is of a merely ministerial character." *Kendall vs. U. S.*, 12 Pet., 610.

"*Retrospective laws* which do not impair the obligation of contracts, or partake of the character of *ex post facto* laws, are not condemned or forbidden by any part of" the Constitution. *Washington, J.,* in *Satterlee vs. Matthewson,* 2 Pet., 413.

"*An Act of Congress,* that a certain bridge across the Ohio River is 'declared to be a lawful structure, and shall be so held and taken to be, anything in the laws of the United States to the contrary notwithstanding," *supercedes the effect and operation of the decree of the court* previously rendered, declaring it ["] an obstruction to navigation and directing its removal." *Pa. vs. The Wheeling Bridge Co.,* 18 How., 421.

Natural and Necessary Limitations upon the Law-making Power. *E.g., With regard to the retroaction of laws.*

"*A legislative act cannot declare what the law was,* but only what it shall be." *Headnote, Ogden vs. Blackledge,* 2 Cr., 272.

"*A subsequent legislative declaration* as to what was the true intent and meaning of a statute *is not conclusive.* The utmost effect to be given to it is to regard it as an alteration of existing law in its application *to future transactions.*" *Town of Koshkonong vs. Burton,* 104 U. S., 668.

"*Both in principle and in authority* it may be taken to be established that a legislative body may by *statute declare the construction* of previous statutes so as to bind the courts in reference to all transactions occurring after the passage of the law, and may in many cases thus furnish the rule to govern the courts in transactions which are passed, *provided no constitutional right of the party concerned is violated.*" Miller, J., in *Stockdale vs. Atlantic Ins. Co.,* 20 Wall., 331.

"*It may well be doubted* whether *the nature of society and of government* does not prescribe some limits to the legislative power; and, if any be prescribed, where are they to be found, if the property of the individual, fairly and honestly acquired, may be used without compensation?" *Marshall,* in *Fletcher vs. Peck,* 8 Cr., 135.

Upon ground of public policy:

"*An agreement* to abstain in all cases from resorting to the courts of the United States is void *as against public policy,* and a statute of the State of Wisconsin requiring such an agreement is in conflict with the Constitution of the United States, *and void." Headnote, Doyle vs. Continental Ins. Co.,* 4 Otto (94 U. S.), 535, reaffirming 20 Wall., 445.

"Contracts permissible by other countries are not enforceable in our courts, if they contravene *our laws, our morality, or our policy." Oscanyon vs. Winchester Rep. Arms Co.,* 13 Otto (103 U. S.), 261, 277.

In England, similarly,

"*It was formerly held by Lord Coke* and others, that the *lex non scripta might,* in some imaginable cases, *control the statute law, if* that law were *against common right and reason,* or repugnant or impossible to be performed"; and, though "these *dicta* have been treated rather as a warning than an authority," they are *accepted to mean* that *the courts will read right reason and purpose into statutes* wherever it is possible to do so. *Blackstone* declared the *"Law of Nature"* to be *"superior in obligation* to any other"; English judges have declared it to be *"a part of the Laws of England";* have affirmed that "the law of England *will not sanction what is inconsistent with humanity";* have even decided that "principles of *private justice, moral fitness,* and *public convenience,"* "when applied to a new subject, *make common law without a precedent."* (See Herb. *Broom,* "Commentaries on the Common Law," 8th. ed., pp. 8 and 20-22, *with cases there cited).*

Very well stated by Chancellor *Walworth* in *Salters vs. Tobias,* 5 Paige, 344. "*In England,* where there is no constitutional limit to the powers of Parliament, a declaratory law forms a new rule of decision and is valid and binding upon the courts, not only as to cases which may subsequently occur but also as to pre-existing and vested rights. But *even there* the courts will not give it a retrospective operation, so as to deprive a party of a vested right, *unless the language of the law is so plain and explicit as to render it impossible to put any other construction upon it."*

Constitutional Limitations: the *complex system of our law.*

I. *In the case of Congress* there are limitations arising from

    (1) The *explicit character of the grant* of powers to it in the Constitution, which [puts] limits to these powers and to such as may reasonably be implied as incident to them.

    (2) The *explicit prohibitions* of the Constitution.

    (3) *The implied restrictions imposed by the* federal *Bill*

of Rights (the first eight amendments to the Constitution).

II. *In the case of the state Legislatures.* These limitations *will be considered in a subsequent lecture* (Lecture VI.).

To Whom is the Constitution addressed? To the Courts or only to (the conscience of) the Legislature?

It is addressed to each one of the authorities which it *constitutes,* to the courts as much as to either of the others. So far as the courts are concerned, the argument is, summarily, as follows.

The Constitution is part of the law of the land, of which the courts are bound to take notice as much as of other law, but which, because of its *peculiar character and derivation,* they are bound to regard as *supreme. The judges are bound,* indeed, *by oath* to maintain the Constitution.

It is a Constitution which establishes limits to the powers of legislation: the establishment of such limits is, in fact, one of its principle and most notorious objects; and its provisions are meant to be paramount.

It is the province of the courts to say what the law is; and the judicial power is expressly declared to extend to *cases arising under "this Constitution,"* as well as under the laws and treaties which shall be made by the properly constituted authorities.

The courts, moreover, *are an independent and coördinate department* of the government, with their own distinct constitutional standing, *acting for the country,* and not as servants of the Legislature.

If the Legislature refuses obedience to the Constitution, it destroys the validity of the very instrument under which it itself acts, and therefore *abrogates its own authority.*

See *Marbury vs. Madison,* 1 Cr., 176; *Trevett vs. Weeden* in *Coxe,* "Judicial Power and Unconstitutional Legislation," p. 234; and *Bayard vs. Singleton,* Ibid., 248. The last named cases (Rhode Island and North Carolina) bearing date respectively *Sept., 1786,* and *May, 1787.*

Nature of the restraint exercised by the courts: confined to *the determination of individual rights*[.] *Determinative,* therefore, and *in no sense superintendent. Confined to the sphere of its ordinary and proper duties.*

Case law, nevertheless, has been powerfully instrumental in *building up the political practice* of the government. *Creat-*

ing interpretation authoritative for individual litigants, the courts have also, of course, created interpretations *authoritative for Congress* as well.

Analysis of Cases:

Although constitutional cases affecting the powers of Congress are very numerous in the reports, *there is no case* in which the decision is unfavourable to Congress which is *not concern*[ed] *with the jurisdiction of the federal courts* themselves *until the Dred Scott Case (Dred Scott vs. Sanford,* 19 How., 393, 447: 1857). Until then the courts did little more than assert and define their own exclusive and independent functions. *E.g., The United States vs. Ferreira,* 13 How., 47, (December Term, 1851). *Congress having,* in execution of a treaty entered into in 1819 between the United States and Spain, laid upon the judge of the territorial court of Florida the duty of passing upon claims for losses, *Held,* That this was no judicial function: the judge was merely a commissioner; and there could, therefore, be no appeal to the Supreme Court.

Since the war, the cases have covered a much wider field, *it having become necessary,* particularly, *to determine the effect of the post-bellum Amendments* upon the powers of Congress, and to restrain the Congress from excessive interference with the prerogatives of the States.

The vast majority of the constitutional *cases have affected,* not the powers of Congress, but *the powers of the state legislatures.*

See volume 131 of the U. S. Reports (closing the century (1889), where, in an *Appendix*, the cases in which laws, whether federal or state, have been declared unconstitutional are enumerated, with more or less completeness.

See also Coxe, pp. 8 ff.

30 March, 1894

V. *Constitutional Law.*
The Courts and the Executive.

Principle of the Coördination of Departments: a constitutional principle only by inference: each Dept. deriving its powers in kind (though, except in the case of Congress, not in item) directly from the Constitution itself.

☞ *Read Article III. of Const.*

The Courts have been most scrupulous, and even punctilious, *in dealing with the Executive,* to give it the utmost latitude

and independence. They have established a jurisdiction derived by inheritance from the King's bench in England[.]
The General Principle, That the courts will not interfere with the Executive in *the exercise of its judgment or discretion* in any particular; and that they will *construe its 'discretion' most liberally*, as including all ordinary executive or departmental functions.

They will not undertake to command executive officers in the performance of their duties *except in cases* of acts which are *manifestly merely ministerial in character*.

Thus, in *Marbury vs. Madison*, 1 Cr., 170, C. J. Jay says, "*The province of the court* is, solely, *to decide on the rights of individuals*, not to inquire how the Executive, or executive officers, perform duties in which they have a discretion. Questions in their nature political, or which are, by the constitution and laws, *submitted to the Executive, can never be made in this court*."

Again, *in Cox, Secretary, vs. U. S., ex rel*. McGarrahan, the *general principle* is very succinctly stated. "The writ of mandamus cannot issue to an executive officer, where discretion and judgment are to be exercised by the officer. *It can only issue in cases where the act required to be done is merely ministerial* in character, and where the relator is without any other adequate remedy." 9 *Wall.*, 298.[5]

The Secretaries Proxies of the President, and therefore members of the constitutional Executive.

Thus, *in U. S. vs. Eliason*, 16 Pet., 291, it is held, that "the Secretary of War is *the regular constitutional organ of the President* in the administration of the military establishment of the nation; and rules and orders publicly promulgated through him must be received as acts of the Executive, and as such are binding upon all within the sphere of his legal and constitutional authority."

The functions and privileges of executive officers are very fully characterized in *Commissioners of Patents vs. Whiteley*, 4 Wall., 522, in which C. J. Taney holds the following language: "*In general*," executive duties, "whether imposed by act of Congress or by resolution, are not mere ministerial duties. *The head of an Executive Department*

---

[5] The principle underlying in all of the cases is, that neither questions of expediency nor questions of fact, but only questions of right, shall be brought on these writs. This principle is applicable whatever be the rank or character of the officer who is to be tried. Goodnow [*Comparative Administrative Law*], II., 205, and cases there cited. [WW's note]

of the Government, in the administration of the various and important concerns of his office, *is continually required to exercise judgment and discretion.* He must exercise his judgment in expounding the laws and resolutions of Congress under which he is required to act. . . . If a suit should come before this court, which involved the construction of any of those laws, the court would certainly not be bound to adopt the construction given by the head of the Department. And if they supposed his decision to be wrong, they would, of course, so pronounce their judgment. *But this judgment,* upon a construction of the law, *must be given in a case in which they have jurisdiction,* and in which it is their duty to interpret the acts of Congress, in *order to ascertain the rights of the parties* before them. *The court could not entertain an appeal from* the decision of *one of the Secretaries, nor revise his judgment* in any case, where the law authorized him to exercise judgment or discretion. *Nor can it by mandamus act directly upon the officer,* and guide and control his judgment or discretion in the matters committed to his care, in the ordinary exercise of his official duties. . . . The interference of the courts with *the performance of the ordinary duties of the Departments* would be productive of nothing but mischief, and we are quite satisfied that such a power was never intended to be given to them."

These principles are as applicable to Injunction as to Mandamus. See *Gaines vs. Thompson,* Secretary of the Interior, 7 Wall., 347; where the *leading cases are all cited.*

The power of the courts, moreover, in this field as in others, is *limited by the Constitution* (in the case of the Supreme Court) *and by the Judiciary Act* (in the case of the inferior courts).

In *Marbury vs. Madison,* 1 Cr., 173, it is held that *Congress cannot confer upon the Supreme Court any original jurisdiction,* beyond what is explicitly allowed it by the Constitution, and that the issuing of a writ of *mandamus* by the court in the case under consideration would be an act of original jurisdiction, and under the Constitution invalid. (*President Adams* had signed the commissions of certain Justices of the Peace for the District of Columbia, and they had been duly authenticated by seal, etc., *but Secretary Madison* refused to deliver them).

In M'Intire vs. Wood, 7 Cr., 504, "It was decided that the power of the circuit courts to issue *writs of mandamus is confined to such matters as they have original jurisdiction over by the Judiciary Act* of 1789." The language of the court is as follows: "Had the eleventh section of the Judiciary Act covered the whole ground of the Constitution, there would be much reason for exercising this power in many cases, wherein some ministerial act is necessary to the completion of an individual right, arising under the laws of the United States, and the fourth section of the same Act would sanction the issuing of the writ for such purposes. *But, although the judicial power of the United States extends to all cases* arising under the laws of the United States *the legislature has not thought proper to delegate the exercise of that power to its Circuit Courts, except* in certain specified cases. When questions arise under those laws in the state courts, and the party who claims a right or privilege under them is unsuccessful, an appeal is given to the Supreme Court, and this provision the legislature has thought *sufficient*, at present, *for all the political purposes intended* to be answered by the clause of the Constitution which relates to this subject."

See, to the same intent, *Kendall vs. U. S.*, 12 Pet., 524, where the the [*sic*] jurisdiction not yet communicated to the courts by Congress is spoken of as *"a dormant power*, not yet called into action and vested in those courts."

Some Specific instances, showing how far the courts have gone in their reluctance to interfere with the Executive.

U. S. vs. Guthrie, 17 How., 384. "A writ of mandamus should not be issued to the Secretary of the Treasury, commanding him to pay to a judge of a Territory his salary for the unexpired term of office from which he has been removed by the President, and another person appointed thereto."

Reeside vs. Walker, 11 How., 272. "A mandamus will not be issued to the Secretary of the Treasury to compel the *payment of a debt* from the United States for which no appropriation has been made by law."

Brashear vs. Mason, 6 How., 92. "A mandamus will not lie to compel the Secretary of the Navy to pay an officer in the navy a sum which may be shown to be due," inasmuch as the Secretary is *"obliged to inquire into the condition of the fund*, and the claims already charged upon it, in order to ascertain *if there is money enough* to pay all the accruing demands, and, if not not [*sic*] enough, how it shall be *apportioned among the parties* entitled to it. . . . *At most the Secretary is but a trustee* of the fund for the benefit of all those who have claims chargeable upon it, and, *like other trustees*, is bound to administer it with a view to the rights and interests of all concerned." ☞ *Unlike* other trustees, he is *not subject to the supervision of the courts* in the administration of this trust.

Decatur vs. Paulding, 14 Pet., 497. "A mandamus would not lie from the circuit court of this District to the Secretary of the Navy to compel him to pay to the plaintiff a sum of money claimed to be due her as a pension under a resolution of Congress. There was *no question as to the amount* due, if the plaintiff was properly entitled to the pension; and it was *made to appear* in this case *affirmatively*, on the application, *that the pension fund was ample* to satisfy the claim. The fund also was under the control of the Secretary, and *payable to his own warrant.* . . . The court say, that the duty required of the Secretary by the resolution was to be performed by him *as the head of one of the executive departments* of the government *in the ordinary discharge of his official duties*," and reiterate the general principle of non-interference with official discretion. (The above is the language of the court in *Brashear vs. Mason*, quoting Decatur vs. Paulding.)

The same principles are *held* also *by the state courts*:

"The court has no power to award a mandamus, either to compel the performance of any duty enjoined on the executive by the constitution, or to direct the manner of its performance." *State vs. Governor*, 25 N. J., 331.

Hawkins vs. The Governor, 1 Ark., 570. "The Governor of the State is not amenable to the judiciary for the manner in which he performs, or for his failure to perform, his legal or constitutional duties. *The constitution assigns to him no ministerial duties* to be performed, *nor can the law enjoin upon him any such duty*."

(Sutherland)[6]

People vs. The Governor, 29 Mich., 320. The constitutional *duties of the Governor "will be presumed to have*

---

[6] Commonly referred to as the "Sutherland case" because it was The People on the Relation of John L. Sutherland and Others *v.* the Governor, decision on which was rendered by Justice Thomas M. Cooley of the Michigan Supreme Court on May 12, 1874. [Eds.' note]

been done," because of the exalted nature of the confidence reposed in him; and his duty "can seldom be considered as merely ministerial[.]" *"The governor of a state occupies a position analogous* rather *to the president* of the Union than to the heads of the executive departments of the federal government; and a decision that the latter may be compelled by mandamus to perform a mere ministerial duty is not in point where the writ is sought against the governor." *Not affected by the voluntary appearance of the governor.*

Mauran vs. Smith, Gov'r., 8 R. I., 192. No mandamus can issue against the governor as commander-in-chief to perform a duty imposed upon him in that capacity by statute.

State vs. Warmouth, 22 La. An., 1. *"Even though the act* he is required to perform *be purely ministerial* in its character." *The question* whether it be merely ministerial *is to be decided*, not by the courts, *"but by the chief executive himself."*

Rice vs. Austin, Gov'r., 19 Minn., 104. "The judicial and executive departments of our state government having been made distinct and independent by our state constitution, neither can enforce the performance of its duties by the other."

On the other hand:

Marbury vs. Madison, 1 Cr., 170. "If *there be no* such *question* as the exercise of *executive judgment* or discretion, if it be not a case of intermeddling with a subject over which the Executive can be construed as having exercised any control, there is *nothing in the exalted station of the officer which shall bar* the citizen from asserting, in a court of justice, his legal rights, or shall forbid a court to listen to the claim, or to issue *a mandamus* directing the performance of a duty, not depending on executive discretion, but on particular acts of Congress, and the general principles of law." *The Supreme Court, however*, is *not the proper forum* in which to apply for such an act of original jurisdiction.

Kendall vs. U. S., 12 Pet., 324. *Held*, that "the authority to issue a writ of mandamus to an officer of the United States, commanding him to perform a specific act, required by a law of the united States, is within the scope of the judicial powers of the United States, under the

Constitution" (though not within the jurisdiction of the courts except by grant of the Judiciary Act).

It being *claimed that the Secretary was subject to the control and commands of the President* alone in the performance of his duties, *Held,* That the court *could not sanction that doctrine* because "it would be vesting in the President a dispensing power which has no countenance for its support in any part of the Constitution, . . . a principle wh. if carried out in its results to all cases falling within it, would be clothing the President with a power to control the legislation of Congress, and paralyzing the administration of justice."

Little vs. Barreme, 2 Cr., 170. "The commander of a ship of war of the United States, in *obeying his instructions from the President* of the United States acts *at his peril.* If those instructions are not strictly warranted by law, he *is answerable in damages* to any person injured by their execution. . . . The Act of the 9th. of February, 1799, did not authorize the seizure upon the high seas of any vessel sailing from a French port; and orders of the President of the United States could not justify such a seizure."

"*The refusal of the* United States *Secretary of the Interior to issue a patent* for lands after all questions of discretion had been decided in favour of the applicant, has been held to be the violation of a ministerial duty and may be overcome by application to the court." *Goodnow,* quoting *U. S., vs. Schurz,* 102 U. S., 378.

Circuit Court Cases:

Milligan vs. Hovey, 3 Biss., 13. *The members of military commissions, and officers of the United States army,* engaged in the trial of persons not in the military service, "are *liable for arrest and imprisonment* ordered by them" in States "where the courts are undisturbed," "even though ratified and approved by the Executive Department of the Government."

Durand vs. Hollins, 4 Blatch., 452. ["]*On the other hand, the interposition of the President* to protect *abroad* the lives and property of citizens of the United States, is *a matter resting in his discretion;* and, in all cases where a public act or order rests in executive discretion, neither he nor his authorized agent is personally civilly responsible for the consequences."

Result in respect of the powers of *the several Comptrollers. (See* "The Comptrollers and the Courts," by *E. I. Renick*, Pol. Sci. Quarterly, V., 214).

Until the establishment of the Court of Claims and the later investiture of the District and Circuit Courts of the United States with a claims jurisdiction, *the comptrollers* of the Treasury were *practically independent and irresponsible* judges. "The comptroller was not required to conform to the directions of those superior to him in rank. He was *not amenable to the courts. He was beyond even the reach of a mandamus;* for in all cases of payment of money he was supposed to exercise '*discretion.*' From his decision adverse to a claimant there was *no appeal except to Congress.*"

Special laws, creating the Court of Claims and giving jurisdiction in such cases to the lower courts of the United States, *have now remedied this* state of affairs.

State Cases:

Questions of fact may be considered upon mandamus or quo warranto, where an administrative authority has decided against *a title to office. Goodnow*, quoting *State vs. Garesche*, 65 Mo., 480; People vs. Pease 27 N. Y., 45.

Courts will also decide what is 'cause' when an administrative authority has removed an officer who can be removed only for cause. *People vs. Board of Police*, 72 N. Y., 415.

In many States special statutes authorize appeals from the decisions of tax assessors.

There may be habeas corpus proceedings, too, *to test* cases of *inter-state rendition*. See *People vs. Curtis*, 50 N. Y., 321, and *People vs. Brady*, 56 N. Y., 182.

(*Compare*, with reference to these state cases, *F. J. Goodnow*, "Comparative Administrative Law" II., *Chap. V.*, esp. pp. 205-210.).

The courts are *inclined to be much freer with minor authorities.*

Gilchrist vs. Collector of Charleston, 1 Am. Law Journal, 429. "A circuit court of the United States has power to issue *a mandamus* to a collector, *commanding* him to grant *a clearance.*"

U. S. vs. Mayor of Burlington, 2 Am. Law Reg., N. S., 394. "The *federal courts* have power to issue a *mandamus* to a municipal corporation to compel it *to perform a duty*, although such duty is *created by state laws only.*"

U. S. vs. Jefferson Co., 6 Rep., 486. "*Mandamus* lies from a circuit court *to compel* officers of *a municipal corporation,* against which the court has rendered judgment, *to levy a tax* to provide means to pay the judgment." See *U. S. vs. Keokuk*, 6 Wall., 514.

Also to compel "the *supervisers* of a county, charged by law with the duty of levying a special tax to pay bonds and coupons for the erection of county buildings, *to discharge that duty* in order to pay judgment for such coupons." *Jenkins vs. Culpeper Co.*, 1 Hugh., 568.

But,

"*Mandamus will not lie* to compel officers of a municipal corporation to levy a tax, *unless the legislature has made it the duty* of such officers to levy it." *U. S. vs. New Orleans*, 2 Woods, 250.

VI. *Constitutional Law.*
The Federal Government and the States.

Constitutional Limitations upon the powers of the several States, arising from,

1. The existence of such *powers of Congress* as are *in their nature exclusive*;
2. *Explicit prohibitions* of the *federal Constitution.* (*Particularly* Article I., section x.)
3. *Implicit prohibitions of the federal Constitution.* (*E.g.,* against the exercise of any power, the taxing power, for example, in such a way as to hinder or embarrass the action of the federal government.)
4. The *express prohibitions of the state constitutions*;
5. The *implied prohibitions* contained *in the Bills of Rights* embodied in the state constitutions;
6. *Detailed directions*, as to procedure, forms of legislation; length of legislative sessions, etc., in state constitutions.

Real Scope of our state constitutional law very much greater, nevertheless, than that of the federal government.

We are *too apt to think of our constitutional law as predominantly federal*,—a view due, no doubt, to the presidency of the federal courts over the entire system. *The state part* of our constitutional law is in reality *much the largest*, and, so far as our daily interests are concerned, *much the more important.*

The States control the whole range of *civil and religious rights*; the *education* of the people; the regulation of the *suffrage*; the laws relating to *marriage* and to the *relations of husband and wife, parent and child, guardian and ward;* the powers of *masters over servants,* and the whole law of *principle and agent; partnership, debt, credit, insurance; corporations,* both private and municipal; the possession, distribution, devolution, and use of *property;* all *contract* relations; the exercise of *trades; criminal law;* etc., etc., etc.

Comparison of leading topics of legislation in England. (*Read "The State,"* page 487).

The States ante-date the Union; and new States come into the same heritage of historical power that the or[ig]inal States enjoy.

The courts are constantly arguing back to the historical derivations of state power, and to the general powers of government, as exercised, for example, in England. *Thus,* in

The Slaughter House Cases, 16 Wall., 36, the court holds, *not only* that *the general police powers* exercised by all governments belong to the States, as the repositories of general governmental powers, but also that *direct inferences may be drawn from the authority and practice of Parliament.* "The *Parliament of Great Britain,* representing the people in their legislative functions, *and the legislative bodies of this country* have, from time immemorial to the present day, continued to grant to persons and corporations exclusive privileges; . . . privileges which come within any just definition of the word monopoly, . . . and the power to do this has never been questioned or denied."

In Calder vs. Bull, 3 Dal., 386, it is held that *the state legislatures retain all the powers of legislation* delegated to them by the state constitutions, which are not expressly taken away by the Constitution of the United States.

And in *Texas vs. White,* 7 Wall., 700, it is held that *Texas came in upon just the same footing* exactly. "Under the Constitution, although the powers of the states were much restricted, still, all powers not delegated to the United States, nor prohibited to the States, are reserved to the states respectively or to the people. And we have already had occasion to remark at this term that '*the people of each state* composed *a state,* having its own government, and *endowed with all the functions essential to separate and independent existence,*' and that 'without the states in the Union, there could be no such political body as the United States.' *Lane Co. vs. Oregon.* (71-81) Not only, therefore, can there be *no loss of separate and independent autonomy* to the states, through their union under the Constitution, but it may be not unreasonably said that the preservation of the states, and the maintenance of their governments, are as much within the design and care of the Constitution as the preservation of the Union and the maintenance of the federal government."

States made out of Territories, therefore, *a fortiori*, not only lose nothing by the change, but *actually gain "separate and independent autonomy."*

Subsequent Process of Subtraction:

Gibbons vs. Ogden, 9 Wheat., 1 (involving a question of interstate commerce,—a grant of exclusive rights of navigation on the Hudson to Livingston): "When *these allied sovereigns converted their league into a government*, when they converted *their Congress of Ambassadors*, deputed to deliberate on their common concerns, and to recommend measures of general utility, *into a legislature*, empowered to act on the most interesting subjects, *the whole character in which the states appear, underwent a change*, the extent of which must be determined by a fair construction of the instrument by which that change was effected." (*Marshall*, p. 187).

The Subtraction Permanent:

Texas vs. White, again: "The constitution, in all its provisions, looks to *an indestructible Union, composed of indestructible states.*"

"When, therefore, *Texas* became one of the United States, she *entered into an indissoluble relation*. All the obligations of perpetual union, and all the guarantees of republican government in the Union, attached at once to the State. *The Act* which consummated her admission into the Union was *something more than a compact*; it was the *incorporation* of a new member into the political body. *And it was final.* The union between Texas and the other States was *as complete*, as perpetual, and as indissoluble *as the union between the original states*. There was no place for reconstruction, or revocation, except through revolution, or through *consent of the states.*"(!)

The "Supreme Law of the Land":

Article VI. of the Constitution: "This Constitution, and the laws of the United States which shall be made in pursuance thereof, and all treaties made, or which shall be made, under the authority of the United States, shall be the supreme law of the land; and the judges in every state shall be bound thereby, anything in the constitution or laws of any state to the contrary notwithstanding." *See comments* in *Ableman vs. Booth*, 21 How., 506. (517 ff.)

Hence the presidential position and power of the courts of the United States.

Digression with regard to
The Peculiar Position of Treaties under this clause:

"*A treaty is in its nature a contact* between two nations, not a Legislative Act. It *does not generally effect, of itself, the object to be accomplished*, especially so far as its operation is infraterritorial; but is *carried into execution by the sovereign power* of the respective parties to the instrument.

"*In the United States a different principle* is established. Our Constitution declares the treaty to be *the law of the land*. It has, consequently, to be regarded in courts of justice as *equivalent to an Act of the Legislature*, whenever it operates of itself without the aid of any legislative provision." *Foster vs. Neilson*, 2 Pet., 253, 314.

"The treaty is therefore a law made by the proper authority, and *the courts of justice have no right to annul or disregard any of its provisions*, unless they violate the Constitution of the United States. It is *their duty to interpret it and administer it* according to its terms." *Doe vs. Braden*, 16 How., 635, 657.

Whenever, however, it is in the nature of *a contract*, engaging to do a particular thing, "*the legislature must execute the contract before it can become a rule of court.*" *Foster vs. Neilson.*

"So far as the provisions of a treaty can become the subject of judicial cognizance in the courts of the country, they are *subject to such Acts as Congress may pass* for their enforcement, modification, or repeal." *Edye vs. Robertson*, ("Head Money Cases"), 112 U. S., 580.

"*Congress may pass any law*, otherwise constitutional, *notwithstanding it conflicts* with an existing treaty with a foreign nation.

"*If* an Act of Congress is *plainly in such conflict, a court cannot enquire* whether, in passing such an Act, Congress had or had not an intention to pass a law inconsistent with the provisions of the treaty." *Ropes vs. Clinch*, 8 Blatch 304.

"*An Act of Congress* imposing taxes on tobacco *must pre-*

vail over the tenth article of the *treaty* with the Cherokee Nation." *The Cherokee Tobacco Case,* 11 Wall., 618.

The Question of Concurrent Powers:

Many of the most interesting constitutional ques[tions] are raised by the inquiry, What powers of Congress are by their nature exclusive?

The general rule may be stated to be, that the *powers of Congress are exclusive so far,* and only so far, *as they are exercised. The States must withdraw where Congress enters.*

Thus, in a case affecting *bankruptcy laws,* the Supreme Court has held that "it is *not the mere existence of the power, but its exercise,* which is incompatible with the exercise of the same power by the states. It is not the right to establish these uniform laws [of bankruptcy][7] but their actual establishment, which is inconsistent with the partial acts of the states. It has been said that Congress has exercised this power, and, by doing so, has extinguished the power of the states, which cannot be revived by repealing the law of Congress. We do not think so. If the right of the states to pass a bankruptcy law is not taken away by the mere grant of that power to Congress, it cannot be extinguished, it can *only* be *suspended, by the enactment* of a general bankruptcy law. *The repeal* of that law cannot, it is true, confer the power on the states; but it *removes a disability* to its exercise, which was created by the Act of Congress." *Marshall* in *Sturges vs. Crowninshield,* 4 Wheat., 196.

Some powers there are which are *not* made *exclusive even by their exercise,* notably *the power to tax.* Congress and the states *may even tax the same things at the same time.*

Both the federal government and *the governments of the states must take care,* however, *not to exercise this power* of taxation *in such a manner as to injure or hamper each other.* "*The power to tax involves the power to destroy;* that power to destroy may defeat and render useless the power to create"; and "there is a plain repugnance in conferring on one government a power to control the constitutional measures of another, which other, in respect to those very measures, is declared to be supreme over that which exerts the control." *Marshall* in *McCulloch vs. Maryland,* 4 Wheat., 413.

The United States, therefore, *cannot tax state agencies,* securities, properties, or public salaries; and *neither can a*

[7] WW's brackets. [Eds.' note]

state tax federal agencies, properties, salaries, treasury notes, revenue stamps, or etc., etc. (*See*, among a great many other cases, *McCulloch vs. Maryland*, 4 Wheat., 316; *Osborn vs. The Bank of the U. S.*, 9 Wheat., 738; *United States vs. Railroad Co.*, 17 Wall., 322; *Ward vs. Maryland*, 12 Wall., 418; *Dobbins vs. Commissioners*, 16 Pet., 435; *Bank Tax Case*, 2 Wall., 200).

Guarantee of a Republican Form of Government:

Its historical interpretation. The limitations thrown about federal interference in such cases as *Luther Vs. Borden*, 7 How., 1.

Conclusion:

The *Supremacy of the federal government strictly limited*, and *strong presumptions* established *against it.*

The Presumptions:

I. *In the case of the States*, the presumption is, as a rule, *in favour of their right* to exercise any power of government whatever.

Thus, *Denio*, C. J., in *People vs. Draper*, 15 N. Y., 543, 544, in speaking of the power of state legislatures, says, "*Plenary power in the legislature for all purposes of civil government is the rule. A prohibition to exercise a particular power is an exception.*" Not that every prohibition must be express. "The frame of the government; the grant of legislative power itself; the organization of the executive authority; the erection of the principal courts of justice, create *implied limitations* upon the law-making power *as strong as though a negative was expressed* in each instance; but independently of these restraint[s] express or implied, *every subject within the scope of civil government*, is liable to be dealt with by the legislature."

Redfield, C. J., in *Thorpe vs. Rutland and Burlington R. R. Co.*, 27 Vt., 142, 143: "It has never been questioned, so far as I know, that the *American legislatures have the same* unlimited *power* in regard to legislation *which resides in the British Parliament*, except where they are restrained by written constitutions. That must, I think, be conceded to be *a fundamental principle* in the political organization of the American States."

Always the courts of the United States adopt and follow the decisions of the state courts in questions which concern merely the constitution and laws of the state." *Luther vs. Borden*, 7 How., 1.

II. *In the case of the federal government*, the presumption is *just the other way.* It is *a government of enumerated powers*; and some plain warrant must be found in the Constitution for everything that it does.

No exigency can warrant any *change or suspension* of the principles or provisions of that instrument. "The government, within the the [sic] Constitution, *has all the powers granted* to it *which are necessary* to preserve its existence," and these can neither be suspended nor added to. *Ex parte Milligan*, 4 Wall., 2.

Recast, 13 April, 1894.

VII. *Constitutional Law.*
Interstate Commerce.

An *admirable discussion* of the whole subject *in Pomeroy*'s "Introduction to the Constitutional Law of the United States," pp. 269-337.

Historical Explication of the Power to Regulate Commerce:
One of the primary objects of the Union, and the power is granted among the first of those explicitly given to Congress. *Const., I., viii.*

There had been *tariff wars between the States* which threatened to divide and antagonize them, and it was unquestionably *the purpose* of the framers of the Constitution *to throw the States into one community* in respect of all the movements of commerce and intercourse.

The Group of Constitutional Provisions affecting this matter:
Congress is *given power* "to *regulate commerce* with foreign nations, among the several States, and with the Indian tribes; to *establish uniform laws* on the subject *of bankruptcy* throughout the United States; to *coin money*, regulate the value thereof, and of foreign coin; and to *fix the standards of weight and measure*"; but it is expressly provided that "*no preference shall be given* by any regulation of commerce or revenue to the ports of one State over those of another; nor shall vessels bound to or from one State be obliged to enter, clear, or pay duties in another." (A *reminiscence* of *the old navigation laws* which had been so burdensome to the colonies).

On the other hand, the *States* are expressly *prohibited* to lay *duties* upon imports or exports ("except what may be absolutely necessary for executing" their "inspection laws"); to impose any *tonnage duties*; emit *bills of credit*; make anything but gold or silver *legal tender* in payment of debts or *pass any law impairing the obligation of contracts.*

It is *evident* from these provisions that special *pains were taken* to make specific provision *for a uniform national regulation* of all internal, as well as of all foreign, commerce and intercourse, to the end *that we might be in these re[s]pects one people.*

What does the Term Commerce Include?

It is *not limited to the exchange of economic goods*, but embraces also everything incident to that exchange. It therefore *includes navigation*, the control of waterways, of the interstate *carrying business* whether on water or on land, and of the *transmission of messages by telegraph.* "It is not only the right but the duty of Congress to see to it that *intercourse among the States* and the *transmission of intelligence* are not obstructed or *unnecessarily encumbered* by state legislation." *Pensacola Tel. Co., vs. W. U. Tel. Co.*, 96 U. S., 1, 9.

Persons, moreover, as well as goods, are *objects of commerce*, and no State can lawfully lay a tax upon the introduction of passengers. *Passenger Cases*, 7 How., 283; *Henderson vs. Mayor of New York*, 92 U. S., 259.

The commerce contemplated, however, is of course *interstate or foreign* commerce. Congress may not assume to regulate such commerce as is confined within the limits of a single State or the use and traffic of *a stream "whose navigable waters are exclusively within the limits of a State*, and which does not, by connecting with other waters, afford a continuous highway over which commerce is or may be carried on with other States or with foreign countries." *Veazie vs. Moor*, 14 How., 568.

How far is the Power Concurrent, how far Exclusive?
What may the States do?

Here the *leading case* is *Gibbons vs. Ogden* (9 Wh., 1), which involved the question of the right of New York to grant the exclusive privilege of navigating the waters of the State for a term of years[.] *The power* of Congress, *it was held* (Marshall), "is the power to regulate; that is, to prescribe the rule by which commerce is to be governed. This power, like all others vested in Congress, *is complete in itself*; may *be exercised to its utmost* extent, and *acknowledges no limitations* other than are prescribed in the Constitution." It was *not held*, however, *that the mere grant* of this great power to Congress *ousted the States* of all right to act in the absence of Congressional Regulation. It was *decided, simply,* that, *so far as Congress had acted the State was ousted;* and that, inasmuch as *the plaintiff* was acting as *a licensee under* the coasting trade *laws of the United States,* no state statute could interfere with or curtail his privileges in any way.

Step by step this modest doctrine has been steadily *outgrown,* until, now, *the accepted judicial view* is firmly established to the effect that *"whenever the subjects* over which the power to regulate commerce is asserted *are in their nature national,* or *when they admit of one uniform system or plan of regulation,* they are within *the exclusive* control of Congress." (*Reading R. R. Co., vs. Pa.,* 15 Wall., 232).[8] And that *even when Congress has not legislated* in the matter. *The inaction of Congress* "when considered with reference to its legislation with respect to foreign commerce," must be regarded as "virtually a declaration that law-making is not requisite, but commerce shall be allowed to take its natural course." (*Welton vs. Missouri,* 92 U. S., 275). Comp. Hare, 469. *"By refraining from action Congress* in effect *adopts* as its own regulations those wh. *the Common Law, or the Civil Law* where that prevails, *has provided* for the government of such business"; . . . and *"congressional legislation* is only necessary to cure defects in existing laws, . . . *and to adapt* such laws to new developments of trade." (Cooley, 71, generalizing from *Hall vs. De Cuir,* 95 U. S., 485, 490.)

All navigation on the high seas, even though in the individual case it be confined to trade and passage *between ports of the same State,* is within the exclusive jurisdiction of the United States, inasmuch as "navigation on the high seas is *necessarily national in its character."* (*Lord vs. Steamship Co.,* 102 U. S., 541).

The right of a State to authorize *the construction of a bridge across a navigable stream* furnishes a nice test of theory. If *the usefulness of the bridge to national commerce* is greater than the usefulness of the stream, the State may be justified in authorizing its construction; but otherwise it is not. (*Wheeling Bridge Case,* 13 How., 518). And *in any case Congress may authorize such a bridge,* making sovereign judgment of its usefulness to commerce. (*18 How.,* 421).

---

8 Above "15 Wall., 232," Wilson wrote "82 U. S. 271 Justice Strong" [Eds.' note]

Where the specific *subjects* of regulation are *"local in their nature or operation*, or constitute mere aids to commerce, *the States may provide* for their regulation and management, *until Congress intervenes* and supercedes their action." (*Pomeroy*, 307, n., based on *Caldwell vs. Am. Bridge Co.*, 113 U. S., 105).

Where the subjects of legislation *are matters of internal police or sanitation* state regulations may stand even to the exclusion of the power of Congress. *Quarantine laws*, therefore, are within the sanitary powers of the States, and laws of *harbour police*; and even *laws regulating pilots*, in the absence of Congressional regulation on that head. (*See the cases* cited by *Cooley*, p. 74, ed. 1880, and *The Slaughter House Cases*, 16 Wall., 36).

But the best illustration of the theory in this connection may be found in the very interesting cases affecting *the right of the States to control the sale of intoxicating liquors.*

The State of Maryland sought to compel every importer of *foreign goods by the bale or package*, or of spirituous liquors, and every person who should sell the same by the wholesale, to take out a license and pay fifty dollars therefor. *Congress had legislated* concerning the introduction of merchandise from foreign parts; *the license* required *would operate as a serious restriction upon what Congress permitted*; and it did *not* appear that the license was required as a *measure of police* regulation in the interest of public morals or order. *Held*, in the case of *Brown vs. Maryland*, 12 Wheat., 419, that this was an *unlawful restriction*; and that the *power of a State to tax commences*, not "the instant when the article enters the country, but *when* the importer has so acted upon it that *it has become incorporated and mixed up with the mass of property in the country.*" The importer, in brief, cannot be prevented by a State from selling *in the original bulk or package*, and so getting what he imports into the general mass of property in the country.

In Bartemeyer vs. Iowa, 97 U. S., 32, 33 (as well as in other cases) it was held that, "as *a measure* of police regulation *looking to* the preservation of *the public morals*, a state law prohibiting the manufacture and sale of intoxicating liquors is not repugnant to any clause of the Constitution of the United States." This was *sustained in a case where it was* made to appear that the liquor was *manufactured for sale outside* of the State: *Kidd vs. Pearson*, 128 U. S., 1. And in *Mugler vs. Kansas* it was decided that *the places* where liquor was sold *might be declared a nuisance*, and "abated" as such. (*123 U. S.*, 623.)

"*Original Package*["] *Case, Leisy vs. Hardin*, 135 U. S., 100 (108). *Head Notes* 1-4: "*A citizen of one State* has *the right to import* beer into another State, *and the right to sell* it there in its original packages. *Up to such sale, the State has no power to interfere*, by seizure or any other action, to prevent the importation and sale by a foreign or non-resident importer. *The right of transportation* of an article of commerce from one State to another *includes the right* of the consignee *to sell* it in unbroken packages at the place where the transportation terminates. It is *only after* the importation is completed and *the property imported is mingled* with and becomes a part of the general property of the State by a sale by the importer, *that the state regulations can act* upon it."

This, notwithstanding the fact that *Congress had not acted* at all with reference to interstate commerce in such a way as even by implication to assume jurisdiction; *and notwithstanding* the fact that *the state legislation* drawn in question had no purpose of trade restriction but *an object of morals and police*. The case *therefore differs* quite widely *from Brown vs. Maryland*, upon which the majority of the court relied. "*So-called original packages*" of any size might thus be made to defeat the acknowledged police powers of the States.

What may Congress Do?. (Following *Pomeroy*, 333) "Congress has power to pass laws regulating,

"(1) *Places* where traffic and intercommunication with foreign nations and among the several States may be" carried on. E.g., it may regulate the *registration and clearage* of vessels, the *improvement of harbours*, the establishment of *lighthouses, piers, breakwaters*, etc., etc.

"(2) *The means and instruments* by which traffic and intercommunication may be carried on." E.g., the regulation of the *coasting trade*, the "*navigation laws*," rules regarding the *number of passengers* to be carried and the *strength and quality of crews*, the *inspection* of boilers, etc., etc. Also the construction of *interstate bridges, roads, canals*, and *railroads*.

"(3) *The subject-matter of commerce*." Importation and exportation.

"(4) Statutes relating to the *liability of shipowners* and others engaged in commerce, either declaring, altering, or supplementing the rules of the Common Law, or general Law Merchant."

"*Alexander Hamilton maintained* that, under this grant of power, Congress may pass uniform rules respecting *marine insurances, foreign bills* of exchange, *bottomry bonds, etc.,* which he urged were inseparable concomitants and instruments of commerce." (*Pomeroy,* 337.)

N.B.

Total number of cases decided *against the States* by the Supreme Court during the first century of its existence, 177 (see *Brinton Coxe,* 22). Of these only a few less than fifty (47) are cases *touching commerce.* Sixty-three (47 + 63 = 110) concern the obligation of contracts.   20 April, 1894

VIII. *Constitutional Law.*
The Obligation of Contracts.

Excellent analysis and discussion *in Pomeroy,* secs. 538-627.
The very great prominence of this provision in adjudication. *Sixty-three* out of the one hundred and seventy-seven *decisions* rendered against the States by the Supreme Court during the first century of its existence turned upon questions arising under this clause; *besides almost innumerable others decided in favour of state power.*

Scope of the Prohibition. "No State shall pass any law impairing the obligation of contracts." Art. I., sec. x.

> *Very little importance* seems to have been *attached* to this provision *at the time of the framing* and adoption *of the Constitution*; and it passed without much comment. *The Federalist* alluded to it in passing as a "constitutional bulwark in favour of *personal security and private rights*" against any legislation that might be attempted "contrary to the first principles of the social compact, and to every principle of sound legislation." "*Apparently nothing was in view at the time except to prevent the repudiation of debts and private obligations*, and the disgrace, disorders, and calamities that might be expected to follow" (*Cooley,* 300)

But *radical adjudication* has given it the widest possible scope. *The term "contract," as we shall see, has been given the broadest possible significance; and the word "law"* has been construed to include every authoritative action of the State or its agents.

"*The term 'law' is broad enough*," says Judge Hare (p. 732), "to include every rule of property or conduct enacted by the sovereign power of a State or by virtue of an authority which it has conferred; and hence, whether an antecedent obligation is impaired *by the people, the legislature, the judiciary, or the executive*, the federal tribunals may afford redress." It *ranges* therefore *from a constitutional amendment* to *a judicial judgment.* The State can *do* nothing to impair, &c.

Thus, when the *State of Ohio* had incorporated a bank with the express provision that it should not be taxed beyond a certain limit, no subsequent action of the State, though it were a constitutional amendment, could authorize its taxation beyond that limit. *Dodge vs. Woolsey*, 18 How. 331. Neither could the liability of the property of the *Northwestern University* to taxation be extended under the terms of a general constitutional provision as amended after the institution of the University. *Northwestern Univ. vs. The People of Ill.*, 99 U. S., 309.

In brief, there is *no legitimate means* by which a State can take away from the force or diminish the advantage of existing contracts. It becomes *very important* indeed, therefore, *to determine* the question,

What is a "Contract" under the meaning of this clause?

When strictly employed, the word Contract means (not a two-sided transaction which creates rights *in rem*), but *a two-sided act* which gives rise to *rights in personam*, i.e., to *Obligations, to which the State will give effect.*

But the Supreme Court has not confined itself to this strict conception. It has gone the length of holding that

A Grant (or Conveyance) is a Contract.

"*A contract* is a compact between two or more parties, and is *either executory or executed*: . . . *A contract executed* is one in which the object of the contract is performed; and this, says Blackstone, *differs nothing from a grant*. . . . Since, then *a grant is in fact a contract executed*, the obligation of which still continues, and since the *constitution uses the general term* contract, without distinguishing between those which are executory and those which are executed, it *must be construed to comprehend the latter* as well as the former. . . . If, under a fair construction of the constitution, grants are comprehended under the term contracts, *is a grant from a State excluded* from the operation of the provision? Is the constitution to be considered as inhibiting the State from impairing the obligation of contracts between two individuals, but as excluding from that inhibition contracts made with itself? *The words* themselves *contain no such distinction.* They are general, and are applicable to contracts of every description." *Neither*, in the opinion of the court, *did the circumstances* under which this provision of the Constitution was made *warrant* the drawing of *such a distinction. Marshall* in *Fletcher vs. Peck*, 6 Cr., 135-138.

And yet *this is confounding two very distinct sorts of jural relationships.* Though primitive society do [no] doubt confounded them, *modern jurisprudence* has *very sharply distinguished conveyances* from *contracts*, rights of property (*in rem*) from rights against one person, a few persons, or a definite group of persons (*in personam*). *Proprietary rights* and *Obligations* cannot legitimately be brought under the same conception; and *the Constitution contains provision for the protection of property quite apart* from those which protect the contractual rights which are the very gist of certain jural relationships. *In proprietary rights* the *in personam relationship* in which they may have arisen is *quite swallowed up* and *subordinated.* A State must keep its contracts; but its relation to property is separately determined and regulated.[9]

Am. v.

A Charter is a Contract.

Even though it grant franchises involving the exercise of powers which the State alone possesses and which *the State alone*, therefore, *can delegate.*

Leading Case, Trustees of Dartmouth College vs. Woodward, 4 Wheat., 518. "*The charter* granted by the British crown to the trustees of Dartmouth College, in the year 1769, *is a contract* within the meaning of that clause of the Constitution which declares that no State shall make any law impairing the obligation of contracts. The charter was *not dissolved by the Revolution.* An act of the state legislature of New Hampshire, altering the charter, without the consent of the corporation, in a material respect, is an act impairing the obligation of the charter, and is unconstitutional and

---

[9] So far has the Supreme Court gone in this matter, that in *New Jersey vs. Wilson*, 7 Cr., 164, (following *Fletcher vs. Peck*) it was held that a grant of lands to Indians exempt from taxation made the exemption part of the "contract" of the grant; and that a subsequent sale of the lands by the Indians, with the consent of the legislature, which was given without mention of the exemption from taxation, transferred the exemption along with the title. *The subsequent taxation of the owners of these lands* was *unconstitutional*, as impairing the obligation of contracts. [WW's note]

void. Under its charter, Dartmouth College was a private and not a public corporation. That a corporation is established for purposes of general charity, or for education generally, does not, *per se*, make it a public corporation, liable to the control of the legislature." ☞ And yet the only consideration for the charter was the public good as embodied in education!

It has long been settled that a State may grant to a private corporation its own rights of eminent domain by charter, and so bind itself in the matter that it cannot afterwards withdraw the gift or interfere with its use. *For example*, the right of eminent domain may be granted *to a railway company*, and *even to a street railway company*, for private profit, in such a way that the State or municipality cannot even authorize parellel lines while the period of the charter lasts. (See *The Richmond R. R. Co. vs. The Louisa R. R. Co.*, 13 How., 71; and, with reference to exclusive *bridge franchises, The Binghamton Bridge Case*, 3 Wall., 51, and *The Charles River Bridge vs. The Warren Bridge*, 11 Pet., 420).[10]

All collateral stipulations of a charter, too, constitute part of the contract which must not be "impaired." *Thus* a provision in the charter of a bank that its *notes* shall be *receivable for taxes* is a contract with the holders of those notes and cannot be abrogated. *Farman vs. Nichol*, 8 Wall., 44. *A State cannot appropriate the assets of a bank* of which it is itself sole owner for the payment of the general indebtedness of the State, to the prejudice of the bill holders and other creditors. *Barings vs. Dabney*, 19 Wall., 1.

Not only so, but *the collateral agreements may include* the provisions of *general statutes*, under which the corporations were formed. Thus, *a general banking law* setting off six *per cent.* of semi-annual dividends in lieu of taxes, is part of the contract of the charters formed under it, and further taxation is unconstitutional. *Piqua Bank vs. Knoup*, 16 How., 369.

Even contracts whose consideration is no longer legal, e.g., a contract made for the sale of a slave when slavery was legal, cannot be invalidated either by statute or constitution. *White vs. Hart* 13 Wall., 647.

10 *Reference* to the case of *The Charles River Bridge* vs. The Warren Bridge, 11 Pet., 420. *Decides*, chiefly, the following points: 1. That *a State may divest any vested rights* it pleases, *so no contract be impaired*. 2. That in case of charter or any other grant of a public privilege, the assurance that another charter impairing the value of the first will not be granted *is never to be implied. Public powers* or interests are *not to be abandoned* or given away *by implication*: the construction must be strict. [WW's note]

These principles apply, however, *only to private corporations and persons.* The charter of a public corporation is not a contract. This principle was stated in the *Dartmouth College case*, and in the case of *East Hartford vs. The Hartford Bridge Co.*, 10 How., 511, it was directly decided.

A public office is *not held by contract*, the official is merely an agent of the State, and his authority may be revoked by law at any time, in any way. *Butler vs. Pennsylvania*, 10 How., 402.

But "*a contract* between a State and a party, whereby he is to perform *certain duties* for a *specific period*, at a *stipulated compensation*, is within the protection of the Constitution; and, on his executing it, he is entitled to that compensation, although before the expiration of the period the state repealed the statute pursuant to which the contract was made." *Hall vs. Wisconsin*, 103 U. S., 5.

Licenses, moreover, are mere naked permission, *revocable at will.* "A license from a state authorizing a person to do some act which is generally forbidden, is *a mere permission which excepts the individual from the operation of laws that would otherwise prohibit him*, as well as other citizens, from doing the specific act." *Pomeroy*, 451. See *Phalen vs. Virginia*, 8 How., 163.

"*A license* authorizing a person *to retail spirituous liquors*, does not create any contract between him and the government. It *bears no resemblance to an act of incorporation* by which, in consideration of the supposed benefit to the public, certain rights and privileges are granted by the legislature to individuals, *under which they embark their skill, enterprise, and capital.* The statute regulating licensed houses has a very different scope and purpose. It was intended *to restrain and prohibit* the indiscriminate sale of certain articles deemed to be injurious to *the welfare of the community. . . . a mere police regulation* intended to regulate trade, prevent injurious practices and promote the good order and welfare of the community, and liable to be modified and repealed whenever, in the judgment of the legislature, it failed to accomplish these objects." *Calder vs. Kurby*, 3 Gray, (Mass.), 597.

It is hard to see a fundamental difference between these cases and those of certain corporate franchises. The *right to use public ways*, or to exercise in any other way the right of eminent domain, is as much "*an act which is generally forbidden*" as the sale of spirituous liquors. Such a franchise is *a right in rem to the exercise of a public power;* and the exercise of such rights is certainly *founded solely on considerations of public welfare and convenience.*

If the State's *power to tax,* and its power to exercise the right of eminent domain may be bartered away, *why* may *not its police power* also? *This question certainly demands reöpening:* and the point at which it should be reopened is the question of *"an executed contract"* being upon the same footing with one that is "executory" in the meaning of the Constitution.

Mr. Pomeroy regards this as a question of state sovereignty (see, for example, p. 457), and greatly rejoices in the decisions of the Supreme Court against the powers of the States. *But there is no contest or collision* here between state and federal authority. If these decisions stand, the States are not simply subordinated: these powers which are denied to them are *gained by nobody. They are simply annihilated.*

The only question remaining is this, *What is included in the "Obligation"* of a Contract?

It is *not simply "what the parties have,* in terms, *agreed to do or forbear;* but is the legal effect given to those agreements by *the whole of the existing law applicable* to such contract; it includes the rights and duties which the whole existing law creates from the fact of such contract being made" *Pomeroy,* 491.

Thus, an insolvent law discharging creditors from their liabilities is void as against previous obligations. *Sturges vs. Crowninshield,* 4 Wheat., 122. But *valid as to contracts subsequently entered into. Ogden vs. Saunders,* 12 Wheat., 213.

The obligation also includes, of course, *substantial remedy.* "In *modes of proceeding* and *forms* to enforce the contract the legislature has the control, and may enlarge, limit, or alter them, provided it does not deny a remedy, or so embarrass it with conditions or restrictions as seriously to impair the value of the right." *Penniman's case,* 103 U. S., 714. See also *Bronson vs. Kinzie,* 1 How., 511.

Bonds bought under a statute authorizing the issue and taxation to pay the same: in such a case the empowering statute cannot be withdrawn without impairing the obligation of contracts; and a *mandamus* will lie to compel taxation for the purpose of paying such bonds. *Von Hoffman vs. City of Quincy,* 4 Wall., 535.

A State's only escape from these restrictions is to resort to *con-*

fiscation, with compensation,—to resort to the very power she is said to be at liberty to barter away!

"*All property is held* by tenure *from the State*, and *all contracts* are made *subject to* the right of *eminent domain*, a franchise not being distinguishable from other property." *West River Bridge vs. Dix*, 6 How., 507.

27 April, 1894

See 'Coupon Cases' and the Va. debt cases, 135, U. S., 662 (McGahey v. Va., &c. &c.).

IX. *Constitutional Law.*
Individual Liberty.

This is the *branch* of constitutional law which *deals with individuals separately*, and with which, therefore, lawyers will most frequently be called upon to deal. It is the more necessary to have a solid

Theoretical Basis for the principles we shall adopt. A theory of state action necessary to support a consistent practice and body of precedent.

The Theory of the Weal State: An ideal, not of organization (such as *we* are apt to demand), but *of motive. All functions are legitimate* for the State *whose object is* the promotion of *the interests of the State* and of its members. No new or certain means of *determining* the common good is supplied: all is left to the discretion of an unchecked Administration. Under this conception *the Administration* is *the embodiment* at once *of the judgment and of the power of the Community.*

The Theory of the Law State: That *the State* is not a natural and inevitable association, with laws of life springing from its own nature, but *an artificial arrangement effected by law.* The ideal of this theory is "*a government not of men but of laws*"; in which laws both originate political power and limit individual privilege, and there is *neither authority nor liberty without them.*

The Theory of the Constitutional State: A State in which, *by one process or another*, whether by the establishment of well understood customs or by the definitive enactment of fundamental laws, or by both these means combined, *a definite set of imperative rules* is recognized and maintained in the *adjustment of the powers of the government to the life of the Community* and the free activity of the individual.

In all States, and at all times, the *power and authority* of Government *have rested upon* the *consent* of the governed;

but generally that consent has been vague, its extent defined
and ascertained from time to time by experiment. *A "constitutional" State is one in which* that assent, that *agreement
of wills between Government and Community*, has been rendered *definite both in content and purpose*.

Looking only to our written constitutions, and remembering the
deliberate manner of their formulation and adoption, we can
easily conceive *our governments the creations of law*, and
adopt the theory of the Law State as the basis of our legal
thought.

We have only to examine *our Bills of Rights*, however, our
"Constitutions of Liberty," to *disabuse our minds* of that idea,
and perceive that *we have "constitutional" governments* in the
sense of our definition. We shall there find our constitutional
life evidently *resting on old foundations*, upon precedents and
old understandings which are *only implicit in the language* of
the fundamental law.

The only idea of Liberty which *the lawyer* may legitimately hold
is *the idea of a definite adjustment* of precedent or enactment *between the power of Government and the free activity
of the individual*. This will more clearly appear by means
of the Question,

How far does the mere Statement or Enumeration *of individual
rights* in a constitution, or in any fundamental charter,
avail to render them positive and practicable rights?

Stated in more general or abstract terms (as, e.g., all citizens shall be inviolable in their persons and property), they
do not constitute any real check on administrative action.
*Their value and validity depend upon the admission and
definition of exceptions*, upon the establishment of such
definite lines of positive law as shall separate those invasions
of individual right which are accepted as necessary to the
order and energy of the State from those which are unnecessary, arbitrary, and tyrannical. *Positive law* or undisputed
custom *must make all such invasions regular*, that is, deliberate and just and impartial in process, *and* must *restrict
them to necessary cases*.

Our general idea is, That *every man* should be *suffered to do,
and to be, what he can*.

Really, however, there are *two aspects* under wh. the rights
and liberties of every man must be viewed. *Under the one* he
is predominantly *a unit*, a separate being, self-centred and free
(though of course no man is wholly such); *under the other*

he is *a fraction* of Society, a social being bound up with other men in every interest and effort of his life. *Under the first* of these aspects we may range and discuss the items of what we call *Individual Liberty*: *under the second,* what the Constitution classes as *"rights and immunities."* Such a classification is of course more or less arbitrary.

Every man has the right to be, to sustain himself by the satisfaction of his physical wants, and *to use his* intellectual and spiritual *faculties. If he could live alone. The practical Question* is, *How far are these rights compatible with the existence of Society?* Let us *examine the items*, and answer the question with regard to each according to the adjustments effected by the particular understandings of our system.

(1) *Inviolability of Person*: exemption from arrest or detention. Here *the general features* of our understanding with Government are too well known to need the citation of cases. The general rule is, that *no one shall be arrested without a warrant* issued upon *probable cause,* stated in the warrant itself, *supported by oath or affirmation,* and *clearly designating the person* to be seized. The probable cause, too, must be some unlawful action. *And yet* "Any one may arrest another whom he sees committing or attempting to commit a felony or forceable breach of the peace; and a peace officer may arrest, on reasonable grounds of suspicion of felony." (*Cooley*, 213). *The rule*, i.e., *does not prevent* the use of force upon individuals for *the accomplishment of any regular or legitimate object of government*. It *simply prevents malicious, unreasonable, arbitrary, unregulated interferences* with individual liberty. *Note* the forceable overcoming of passive resistance, the use of *corporeal punishment* in the public schools, *compulsory vaccination,* etc., etc.

The detention of individuals, even their indefinite detention, to await the convenience, and the dockets, of courts, not unlawful. *Habeas Corpus proceedings* require *nothing more than* the immediate *establishment of probable cause*; and *the law freely determines* the cases in which *bail* shall be accepted.

We are simply put on parol. We are *subject to subpoena, to draft,* etc., and remain free only so long as we *keep the conditions of our freedom.* These conditions the law establishes.

(2) *Freedom of Movement and of Settlement,* in order to seek the best conditions of development.

Here, again, the limitations are well known. Considerations of public safety must justify the denial of the right of *expatriation in time of war*, when it may be used to escape military duty. Systems of *poor relief* necessitate restrictions upon the movements of those who have no means to support themselves, and are likely to become a public charge. *Sanitary regulations* properly include internal quarantine upon occasion, etc., etc. Such are the recognized powers of every government. *The courts can prevent nothing but unjust discrimination* in the use of them.

(3) *Freedom of Economic Effort.* In general, of course, every man has the right to make his living in any way he sees fit. Thus *monopolies are in general illegal*, in case of "such ordinary vocations as can be left open to all to the common benefit," as violating the principle of equitable equality. (See *Broom*, "Constitutional Law," 500). *But, if the public interest can be better served by a monopoly* than by free competition, there is no constitutional principle which forbids. (*State v. Milwaukee Gas Co.*, 29 Wis., 454; *Slaughter House Cases*, 16 Wall., 36; *New Orleans Gas Co. v. Louisiana Light Co.*, 115 U. S., 650; *Boston and Lowell R. R. Co. v. Salem and Lowell R. R. Co.*, 2 Gray, 9).

These principles *would justify the regulation and even the assumption of "natural monopolies"* by Government. ☞ *"Natural Monopolies"* are characterized by the following features: 1. What they supply is a necessary, in the literal or in the social sense of that word; 2. They occupy peculiarly favoured spots or lines of land; 3. The article or convenience they supply is necessarily used in connection with their fixed plant; 4. It can be increased without any proportionate increase in their plant or capital; 5. Certainty and organization, such as can be secured only by unity of management, are paramount considerations in their business, if it is to be made efficient. (See *T. H. Farrar*, "*The State in Relation to Trade*," in the "English Citizen Series," p. 71).

Compulsory education is one notable instance of the interference of the State with the economic liberty of the individual; inasmuch as it in effect compels the parent, who by the common law has a right to the child's services, to give them up for a considerable time, in order that the child may be put upon a higher plane of economic endeavour, and perhaps rendered permanently unserviceable in the parent's occupation.

Then there is *the system*, everywhere regarded as legitimate, *of requiring professional licenses* in *law, medicine,* etc, including requirements of *educational training, both general and technical,* on the part of those who would enter such callings. (See *Bradwell v. State,* 16 Wall., 130).

There is, besides, the system of regulating certain non-professional occupations: e.g., requiring *license* or permission in cases *where the occupation involves danger* to the health or lives of others; regulating trades that involve *risks, inconveniences,* or *nuisances* to the public; regulating certain undertakings *in the interest of the working classes* (e.g., forbidding *the truck system* of paying wages, and work on Sundays or holidays; determining *the length of the labour day*; restricting the *labour of women and children*; enforcing the observance of certain safeguards, like the *fencing in of* dangerous *machinery*; imposing *insurance against accidents* on employers, etc., etc.). See *The License Tax Cases,* 5 Wall., 462; *Lincoln v. Smith,* 27 Vt., 328; *Reynolds v. Geary,* 26 Conn., 179; *Wilkerson v. Rust,* 57 Ind., 172; (etc.).

Note, also the regulation of such semi-public callings as that of *inn keepers and common carriers*; the *compulsory labour of the able-bodied poor,* who might become a public charge, etc.

(4) *Use of Personal Possessions,* well understood to be restricted to such use as does not conflict with the *general convenience*. The *doctrine of nuisance*.

(5) *Intellectual Liberty*: Freedom of *Belief and opinion*. The *Constitution* provides, *Art. VI.,* cl. 3, That "no religious test shall ever be required as a qualification to any office or public trust under the United States." *The First Amendment* adds that Congress shall not abridge freedom of speech or of the press, and that it "shall make no law respecting an establishment of religion, or prohibiting the free exercise thereof." *Most of the State constitutions* contain similar provisions. It will be *best to discuss this* matter *under* the next Topic, of "*Rights and Immunities*," in connection with the social right of *freedom of speech*; for here the social aspect would seem to predominate.

(6) *Home Privacy,* we all recognize to be *subject to* such regulated invasions as may be necessary in *searching for stolen goods*, for *criminals*, etc.; for *breaking up gaming*, making *tax assessments,* effecting *sanitary inspection*, etc., etc. *We*

pray for, but have not yet obtained, *protection against the* invasions of the *newspaper reporter*.

4 May, 1894

X. *Constitutional Law.*
Citizenship: Rights and Immunities.

Last time considered *man* as nearly as might be *as a unit*, possessing rights in a sense independent of the action, or even the existence, of Society. Found him, nevertheless, limited on every side by social conditions. The mere abstract statement of rights does not secure them. *Now advance* to the question,

How far are Individual Rights dependent upon the action of the State for their realization? To what extent are they made effectual, and even given existence, by the power and purpose of Society?

The fundamental relationship, with respect to social privilege, is

Citizenship. This, stated in its most general terms, means simply *a title to equal consideration* with others, *a right to equal private privileges* under the law. It is participation in the advantages of associated effort and political order.

The XIV Amendment declares that "All persons born or naturalized in the United States, and subject to the jurisdiction thereof, are citizens of the United States and of the State wherein they reside."

This means that, so far as the jurisdiction of the general government extends, all persons born or naturalized within the territory of the Union shall *enjoy the same protection and the same private rights under federal law*, without discrimination; and that, similarly, *within the States* of their residence, they shall *stand upon the common footing of privilege under the laws* of their States. It neither confers nor enlarges either any powers of government or any individual privileges. *It simply defines* the two complimentary spheres of citizenship.

Citizenship of a State includes only full membership of its community, subject to its laws. *Citizenship of the United States includes*, in like manner, only "the rights which are essential to the relations of the people as citizens of the United States to the government and to each other as natives of the same country; and among them that of assembling to petition Congress for a redress of grievances, and of passing

freely through the State or from State to State, for the transaction of business or any other lawful purpose, and also of
making their abode in any State under the equal protection
of its laws." (*Hare*, 519). For an exposition of this matter,
see *The Slaughter House Cases*, 16 Wall., 36; *United States
v. Cruikshank*, 92 U. S., 542; *Crandall v. Nevada*, 6 Wall.,
35; *Presser v. Illinois*, 116 U. S., 252. *Elk v. Wilkins*, 112
U. S., 94; *U. S. v. Osborne*, 6 Sawyer, 406.

Property. The right to own property seems to come nearer than
any other social right to being a natural right. It *is, in reality,*
beyond the sphere of mere physical dominion, *purely a social right,* though based ultimately, no doubt, upon the natural right of self-sustenance. *How much property will Society assure a man safe title to*; and how far will it suffer
him to exercise rights of absolute dominion under that title?
These are the crucial questions. *Only that is Property to wh.
the law guarantees title.* "Property and law," says Bentham,
"are born and must die together. Before the laws there was
no property; take away the laws all property ceases." *The
right* to property, therefore, is *a social, not a natural, right.*

What is property, and both the nature and extent of property rights are *determined among us* principally *by the common law,* partly by statute. "A person has *no property*, no
vested interest, *in any rule of the common law. . . .* Rights
of property, which have been created by the common law,
cannot be taken away without due process; but the law itself
as a rule of conduct may be changed at the will, or even at
the whim, of the legislature, unless prevented by constitutional limitations." *Munn v. Illinois*, 94 U. S., 113.

Constitutional Guarantees: The Vth. Amendment provides
that "no person shall be deprived of life, liberty, or property
[*by Congress*][11] without due process of law," and *the XIVth.
Amendment* extends the same prohibition to the States.

"*Due process of law*" means simply that *all men shall be
dealt with alike.* It is synonymous with the words, "*the law
of the land,*" used in the 39th. cap. of *Magna Carta.* "By the
law of the land" said *Webster*, in the Dartmouth College
Case, "is most clearly intended the general law,—*a law which
hears before it condemns, which proceeds upon inquiry, and
renders judgment only after trial.* The meaning is that every
citizen shall hold his life, liberty, property, and immunities
under the protection of the general rules which govern so-

11 WW's brackets. [Eds.' note]

ciety." The provision was *"intended to secure the individual
from the arbitrary exercise of* the *powers* of government, un-
restrained by the established principles of private right and
distributive justice." (*Bank of Columbia v. Okely*, 4 Wh.,
235).

Any legislation, therefore, is *permissible* wh. *does not
take away vested rights*, change the character or consequences of *past transactions*, or *deprive of remedy* in the
courts for the breach of acquired rights or the enforcement
of established claims. (*See Railroad Co. v. Hecht*, 95 U. S.,
168)

We recognize that *the rights of property may legitimately
be limited*, e.g., *by forest*, mining, hunting, fishing, and
building *laws*, and by various *agricultural regulations*; by
the *exaction of contributions* or services by the State from
property owners; *by the privilege* of the public authority
to destroy property to meet an exigency (e.g., to tear down
houses *to prevent the spread* of a conflagration); and by the
right of eminent domain or expropriation, which, under our
system of law belongs alike to the State and the federal
governments. *Kohl v. United States*, 91 U. S., 367.

The Suffrage. The constitutional provisions: Art. I., sec. 2, "The
electors in each State shall have the qualifications requisite
for electors of the most numerous branch of the state legislature." *Id., sec. 4*, "The times, places, and manner of holding
elections for Senators and Representatives shall be prescribed
in each State by the legislature thereof; but the Congress may
at any time by law make or alter such regulations, except as
to the places of choosing Senators." *Amendment XIV., sec.*
2, with reference to the proportion of Representatives to be
allotted each State in case of the exclusion of male citizens
of full age from the franchise on any ground "except for
participation in rebellion, or other crime." *Amendment XV.,
sec. 1*, "The right of citizens of the United States to vote
shall not be denied or abridged by the United States or by
any State on account of race, color, or previous condition
of servitude."

"Mere citizenship of the United States *does not involve the
right of suffrage. . . .* The United States have no power or
authority to interfere with *the discretion of the States* in determining what class of persons possess the 'qualifications'
for electors. The state laws may throw open the doors as
wide as possible, or may place any limitation which is not

inconsistent with a republican form of government." *Pomeroy*, sec. 209. *See United States v. Cruikshank*, 92 U. S., 548, which should be read through by every careful student; *Minor v. Happerstett*, 21 Wall., 162; *Ex parte Yarmouth*, 110 U. S., 621.

The principle is plain enough. The right of *suffrage is a right to take part in the conduct of the government*: not a right to life, liberty, or property, but a right to have a voice in the determination of policy: *not a private, but a public privilege*. The case of *Minor v. Happerstett*, quoted above, discusses the connection between citizenship and the suffrage in regard to women.

Freedom of Speech and of the Press.

A. V. *Dicey*, "The Law of the Constitution," Lect. VI., II., *quoting* Odgers, "Libel and Slander," Introd., p. 12: " 'Our present law permits any one to say, write, and publish what he pleases; but if he make *a bad use of this liberty*, he must be punished. If he unjustly attack an individual, the person defamed may sue for damages; if, on the other hand, the words be written or printed, or if treason or immorality be thereby inculcated, the offender can be tried for the misdemeanor either by *information or indictment*.' Any man may therefore say or write whatever he likes, subject to the risk of, it may be, severe punishment if he publishes any statement (either by word of mouth, by word, or print) which he is not legally entitled to make.

"*The truth of the matter* is very simple when stripped of all ornaments of speech, and a man of plain common sense may easily understand it. It is neither more nor less than this; that *a man may publish anything which twelve of his countrymen think is not blameable*, but that he ought to be punished if he publishes that which is blameable (i.e., that twelve of his countrymen think is blameable].[12] This in plain common sense is the substance of all that has been said on the matter." *Rex v. Cutbill*, 27 St. Tr., 642, 675, *cited in Dicey*.

Some of our own decisions have been *most illiberal* in their attitude towards individual criticism. *Thus, in King v. Root*, 24 Wend., 113, it was held that, in ordinary cases of slander, the term maliciously means intentionally and wrongfully, without any legal ground of excuse. "*Malice* is *an implication of law* from the false and injurious nature of

---

12 WW's brackets. [Eds.' note]

the charge." This narrows even the discretion of the twelve fellow countrymen very materially.

How much freedom of the press and of speech is a matter, *not of private privilege, but of public opinion and policy* appears in striking form in the cases which deal with the expression of *religious opinion.* In *The People v. Ruggles,* 8 Johnson (N. Y.), 290, it is held (by Kent, C. J.) that *Christianity is a part of the Common Law,* and its support indispensable to stable and enlightened government; and, therefore, that blasphemy is an offence against the Common Law. The case of *Commonwealth v. Kneeland,* 20 Pick. (Mass.), 206 (1838), *supports a statute* directed against "the denial of God, his creation, government, or final judging of the world made wilfully, that is, with the intent and purpose to calumniate and disparage him and impair and destroy the reverence due to him," as blasphemy; *and upholds an indictment based on the words,* "The Universalists believe in a god, which I do not; but believe that their god, with all his moral attributes (aside from nature itself) is nothing more than a mere chimera of their own imagination," *the jury,* of course, *being satisfied of the intent.*

The English statute 9 & 10 Will. III., c. 35, amended by 33 Geo. III., c. 160, makes the denial "of the truth of Christianity or of the authority of the Scriptures by 'writing, printing, teaching, or advised speaking' on the part of any person who has been educated in or made profession of Christianity *in England,*" a criminal offence subject to very severe penalties. *See Dicey,* second edition, p. 259, and authorities there cited.

With regard to what we call *freedom of the press,* the principles of our system are very simply and clearly stated in *Commonwealth v. Blanding,* 3 Pick., 304: "The provision in the constitution securing freedom of the press, was intended to prevent any *previous* restraints upon publications, and not to affect prosecutions for the abuse of such liberty."

It is simply *a question between two systems:* (1) *That of* many of the continental countries of Europe which require a *previous license* for the publication of books or periodicals, subject the press to an exceptional system of supervision, *and* assign *special tribunals* for the trial of cases arising under the special press laws; *and* (2) *Our own,* under which the press stands upon no peculiar footing either of special obligation or of special privilege; but the whole matter of the *expression of opinion* and the allegation of fact is *left to be dealt with under the ordinary law of libel and slander* and *by the ordinary tribunals.*

Assembly and Petition. "The right of the people peaceably to assemble, and to petition the government shall not be curtailed." This, again, however, is merely an individual privilege. *Amendment I.* (*Bill of Rights,* 3).

"*No better instance* can be found of the way in which in England [as in this country, in respect of individual right][13] the constitution is built up upon individual rights than our rules as to public assemblies. *The right of assembling is nothing more than a result* of the view taken by the Courts as to *individual liberty of person and individual liberty of speech.* There is no special law allowing A, B, and C to meet together either in the open air or elsewhere for a lawful purpose, but the right of A to go where he pleases so that he does not commit a trespass, and to say what he likes to B so that his talk is not libellous or seditious, the right of B to do the like with regard to A, and the existence of the same rights of C, D, E, and F, and so on *ad infinitum,* leads to the consequence that A, B, C, D, and a thousand or ten-thousand other persons may (as a general rule) meet together in any place where otherwise they each have a right to be for a lawful purpose and in a lawful manner." *Dicey,* Lect., VI., III.

In the case of Crandall v. Nevada, 6 Wall., 35, it was held that "The United States has the right to require the service of its citizens at the seat of government. *Citizens have a right to approach the seat of government,* the *ports of entry,* and the various *federal offices* within the State." The power to tax is unlimited in degree: *a tax on passengers going out of the State is illegal,* because it might destroy the right of transit. This is only in affirmance of the principles of free individual movement just quoted.

The right to bear arms is fully examined in *Presser v. Illinois,* 116 U. S., 252. It is known, in our own case, to rest upon the desire to provide *an efficient militia,* to take the place of a standing army; and it is *based in all cases upon considerations of public advantage,* never of course upon considerations of private power. The accumulation of arms, and the bearing of concealed weapons may be forbidden constitutionally.

Thus all individual rights are seen to rest upon considerations,

---

13 WW's brackets. [Eds.' note]

not so much of absolute private advantage or abstract conceptions of equality, as upon broad grounds *of convenience.* Individual rights could hardly be effectual unless there were a Society to recognize and enforce them: and they must always depend, accordingly, upon the state of opinion and the stage of social convention. *They are institutional.*

10 May, 1894.

WWT body of notes with some shorthand additions (WP, DLC).

Notes for a Course in the History of English Common Law

[March 6, 1894-May 7, 1900]

Contents:

WWT and WWhw notes for lectures on the following topics, with composition dates when given: *"Nature of the Course"* (March 6, 1894), printed at this date; *"II. Anglo-Saxon Law."* (March 12 and 13, 1894); *"III. Anglo-Frankish Law."* (March 28, 1894); *"IV. English Law: Its Parts and their Genesis."* (April 2, 1894), printed at this date; *"V. The Science of Case Law."* (April 5, 1894); *"VI. The Law of Real Property."* (April 19, 1894); *"VII. The Ecclesiastical Courts: Their Jurisdiction and Influence."* (April 25, 1894); *"VIII. The Law of Contract."* (May 2, 1894); *"Crime and Tort."* (April 16, 1898); and *"*EQUITY: Its History and Character"* (May 7, 1900).

Loose pages (WP, DLC).

Notes for a Classroom Lecture

6 March, 1894

ENGLISH COMMON LAW.

Nature of the Course: A sketch in broad outline of the main forces of development and of the leading principles developed.

The Topics of the Course:
  I.   Outline of Periods and Forces.
  II. Anglo-Saxon Law: Character and Sources.
  III. Anglo-Frankish Law: Character, Development, and Sources.
  IV. English Law, Common and Statutory.
  V.   The Field of the Common Law (determined by the administrative provisions of Henry II.).
  VI. The Science of Case Law.
  VII. The Law of Real Property: History.
  VIII. The Law of Real Property: Principles.
  IX. The Ecclesiastical Courts: Jurisdiction and Influence.
  X.   Contracts.
  XI. Torts.

I.

Outline of Periods and Forces

I. *The Anglo Saxon Period* (To the Norman Conquest).

Chiefly *notable for the genesis of a State* which should be made ready to the hand of the Norman and the Angevin for the subsequent purposes of English history.

The law customary and, except for the jurisdiction of the Witenagemot, *wholly in the hands of the local moot courts,—* only certain "dooms" being codified.

The law of this period *ought, nevertheless, to be carefully scrutinized,* so far as our materials serve, because there is *no break in the continuity* of the law at the Norman Conquest, at any rate in respect of private law; but only the addition of a few new elements, and of a new system of administration. *This system did,* indeed, *modify the entire structure* of the English law; *but the process* of modification *was slow,* in some things almost insensible, and *caused no breach* of continuity, but only an accelerated rate of development along particular lines.

The influence of the Roman law during this period, even if it can be shown to have had any, was *quite unimportant,* and the body of law which grew up may be said to have been more *purely Germanic* than any other of the same period.

II. *The Anglo Frankish Period*, or *The Period of Organization and Determinate Formation.* (*1066-1307*, Accession of Edward II.).

William the Conqueror subdues the State to the Crown, defines jurisdictions, and determines the larger features of public law.

Henry II., by his reconstruction of *the administration of Justice*, made English law Common Law, and produced *an English Jurisprudence* which was henceforth to be woven out of common precedent by the labour of *trained professional judges.* "Then begins the process which makes the custom of the king's court the common law of England." (Maitland).[1] *Language* of the courts, *French*: hence its terms.

Chronological Analysis:

William, 1066-1087. *Domesday Book*, 1086. *Lanfranc.*
William II., 1087-1100.⎫
Henry I., 1100-1155   ⎬*Lanfranc and Anselm.* (1093)
Henry II., 1154-1189. *"Glanvill,"* 1187. *Becket.*
Richard I., *The "beginning of legal memory."* 1189-1199.
John, 1199-1216. *Magna Carta*, 1215. *Vacarius* at
   Oxford.
Henry III., 1216-1272. *"Bracton,"* 1250-'58. *Montfort.*
Edward I., 1272-1307. *Administrative, fiscal, legal
   reforms.* Parliament (*Commons*) *summoned* "ad
   faciendum," to enact.

Subdivision of the Period:
1. *"From the Norman Conquest to Glanvill* (1188) *and the
   Beginning of Legal Memory"* (Accession of Richard I.,
   since when there has been a *continuous record of the
   judgments of the courts* at Westminster). *Including a
   Glance at Norman Law* (Henry II.).
2. *Richard I. to the Accession of Edward II.* (1189-1307).
   "Glanvill to Bracton." (1188-1256).

This is the period of the Roman Influence. Powerful from the
middle of the twelfth to the middle of the thirteenth century.
Shows unmistakably in Glanvill and Bracton. "Logic, method,
spirit, rather than matter" (Maitland); though Bracton does
fill in the gaps of precedent with principles borrowed from
the Roman Law.
   During this period English law was so innoculated with
Roman law *as afterwards to be entirely protected* against the
infection. *See* "Social England," vol. I., p. 284, and "The
Political Science Quarterly," vol. IV., p. 517.

III. *The Period of English Law.* 1507-1532.
May be subdivided as follows, the first subdivisions being essential, the others hardly more than convenient:
1. *Period of the Year Books,"* Edward II., 1307, to Henry VIII.,
   1535. (This date refers to the Year Books, Henry's death
   occurring, 1547).
   During this time *parliamentary procedure and authority
   took shape* (fourteenth century), and *we emerge from the
   Middle Ages into modern England.* The first fairly "modern"
   law book, that of *Littleton on "Tenures,"* written (in French)
   temp. Edward IV. (1481), "the most perfect and absolute
   work that ever was written in any human science," says
   Coke.

2. *Edward VI., 1547, to the End of the Stuarts,* (Charles I., 1649), or to Coke (Commentaries, 1628)

3. *Cromwell, 1649, to George III.,* 1760, or Coke to Blackstone, (1628-1765-'9).

4. *George III., 1760, to the Reform Bill, 1832,* or Blackstone to Bentham, (1765-1832).

(*Comp.* F. W. Maitland, Political Science Quarterly, IV., 504, "Materials for English Legal History.")

WWT MS. in body of lecture notes described at March 6, 1894.
¹ See the authorities and works listed in the Editorial Note, "Wilson's Teaching at Princeton and the Johns Hopkins, 1893-97."

To Horace Traubel

My dear Sir,   Princeton, New Jersey, 7 March, 1894.

Allow me to acknowledge with sincere thanks your letter of yesterday, and the check enclosed, for twenty dollars ($20), in payment of my expenses on the occasion of my addressing the Contemporary Club.

My interest in the Club is sincere, and it always gives me pleasure to think that I have been of any service to it.

Very truly Yours,   Woodrow Wilson

WWTLS (in possession of Charles E. Feinberg) with canceled check endorsed by Wilson.

To Herbert Baxter Adams

My dear Dr. Adams,   Princeton, New Jersey, 13 March, 1894.

I trust that my delay in writing has not caused you any inconvenience. To speak without reserve, it has gone hard with me to decline the volume you proposed to me.¹ That particular volume, and the whole scheme, have great attraction for me; and the temptation to undertake the job was very great, in spite of the inadequacy of the pay. I wanted the subject, not the money. But here at home, in the immediate presence of the other work I have begun, I have realized the "must" of the case. I must decline,—with genuine regret, and with renewed apologies for being so long about it.

With the warmest regard.

Most siocerely [sincerely] Yours,   Woodrow Wilson

WWTLS (H. B. Adams Papers, MdBJ).
¹ While Wilson was in Baltimore, Adams had asked him to write a book on the American federal government for Adams's projected "American Citizen Series," which Macmillan and Company was to publish. The series under Adams's editorship never materialized.

To Francis Fisher Browne[1]

My dear Mr. Browne,　　　Princeton, New Jersey, 13 March, 1894.

I wish that I might undertake the article you want on English at Princeton. There is not very much to say about it, I am sorry to say; and I am tempted to declare that Princeton might, without great impropriety, be left off your list; but what may be said I should like to say. But a multitude of engagements forbid. If you will have the truth, whatever it is, however, there are others here besides myself who can "do" you the piece. I hope that Dr. Murray, the head of the Department, would be willing to undertake it, and there are few men more scholarly or capable. Suppose you write to him and see.[2]

Most Cordially Yours,　　Woodrow Wilson

WWTLS (de Coppet Coll., NjP).
　[1] Editor of the Chicago *Dial*.
　[2] Neither Dean Murray nor anyone else at Princeton contributed to the *Dial*'s series on the teaching of English in American colleges and universities.

An Announcement

[March 14, 1894]

Examinations in Jurisprudence, for those conditioned, or absent from the regular examinations, will be held, not on Monday, but on Tuesday evening, March 20th, at 8 o'clock in Professor Fine's Room.　　WOODROW WILSON.

Printed in the *Daily Princetonian*, March 14, 1894.

A Newspaper Report of Wilson's Delivery of "Democracy"

[March 23, 1894]

WOODROW WILSON!

A Thoughtful, Scholarly Lecture.

DEMOCRACY HIS SUBJECT

When Prof. Woodrow Wilson stepped before the footlights at Stokes Hall last evening[1] the audience saw a man of medium height who could not by any means be called handsome. But his eyes gleam pleasantly through his spectacles, and he has a clear, distinct voice of good compass. He is not a speaker and makes no attempt at oratory.

He reads his manuscript closely.

The lecture bristled with thought and step by step lead up so logically to its conclusion, that it took no effort to follow him. His effort was in the purest, simplest English—natural, without the pyrotechnics that muddy ideas.

It was a clear, perspicuous description, explanation and definition of democracy.

It was a lecture by a man of thought, for thoughtful men.

There was no effort to gain applause.

His lecture is scholarly, and yet is couched in the purest simple English.

Printed in the *Durham*, N. C., *Daily Globe*, March 23, 1894; some editorial headings omitted.
[1] Wilson delivered his address, "Democracy," printed at Dec. 5, 1891, Vol. 7, in the Trinity College Lecture Series.

From Stockton Axson

My dear Brother Woodrow: [Burlington, Vt.] March 23, 1894.

I owe you all sorts of apologies for so long neglecting to answer your kind note. Great pressure of work and poor health are my only excuse.

I wish that I could go to Princeton and spend the holidays with you all. It would be a double pleasure to me—first to get away from Burlington, and secondly to see and be with you all. But I feel that I ought not to go to the expense which the journey would necessitate. It would cost me thirty dollars or more to make the trip and this seems too much to expend on a five day's relaxation. So I have made up my mind to remain in Burlington.

I improved in health considerably during February and the early part of this month, but I seem to be getting back into a bad way again. It is discouraging but must be endured without whining I suppose.

I hope that you all keep well and happy—the latter condition being very dependent upon the former I find. I imagine that you must be lecturing in New York now,[1] which of course must entail a good deal of additional labor.

Please give my best love to all.

Ever affectionately yours   Stockton Axson

ALS (WP, DLC).
[1] That is, to give his annual series of lectures on constitutional law at the New York Law School, about which see the Editorial Note, "Wilson's Lectures at the New York Law School," Vol. 7.

From Dodd, Mead & Company

Dear Sir: New York, March 30th, 1894

We have been trying to persuade Mr. Schouler, whose History of the United States we publish, to write in the same proportion two or three volumes covering the period preceding the constitution, and one on the war, thus making his history complete. He has finished, as you will doubtless remember, his original plan, which was to write the history of the United States from the adoption of the Constitution to the beginning of the Civil War. He has consented to write on the later period, following his present fifth volume with one on the Civil War. But he wishes to revise his work, practically re-writing the first two volumes and making in the others important changes.

With all this before him and at his time of life and with health not of the best, he is unwilling to undertake more, but has consented to our asking you to write a history upon the general lines of his work, covering the settlement and colonial and revolutionary periods. We may say that we have under consideration in connection with Mr. Schouler's revision an elaborate illustration of his history on the plan somewhat of the new edition of Green's short history. We feel that whether illustrated or not this work if rounded out in the way proposed will fill a place at present unoccupied, giving a history sufficiently popular for general reading, and yet having the weight of scholarship and authority and covering upon one plan the whole ground.

We hope you will take the matter into favorable consideration, and if you are inclined to do so, we will be glad to meet you either in Princeton or at our office to go more fully into details.

Awaiting your reply,[1] we are

Your very truly,   Dodd Mead & Company

TLS (WP, DLC).
[1] Wilson's reply is missing, but in it he undoubtedly declined the invitation.

From John Adams Wilson

Dear Woodrow: Franklin, Pa. March 30th. 1894

Do not think for a moment that I have forgotten to answer your letter. I have been expecting to get to Princeton each week since you wrote, but something has always happened to pervent [prevent]. I had made my entry for the big Pigeon Shoot[1] in New York next Tuesday, and as a matter of course supposed I would be on hand, but I will not be. Our President,[2] Mr. [Charles] Miller went South about six weeks ago and was expected home tomorrow. He has his Private car and his whole family with him. When they struck the cold weather at Omaha on Tuesday of this week, it must have been a little too much for them, so they turned around and will be in Sanfrancisco tomorrow and then take a tour of California for the next four weeks. This means that I will have to keep pretty close to the Office during that time. Last week Tuesday I left here and went to Savannah and returned Saturday of the same week. I will get to see you as soon as I can.

If convenient, I wish you would see Altman of the Ball Nine[3] and tell him I would like to have him spend his Summer vacation in Franklin[.] He will want to play ball and as he is not burdened with wealth, will as a matter of course want to make a little out of it. The College men all over the country, are trying to get a line on men who play for money during vacations with a view of barring them the following year. I think it would be much better for Altman to be with one who would protect him, and the College at the same time.

The Princeton Club gives a Banquet at the Duquesne Club Pittsburgh, on the evening of April 9th. Cannot you make it convenient to be there then? If you can come let me know and I will be on hand.

Hope you are well and happy.

                    Affectionately yours   Jno. A. Wilson.

Tell Altman, he will not be expected to play ball for fun if he comes here.   J. A. W.

TLS (WP, DLC) with WWhw notation on env.: "Ans."
  [1] The New York newspapers did not mention this affair.
  [2] Of the Galena Oil Works, Ltd., of Franklin, Pa.
  [3] Owen Randolph Altman, '97.

Notes for Classroom Lectures

                                        2 April, 1894

ENGLISH COMMON LAW.

IV. English Law: Its Parts and their Genesis.

I. *The Body of English Law*: Its several members and their development.

From the opening of the fourteenth century the body of law in England becomes definitely *national and organic* in character. The period of the interfusion of systems and the readjustment of administration is past. *Henceforth there is a homogeneous body of English law.* It has *many members, however*; and in order to understand these adequately it is necessary to consider the development of Parliament and the courts.

I. *Parliament* assumed both its *formal shape* (i.e., its division into two Houses) and its *essential powers*, of assent to all law-making, *in the course of the fourteenth century*.

II. *The Courts of Law*, some of which are older, while others are younger, than Parliament, were *all* of them *in modern shape by the middle of the fourteenth century*.

Of these

(1) *The Court of Exchequer*, organized finally by Roger of Salisbury, is *the oldest*, dating, in germ at least, it would seem, from the conquest.

The Exchequer had *both civil and equitable jurisdiction*. First of all *a court of accounts*, organized to superintend the *financial business of the Crown*, it came at length to handle *all pecuniary suits in which the Crown was concerned*; and finally, by *the fiction* of *quo minus* (by which any plaintiff who could call himself a debtor of the Crown could complain of any injury alleged to render him less able to meet his obligations to the king) it gained *jurisdiction over personal actions of all kinds*. Its jurisdiction fixed since *1311*.

(2) *The Court of Common Pleas*, mentioned in *Magna Carta*, and given its *distinct organization and separate staff of judges under Henry III. and Edward I.*, theoretically heard all suits between common (i.e., not specially privileged) *suitors in ordinary matters*, and for long enjoyed exclusive *jurisdiction over real actions*.

(3) *The Court of King's Bench*, was theoretically the king's own court. It took distinct and separate shape at the same time that the common pleas were given their separate tribunal (*temp. Henry III. and Edward I.*). "*Its jurisdiction*, both civil and criminal, was very great, and its business *comprised all that of the old Curia Regis which was not transferred to the Courts of Exchequer and Common Pleas*. It had special jurisdiction over all inferior courts," magistrates, "and *civil corporations*, and 'protected *the liberty of the subject* by speedy and summary interposition.'" By the *fiction of a trespass* on the part of the defendant, it got jurisdiction over *all personal actions*; so that the three law courts had identical jurisdiction in this field.

(4) *The Court of Chancery. After Henry* II. there could be *no suit without a writ.* The preparation of *special writs* was entrusted (to meet unusal cases) to the *clerks in Chancery,* in the time of Edward I. In 1280 it was arranged that all "matters of grace" should be reported on by the Chancellor before going to the king. Finally, *in 1348 the Court of Chancery was established* by an ordinance which gave the Chancellor authority to dispense justice in *"matters of grace."* (We shall look into the history of Chancery more particularly hereafter.)

Comp. Digby, 319 ff.1

(5) *The Ecclesiastical courts* had been allowed an inclusive jurisdiction ever since *before the Conquest,* and the separation of civil and ellesiastical [ecclesiastical] jurisdiction effected by the Norman and Angevin sovereigns *left many important causes in their keeping.* They continued in a wide "indulged" jurisdiction, acting according to *the canon law, pieced out and supplemented by the Civil Law,* in respect of *such crimes as* must be treated *pro reformatione morum* or *pro salute animae, e.g., heresay* [heresy], *adultery, fornication,* etc.; and *such civil matters as tithes, benefices, marriage and divorce, testaments* and their incidents, etc. *See Hale,* pp. 26 ff.

(6) *The Courts of Admiralty,* established *temp.* Edward III., *about 1350,* and held before the Lord High Admiral or his deputy. They possessed both *civil and criminal jurisdiction,* and took cognizance of all *"crimes and offences committed either upon the sea or on the coasts out of the body or extent of any English county.* ["] E.g., "depredations and piracies, offences of masters and mariners upon the high seas; maritime contracts made and to be executed upon the high sea; matters of prize and reprisal upon the high sea," etc., etc. (Hale, p. 32 ff.)

These courts, it will be observed, *fall into two groups:* I. The *Courts of Law;* and II. The *Chancery, Admiralty, and Ecclesiastical* Courts. The courts of the *second group* are *no less characteristic* of the English system of justice, *no less national,* than those of the first group; *but they differ in procedure* and *in* the derivation of the *pri[n]ciples* of

---

1 With one exception, full bibliographical references to all authorities cited by Wilson in these notes are listed in the Editorial Note, "Wilson's Teaching at Princeton and the Johns Hopkins, 1893-97." The exception is John Indermaur, *Principles of the Common Law,* 6th edn. (London, 1891).

law which they recognize and administer so much that English law may be said to consist of *three distinct members* or branches: viz., *Common Law, Equity, Civil Law*, though the two latter have much in common, and no one of the members is strictly exclusive of the other two. The Chancery, the admiralty, and the ecclesiastical courts alike *have drawn suggestion* and specific principles *from the law of Rome*; but *in the ecclesiastical courts* the principle vehicle of the Roman is *the Canon law*; *in the admiralty courts* the chief suggestions come from *the maritime law* which has only passed through the Roman codes; *the Chancery Courts* resort only covertly and upon exigent occasion to the *Corpus Juris*; and *the Common law courts are not unaffected* by the practice and precedents of the other courts. *All alike are affected by statute.*

It becomes necessary, therefore, to determine more clearly—

II. *The Nature and Field of the Common Law.* (*"Lex terrae"*— Magna Carta, 29—*"Lex Angliae, or terrae Angliae, or regni Angliae; "Lex et consuetudo regni"*).

"The common municipal law of this kingdom, which has the superintendence of all . . . particular laws . . . , and is *the common rule for the administration of common justice* in this great kingdom" (*Hale*, p. 47).

The law "which asserts, maintains, and, with all imaginable care, provides for the safety of the king's royal person, his crown and dignity; and all his just rights, revenues, powers, prerogatives, and government; as the great foundation (under God) of the peace, happiness, honour, and justice of this kingdom. And this law is also that which asserts the rights, and liberties, and the properties of the subject; and is the just, known, and common rule of justice and right, between man and man, within the kingdom." (*Ibid.*).

A. *The General Common Law*: "That law by which proceedings and determinations, in the king's ordinary courts of justice, are directed and guided. This directs the course of the descents of lands, and the kinds; the natures, and the extents and qualifications of estates; . . . the manner, forms, ceremonies, and solemnities of transferring estates from one to another; the rules of settling, acquiring, and transferring, of properties; the forms, solemnities, and obligation of contracts; the rules and directions for the exposition of wills, deeds, and acts of Parliament; the process, proceedings, judgments, and executions of the king's ordinary courts of justice; the limits, bounds, and extents of courts, and their jurisdictions; the several kinds of temporal offences and punishments at common law, and the manner of the application of the several kinds of punishments"; etc. (*Hale*, p. 22).

Summarized, this would seem to *come to the following*:

1 *The law of Real Estate*, its tenure, inheritance, alienation, &c.
2 *Contracts*, their obligation, forms, etc.
3 *Hermeneutics*.
4 *Jurisdiction*, Process, and Procedure of the Courts.
5 *Tort, and Damages*.
6 *Crime, and Punishment*.

Of the accepted text writers, Broom conforms most nearly to this table of contents: Courts (their jurisdiction and mode of procedure); Enforceable rights; Ordinary Remedies; Extraordinary Remedies; Contracts (including landlord and tenand [tenant]; Torts; Criminal Law.

Holmes includes: Crime; Tort; Bailment; Possession and Ownership; Contracts; Successions; *taking in* more of the law of *real property* than Broom.

Indermaur confines himself to: Contracts (including bailments, mercantile contracts, etc.); Torts; Damages; Evidence. *Hale makes it even more inclusive* than the above enumeration would indicate; *for, besides all that*, it would seem, *it includes* "the laws applicable to matters of very great moment," which, though assuming "divers denominations, yet are but branches and parts of it; *like as the same ocean*, though it many times receives a different name from the province, shire, island, or county to which it is contiguous, yet these are but parts of the same ocean." Pp. 22, 23. So that there are, besides its general body,

B. *Particular Branches of the Common Law*, which are such because *leges non scriptae*, inasmuch as, though written, they do not draw their authority from the writing, but from long and immemorial usage, or "*by the strength of custom* and reception in this kingdom," *by special commission* from the Crown, or *from the superintendant sufferance of the common law courts. These* branches *are*:

Extensions of Common Law $\left\{\begin{array}{l}\textit{Lex Prerogativa} \\ \textit{Lex forestae,} \\ \textit{Lex Mercatoria} \text{ (whose} \\ \quad \text{sources, general).}\end{array}\right.$

Indulged Jurisdictions $\left\{\begin{array}{l}\text{The Ecclesiastical juris-} \\ \quad \text{diction} \\ \text{The Admiralty jurisdic-} \\ \quad \text{tion} \\ \text{Jurisdiction of the Courts} \\ \quad \text{martial}\end{array}\right.$

(not to meddle with
anything determina-
ble by common law)
(*Hale*, p. 40 ff.)

Doctrine of the Superintendence of the common law courts.
"As the laws and statutes of the realm have prescribed to
those courts their bounds and limits, so *the courts of common law have the superintendency over those courts*, to keep
them within the limits and bounds of their several jurisdictions," *issuing* "*their prohibitions* to restrain them," *and
uttering the* only authoritative *interpretation* of the statutes
from which they draw their jurisdictions. (*Hale*, 45).
Sir Matthew Hale would thus *seem to make* "Common Law"
synonymous with the whole body of the lex non scripta,
whether derived from the custom of England or from the
texts of foreign law.
The Usual Antitheses:

(1) *The Common Law,—the Civil Law.* The law and custom of England, i.e., built up by the practice of the
courts of common law; and that body of foreign law,
whose ultimate source is the texts of the *Corpus Juris*,
which has filtered into all the continental systems, deeply impregnating them, and which has in some measure
affected the law of England through the practice of the
Chancery, the ecclesiastical, and the admiralty courts.

(2) *Common Law,—Equity.* I.e., the common law, and
that particular mixture of modified common law, natural equity, exceptional remedies, and Roman law
which has come in through the peculiar practice of the
Courts of Chancery.

"*In conformity with our most approved Commentators*, I
have mentioned *maxims* as an important element of our
common law. *Of these* maxims, which embody principles of

much value, when their application is rightly understood, *many have been derived from the Roman or Civil Law*; and, although it be true . . . that this law forms no rule binding in itself upon the subjects of these realms; yet, *in deciding a case upon principle*, where no direct authority can be cited from the books, *our Courts will listen to* arguments drawn from *the Institutes and Pandects* of Justinian, *and will rejoice* if their conclusions are shown to be in conformity with that law, which is 'the fruit of the researches of the most learned men, the collective wisdom of ages, and the groundwork of the municipal law of most of the countries of Europe.[']" Broom, *"Commentaries on the Common Law,"* 8th ed., p. 20.

   The most common antithesis: Common Law,–Statute Law. W[herein]. C[onsider].,

III. *The Relations and Antitheses of Common and Statute Law.*
   By Hale they are *carefully distinguished*, the Common law being *par excellence* the *lex non scripta*, the law which does not derive its authority from enactment. He is *obliged*, however, *to include certain older statutes*. All statutes or enactments passed *before the beginning of legal memory* (1 Rich.I., whose reign began 6 July, 1189,–crowned, 3 Sept.), and not since altered or repealed by contrary statutes *or custom*, are part of the Common Law. (Hale, p.p. 1-5).
   Even as regards the time Henry III.–Edward II., moreover, the statutes remaining were many of them *"made but in affirmance of the common law*; and . . . *the rest* of them, that made a change in the common law, are yet *so antient*, that they now seem to have been, as it were, a part of the common law; *especially considering the many expositions that have been made of them* in the several successions of times, whereby as they became the great subject of judicial resolutions and decisions, so those expositions and decisions, together also with those old statutes themselves, *are as it were incorporated into the very common law*, and become a part of it." "Many provisions there may have been of those times, moreover, which are not now extant." (Hale, p. 9).
   Broom does not scruple to include statutes without distinction within the Common Law, which he makes to consist *both of lex* scripta and of *lex non scripta*. (p. 2). The leading *maxims with regard to the interpretation of statutes*, moreover, would seem to bear out the view, inasmuch as they seem to assume that statutes are in all cases supplementary,

ancillary, to the common law. *Viz.*, (*1*) What was the common law before the making of the act? (*2*) What was the mischief and defect against which the common law did not provide? (*3*) What remedy has Parliament devised and applied? (*4*) The true reason of the remedy. (P. 5) *In brief,* there is substantial *antithesis* between common and statute law *only where statutes alter* the very *system and principle* of the common law; not where they simply seek its amendment or its adjustment to new conditions.

> *The Materials of the Common Law*, therefore, are *both old practice* and *new and deliberate adjustments* of the law by enactment, its application being subject to betterment alike by decision and by statute: by legislative, as well as by judicial accommodation or extension.

> *The process* by which these several elements are worked into a common body and system is *the process of interpretation* and application; and no statute has become a part of the common law which has not been *so knitted into the body of its principles* by the careful stitches of successive generations of judges *as to have become almost indistinguishable* from the material with which it has been combined.

> *In its widest scope,* too, *Common Law partakes of* the rich matter of *all right reason. Blackstone* declared the "*Law of Nature*" to be "superior in obligation to any other"; English *judges* have pronounced it "*a part of the Laws of England*"; have affirmed that "*the law of England will not sanction what is inconsistent with humanity*"; have even decided that "principles of *private justice, moral fitness,* and *public convenience*," "when applied to a new subject, *make common law without a precedent.*" (Broom, pp. 20-22, with cases there cited).

> *Thus freely have the king's judges,* commissioned by Henry II., *made use of all sources and all means* to develop for the realm an all-serviceable Common Law. At the least we may say, that until the fourteenth century had finished its work, there was practically no distinction between common and statute law.

WWT MS. in body of notes described at March 6, 1894.

A News Item

[April 6, 1894]

Sunday, April 8, . . .

12.15 P.M.—Laymen's Conference[1] in the Faculty Room. Addressed by Prof. Woodrow Wilson.

Printed in the *Daily Princetonian*, April 6, 1894.
[1] The Laymen's Conference of Princeton University, founded in 1893 by Princeton undergraduates, included in its membership students, faculty members, and townspeople. The Laymen's Conference maintained a reading room, with daily newspapers and periodicals, for the workingmen of the town. It also held meetings in the Faculty Room of Nassau Hall on Sundays after chapel to hear speeches on and discuss "the sources and causes of evil, injustice and poverty in the world, and the best methods of dealing with them, believing that in thus serving man, we are best serving God and accomplishing the most for His Kingdom." From *The Laymen's Conference of Princeton University* (Princeton, 1893), p. 4. The organization was functioning as late as the academic year 1895-96.

A Newspaper Report of an Address

[April 13, 1894]

PHILADELPHIAN SOCIETY

Prof. Woodrow Wilson addressed the meeting in Murray Hall last night. He read the 24th chapter of Proverbs and interpreted the spirit of the passage for college life, the subject of his address being the "University Spirit." Evils are never cured by physical force but by the spirit. It is sentiment which has stopped cheating in examinations, a result which could not be accomplished by physical force. The true university spirit has five important characteristics. First, it has an eager curiosity about a great many things, not a nervous curiosity, but an earned [earnest] desire for knowledge. Second, it has the spirit of wisdom, that wisdom which is received from many counsellors and does not eagerly grasp new things, but compares them with the old. Third, the religious spirit is a characteristic of university spirit. It is not content with a material explanation of life, but looks for a connection between itself and the forces of the universe. It hears with the heart as well as the head. Fourth, this spirit aims toward an ideal. It is not content with success without an image back of it. This image is God and satisfies a man because it is compatible with his spirit. In the last place, the real university spirit is broad and tolerant. Christianity in its widest sense must be cultivated to attain this end. It does not permit a man to be wise in his own conceit and its only ideal is that which comes from God.

Printed in the *Daily Princetonian*, April 13, 1894.

To Robert Bridges

My dear Bobby,　　　　　　　　[Princeton, N. J.] 22 April, 1894

I was sorely disappointed not see you yesterday. My little calls at your office cheer me greatly, and I hate to let an opportunity go by of seeing you. But yesterday I really did not have an opportunity. I understood you to say a week ago that I had better "let things take their natural course" with regard to the History, and I thought I ought probably to take Mr. Scribner's continued silence as a hint that he was not much interested,[1] and so I went to see the *Century* people. I saw only Robt. U. Johnston;[2] and he was evidently unable to say anything binding; but he gave me all the encouragement he could, and I am to see Gilder and Scott[3] next Saturday by appointment, to talk the whole matter over. Of course, therefore, the matter is in a *very* early initial stage. I can only surmise what may come of it, and I shall be quite as slow as may be decent in coming to terms with them.

I wanted specially to see you to tell you how much Mrs. Wilson and I admire the dedicatory poem of your book[4] (I don't mind admitting the tears it brought to my eyes) and enjoy the light touch and the insight of the sketches.

　　　　　　Affectionately Yours,　　Woodrow Wilson

ALS (WP, DLC).
[1] Wilson had talked with Bridges about the possibility of publishing his "Short History of the United States" in serial form in *Scribner's Magazine.*
[2] Robert Underwood Johnson, at this time associate editor of the New York *Century Magazine.*
[3] Richard Watson Gilder, editor of the *Century Magazine,* and Frank Hall Scott, president of the Century Company.
[4] In Bridges's *Overheard in Arcady* (New York, 1894), dedicated to his mother.

From the Minutes of the Princeton Faculty

　　　　　　　　　4 5′ P.M. Wednesday, April 25th, '94

. . . Professors Perry, W. Wilson and Sloane were appointed a Committee to select a Question for the Lynde Debate. . . .[1]

At the request of the Dean it was Resolved That a Committee be appointed to investigate the matter of Clubs in College and to report at the next meeting of the Faculty.

Professors Duffield, W. Wilson, Magie & Hibben were appointed the Committee.[2]

[1] The committee set the following question: "Resolved, That the Federal Senators should be elected by Popular Vote." The debate took place in newly dedicated Alexander Hall on June 12, and the winners, all members of the Class of 1894, were Benjamin William M'Cready Sykes, Donald MacColl, and Charles Roger Watson. For the nature of the Lynde Debate, see n. 1 to Wilson's diary entry of June 23, 1876, Vol. 1, p. 145.
[2] The committee's report is printed at May 2, 1894.

A News Item

[May 1, 1894]

The catalogue of the New York Law School for 1893-94 has just been issued, with the prospectus for 1894-95. This school is now in the third year of its existence, and its successful establishment upon the special plan of continuing Professor Theodore W. Dwight's method of legal instruction, has been viewed by the friends of that method with special interest. The number of college graduates in the school this year is 203, or about forty per cent. of the whole number of students. Of these, 42 are from Yale, 37 from Princeton, 19 from Columbia, 16 from the New York City College, 9 from Amherst, 8 from Harvard, 7 from Rutgers.

Among the special lecturers in the school for this year are Prof. Woodrow Wilson of Princeton, Prof. Chas. E. Hughes, lately of Cornell University Law School, and Hon. William W. Goodrich, the admiralty lawyer of New York City.

A new announcement for the coming year shows that six free scholarships have been established in the school, each of which will entitle its recipient to free tuition during an attendance of two years. Three of these scholarships will be awarded each year, beginning with October, 1894.

Printed in the *Daily Princetonian*, May 1, 1894

From the Minutes of the Princeton Faculty

4 5′ P.M., Wednesday, May 2nd, 1894.

. . . The Committee appointed to consider the subject of Clubs in College (V. p. 556) made the following report which was adopted in the form of a resolution: Resolved That the Faculty announce that no Club of Sophomores will be allowed to lease or manage any property for Club purposes, and further that in the future no Club of Sophomores will be allowed to elect successors from the Freshman Class. . . .

From Charles Scribner

My dear Mr. Wilson, [New York] May 9, [189]4

It was too bad that we missed one another. I wanted to talk with you about your plan which Bridges imparted to me. So far as the Magazine is concerned I fear we could not take up the serial publication of such a work to a sufficient extent to justify bringing it to us and I suppose the book is bound up with the magazine publication. If the latter is not the case I should be glad to make a try for it. This will serve to let you know about how we should probably stand in the matter. It is needless to add that it would give me great pleasure to talk the matter over with you, at any time you could call.

Yours sincerely   Charles Scribner

ALS (Letterpress Books, Charles Scribner's Sons Archives, NjP).

To Charles Scribner

My dear Mr. Scribner,   Princeton, N.J. 11 May, 1894

I am very much obliged to you for your kind note of the 9th. I don't know any house I should rather have publish my history, when it is done, than your own; but the writing of it is but just begun; it will probably occupy me several years, and I feel that arrangements for its publication as a book would just now be premature.

I have learned to be shy about putting what I write *first* into *plates*, where errors both of statement and of treatment stand fast, as judgments against one. Moreover, I am taking this work very seriously indeed, and wish to perfect its form by the most careful study. It has been my wish, therefore, to carve from it some twenty-four historical essays for publication throughout a couple of years in a magazine: in order that what I was writing should be subjected to the test of exposure to the air, and to the scrutiny of critics: in order that I might myself see it in cold print: and in order that its quality should be advertised and the book come at last like a friend, rather than like a stranger. It was my idea, too, that in this way much of the expense of an illustrated edition could be carried, and a couple of years of editorial care go into the choice of illustrations, which would themselves be vehicles of history.

I have thus stated my whole thought as to the plan of publication in order that you might understand exactly why I do not yet wish to enter into any negotiations looking towards the publication of my work as a book.

I am none the less obliged to you for your kind offer to take the matter under consideration.

Most sincerely Yours,   Woodrow Wilson

ALS (Charles Scribner's Sons Archives, NjP).

A Final Examination

May 14, 1894.

EXAMINATION IN

ENGLISH COMMON LAW.

1. Of what materials is English common law made up? What has been the process of its growth, and what are its field and character?

2. Outline the several periods chiefly to be distinguished in the development of English law, and indicate briefly the character of each period.

3. Describe the administrative reforms of the time of Henry II., and their effect both upon the administration and upon the substance of the law.

4. What was the origin of the civil jury, and by what steps did it come to its present character and development?

5. What were the effects of the conquest upon the system of land tenure in England? What were the characteristic features of the feudal land system in England?

6. What was the occasion and what were the consequences of the Statute of Uses?

7. What is the doctrine of 'consideration' of the English law of contract? Illustrate its operation and account for its establishment.

Text-book.

8. Describe the rise and character of the 'country gentleman.'

9. What causes led to the concentration of estates and to the decay of the free yeomanry of England?

10. Trace the causes and the results of the rise of manufactures in England.

To be answered by those who were absent from the regular written recitation:

11. Why were the great vassals in England strong enough to force a constitutional government upon the Crown, but not strong enough to destroy its power?

12. What civil, fiscal, and economic privileges did the landed gentry enjoy in the eighteenth century?

13. What was the reform of 1832, and why has it led to still more radical changes?

"I pledge my honor as a gentleman that, during this examination, I have neither given nor received assistance."

Printed examination (WP, DLC).

To Charles William Kent

My dear Kent,   Princeton, New Jersey, 29 May, 1894.

It distresses me very deeply that the University of Virginia should think, even through a minority of its Faculty, of admitting women to its courses.[1] I have had just enough experience of co-education to know that, even under the most favourable circumstances, it is most demoralizing. It seems to me that in the South it would be fatal to the standards of delicacy as between men and women which we most value. For that is just its result. It is bad enough when the life outside the class room is separate, absorbed by the various life, and dominated by the conventions, of a city. Intimate intercourse such as would necessarily characterize the system at the University of Virginia would emphasize its worst evils. I do not mean that it leads to vice; though occasionally it does; but it *vulgarizes* the whole relationship of men and women. To say more than that would be only to give particular instances. The generalization is a *fact* itself, and of my own observation.

Besides, where is the necessity? Women now have excellent colleges of their own; where their life can be such as is fit for women. What an age this is for going out of its way to seek change!

I wish I could write all my heart contains on the matter. As it is, I can only pray that the University may be led away from such gratuitous folly!

In haste,   Your Sincere friend,   Woodrow Wilson

WWTLS (Tucker-Harrison-Smith Coll., ViU).
¹ Kent's letter, to which this was a reply, is missing.

A Biographical Sketch of Wilson¹

[c. June 11, 1894]

WOODROW WILSON

Has constantly followed out the line of study which he planned when he was a student at Princeton, devoting himself particularly to the study of the development of institutions. He has gained a wide recognition and reputation as a writer of books and essays, as a college professor, and as a public lecturer on literary and political subjects. He returned to Princeton as professor in 1890, and is one of the most influential members of the Faculty; his elective classes are among the largest of the college. He has also taken a great interest in the athletic sports of the University, and has been a member of the Graduate Advisory Committee. His books on "Congressional Government" and "The State" have become acknowledged authorities, both in this country and in England. The principal dates in his career are as follows: He studied law in the University of Virginia, 1879-81. Practised law in Atlanta, Ga., 1882-83, but finding the study of the law, especially in connection with the systematic study of politics, more attractive than the practice, entered the Johns Hopkins University as a graduate student of history and politics, in the autumn of 1883. Was a student in Johns Hopkins University, 1883-85, holding the appointment of Fellow in History there, 1884-85. Took the degree of Ph.D. in the same institution in regular course, upon examination in June, 1886. Associate in History in Bryn Mawr College, 1885-86, and Associate Professor, 1886-88; Professor of History and Political Economy in Wesleyan University, Middletown, Conn., 1888-90; since 1887 Lecturer on Administration in Johns Hopkins University; Lecturer on Constitutional Law in the New York Law School. He was married, June 24, 1885, to Miss Ellen Louise Axson. Three children: Margaret, born April 16, 1886; Jessie Woodrow, born August 28, 1887, and Eleanor Randolph, born October 16, 1889. He is a Presbyterian and a Democrat, "but ready to vote at any time against Maynards and race-track candidates for State Legislatures."[2]

Printed in *The Class of 1879, Princeton College, Quindecennial Record, 1879-94* (New York, 1894), pp. 118-19.

[1] This sketch, although probably written by Robert Bridges, a member of the committee that prepared the Class of 1879's book for its quindecennial celebration, was undoubtedly a paraphrase of Wilson's own report.

[2] An entrenched and corrupt Democratic organization allied with race-track interests obtained passage by the New Jersey legislature in 1893 of bills permitting towns and counties to legalize race-track betting. Vetoed by Governor George T. Werts, the bills were re-enacted over his veto. This set off a state-wide furor led by ministers and the Anti-Race Track League, which culminated in a Republican landslide in the state elections of 1894. "Maynard" was Isaac H. Maynard, Democrat, former Deputy Attorney General of the State of New York, who had been involved in an election scandal in 1891-92.

Notes for an After-Dinner Speech[1]

[c. June 11, 1894]

The Glories of '79

Who shall say that the product of a university is better than that of a college?[2]

True, a great interval separated '79 from the classes which accompanied her, and no teaching body is calculated for genius.

Nature provides every class with one poet [the class poet, Edward Parker Davis]: we provided ourselves with 2 and the poetry of Robert Bridges has become the private cult of a special sect in England. The same people in many instances no doubt that worship Walt Whitman.

My own relations peculiarly satisfactory to me as I look back. I flatter myself I was not looked down upon by Jack Davis nor too much looked up to by Ridge Wright (and Billy Wilder). Some of my chums will wonder to learn that I am now a member of the Disciplinary Committee and a terror of the unrighteous.

In 20 years, boys, we have changed from green to gray.
The things that have kept us together: Billy Isham[3]
                       The Class Committee[4]
                Our own sense of comradeship
Much of all this is represented by
    (*Toasts*)   Our Class Prex.[5]
                Our Trustees (Cuyler?)[6]
                Our Youth (Wright)[7]
It has been the spirit of bounding vitality and shows itself in
    Our Public Spirit (Pitney)[8]
    (Woodberry—Lord)[9]
    Our Professional Devotion (Davis)[10]
    Our Silent Partners (Sheldon)[11]
Tom Hall[12]
Riker[13]
McNair[14]

Transcript of WWsh and WWhw notes on two loose pages in *The Class of 1879, Princeton College, Quindecennial Record, 1879-94* (New York, 1894), in the Wilson Library, DLC.

[1] These were Wilson's notes for his speech as toastmaster at the Class of 1879's dinner at the Princeton Inn on June 11, 1894.

[2] A reference to the preparations, now in progress, to change Princeton from a college into a university.

[3] A reference to the famous Isham dinners, about which see Alexander J. Kerr, "The Isham Dinners," *Fifty Years of the Class of 'Seventy-Nine Princeton* (Princeton, N.J., 1931), pp. 199-206.

[4] Abram Woodruff Halsey, Robert Bridges, Cornelius Cuyler Cuyler, John Farr, and Cyrus Hall McCormick.

[5] Halsey.

[6] Cuyler had been mentioned for election to the Board of Trustees. His election occurred in 1898.

[7] No doubt a reference to J. Ridgway Wright's youthful appearance.

[8] A humorous reference to the following portion of Mahlon Pitney's sketch in the quindecennial record, page 85: "He says that he has 'neither filled nor tried to fill any office. Have been "mentioned" once or twice in connection with public office, but this was entirely without my procurement, and did not result in any serious popular uprising.' "

[9] John McGaw Woodbury, a surgeon of New York, and Frank Howard Lord, treasurer of a New York lumber company.

[10] Most probably Edward Parker Davis, prominent physician of Philadelphia and one of Wilson's close friends. Wilson could have been referring to John D. Davis, then Professor of Semitic Philology and Old Testament History in Princeton Theological Seminary.

[11] A silent partner, that is, as a lawyer advising trust companies and railroads.
[12] Pastor of the Fourth Presbyterian Church of Chicago.
[13] Adrian Riker, lawyer of Newark.
[14] Theodore M. McNair, Presbyterian missionary in Japan.

To Robert Bridges

My dear Bobby,   Princeton, N.J. 13 June, 1894

I enclose my check for $362.00. I have not deposited the cash yet; but will, in time to meet the check.[1]

What a good time we did have—and how Mrs. Wilson and I did enjoy "the gang"![2]

In haste,

As ever,   Most affectionately,   Woodrow Wilson

ALS (WP, DLC).
  [1] Perhaps Wilson had collected the money at the Class of 1879's dinner to pay for the quindecennial record, cited earlier.
  [2] The Wilsons had probably invited the "Witherspoon Gang"—members of the Class of 1879 who had roomed with Wilson in Witherspoon Hall—to dinner during the commencement period.

To Frank Irving Herriott[1]

My dear Mr. Herriott,   Princeton, New Jersey 14 June, 1894.

I am very much obliged to you for your letter of yesterday. Hart and I must have drawn from the same source in regard to the civil service. I am glad other men make mistakes, as well as I.

No, I do not expect to touch "Congressional Government" again. I think it must stand as it is. It was intended as a monograph simply, not as a text or manual; and a book like that must be left to represent, not two periods of a man's thought, but only that one in which it was written.

With warmest regards,

Most sincerely Yours,   Woodrow Wilson

WWTLS (Ia-HA).
  [1] A former student of Wilson's, Herriott had taken his Ph.D. at the Johns Hopkins in 1893 and was in 1893-94 editor of the Philadelphia *University Extension Magazine*.

An Essay on Education

[c. *June 20, 1894*]

UNIVERSITY TRAINING AND CITIZENSHIP.

It is hard, amidst a multitude of counsellors, to make up our own ideal of what a university should be. We have been so often bidden, by young and old alike, to make our university instruction like that of Germany, that we have more than half consented to try the experiment. And yet we are by no means sure of our purpose in that direction. Once and again we have been made to think a good deal about the advantage that a young fellow gets from reading widely and systematically with a tutor, as the men do at the English universities. We like the close contact between teacher and pupil, and the rather liberal and unscholastic way of handling many books, which such a method of instruction seems to secure. The French system, too, we can appreciate and wish for when we are in the humour. We like the French spirit and sense of form, and we hold our judgments open to suggestions as to the best way of imparting vitality of that sort to our own instruction. All the while, however, it is our temper to put varied and vexatious restrictions on these, as on other, international exchanges. There is a very heavy duty on imported ideals. It costs us more than they are worth to subject them to our customs and get them fairly on the market. There is no great demand for them. The young men who really want them go abroad, if they can, to get them.

And yet we have no university ideal of our own. We are not even sure that we wish to create one. We ask ourselves, Do we want universities of a distinctively American type? It is the first impulse of most scholarly minds to reply with a plain and decided negative. Learning is cosmopolitan, and it would seem at first thought like stripping learning of its freedom and wide prerogative to demand that the universities where it makes its home should be national. Let the common schools smack of the soil, if they must, but not the universities! Must not the higher forms of scholarship follow everywhere the same method, in the same spirit? May not its doctrines constitute always a sort of international law of thought? Is it not a kind of freemasonry which has everywhere like degrees and a common ceremonial? Certainly truth is without geographical boundary, and no one could justly wish to observe a national bias in the determination of it.

It must be remembered, however, that scholarship is something more than an instrument of abstract investigation merely. It is also an instrument and means of life. Nations, as well as individuals, must seek wisdom: the truth that will make them free. There is a learning of purpose as well as a learning of science; for there is a truth of spirit as well as a truth of fact. And scholarship, though it must everywhere seek the truth, may select the truths it shall search for and emphasize. It is this selection that should be national. It is a question of emphasis and point of view; not a question of completing the circle and sum of knowledge. A wise man will choose what to learn; and so also will a wise nation. Not all learning, besides, is without a country. All physical science is international, so are also all formal parts of learning; and all philosophy, too, no doubt, and the laws of reasoning. But there is, besides these, a learning of purpose, to be found in literature and in the study of institutions; and this it is which should be made the means of nationalizing universities, being given the central and coördinating place in their courses of instruction.

In order to be national, a university should have, at the centre of all its training, courses of instruction in that literature which contains the ideals of its race and all the nice proofs and subtle inspirations of the character, spirit, and thought of the nation which it serves; and, besides that, instruction in the history and leading conceptions of those institutions which have served the nation's energies in the preservation of order and the maintenance of just standards of civil virtue and public purpose. These should constitute the common training of all its students, as the only means of schooling their spirits for their common life as citizens. For the rest, they might be free to choose what they would learn. Being thus prepared for their common life together by schooling in the same ideals of life and public action, they might the more safely be left to prepare for their individual and private functions separately and with undisturbed freedom.

It is the object of learning, not only to satisfy the curiosity and perfect the spirits of individual men, but also to advance civilization; and, if it be true that each nation plays its special part in furthering the common advancement, every people should use its universities to perfect it in its proper rôle. A university should be an organ of memory for the State for the transmission of its best traditions. Every man sent out from a university should be a man of his nation, as well as a man of his time.

This idea of a balance between general and special training has been temporarily lost sight of by the necessity to make room for the modern scientific studies. We have adopted the principle that a student may freely choose his studies, and so make the most of his natural tastes and aptitudes; and the length we go in applying the principle is determined, it would seem, rather by historical accident than by reasoned policy. If we are conservative, we insist that at least every Bachelor of Arts shall submit to a drill in both Greek and Latin. If we are 'liberal,' we permit the substitution of a modern language for one of these. If we are radical, we give the pupil *carte blanche*, and let him choose for himself what training he will have. But, whether we be conservative, 'liberal,' or radical, we are willing to confer other degrees besides Bachelor of Arts, and, under another label, to send men forth from the university who have taken nothing from it but a drill in laboratories and instruction in the use of tools. We have lost all idea of a common standard of training for all the men alike who seek to be accredited to the world by an academic degree.

Not only so, but in our controversies about the matter we have allowed ourselves to be driven into an awkward and even untenable position. We debate the relative values of a classical training and a scientific, as if it turned wholly upon the question of the development of the individual mind as a good working instrument. Can the man who has received a purely scientific training, from which all the nice discriminations of taste and of delicate judgment that come from the critical study of languages have been left out, use his mind as well as the man who has had these; as well as the man who has been schooled to submit his faculties to the subtle and refining influences of style and syntax, the elevating influences of delicate feeling, and the vivid passion of poet and orator? The question cannot be answered. The one may use his mind quite as well as the other: it depends upon what he uses it for. He uses it differently: that is all. The values represented by the difference cannot be satisfactorily assessed.

The difference is even very difficult to express. But no doubt it can be illustrated. The man who has been trained only in science or in technical and narrow lines—however well equipped or variously within those lines—is confined to them, not because he lacks knowledge, but because he lacks sympathy and adaptability. The scientific spirit and method, in academic instruction, hold their votaries very rigorously to a single point of view, and the more this spirit and method are submitted to and served, the more restrictive does their mastery become. It is presently impossible for those who are their willing and habituated subjects to understand whereof other men speak when they urge considerations which cannot be subjected to exact tests or modern standards. The men who have been inducted into literature and language, on the other hand, while they have obtained little marketable knowledge, have obtained both drill and an opened view of life. They have, so to say, breathed and analyzed the common air of thought that the better minds have lived in from the first. They have, in greater or less degree, become citizens of the intellectual world, and have examined with some critical care and a little discrimination the documents by which that citizenship is evidenced and secured. They cannot, however, make themselves so immediately useful in the practical tasks of the world of business as the men of the laboratories, the shops, or the purely professional schools; and they are thought, by those who have special training or capacity, to know nothing. They can use their minds, but there is nothing in them to use. They possess, at most, only a point of view. They are like good soils that have been prepared for planting, but as yet contain no edible harvest. The best light of the world has shone upon them; they have been watered by the tears of old songs, quickened by the passion of deeds done long ago; but no merchantable thing has yet been sown in them, and the man of science brings his quick crop first to market.

Certainly we have come to the parting of the ways, and there is nothing for us but to choose a direction. The graduates of our universities no longer go forth with a common training which will enable them to hold together in a community of thought. Some of them are trained in science, some in letters; some well and broadly trained, many ill and narrowly, with a hard technicality and mean contraction of view. Scarcely one of them has been fully inducted into the learning which deals with the common experiences, the common thoughts and struggles, the old triumphs and defeats of the men of his race in the past; their dreams and awakenings; their ambitions, humours, confidences, liberties, and follies: the intimate stuff of their minds and lives in past generations, when others were in like manner graduated from college and brought face to face with life and the unthinking mass of men.

The study of institutions and of English literature furnishes the only practicable common ground for the various disciplines of the modern university curriculum; but fortunately it has much more to commend it than its practicability. It would furnish also an ideal principle of unity. Such studies are practicable because they are not open to any serious utilitarian objection. They do not involve the long and tedious acquisition of any dead language: their tools are of easy use by any one. They bear directly upon such practical matter as a man's usefulness as a citizen and his influence and acceptability as a member of society. He can understand other men so much the better, command their sympathy the more readily, aid them and obtain their aid the more efficiently, for comprehending affairs and appreciating the common movements of sentiment and purpose. Such a community of plan is ideal because the great spiritual impulses and values which young men get when properly trained in the classics can be gotten in part from the splendid and various literature of our own tongue, rich as it is with treasures both new and old; because men trained to the exact standards and accustomed to the precise measurements of science, its cold dispassionateness and cautious reserve of judgment, can get from that literature an imagination for affairs and the standards by which things invisible and of the spirit are to be assessed; and because the men trained in the classics can get by it their pilotage into the modern world of men and ideas. It makes the classicist more practical and the scientist less narrow and pedantic; it is capable of giving to things technical an horizon and an elevation of spirit, and to things merely scholarly or æsthetic a thrill and ardour and discipline of life.

Every university, therefore, which would educate men as well as drill them, should make the reading of English literature in many sorts and much variety, under energetic and quick-witted tutors, compulsory from entrance to graduation; and the study of institutions under suggestive lecturers compulsory throughout at least the latter half of every course for a degree. It can be done, and sooner or later it must be done, if only to prevent disintegration and the utter separation and segregation of educated men in respect of their ideals of thought and conduct.

But this is the view only from inside the university. The greater arguments, from without, are supplied by the life of the modern world and the exigencies of national existence. The world in which we live is troubled by many voices, seeking to proclaim righteousness and judgment to come; but they disturb without instructing us. They cry out upon this point or upon that, but they have no whole doctrine which we can accept and live. They exaggerate, distort, distract. But they are dangerous voices, for all they are so obviously partial and unwise, because we have no clearly conceived standards of common thought to which to hold them. Those who hear are as ignorant and as fanatical as those who speak. A college man who has studied only the classics can no more criticise them than the man who has studied only science or the man who has studied nothing at all. Even the man who has read political economy and history has nowadays, very likely, read no literature. He can only cry out from his corner that these would-be teachers now everywhere on the platform are guilty of errors in logic and misconceptions of historical fact in all their revolutionary talk; and no one cares to listen to his pedantic and scholastic corrections: for these, they say, are matters of life and death, in which we need, not dialectic, but deliverance.

There is no corrective for it all like a wide acquaintance with the best books that men have written, joined with a knowledge of the institutions men have made trial of in the past; and for each nation there is its own record of mental experience and political experiment. Such a record always sobers those who read it. It also steadies the nerves. If all educated men knew it, it would be as if they had had a revelation. They could stand together and govern, with open eyes and the gift of tongues which other men could understand. Here is like wild talk and headlong passion for reform in the past,—here in the books,—with all the motives that underlay the perilous utterance now laid bare: these are not new terrors and excitements. Neither need the wisdom be new, nor the humanity, by which they shall be moderated and turned to righteous ends. There is old experience in these matters, or rather

in these states of mind. It is no new thing to have economic problems and dream dreams of romantic and adventurous social reconstruction.

And so it is out of books that we can get our means and our
self-possession for a sane and systematic criticism of life: out of
our own English books that we can get and appropriate and forever recreate the temper of our own race in dealing with these so
hazardous affairs. We shall lose our sense of identity and all
advantage of being hard-headed Saxons if we become ignorant
of our literature, which is so full of action and of thoughts fit for
action. We must look to the universities to see to it that we be not
denationalized, but rather made more steadfast in our best judgments of progress. To hear the agitators talk, you would suppose
that righteousness was young and wisdom but of yesterday. How
are the universities correcting the view, and aiding to make this
nonsense ridiculous? How many of their graduates know anything
clearly to the contrary? How many of them know when to laugh?

Of all things that a university should do for a man, the most
important is to put him in possession of the materials for a systematic criticism of life. Our present methods of training may
easily enough make *tabula rasa* of a man's mind in respect of
such matters. The reasoning of the scientific method, for all but
a few constructive minds, is analytical reasoning. It picks things
to pieces and examines them in their ultimate elements. It is
jealous, if not quite intolerant, of all traditional views; will receive
nothing, but test everything; and its influence is very marked
and pervasive. It produces, for one thing, an overweening confidence in the pure reasoning faculty. Now, it happens that the
pure reasoning faculty, whose only standard is logic and whose
only data are put in terms of determinable force, is the worst
possible instrument for reforming society. The only thing that
makes modern socialism more dangerous than like doctrine has
ever been is, that its methods are scientific and that the age also
is scientific. Two-thirds of our college graduates are not taught
anything that would predispose them against accepting its logic
or its purpose to put all things into a laboratory of experiment
and arbitrarily recombine the elements of society.

The 'humane' spirit of our time is a very different thing from
the *human* spirit. The humanity which we nowadays affect is
scientific and pathological. It treats men as specimens, and seeks
to subject them to experiment. It cuts cross-sections through the
human spirit and calls its description of what is thereby disclosed
moral essays and sociological novels. It is self-conscious and
without modesty or humour. The human spirit is a very different

thing. It has a memory and a sense of humour. It cannot read Ibsen after having read Shakespeare, any more than it can prefer sugar and butter and flour and sweets separately, in their individual intensity, to their toothsome and satisfying combination in pudding. Its literature is that which has the one flavour for every generation, and the same broad and valid sagacity. It regards the scientific method of investigation as one, but only one, method of finding out the truth; and as a method for finding only one kind of truth. It sees the telling points of the socialistic argument, but it knows some old standards of justice that have outlived many programmes of reform and seem still sound enough to outlast these also. "It's a mad world, my masters!" but it takes a nice balance of judgment and a long view of human nature to determine where the madness lies.

The worst possible enemy to society is the man who, with a strong faculty for reasoning and for action, is cut loose in his standards of judgment from the past; and universities which train men to use their minds without carefully establishing the connection of their thought with that of the past, are instruments of social destruction. Of course no man's thought is entirely severed from the past, or ever can be. But it is worth while to remember that science is no older than the present century, and is apt to despise old thought. At least its young votaries are: not because they are 'scientists,' but because they are only scientists. They are as much pedants, in their narrowness, as the men trained exclusively in the classics, whose thought is all in the past.

The training that will bring these two extremes together can be obtained by a thorough familiarity with the masterpieces of English thought and with the efforts of human genius in the field of institutions. A body of men thus made acquainted with their species is needed, to give us, at the centre of our political and social life, a class with definite and elevated ideals and a real capacity for understanding the conditions of progress: a power making for stability and righteousness against the petty and ineffectual turbulence of revolution.

We mistake the service of literature when we regard it as merely æsthetic. A literature of such variety as our own is nothing less than the annals of the best thought of our race upon every topic of life and destiny. Even our poets have had an eye for affairs; their visions have been of men and deeds. And, as for reading in the literature of institutions, no self-governing people can long hold together in order and peace without it. It is noteworthy that what remains the greatest text-book of English law, invaluable in spite of all the modern changes which have been hurried forward in the century since it was written, was written for laymen. Blackstone intended his lectures for the gentlemen of England: to enable the men of Oxford to take a place of intelligent authority in society when they should come into their own. With the spirit of our sane literature in us, and the strong flavour of our institutional principles present in all that we do or attempt, we shall be broad men enough, be our special training, in tools or books, what it may. Without this, we can but go astray alike in our private judgments and our public functions.

It would not be necessary to erect a new university to try the experiment of such a synthesis of university courses; though that would be worth doing, were the means made sufficient for a really great object-lesson in the right motives of education. Anybody can establish the modern sort of university, anywhere. It has no necessary nationality or character. But only in a free country, with great traditions of enlightened sentiment and continuous purpose, can a university have the national mark and distinction of a deliberate espousal of the spirit of a noble literature and historic institutions. Such a university would be a National Academy,—the only sort worth having. The thing can be done, however, without troubling a millionaire to appropriate to himself the glory of a unique function of greatness in the development of education. It can be done by only a comparatively slight readjustment of subjects and instructors in the greater of the universities we already have. It can even be done upon no mean scale by every college whose resources are at all adequate to the ordinary demands of education.

It may be made the basis for the synthesis now so sadly lacking in university plans. Better than any other discipline, it can be made the meeting point for all degrees: where candidates in every sort may get their liberalizing outlook upon the world of thought and affairs. More worthily than any other can it be made the means of nationalizing the men whom the universities send forth to represent the power and worth of education. In no better way can an American university obtain a distinguishing function in the world.

As a practical means of university reorganization, such a plan would sacrifice nothing of our present academic freedom. The study of the literature and institutions of our stock could be made the common feature of all the schools of a modern university without cutting off any essential part of the separate groups of studies we have been at such pains to develop. It would not prevent, or even embarrass, specialization. It is susceptible of being joined alike to classical studies and to technical training; and it would not be incongruously joined to either. It would serve ideally, besides, as the centre of those compromise and middle courses of study, half way between the classical and the scientific, which the peculiar conditions of the day have constrained the colleges to offer. It would make all courses in a good sense 'liberal' without requiring any wholesale reconsideration of the provisions we have already made to train men for the special tasks of practical life.

The serious practical question is, How are all the men of a university to be made to read English literature widely and intelligently, as this plan presupposes? For it is reading, not set lectures, that will prepare a soil for culture: the inside of books, and not talk about them; though there must be the latter also, to serve as a chart and guide to the reading. The difficulty is not in reality very great. A considerable number of young tutors, serving their novitiate for full university appointments, might easily enough effect an organization of the men that would secure the reading. Taking them in groups of manageable numbers, suggesting the reading of each group, and by frequent interviews and quizzes seeing that it was actually done, explaining and stimulating as best they might by the way, they could not only get the required tasks performed, but relieve them of the hateful appearance of being tasks, and cheer and enrich the whole life of the university.   WOODROW WILSON.

Printed in the New York *Forum* (Sept. 1894), 107-14.

From Cuyler, Morgan & Company[1]

Dear Sir: New York. June 22nd 1894.

We are in receipt of the Charlotte Columbia & Augusta coupon due Jan. 1st '94, & will collect & remit you proceeds of the same together with the proceeds of bond, sold for your account @ 104 3/4 as per enclosed contract, upon receipt of the funds from Baltimore, probably on the 26th inst.[2]

Yours very truly,   per pro Cuyler, Morgan & Co.

D. P. Kingsford

ALS (WP, DLC). Enc.: statement of bond sale in amount of $1,045, dated June 22, 1894.
   [1] A New York brokerage firm, of which Cornelius Cuyler Cuyler, '79, was the senior partner.
   [2] The check was forwarded to Wilson in Cuyler, Morgan & Co., to WW, June 26, 1894, printed and handwritten letter (WP, DLC).

Notes for Three Lectures[1]

I.

Nature of the State and Its Relation to Progress.[2]

INTRODUCTION: *An Age of Science* seems about to give place to *an Age of Right*: for which Science is responsible, inasmuch as it has produced modern social (cities) and industrial conditions.

Revival of Altruism, of public altruism and a public conscience. *Danger* that it may degenerate into *Sentimentalism*, and a relaxation of public order.

Imperative need to examine with the utmost candour and thoroughness *the factors and instruments* we are dealing with; and, above all,

The *NATURE of the STATE*

A State is "A People" independently "organized for Law within a definite Territory." The part of this definition which at present needs emphasis is the "organized for Law." The State can express and realize its life only through the instrumentality of Law. In order to understand the nature of the State, therefore, it is necessary for us to comprehend, first of all, the

Law: Its Character.

Nature and Field of LAW.—whence it arises and what it accomplishes.

To some, Law wears the appearance of being framed and enforced by *the arbitrary will of rulers*; and *there are cases* of the imposition of law for generations together upon cowed subject populations, by a minority established in power by conquest and maintained in power by armed and organized force. But even in such cases the law thus arbitrarily imposed will be found *to penetrate but a very little* way into the daily life of the people,— *unless*, indeed, by degrees and in the long run, *an organic habit of submission* and accommodation has been established. Not dissimilarly, it seems to others an instrumentality of reform: a choice of leading minds.

For Law is an organic product, the result of the association of men with each other, and the consequent institution of certain definite relationships between them.

[1] Prepared for lectures at the third annual session of the School of Applied Ethics sponsored by the Ethical Culture Society at Plymouth, Massachusetts, which Wilson gave on July 13, July 16, and July 17, 1894. Fairly full newspaper accounts of these lectures are printed at July 14 and 17, 1894. [Eds.' note]

[2] There is a WWT partial outline of this lecture in WP, DLC. [Eds.' note]

The associated life out of which the law springs *produces many things,*—natural ties; ties of habit and affection; ties of interest; a developed set of rules of social morality.

Law takes up whatever is in this wise *completed* and rendered universal, made ready to be reduced to a uniform rule of conduct and provided with an invariable compulsive standard or sanction.

It is also itself a modifying force: disciplinary, evolutionary, crystalizing, and *constructive*: definitive.

Law, therefore, is that portion of the established social habit which has gained distinct and formal recognition in the shape of uniform rules backed by the power and authority of Government.

Not necessary to blink the fact, already alluded to, that *this habit may be produced by* forces of *coercion* as well as by forces of freedom.

Law: Its Elements

Historical Nature of Law:—*A product* of Society, not only, put [but] of *Political Society.* It is,—

    1. *A Principle (and Force) of Order and Peace*: for it is

    2. *The Result of Union (association) and Variety,*—ordering the interplay of rival forces, *reconciling and co-ördinating* interests.

Participant and Originative Factors: The family; the individual; the Church; orders and classes; corporations; communes; provinces; States; the Society of States.

Objects of Law: Religion, Justice, Morality, Commerce, Industry, Science, Art.

Law is, thus,

    1. *A body of Principles*, a mirror of prevalent conceptions;

    2. *An Active Force*, involving

    An Ought, for the majority,[3]

    A Must for the minority.

θέμις, *Recht, Jus*: their derivations and significance.

A movement from Status to Contract. The history of Law had been a history of *differentiation and recombination,*— of a conflict of forces and compromise of interests, resulting from *progressive individualization plus varying association,*—new candidates for Rights constantly arising: necessarily, therefore, a movement into the field of contract and accommodation.

---

[3] It will have no moral compulsion unless it conforms to 1., and is really *a mirror of prevalent conceptions.* [WW's note]

The ORGANIC IDEA, nevertheless, *may mislead*: for *not all* of the organic associations of a People are summed up in *the State*. It is the completed and the universalized work of all the non-political forces, the conditions which they have brought into universal recognition, and only these, that can be taken up by the State, and embodied in law.

Properly conceived the *ORGANIC IDEA* is *only this*: That every State is the historical form of the organic common life of a particular people, some form of organic political life being in every instance commanded by the very nature of man. No nation has ever been without an organic common life; nor can any nation ever break the continuity of its organic common life without instantly ceasing to be a nation.

> *The State, therefore, is an abiding natural relationship*: neither a mere convenience nor a mere necessity, neither a mere voluntary association nor any other artificial thing, but *the eternal, natural embodiment and expression of a higher life than the individual*, namely that common life which gives leave to the individual life, and opportunity for completeness
>
> *Each nation has its own State*, i.e., its own form of organic life, its own functional characteristics, *produced by its own development*, expressive of its own character and experience in affairs.

The STATE'S RELATION to PROGRESS:

What is Progress? Civilization has *two elements*:

> (a) *A material element.* It consists in an assured mastery over nature, which, instead of subordinating our strength to hers, is subordinated to our knowledge of her powers and our means of using them.
>
> (b) *An immaterial element*, which consists in an assured and equitable order: a stable system of government and authority, in which law is clearly developed, regularly obeyed, and, as nearly as may be, accommodated to existing needs and conditions.

Its Vehicles are

> *Struggle*, with its discipline;
> *Religion*, with its ideals of duty;
> *Education*, with its enlightenment, and its instruction in means.

Relation of the Masses to Progress, is passive, depending upon the effect wrought by the discipline of life and the enlightenment of education and experience. There cannot be progress without the masses, but they are its material, not its effective cause. Progress works upon them, rather than by means of them.

Relation of the Individual to Progress, may be active, but only so far as he can work upon and school the common thought, and so make institutional change practicable.

How far may LAW be the vehicle of Progress? Only so far as *effort of one kind or another has brought to a common recognition such principles of action as may be universalized in their application, and enforced in the region of actual transaction* between man and man.

Two Questions to be asked of LAW:

1. *As to its Expediency:* Is it suited to its object, to the purposes of its originators? E.g., laws in restraint of public meeting, freedom of opinion, etc.

2. *As to its Justice:* Does it correspond with actual fact (e.g., witchcraft) and with moral truth? For instance, in a case of conviction, (a) Does the act of the accused come within the terms of the law? (b) Does the punishment announced accord with true views as to desert and responsibility?

But note,

The Causal Relationship between Justice and Expediency in the sphere of Law.

Only that is expedient which is just. But this is only another way of saying that *only that is expedient which tallies with prevalent standards of judgment* as to conduct and its responsibilities. Justice and expediency, consequently, have shifting boundaries,—shifting with ethical conceptions and social developments.

The standard cannot be the same for the State as for the individual; for they are not similarly made up. *The State is a complex* of individual forces. *It must depend upon average judgments, and follow a utilitarian Ethic.*

2 *July, 1894.*

II.

The Organs of the State and Its Means of Advancement.

INTRODUCTION: *Danger of confounding the "State,"* i.e., "a people *organized," with Society,* the field of individual initiative and endeavour, and of combination in small groups as contrasted with universal organization for common and general objects.

We may be helped to a vivid perception of the difference by asking the following questions:

Are the People, the whole body of citizens, *an Organ of the State*? Certainly not, for they cannot have *the same purpose at the same time*. Is the environment an organ of the body? Does the force wh. results from a correlation of forces consist of the forces correlated?

Is the Press an "estate of the realm," an organ of the State? No: for the same reason. It is but a number of voices speaking the opinions of a number of (aggregate) persons. *It is not organic.*

Is the Platform an organ of the State? ("The Platform: Its Rise and Progress"!).[4]

A set of closely interrelated and uniformly coöperative organs necessary to organic life: in the State, consultation and a single, united will and purpose. "Public Opinion" is not of organic action or of governing efficacy until it passes through a set of coördinating organs.

ORGANS *of the* STATE:

The LEGISLATURE, is a *Law-making, not* a *Programme-making* organ. It is its function, not to beckon on and originate, so much as to recognize, accept, and formulate the practical judgments of Expediency wh. have emerged to the common view out of the experiences of Society. Legislation consists in *the consultative choice of the rules which shall be universal* in respect of men's dealings with each other.

Natural, and indeed inevitable, *presidency and leadership of the Legislature* wherever there is progress and a deliberate search after better rules of common action.

Law is undoubtedly, in the modern State, the *instrumentality of reform*: but not all change is reform. The fundamental question of legislation is this, *How may power*, the forces which stir and press forward in Society, *be made to serve Permanence. Law is stable equilibrium.* *Fundamental Question of Legislation:*

It is *one of the first duties* of legislators, one of the indispensable maxims of legislation, that *a careful continuity* be observed in the movements of law; that strict faith be kept with the past. *Stable Equilibrium.* *Continuity.*

The vehicles of Progress, as we have seen, are *Struggle, Religion, Education. Legislation is* the means and vehicle of *reconciliation and order*. Hence the principle (by no *Reconciliation.*

4 Henry L. Jephson's book by that title, published in 1892. [Eds.' note]

means confined to our own constitutions) against retro-active laws.

Besides:

While the chief functions of legislation are these of recon-ciliation, completion, discipline, and order, however, *the State has also functions of ministration* of which legisla-tion is of course its primary instrumentality.

The State may, and does, *assist Society*

(1) *Physically,* by *Sanitation, hospital assistance,* the *authentication of physicians, apothecaries,* etc.

(2) *Economically,* by constituting and regulating *Cor-porations;* by *protection* of person and property, not only against the wrongful acts of individuals, but also against the powers of nature (fire, water, etc.); by *public roads, posts, coinage, weights* and measures; by *public works* of various sorts (gas and water works, among the rest); by *poor relief; forestry* and the *protection of game; patents; saving banks; statistics; drainage;* and *breeding.*

(3) *Spiritually,* by *Education* (including public art gal-leries and museums, industrial exhibitions and training schools, and the prosecution of practical research by such institutions as the Smithsonian).

I.e. It is *a convenience as well as a discipline.*

By *the repression of vice.*

By *sumptuary laws* (?).

The EXECUTIVE (or, more properly, *the* ADMINISTRA-TION), like the Courts, is *an organ of discretion and ad-justment.* It is its part to adjust the law to individual and concrete cases.

The real function of the Administrative is not merely ministerial, but *adaptive, guiding, discretionary.* It must accommodate and realize the law in practice. It may, it *must, discriminate.* It *may meet, if not anticipate, ethical judgments,* and apply them, as they cannot be applied in any general rule, such as the legislature frames.

Law vs. Ordinance. E.g., the so-called "McKinley Ad-ministrative Act."[5]

Vital importance of the temper and method of the Ad-ministration in the execution of the ministrant functions mentioned above. This becoming the chief field of ad-ministrative action in the modern State.

The COURTS have functions of *accommodation* comparable

---

[5] That is, the Customs Administrative Act of 1890, which prefaced the Mc-Kinley Tariff Act of that year. The Administrative Act, designed to make enforce-ment of the customs laws more efficient and uniform, established a Board of General Appraisers empowered to determine the classification and appraisal of imports. [Eds.' note]

to those of the Administration, except that they are not exercised upon their own initiative, lie for the most part within the field of Private law, and form no part of a constructive or guiding policy. Their functions made clear under the following heads:

Interpretation. Not only *grammatical* (adhering as nearly as may be to the real meaning of the terms and sentences of the law) *and logical* (reading away inconsistencies, and giving right of way to the dominant purpose or principle of the law), but *also Systematic.* Every law must be interpreted, that is, *with reference to the general principles of the sytem* [system] of law of which it forms a part; with reference to its own individual history, as respects the law supplanted by it, the course of repeal, modification, etc.; with reference to its direct relation to other cognate provisions; etc.

Example: the most fully established contract would be denied enforcement if it involved the performance of an *immoral act*, or of any *malum* elsewhere in the same system of law made *prohibitum.*

The question of Intention of the legislature, and its many delicacies and difficulties.

Constructive Inference, where there is no specific law either customary or statutory which is applicable. *This is the process of analogy*: of putting laws together, for the purpose of getting some so to say *systematic suggestion* as to the filling in of the gap.

Here the courts come upon *the field*, oftentimes, *of the most general principles,*—those fundamental doctrines and conceptions common to all systems, or at any rate natural inferences from the general reasoning of the particular system concerned.

Equity, typified in the functions of the Roman Praetor and the English Chancellor. *An effort to cure the defects of a rigid system*, difficult to alter or to liberalize, *by relaxing its formal requirements and affording substantial relief,*—without, however, doing violence (at any rate, at once or by intention) to the essential principles of the established law.

It has *usually* been *Modes of Redress* and *Rules of Evidence* that have had to *bear the brunt of criticism* and have represented to the lay mind the attude [attitude] of the law towards Society. *But these are merely means of approach* to the principles of the law. They are not themselves the vehicles of its ethical judgments.

The Functions of LEGAL SCIENCE.

Principally (from our present point of view) to make *a practical study of the conditions* of the life of law and of the forces which originate it. It should establish the connections between law and the growth of moral ideas: the development of institutions. *To study law as* at one and the same time *a product and a factor* of social life. *It is thus that we see* what means, and *what means only*, the State possesses of promoting the Advancement of Society.

5 July, 1894

III.

Political Liberty, Political Expediency, and Political Morality in the Democratic State.

INTRODUCTION: The *fundamental error* of conceiving *liberty* to consist of *as little government as possible*, and of "scientific anarchy" as its ideal. This idea is simply a product of the reaction against a system under which a very few persons determined the rights of all,—not against institutions, but against tutelage.

LIBERTY is to be *found only where there is the best order*. The *machine* free that runs with perfect adjustment; the *skein* free that is without tangle; the man free whose powers are without impediment to their best development.

Bondage of the kite and of *the sailing vessel*, held fast by an external force: *freedom of the steamer*, having an originative force in its own bowels. But the kite and the sailing vessel may *also sail "free"* if they be perfectly adjusted to the force that controls them, and use it for the passage they are attempting.

Political Liberty, therefore, is *also an adjustment*: It is *a reasonable accommodation* between individual right and public power: *a properly adjusted balance* between the forces of individual character and public convenience.

"How false is the conception, how frantic the pursuit," *exclaims Ruskin*, "of that treacherous phantom which men call Liberty. . . . There is no such thing in the universe. There can never be. The stars have it not; the earth has it not; the sea has it not; and we men have the mockery and semblance of it only for our heaviest punishment.

"The enthusiast would reply that by Liberty he meant the

Law of Liberty. Then why use the single and misunderstood word? If by liberty you mean chastisement of the passions, discipline of the intellect, subjection of the will; if you mean the fear of inflicting, the shame of committing, a wrong; if you mean respect for all who are in authority, and consideration for all who are in dependence; veneration for the good, mercy to the evil, sympathy with the weak; if you mean watchfulness over all thoughts, temperance in all pleasures, perseverance in all toils; if you mean, in a word, *that Service which is* defined in the liturgy of the English church to be *perfect Freedom*, why do you name this by the same word by which the luxurious mean license, and the reckless mean change; by which the rogue means rapine, and the fool, equality, by which the proud mean anarchy, and the malignant mean violence? Call it by any name rather than this, but *its best and truest* is, *Obedience*. Obedience is, indeed, founded on a kind of freedom, else it would become mere subjugation, but that *freedom is only granted that obedience may be more perfect*; and thus, while a measure of license is necessary *to exhibit the individual energies of things*, the fairness and pleasantness and perfection of them all consist in their Restraint. *Compare a river* that has burst its banks with one that is bound by them, and the *clouds* that are scattered over the face of the whole heaven with those that are marshalled into ranks and orders by its winds. So that though restraint, utter and unrelaxing, can never be comely, this is not because it is in itself an evil, but only because, when too great, it overpowers the nature of the thing restrained, and so counteracts the other laws of which that nature is itself composed. And *the balance wherein consists the fairness of creation* is between the laws of life and being in the things governed and the laws of general sway to which they are subjected; and *the suspension or infringement of either kind of law*, or, literally, disorder, is equivalent to, and synonymous with, *disease*; while the increase of both honour and beauty is habitually on the side of restraint (or the action of superior law) rather than of character (or the action of inherent law). The noblest word in the catalogue of social virtue is 'Loyalty,' and the sweetest which men have learned in the pastures of the wilderness is 'Fold.'

"Nor is this all; but we may observe, that *exactly in proportion to the majesty of things* in the scale of being, is *the completeness of their obedience* to the laws that are set over them. Gravitation is less quietly, less instantly obeyed by a *grain of dust* than it is by the *sun and moon*; and the *ocean* falls and flows under influences which the *lake and river* do not recognize. So also in estimating the dignity of any action or uccupation of men, there is perhaps no better test than the question 'are its laws strait?' For their severity will probably be commensurate with the greatness of the numbers whose labour it concentrates or whose interest it concerns."[6]

In confirmation of this, note *our* instinctive *homage* to *the equable and elevated* in character, demeanour, utterance, —*not the quick* shot, *but the* steady and *crack shot.* The *impotency of irregular force.* The *absence of dignity from an accident.*

We rightly conceive *the highest freedom* to consist in *Self*-government, self-direction, a *self-originated rectitude and adjustment,* a self-sustained order.

Modern Constitutions of Liberty, as contradistinguished from *Constitutions of Government:* The *Differences,*

(1) *In Age,* the deliberate recognition and formulation of liberty being comparatively modern.

(2) *In Character:* Organization vs. Restraint of government. *Negative* statement, accordingly, of the items of privilege. *"Bills of Rights"* are meant, not to keep the hands of government off, but *only to prevent irregular and arbitrary* exertions of power.

(3) *In Source.*

(4) *In distinctness* and sharpness of definition or statement. The *Restraints* exercised upon government *needing* very *much more explicit* statement than the organization of government, wh. may be merely habitual.

The historical contradiction of Socialism, which seeks to give precedence to organization.

A *"constitutional" government,* one which is restrained by the recognition of Liberty: of an adjustment and balance between the freedom of the individual and the authority of the government.

POLITICAL EXPEDIENCY: Whose field is *the field of statesmanship.*

The Law of Progress, in Society, is *the law of Modification:* and this law furnishes *the standard* of Political Expediency.

Modification in the modern Democratic State *means the*

---

[6] From John Ruskin, *Seven Lamps of Architecture,* Chap. 7, Sects. 1-3. [Eds.' note]

adjustment and accommodation of the general opinion and purpose to changing social conditions: —law following after and resulting from such changes, like a chemical precipitation.

Note that in this conception of Progress "the *general opinion*" means the *organic* opinion, the efficient opinion, *formed by the concert and prevalence of commanding minds*, not commanding numbers. Persuaded, not commanding, numbers.

The general opinion
1688
1788
1861
Revolution

Revolution can never be expedient: for it destroys the atmosphere of opinion and purpose which holds institutions in equilibrium.

Revolution *may be necessary as death* is necessary: a death and re-birth: a destruction and reconstitution.

What is expedient Speech? Not that which creates distemper and overheats the judgment; but that which points out the best means of accommodation and of progress by means of accommodation.

POLITICAL MORALITY: *has no other standard than that of Expediency*, as already expounded. *The individual Ethic* is *absolute*, but *the social* Ethic is *utilitarian*.

"*Sin is the transgression of the law*," of the law, that is, *of political progress*.

Morality is the science of relationships, of the best adjustments, on the one hand, of man to God, and, on the other, of man to his fellow men. It is immoral, therefore, to act as if regardless of these relationships. *Progressive morality is an improvement of relationships*, from step to step; and is *always* a *conservative, never* a *radical*, or revolutionary, process.

The LAW OF ENDEAVOUR: is *to create and enlighten social movement.*

The law of instruction, of illumination, whether by action or by speech. *Leadership is necessary* in order to make an effective place in a political system for enlightening speech. Speech must be made sure of a hearing, irrespective of party.

Leadership: constitutional statesmen.

Effective speech comes from a true vision of affairs, such as will appeal to those who know and have their eyes open, as well as to those who simply feel and have their hearts open. When what is seen with such vision is put with the words, the *imaginative and illuminative words*, of insight, and with a feeling for human nature as it is (not as it may become) and a sagacious *appreciation of* the existing *situation*: then it carries: carries reform, and creates morality.

"Slight those who say, amidst their sickly healths,
Thou livest by rule. What doth not so but man?
Houses are built by rule and Commonwealths.
Entice the trusty sun, if that you can,
From his ecliptic line; beckon the sky.
Who lives by rule then, keeps good company.

"Who keeps no guard upon himself is slack,
And rots to nothing at the next great thaw;
Man is a shop of rules: a well-truss'd pack
Whose every parcel underwrites a law.
Lose not thyself, nor give thy humours way;
God gave them to thee under lock and key."

George Herbert.[7]
10 July, 1894.

WWT MSS. with WWhw and WWsh additions (WP, DLC).
[7] From "The Church Porch" in *The Temple*. [Eds.' note]

To Ellen Axson Wilson

My own darling,   New York, 12 July, 1894

I have a few minutes this morning, before my train starts, which I cannot let go without a line to you, to satisfy my heart. My heartstrings have been very tense and painful since I left my sweet home last night. You were so brave in your anxiety, and so generously solicitous to have me go away without any strain of anxiety, that it was almost like an ordinary leave taking. But I knew, nevertheless, how heavy your heart was, and how anxious: and to leave you so made me sad beyond expression. I shall be with you *every minute* in my thoughts, my precious Eileen, loving you and longing for you, thinking *of* you and *for* you, blessing you and *living because of you*, in a way and with an intenseness beyond all expression. I would turn back to you this moment if I could. Do not wait at home till Wednesday because I might come, remember, but get to the shore as soon as possible.[1]
With a heartful of all love,   Your devoted   Woodrow

Love to Stock and dear Maggie[2]

ALS (WC, NjP).
[1] Ellen planned to take the family to Belmar on the New Jersey shore. Wilson had to go to Colorado Springs, Colorado, for another series of lectures immediately after completion of his lectures in Plymouth. Ellen did not heed his

advice about leaving at once for the shore. She remained in Princeton and saw her husband between his return to Princeton on July 18 and his departure for the West on the following day.

2 Ellen's sister, Margaret Axson, was spending the summer with the Wilsons.

From Ellen Axson Wilson

Princeton, N.J. Friday
My own darling,   [Thursday, July 12, 1894]

I have a very good report to make today! At eight o'clock Maggie had less than 101 degrees of fever, at nine the same, and at two, —a short time ago,—so far from having risen as usual, it was but a fraction over 99°! I begin to hope we may break it up promptly after all. She is perfectly comfortable still & has eaten some broth. So you see you must not be uneasy about us at all. I am perfectly well & in excellent spirits.

I really have scarcely a moment to write though for this is Annie's[1] day out, and besides Maggie is not sleeping as she did before, so I feel that I must stay with her most of the time, read to her &c., & keep her from feeling lonely and possibly homesick. We are all well.

Your letter has just been received, giving me a delightful surprise. I am *so* glad to be able to relieve your anxiety, dearest!

Ah I love you my darling more than words can tell,—with all my heart I am,   Your own   Eileen.

ALS (WC, NjP).
1 Presumably a new nursemaid.

To Ellen Axson Wilson

My own darling,   Hotel Pilgrim, Plymouth, Mass., 13 July, 1894

I arrived here all right last night, after a most tedious but not unamusing journey. How diverting New England is—and how unlike the United States! I have a comfortable room, looking right out on the water: the "historic spot" is right under my eyes, and is most interesting. This morning, 10:40 to 11:40, I delivered my first lecture, with some confidence, and with sufficient success: *that* is over! The other two come at the same time on Monday and Tuesday. By that time you will be at Belmar (by the way, give me the exact address there): For my comfort is completed by your letter, just received. Oh, how relieved I am, and how happy! Such a good—such a wonderfully good report! I have no words in which to say how thankful and how happy I am! And then the assurance that you are perfectly well [and] love me! I know perfectly well that you love me—have I not had proofs

enough of it to make a man proud for a life time and happy beyond disturbance? And yet every word of love you speak or write
is as precious to me as if it revealed your heart to me for the first
time. It gives me a new thrill of *life*. Ah, my sweet one, you are
all the world to me!

I am quite well, and shall continue so, I feel sure, so long as
all goes well with you.

Lots of love to dear Maggie, Stock, and the chicks, and for yourself, the whole heart of   Your own   Woodrow

ALS (WC, NjP).

A Newspaper Report of a Speech

AT THE SCHOOL OF ETHICS.

Plymouth, July 14, 1894.

As the lectures go on at the Plymouth School it becomes more
and more evident that their coordination is the happiest feature
of this year's session. Nothing is remote from the one aim of enlightening the subject of the labor troubles of the day, and in the
light of this aim even such details as those of ancient life, which
in the Old Testament have so generally seemed dry and unprofita-
ble, become luminous with new interest.[1] Over one hundred
tickets have been sold, more than half of which have been for
the whole course; and this, together with the fact that the attendance has been almost entirely that of visitors rather than
residents in Plymouth, shows that the value of the session is being appreciated. The high-school hall is a great improvement over
last year's meeting place, the light and ventilation and seats giving comfort and pleasure in listening even during the hot days. . . .

In the department of ethics Professor Wilson of Princeton gave
his first lecture on Friday. He spoke with brightness and rapid
interest of the nature of the state and its relation to progress.
Administration was an organ of adjustment, a housekeeping process, the application of general purpose to special cases. We cannot follow the English idea of principles which take no account
of exceptions. Law cannot be the same for a lunatic as for the
majority because law presupposes freedom of choice. Sending
bouquets and canary birds to penitentiaries is wrong, because the
pity is based on the idea that men could n't help being there. The
state is organized not for philanthropy but for making general
rules and administering them. Law is not arbitrary choice by
rules or rulers or legislators, but an organic product coming
from within a people. Much comes which cannot be so general

as to be cast into the form of law, such as rules of etiquette, the ties of affection stronger than steel, without which a man is an enemy to society (a bachelor being "an amateur in life"), ties of interest and business—these cannot be made uniform. Political interests being those which affect everybody in the same way, law becomes a principle of peace. The law must be enforced, but if as many bayonets are needed as there are individuals it ceases to be law. It is at once a product of union and variety. It must mirror general convictions or it can't be obligatory or strong. That which is for the minority a *must*, becomes for the majority an *ought*. It is a union of the Greek idea of divine suggestion with the German idea of rectitude, and the Roman idea of justice, or a yoke binding together, the nexus of society. The lecturer criticized the present tendency to regard the state as an organism when it is only like one. The state is not a body. It can be separated as the body cannot. It need not do everything through one instrumentality as the body essentially does. Hence the Socialistic idea which straps every man into his place cannot be admitted; nor is individual life higher than the social life. Robinson Crusoe lost his liberty the moment he was alone in bondage to nature. Society is the means by which we realize our highest faculties. Society makes men of us. The relation of the State to progress is that it makes man a political being; it is a civil-making [process]. On its material side, progress is an increasing command over nature, and on its spiritual side, civilization consists in an assured and equitable order. We ask of law: First, that it be true. Witchcraft did exist as a universal conviction, hence law against it was for the time true. Second, that it be convenient. Speeches may be iniquitous, but if they are shut up, will do more harm in bursting their bottle. Lincoln observed this when he told about an opponent who lifted up his eyes and opened his mouth and left the consequences to God. The standard of law is not absolute right and wrong, but general conviction. . . .

Printed in the *Boston Evening Transcript*, July 16, 1894; some editorial headings omitted.

1 The central theme of the Ethical Culture Society's session of 1894 at Plymouth was the labor problem, and the lecturers included, in addition to Wilson and others, Professor Henry Carter Adams of the University of Michigan, President Elisha Benjamin Andrews of Brown, Professor John Bates Clark of Amherst, Professor Franklin Henry Giddings of Bryn Mawr, who was about to go to Columbia, Professor Richmond Mayo-Smith of Columbia, Dr. Elgin Ralston Lovell Gould of the Johns Hopkins, and Professor Jeremiah Whipple Jenks of Cornell; and—from the ranks of the theologians—Professor Henry Sylvester Nash of the Episcopal Theological School, Cambridge, Massachusetts, and Crawford Howell Toy, Hancock Professor of Hebrew at Harvard.

To Ellen Axson Wilson

My own darling,   Plymouth, Mass., 14 July, 1894

Your letter has not come yet: but I have no doubt it will come very soon. I wont wait for it to come before writing my own for fear of being cut out of a mail: for "Hotel Pilgrim" is three miles and a half from the Post Office, and letters can be sent in only at certain times.

This afternoon I shall go to Boston, not to see anyone, for everyone will, I take it for granted, be out of town "over Sunday,"—but because I can go by boat, and follow the coast Miles Standish followed when he felt his way around into Boston harbour. The trip will take four hours—3 to 7, and I shall return tomorrow morning, probably. I have found some old acquaintances here—and of course made a few new ones: but it is emphatically a New England crowd, and very hard to feel at home with. The lecture audience is most interesting—full of faces that it is a pleasure to dwell upon—so full are they of the records of character and thought. The majority are women; but not a large majority: there are also many men (the total number of the audience being, probably, about 110). The women's faces are, on the whole, the more interesting: at any rate, there are more interesting faces among the women than among the men. I feel sure, as I look at the audience, that the average of intelligence among them is perhaps higher than in any other audience I ever spoke to—at least the sort of *prepared* intelligence needed for such lectures as they have gathered to hear—and of course that is very inspiring.[1]

We had a land breeze yesterday and were very uncomfortable; but the wind has got around to-day and we are much happier. I am quite well, as usual. I love you with a passion that is consuming. I admire you and delight in you with an ardour that is unspeakable. I am altogether,   Your own   Woodrow

Love without stint to Stock., Maggie, and the precious chickens.

ALS (WC, NjP).
[1] A contemporary reporter confirmed Wilson's observation, as follows: "The school has made a definite place for itself. It is not the picnic, piano-in-the-parlor summer school, neither is it the summer repetition of a college course. It is rather . . . a meeting-place for scholars. Students are in attendance from Harvard, Cornell, Wellesley, Vassar, University of Georgia and other colleges, and several clergymen and teachers are present. . . . The aim is that here all the sciences of conduct may be assembled that they may act and react on one another, that a new group of studies may be created, and that this hegemonic idea may strike root and be transplanted. Incidentally the school is an inter-collegiate institution and gathers men of active professional pursuits, offering a summary of the latest results of science and providing its hearers with the most recent bibliography. Thinkers who are also workers and workers who are also thinkers are gathered together for conference as well as instruction, so that it is not too much to say that here may grow a monument to the Pilgrims and

what they stand for, and that hither may come a new race of pilgrims—pilgrims from all over the country, to be baptized in the spirit of the fathers of the republic." *Boston Evening Transcript*, July 13, 1894.

From Ellen Axson Wilson

My own darling   Princeton, N.J. Friday [July 14, 1894]

I feel as though I am treating you very badly to put you off with such wretched little notes, yet somehow I have not been able to find any quiet moments to myself for writing today; tonight it is so intolerably hot indoors by a lamp that I feel forced to be brief. It is, they say, the hottest day of the season. I am not at all exhausted by it however and am in excellent spirits in spite of it because Maggie is doing so finely. She has been *free* from fever all day! Isn't that good? The doctor says it is a treacherous thing and we cannot be sure yet that it is broken up, but that it does look as if it were.

I think I will plan to leave when you do next week. Stock of course is free to go now whenever he wishes, but I don't believe he cares much to be in the city in this weather. We are all well. There has been no mail of consequence.

And now good-night, dear, and God bless you. I love you with all my heart and with all my thoughts. As ever

Your devoted   Eileen

ALS (WC, NjP).

To Ellen Axson Wilson

My own darling,   Young's Hotel, Boston, 15 July 1894

I did not come to Boston by boat, after all. It was storming, and I thought it best to come by rail. But I go back by boat this morning, the weather being all that could be desired. Last night I went to a light opera, "The Mikado,"[1] and you must remind me, when I get home, to tell you about the performance. Some very interesting things happened: but the whole interest was in particulars which it would take all morning to tell with a pen.[2]

I am taking things in a vacation spirit. I could be surer, a little bit, of my spirits, if I had gotten a second letter from you before leaving: but, even as it is, I am having a good time—somewhat deliberately, it may be, but none the less really. It is such a comfort to carry my love for you with me everywhere—oh, if I could only carry you yourself! I do, in one sense. I seem to have a vivid realization of you all the time: so that whatever I enjoy I enjoy *as if* you were with me—and with a very keen sense of dependence on you. I could not enjoy it half so much—I could not enjoy it at all—if I did not have you to think about, as a sort of standard and completion of it all. Ah, my queen, you are, in a sense fairly *literal, all the world to me*: for me, all the world is ruled by thoughts of you—and in all that I do, as in all that I am, I am

Your own   Woodrow

Love unbounded to Stock, Maggie, and our precious little girls.

ALS (WC, NjP).
1 Presented by a company of actors under the leadership of John and Marion Mason at the Park Theatre in Boston.
2 Wilson was referring to the following events: Shortly before the matinee performance of "The Mikado" was scheduled to begin on July 14, the Masons were arrested on a bad debt charge. (They had attempted to pawn jewelry in Boston on which money was still owed to a New York jeweler, and the jeweler had come to Boston and requested their arrest.) The Masons were released on $2,000 bail after a hearing and began the matinee half an hour late. At the evening performance, Mason made a speech "in which he thanked the public for its appreciation, and said that in the afternoon, for the first time in his life, he had nearly failed to keep an appointment, and thanks were due to his lawyer, his backers and his brother that he was able to return to the theatre and sing his part." *Boston Daily Advertiser*, July 15, 1894.

From Ellen Axson Wilson

My own darling,   Princeton, N.J. Sunday [July 15, 1894]

Your Friday note reached me yesterday,—and was altogether welcome, with its account of pleasant environment and the successful lecture;—I am *so* glad, dearest, that you are enjoying yourself.

We are *all* well and happy. For Maggie too is practically herself again,—has had no fever now for three days and a half, was down and out today. We *could* go to the beach tomorrow but we won't go until Thursday, not only because we want to see you but because I couldn't think of going with a bag of soiled clothes to be 'done up' at the usual fancy rates prevailing at summer resorts. So we confidantly expect to see you this week here, let me know just when you will arrive. It is still intensely hot but I am not used up by it,—only frightfully lazy,—which is my only good excuse for not sending you a long letter today as I intended. It seemed impossible to leave the trees—where life was really quite endurable, —& come in and write. I was just beginning tonight when Stock asked me to let him read his "Hamlet."[1] Of course I consented & now it is half past ten & he is waiting to mail this,—so I must close abruptly.

His "Hamlet" is I think quite good by the way,—(it is not finished yet,) entirely clear and well expressed in spite of some subtilty in the thought. I have been extremely sorry for him,— trying to work in such weather.

Good-night, dear love,—believe me, darling, I love you as much as you wish to be loved and am altogether

Your own   Eileen

ALS (WC, NjP).
  [1] Stockton Axson's purpose in preparing this essay is unknown.

To Ellen Axson Wilson

My own darling,   Plymouth, Mass., 16 July, 1894

Your second letter, with its delightful news of Maggie's freedom from fever, reached me this morning. I must have 'spent Sunday' somewhere. Ah, how it does relieve me; and yet how desperately lonely I am without you! I have made some delightful acquaintances,—almost friends,—here, among them at least one woman who is altogether delightful;[1] I have nothing to complain of, and everything to make me glad I came; but, ah me! nothing ever compensates me for my loss of you. I long for you, —for the sweet companionship I have grown strong and happy on,—all the time: and nothing wholly comforts me—or can.

My second lecture 'came off' this morning—with reasonable success. I was not feeling in perfect form, because of a slight disturbance of my bowels, due no doubt to *clam broth*, and I am afraid it was evident I laboured a little. But, no matter: the audience seemed well enough pleased

I came back from Boston by boat, as I planned to do, and, though the boat was both crowded and very slow, I enjoyed the four and a half hours very much indeed, seeing the coast well enough, in spite of a slight haze, and getting a very keen imaginative appreciation of certain historical events.

It's astonishing, by the way, what a self-conscious little town this is: it is rather spoiled by it, indeed.

Love to all the dear ones, and for yourself, the unbounded, unspeakable admiration and love of

Your own   Woodrow

ALS (WP, DLC).
  [1] She was, undoubtedly, Nancy Saunders (Mrs. Crawford Howe) Toy, wife of the Hancock Professor of Hebrew at Harvard, who was also lecturing at the School of Applied Ethics.

A Newspaper Report of Two Speeches

AT THE SCHOOL OF ETHICS.

Plymouth, July 17, 1894.

Professor Wilson's visit has been the special feature of these first days. His agile mind and wit have lighted the subjects he has treated, and the sanity and depth of his opinions have given them special power. Yesterday and today he has been speaking of the organs of the state and its means of advancement, and of polical [political] liberty, political expediency and political morality in the democratic state. At the outset he opposed the notion that the state and society were interchangeable terms, that the difference was not one of kind but of degree, so that no function in itself was foreign to the state. People who think they represent society confound the two, but the truth is that no company of persons, no party or press represents society. The bulk is not thoughtful, society does not think save through all those who represent greater or less portions of it.

Only those specially trained to think can think with open mind in the spirit of John Robinson;[1] most thought is habitual in formulae furnished. It is an error to think of the people as an organ of the state, because no man living can say what is the mandate of the people. Witness the variety of opinion as to what the people said in the last election. To speak literally of the government of the people is to use a kind of metaphysics confounding to the intellect. We cannot conceive of a sovereignty that is inaudible and indefinable. It is easy to lose everything in a weak analysis. The press consists of organs but it is not an organ. It is an absurdity, the title of a book called "The Platform—Its Rise and Progress," as if one could see a platform ranging about. Morrison Swift[2] is simply *his* voice of the state though he claims to be *the* voice of the state. And others may learn by the same rule. The state consists of concerted thought and coöperative action through common convictions. The only organs of the state are the legislature, the court and the executive. The legislature is not a programme-making but a law-making power. You must convert the people to a programme before it can be made a law, and it is for the people that legislation is conducted, not by philosophers.

The fundamental problem is how power may be made to serve permanency—just as in the effort to be better, men must not be fools in the process; so, to reconstruct the state we can't take it down, we must do it gradually and have something to live in while the house is remodelled. The elements of permanence are:

1. Continuity—faith in the past; it is folly and bad morals to sweep

away a system, even though a new one may be the goal of effort.
2. Reconciliation: in Burke's phrase we can't use force first and
reconciliation afterward. People must get used to differences of
opinion, and not get nervous about struggles since these are constituent progress. Free organization is safe, and the wall which
extreme opinions must meet is sufficiently fatal to allow us to
refrain from making it more painful for them. 3. Religious conviction. No man of power but is a man of faith. The pure agnostic
need not be feared. He makes himself safer than we could make
him. Agnosticism is in its nature innocuous. 4. Education. By
these things we carry the race surely forward. The legislative and
administrative functions are to be distinguished. Administration
may take cognizance of ethical differences, render or withhold
punishment on the basis of justice. Equity means elasticity, and
originally meant the accommodation of law to unforseen cases so
as to give every man substantial justice.

Here is where the legislature and court come into contact,
where the State learns. Hence legislation must be guided by administration, for it is sad folly to put through a mere grogramme
[programme] as if it were a law. Government must be adjusted
to those experiences which can be obtained only by the experi-
encing part of government.[3] Today the subject of political liberty
was discussed and its foundation in obedience illustrated. The
idea that liberty consists of as little government as possible was
a mistake. Liberty consists in the best mode of restraint, that
which frees what is best in men. Perfect adjustment is the means
of ease of movement. Men are never so free as in serving good
purposes. There is no dignity about an accident; it is either tragical or ridiculous. Expertness consists in a state of mind, a consciousness that you know growing out of subjection to the thing
to be known. Ruskin's rhetoric in the "Lamp of Obedience" is
sound truth. We are to "compare a river which has burst its banks
with one that is bound by them" to gain a true notion of obedience.
Of this liberty adjustment is the only test. Organization of government realizes liberty in those respects in which it restrains.
Deprivation of life-liberty and property is forbidden under one
exception, that it be under due process of law. There is a science
of accommodation, and political liberty must be realized from its
origin in reactions through the frontiers determined by Government, and through the law of expediency. It is immoral to break
the law of practicability. Professor Wilson ended by quoting
Herberts's poem containing the lines—

"Man is a shop of rules, a well-trussed pack
Whose every parcel underwrites a law." . . .

Printed in the *Boston Evening Transcript*, July 18, 1894; some editorial headings omitted.

¹ Pastor of the Pilgrim congregation at Leyden.

² Morrison Isaac Swift of San Francisco, anarchist, socialist, and prolific pamphleteer.

³ The *Boston Daily Globe*, July 17, 1894, gave the following additional report: "In his second lecture Prof Wilson discussed 'The Organs of the State in Relation to Progress.' 'Although a free trader,' said the speaker, 'I should deem it not merely inexpedient but immoral to sweep away at once all protection, because of the enterprises undertaken in the past on the supposition that such protection was to be guaranteed.' "

To Ellen Axson Wilson

Broad St. Station, Phila.

My own darling,   Thursday 11:20 AM [July 19, 1894]

I am so intensely, so *painfully* ashamed of myself, for leaving you with your [baggage] checks in my own pocket. I hope you understood my telegram.¹ The agent at Princeton telegraphed to the agent at Belmar to let you have the trunks upon identifying them. He was to forward the checks himself, to their agent at B., so that you have no more to do with *them*. How it cuts me to the quick to think of causing you inconvenience and anxiety by my own unspeakable stupidity! I love you—oh I love you. I am well—though worried. Forgive me and love me. The house is all right. My train goes in a few minutes. With all my being

Your own   Woodrow

ALS (WC, NjP).
¹ It is missing.

Four Letters from Ellen Axson Wilson

My own darling,   [Belmar, N.J.] Friday [July 20, 1894]

Your sweet little note is just at hand. Am *so* sorry you were worried about the checks. The idea of asking me to "forgive" you! —as if it was not as much or more my fault. I was scarcely worried at all. I had one moment of panic & then I reflected that I could almost certainly get them by identifying & unlocking them; —but they did not even make me do the latter. Dr. Purves very kindly met me and we had the trunks sent up at once.

We are very comfortable here. The children have a large room facing the ocean. Ours is quite small but a corner one so there is a fine breeze through. I have a fine view of the ocean from the side window. Table is very good & the house neatly kept. It is really quite a nice place; of course not like dear old Sagg¹—much more commonplace; but after all it *is* nice to be so close to the water, & I think it is *much* better to come here than there for a short time. It seems it is hot every morning until eleven but then the sea-breeze comes & it is delightful. It is ten minutes of eleven now & it is just beginning.

I meant to write a long letter but it is *impossible* with this (so-called) ink; will get some this afternoon & try and do better to-morrow.

Ah *darling how* I love you. It seems to me my heart is fairly melting with love for you. I am homesick for you my own Wood-row, my life, my all! With all *my* being,

Your own   Eileen

I have a little room for Ed next to mine—ten dollars a week

ALS (WP, DLC).
¹ That is Sagaponack, near Bridgehampton, Long Island, where the Wilsons had vacationed in earlier years.

My own darling,   [Belmar, N.J.] July 21 1894.

How I wonder where you are now, how things are going with you and when I can get a telegram, at least!—not before Monday I fear! I wish *that* Colorado were as accessible as *this*. By the way, I have discovered why it is called "Colorado,"—it was the Colorado state building at the Centennial;—afterwards taken down and brought here. Another of the hotels had the same history. It is very cool today even now at nine in the morning so I think there must have been a cool change inland.

The children are supremely happy—Maggie remarks at frequent intervals "Sister, *isn't* it *lovely* here!" I am enjoying it too in spite of Mrs. Purves who certainly is wearing, but I am already learn-ing how to avoid her in the most natural manner by keeping dif-ferent hours. She is busy for hours every day in her room dressing and undressing her children. They dress completely three times a day!

It seems she has been exercising herself about my coming in a manner equally foolish and kind-hearted. Another very bright woman has been giving me a most comical account of it,—of course before Mrs. Purves; poking good-natured fun at her. It seems she wrote letter after letter to me and tore them up, fearing they misrepresented in some way, reading them to this lady to see if she thought them all right, interviewing the landlady again & again about a new bed &c. &c., superintending the cleaning of the rooms herself, and finally buying, and making, herself a cur-tain for my room. She was in a perfect fever of anxiety for fear I shouldn't be pleased, and she would be "responsible." She told

Mrs. Moses with infinite relief night before last that "Mrs. Wilson was delighted with every thing";—then added with a sudden return of terror "Oh, if I could only be sure it would last!" Mrs. M's last words to me that night were "Well, goodnight, may you find your bed all we have hoped!"—Poor thing, I was greatly touched by her would-be kindness,—though naturally a little bored too at having such a "to-do" made over me.

I feel an infinite pity for both Dr. and Mrs. Purves and what seems to me the steadily accumulating tragedy of their lives. She is intensely worried about his health—and I fear with reason. The work and especially the worry of the last years have begun to tell on him sadly. He is suffering from insomnia and great nervousness and depression of spirits. And what do you think he said to her yesterday morning;—she was making some plan for next fall, when he suddenly said "I don't know whether you will have me with you that long." "George," she cried, "what *do* you mean!" "Oh, I don't know," he said, ["]but I feel dreadfully."[1] Of course she had to tell some one—probably *everyone*—about it, but five minutes after she had told me, crying bitterly, she veered off as usual to her servants & spent an hour giving details of their quarrels with each other! Poor thing, in a certain sense she is no more "responsible" than Mrs. West[2] and that is what makes the situation so hopeless.

Somehow all this fills me with an infinite tenderness for *you*, my *darling*,—and remorse that I have so often suffered you to be worried about little things. I feel that I have taken very poor care of you, my priceless treasure,—and I *am* altogether "responsible." Oh for the "great heart-word["] that would tell you, Woodrow, with what a passion of love my heart is overflowing. I would gladly *die* for you,—I pray God that I may *live* for you to better purpose.

With all my heart & soul & mind believe me dear

Your little wife   Eileen

Love to the family.[3]

ALS (WP, DLC).

[1] He was probably suffering from the diabetes from which he died in 1901.

[2] Mrs. Andrew Fleming West, who had been suffering from mental illness since the birth of her son, Randolph, on August 7, 1890.

[3] Wilson was to stay in Colorado Springs with his first cousin, Harriet Woodrow Welles, and her husband, Edward Freeman Welles, a mining and stock broker.

My own darling,   [Belmar, N. J.] July 22 1894

It is hard to believe the above date is the correct one today so cold is it. We have on thick flannels and are shivery at that. We had quite a storm last night[,] at least so people say,—I slept through it! The sky is still lowering and the sea grey and storm-swept. I have never seen such high waves before and I am glad to have the opportunity,—though I shall be still more glad to see again blue sky and bluer sea. We had a glorious day yesterday, it was perfect on the beach. I lay basking on the sand most of the morning after writing to you. Early in the afternoon Ed came: he said he left it 78° in New York! I am afraid you have had a very hot journey. Ah, how impatient I am getting for that telegram. The children, including Maggie are quite well. Margaret was slightly "upset" yesterday but seems all right today,—now it is my turn,—nothing of consequence however. The water—a strong iron —is said to affect everyone when they first come.

There is a very nice woman here from Reading who knows the Hibben's, &c.—she *was* from Chambersburg.[1] She also knows Mr. [Albert] Shaw's wife[2] very well. (She was a Reading girl it seems.) The town seems to have been very much astonished that "the poor little thing" should have made such a fine match,— especially that she should have married a literary man. She is an insignificant, uneducated little person with a vulgar Mama —divorced from her husband. But she is said to have a sweet disposition. I trust she has sense & tact too, it seems to me Mr. Shaw's wife would need to be well endowed with those us[e]ful articles. I wonder if the marriage was all accident or if he really "looked below the surface" and discovered various fine qualities which the community failed to perceive beneath her insignificant exterior.

By the way, I had a letter from Jessie Brower yesterday,[3] and she insists upon your making her a visit on your way back,— says she will never forgive you if you don't. Perhaps you had better spend a few hours!—a *most* unselfish suggestion for me to make— that last! for I am already so homesick for you that I can hardly endure it! Of course it will be better when the letters begin to come; even the telegram will be a great help. Oh, you *darling*! I love you so that it *hurts*! My heart fairly yearns over you—my Woodrow, my own, my incomparable one! What would I not give to clasp you close, close in my arms *now*!

But I must not indulge too much in such longing—you are too far away. May God bless you, dear heart, & bring you safely back to   Your own   Eileen.

ALS (WC, NjP).
¹ That is, the "nice woman," not Jenny Davidson (Mrs. John Grier) Hibben, who came from Elizabeth, N. J.
² The former Elizabeth L. Bacon of Reading, Pa.
³ It is missing.

My own darling,   [Belmar, N. J.] July 23/94

At last the telegram[1] has arrived and I feel immensely better! —*so* glad and thankful to know that my darling is safe and well.

Things are looking brighter here too; it seemed as stormy as ever when we rose, but now at nine it is already beginning to clear & to grow warmer. Perhaps by eleven the children may be able to bathe after all—though I think I will wait 'till tomorrow. They were counting on beginning today and I am sorry for their disappointment. However they are very happy just now over some toy balloons,—the first they have ever had,—and perhaps that is joy enough for one day. I am over my little trouble of yesterday,— so all is now well with the whole party.

I am having a good time reading the "Herodotus";—am bored that I did not bring the second vol. for I am already nearing the end of the first. Shall have any number of good stories to tell you from him,—if I can remember them so long! Am also enjoying the "Homer" (Lang's)[2] very much,—quite an appropriate thing to read by "the loud-sounding sea."

All the children send love and kisses to Papa, and I send "more of both than anybody knows"—even *you* perhaps! Oh I love you, *love you, love* you, Woodrow my darling, and I am in every heart-throb   Your own   Eileen

ALS (WC, NjP).
  [1] It is missing.
  [2] *The Iliad of Homer*, translated by Andrew Lang *et al.* (London, 1883).

To Ellen Axson Wilson

My own precious darling,   Colorado Springs, 23 July, 1894

How far, how terribly far away from you I am,—and yet how very, very near! I could not be nearer if you were locked fast in my arms. Somehow the intensity of my feeling for you seems to increase with the distance: or, rather,—for this, I think, is the truth of the matter—it increases with the variety of my experiences. Every new country I see, and every new community, makes me love my own sweet home and admire my matchless little wife so much the more. It is just your matchlessness that *excites* me to love you more and more. You are not a *type*. I don't see anyone who reminds me of you. I have not married the sweetest of her kind, but one sweet after her own kind, and inimitable. To have married a woman who was simply the perfection of a certain type would be to have married a sort of *generalized* woman, and to be constantly exposed to the chance of meeting some other woman of the same type to whom one might almost as well be married. But you are like nobody but yourself. You suggest no other woman, and no other woman suggests you. Nobody else, accordingly, could possibly excite in me emotions at all like those you excite. You are my own incomparable queen: you can never so much as come into comparison with any[one] else,—and my love for you exceeds all bounds!

I have been most affectionately received here, and have a *very* comfortable room. As I sit, I have only to lift my eyes to look up to Pike's Peak and these singular mountains. I cannot describe this country yet: it is too unlike anything I ever saw before—and too unlike what I expected to see. Neither my impressions nor my vocabulary have adjusted themselves. I am both disappointed and strangely impressed. I am more than a mile higher than you are (6000 ft.) and the peak in front of me is some 9000 ft. higher still; and I breathe an air very different from any I ever breathed before: one seems to have to breathe *a little more.*

I am to lecture[1] in the *evenings,* it seems—Mondays, Wednesdays, and Fridays—just about the time that you go to bed!—for when it is ten with you it is only eight here.

I must set to now—while uninterrupted—and begin my preparation for this evening. Oh, how I love and long for you, my Eileen!

Your own   Woodrow

ALS (WC, NjP).

[1] Wilson was lecturing, along with Hamlin Garland, among others, at the third annual Summer School of Colorado College. Wilson gave six lectures between July 23 and August 3, repeating substantially the lectures he had given at the Brooklyn Institute of Arts and Sciences in November and December 1893 and using the notes printed at November 15, 1893. Brief reports and announcements of his lectures appeared in the *Colorado Springs Gazette*, July 24, 25, 27, 28, and 29, and August 1 and 2, 1894.

A News Item

[July 24, 1894]

Dr. Woodrow Wilson at the Summer School.

If all of Dr. Wilson's lectures can be judged by his first, his course in the Summer School will be one of more than usual attractiveness.

Dr. Wilson is a man of very prepossessing manners upon the platform, an extremely pleasant speaker, and best of all has something to say. His subject last evening was "What is Constitutional Government?" and he discussed the subject in a very able manner and in a style entirely his own.

The next lecture of his course will be given in the College chapel on Wednesday evening at 8 o'clock on the subject "Political Liberty: What it is and Whence we Have Derived it."

Printed in the *Colorado Springs Gazette*, July 24, 1894.

From Ellen Axson Wilson

My own darling,   [Belmar, N.J.] Tuesday [July 24, 1894]

I am late about writing today & must make great haste to avoid missing the mail. The fact is I am in some trouble, though it is nothing serious. The children all have dirrhoeah again (!)— how *do* you spell it?—and except Margaret, who has but a slight touch of it, are worse than at first. Jessie and Nellie are vomiting too & Nellie has fever, which decided me to send this morning for the doctor. I think it will be soon controlled now that they have medecine & are on milk and lime water diet. But I have about decided to go home on Thursday if Nellie is well enough. I can't reconcile myself to wasting money staying here when it is doing them harm rather than good. If we were here for the summer they might reap some benefit after they had succeeding in getting acclimated, but since our stay is to be short in any event, it seems to me the shorter the better. Am only sorry to take Maggie away for it seems to suit her perfectly. She is looking much better. None of them have had a bath yet for the cold weather & the rain continued yesterday after all. But it really is clearing & getting warmer today, so I hope we will have one or two baths at least before we go.

Don't be worried about them, darling;—it is not *at all* serious; only it seems better by going away to get rid at once of the exciting cause of the trouble.

There is no mail of consequence for you yet.

Remember me kindly to the family.

I love you, Woodrow, dearest, devotedly, *passionately*—I am always & altogether   Your own   Eileen.

ALS (WP, DLC).

To Ellen Axson Wilson

My sweet, sweet love,   Colorado Springs, 24 July, 1894

The first lecture of the course was delivered last night to an audience of about sixty persons, who seemed to enjoy it as much as so small an audience could. The attendance on the School, it seems, is smaller than was expected, on account of the interruption of travel occasioned by the strikes[1]—and the people of the "Springs" do not affect lectures of the serious kind. I have received an invitation from a lady representing "about two hundred women of Denver, representing those most prominent in art, literature, politics, and society," to deliver "one or more" of my lectures in that city.² I don't know whether to accept or not. Women, you know, have the franchise in this State, and I am a bit shy of figuring 'under the auspices' of this Club. Still, I want to see the city of Denver. But *what* lecture?

To-day I go out to lunch with the Slocums (Mr. Slocum is President of the College),³ and this evening to a reception. These are the penalties of a visit to a strange place. This morning Hattie and I rode out into one of the cañons, and saw sights which I must certainly try to describe to you when I can. They are too much for me as yet.

I received your first letter yesterday, my darling. How sweet a letter it is—and how sweet a refreshment it brought me. My darling, my darling—my queen: how passionately I love you: how my whole life centres in you! Hattie sends her love to you and the chickens. Kiss them all for me, and keep for yourself all the love of all my nature for my matchless little wife!

Your own   Woodrow

ALS (WC, NjP).

¹ The great railroad strike of 1894, which began with a strike by the employees of the Pullman Palace Car Company of Chicago and spread throughout the Middle West and Far West after the American Railway Union under Eugene V. Debs boycotted all trains which pulled Pullman cars.

² Probably from a Mrs. Platt, president of the Women's Club of Denver, whose letter is missing. As the documents will soon reveal, Wilson spoke to the Women's Club on July 31 on "The Origin and Derivation of Our Political Liberty."

³ The Rev. Dr. William Frederick Slocum, President of Colorado College, 1888-1917.

From Ellen Axson Wilson

My own darling,   Belmar [N. J.], July 25 [1894]

The children are better today on the whole so that the doctor says they will be able to travel tomorrow. None of them have fever today though they were *all* vomiting again early this morning, and Margaret, who seemed nearly well yesterday, was suffering a good deal of pain. But the other trouble is partially checked and they all seem *quite* bright this afternoon (3 P.M.) We shall leave tomorrow at 12.40, reach Princeton about three. I wrote to Annie yesterday to be there; my only trouble in the matter is Mrs. Purves who, of course, makes a high tragedy of the whole affair. I shall leave Maggie and Ed until Sat. afternoon when his week ends, for it is doing her the *greatest* good and I want her to have a few more baths. She has had but one so far, thanks to the weather: but it—the said weather—is *perfect* now.

I shall have time to get your first letter before I leave tomorrow and oh how eager I am for it! It seems scarcely possible that it is not yet a week since I saw you. Nearly a third of the time has gone anyhow,—in four more days it will be half—and that is always a great point gained!

I had the most extraordinary dreams last night,—thanks to Greek history;—I had turned Amazon and was hewing down my enemies on all sides,—enjoying it hugely, too,—filled with

"the stern joy that warriors feel
In foemen worthy of their steel!"[1]

I imagine the Greeks themselves would have looked for great calamities upon the country when their *women* even dreamt such dreams. Here is Jessie Brower too predicting "another French Revolution"![2] 'The omens are bad,' as Herodotus would say.

He himself is responsible in this case however. I have read his first volume, the "Thucydides," the "Xenophon," & a good deal of the "Iliad" since I came here.

But as this is my last day at the sea I must go and *"drink it in"*! With a heart full, *full* of love for my precious one believe me Woodrow dear,   Your ever devoted wife,   Eileen

ALS (WC, NjP).
[1] From Scott's "The Lady of the Lake."
[2] A reference in her missing letter to the violence of the Pullman and railroad strikes in Chicago.

To Ellen Axson Wilson

My sweet, sweet Nellie,   Colorado Springs, 25 July, 1894

How your letters do warm and cheer me! I carry them about with me, riding, calling, or lecturing, as I would a charm. They have come directly from your hand; they seem warm with your own charm and sweetness; they are like a bit of home carried next my heart; and they keep off all bad humours: discouragement or timidity or weakening loneliness. It makes me brave, confident even, and full of a calm spirit of strength to have about me the evidences of your love. You are like a sweet spirit always at my side, whose love acts upon me like an inspiration. Oh, my priceless treasure!

What you say about Dr. Purves's health and the hopeless tragedy that is doubtless his real disease, is beyond all measure deplorable and pathetic. It fills me with a deep sorrow. Oh, if she should indeed kill such a man! How unfathomable such a providence is! But how, my darling, *can* you draw such a moral from it—that you have not taken enough care for me, to shield me from worry and the wear and tear of life! Oh, my sweet love, don't chide yourself for nothing. *You* are the sweetest, the dearest, the most helpful, the most indispensable and *completing* wife a man ever had—to make him ashamed of deserving her so little.

My first lecture has been so much talked about and has received so much praise that I am made the more nervous about the second one to-night. It will probably be more numerously attended, a good deal; may it meet expectations!

The luncheon passed off very agreeably indeed yesterday; and afterwards I was taken another ride through this wonderful country. By the time the reception of the evening was over I was thoroughly tired out, as you will readily believe. To-day I am studying my evening's lecture and resting as much as possible. I have not planned any expeditions into the mountains yet: but they will come presently, no doubt. The trouble is, that in this colossal region the distances are all so magnificent that every trip that is worth while is both expensive and fatiguing: consuming all the valuables, time, strength, and money.

I am perfectly well, my darling: no one seems to *get* sick here: and my spirits are in proportion to my consciousness of your love, and presence with me. All send love. Love unbounded to the chickens and Maggie, and for yourself the heart and life of

Your own   Woodrow

ALS (WC, NjP).

From Ellen Axson Wilson

My dearest W.   [Princeton, N. J.] Thursday aft. [July 26, 1894]

We have reached home safely. All the children much better, and happy to be back. Will write tonight. Send only a line now for fear of missing today's mail.   Ever yours   E. A. W.

API (WP, DLC).

To Ellen Axson Wilson

My own darling,   Colorado Springs, 26 July, 1894

Things are going very normally with me—even in this abnormal country. The second lecture was not quite so successful as the first—though fully twice as many persons heard it—because I did not speak with quite so much ease and confidence. The subject— Political Liberty—was *very* difficult to handle and illustrate, and I could not speak as directly and simply upon it as I can upon the other topics of the course. It will be interesting to see how big the audience is next time!

This morning Hattie and I took a drive through the Garden of the Gods: which, I must say, is most appropriately named. A more beautiful and extraordinary place I never saw. The only expedition away from here that I have planned is one to Glenwood Springs. It will take two days: one going, another coming back; I can go one way and return another and see *en route* almost all the most striking parts of the Rockies. Here, you know, one is not *in* the Rockies at all, but just on the eastern edge of them. This is the point at which the plains, having risen gradually and quite imperceptably from the Mississippi to the extraordinary height of six thousand feet, break suddenly into the great peaks and masses of this stupendous range. I want to get *among* the huge structure, and feel their terrible grandeur. Oh, my love, how I wish for *you*, my little artist and poet! It almost tortures me to think of the deep wonder and excitement that would spring into your eyes, if *you* could but see what I am seeing. It makes me feel so *selfish* to see it without you—who could enjoy it, perhaps, with a purer rapture than any one else in the world. I try to see *for* you, and store up impressions for you: but I know all the while that I cannot see it as you would. You would find as much more in it than I do as you found in the Fair. I *must* get you out here by hook or by crook, if I have to write half a dozen articles to do it, send Ed. with you, and stay at home myself with the children. I could almost wish you were a lecturer!

Oh, my sweet one, how these passionate expressions of love in your letters exalt and delight and stay me! If you could only know how wholly, how reverently, and how passionately I am

                                        Your own   Woodrow

ALS (WC, NjP).

From Ellen Axson Wilson

My own darling,   Princeton, N. J. July 27/94

Arn't you sorry for me?—still no letter from you! I thought it certainly would have reached Belmar before I left yesterday afternoon. Surely though it will come this afternoon. This has been one of the longest weeks I ever spent, and all for want of letters. But how thankful I am that the telegraph was invented!—what should I have done without the little message that told me at least of your safty.

We are all *well* again! Jessie and Nellie seemed better when we left Belmar but Margaret was quite wretched—had been crying with pain much of the morning, beside the other troubles. But she seemed like another person when we had reached home, and today the last trace of the trouble has disappeared and they are all quite as well and lively as ever, and delighted to get home. I am *quite* well again—had another turn myself the last two days at Belmar. Ed is to come home tomorrow, but Maggie is to stay out her two weeks,—thanks to Mrs. Purves who insisted on keeping her in their rooms with her children for those four days. I was glad to consent for she is having a famously good time & it seems to be doing her a world of good. So for her sake I am glad I went after all,—now that the others are all right again,—but glad too to save the second $38.00.

It is intensely hot here and has been straight along, they say. There "hasn't been such a summer for many years"; still the *quality* of the heat is more endurable than it was earlier in the month and I am bearing it finely.

Prof. Wilson's[1] second little girl, Grace, was buried day before yesterday;—a rapid case of typhoid fever, she was sick but ten days. They are said to be perfectly overwhelmed by it. It is reported that another of them has it but I trust it is a mistake. There are no cases of typhoid in the town.[2]

You get positively no mail at all! I never saw such a dearth. There is a circular from the "Omaha & St Louis" threatening dire vengeance if the *bonds* & *unpaid coupons* are not deposited before Aug. 15.[3] But yours *were* sent, were they not? We must forfeit $50.00 on each bond if they are not received before then.

The only letter needing to be answered is one from Mr. Sheldon asking your private opinion of McKenzie the baseball captain—I mean as to his character & ability.[4] He has applied for a place in their office. This letter came just before I left B. & I am sorry to say I have misplaced it temporarily: but I have given all its contents.

I love you, dear, with all my strength. I think of you all day & dream of you by night.

I am altogether   Your own   Eileen.

ALS (WC, NjP).
    [1] Frederick Newton Willson, Professor of Descriptive Geometry, Stereotomy, and Technical Drawing at Princeton.
    [2] The Willsons lived at Stony Brook, not in Princeton.
    [3] This circular is missing.
    [4] Edward W. Sheldon's letter concerning Charles Stephens Mackenzie, '94, is missing.

To Ellen Axson Wilson

My own darling,   Colorado Springs, 27 July, '94

I spend 'lecture days' as quietly as possible 'at home,'—so that there is nothing to write about to-day except anxiety as to how I shall make out to-night; and with that subject you are already painfully familiar. I don't see why I should ever consent to give a course of lectures *any*where!

Last night we went out to dine with a Mr. and Mrs. Kennedy who have a son in Princeton.[1] I suppose I was the 'guest of honour[']: I was placed by the side of the hostess, but on her *left*: her daughter was on her right hand; neither did Mrs. Kennedy go out with me to dinner. It was altogether a singular and unconventional affair. The first thing brought to each guest was a plate full of dinner *á la* Mrs. Coales:[2] then salad: then dessert. The people seemed most refined, nevertheless. They are probably only old-fashioned and not accustomed to giving dinners *of late*. I am the last person of my acquaintance to think less of them for a breach of fashion. The other invited guests were cultivated and agreeable in a most unusual degree, and I enjoyed the evening very much indeed. The people here have a way of inviting one to their houses without first calling upon him: but I suppose one must waive the irregularity and call on them.

So far as I have met the people here, they seem to be all of them eastern people but recently settled here. It is, therefore, not in character and make up western people at all, but are simply living in the West. No one, indeed, more than twenty-one *could* be a native of "Colorado Springs." It was 'laid out' in 1871.

I keep very well: I suppose every one keeps well here who was not ill when he came. I love you with a devotion, a longing, a passion, beyond all utterance. I am in every pure movement of my heart consciously and altogether

                         Your own   Woodrow

Love to Maggie and the chicks

ALS (WC, NjP).
  [1] Matthew and Mary Jane Cameron Kennedy, parents of Richard Lea Kennedy, '95.
  [2] Mary Anna Coale, proprietress of "The Betweenery" at Bryn Mawr College when the Wilsons lived and boarded there, 1885-87.

From Ellen Axson Wilson

My own darling,   Princeton, N. J. July 28/94

Your letter came at last yesterday afternoon—it is impossible to say with what delight it was received. I suppose I shall get another this afternoon from Belmar. It is a severe penalty for coming home that I must wait for them all to be forwarded from there for some days. But otherwise it was a good thing, for the children are still perfectly well and happy in spite of the extraordinary heat.

The other little Wilson child *has* the fever but is not dangerously ill at present. Annie's mother is very ill and she has gone home for a month, or as much longer as may be necessary, and I have little Mary; who will do very well. They do not think Annie's mother will ever be better.

I am ashamed of myself to have let the heat make me so lazy about writing this morning, that now I must either content myself with this hasty scribble or else fail to make this afternoon's mail—and as it is Saturday that would never do. Miss Ricketts has made me a long & very pleasant visit too.

So goodbye for today, *my* matchless darling. It is just your matchlessness that excites me to love *you* more & more. I have certainly never seen anyone to remind me of you. All the selected good & great qualities of all the other men I ever saw combined would never equal you,—because they just wouldn't be *you*! No one could discover the *combination*. It is nature's own secret,— that subtile alchemy by which for once she made an *altogether* admirable & lovable man,—one to be honoured and enjoyed and gloried in and loved equally. Ah how tenderly devotedly, passionately he is loved nobody knows except

His little wife,   Eileen.

ALS (WC, NjP).

To Ellen Axson Wilson

My own darling,   Colo. Sprgs. 28 July, 1894

I am just about to leave for Glenwood Springs thr. the mountains and have been kept by a caller till the very eve of train time. I am perfectly well—the third lecture went very well indeed—and I love you with a passion beyond all words.

Your own   Woodrow

ALS (WC, NjP).

From Ellen Axson Wilson

My own darling,   Princeton, N. J. July 29/94

Your second letter came duly to hand yesterday afternoon. I hope you *can* go to Denver. I want you to have as many experiences as possible on this trip. I have been racking my brain to remember whether you decided to take or leave your written lectures. I know it was under discussion. How I hope you have one!

Am glad you are enjoying the strange sights &c. Arn't you glad now that you "braced up" & went? I am; especially since by going I trust you will escape all this frightful weather. It is 98°, I believe. And the drought is becoming alarming. We are all well however in spite of it. The children's appetites are something extraordinary, considering the heat, and they are very bright and happy.

Ed is at home again and reports Maggie as "all right."

I love, my darling, with all my heart, though I havn't strength of mind enough to write much about it in such weather.

Believe me, dear, now & forever,   Your own   Eileen.

ALS (WC, NjP).

To Ellen Axson Wilson

My own darling,   On the cars, Colorado Midland 29 July, 1894

Here I am on my way back from Glenwood Springs, and I must try to write you a line or two on the cars, to be mailed at the first opportunity.

I had a glorious ride yesterday, thr. extraordinary gorges and amidst the most stupendous scenery I ever imagined—how I did wish for you! To-day the scenery is equally grand (I am returning by a different route) but scarcely so extraordinary. I am perfectly well—excited with new emotions—gradually filling up with new ideas and realization of our continent,—and always, with an unspeakable devotion   Your own   Woodrow

ALS (WC, NjP).

From Ellen Axson Wilson

My own darling,   Princeton, N. J. July 30/94

I know that you will be glad to hear that it is a little cooler here today! We had a nice little shower last night and a very comfortable night after it. We *hoped* for a fine storm, there seemed very elaborate preparations a-making in the shape of (distant) thunder and lightening; but we missed most of it.

Here is at last a letter that needs an immediate answer; one from Amasa Parker, editor of the Albany Law Journal asking to publish your paper to be read before the "Am. Bar Ass."[1] They wish the article *at once*, though it would not be published until Aug. 25,—after the meeting.[2] I know you havn't it ready, so I suppose I had better answer it for you.

We are all well still. There is absolutely no news of any sort; the arrival of your letter is the one and only *event* of the day, and that has not as yet "transpired" today. Ah me, what would I not give if the next message could be brought "en personne"! My longing for a sight of your dear face is so great that it has become a permanent heart-ache. Oh my love, my love!—but this will never do; you are still too far away in time & space for such indulgence, I must 'brace up.' With all the love you want,

Your own   Eileen.

ALS (WC, NjP).

[1] The paper that Wilson would entitle "Legal Education of Undergraduates" and deliver before the American Bar Association on August 23, 1894. It is printed at this date.

[2] The *Albany Law Journal* did not publish his paper, inasmuch as Wilson was not prepared to meet the early deadline.

To Ellen Axson Wilson

My own darling,   Colorado Springs, 30 July, 1894

Oh, how dismal and distressing it is to be so far away when my little darlings are sick and my precious little wife in trouble! I am not only troubled—I am dismayed—that your trip, from which I had hoped so much refreshment for you, should have been so sad a failure,—and that, instead of getting pleasure out of it, you got only distress. Oh, my darling, how sorry, how troubled I am about it all! And you are so sweet and wise and self-possessed through it all! Ah, how I do admire and wonder at you, my pride! I promise, for my part, to be as calm and undisturbed as I can: but you will allow that it is very much harder *away* from the trouble—where one can be of no use, and where there is no *immediate* news. I am not so reasonable as you are, or so wise.

I got 'home' very tired last night, but very well satisfied with the trip. The route I took returning was very much less beautiful than the one by which I went, but it showed me very different aspects of the great mountains and was no less instructive. What an eye-opener this extraordinary region is! I shall not miss the Alps so much hereafter.

I go to Denver to-morrow, to lecture in the evening to lecture [*sic*] on 'Liberty' to a women's club there. I am to be entertained by the President of the Club—worse luck!—and it is quite possible I shall be cut out of writing my letter; but I will *try* not to be.

I don't know *how much* they mean to entertain me. I can't imagine why I consent to do this sort of thing—and for nothing, too;—but such is your husband—hungry—*too* hungry—for reputation and influence. Don't be disturbed if my letters skip a day.

I mean to leave here Saturday night [August 4]. I shall reach Chicago on Monday morning; stay with Jessie till the next afternoon; get to Chillicothe[1] Wednesday morning; leave there sometime Thursday; reach N.Y., I suppose, and Princeton, I devoutly hope, some time on Friday. Oh, what would I not give to go straight home, by the quickest trains! I long for you intolerably, my darling. I feel as if I could not stand another week away from you. If I *dared* I would try to tell you now how much I love you: but it would break my heart to strain it so, and I could not collect myself for the lecture. Oh, my love, my queen, my Eileen!

Your own   Woodrow

ALS (WC, NjP).
[1] To visit his Woodrow relatives there.

From Ellen Axson Wilson

My own darling,   Princeton, N. J. July 31/94

Your letter—that of the 26th—came by the morning mail today.

I am sorry you did not feel satisfied about your lecture, but I have no doubt the *audience* were.

I am delighted indeed that you are getting so much enjoyment and stimulation from these new and wonderful sights. I *do* enjoy it intensely through your eyes.

How sweet it is in you to be so wild for me to see them too! You don't know, darling, how much I appreciate all that thought for me. But that particular sort of pleasure—the pleasures of freedom and travel arn't for mothers;—and having bartered them for something better, they certainly have no cause for dissatisfaction. It seems to me that one of the greatest sources of mischief in this world is that *dishonesty* in people which makes them unwilling to pay the just price for their happiness. They fail to enjoy the good the gods have sent because forever discontentedly striving after other wholly incompatible delights. And if the discontent leads them, as too often it does, to neglect the *duties* which lie at the foundation of all their *joys* then indeed they have made an unmitigated failure in their art of living. Don't you think that to grasp clearly "the great & beautiful doctrine of compensations" would save most people a world of vexation and might have very wide-reaching consequences of many sorts? It might even handicap a "walking delegate" or two! But what a very uncalled for sermon!

I have seen today a *paper*;—the first one since I saw you. I feel entirely behind the times,—didnt even know about Cleveland's letter; wish I had seen it.[1] As far as I can make out it seems to have been a splendid political move,—going far towards shifting the responsibility for the situation from the party at large and himself as its head, and distinctly fastening it where it as distinctly belongs, upon the "sugar senators" &c. Don't you think it may go far towards saving the party in the next election? Is or is not a President justified by law and precedent in "influencing legislation" in that particular way? For once our legislation too seems to have a dramatic element in it. This trial of strength & endurance between House & Senate is positively exciting.

The weather is more tolerable today, & we are to expect a cold wave after 36 hours! Somehow merely to be beginning another month is encouraging. We are all quite well, and we all love you as much as we *can* love! I wonder if you know how much that means in the case of   Your little wife,   Eileen.

ALS (WC, NjP).

[1] The Wilson tariff bill, having been approved by the Senate with a number of amendments increasing the rates, was sent to conference committee on July 7, 1894. After twelve days, the committee reported that it could not reach agreement, and Representative Wilson, chairman of the House conferees, appeared before the House of Representatives to request permission for further conference with the Senate's committee. At the conclusion of his speech, Wilson read a letter addressed to him by President Cleveland on July 2, urging the House conferees to fight for the original Wilson bill and asserting that any abandonment of the principles upon which it rested would constitute "party perfidy and party dishonor." Angry senators, including Democrats, replied that the President had impugned their political integrity and meddled in legislative matters. As it turned out, the House conferees capitulated to their Senate colleagues on August 16. The President permitted the measure, known as the Wilson-Gorman Tariff Act, to become law without his signature.

A Newspaper Editorial

[July 31, 1894]

PROF. WILSON AT UNITY.

Dog days, dull times and everybody out of town are not enough to discourage the reform branch of the Woman's club of this city. Finding that the sinews of war are necessary, even in times of peace, the department has arranged for two lectures, to be given on Tuesday and Friday evenings of this week at Unity church. It is unfortunate that they come so near together, but there is no choice in the matter, and after all one cannot have too much of a good thing.

This evening Prof. Woodrow Wilson of Princeton college will

deliver his famous address on "The Origin and Derivation of Our Political Liberty." The subject is one full of interest to the general public, and perhaps especially so to our women voters who are making a careful study of all things appertaining to politics. Prof. Wilson is an orator of unusual ability, and we bespeak a crowded house for him.

On Friday night Mr. Samuel Parsons will speak on "Landscape Gardening." . . . Both gentlemen have been at the Summer college at Colorado Springs, where they have been very cordially received, and merely stop over in Denver on their way to their Eastern homes. . . .

Printed in the Denver, Colorado, *Rocky Mountain News*, July 31, 1894.

A Newspaper Report of a Speech

[August 1, 1894]

POLITICAL LIBERTY.

A small and select audience gathered at Unity church last night to listen to Professor Woodrow Wilson of Princeton college, who addressed the reform department of [the] woman's club on "The Origin and Derivation of Our Political Liberty." American conceptions of liberty, he said, had been originally taken from other races than the Anglo-Saxon, from French writers, in fact, who wer[e] great theorists about liberty, even before they had enjoyed any of its benefits. Freedom he defined as lack of friction; perfect adjustment of all parts of the body politic. When some part of the body politic was out of gear with the rest, and running contrary to the interests of the rest, there was trouble and a measure of liberty was lost. The American constitution of liberty provided that no man should be deprived of life or property without due process of law.

"I say that my life and my property are free in this country, and so they are," he said. "Yet the government can condemn any piece of property it desires and take it, and the government can draft me into the army and sacrifice my life if necessary. What is the safeguard? None of these things can be done without due process of law. If, then, you touch a man's property without due process of law, you are warned beforehand. You know what will happen."

He was very much pleased, the professor said in this connection, in talking with a locomotive engineer the other day, to hear him say that he was against strikes, because in a strike everybody was so mad that they couldn't settle anything. It was very encouraging, the speaker thought, when these men began to learn this. Law must strike the average man, must not be greatly above or below the general sentiment of the community. Prohibition was possible only in a community that didn't need it. Constitutional liberty had existed only since Runnymede, when the barons forced King John to recognize that there was something else in England besides the government. The government and the state were not identical. The state was an organized body of people within a given territory. The government was a small body of poeple [people] organized for the purpose of governing the state. If the government misrepresented the state liberty was lost.[1]

Printed in the Denver, Colorado, *Rocky Mountain News*, Aug. 1, 1894.
  [1] There is a brief WWhw outline of this speech entitled *"Political Liberty: Speaking analysis"* in WP, DLC.

To Ellen Axson Wilson

My own darling,   Colorado Springs, 1 Aug., 1894

And so I was deprived of the pleasure and the privilege of writing to you yesterday. I never get over the feeling that it is a *privilege* of the rarest sort to address love letters to you. I am so proud of it: it gives me a sort of impression of of [sic] having everything to live for and everything to live up to! The best thing about me is that I am your accepted lover and confidant, my queen.

Yesterday was a very full day for me. Mrs. Platt, with whom I stayed in Denver, the President of the Women's Club, is a very intelligent and agreeable woman indeed; her house is elegant, and her hospitality most cordial and home-like; and I enjoyed myself as much as I can among strangers. The whole afternoon was consumed in finishing lunch and driving round and about the city. It is a really beautiful place, full of the most elegant residences. It gives one a singular impression, however. It seems a sort of museum or experiment ground in all the modern styles of dwelling architecture. Every style that architects have conceived since 1879 is here to be seen within the compass of a few city blocks. You seem to be in a sort of architectural exhibit, such as the World's Fair might have contained, had there been space and means enough.

In the evening came the lecture, "before a small but select audience" (25¢ admission) in Unity Church. Enter to the platform two ladies followed modestly by the lecturer of the evening. He is introduced in a few laboriously chosen words by one of the ladies, a sweet and delicate looking person; he rises and bows to her deferentially: begins his lecture as collectedly as may be under the circumstances; and she and her companion withdraw to the front pew. The lecture is on Political Liberty; it is soon concluded; the lecturer holds a levee at the foot of the pulpit; is then carried off to "the Club" by two Princeton men; and gets back to Mrs. Platt's about eleven a very tired man. That's the Denver visit. It took me three hours to get back this morning—I went to a lunch here as soon after getting back as possible—and now I must take a nap before my lecture. With a heart full to overflowing with thankfulness that you are all well—and fairly breaking with love and longing,   Your own   Woodrow

ALS (WC, NjP).

From Ellen Axson Wilson

My own darling,   Princeton, N. J. August 1/94

Just a hasty note today for it is after two and I want this to make the usual mail—the half past two.

We are all quite well *and comfortable*! We had a thunderstorm last night and it was positively cool all the evening. It was such a luxury that I couldn't bear to go to bed but sat up until half past eleven reading;—had down a dozen "Britannicas" & three or four "Century dictionaries";—so you see I had come to life very decidedly. Have been so busy this morning too about various little matters that I could not get time to write.

Your only mail is a letter from Mr. Riggs,[1] saying that the Peabody course is filled up,—they having planned to have it scientific this year.

I have a letter from Mrs. [Edwin Seelye] Lewis asking me to let the children take music lessons from her next winter. Imagine!

But I received a paper from Nashville giving terrible news. Robert Ewing, Cousin Hattie's oldest boy is dead—killed!—but I will enclose the paper. I feel quite overcome by this. It will almost break her heart; she is such a devoted mother,—such a great-hearted woman; and Rob was the very apple of her eye—the dearest of all.

I love you, dear, more than words can say & am in every heart-throb   Your own   Eileen.

ALS (WC, NjP). Enc.: undated clipping describing the accidental death of Robert Ewing, Jr., in Tracy City, Tenn.

[1] Lawrason Riggs, Princeton '83, a Baltimore lawyer and trustee of the Peabody Institute of that city. His letter is missing.

To Ellen Axson Wilson

My precious Eileen,   Colorado Springs, 2 Aug., 1894

The fifth lecture has been delivered; there is but one more; day after to-morrow (before you receive this letter) I shall *start* for home: alas, it will be only a start: but then there will almost immediately be *less* of this immense continent between us: I shall be *coming* to you. Oh, my sweet, sweet love, how my heart pulls and urges me: what a loadstone you are! You are not only the sweetest woman I ever knew, and the most interesting: you are also the most *engaging*. It is so *dull* to be away from you. Life is so much more *commonplace* without you. That is one of the depressing and degrading things you have saved me from: a commonplace life. It is so fresh and sweet and interesting where you are. God bless you, darling, for all that you have been and are to me. The best of it all is, that I do not have to be separated from you to realize it as keenly, and as consciously rejoice in it when I am with you without intermission as when we are separated. Only, it makes the pain, the effort of separation so much the greater. My incomparable darling! My queen and delight!

I am rejoiced to say that I not only keep my audience here, but draw new people at every lecture, till now I have quite a 'following.' One man expressed his enthusiasm by exclaiming 'Why, that fellow is a whole team *and the dog under the wagon!*' The best part of all this is, that you will be as much rejoiced by it as I am. Nothing fills me with quite so sweet a feeling as the knowledge of that fact: the fact, the wonderful fact, of your great love for me: and nothing is quite such an inspiration as your belief in my success and enthusiasm because of it. I was not entirely 'making up out of my head' when I wrote of Edith's 'management' of John Hart.[1] You have yourself just as surely produced the conditions of my success: you are *my* 'manager': my sweet and stimulating atmosphere. Oh, Eileen, I am afraid I shall hurt you with kisses & caresses when I get you in my arms again!

I still have numerous little expeditions to make to 'points of interest' about here wh. I have not yet seen: so that the remaining hours (note that word!) of my stay will be crowded with tourist business. I will *try* to describe this wonderful country to you when I get back! I am quite well—quite comfortable in spirits —and *desperately* in love with you.   Your own   Woodrow

ALS (WC, NjP).
[1] In "The World and John Hart," printed at Sept. 1, 1887, Vol. 5.

From Ellen Axson Wilson

My own darling,　　　　　　　Princeton, N. J. Aug. 2, 1894

Your little note of the 28th came this morning;—I suppose after today they will come directly to Princeton and save me twenty-four hours of waiting. And, by the way—it has just occurred to me at this moment that this is the last letter you will have time to receive before starting homeward! How charming! it seems to make your return nearer. I wish I knew just when to expect you; the pause in Chicago and the detour to Chilicothe throw me quite out of my reckoning; alas! I fear that at best it cannot be before Saturday week!

The weather today is really charming; I have been up to the Library and renewed my old amusement of looking at houses! I have found one that I *think* I like better than any yet. And it "fits the plan" too![1]

Maggie returns this afternoon. Ed will go to the Junction for her.

The children are very happy over a croquet set I have bought them to atone for their disappointment in not being able to bathe. It cost only a dollar. I had no idea they were so cheap or they might have had one long ago. You would be surprised to see how well Nellie plays for such a baby—much better than Jessie.

I overheard a funny speech of Jessie's the other day. She had said something about being "alive" and Ed had asked her how she knew she was alive. She didn't answer, but retorted by asking him if he was "civilized" (!) and how he knew that he was civilized. They, and all of us are *quite* well. Nellie is extraordinarily disfigured by the heat but even that is getting a little better.

I am so glad that you keep well, darling, and delighted that you are taking the trip to the Springs. I trust you are going up Pike's Peak too as far as the railroad will carry you. I hope you will see all you possibly can while you have the opportunity. What about the Denver trip? How much you will have to tell me about when you return,—and ah, how happy I shall be to listen! It seems to me I shall be too happy to breathe when I am once again within sound of your dear voice and touch of your hand. My darling, my darling! I love you with the smiles, tears, breath of all my life. I am always and altogether

Your little wife　　Eileen.

ALS (WC, NjP).
　[1] This is the first indication in the documents that the Wilsons had begun to plan to build a home of their own. The subject will loom large in Volume 9.

To Ellen Axson Wilson

My precious darling,   Colorado Springs, 3 August, 1894

The exceptional has happened this morning: it is wet and foggy—a thing that almost never happens here—; the mountains are not to be seen; and I am cut out of seeing some extraordinary places we were to drive to to-day. Perhaps it's just as well, since I am quite tired this morning. We went to a concert last night at a magnificent Casino about two miles out of town; coming back (it was raining the while) I had to stand up for about an hour in a packed trolley car; we got home damp and disconsolate, and staggered to bed at midnight. The concert was not superlatively good, either.

It distresses me beyond measure, my sweet one, that you should be suffering from such terrible heat. Reports of it reached me in the papers before your letters told of it, of course, and it made me desperately anxious to think of your going home from the seashore in such a season. Of course you took the right step under the circumstances, but I have not been happy thinking of my dear little sensitive plant wilting in Princeton. You seem to be bearing it very well from what you say; but I don't like to think of it. I hope from the bottom of my heart that a relief has come before this. What *is* poor Stock doing in the midst of the fiery furnace in Philadelphia![1] It *hurts* me to think of him. Surely he will get off to the mountains, or to the Maine woods.

To-morrow night, Eileen, I start *home*ward. Oh, how my heart leaps at the thought! I don't know the eastern schedules yet, but I hope,—and mean, if I can,—to be *at home*, in your arms, one week from to-night,—about four days after this letter reaches you. When you get it I shall be in Chicago. When I get started I suppose I shall be obliged to stop writing. I will telegraph from Chicago of my arrival, and from Chillicothe,—so that to-morrow will be my last regular letter, in all probability. Oh, my precious love, how my heart throbs at all this: what an exciting prospect it is, that I am going back to you! You are my chief refreshment and, it sometimes seems to me, my *whole* inspiration. I wish you could know how constantly I live *with reference to you*,—so that thoughts of you seem part of every plan and of every experience. You are literally part of my life—the chief part of it! My heart clings *to* you and *about* you with a passion and dependence which seem the whole force of

Your own   Woodrow

ALS (WC, NjP).
[1] He had begun his work as lecturer for the American Society for the Extension of University Teaching.

From Ellen Axson Wilson

My own darling,   Princeton, N. J. Aug 3/94

I had *three* letters from you yesterday—one by each mail!—a red letter day indeed, only it must of course be followed by several "lean" days. I see from the one which came last night—direct from Col.—that if I write now to Chicago you can get one more message from home before your return.

Am sorry darling that you were so troubled about us all; you know it was never serious; the expense was really what turned the scale in favour of returning; the thing was not *paying*! Am delighted you enjoyed the mountain trip so much;—have no doubt that you will be glad afterwards that you went to Denver too: it will be another experience; besides it will help the college as well as extend your own reputation.

Give my best love to dear Jessie [Brower] and Helen [Bones]. Tell them I meant to write them long ago but—the heat! Tell Helen we all miss her sadly and she must be sure to come back *soon*. Will she go abroad this Fall?

Maggie has returned looking very well—plumper I think. And the sun-burn is quite becoming. Stock is in New York—says [Robert Johnston] Finley's flat is the coolest place he has found this summer. They are going to Atlanta on a little trip; Finley has gotten passes. Stock says his lectures seemed to be very well received. Ed has struck up a friendship with young Pell who seems quite a nice boy—if he was dropped![1] He is a Virginian from Fairfax & is going abroad to study art in a year or two.

By the way, did you see in the paper before you left about a distinguished clergyman who, having lost two daughters within a week, died himself, literally of a broken heart, half an hour after the death of the second? I learn that it was young Teale's father and sisters![2]

And now goodbye, dearest, till the slow week rolls round and brings you to my arms. May God bless and keep you safe and well through all those great stretches of travel, and bring you safely back to home & to me. We are all well and love you with our whole hearts.   Ever your devoted little wife   Eileen

ALS (WC, NjP).

[1] William Black Pell, a special student in the Academic Department during the academic year 1893-94. He was readmitted as a freshman in 1894 and was graduated with the Class of 1898.

[2] "Young Teale" was Arthur Rogers Teal, '95; his father, the Rev. John W. Teal of Elizabeth, N. J.

Three Letters to Ellen Axson Wilson

My own darling,   Colorado Springs, 4 Aug., '94

How exciting it is to be writing my last letter before starting for home! It fills me with an unspeakable delight merely to be getting *nearer* to you, whether in time or in space. You are the centre of my life, and I seem to lose force in direct proportion to my distance from you. Oh, how sweet it is that we *cannot* be separated at all *in spirit*! That fact makes the other separation at once painful and endurable. It would be intolerable, were it not so; and yet the very inseparability of our hearts makes absence the more keenly painful, because of the temporary breach of intimate intercourse which it involves. I have learned to depend so, for comfort and inspiration, upon intimate association with you *from hour to hour*, that when I am away from your side I feel maimed and imperfect. Your sweet spirit has become necessary, not only to my pleasure, but even to my completeness; and I cannot think of doing anything of any magnitude without bringing your help into the reckoning. Oh, my Eileen, my Eileen, my love, my wife, my queen! I am coming home to *you*!

It is still early in the morning, I am about to take another drive out to the Garden of the Gods, the choice spot of all these parts, as it seems to me. I could not go away without another glimpse of the exquisite place. At one o'clock Hattie is to have some company to meet me at luncheon; after they are gone, I must make a call; and then there will be nothing more for me to do here except pack my bags and wait for my train! It leaves at 9:42 this evening. How my heart throbs at the prospect!

I have certainly been most cordially received by all sorts of people here; and I think I *must* say that I have considerably advanced my reputation by coming here. My lectures have drawn increasing audiences of the best quality; they have been the feature of the Summer School; and the enthusiastic comments upon them compel even me to pronounce them an unqualified success. *You* know how much that is for me to say; and I say it for your delight—my precious, matchless little wife.

Eileen, my treasure, my heart yearns for you almost to breaking, and I am altogether   Your own   Woodrow

My own darling,   Chicago, 7 Aug., 1894

I have nothing to say: I have simply found myself alone for a few minutes and want to send you a love message. The impatience to have you in my arms is growing upon me as usual as the end of our separation draws near, but a line of passionate love speech is better than nothing. I am quite well. I love you beyond all words, and I mean to be with you, God willing, Friday *morning*!   Your own   Woodrow

Congress Hall.
My own darling,   Saratoga Springs, N.Y.   22 August 1894

This convention[1] grinds so unceasingly that it seems that I am to have almost no time at all to write,—what with sessions morning, afternoon, and night! Judge Cooley's address this morning occupied *two hours and ten minutes*! He was not well enough to be present himself; but he sent the stupendous thing on and it was read by another man. It would probably have killed the delicate little gentleman to read all that aloud himself! It was what is usually called "a very able discussion of the subject"; though I must say that it did not seem to me to have any very distinct or separate subject; and the treatment was throughout extremely—to me, painfully—obvious![2]

This afternoon—within a few minutes from "the present writing"—our Section[3] gets to work; but I am not 'on,' as you know, till to-morrow afternoon. Judge Dillon,[4] who *is* on will probably have something showing the same sort of ability as Judge Cooley's! But, that's what I came for; and I am enjoying myself, meeting some very engaging and interesting men, and the movement —amusing enough for a few days—of a great resort. I am quite well, though still a trifle stiff. I love you in everything that I think, in everything that I see, in everything that I do. You are my life and my inspiration. Everything that happens—to us both or to me alone—seems but to deepen and intensify my devotion to the sweetest of all sweet women   Your own   Woodrow

We met Stock all right, and he took charge of M.[5] Father is in the White Mountains!

ALS (WC, NjP).
[1] The seventeenth annual meeting of the American Bar Association, which met at Saratoga Springs, August 22-24, 1894.
[2] This was Judge Cooley's presidential address, which was presented by Judge Samuel F. Hunt of Cincinnati. A reading of Cooley's address might well tempt one to agree with Wilson's judgment. It was a leisurely review of noteworthy changes in statutory law by Congress and the several states, followed by an equally long section entitled "The Year in Its Constitutional Aspects: the Lawyer as a Teacher and Leader." This portion covered, among other things, labor unrest and strikes, Coxey's army, agitators, anarchists, and other "foes to the human race." Most of Cooley's remarks about lawyers as public teachers consisted of a condemnation of proposals for compulsory arbitration of labor disputes. The address is printed in *Report of the Seventeenth Annual Meeting of the American Bar Association* . . . (Philadelphia, 1894), pp. 181-243.

3 The "Section of Legal Education," which held its first session at 3 P.M., the proceedings of which are printed in *ibid.*, pp. 351-63.

4 Former Judge John Forrest Dillon, whose paper, "The True Professional Ideal," is printed in *ibid.*, pp. 409-22.

5 Wilson and Margaret Axson met Stockton Axson in New York, and they went together to Saratoga Springs.

From Ellen Axson Wilson

My own darling, Princeton, N. J. Aug 22/94

How very fortunate you and little Maggie are in the matter of weather! It is quite ideal for sightseeing, for travelling—indeed for doing anything. I hope you enjoyed your journey and will also enjoy everything at the end of it,—that this trip will be as successful as the last two.

We are getting on very well. Margaret had a good night—was not at all croupy. She coughed a little towards morning but it was only the ordinary hack. In fact they are *all* coughing in that way; it is too bad that any change in weather even a change for the better should give them cold. I have let them go out though with the usual misgivings on the subject;—it is really much warmer and pleasanter out of doors than in.

There is no mail & nothing whatever has happened. Mrs. Hinton[1] wrote to ask us to take tea Friday night. Of course as you were absent I declined. I hope the poor things will feel that they have done their duty by us and not trouble to renew the invitation.

I am missing you terribly this time, my darling; I am so lonely I don't know what to do. I believe I am naughty and silly enough to be even a little miserable for want of you. But after all that isn't a very serious trouble—is it?—when you are to be back on Sat! I suppose it must be described as a mere *luxury* of sadness —like the young poet who was "sad as night for very wantonness."

I love you dear—I am as ever,

Your devoted little wife, Eileen

ALS (WP, DLC).
1 Mary E. Hinton of 78 Canal Street, wife of Charles Howard Hinton, Instructor in Mathematics. Mrs. Hinton thought of herself as a considerable authority on poetry.

To Ellen Axson Wilson

My own darling, Saratoga Springs, N. Y. 23 August, 1894

Your little letter of yesterday has at once comforted and disturbed me,—disturbed me because of its confession of wretchedness. I know what that means, my sweet one, for I have felt it myself ever since leaving you. I think, in the case of both of us, it must be the after effect of that afternoon of unhappiness: an additional warning to us not to be so foolish again! Oh, how I love you, how deeply, how desperately, and what a keen pang it gives me to think that I ever,—even though unintentionally caused you a moment of unhappiness! May God make me a better man, and so a better lover! I love you, I yearn for you more than I dare trust myself to try to say: I mean to try and *show* you how much, instead, when I get back! My queen, my darling!

I am afraid you must expect a crowded house Saturday night. I have just had a note from father which seems to indicate that he will go down with me on the 5 o'clock train (Princeton, 6:37); and I suppose Stock. and Maggie will go down then, too.

The four sessions of the Ass'n I have so far had to attend have aggregated 12½ hours (it is now 2:30 P.M., the second day) but it has been progressively interesting.

It is now within about an hour of my own ordeal. I shall love you through it all and read so much the better!

Your own   Woodrow

ALS (WP, DLC).

EDITORIAL NOTE
WILSON'S ADDRESS ON LEGAL EDUCATION

Wilson's address before the "Section of Legal Education" of the American Bar Association on August 23, 1894, printed below, was one of the most significant and self-revealing speeches that he had made to this date.

It was significant, first, for what it revealed about Wilson's reactions to the domestic upheavals of 1893-94—the march of Coxey's Army, the Pullman and railroad strikes, and the severe repressive measures taken by the courts, state governments, and, particularly, President Cleveland to quell various outcroppings of popular unrest.

Wilson's strictures against the reactions of lawyers and the courts to the national crisis were made, not in a vacuum, but at a meeting where numerous speeches reflected the concern, fear, and demands of a conservative legal community for all measures necessary to prevent violent upheaval. In this context, Wilson's remarks, which can only be characterized as courageous, placed him squarely on the side of the moderates who blamed reactionary judges and lawyers as much if not more than agitators and strikers for the crisis. Thus Wilson was reiterating, eloquently if cryptically, the theme of his first lecture on Burke, printed at August 31, 1893, and discussed in the Editorial Note, "Wilson's First Lecture on Burke"—that society had to respond sensitively to changing needs by constructive reforms if revolution was to be avoided.

Wilson's address is significant, second, because he reiterated even more clearly and emphatically than before his vigorous dissent against slavish adherence to the case method of study in vogue in professional law schools (a matter discussed in the Editorial Note, "Wilson's Plans for a School of Law at Princeton," Volume 7), and his conviction that professional legal training could ill afford to neglect the broader historical, philosophical, and sociological context of legal development.

The address is important, finally, because in defining what he thought was an ideal undergraduate pre-legal curriculum, Wilson was in fact describing his own pre-law course at Princeton.

Although the invitation to Wilson to participate in the American Bar Association's program had been extended in February 1894, Ellen Wilson's letter to her husband of July 30 makes it clear that he had not prepared his address by this date. He therefore must have prepared it soon after his return to Princeton from Colorado on August 10. No manuscript copy of the speech seems to have survived.

An Address

[[c. Aug. 23, 1894]]

LEGAL EDUCATION OF UNDERGRADUATES.

At no time, it must seem to every thoughtful man, has the study of the law in a broad and enlightened spirit been of more vital importance to society than it is at present. For society and its established principles of conduct and authority are being subjected nowadays to a peculiarly sharp and disturbing scrutiny. Men of every calibre and all dispositions have assumed the *rôle* of critics. Society does not suit one because it has loitered too long on the way to perfection. It displeases another because it has been all too energetic in its mistaken zeal for change. Some censure it because it is not altruistic; others, because it has not noted and acted upon radical practical changes in modern life. On one hand it is condemned for its lack of heart and humane feeling; on another, for its lack of practical sagacity. It is bidden, in some quarters, to make the individual freer, in others to take him more thoroughly in hand for his discipline and guidance. Some want the State to regulate monopolies, others wish it to assume the entire management of them out of hand. Every one knows that the relations—even the legal relations—now existing between capitalists and laborers are seriously amiss, and every one has his own remedy for the evil. None of the critics of society stop short with censure; each has his reform to propose; each comes with the draft of a new law in his hand. There is an accumulating clamor for legislation, for changes in the law—an almost pathetic faith that new machinery for the voter and new rules for the courts will surely bring regeneration and progress.

The lawyer, meanwhile, is everywhere sadly discredited. The world is in search of prophets, not barristers. It wants change, not a judgment. The lawyer will stickle for form and regularity, will demand exactness of phrase and certitude of provision, workable laws and rules susceptible of being consistently and equitably administered. He has puzzling points in his head, too, about the practicability of getting at certain vague rights upon which philanthropists insist. And so reformers shun him and deem his counsel disheartening. It must be granted, moreover, that they are not without striking instances, drawn out of authentic history, of lawyers having acted as very stubborn and very stupid obstructionists, and having refused to take any part in necessary, nay inevitable, changes in the law which they might have moderated and shaped to temperate uses had they not resisted them and so rendered them the more inapt and extreme. The prophets, therefore, go without their counsel and lend countenance to the improving of statutes by any hopeful man, with or without experience in such critical matters, who is of their creed and vision.

No doubt much of this new ardor for reform is sound and just, an earnest of quick health in the social body, and a signal of hope. No man among us is so blind as not to see that the law limps sadly at many points; that it has not at all kept pace with the swift and radical changes that have transformed industrial society beyond recognition almost within a single generation. I do not doubt that the law of contract and association and taxation and tenure needs amendment and remodeling. But I deprecate the haste, the ignorance, the intemperance, the fatuity of many of those who are seeking our suffrages as reformers. I believe that we shall run upon irreparable disaster unless we ponder very seriously the proper means and practicable measures of reform. I feel sure, therefore, that nothing will steady us like a body of citizens instructed in the essential nature and processes of law and a school of lawyers deeply versed in the methods by which the law has grown, the vital principles by which, under every system, it has been pervaded, its means of serving society and its means of guiding it. We need laymen who understand the necessity for law, and the right uses of it, too well to be unduly impatient of its restraints; and lawyers who understand the necessity for reform and the safe means of affecting it, too well to be unreasonably shy of assisting it. The worst enemy to the law is the man who knows only its technical details and neglects its generative principles, and the worst enemy of the lawyer is the man who does not comprehend why it is that there need be any technical details at all. There is critical danger that the law may cease or fail to be a liberal profession and lose its guiding place in society accordingly; and I know of no measure so well calculated to deliver us from that danger as the proper establishment of law studies as a university discipline, no more to be confined to technical and professional schools than the study of science. Law is a branch of political science, and in this day especially we need to insist in very plain terms upon its study as such. In the presence of many new and strange questions, our courts are puzzled and disconcerted. Called upon to find principles of law or procedure for the amazing developments of an industrial society which seems constantly to shift and change under their very eyes, they either strain old analogies and wrest old precedents to strange uses or else cut the knot with some sharp remedy which seems to damage as many rights as it preserves. We need lawyers now, if ever, who have drunk deeper at the fountains of the law, much deeper, than the merely technical lawyer, who is only an expert in an intricate and formal business; lawyers who have explored the sources as well as tapped the streams of the law, and who can stand in court as advisers as well as pleaders, able to suggest the missing principles and assist at the adaptation of remedies. Such men we shall get when we recognize law as a university study. You must begin to make your lawyer, in short, on the other side of the law school. There are other reasons, to be sure, for teaching undergraduates to understand law. Every business man must wish such a training, for his business runs everywhere amidst the intricacies of the law. Every minister should know as intimately as possible the function that law performs in society, for our ministers are nowadays our reformers, and they make but a silly exhibition of themselves when they talk as if law could be recast to-morrow upon the lines of the nearest text. Every citizen should know what law is, how it came into existence, what relation its form bears to its substance, and how it gives to society its fibre and strength and poise of frame. But our concern is with the lawyer, and it is certainly he more than any other who needs to be versed in the philosophy and the history of law. In the Law School he cannot get this view of his great subject. Time does not serve. Details, niceties, special statutes, entangled decisions crowd into the foreground. He is too near the mass of the law and too much engaged with a critical scrutiny and nice discrimination of its multifarious parts to take his distance, observe whence it came and whither it is tending, what its greater proportions are and its commanding principles. He must see all this first, and then the details will not confuse or mislead him. What the instruction given him in college should be, how arranged, how imparted, how emphasized, is the important and difficult question. One thing is plain: it must be put in its right place among his other studies. It must be made evident from its position, its method, its outlook, that it is an integral portion of political science. In law the principles of social relationship— elsewhere in solution, in philanthropy, in social intercourse, in political economy—are brought to a sharp crystalization. It is that portion of the established social habit which has gained distinct and formal recognition in the shape of uniform rules, backed by the authority and the power of government, and all the influences that move and mould society serve to explain and animate and prophesy for law. The lawyer should know what these influences are, how they are to be recognized and their force reckoned, how they are to be dealt with and directed. The man who teaches law to undergraduates should be a political scientist and—what nowadays we recognize as a different thing—a sociologist; and I do not hesitate to add that the teacher of sociology and political science should have a thorough acquaintance with the principles which govern the life of law. The statical forces of law which hold society steadfast, and the dynamical forces of politics and morals and industrial motive, which subject it to almost constant change, are not to be separated as if they had no causal connections. Austin has done us the great disservice of putting his analysis of law into such terms as to create the very general impression among lawyers who do not think, but swallow formulas, that law is somehow made independently of the bulk of the community, and that it is their business to accept and apply it as it is without troubling themselves to look beyond the statute or decision in which it is embodied. I do not see how any one can possibly understand the law or know anything of it, except *memoriter*, without getting a clear idea of how it is in fact generated in society and adapted from age to age to its immediate needs and uses.

For my own part, I have a very clear notion of the field which ought to be covered in the undergraduate instruction of young men who expect to become lawyers. They ought, in the first place, to be taught very carefully the differences between the two great bodies of law which we call public and private. Public law is a thing of polity; private law, a product of the essential relationship existing between man and man in any society, no matter what its political constitution. The student, as well as every other citizen, ought to know the nature and organization of the government he lives under and the principles, whether of liberty or authority, which regulate the relations of individuals to the State. But the student of the law should go further than the citizen, and scrutinize those conceptions of jural relationship which are in a sense independent of polity. He should be very carefully grounded in the principles of general jurisprudence before he undertakes to master any particular system of law. For the time, the explicit provisions of particular systems should serve his thought simply as illustrations, concrete examples and verifications. It is possible—and I need not say how desirable—that he should be made familiar with a sketch, general, of course, and yet not too general, of the history of law; its genesis and form in the childhood of States, its development in classical instances in antique States, its passage through the strange crucible of the middle ages, and the circumstances of its development in the societies of modern Europe. But that is not enough. He should not be left with nothing but this sketch, which can hardly do more than provoke his curiosity upon a hundred and one points left undeveloped. He must be given, besides, two bodies of law for his more particular examination, in respect of their individual character and the way they came about; one a system aged and completed, the other a system of our own time and as yet unfinished. The former can be none other than the splendid system of Rome, which no lawyer can contemplate without emotion or examine without instruction; the other, if one had the knowledge and the foreign taste, might be the law of France or the law of Prussia, but I should think it ought to be the common law of England. We know much less about how the common law was begotten and bred and brought to maturity than French and German scholars know of the derivation and growth of their own systems, to our shame be it said; but there is the more reason that we should bestir ourselves to put together what we do know, extend it and complete it; and nothing is quite so stimulating or so instructive to the young student as to be present at such a process of investigation and take part in it where he can. That is the lesson of modern educational methods.

I need not say, after this survey of the field, that the method of instruction should at every step be both historical and comparative. No other method has the slightest claim to be called philosophical. For by the philosophy of law I do not mean its metaphysics; I mean its rational explanation; and no explanation of law can be rational which does not make it clear why and how law came into existence, what are the essential and what the accidental contrasts and divergencies between particular systems, and what the principles are which everywhere prevail and under whatever circumstances, as if by a sort of radical necessity.

And here let me pay my compliments in passing to the question whether the law, when taught as a profession, should be taught by the inductive use of cases or by the deductive use of principles already extracted from the cases and formulated in texts. The teaching of law as a profession should no more be irrational than the teaching of it as part of a liberal education or as a preparation for law studies. The case method, therefore, falls short and is slavish if it stops in each instance with the first case in a series. Where did the court get their principle from in the first case, if there was, indeed, neither statute nor precedent; and, if there was a statute, what guided them to its interior meaning? Such are the questions which reveal to the student, when successfully answered, the real genesis and significance of law. In like manner, the text-book method is neither philosophical nor really instructive unless the principles made use of are challenged, cross-questioned, and made to give a rational account of themselves. It is only when principle is thus realized as a living and necessary thing, with as clear a pedigree and explanation as a horse or a king, that it can become really a part of the lawyer's thought and judgment and professional equipment. The first case, of course, came to the judges out of a special set of circumstances in the community around them, and they were able to decide it because they understood the conditions out of which it had arisen and knew what those conditions demanded. They pluck out the heart of a statute in the same way, by understanding what gave rise to its enactment and what it is that it is intended to accomplish. The judge, after all, if he be of the sort we quote and make a veritable authority of, is a seer and a man who might have been a statesman or a professor of political science! The "common" law we believe to have arisen out of *custom*, out of the life of the people; and have not all our writers upon the common law, from astute Sir Matthew Hale down to formal Mr. Broom,[1] assumed that statutes are made but in supplement to it or amendment of it, as if it were complete and they exceptional? This is plainly the assumption of the celebrated maxims with regard to the interpretation of statutes: "What was the common law before the making of the act?" "What was the mischief and defect against which the common law did not provide?" "What remedy has the legislature devised and applied?" "The true reason of the remedy?" And have you not noted the result of this process of interpretation, the new law held up to the standard of the old and treated as if it were meant, of course, to be fitted into it? Old

---

[1] The works of both authorities are cited in the Editorial Note, "Wilson's Teaching at Princeton and the Johns Hopkins, 1893-97."

statutes disappear, as it were by digestion, into the general body of principles; or, rather, for the process is deliberate, they are kneaded into the mass by much pressing and handling in the courts, until writers are sorely puzzled to distinguish common from statute law. New statutes, too, immediately begin to feel and yield to the same process. In time they, too, will be so knitted into the body of the law by the careful stitches of successive generations of judges as to have become fairly indistinguishable from the material with which they have been combined. Through the courts they are being played upon and weather-beaten by the practical conditions of the economic and moral life of the community, and so are being steadily moulded by forces which the student must afterwards re-examine if he would comprehend and veritably master the law which is their product.

To take a definite example, in order to make my meaning clearer, it is a favorite idea of mine that commercial law should be taught along with *the history of commerce*, which will make it plain what gave rise to the relations of business with which the law deals, how the forms of commercial negotiation and of commercial paper came into existence, and how statutes and all the imperative regulations of the law have come after the fact, fixing obligations already habitually recognized, or at any rate ready to be put into form, and so simply serving merchants, not inventing transactions for them. One portion of our law we already study in this way—the law of real property. It has retained forms and phrases which we cannot understand without turning back to examine the feudal system and the social conditions of the middle ages; and so we are happily obliged to give heed to its genesis. We ought to do the same for every portion of the law.

I shall not need to argue, after what I have said, that the studies I have outlined properly find a place in the curriculum of a college. They are liberal studies, not technical. I am careful, in my own lecturing, to treat such subjects as strictly as possible as a part of political science—to exhibit law as an instrument of society, and not as the subject-matter of a technical profession. I am punctilious to give out as little as may be of such law as could be used in court to win a case with. If you say that such studies, though no doubt very interesting, and even stimulating and enlightening, are only for the man who has the time for them; that they are a luxury, and are but so much the more added to what the lawyer will in any case be obliged to learn, I reply that you are mistaken; that such studies, besides being in themselves a liberal education, really save time. It saves time to become more than a lawyer and be a jurist. You have just so much

the readier and more various means of ascertaining and enforcing the methods and the arguments by which to win cases, if
that is all you want; and you will the sooner get the best sort
of practice. Mr. James Bryce was for twenty-three years professor
of the civil law at the University of Oxford, taking up the office in
1870, and laying it down last year; and during all of that time, I
believe, he continued in the active practice of his profession as
a barrister. He says very frankly, in his interesting valedictory
lecture, that his knowledge of Roman law has seldom, if ever,
been of direct and immediate service to him in his practical law
business; and he doubts whether any of his pupils has ever found
occasion to use it in court. But he confidently expresses the opinion that a student who, out of three years devoted to law study,
has given one year to Roman law and two to English, will, at the
end of the period, know as much English law as the man who has
given all three of the years to studying nothing else; and he in-
timates that the student of Roman law will know English law
more discriminatingly and with an easier mastery. That is what
I mean by saving time; *saving subsequent time*. The more various the apparatus of study, the easier the study. And so I believe that, by teaching law to undergraduates thus historically
and comparatively, and as a part of general political science, as
if it were stuff of society, with a wealth of instructive experience
wrapped up in it, a material and vehicle of life, I am making,
so far as I succeed, not only enlightened men, but also successful
lawyers.

I do not hesitate to say, moreover, that in general view and
method professional instruction in law should be of the same
kind. Just in proportion as you give, along with every principle,
its history and its rational explanation, just in that proportion
do you increase the ease and rapidity with which the pupil will
master it, and the certainty that he will retain and be able to
make accurate use of it. Of course, professional instruction in
law must be very different in detail. It must deal with the law
as a practical science and must expound with not a little minute-
ness the ways in which it is to be applied to business and to the
changing and infinitely various circumstances of all the formal
dealings of society. It is inevitable, as I have already said, that it
should be technical, and that its technicalities should even crowd
the foreground of every exposition. But what of the background?
what of the light in which all these details are to be exhibited,
the setting and the reasonable order in which they are to be
placed? What of the accompanying comments and the accompanying outlines of development? It is absolutely necessary

that these countless technical niceties should be given *their significance*, their connection with the principles whose servants and attendants they are, and to which they should always be obedient. To do this saves time, I urge again, as well as makes better, more masterful and sure-footed lawyers. A technicality is difficult only so long as it is unexplained and has to be kept sticking to the memory by external and artificial pressure. So soon as you explain it you bring out its adhesive quality and it will not leave you so long as you continue to understand it. There's no glue like comprehension! I have observed that the young American very keenly relishes a technicality and makes no difficulty of it at all, if you will but show him how it points a principle or sums up an experience. He likes the intellectual art of navigating a subtlety amidst practical difficulties.

We do not in this country recognize, at any rate in any formal manner, the distinction drawn in the old country between attorneys and barristers. Our barristers are their own attorneys, and are in fact very much more engaged in most instances in attorney work than in the conduct of actual litigation. It is for this reason, no doubt, that our law schools have come to confine themselves so exclusively to a very technical course of training. It is not clearly enough realized, I venture to think, however, that this is the case; that we devote our instruction to the preparation of attorneys, who direct the *business* of the law and must be technical experts, and neglect to provide ourselves, in any systematic way, with barristers, who handle the *principles* of the law in argument, and who must possess a knowledge of legal reasoning at once comprehensive and flexible. We must not forget, either, that we need judges—under our system of government a great many—and that we get so many illiberal judgments from our courts because we have so many mere attorneys on the bench. A barrister, let it be said very frankly, has a much higher function than the attorney—as the judge has, by common consent, a higher function than either. Any exact and painstaking man may make a fairly good attorney; but a man who would plead cases must, if he would master his part, be a man capable of making law for the court—making it, I mean, as courts make it, by systematic interpretation. Systematic interpretation is the reading together, as the premises for a conclusion, of different parts of a body of law. It is driving precedents into court, not tandem, but abreast, to beat a new road and pick the court up to take them into a fresh country. It is bringing the thought of a system of law to a new focus, and so effecting a new illumination. A few men we always have who can do this. They are always men who have somehow gotten a wide outlook upon men and books; who have given themselves a large equipment and diligently multiplied their resources. They have not in all cases gotten these things from a class-room or the guidance of any teacher. Sometimes they have conquered their territory for themselves, unassisted, because they had the instinct of mastery, and the courage, and the initiative. But systematic study under the right sort of stimulation and suggestion must be credited with most such master practitioners, I believe. It is worth while considering whether we could not deliberately produce them in somewhat greater numbers by a partial change in the method and point of view of our instruction in the law schools. Many a young fellow, not yet awakened or stimulated by a liberal course of preparation for professional studies would discover the life and power of the law for himself if you would but once make the necessary suggestions to his mind, if you would but enable him to see the law as a thing full of life and growth, quick with questions waiting to be answered out of accessible books and by means of study sure to yield tremendous increase of forensic power.

But the best hope is from the colleges. We must invite undergraduates to become jurists, and systematically show them how it can be done. It is the proper function of universities, certainly, to train citizens; and while training citizens you can provoke jurists. It is in this sense that our young men must be made to become lawyers before entering law schools. Our Committee on Legal Education, in their admirable report,[2] insist, with irresistible show of reason, that we must give over devoting our attention so exclusively to the detail of highly specialized portions of the law and return to the earlier and better method of giving the student, first of all, at any rate, and as a foundation for everything that is to follow, a unified and comprehensive view of the law as a whole, displayed and connected as a system, its parts shown in their due proportions and relations, and its entire body erected for a single view. In my opinion, only the coöperation of the colleges can make this possible. We all remember that Blackstone's Commentaries were first of all what we should call a course of college lectures. To view the law as a whole, in its philosophical and historical relationships and for the purpose of discovering its whole significance is the function, not of the professional

2 Since the Committee on Legal Education reported very briefly to the meeting in 1894 to the effect that it would defer making its formal report, this report seems to have been the one printed under the names of Austin Abbott, George M. Sharp, Henry Wade Rogers, Charles A. Graves, and William Wirt Howe in *Report of the Eighteenth Annual Meeting of the American Bar Association* . . . (Philadelphia, 1895), pp. 309-33.

expert, but of the political scientist. The means and the spirit for such study must be supplied by the universities; the law schools must welcome and carry forward their employment. When we have universities investigating and teaching law as a science, we may ask the law schools to adopt the spirit of the universities, and to transmit the results of such study while carrying forward their own proper function of imparting law as an art. The undergraduate must determine what the law student is to be.

Printed in *Report of the Seventeenth Annual Meeting of the American Bar Association* . . . (Philadelphia, 1894), pp. 439-51.

From Ellen Axson Wilson

My own darling   Princeton, N. J. Aug 23/94

I do not know whether this will reach you before you leave Saratoga but will adventure a line at any rate to let you know if possible that the children are all better. They had a very good night indeed, coughed scarcely at all and seem almost well to-day. The weather is still charming but warmer.

There is no news and no word as yet from you or Maggie,—I am hoping for a letter this afternoon. I went yesterday to see Mrs. Armstrong[1] &, to fulfil my promise, Mrs. Miller's sister.[2] Such a bore to put on one's best things,—and *gloves*,—actually! and begin the old business of calling. Mrs. Miller I am glad to say reports herself almost through her hard task.[3]

And now goodbye dear for a little space. I love and honour you "with my soul, and my heart, and my duty, and my life, and my living, and my uttermost power" and I am now and always,

Your devoted little wife,   Eileen.

ALS (WC, NjP).

[1] Dean Murray's daughter, Mabel Chester Murray (Mrs. Andrew Campbell, Jr.) Armstrong, of Middletown, Conn.

[2] The wife of the Rev. John Miller of 38 Washington Street. Her sister was probably visiting her.

[3] A mysterious reference.

ADDENDUM

To Horace Elisha Scudder

My dear Mr. Scudder,   Middletown, Conn., 31 March, 1889

I was sincerely gratified to see your handwriting again.[1] It does me an immense amount of good to know that you are interested in my fortunes and follow my movements.

Yes, the move from Bryn Mawr was distinctly to my advantage —palpably so pecuniarily, for the Bryn Mawr salaries are quite paltry—but even more so in other respects. There was a plentiful lack of inspiration in teaching young women politics; and the "administration" of the college inclines more, I discovered, to new educational "fads" than to tested educational wisdom. In college phrase, it was "very fresh." Here I have, not inspiring classes, but goodly numbers of very sturdy, earnest men, who are capable of worthy work and elevating enthusiasm, who mean business and respect business. The atmosphere here is altogether wholesome, the spirit at once sober and progressive. I am braced and comforted. My source of stimulation is my connection with the Johns Hopkins. I deliver twenty-five lectures there each winter: have just returned from a six weeks' stay in Baltimore.

The book on the State announced in the *Nation* is not yet quite ready for the publisher. It is one of those inconvenient things, a *fact* book, and its facts concern systems of government and administration, foreign and domestic: with these systems legislatures are forever tinkering, and whenever they tinker I have to re-write. The Local Government Act in England spoiled all my remarks about local administrative arrangements there,—and if those unstable Frenchmen don't pull themselves together very speedily my whole chapter on France will be knocked into a cocked hat by that knave Boulanger! (My emotion must excuse the above blot!) I hope to be rid of the burden (till revised editions become necessary!) by the 1st May. I could not look with any complacency on the three or four years spent on this textbook—and the months to be spent on a smaller one for schools— were the work not part of a deliberate course of training. I undertook the job as the one most likely to afford me the discipline of close, drudging contact with facts so necessary in preparation for the thought books I mean hereafter to write. I shan't want any more of the same sort. I am now, I trust, supplied with the wished-for habit.

Yes indeed, I read Mr. Bryce's book immediately, and have expressed my opinion on it quite at length in the March *Political*

Science Quarterly. Your own *Atlantic* notice[2] of it I read with pleasure and agreement. It is a book which compels admiration, at the same time that it has the healthy capacity of provoking criticism. Its lack of executive coherence and compactness in method and of executive speed in statement, which you note, are unquestionably among its chief defects. No man can receive such a book into his mind *as a whole*: it must, therefore, lack individuality. It is a work full of information, of insight, of sagacity, but not of power—But you do not need to have it explained to you what it is!

I have had a score of occasions to thank you in my heart—and in my conversation with my confidants—for the letter that you wrote me in '86[3] in answer to my outpour of confidence touching the work upon which my mind is set,[4] towards which I am steadily bending every energy of thought I possess. I am realizing more and more fully year by year the value of *patience* in thinking, the gain of "waiting, on the slowness of my thought"—at the same time that I am eager to be at the work I have planned. My enthusiasm grows rather than abates: but it is becoming chastened, not heady and impatient.

I wish I did sometimes find occasion to visit Boston, and I hope I shall; but my one visit there has so far been all. I hope that you will give my kindest regards to Mr. Houghton, and that you will accept for yourself the assurance that your friendship is both an encouragement and a stimulation, as well as a source of the deepest gratification to me.

Most cordially Yours,   Woodrow Wilson

TCL (Houghton Mifflin Letter Files, MH).
    [1] H. E. Scudder to WW, March 25, 1889, Vol. 6, pp. 164-65.
    [2] "A Bird's-Eye View of the United States," *Atlantic Monthly*, LXIII (March 1889), 418-24.
    [3] H. E. Scudder to WW, June 6, 1886, Vol. 5, pp. 287-89.
    [4] WW to H. E. Scudder, May 12, 1886, Vol. 5, pp. 218-21.

INDEX

NOTE ON THE INDEX

THE alphabetically arranged analytical table of contents at the front of the volume eliminates duplication, in both contents and index, of references to certain documents, such as letters. Letters are listed in the contents alphabetically by name, and chronologically within each name by page. The subject matter of all letters is, of course, indexed. The Editorial Notes and Wilson's writings are listed in the contents chronologically by page. In addition, the subject matter of both categories is indexed. The index covers all references to books and articles mentioned in text or notes. Footnotes are indexed. Page references to footnotes which place a comma between the page number and "n" cite both text and footnote, thus: "624,n3." On the other hand, absence of the comma indicates reference to the footnote only, thus: "55n2"—the page number denoting where the footnote appears. The letter "n" without a following digit signifies an unnumbered descriptive-location note.

An asterisk before an index reference designates identification or other particular information. Re-identification and repetitive annotation have been minimized to encourage use of these starred references. Where the identification appears in an earlier volume, it is indicated thus: "*1:212,n3." Therefore a page reference standing without a preceding volume number is invariably a reference to the present volume. The index supplies the fullest known forms of names, and, for the Wilson and Axson families, relationships as far down as cousins. Persons referred to in the text by nicknames or shortened forms of names can be identified by reference to entries for these forms of the names.

A sampling of the opinions and comments of Wilson and Ellen Axson Wilson covers their more personal views, while broad, general headings in the main body of the index cover impersonal subjects. Occasionally opinions expressed by a correspondent are indexed where these appear to supplement or to reflect views expressed by Wilson or by Ellen Axson Wilson in documents which are missing.

INDEX

AND WOODROW WILSON

life stands still when WW is gone, 3;
WW the dearest, noblest, tenderest,
most perfect, most wonderful husband in the world, 3; danger of
taking separation all too tragically,
7; WW an instrument fit for the
gods—steel of the finest temper,
strongest yet keenest and most beautiful of weapons! 12; longs for WW
with a longing unspeakable, 74;
dreams of WW, 74; love increasing
all the time, 293; WW in danger of
suffocation when he returns, 475;
vivid dream of WW, 476

OPINIONS AND COMMENTS

Princeton trustees: selfish lethargy in
the matter of salaries, 16
William Milligan Sloane disgusting
with ladies: his flattery so fulsome
and so artificial, 474
Henry Cabot Lodge: a contemptible
hypocrite, 491
pleasures of freedom and travel are